P9-AFE-393

THE GLORIES OF MARY

N
LF

THE

GLORIES OF MARY

Translated from the Italian of

ST. ALPHONSUS MARIA DE LIGUORI,

BISHOP OF ST. AGATHA OF THE GOTHS, AND
FOUNDER OF THE CONGREGATION OF THE MOST HOLY REDEEMER

REVISED BY THE RIGHT REV. ROBERT A. COFFIN
LATE BISHOP OF SOUTHWARK

TAN BOOKS AND PUBLISHERS, INC.
Rockford, Illinois 61105

We hereby approve of this Translation of the *Glories of Mary*, and cordially recommend it to the Faithful.

NICHOLAS CARD. WISEMAN,

ARCHBISHOP OF WESTMINSTER.

Given at Westminster on the Feast of Saint Alphonsus de Liguori, A.D. 1852.

Second Edition.

We heartily recommend this Translation of the *Glories of Mary* to all the disciples of her Divine Son.

✠ HENRY E.,

ARCHBISHOP OF WESTMINSTER.

Aug. 11, 1868.

Originally published by Burns, Oates & Washbourne Ltd., London. Reprinted under arrangement with Burns, Oates & Washbourne by TAN Books and Publishers, Inc., in 1977, 1978, 1980, and 1982.

Library of Congress Catalog Card Number: 79-112485.

ISBN: 0-89555-021-0.

Printed and bound in the United States of America.

TAN BOOKS AND PUBLISHERS, INC.
P.O. Box 424
Rockford, Illinois 61105

1977

NOTICE.

THE present edition of the *Glories of Mary* has been revised and corrected in so far as was necessary.

The Translator of the first edition bestowed much pains and labour in verifying the numerous quotations which occur in the work ; he carefully compared and corrected all the quotations with the originals from which they are taken. In the few instances in which he was unable to procure the authors or to find the quotations, he put this sign †; not to denote that they do not exist, but simply to indicate that he did not pledge himself to them.

In 1862 the Rev. Father Dujardin, C.SS.R., published a French Translation of the *Glories of Mary*. In his preface he states that he has carefully verified all the quotations, and that he vouches for their exactitude.

We have therefore gladly availed ourselves of that portion of his work, and have collated all the quotations and references given in the first English edition with those given by Father Dujardin.

Some of the Indulgences granted to certain devotions have been corrected on the authority of the *Raccolta*.

It may be remarked here that in older editions of the works of St. Anselm, the treatise *de Excellentia Virginis*, so often quoted by St. Alphonsus, is attributed to him, but in later editions it is given as the work of another author.

St. Mary's, Clapham,   R.A.C., C.SS.R.
    August 17, 1868.

* *Œuvres complètes de St. Alphonse de Liguori*, traduites de l'Italien par Léopold J. Dujardin, de la Congrégation du Très-Saint Redempteur. *Gloires de Marie*, tomes vii. viii. Casterman, Tournai.

THE AUTHOR'S PROTEST.

In obedience to the decrees of Urban the Eighth, I declare that I have no intention of attributing any other than a purely human authority to the miracles, revelations, favours, and particular cases recorded in this book ; and the same as regards the titles of Saints and Blessed, applied to servants of God not yet canonised, except in those cases which have been confirmed by the Holy Roman Catholic Church and the Apostolical See, of which I declare myself to be an obedient son ; and therefore I submit myself, and all that I have written in this book, to her judgment.

CONTENTS.

PART I.

CHAP. I. *Hail, Holy Queen, Mother of Mercy:*

CHAP. II. *Our Life, our Sweetness.*

CHAP. III. *Our Hope.*

PART II.

DISCOURSE I. *Of Mary's Immaculate Conception.*

DISCOURSE II. *Of the Birth of Mary.*

DISCOURSE III. *Of the Presentation of Mary.*

PART III.

THE AUTHOR'S PRAYER

Jesus and Mary.

———

MY most loving Redeemer and Lord Jesus Christ, I, thy miserable servant, well knowing what pleasure he gives Thee who endeavours to exalt thy most holy Mother, whom Thou lovest so much; knowing, too, how much Thou desirest to see her loved and honoured by all, have determined to publish this work of mine, which treats of her glories. I know not, however, to whom I could better recommend it than to Thee, who hast her glory so much at heart. To Thee, therefore, do I dedicate and commend it. Accept this little homage of the love I bear Thee and thy beloved Mother. Do Thou protect it, by showering down on all who read it the light of confidence and flames of love towards this Immaculate Virgin, in whom Thou hast placed the hope and whom Thou hast made the refuge of all the redeemed. And as a reward for my poor labour, grant me, I beseech Thee, that love towards Mary, which, by the means of this book, I desire to see enkindled in all who read it.

And now I turn to thee, O my most sweet Lady and Mother Mary. Thou well knowest that, after Jesus, I have placed my entire hope of salvation in thee: for I acknowledge that everything good—my conversion, my call to renounce the world, and all the other graces that I have received from God—all were given me through thy means. Thou knowest that in order to see thee loved by all as thou deservest, and

B

also as some mark of gratitude for the many benefits thou hast conferred upon me, I have always endeavoured in my sermons, in public and in private, to insinuate into all thy sweet and salutary devotion. I hope to continue doing so until my last breath, but my advanced years and feeble health admonish me that I am near the end of my pilgrimage and my entry into eternity; and therefore I wish, before dying, to leave this book to the world, in order that in my place it may continue to preach thee, and encourage others to announce thy glories, and the tender compassion thou showest to thy clients. I trust, my most beloved Queen, that this little gift, which is one of love, though far beneath thy merits, will yet be acceptable to thy most gracious heart. Extend, then, that most sweet hand with which thou hast drawn me from the world and delivered me from hell, and accept it and protect it as thine own. But at the same time thou must know that I expect a reward for my little offering; and that is, that from this day forward I may love thee more than ever, and that every-one into whose hands this work may fall may at once be inflamed with love of thee; and that his desire of loving thee, and of seeing thee loved by others, may be increased, so that he may labour with all affection to preach and promote, as far as he can, thy praises, and confidence in thy most powerful intercession. Amen.

Thy most loving though vile servant,

ALPHONSUS DE LIGUORI.

TO THE READER.

In order that my present work may not be condemned by the over-critical, I think it well to explain certain propositions that will be found in it, and which may seem hazardous, or perhaps obscure. I have noticed some, and should others attract your attention, charitable reader, I beg that you will understand them according to the rules of sound theology and the doctrine of the holy Roman Catholic Church, of which I declare myself a most obedient son. In the Introduction, at page 7, referring to the sixth chapter of this work, I say that it is the will of God that all graces should come to us by the hands of Mary. Now, this is indeed a most consoling truth for souls tenderly devoted to our most Blessed Lady, and for poor sinners who wish to repent. Nor should this opinion be looked upon as contrary to sound doctrine, since the father of theology, St. Augustine,[1] in common with most writers, says, that Mary coöperated by her charity in the spiritual birth of all members of the Church. A celebrated writer, and one who cannot be accused of exaggeration or of misguided devotion, says,[2] 'that it was, properly speaking, on Mount Calvary that Jesus formed His Church:' and then it is evident that the Blessed Virgin coöperated in a most excellent and especial manner in the accomplishment of this work. And in the same way it can be said, that though she brought forth the Head of the Church, Jesus Christ, without pain, she did not bring forth the body of this Head without very great suffering ; and so it was on Mount Calvary that Mary began, in an especial manner, to be the Mother of the whole Church. And now, to say all in a few words : God, to glorify the Mother of the Redeemer, has so determined and

[1] Mater quidem spiritu, non capitis nostri, quod est ipse Salvator, ex quo magis illa spiritaliter nata est ; quia omnes, qui in eum crediderint, in quibus et ipsa est, recte filii sponsi appellantur ; sed plane mater membrorum ejus (quod nos sumus), quia cooperata est charitate, ut fideles in ecclesia nascerentur, quæ illius capitis membra sunt.—*Lib. de Sancta Virginitate*, cap. vi.

[2] Mons. Nicole, Istruzioni teologiche e morali sopra l'Orazione Domenicale, Salutazione Angelica, &c. Istruzione 3, c. 2.

disposed, that of her great charity she should intercede in behalf of all those for whom His Divine Son paid and offered the superabundant price of His precious blood, in which alone " is our salvation, life, and resurrection." On this doctrine, and on all that is in accordance with it, I ground my propositions[3]—propositions which the Saints have not feared to assert in their tender colloquies with Mary and fervent discourses in her honour. Hence St. Sophronius says, that ' the plenitude of all grace which is in Christ came into Mary, though in a different way ;'[4] meaning that the plenitude of grace was in Christ, as the Head from which it flows, as from its source ; and in Mary, as in the neck through which it flows. This opinion is clearly confirmed and taught by the angelical Doctor, St. Thomas, who says : 'Of the three ways in which the Blessed Virgin is full of grace, the third is that she is so for its transfusion into all men ;' and then he adds : 'This plenitude is great in any Saint when there is as much grace as would suffice for the salvation of many, but it is in its highest degree when there is as much as would suffice for the salvation of the world ; and it was in this degree in Christ and in the Blessed Virgin : for in all dangers thou canst obtain salvation of this glorious Virgin ; and therefore it is said in the sacred Canticles that " a thousand bucklers," that is to say, means of protection against dangers, " hang upon it." Also, in every work of virtue thou canst have her for thy helper, for she says, in the words of Ecclesiastes, " In me is all hope of life and virtue." '[5]

[3] In Chapters vi. vii. viii. ix.

[4] In Mariam vero totius gratiæ, quæ in Christo est plenitudo venit, quamquam aliter.—Int. op. S. Hieron. *Serm. de Assump. B.V.*: ap. Coutenson, *Theol. Ment. et Cord.* l. 10. d. 6. c. 1.

[5] Dicitur autem beata Virgo plena gratiæ, quantum ad tria ... Tertio, quantum ad refusionem in omnes homines. Magnum enim est in quolibet sancto, quando habet tantum de gratia, quod sufficit ad salutem multorum : sed quando haberet tantum, quod sufficeret ad salutem omnium hominum de mundo, hoc esset maximum, et hoc est in Christo et in Beata Virgine. Nam in omni periculo potes salutem obtinere ab ipsa Virgine gloriosa. Unde Canticorum iv. " mille clypei," id est remedia contra pericula, " pendent ex ea." Item, in omni opere virtutis potes eam habere in adjutorium, et ideo dicit ipsa Ecclesiastici xxiv. " In me omnis spes vitæ et virtutis."—*Exp. in Salut. Ang. Opusc.* 8.

INTRODUCTION,

WHICH IT IS NECESSARY TO READ.

MY beloved reader and brother in Mary. Since the devotion that led me to write, and moves you to read, this book, makes us happy children of the same good Mother, should you hear it remarked that I might have spared myself the labour, as there are already so many celebrated and learned works on the same subject, I beg that you will reply, in the words of the Abbot Francone, that ' the praise of Mary is an inexhaustible fount, the more it is enlarged the fuller it gets, and the more you fill it so much the more is it enlarged.'[1]   In short, this Blessed Virgin is so great and sublime, that the more she is praised the more there remains to praise ; so much so, says an ancient writer, ' that if all the tongues of men were put together, and even if each of their members was changed into a tongue, they would not suffice to praise her as much as she deserves.'[2]

I have seen innumerable works, of all sizes, which treat of the Glories of Mary ; but finding that they were either rare, voluminous, or did not answer the object I had in view, I endeavoured to collect, from as many authors as I could lay my hands on, the choicest passages, extracted from Fathers and Theologians, and those which seemed to me to be the most to the point, and have put them together in this book, in order that the devout may with little trouble and expense be able to inflame themselves with the love of Mary, and more

---

[1] Laus Mariæ fons est indeficiens, qui quanto longius extenditur, tanto amplius impletur; et quanto amplius impletur, tanto latius dilatatur.—*De Grat.* lib. vii.

[2] Etiamsi omnium nostrum membra verterentur in linguas, eam laudare sufficeret nullus.—Int. *Op. St. Aug.* in App. tom. v.

particularly to furnish priests with matter for their sermons, wherewith to excite others to devotion towards this Divine Mother.

Worldly lovers often speak of and praise those whom they love, in order that the object of their affections may be praised and extolled by others. There are some who pretend to be lovers of Mary, and yet seldom either speak of or endeavour to excite others to love her : their love cannot be great. It is not thus that true lovers of this amiable Lady act ; they desire to praise her on all occasions, and to see her loved by the whole world, and never lose an opportunity, either in public or private, of enkindling in the hearts of others those blessed flames of love with which they themselves burn towards their beloved Queen.

That everyone may be persuaded how important it is, both for his own good and that of others, to promote devotion towards Mary, it is useful to know what Theologians say on the subject. St. Bonaventure says, that those who make a point of announcing to others the glories of Mary are certain of heaven ; and this opinion is confirmed by Richard of St. Lawrence, who declares, ' that to honour this Queen of Angels is to gain eternal life ;'[3] and he adds, ' that this most gracious Lady will honour in the next world those who honour her in this.'[4] And who is ignorant of the promise made by Mary herself, in the words of Ecclesiastes, to those who endeavour to make her known and loved here below, "they that explain me shall have life everlasting ;"[5] for this passage is applied to her by the Church, in the office of the Immaculate Conception. ' Rejoice, then,' exclaims St. Bonaventure (who did so much to make the glories of Mary known), ' rejoice, my soul, and be glad in her for many good things are prepared for those who praise her ;' and he says that the whole of

[3] Honorare siquidem Mariam, thesaurizare est sibi vitam æternam.—*De Laud. V.* l. 2.
[4] Glorificabit in futuro servientes sibi et honorificantes se in præsenti.—*Ib.*
[5] Qui elucidant me, vitam æternam habebunt.—*Eccl.* **xxiv.** 31.

the sacred Scriptures speak in praise of Mary :[6] let us therefore always with our hearts and tongues honour this Divine Mother, in order that we may be conducted by her into the kingdom of the blessed.

We learn from the revelations of St. Bridget, that the blessed Bishop Emingo was in the habit of always beginning his sermons with the praises of Mary. One day the Blessed Virgin herself appeared to the Saint, and desired her to tell him, that in consequence of his pious practice, 'she would be his mother, that he would die a holy death, and that she would herself present his soul to God :'[7] he died like a Saint in the act of praying, and in the most heavenly peace. Mary also appeared to a Dominican friar, who always concluded his sermons by speaking of her; when on his deathbed the Blessed Virgin defended him from the devils, consoled him, and then she herself carried off his happy soul.[8] The devout Thomas à Kempis represents us Mary recommending a soul who had honoured her to her Son, and saying, 'My most loving Son, have mercy on the soul of this servant of Thine, who loved and extolled me.'[9]

Next, as to the advantage of this devotion for all, St. Anselm says, that as the most sacred womb of Mary was the means of salvation for sinners, the hearing of her praises must necessarily convert them, and thus also be a means of their salvation : 'how can it be otherwise than that the salvation of sinners should come from the remembrance of her praises, whose womb was made the way through which the Saviour came to save sinners ?'[10]

And if the opinion is true, and I consider it as indubitably so (as I shall show in the sixth chapter), that

---

[6] Exulta, anima mea, et lætare in illa, quia multa bona sunt laudatoribus præparata. *In Ps.* xliii. *B.V.* Omnes scripturæ loquuntur de ea. *Serm.*13, *in Hex.*
[7] Revel. lib. iii. cap. xiii.   [8] Ap. P. Auriem, Aff. scamb. p. 1, c. 13.
[9] Fili mi amantissime, miserere animæ famuli tui amatoris et laudatoris mei.—*Pars* 3, *Serm.* 2, *ad Nov.*
[10] Quomodo fieri potest, ut ex memoria laudum ejus salus non proveniat peccatorum, cujus uterus factus est via ad sanandum peccatores venienti Salvatori ?—*S. Ans. de Exc. V.* cap. 1.

all graces are dispensed by Mary, and that all who are saved are saved only by the means of this Divine Mother, it is a necessary consequence that the salvation of all depends upon preaching Mary, and exciting all to confidence in her intercession. It is well known that it was thus that St. Bernardine of Sienna sanctified Italy, and that St. Dominic converted so many provinces. St. Louis Bertrand never omitted in his sermons to exhort all to love Mary ; and how many others have done the same.

I find that Father Paul Segneri the younger, who was a very celebrated missioner, in every mission preached a sermon on devotion to Mary, and always called it his beloved sermon. And in our own missions, in which it is an inviolable rule to do the same, we can attest, with all truth, that in most cases no sermon is more profitable, or produces so much compunction in the hearts of the people, as the one on the mercy of Mary. I say, on her mercy ; for, in the words of St. Bernard, ' we praise her virginity, we admire her humility ; but because we are poor sinners, mercy attracts us more and tastes sweeter ; we embrace mercy more lovingly ; we remember it oftener, and invoke it more earnestly ;'[11] and for this reason I here leave other authors to describe the other prerogatives of Mary, and confine myself for the most part to that of her mercy and powerful intercession ; having collected, as far as I was able, and with the labour of many years, all that the holy Fathers and the most celebrated writers have said on this subject ; and as I find that the mercy and power of the most Blessed Virgin are admirably portrayed in the prayer ' Salve Regina,' the recital of which is made obligatory for the greater part of the year on all the clergy, secular and regular, I shall divide and explain this most devout prayer in separate chapters. In addition to this, I thought

---

[11] Laudamus virginitatem, humilitatem miramur ; sed miseris sapit dulcius misericordia ; misericordiam amplectimur carius, recordamur sæpius, crebrius invocamus.—*Serm. 4, de Ass.*

that I should be giving pleasure to Mary's devout clients, by adding discourses on the principal festivals and virtues of this Divine Mother, and by placing at the end of the work the devotions and pious practices most used by her servants, and most approved of by the Church.

Devout reader, should this work, as I trust it will, prove acceptable to you, I beg that you will recommend me to the Blessed Virgin, that she may give me great confidence in her protection. Ask this grace for me; and I promise you, whoever you may be, that I will ask the same for you who do me this charity. O, blessed are they who bind themselves with love and confidence to these two anchors of salvation, Jesus and Mary. Certainly they will not be lost. Let us then both say, devout reader, with the pious Alphonsus Rodriguez, 'Jesus and Mary, my most sweet loves, for you may I suffer, for you may I die; grant that I may be in all things yours and in nothing mine.'[12] Let us love Jesus and Mary, and become Saints; we can neither expect nor hope anything better. Farewell, then, until we meet in Paradise, at the feet of this most sweet Mother and of this most loving Son; there to praise them, to love them face to face for all eternity. Amen.

[12] Jesu et Maria, amores mei dulcissimi, pro vobis patiar, pro vobis moriar, sim totus vester, sim nihil meus.—*Ap. Auriem, Aff. sc.*

Prayer to the Blessed Virgin

TO OBTAIN A GOOD DEATH.

———

Mary, sweet refuge of miserable sinners, when my soul is on the point of leaving this world, O, my most sweet Mother, by that sorrow which thou didst endure when assisting at the death of thy Son on the cross, assist me with thy mercy. Drive the infernal enemy far from me, and do thou come and take my soul to thyself, and present it to the eternal Judge. My Queen, abandon me not. Thou, after Jesus, hast to be my comfort in that terrible moment. Entreat thy beloved Son, in His goodness, to grant me the grace to die clinging to thy feet, and to breathe forth my soul in His wounds, saying, 'Jesus and Mary, I give you my heart and my soul.'

THE GLORIES OF MARY.

PART THE FIRST.

ON THE SALVE REGINA:

IN WHICH THE MANY AND ABUNDANT GRACES DISPENSED BY THE
MOTHER OF GOD TO HER DEVOUT CLIENTS ARE TREATED
OF, UNDER DIFFERENT HEADS, TAKEN FROM
THE SALVE REGINA.

CHAPTER I.

HAIL, HOLY QUEEN, MOTHER OF MERCY!

SECTION I. *How great should be our confidence in Mary,
who is the Queen of Mercy.*

As the glorious Virgin Mary has been raised to the
dignity of Mother of the King of kings, it is not without reason that the Church honours her, and wishes
her to be honoured by all, with the glorious title of
Queen. 'If the Son is a King,' says an ancient writer,
'the Mother who begot him is rightly and truly considered a Queen and Sovereign.'[1] 'No sooner had Mary,'
says St. Bernardine of Sienna, 'consented to be Mother
of the Eternal Word, than she merited by this consent

---

[1] Siquidem is ipse qui ex Virgine natus est, rex est, et ipse Dominus Deus.
Mater, quæ ipsum genuit, Regina, Domina, et Deipara proprie ac vere prædicatur.—*Serm. de Deip. int. op. S. Athan*

to be made Queen of the world and of all creatures.'² 'Since the flesh of Mary,' remarks the Abbot Arnold of Chartres, 'was not different from that of Jesus, how can the royal dignity of the Son be denied to the Mother?'³ 'Hence we must consider the glory of the Son, not only as being common to, but as one with, that of His Mother.'⁴

And if Jesus is the King of the universe, Mary is also its Queen. 'And as Queen,' says the Abbot Rupert, 'she possesses, by right, the whole kingdom of her Son.'⁵ Hence St. Bernardine of Sienna concludes that 'as many creatures as there are who serve God, so many there are who serve Mary: for as angels and men, and all things that are in heaven and on earth, are subject to the empire of God, so are they also under the dominion of Mary.'⁶ The Abbot Guarricus, addressing himself to the Divine Mother on this subject, says: 'Continue, Mary, continue to dispose with confidence of the riches of thy Son; act as Queen, Mother, and Spouse of the King: for to thee belongs dominion and power over all creatures.'⁷

Mary, then, is a Queen: but, for our common consolation, be it known that she is a Queen so sweet, clement, and so ready to help us in our miseries, that the holy Church wills that we should salute her in this prayer under the title of Queen of Mercy. 'The title of Queen,' remarks B. Albert the Great, 'differs from that of Empress, which implies severity and rigour,

---

² Hæc autem Virgo in illo admirando consensu meruit dominum et primatum totius orbis.—Tom. iv. 90.

³ Nec a dominatione et petestate filii Mater potest esse sejuncta. Una est Mariæ et Christi caro.—De Laud. Virg.

⁴ Filii gloriam cum Matre non tam communem judico, quam eamdem.—Ib.

⁵ Prædicabitur de te quod sis . . . . Regina cœlorum totum jure possidens Filii regnum.—In Cant. l. 3.

⁶ Tot creaturæ serviunt gloriosæ Virgini, quot serviunt Trinitati ; omnes namque creaturæ, sive angeli sive homines, et omnia quæ sunt in cœlo et in terra, quæ omnia sunt divino imperio subjugata, gloriosæ Virgini sunt subjectæ.—Tom. iv. Serm. 5, de B.V. c. 6.

⁷ Perge, Maria, perge secura in bonis filii tui, fiducialiter age tamquam Regina, Mater regis et sponsa ; tibi debetur regnum et potestas.—Serm. 3, in Ass. B. M.

in signifying compassion and charity towards the poor.'
' The greatness of kings and queens,' says Seneca, ' consists in relieving the wretched ;'[8] and whereas tyrants,
when they reign, have their own good in view, kings
should have that of their subjects at heart. For this
reason it is that, at their consecration, kings have their
heads anointed with oil, which is the symbol of mercy,
to denote that, as kings, they should, above all things,
nourish in their hearts feelings of compassion and benevolence towards their subjects.

Kings should, then, occupy themselves principally
in works of mercy, but not so as to forget the just
punishments that are to be inflicted on the guilty. It
is, however, not thus with Mary, who, although a Queen,
is not a queen of justice, intent on the punishment of
the wicked, but a queen of mercy, intent only on commiserating and pardoning sinners. And this is the
reason for which the Church requires that we should
expressly call her ' the Queen of Mercy.' The great
Chancellor of Paris, John Gerson, in his Commentary
on the words of David : "These two things have I
heard, that power belongeth to God, and mercy to thee,
O Lord,"[9] says, that the kingdom of God, consisting in
justice and mercy, was divided by our Lord : the kingdom of justice He reserved for Himself, and that of
mercy He yielded to Mary, ordaining at the same time
that all mercies that are dispensed to men should pass
by the hands of Mary, and be disposed of by her at
will. These are Gerson's own words : ' the kingdom
of God consists in power and mercy ; reserving power
to Himself, He, in some way, yielded the empire of
mercy to His Mother.'[10] This is confirmed by St. Thomas,
in his Preface to the Canonical Epistles, saying, ' that

---

[8] Hoc reges habent magnificum, prodesse miseris.

[9] Duo hæc audivi, quia potestas Dei est, et tibi, Domine, misericordia.—
Ps. lxi. 12, 13.

[10] Regnum Dei consistit in potestate et misericordia : potestate Domino
remanente, cessit quodammodo misericordiæ pars Christi Matri sponsæque
regnanti.—*P.* 3, *Tr.* 4, *s. Magnif.*

when the Blessed Virgin conceived the Eternal Word
in her womb, and brought Him forth, she obtained
half the kingdom of God; so that she is Queen of
Mercy, as Jesus Christ is King of Justice.'[11]

The Eternal Father made Jesus Christ the King of
justice, and consequently universal Judge of the world:
and therefore the royal prophet sings: "Give to the
King Thy judgment, O God, and to the King's Son
Thy justice."[12] Here a learned interpreter takes up the
sentence, and says: ' O Lord, Thou hast given justice
to Thy Son, because Thou hast given mercy to the King's
Mother.' And, on this subject, St. Bonaventure, para-
phrasing the words of David, thus interprets them:
' Give to the King Thy judgment, O God, and Thy
mercy to the Queen His Mother.'[13] Ernest, Archbishop
of Prague, also remarks, ' that the Eternal Father gave
the office of judge and avenger to the Son, and that of
showing mercy and relieving the necessitous to the
Mother.'[14] This was foretold by the prophet David
himself; for he says that God (so to speak) consecrated
Mary Queen of mercy, anointing her with the oil of
gladness (" God hath anointed thee with the oil of
gladness").[15] In order that we miserable children of
Adam might rejoice, remembering that in heaven we
have this great Queen, overflowing with the unction of
mercy and compassion towards us; and thus we can
say with St. Bonaventure, ' O Mary, thou art full of
the unction of mercy and of the oil of compassion;'[16]
therefore God has anointed thee with the oil of gladness. And how beautifully does not B. Albert the
Great apply to this subject the history of Queen Esther,

[11] Quando filium Dei in utero concepit, et postmodum peperit, dimidiam
partem regni Dei impetravit, ut i sa sit Regina misericordiæ, ut Christus est
Rex justitiæ.
[12] Deus, judicium tuum Regi da, et justitiam tuam filio Regis.—*Ps.* lxxi. 2.
[13] Deus, judicium tuum Regi da, et misericordiam tuam Reginæ Matri ejus.
—*In Ps.* lxii. *de B. V.*
[14] Pater omne judicium dedit Filio, misericordiæ vero officium dedit Matri.
[15] Unxit te Deus oleo lætitiæ.—*Ps.* xliv. 8.
[16] Maria plena est unctione misericordiæ et cleo pietatis.—*Speculum B. M
Virg.* lect. 7.

who was herself a great type of our Queen Mary. We read, in the 4th chapter of the Book of Esther, that in the reign of Assuerus, a decree was issued, by which all Jews were condemned to death. Mardochai, who was one of the condemned, addressed himself to Esther, in order that she might interpose with Assuerus, and obtain the revocation of the decree, and thus be the salvation of all. At first Esther declined the office, fearing that such a request might irritate the king still more ; but Mardochai reproved her, sending her word that she was not to think only of saving herself, for God had placed her on the throne to obtain the salvation of all the Jews : "think not that thou mayst save thy life only, because thou art in the king's house, more than all the Jews."[17] Thus did Mardochai address Queen Esther. And so can we poor sinners address our Queen Mary, should she show any repugnance to obtain of God our delivery from the chastisement we have justly deserved : 'Think not, O Lady, that God has raised thee to the dignity of Queen of the world, only to provide for thy good ; but in order that, being so great, thou mightest be better able to compassionate and assist us miserable creatures.'

As soon as Assuerus saw Esther standing before him, he asked her, with love, what she came to seek. ' What is thy request ?' The queen replied, " If I have found favour in thy sight, O king, give me my people, for which I request."[18] Assuerus granted her request, and immediately ordered the revocation of the decree. And now, if Assuerus, through love for Esther, granted, at her request, salvation to the Jews, how can God refuse the prayers of Mary, loving her immensely as He does, when she prays for poor miserable sinners, who recommend themselves to her, and says to Him, ' My King and my God, if ever I have found favour in Thy

[17] Ne putes, quod animam tuam tantum liberes, quia in domo Regis es præ cunctis Judæis.—*Est.* iv. 13.

[18] Quæ est petitio tua ?... Dona mihi... populum meum pro quo obsecro. —*Esth.* c. vii. 2, 3.

sight' (though the Divine Mother well knows that she
was the blessed, the holy one, the only one of the
human race who found the grace lost by all mankind
well does she know that she is the beloved one of her
Lord, loved more than all the saints and angels together), ' give me my people for which I ask.'   If
thou lovest me, she says, ' give me, O Lord, these sinners, for whom I entreat Thee.' Is it possible that God
should refuse her? And who is ignorant of the power of
the prayers of Mary with God? "The law of clemency
is on her tongue."[19]   Each of her prayers is, as it were,
an established law for our Lord, that He should show
mercy to all for whom she intercedes. St. Bernard asks
why the Church calls Mary ' the Queen of Mercy'? And
he replies, that ' it is because we believe that she opens
the abyss of the mercy of God to whomsoever she wills,
when she wills, and as she wills ; so that there is no sinner, however great, who is lost if Mary protects him.'[20]

But perhaps we may fear that Mary would not deign
to interpose for some sinners, on account of their being
so overloaded with crimes? Or perhaps we ought to be
overawed at the majesty and holiness of this great Queen?
' No,' says St. Gregory the Seventh ; ' for the higher and
more holy she is, the greater is her sweetness and compassion towards sinners, who have recourse to her with
the desire to amend their lives.'[21]   Kings and queens,
with their ostentation of majesty, inspire terror, and
cause their subjects to fear to approach them : but what
fear, says St. Bernard, can the miserable have to approach this Queen of Mercy, for she inspires no terror,
and shows no severity, to those who come to her, but
is all sweetness and gentleness. ' Why should human
frailty fear to go to Mary? In her there is no austerity,

---

[19] Lex clementiæ in lingua ejus.—*Prov.* xxxi. 26.
[20] Quod divinæ pietatis abyssum, cui vult, quando vult, et quomodo vult,
creditur aperire ; ut quivis enormis peccator non pereat, cui sancta sanctorum patrocinii sui suffragia præstat.—*S. Bern. in Salve Reg.*
[21] Maria quanto altior et sanctior, tanto clementior et dulcior circa con-
versos peccatores.—Lib. i. Ep. 47.

nothing terrible : she is all sweetness, offering milk and wool to all.'[22] Mary is not only willing to give, but she herself offers milk and wool to all : the milk of mercy to animate our confidence, and the wool of her protection against the thunderbolts of Divine justice.

Suetonius[23] relates of the Emperor Titus that he could never refuse a favour, so much so that he sometimes promised more than he could grant, and when admonished of this he replied, that a prince should never send away any person whom he admitted to his audience dissatisfied. Titus spoke thus, but in reality he must often have deceived or failed in his promises. Our Queen cannot deceive, and can obtain all that she wills for her clients. Moreover, ' our Lord has given her so benign and compassionate a heart,' says Lanspergius, ' that she cannot send away anyone dissatisfied who prays to her.'[24] But how, to use the words of St. Bonaventure, canst thou, O Mary, who art the Queen of Mercy, refuse to succour the miserable ? And ' who,' asks the Saint, ' are the subjects for mercy, if not the miserable ? And since thou art the Queen of Mercy,' he continues, ' and I am the most miserable of sinners, it follows that I am the first of thy subjects. How, then, O Lady, canst thou do otherwise than exercise thy mercy on me ?'[25]

Have pity on us, then, O Queen of Mercy, and take charge of our salvation. ' Say not, O holy Virgin,' exclaims St. George of Nicomedia, ' that thou canst not assist us on account of the number of our sins, for thy power and compassion is such, that no number of sins, however great, can outweigh it. Nothing resists thy power, for our common Creator, honouring thee as His

[22] Quid ad Mariam accedere trepidet humana fragilitas ? Nihil austerum in ea, nihil terribile ; tota suavis est, omnibus offerens lac et lanam.—*Super Sign. Magn.*

[23] Tit. c. 8.

[24] Adeo feci eam . . . benignam, ut neminem a se redire tristem sinat.— *Op. Mix.* lib. i. *Alloq.* can. 12.

[25] Tu es Regina misericordiæ, et qui misericordiæ subditi nisi miseri ? Sed Regina misericordiæ es, et ego miserrimus peccatorum, subditorum maximus. Quemodo ergo, Domina, non exercebis in memetipsum tuæ miserationis effectum ? —*Stim Am.* p. 3, *in Salv. Reg.*

Mother, considering thy glory as His own;'[26] and the Son, ' exulting in it, fulfils thy petitions as if He were paying a debt;'[27] meaning thereby, that although Mary is under an infinite obligation to the Son for having chosen her to be His Mother, yet it cannot be denied but that the Son is under great obligation to her for having given Him His humanity ; and therefore Jesus, to pay as it were what He owes to Mary, and glorying in her glory, honours her in a special manner by listening to and granting all her petitions.

How great, then, should be our confidence in this Queen, knowing her great power with God, and that she is so rich and full of mercy, that there is no one living on the earth, who does not partake of her compassion and favour.   This was revealed by our Blessed Lady herself to St. Bridget, saying, ' I am the Queen of heaven and the Mother of Mercy; I am the joy of the just, and the door through which sinners are brought to God.   There is no sinner on earth so accursed as to be deprived of my mercy ; for all, if they receive nothing else through my intercession, receive the grace of being less tempted by the devils than they would otherwise have been;'[28] ' No one,' she adds, ' unless the irrevocable sentence has been pronounced' (that is, the one pronounced on the damned), ' is so cast off by God, that he will not return to Him, and enjoy His mercy, if he invokes my aid.'[29]   ' I am called by all the Mother of Mercy, and truly the mercy of my Son towards men has made me thus merciful towards them ;'[30] and she con-

[26] Habes insuperabilem potentiam ; habes vim inexpugnabilem. Ne rogo multa nostra peccata, immensam tuæ miserationis vim superent . . . Nihil enim resistit tuæ potentiæ . . . . quippe suam Filius tuus, tuam existimat gloriam.—*Or. de Ingressu B. V.*

[27] Eaque tanquam Filius exultans, postulata ceu debitor implet.—*Ib.*

[28] Ego Regina cœli, ego mater misericordiæ : ego justorum gaudium, et aditus peccatorum ad Deum.   Nullus est adeo maledictus, qui quamdiu vivit careat misericordia mea ; quia propter me levius tentatur a dæmonibus, quam alias tentaretur.—*Rev. lib. vi. cap. 10.*

[29] Nullus ita alienatus est de Deo, nisi omnino fuerit maledictus, qui, si me invocaverit, non revertatur ad Deum, et habebit misericordiam.—*Ib.*

[30] Ego vocor ab omnibus mater misericordiæ, vere filia misericordia Filii mei misericordem me fecit.—*Rev. lib. ii. cap. 23.*

cludes by saying, 'and therefore miserable will he be, and miserable will he be to all eternity, who, in this life, having it in his power to invoke me, who am so compassionate to all, and so desirous to assist sinners, is miserable enough not to invoke me, and so is damned.'[31]

Let us, then, fly, and fly always, to the feet of this most sweet Queen, if we would be certain of salvation ; and if we are alarmed and disheartened at the sight of our sins, let us remember that it is in order to save the greatest and most abandoned sinners, who recommend themselves to her, that Mary is made the Queen of Mercy. Such have to be her crown in heaven ; according to the words addressed to her by her Divine Spouse : " Come from Libanus, my spouse ; come from Libanus, come : thou shalt be crowned . . . . . from the dens of the lions, from the mountains of the leopards."[32]   And what are these dens of beasts, but miserable sinners, whose souls have become the home of sin, the most frightful monster that can be found. 'With such souls,' says the Abbot Rupert, addressing our Blessed Lady, ' saved by thy means, O great Queen Mary, wilt thou be crowned in heaven ; for their salvation will form a diadem worthy of, and well becoming, a Queen of Mercy.'[33] On this subject read the following

EXAMPLE.

We read, in the life of Sister Catherine of St. Augustine, that in the place where she resided, there was a woman, of the name of Mary, who in her youth was a sinner, and in her old age continued so obstinate in wickedness, that she was driven out of the city, and reduced to live in a secluded cave ; there she died, half consumed by disease, and without the sacraments, and

---

[31] Ideo miser erit, qui ad misericordiam, cum possit, non accedit.—*Rev.* lib. ii. cap. 23.

[32] Veni de Libano, sponsa mea, veni de Libano, veni, coronaberis . . . . de cubilibus leonum, de montibus pardorum.— *Cant.* iv. 8.

[33] De talium leonum cubilibus taliorumque pardorum montibus tu, amica mea, coronaberis . . . Eorum salus corona tua erit.– *In Cant.* lib. iii.

was consequently interred in a field like a beast. Sister Catherine, who always recommended the souls of those who departed from this world, with great fervour, to God, on hearing the unfortunate end of this poor old woman, never thought of praying for her, and she looked upon her (as did everyone else) as irrevocably lost. One day, four years afterwards, a suffering soul appeared to her, and exclaimed : ' How unfortunate is my lot, Sister Catherine ! thou recommendest the souls of all those that die to God : on my soul alone thou hast not compassion.' ' And who art thou ?' asked the servant of God. ' I am,' she replied, ' that poor Mary, who died in the cave.' ' And art thou saved ?' said Catherine. ' Yes,' she answered, ' by the mercy of the Blessed Virgin Mary.' ' And how ?' ' When I saw myself at the point of death, loaded with sins, and abandoned by all, I had recourse to the Mother of God, saying, Lady, thou art the refuge of abandoned creatures : behold me, at this moment, abandoned by all ; thou art my only hope ; thou alone canst help me : have pity on me. The Blessed Virgin obtained me the grace to make an act of contrition. I died, and am saved ; and besides this, she, my Queen, obtained that my purgatory should be shortened, by enduring, in intensity, that which otherwise would have lasted for many years : I now only want a few masses to be entirely delivered ; I beg thee to get them said ; and on my part, I promise always to pray for thee to God and to Mary.' Sister Catherine immediately had the masses said ; and after a few days that soul again appeared to her, shining like the sun, and said : ' I thank thee, Catherine : behold, I go to Paradise, to sing the mercies of my God, and to pray for thee.'

PRAYER.

O, Mother of my God, and my Lady Mary : as a beggar, all wounded and sore, presents himself before a great queen, so do I present myself before thee, who art the Queen of heaven and earth. From the lofty throne on which thou sittest, disdain not, I implore thee, to cast thine eyes on me, a poor sinner. God has made thee so rich that thou mightest assist the poor, and has constituted thee Queen of Mercy in order that thou mightest relieve the miserable. Behold me then, and pity me : behold me, and abandon me not, until thou seest me changed from a sinner into a saint. I know well that I merit nothing ; nay more, that I deserve, on account of my ingratitude, to be deprived of the graces that, through thy means, I have already received from God. But thou, who art the Queen of Mercy, seekest not merits, but miseries, in order to help the needy. But who is more needy than I ?

O, exalted Virgin, well do I know that thou, who art Queen of the universe, art already my queen ; yet am I determined to dedicate myself more especially to thy service, in order that thou mayest dispose of me as thou pleasest. Therefore do I address thee in the words of St. Bonaventure :[34] 'Do thou govern me, O my Queen, and leave me not to myself.' Command me ; employ me as thou wilt, and chastise me when I do not obey ; for the chastisements that come from thy hands will to me be pledges of salvation. I value more the being thy servant than being ruler of the earth. " I am thine ; save me."[35] Accept me, O Mary, for thine own, and as thine, take charge of my salvation. I will no longer be mine ; to thee do I give myself. If, during the time past I have served thee ill, and lost so many occasions of honouring thee, for the future I will be one of thy most loving and faithful servants. I am determined that from this day forward no one shall surpass me in honouring and loving thee, my most amiable Queen. This I promise ; and this, with thy help, I hope to execute. Amen.

[34] Domina, me totaliter tuæ dominationi committo, ut me plenarie regas et gubernes. Non mihi me relinquas.—*In Salve Reg.*
[35] Tuus sum ego, salvum me fac.—*Ps.* cxviii. 94.

SECTION II. *How much our confidence in Mary should be increased from the fact of her being our Mother.*

It is not without a meaning, or by chance, that Mary's clients call her Mother ; and indeed they seem unable to invoke her under any other name, and never tire of calling her Mother. Mother, yes ! for she is truly our Mother ; not indeed carnally, but spiritually ; of our souls and of our salvation. Sin, by depriving our souls of Divine grace, deprived them also of life. Jesus our Redeemer, with an excess of mercy and love, came to restore this life by His own death on the cross, as He Himself declared : " I am come that they may have life, and may have it more abundantly."[1] He says more abundantly ; for, according to theologians, the benefit of redemption far exceeded the injury done by Adam's sin. So that by reconciling us with God He made Himself the Father of Souls in the law of grace, as it was foretold by the prophet Isaias : " He shall be called the Father of the world to come, the Prince of Peace."[2] But if Jesus is the Father of our Souls, Mary is also their Mother ; for she, by giving us Jesus, gave us true life ; and afterwards, by offering the life of her Son on Mount Calvary for our salvation, she brought us forth to the life of grace.

On two occasions, then, according to the holy Fathers, Mary became our spiritual Mother. And the first, according to Blessed Albert the Great,[3] was when she merited to conceive in her virginal womb the Son of God. St. Bernardine of Sienna says the same thing more distinctly, for he tells us, ' that when at the Annunciation the most Blessed Virgin gave the consent which was expected by the Eternal Word before becoming her Son, she from that moment asked our salvation of God with intense ardour, and took it to heart

[1] Veni, ut vitam habeant, et abundantius habeant.—*Joan.* x. 10.
[2] Pater futuri sæculi, princeps pacis.—*Is.* ix. 6.
[3] De Laud. B. M. l. 6, c. 1.

in such a way, that from that moment, as a most loving mother, she bore us in her womb.'[4] In the second chapter of St. Luke, the Evangelist, speaking of the birth of our Blessed Redeemer, says that Mary " brought forth her first-born son."[5] Then, remarks an author, ' since the Evangelist asserts that on this occasion the most Holy Virgin brought forth her first-born, must we suppose that she had afterwards other children?' But then he replies to his own question, saying, ' that as it is of faith that Mary had no other children according to the flesh than Jesus, she must have had other spiritual children, and we are those children.'[6] This was revealed by our Lord to St. Gertrude,[7] who was one day reading the above text, and was perplexed and could not understand how Mary, being only the Mother of Jesus, could be said to have brought forth her first-born. God explained it to her, saying, that Jesus was Mary's first-born according to the flesh, but that all mankind were her second-born according to the Spirit.

From what has been said, we can understand that passage of the sacred Canticles : " Thy belly is like a heap of wheat, set about with lilies,"[8] and which applies to Mary. And it is explained by St. Ambrose, who says : ' That although in the most pure womb of Mary there was but one grain of corn, which was Jesus Christ, yet it is called a heap of wheat, because all the elect were virtually contained in it ;'[9] and as Mary was also to be their Mother, in bringing forth Jesus, He was truly and is called the first-born of many brethren. And the

---

[4] Virgo per hunc consensum in Incarnatione filii omnium electorum salutem vigorosissime expetiit et procuravit : et omnium saluti et eorum salvationi per hunc consensum se singularissime dedicavit ; ita ut ex tunc omnes in suis visceribus bajularet, tanquam verissima mater filios suos.—*Tr. de B. V. Serm.* viii

[5] Peperit filium suum primogenitum.—*Luc.* ii. 7.

[6] Si primogenitus, ergo alii filii secuti sunt secundogeniti . . . . Carnales nullos habuit Beata Virgo præter Christum ; ergo spirituales habeat necesse est.—*Spann. Polyanth.* litt. m. t. 6.

[7] Insin. l. 4, c. 3.

[8] Venter tuus sicut acervus tritici vallatus liliis.—*Cant.* vii. 2.

[9] In quo virginis utero . . . acervus tritici . . . germinabat ; quoniam . . . granum tritici generabat . . . Sed . . . de uno grano tritici acervus est factus —*S. Ambr. de Instit. Virg.*

Abbot St. William writes in the same sense, saying, 'that Mary, in bringing forth Jesus, our Saviour and our Life, brought forth many unto salvation; and by giving birth to Life itself, she gave life to many.'[10]

The second occasion on which Mary became our spiritual Mother, and brought us forth to the life of grace, was when she offered to the Eternal Father the life of her beloved Son on Mount Calvary, with such bitter sorrow and suffering. So that St. Augustine declares, that 'as she then coöperated by her love in the birth of the faithful to the life of grace, she became the spiritual Mother of all who are members of the one Head, Christ Jesus.'[11] This we are given to understand by the following verse of the sacred Canticles, and which refers to the most Blessed Virgin: "They have made me the keeper in the vineyards; my vineyard I have not kept."[12] St. William says, that 'Mary, in order that she might save many souls, exposed her own to death;'[13] meaning, that to save us, she sacrificed the life of her Son. And who but Jesus was the soul of Mary? He was her life, and all her love. And therefore the prophet Simeon foretold that a sword of sorrow would one day transpierce her own most blessed soul.[14] And it was precisely the lance which transpierced the side of Jesus, who was the soul of Mary. Then it was that this most Blessed Virgin brought us forth by her sorrows to eternal life: and thus we can all call ourselves the children of the sorrows of Mary. Our most loving Mother was always, and in all, united to the will of God. 'And therefore,' says St. Bonaventure, 'when she saw the love of the Eternal Father towards men to be so great that, in order to save them, He willed the

[10] In illo uno fructu, in uno Salvatore omnium Jesu plurimos Maria peperit ad salutem. Pariendo vitam, multos peperit ad vitam.—*Delrio in Cant.* iv. 13.

[11] Plane mater membrorum ejus (quod nos sumus) quia cooperata est charitate, ut fideles in Ecclesia nascerentur.—*De S. Virginitate,* cap vi.

[12] Posuit me custodem in vineis; vineam meam non custodivi.—*Cant.* i 5.

[13] Ut multas animas salvas faceret, animam suam morti exposuit. -*Delrio in Cant.* i. 6.

[14] Et tuam ipsius animam pertransibit gladius —*Luc.* ii 35.

death of His Son ; and, on the other hand, seeing the love of the Son in wishing to die for us : in order to conform herself to this excessive love of both the Father and the Son towards the human race, she also with her entire will offered, and consented to, the death of her Son, in order that we might be saved.'[15]

It is true that, according to the prophecy of Isaias, Jesus, in dying for the redemption of the human race, chose to be alone. " I have trodden the winepress alone ;"[16] but, seeing the ardent desire of Mary to aid in the salvation of man, He disposed it so that she, by the sacrifice and offering of the life of her Jesus, should coöperate in our salvation, and thus become the Mother of our souls. This our Saviour signified, when, before expiring, He looked down from the cross on His Mother and on the disciple St. John, who stood at its foot, and, first addressing Mary, He said, " Behold thy Son ;"[17] as it were saying, Behold, the whole human race, which by the offer thou makest of My life for the salvation of all, is even now being born to the life of grace. Then, turning to the disciple, He said, " Behold thy Mother."[18] ' By these words,' says St. Bernardine of Sienna, ' Mary, by reason of the love she bore them, became the Mother, not only of St. John, but of all men.'[19] And Silveira remarks, that St. John himself, in stating this fact in his Gospel, says : " Then He said to the disciple, Behold thy Mother." Here observe well that Jesus Christ did not address Himself to John, but to the disciple, in order to show that He then gave Mary to all who are His disciples, that is to say, to all Christians, that she might be their Mother. ' John is but the name of one, whereas the word disciple is applicable to all ; therefore

[15] Nullo modo dubitandum est, quin Mariæ animus voluerit etiam tradere filium suum pro salute generis humani, ut mater per omnia conformis fieret Patri et Filio.—*S. Bon. in Sent.* lib. i. d. 48, a. 2, q. 2.

[16] Torcular calcavi solus.—*Is.* lxiii. 3.

[17] Ecce filius tuus.—*Joan.* xix. 26.

[18] Deinde dicit discipulo : Ecce mater tua.—*Joan.* xix. 27.

[19] In Joanne intelligimus omnes, quorum B. Virgo per dilectionem facta est Mater.—Tom. i. Serm. 51.

our Lord makes use of a name common to all, to show that Mary was given as a Mother to all.'[20]

The Church applies to Mary these words of the sacred Canticles : " I am the mother of fair love ;"[21] and a commentator explaining them, says, that the Blessed Virgin's love renders our souls beautiful in the sight of God, and also makes her as a most loving mother receive us as her children, ' she being all love towards those whom she has thus adopted.'[22] And what mother, exclaims St. Bonaventure, loves her children, and attends to their welfare, as thou lovest us and carest for us, O most sweet Queen ! ' For dost thou not love us and seek our welfare far more without comparison than any earthly mother ?'[23] O, blessed are they who live under the protection of so loving and powerful a mother ! The prophet David, although she was not yet born, sought salvation from God by dedicating himself as a son of Mary, and thus prayed : " Save the son of thy handmaid."[24] ' Of what handmaid ?' asks St. Augustine ; and he replies : ' Of her who said, Behold the handmaid of the Lord.'[25] ' And who,' says Cardinal Bellarmine, ' would ever dare to snatch these children from the bosom of Mary, when they have taken refuge there ? What power of hell, or what temptation, can overcome them, if they place their confidence in the patronage of this great Mother, the Mother of God, and of them ?'[26] There are some who say that when the whale sees its young in danger, either from tempests or pursuers, it opens its mouth and swallows them. This

[20] Joannes nomen est particulare . . . discipulus nomen est commune, utitur ergo hic nomine communi omnibus, ut denotetur, quod ipsa Virgo Maria omnibus dabatur in matrem.—*In Evang.* lib. viii. cap. 17, quæst. 14.

[21] Ego mater pulchræ dilectionis.—*Eccles.* xxiv. 24.

[22] Quia tota est amor erga nos quos in filios recepit.—*Pacciuch. in Ps.* lxxxvi. exc. 22.

[23] Nonne plus sine comparatione nos diligis, ac bonum nostrum procuras, amplius quam mater carnalis?—*In Salv. Reg.*

[24] Salvum fac filium ancillæ tuæ.—*Ps.* lxxxv. 16.

[25] Cujus ancillæ . . . . quæ ait, Ecce ancilla Domini.—*In Ps.* lxxxv.

[26] Quam bene nobis erit sub præsidio tantæ Matris ? Quis nos detrahere audebit de sinu ejus ? Quæ nos tentatio, quæ tribulatio superare poterit, confidentes in patrocinio Matris Dei et nostræ?—*Bellarm. de Sept. Verb.* 1, i. c. 12.

is precisely what Novarinus asserts of Mary : ' When the storms of temptations rage, the most compassionate Mother of the faithful, with maternal tenderness, protects them as it were in her own bosom until she has brought them into the harbour of salvation.'[27]   O most loving Mother ! O most compassionate Mother ! be thou ever blessed ; and ever blessed be God, who has given thee to us for our Mother, and for a secure refuge in all the dangers of this life.   Our Blessed Lady herself, in a vision addressed these words to St. Bridget : ' As a mother on seeing her son in the midst of the swords of his enemies would use every effort to save him, so do I, and will do for all sinners who seek my mercy.'[28] Thus it is that in every engagement with the infernal powers we shall always certainly conquer by having recourse to the Mother of God, who is also our Mother, saying and repeating again and again : ' We fly to thy patronage, O holy Mother of God : we fly to thy patronage, O holy Mother of God.'   O, how many victories have not the faithful gained over hell, by having recourse to Mary with this short but most powerful prayer !   Thus it was that that great servant of God, Sister Mary the Crucified, of the Order of St. Benedict, always overcame the devils.

Be of good heart, then, all you who are children of Mary.   Remember that she accepts as her children all those who choose to be so.   Rejoice !   Why do you fear to be lost, when such a Mother defends and protects you ?   'Say, then, O my soul, with great confidence : I will rejoice and be glad ; for whatever the judgment to be pronounced on me may be, it depends on and must come from my Brother and Mother.'[29]   ' Thus,'

[27] Fidelium piissima Mater, furente tentationum tempestate, materno affectu eos velut intra viscera propria receptos protegit, donec in beatum portum reponat.—V. cap. xiv. exc. 81.†

[28] Ita ego facio, et faciam omnibus peccatoribus misericordiam meam a filio meo petentibus.—Rev. lib. iv. cap. 138.

[29] Dic, anima mea, cum magna fiducia : exultabo et lætabor, quia quicquid judicabitur de me, pendet ex sententia fratris et matris meæ.—S. Bonav. Solil. c. 1.

says St. Bonaventure, 'it is that each one who loves
this good Mother, and relies on her protection, should
animate himself to confidence, remembering that Jesus
is our Brother, and Mary our Mother.' The same thought
makes St. Anselm cry out with joy, and encourage us,
saying : ' O, happy confidence !   O, safe refuge ! the
Mother of God is my Mother.   How firm, then, should
be our confidence, since our salvation depends on the
judgment of a good Brother and a tender Mother !'[30]   It
is, then, our Mother who calls us, and says, in these
words of the Book of Proverbs : " He that is a little
one, let him turn to me."[31]   Children have always on
their lips their mother's name, and in every fear, in
every danger, they immediately cry out, Mother, mother !
Ah, most sweet Mary ! ah, most loving Mother ! this
is precisely what thou desirest : that we should become
children, and call on thee in every danger, and at all
times have recourse to thee, because thou desirest to
help and save us, as thou hast saved all who have had
recourse to thee.

EXAMPLE.

In the history of the foundations of the Society of
Jesus in the kingdom of Naples,[32] we read the following
account of a young Scotch nobleman, named William
Elphinstone.   He was related to king James, and lived
for some time in the heresy in which he was born.   Enlightened by Divine grace, he began to perceive his
errors, and having gone to France, with the help of a
good Jesuit father, who was also a Scotchman, and still
more by the intercession of the Blessed Virgin, he at
length discovered the truth, abjured his heresy, and became a Catholic.   From France he went to Rome ; and
there a friend, finding him one day weeping and in great
affliction, inquired the cause of his grief.   He replied,

---

[30] O beata fiducia, O tutum refugium ! Mater Dei est Mater nostra . . . Qua
igitur certitudine debemus sperare . . . quorum sive salus sive damnatio, de
boni fratris et de piæ matris pendent arbitrio ?—*Or*. li. *ad B. V.*
[31] Si quis est parvulus, veniat ad me.—*Prov*. ix. 4.   [32] *Lib*. v. c. 7.

that during the night his mother, who was lost, appeared to him, and said : 'It is well for thee, son, that thou hast entered the true Church ; for as I died in heresy, I am lost.' From that moment he redoubled his devotion towards Mary, choosing her for his only Mother, and by her he was inspired with the thought of embracing the religious state, and he bound himself to do so by vow. Being in delicate health, he went to Naples for change of air, and there it was the will of God that he should die, and die as a religious ; for shortly after his arrival, finding himself at the last extremity, by his prayers and tears he moved the superiors to accept him, and in presence of the most Blessed Sacrament, when he received it as viaticum, he pronounced his vows, and was declared a member of the Society of Jesus. After this it was most touching to hear with what tenderness he thanked his Mother Mary for having snatched him from heresy, and led him to die in the true Church, and in the house of God, surrounded by his religious brethren. This made him exclaim : ' O, how glorious is it to die in the midst of so many angels !' When exhorted to repose a little, ' Ah,' he replied, 'this is no time for repose, now that I am at the close of my life.' Before expiring, he said to those who surrounded him : ' Brothers, do you not see the angels of Heaven here present who assist me ?' One of the religious having heard him mutter some words, asked him what he said. He replied, that his guardian angel had revealed to him that he would remain but a very short time in purgatory, and that he would soon go to heaven. He then entered into a colloquy with his sweet Mother Mary, and like a child that abandons itself to rest in the arms of its mother, he exclaimed, ' *Mother, mother!*' and sweetly expired. Shortly afterwards a devout religious learnt by revelation that he was already in heaven.

PRAYER.

O most holy Mother Mary, how is it possible that

I, having so holy a Mother, should be so wicked? a Mother all burning with the love of God, and I loving creatures; a Mother so rich in virtue, and I so poor? Ah, amiable Mother, it is true that I do not deserve any longer to be thy son, for by my wicked life I have rendered myself unworthy of so great an honour. I am satisfied that thou shouldst accept me for thy servant; and in order to be admitted amongst the vilest of them, I am ready to renounce all the kingdoms of the world. Yes, I am satisfied. But still thou must not forbid me to call thee Mother. This name consoles and fills me with tenderness, and reminds me of my obligation to love thee. This name excites me to great confidence in thee. When my sins and the Divine justice fill me most with consternation, I am all consoled at the thought that thou art my Mother. Allow me then to call thee Mother, my most amiable Mother. Thus do I call thee, and thus will I always call thee. Thou, after God, must be my hope, my refuge, my love, in this valley of tears. Thus do I hope to die, breathing forth my soul into thy holy hands, and saying, My Mother, my Mother Mary, help me, have pity on me! Amen.

SECTION III. *On the greatness of the love which this Mother bears us.*

Since Mary is our Mother, we may consider how great is the love she bears us; love towards our children is a necessary impulse of nature; and St. Thomas[1] says that this is the reason why the Divine law imposes on children the obligation of loving their parents; but gives no express command that parents should love their children, for nature itself has so strongly implanted it in all creatures, that, as St. Ambrose remarks, 'we know that a mother will expose herself to danger for her chil-

[1] De Dil. Chr. c. 13.

dren,'[2] and even the most savage beasts cannot do otherwise than love their young.[3] It is said that even tigers, on hearing the cry of their cubs taken by hunters, will go into the sea and swim until they reach the vessel in which they are. Since the very tigers, says our most loving Mother Mary, cannot forget their young, how can I forget to love you, my children? And even, she adds, were such a thing possible as that a mother should forget to love her child, it is not possible that I should cease to love a soul that has become my child : " Can a woman forget her infant, so as not to have pity on the son of her womb? And if she should forget, yet will I not forget thee."[4] Mary is our Mother, not, as we have already observed, according to the flesh, but by love ; " I am the Mother of fair love ;"[5] hence it is the love only that she bears us that makes her our Mother ; and therefore some one remarks, ' that she glories in being a Mother of love, because she is all love towards us whom she has adopted for her children.'[6] And who can ever tell the love that Mary bears us miserable creatures? Arnold of Chartres tells us that ' at the death of Jesus Christ, she desired with immense ardour to die with her Son, for love of us ;'[7] so much so, adds St. Ambrose, that whilst ' her Son hung on the cross, Mary offered herself to the executioners,'[8] to give her life for us.

But let us consider the reasons of this love ; for then we shall be better able to understand how much this good Mother loves us. The first reason for the great love that Mary bears to men, is the great love that she

[2] Scimus quia mater pro filiis se offert periculo.—L. vi. Exp. Ev. 4.

[3] Natura hoc bestiis infundit, ut catulos proprios ament. — *S. Ambros. Exam.* l. 6, c. 4.

[4] Numquid oblivisci potest mulier infantem suum, ut non misereatur filio uteri sui? Et si illa oblita fuerit, ego tamen non obliviscar tui.—*Is.* xlix. 15.

[5] Ego mater pulchræ dilectionis.—*Eccles.* xxiv. 24.

[6] Se dilectionis esse matrem merito gloriatur, quia tota est amor erga nos, quos in filios recepit.—*Pacciuch. in Ps.* 86, *Exc.* xxii. n. 5.

[7] Optabat quidem ipsa, ad sanguinem animæ, et carnis suæ addere sanguinem . . . . et cum Domino Jesu corporali morte redemptionis nostræ consummare mysterium.—*De sept. verb. Dom.*

[8] Pendebat in cruce filius, mater persecutoribus se offerebat.—*De Inst. Virg.* c. 7.

bears to God; love towards God and love towards our
neighbour belong to the same commandment, as expressed by St. John: "this commandment we have
from God, that he who loveth God, love also his brother;"[9] so that as the one becomes greater the other
also increases. What have not the Saints done for their
neighbour in consequence of their love towards God!
Read only the account of the labours of St. Francis
Xavier in the Indies, where, in order to aid the souls
of these poor barbarians and bring them to God, he
exposed himself to a thousand dangers, clambering
amongst the mountains, and seeking out these poor
creatures in the caves in which they dwelt like wild
beasts. See a St. Francis of Sales, who, in order to
convert the heretics of the province of Chablais, risked
his life every morning, for a whole year, crawling on
his hands and feet over a frozen beam, in order that he
might preach to them on the opposite side of a river;
a St. Paulinus, who delivered himself up as a slave,
in order that he might obtain liberty for the son of a
poor widow; a St. Fidelis, who, in order to draw the
heretics of a certain place to God, persisted in going to
preach to them, though he knew it would cost him
his life. The Saints, then, because they loved God
much, did much for their neighbour: but who ever
loved God as much as Mary? She loved Him more
in the first moment of her existence than all the
saints and angels ever loved Him, or will love Him;
but this we shall explain at length, when treating of
her virtues. Our Blessed Lady herself revealed to
Sister Mary the Crucified, that the fire of love with
which she was inflamed towards God was such, that if
the heavens and earth were placed in it, they would be
instantly consumed; so that the ardours of the seraphim,
in comparison with it, were but as fresh breezes. And
as amongst all the blessed spirits, there is not one that

---

9 Hoc mandatum habemus a Deo, ut qui diligit Deum, diligat et fratrem
suum.—1 *Joan.* iv. 21.

loves God more than Mary, so we neither have nor can have anyone who, after God, loves us as much as this most loving Mother; and if we concentrate all the love that mothers bear their children, husbands and wives one another, all the love of angels and saints for their clients, it does not equal the love of Mary towards a single soul. Father Nieremberg[10] says that the love that all mothers have ever had for their children is but a shadow in comparison with the love that Mary bears to each one of us; and he adds, that she alone loves us more than all the angels and saints put together.

Moreover, our Mother loves us much, because we were recommended to her by her beloved Jesus, when He before expiring said to her, "Woman, behold thy son!" for we were all represented in the person of St. John, as we have already observed: these were His last words; and the last recommendations left before death by persons we love are always treasured and never forgotten. But again, we are exceedingly dear to Mary on account of the sufferings we cost her; mothers generally love those children most, the preservation of whose lives has cost them the most suffering and anxiety; we are those children for whom Mary, in order to obtain for us the life of grace, was obliged to endure the bitter agony of herself offering her beloved Jesus to die an ignominious death, and had also to see Him expire before her own eyes in the midst of the most cruel and unheard-of torments. It was then by this great offering of Mary that we were born to the life of grace; we are therefore her very dear children, since we cost her so great suffering. And thus, as it is written of the love of the Eternal Father towards men, in giving His own Son to death for us, that "God so loved the world as to give His only-begotten Son."[11] 'So also,' says St.

---

[10] *De Aff. erga B. V.* c. 14.
[11] Sic Deus dilexit mundum, ut filium suum unigenitum daret.—*Joan.* iii. 16.

Bonaventure, 'we can say of Mary, that she has so loved us as to give her only-begotten Son for us.'[12] And when did she give Him? She gave Him, says Father Nieremberg,[13] when she granted Him permission to deliver Himself up to death; she gave Him, when, others neglecting to do so, either out of hatred or from fear, she might herself have pleaded for the life of her Son before the judges; and well may it be supposed that the words of so wise and loving a mother would have had great weight, at least with Pilate, and might have prevented him from sentencing a man to death whom he knew and had declared to be innocent.   But no, Mary would not say a word in favour of her Son, lest she might prevent that death on which our salvation depended.   Finally, she gave Him a thousand and a thousand times, during the three hours preceding His death, and which she spent at the foot of the cross; for during the whole of that time she unceasingly offered, with the extreme of sorrow and the extreme of love, the life of her Son in our behalf, and this with such constancy, that St. Anselm and St. Antoninus[14] say, that if executioners had been wanting, she herself would have crucified Him, in order to obey the Eternal Father, who willed His death for our salvation.   If Abraham had such fortitude as to be ready to sacrifice with his own hands the life of his son, with far greater fortitude would Mary (far more holy and obedient than Abraham) have sacrificed the life of hers.   But let us return to the consideration of the gratitude we owe to Mary for so great an act of love as was the painful sacrifice of the life of her Son, which she made to obtain eternal salvation for us all.   God abundantly rewarded Abraham for the sacrifice he was prepared to make of his son Isaac; but we, what return can we make to Mary for the life of her Jesus, a Son far more noble and beloved than the

---

[12] Sic Maria dilexit nos, ut filium suum unigenitum daret. †
[13] Ut sup.
[14] P. 4. t. 15. c. 41. § 1.

son of Abraham? 'This love of Mary,' says St. Bonaventure, 'has indeed obliged us to love her; for we see
that she has surpassed all others in love towards us,
since she has given her only Son, whom she loved more
than herself, for us.'[15]

From this arises another motive for the love of Mary
towards us; for in us she beholds that which has been
purchased at the price of the death of Jesus Christ. If
a mother knew that a servant had been ransomed by a
beloved son at the price of twenty years of imprison-
ment and suffering, how greatly would she esteem that
servant, if on this account alone! Mary well knows
that her Son came into the world only to save us poor
creatures, as He Himself protested, "I am come to save
that which was lost."[16] And to save us He was pleased
even to lay down His life for us, "having become obedient unto death."[17] If, then, Mary loved us but little,
she would show that she valued but little the blood of
her Son, which was the price of our salvation. To St.
Elizabeth of Hungary it was revealed, that Mary, from
the time she dwelt in the Temple, did nothing but pray
for us, begging that God would hasten the coming of
His Son into the world to save us. And how much
more must we suppose that she loves us, now that she
has seen that we are valued to such a degree by her
Son, that He did not disdain to purchase us at such a
cost. And because all men have been redeemed by
Jesus, therefore Mary loves and protects them all. It
was she who was seen by St. John in the Apocalypse,
clothed with the sun: "And a great sign appeared in
heaven: a woman clothed with the sun."[18] She is said
to be clothed with the sun, because as there is no one
on earth who can be hidden from the heat of the sun—

[15] Nulla post eam creatura ita per amorem nostrum exardescet, quæ filium suum unicum, quem multo plus se amavit, nobis dedit, et pro nobis obtulit.—
S. Bonav. de B.V.M. s. 1.

[16] Salvum facere quod perierat.—*Luc.* xix. 10.

[17] Factus obediens usque ad mortem.—*Phil.* ii. 8.

Et signum magnum apparuit in cœlo, mulier amicta sole.—*Apoc.* xii. 1

"There is no one that can hide himself from his heat"[19] —so there is no one living who can be deprived of the love of Mary. "From its heat," that is, as blessed Raymond Jordano applies the words, 'from the love of Mary.'[20] 'And who,' exclaims St. Antoninus, 'can ever form an idea of the tender care that this most loving Mother takes of all of us,'[21] 'offering and dispensing her mercy to everyone;'[22] for our good Mother desired the salvation of all, and coöperated in obtaining it. 'It is evident,' says St. Bernard, 'that she was solicitous for the whole human race.'[23] Hence the custom of some of Mary's clients, spoken of by Cornelius à Lapide, and which consists in asking our Lord to grant them the graces that our Blessed Lady seeks for them, succeeds most advantageously: they say, Lord, grant me that which the most Blessed Virgin Mary asks for me. 'And no wonder,' adds the same writer, 'for our Mother desires for us better things than we can possibly desire ourselves.'[24] The devout Bernardine da Busto says, that Mary 'loves to do us good, and dispense graces to us far more than we to receive them.'[25] On this subject Blessed Albert the Great applies to Mary the words of the Book of Wisdom: "She preventeth them that covet her, so that she first showeth herself unto them."[26] Mary anticipates those who have recourse to her by making them find her before they seek her. 'The love that this good Mother bears us is so great,' says Richard of St. Lawrence, 'that as soon as she perceives our wants, she comes to our assistance. She comes before she is called.'[27]

[19] Non est qui se abscondit a calore ejus.—*Ps.* xviii. 7.
[20] A calore ejus, id est a dilectione Mariæ.—*Contempl. de V.M.* in prol.
[21] Oh quanta est cura B. Virgini matri de nobis!—Tom. iv. Tit. 15, c. 2.
[22] Omnibus aperit sinum misericordiæ suæ.—Ibid.
[23] Constat pro universo genere humano fuisse sollicitam.—*In Assump. B.M.* Serm. iv.
[24] Ipsa enim majora optat, quam nos optare possumus. †
[25] Plus enim desiderat ipsa facere tibi bonum et largiri aliquam gratiam, quam tu accipere concupiscas.—*Marial.* P. ii. *Serm.* 5, *de Nat. B.V.*
[26] Præoccupat qui se concupiscunt, ut illis se prior ostendat.—*Sap.* vi. 14.
[27] Velocius occurrit ejus pietas quam invocetur.—*Exp. in Cant.* c. xxiii.

And now, if Mary is so good to all, even to the ungrateful and negligent, who love her but little, and seldom have recourse to her, how much more loving will she be to those who love her and often call upon her! "She is easily found by them that seek her."[28] 'O, how easy,' adds the same Blessed Albert, 'is it for those who love Mary to find her, and to find her full of compassion and love!' In the words of the Book of Proverbs, "I love them that love me,"[29] she protests that she cannot do otherwise than love those who love her. And although this most loving Lady loves all men as her children, yet, says St. Bernard, 'she recognises and loves,'[30] that is, she loves in a more special manner, those who love her more tenderly. Blessed Raymond Jordano asserts that these happy lovers of Mary are not only loved but even served by her; for he says that those who find the most Blessed Virgin Mary, find all; for she loves those who love her, nay more, she serves those who serve her.[31]

In the chronicles of the Order of St. Dominic it is related that one of the friars named Leonard used to recommend himself two hundred times a day to this Mother of Mercy, and that when he was attacked by his last illness, he saw a most beautiful queen by his side, who thus addressed him : ' Leonard, wilt thou die, and come and dwell with my Son and with me ?' ' And who art thou ?' he replied. ' I am,' said the most Blessed Virgin, for she it was, ' I am the Mother of Mercy : thou hast so many times invoked me, behold, I am now come to take thee ; let us go together to Paradise.' On the same day Leonard died, and, as we trust, followed her to the kingdom of the blessed.

' Ah, most sweet Mary !' exclaimed the venerable brother John Berchmans, of the Society of Jesus, 'blessed

[28] Facile . . . . invenitur ab his qui quærunt illam.—*Sap.* vi. 13.
[29] Ego diligentes me diligo.—*Prov.* viii. 17.
[30] *In Salve Reg.* s. 1.
[31] Inventa . . . Virgine Maria, invenitur omne bonum ; ipsa namque diligit diligentes se, immo sibi servientibus servit.—*De Contempl. Virg.* in prol.

is he who loves thee! If I love Mary, I am certain of perseverance, and shall obtain whatever I wish from God.' Therefore the devout youth was never tired of renewing his resolution, and of repeating often to himself: 'I will love Mary; I will love Mary.' O, how much does the love of this good Mother exceed that of all her children! Let them love her as much as they will, Mary is always amongst lovers the most loving. Let them love her like a St. Stanislaus Kostka, who loved this dear Mother so tenderly, that in speaking of her he moved all who heard him to love her: he had made new words and new titles with which to honour her name. He never did anything without first turning to her image to ask her blessing. When he said her office, the Rosary, or other prayers, he did so with the same external marks of affection as he would have done had he been speaking face to face with Mary; when the Salve Regina was sung, his whole soul, and even his whole countenance, was all inflamed with love. On being one day asked by a father of the Society who was going with him to visit a picture of the Blessed Virgin, how much he loved Mary,—'Father,' he replied, 'what more can I say? she is my mother.' 'But,' adds the father,' the holy youth uttered these words with such tenderness in his voice, with such an expression of countenance, and at the same time it came so fully from his heart, that it no longer seemed to be a young man, but rather an angel speaking of the love of Mary.'

Let us love her like a blessed Hermann, who called her the spouse of his love, for he was honoured by Mary herself with this same title. Let us love her like a St. Philip Neri, who was filled with consolation at the mere thought of Mary, and therefore called her his delight. Let us love her like a St. Bonaventure, who called her not only his Lady and Mother, but to show the tenderness of his affection, even called her his heart and soul: 'Hail, my Lady, my Mother; nay, even my heart, my soul !'[32] Let us love her like that great lover of Mary, who loved this his sweet Mother so much that he called her the ravisher of hearts ;[33] and to express the ardent love he bore her, added : ' for hast thou not ravished my heart, O Queen ?'[34] Let us call her our beloved, like a St. Bernardine of Sienna, who daily went to visit a devotional picture of Mary, and there, in tender colloquies with his Queen, declared his love; and when asked where he went each day, he replied, that he went to visit his beloved. Let us love her like a St. Aloysius Gonzaga, whose love for Mary burnt so unceasingly, that whenever he heard the sweetest name of his Mother mentioned, his heart was instantly inflamed, and his countenance lighted up with a fire that was visible to all. Let us love her like a St. Francis Solano, who, maddened as it were (but with a holy madness) with love for Mary, would sing before her picture, and accompany himself on a musical instrument, saying, that like worldly lovers, he serenaded his most sweet Queen.

Finally, let us love her as so many of her servants have loved her, who never could do enough to show their love. Father Jerome of Texo, of the Society of Jesus, rejoiced in the name of slave of Mary ; and as a mark of servitude, went often to visit her in some church dedicated in her honour. On reaching the church, he poured out abundant tears of tenderness and love for Mary ; then, prostrating, he licked and rubbed the pavement with his tongue and face, kissing it a thousand times, because it was the house of his beloved Lady. Father Diego Martinez, of the same Society, who for his devotion to our blessed Lady on her feasts was carried by angels to Heaven to see how they were kept there, used to say, 'Would that I had the hearts of all angels and saints, to love Mary as they love her—would that I

---

[32] Ave Domina mea, mater mea ; imo cor meum et anima mea.—*Stim. am Med. in Salut. Ang.*

[33] O raptrix cordium !—*Ib.*

[34] Nonne cor meum, Domina, rapuisti ?—*Ib.*

had the lives of all men, to give them all for her love!
O that others could come to love her as did Charles
the son of St. Bridget, who said that nothing in the
world consoled him so much as the knowledge that
Mary was so greatly loved by God.   And he added,
that he would willingly endure every torment rather
than allow Mary to lose the smallest degree of her
glory, were such a thing possible ; and that if her glory
was his, he would renounce it in her favour, as being
far more worthy of it.   Let us moreover desire to lay
down our lives as a testimony of our love for Mary, as
Alphonsus Rodriguez desired it.   Let us love her as
did those who even cut the beloved name of Mary on
their breasts with sharp instruments, as a Frances Bi-
nanzio and a Radagundis, wife of king Clothaire, or as
did those who could imprint this loved name on their
flesh with hot irons, in order that it might remain more
distinct and lasting, as did her devout servants Baptist
Archinto and Augustine d'Espinosa, both of the Society
of Jesus, driven thereto by the vehemence of their love.

Let us, in fine, do or desire to do all that it is possible for a lover to do, who intends to make his affection known to the person loved.   For be assured that
the lovers of Mary will never be able to equal her in
love.   'I know, O Lady,' says St. Peter Damian, 'that
thou art most loving, and that thou lovest us with an
invincible love.'[35]   I know, my Lady, that among those
that love thee thou lovest the most, and that thou lovest
us with a love that can never be surpassed.   The blessed
Alphonsus Rodriguez, of the Society of Jesus, once prostrate before an image of Mary, felt his heart inflamed
with love towards this most Holy Virgin, and burst
forth into the following exclamation : ' My most beloved
Mother, I know that thou lovest me, but thou dost not
love me as much as I love thee.'   Mary, as it were
offended and piqued on the point of love, immediately

---

[35] Scio, Domina, quia benignissima es, et amas nos amore invincibili.—
Serm. 1 de Nat. B.V.

replied from the image : ' What dost thou say, Alphonsus —what dost thou say ? O, how much greater is the love that I bear thee, than any love that thou canst have for me ! Know that the distance between heaven and earth is not so great as the distance between thy love and mine.'

St. Bonaventure, then, was right in exclaiming : Blessed are they who have the good fortune to be faithful servants and lovers of this most loving Mother. ' Blessed are the hearts of those who love Mary ; blessed are they who are tenderly devoted to her.'[36] Yes ; for ' in this struggle our most gracious Queen never allows her clients to conquer her in love. She returns our love and homage, and always increases her past favours by new ones.'[37] Mary, imitating in this our most loving Redeemer Jesus Christ, returns to those who love her their love doubled in benefits and favours. Then will I exclaim, with the enamoured St. Anselm, ' May my heart languish and my soul melt and be consumed with your love, O my beloved Saviour Jesus, and my dear Mother Mary ! But, as without your grace I cannot love you, grant me, O Jesus and Mary, grant my soul, by your merits and not mine, the grace to love you as you deserve to be loved. O God, lover of men, thou couldst love guilty men even unto death. And canst thou deny Thy love and that of Thy Mother to those who ask it ?[38]

EXAMPLE.

Father Auriemma[39] relates that there was a certain poor shepherdess, whose sole delight was to go to a little chapel of our Blessed Lady, situated on a mountain, and

---

[36] Beati quorum corda te diligunt, Virgo Maria.—*In Ps.* xxxi. *de B. V.* Beati qui devote ei famulantur.—*In Ps.* cxviii. *de B. V.*

[37] Numquam tamen in hoc eximio certamine a nobis ipsa vincetur. Etenim et amorem et honorem redhibet, et præterita beneficia novis semper adauget.—*Pacciuchelli in Ps.* lxxxvi. Exit. 2.

[38] Vestro continuo amore langueat cor meum : liquefiant omnia ossa mea .. Date itaque piissimi, date, obsecro, supplicanti animæ meæ, non propter meritum meum, sed propter meritum vestrum, date illi quanto digni estis, amorem vestrum . . . O amator et miserator hominum, tu potuisti reos tuos et usque ad mortem amare : et poteris te roganti amorem tui et matris tuæ negare ?--*In Depr.* li. *ad B. V.*   [39] *Affetti Scamb.* tom. ii. c. 8.

there, whilst her flocks browsed, converse with and
honour her dear Mother. Seeing that the little image of
Mary (which was carved in relief) was unadorned, she
set to work to make her a mantle ; and one day, having
gathered a few flowers in the fields, she made a garland,
and climbing on the altar of the little chapel, placed it
on the head of the image, saying : 'My Mother, I would
place a crown of gold and precious stones on thy brow,
but, as I am poor, receive this crown of flowers, and
accept it as a mark of the love that I bear thee.' With
this and other acts of homage, the pious maiden always
endeavoured to serve and honour our beloved Lady. But
let us now see how the good Mother on her part recompensed the visits and the affection of her child. She fell
ill, and was brought to the point of death. It so happened that two religious were passing that way, and,
fatigued with their journey, sat down under a tree to rest :
one fell asleep, and the other remained awake ; but both
had the same vision. They saw a troop of most beautiful
ladies, and amongst these was one who in beauty and
majesty far surpassed them all. One of the religious
addressed himself to her : 'Lady, who art thou, and
where art thou going by these rugged ways?' 'I am,' she
replied, 'the Mother of God, and am going with these
holy virgins to a neighbouring cottage to visit a dying
shepherdess who has so often visited me.' Having said
these words, all disappeared. At once these two good
servants of God said, 'Let us go also to see her.' They
immediately started, and having found the cottage of the
dying virgin, they entered it and found her stretched on
a little straw. They saluted her, and she said, 'Brothers,
ask our Lord to let you see the company that is assisting
me.' They immediately knelt, and saw Mary by the
side of the dying girl, holding a crown in her hand, and
consoling her. All at once the virgins began to sing,
and at the sound of this sweet harmony her blessed soul
left her body. Mary placed the crown on her head, and
taking her soul, led it with her to Paradise.

PRAYER.

O Lady, O ravisher of hearts ! will I exclaim with St. Bonaventure :[40] 'Lady, who with the love and favour thou showest thy servants dost ravish their hearts, ravish also my miserable heart, which desires ardently to love thee. Thou, my Mother, hast enamoured a God with thy beauty, and drawn Him from heaven into thy chaste womb; and shall I live without loving thee ? No, I will never rest until I am certain of having obtained thy love; but a constant and tender love towards thee, my Mother, who hast loved me with so much tenderness,'[41] even when I was ungrateful towards thee. And what should I now be, O Mary, if thou hadst not obtained so many mercies for me ? Since, then, thou didst love me so much when I loved thee not, how much more may I not now hope from thee, now that I love thee ? I love thee, O my Mother, and I would that I had a heart to love thee in place of all those unfortunate creatures who love thee not. I would that I could speak with a thousand tongues, that all might know thy greatness, thy holiness, thy mercy, and the love with which thou lovest all who love thee. Had I riches, I would employ them all for thy honour. Had I subjects, I would make them all thy lovers. In fine, if the occasion presented itself, I would lay down my life for thy glory. I love thee, then, O my Mother ; but at the same time I fear that I do not love thee as I ought ; for I hear that love makes lovers like the person loved. If, then, I see myself so unlike thee, it is a mark that I do not love thee. Thou art so pure, and I defiled with many sins ; thou so humble, and I so proud ; thou so holy, and I so wicked. This, then, is what thou hast to do, O Mary ; since thou lovest me, make me like thee. Thou hast all power to change hearts ; take, then, mine and change it. Show the world

---

[40] O Domina, quæ rapis corda.—*Stim. am. Med. in Salve Reg.*
[41] Nunquam quiescam, donec habuero tenerum amorem erga matrem meam Mariam.—*B. John Berchmans, S.J.*

what thou canst do for those who love thee.   Make me a
saint ; make me thy worthy child.   This is my hope.

———————

SECTION IV.   *Mary is the Mother of penitent Sinners.*

Our Blessed Lady told St. Bridget that she was the
Mother not only of the just and innocent, but also of
sinners, provided they were willing to repent.[1]   O how
prompt does a sinner (desirous of amendment, and who
flies to her feet) find this good Mother to embrace and
help him, far more so than any earthly mother !   St.
Gregory the Seventh wrote in this sense to the princess
Matilda, saying : ' Resolve to sin no more, and I promise
that undoubtedly thou wilt find Mary more ready to love
thee than any earthly mother.'[2]   But whoever aspires to
be a child of this great Mother, must first abandon sin,
and then may hope to be accepted as such.   Richard of
St. Lawrence, on the words of Proverbs, "up rose her
children," remarks that first comes 'up rose' and then
children,[3] to show that no one can be a child of Mary
without first endeavouring to rise from the fault into
which he has fallen ; for he who is in mortal sin is not
worthy to be called the son of such a Mother.[4]   And St.
Peter Chrysologus says that he who acts in a different
manner from Mary, declares thereby that he will not be
her son.   ' He who does not the works of his Mother
abjures his lineage.'[5]   Mary humble, and he proud ;
Mary pure, and he wicked ; Mary full of love, and he
hating his neighbour.   He gives thereby proof that he is
not, and will not be, the son of this Holy Mother.   The
sons of Mary, says Richard of St. Lawrence, are her
imitators, and this chiefly in three things : in ' chastity,

———————

[1] Ego etiam quasi sum Mater omnium peccatorum volentium se emendare.
—*Rev.* lib. iv. c. 138.
[2] Pone finem in voluntate peccandi, et invenies Mariam (indubitanter
promitto) promptiorem carnali matre in tui dilectione.—Lib. i. ep. 47.
[3] Surrexerunt filii ejus.—*Prov.* xxxi. 28.
[4] Nec dignus est, qui in mortali peccato est, vocari filius tantæ Matris.—
De Laud. Virg. lib. ii. c. 5.   [5] Qui genitoris non facit opera, negat genus.—*Ib.*

liberality, and humility ; and also in meekness, mercy, and such like'.[6] And whilst disgusting her by a wicked life, who would dare even to wish to be the child of Mary ? A certain sinner once said to Mary, ' Show thyself a Mother ;' but the Blessed Virgin replied, ' Show thyself a son.'[7] Another invoked the Divine Mother, calling her the Mother of mercy, and she answered : ' You sinners, when you want my help, call me Mother of mercy, and at the same time do not cease by your sins to make me a Mother of sorrows and anguish.'[8] " He is cursed of God," says Ecclesiastes, " that angereth his mother."[9] ' That is Mary,'[10] says Richard of St. Lawrence. God curses those who by their wicked life, and still more by their obstinacy in sin, afflict this tender Mother.

I say, by their obstinacy ; for if a sinner, though he may not as yet have given up his sin, endeavours to do so, and for this purpose seeks the help of Mary, this good mother will not fail to assist him, and make him recover the grace of God. And this is precisely what St. Bridget heard one day from the lips of Jesus Christ, who, speaking to his Mother, said, ' Thou assistest him who endeavours to return to God, and thy consolations are never wanting to anyone.'[11] So long, then, as a sinner is obstinate, Mary cannot love him ; but if he (finding himself chained by some passion which keeps him a slave of hell) recommends himself to the Blessed Virgin, and implores her, with confidence and perseverance, to withdraw him from the state of sin in which he is, there can be no doubt but this good Mother will extend her powerful hand to him, will deliver him from his chains, and lead him to a state of salvation. The doctrine that all prayers and works performed in a state of sin are

---

[6] Filii ejus (Mariæ), id est imitatores, maxime in tribus, castitate, largitate, humilitate . . . . mansuetudine, misericordia, et hujusmodi.—*Ib.*

[7] Monstra te esse matrem . . . . monstra te esse filium.—*Ap. Aur. Aff. Scamb.* p. 3, c. 12.

[8] *Ap. Pelb. Stell.* lib. xii. p. ult. c. 7.

[9] Est maledictus a Deo qui exasperat matrem.—*Eccl.* iii. 18.

[10] Matrem, id est Mariam.—*De Laud. B.M.* lib. ii. p. 1.

[11] Conanti surgere ad Deum tribuis auxilium, et neminem relinquis vacuum a consolatione tua.—Lib. iv. c. 19.

sins was condemned as heretical by the sacred Council of Trent.[12] St. Bernard says,[13] that although prayer in the mouth of a sinner is devoid of beauty, on account of its being unaccompanied by charity, nevertheless it is useful, and obtains grace to abandon sin; for, as St. Thomas teaches,[14] the prayer of a sinner, though without merit, is an act which obtains the grace of forgiveness, since the power of impetration is founded not on the merits of him who asks, but on the divine goodness, and the merits and promises of Jesus Christ, who has said, "Everyone that asketh receiveth."[15] The same thing must be said of prayers offered to the divine Mother. 'If he who prays,' says St. Anselm, ' does not merit to be heard, the merits of the Mother, to whom he recommends himself, will intercede effectually.'[16] Therefore, St. Bernard exhorts all sinners to have recourse to Mary, invoking her with great confidence; for though the sinner does not himself merit the graces which he asks, yet he receives them, because this Blessed Virgin asks and obtains them from God, on account of her own merits. These are his words, addressing a sinner : ' Because thou wast unworthy to receive the grace thyself, it was given to Mary, in order that, through her, thou mightest receive all.'[17] ' If a mother,' continues the same Saint, ' knew that her two sons bore a mortal enmity to one another, and that each plotted against the other's life, would she not exert herself to her utmost in order to reconcile them ? This would be the duty of a good mother. And thus it is,' the Saint goes on to say, 'that Mary acts; for she is the Mother of Jesus, and the Mother of men. When she sees a sinner at enmity with Jesus Christ, she cannot endure it,

---

12 Sess. 6. can. 7.
13 *De Div.* s. 81.
14 2a, 2æ, qu. 178. a. 2. ad 1.
15 Omnis enim qui petit, accipit.—*Luc.* xi. 10.
16 Etsi merita invocantis non merentur, ut exaudiatur, merita tamen Matris intercedunt, ut exaudiatur.—*De Exc. Virg.* c. vi.
17 Quia indignus eras, cui donaretur, datum est Mariæ, ut per illam acciperes quicquid haberes.—*Serm.* 3 *in Vig. Nat.*

and does all in her power to make peace between them. O happy Mary, thou art the Mother of the criminal, and the Mother of the judge ; and being the Mother of both, they are thy children, and thou canst not endure discords amongst them.'[18] This most benign Lady only requires that the sinner should recommend himself to her, and purpose amendment. When Mary sees a sinner at her feet, imploring her mercy, she does not consider the crimes with which he is loaded, but the intention with which he comes ; and if this is good, even should he have committed all possible sins, the most loving Mother embraces him, and does not disdain to heal the wounds of his soul ; for she is not only *called* the Mother of Mercy, but is so truly and indeed, and shows herself such by the love and tenderness with which she assists us all. And this is precisely what the Blessed Virgin herself said to St. Bridget : ' However much a man sins, I am ready immediately to receive him when he repents ; nor do I pay attention to the number of his sins, but only to the intention with which he comes ; I do not disdain to anoint and heal his wounds ; for I am called, and truly am, the Mother of Mercy.'[19]

Mary is the Mother of sinners who wish to repent, and as a Mother she cannot do otherwise than compassionate them ; nay more, she seems to feel the miseries of her poor children as if they were her own. When the Canaanitish woman begged our Lord to deliver her daughter from the devil who possessed her, she said, "Have mercy on me, O Lord, thou son of David, my daughter is grievously troubled by a devil."[20] But since the daughter, and not the mother, was tormented,

---

[18] O felix Maria, tu mater rei, tu mater judicis : cum sis mater utriusque, discordias inter tuos filios nequis sustinere.—*Apud S. Bonav. Spec. B.V.* lect. 3.

[19] Ego quantumcumque homo peccat, si ex toto corde et vera emendatione ad me reversus fuerit, statim parata sum recipere revertentem. Nec attendo quantum peccaverit, sed cum quali intentione et voluntate redit.—*Rev.* l. ii. c. 23. Quicunque invocaverit me, ego non dedignor tangere, et ungere, et sanare plagas suas.—*Rev.* l. vi. c. 117. Ego vocor ab omnibus mater misericordiæ, vere filia, misericordia Filii mei fecit me misericordem.—*Rev.* l. ii. c. 23.

[20] Miserere mei, Domine, fili David ; filia mea male a dæmonio vexatur.—*Matt.* xv. 22.

she should rather have said, ' Lord, take compassion *on
my daughter :*' and not, Have mercy on me ; but no,
she said, ' Have mercy on me,' and was right ; for the
sufferings of children are felt by their mothers as if they
were their own.   And it is precisely thus, says Richard
of St. Lawrence, that Mary prays to God when she recommends a sinner to Him who has had recourse to her ;
she cries out for the sinful soul, ' Have mercy on *me !*[21]
' My Lord,' she seems to say, ' this poor soul that is in
sin is my daughter, and therefore, pity, not so much
her, as me, who am her Mother.'   Would that all sinners had recourse to this sweet Mother ! for then certainly all would be pardoned by God.   ' O Mary,' exclaims St. Bonaventure, in rapturous astonishment,
'thou embracest with maternal affection a sinner despised
by the whole world, nor dost thou leave him until thou
hast reconciled the poor creature with his judge ;'[22] meaning, that the sinner whilst in a state of sin is hated and
loathed by all, even by inanimate creatures ; fire, air, and
earth would chastise him, and avenge the honour of their
outraged Lord.   But if this unhappy creature flies to
Mary, will Mary reject him ?   O, no : provided he goes
to her for help, and in order to amend, she will embrace
him with the affection of a mother, and will not let him
go, until, by her powerful intercession, she has reconciled him with God, and reinstated him in grace.

In the second book of Kings[23] we read that a wise
woman of Thecua addressed King David in the following words : " My Lord, I had two sons, and for my
misfortune, one killed the other ; so that I have now
lost one, and justice demands the other, the only one
that is left ; take compassion on a poor mother, and let
me not be thus deprived of both."   David, moved with

[21] Quæ clamat ad Deum pro filia, id est peccatrice anima, cujus etiam per
sonam misericorditer in se transformat, dicens, Miserere mei, fili David.—
De Laud. B.V. l. vi. c. 9.
[22] Maria, tu peccatorem toti mundo despectum materno affectu complect-
eris, foves, nec deseris, quousque horrendo judici miserum reconcilies.—*In Spec.
B.V.* lect. v.
[23] 2 Reg. c. xiv.

compassion towards the mother, declared that the delinquent should be set at liberty and restored to her. Mary seems to say the same thing when God is indignant against a sinner who has recommended himself to her. 'My God,' she says, 'I had two sons, Jesus and man; man took the life of my Jesus on the cross, and now Thy justice would condemn the guilty one. O Lord, my Jesus is already dead, have pity on me, and if I have lost the one, do not make me lose the other also.' And most certainly God will not condemn those sinners who have recourse to Mary, and for whom she prays, since He Himself commended them to her as her children. The devout Lanspergius supposes our Lord speaking in the following terms : ' I recommended all, but especially sinners, to Mary as her children, and therefore is she so diligent and so careful in the exercise of her office, that she allows none of those committed to her charge, and especially those who invoke her, to perish ; but as far as she can, brings all to Me.'[24] ' And who can ever tell,' says the devout Blosius, ' the goodness, the mercy, the compassion, the love, the benignity, the clemency, the fidelity, the benevolence, the charity of this Virgin Mother towards men ? It is such that no words can express it.'[25] ' Let us, then,' says St. Bernard, ' cast ourselves at the feet of this good Mother, and embracing them, let us not depart until she blesses us, and thus accepts us for her children.'[26] And who can ever doubt the compassion of this Mother ? St. Bonaventure used to say, ' Even should she take my life, I would still hope in her ; and, full of confidence, would desire to die be-

---

[24] Mariæ . . . . omnes, potissime autem peccatores, in persona Joannis in filios commendavi . . . . Propterea adeo est diligens adeo sedula, ut officio suo satisfaciens, neminem eorum, quantum in se est, qui sibi commissi sunt, præcipue se invocantium, perire sinat, sed, quantum valet, omnes mihi reducat.—Lib. i. *Alloq.* can. 12.

[25] Hujus Virginis Matris bonitas, misericordia, pietas, amicitia, benignitas, clementia, fidelitas, benevolentia, et caritas erga homines tanta est, ut nullis verbis explicari possit.—*Sac. An. Fid.* P. iii. c. 5.

[26] Beatis illius pedibus provolvamur. Teneamus eam, nec dimittamus, donec benedixerit nobis.—*In Sig. Magn.*

E

fore her image, and be certain of salvation.'[27]   And thus
should each sinner address her when he has recourse to
this compassionate Mother : he should say, 'My Lady
and Mother, on account of my sins I deserve that thou
shouldst reject me, and even that thou shouldst thyself
chastise me according to my deserts ; but shouldst thou
reject me, or even take my life, I will still trust in thee,
and hope with a firm hope that thou wilt save me.   In
thee is all my confidence ; only grant me the consolation
of dying before thy picture, recommending myself to thy
mercy, and then I am convinced that I shall not be lost,
but that I shall go and praise thee in heaven, in company with so many of thy servants who left this world
calling on thee for help, and have all been saved by thy
powerful intercession.'   Read the following example,
and then say if any sinner can doubt of the mercy and
love of this good Mother.

EXAMPLE.

Vincent of Beauvais relates, that, in an English city,
about the year 1430, there was a young nobleman, called
Ernest, who, having distributed the whole of his patri-
mony to the poor, became a monk, and in the monastery to which he retired led so perfect a life, that he
was highly esteemed by his superiors, and this esteem
was greatly increased by their knowledge of his tender
devotion to the most Blessed Virgin.   It happened that
the city was attacked by the plague, and the inhabitants
had recourse to the monastery, in order that the religious
might help them by their prayers.   The abbot commanded Ernest to go and pray before the altar of Mary,
forbidding him to leave it until he should have received
an answer from our Blessed Lady.   The young man,
after remaining for three days in prayer, received an
answer from Mary to the effect, that certain prayers
were to be said : this was done, and the plague ceased.

---

[27] Etiamsi occiderit me, sperabo in eam, et totus confidens juxta ejus ima-
ginem mori desidero, et salvus ero. †

After a time Ernest cooled in his devotion towards Mary : the devil attacked him with many temptations, and particularly with those against purity, and also to leave his monastery. From not having recommended himself to Mary, he unfortunately yielded to the temptation, and resolved to escape by climbing over a wall. Passing before an image of Mary which was in the corridor, the Mother of God addressed him, saying, ' My son, why dost thou leave me ?' Ernest, thunderstruck and repentant, sunk to the ground, and replied, ' But, Lady, dost thou not see that I can no longer resist, why dost thou not assist me ?' ' And why hast thou not invoked me ?' said our Blessed Lady. ' If thou hadst recommended thyself to me, thou wouldst not have fallen so low ; but from henceforth do so, and fear nothing.' Ernest returned to his cell ; his temptations recommenced ; again he neglected to recommend himself to Mary, and at last fled from his monastery. He then gave himself up to a most wicked life, fell from one sin into another, and at length became an assassin ; for having hired an inn, during the night he used to murder the poor travellers who slept there. Amongst others, he one night killed the cousin of the governor of the place. For this crime he was tried and sentenced to death. It so happened that before he was made a prisoner, and whilst evidence was being collected, a young nobleman arrived at the inn. The wicked Ernest, as usual, determined to murder him, and entered the room at night for this purpose—but, lo, instead of finding the young man, he beheld a crucifix on the bed, all covered with wounds. The image cast a look of compassion on him, and exclaimed, ' Ungrateful wretch ! is it not enough that I have died once for thee ? Wilt thou again take my life ? Be it so. Raise thy hand, —strike !' Filled with confusion, poor Ernest began to weep, and sobbing, said, ' Behold me, Lord ; since thou showest me such mercy, I will return to Thee.' Immediately he left the inn to return to his monastery

there to do penance for his crimes; but on the road he
was taken by the ministers of justice, was led before
the judge, and acknowledged all the murders he had
committed. He was sentenced to be hung, without
having even the time given him to go to confession.
He recommended himself to Mary, and was thrown
from the ladder; but the Blessed Virgin preserved his
life, and she herself loosened the rope, and then addressed him, saying, 'Go, return to thy monastery, do
penance, and when thou seest a paper in my hands,
announcing the pardon of thy sins, prepare for death.
Ernest returned, related all to his abbot, and did great
penance. After many years, he saw the paper in the
hands of Mary, which announced his pardon; he immediately prepared for death, and in a most holy
manner breathed forth his soul.

PRAYER.

O my sovereign Queen and worthy Mother of my God,
most holy Mary; I, seeing myself, as I do, so despicable
and loaded with so many sins, ought not to presume to
call thee Mother, or even to approach thee; yet I will
not allow my miseries to deprive me of the consolation
and confidence that I feel in calling thee Mother; I
know well that I deserve that thou shouldst reject me;
but I beseech thee to remember all that thy Son Jesus
has endured for me, and then reject me if thou canst.
I am a wretched sinner, who, more than all others,
have despised the infinite majesty of God: but the evil
is done. To thee have I recourse; thou canst help me:
my Mother, help me. Say not that thou canst not do
so; for I know that thou art all-powerful, and that
thou obtainest whatever thou desirest of God; and if
thou sayest that thou wilt not help me, tell me at least
to whom I can apply in this my so great misfortune.
'Either pity me,' will I say, with the devout St. Anselm,
'O my Jesus, and forgive me, and do thou pity me, my
Mother Mary, by interceding for me, or at least tell me

to whom I can have recourse, who is more compassionate, or in whom I can have greater confidence than in thee.'[28] O, no; neither on earth nor in heaven can I find any one who has more compassion for the miserable, or who is better able to assist me, than thou canst, O Mary. Thou, O Jesus, art my Father, and thou, Mary, art my Mother. You both love the most miserable, and go seeking them in order to save them. I deserve hell, and am the most miserable of all. But you need not seek me, nor do I presume to ask so much. I now present myself before you with a certain hope that I shall not be abandoned. Behold me at your feet; my Jesus, forgive me; my Mother Mary, help me.

[28] Aut miseremini miseri, tu parcendo, tu interveniendo; aut ostendite, ad quos tutius fugiam misericordiores; et monstrate, in quibus certius confida* potentiores?—*In Depr. L. ad B. V.*

CHAPTER II.

OUR LIFE, OUR SWEETNESS.

SECTION I. *Mary is our Life, because she obtains us the Pardon of our Sins.*

To understand why the holy Church makes us call Mary our life, we must know, that as the soul gives life to the body, so does Divine grace give life to the soul; for a soul without grace has the name of being alive, but is in truth dead, as it was said of one in the Apocalypse, "Thou hast the name of being alive, and thou art dead."[1] Mary, then, in obtaining this grace for sinners by her intercession, thus restores them to life. See how the Church makes her speak, applying to her the following words of Proverbs : "They that in the morning early watch for me shall find me."[2] They who are diligent in having recourse to me in the morning, that is, as soon as they can, will most certainly find me. In the Septuagint the words "shall find me" are rendered "shall find grace." So that to have recourse to Mary is the same thing as to find the grace of God. A little further on she says, "He that shall find me shall find life, and shall have salvation from the Lord."[3] 'Listen,' exclaims St. Bonaventure on these words, 'listen, all you who desire the kingdom

---

[1] Nomen habes quod vivas, et mortuus es.—*Apoc.* iii. 1.
[2] Qui mane vigilant ad me, invenient me.—*Prov.* viii. 17
[3] Qui me invenerit, inveniet vitam, et hauriet salutem a Domino.—*Prov* viii. 35.

of God; honour the most Blessed Virgin Mary, and you
will find life and eternal salvation.'[4]

St. Bernardine of Sienna says, that if God did not
destroy man after his first sin, it was on account of
His singular love for this holy Virgin, who was destined
to be born of this race. And the Saint adds, 'that he
has no doubt but that all the mercies granted by God
under the old dispensation were granted only in consideration of this most Blessed Lady.'[5] Hence St. Bernard was right in exhorting us 'to seek for grace, and
to seek it by Mary;'[6] meaning, that if we have had the
misfortune to lose the grace of God, we should seek to
recover it, but we should do so by Mary; for though we
may have lost it, she has found it; and hence the Saint
calls her 'the finder of grace.'[7] The angel Gabriel expressly declared this for our consolation, when he saluted
the Blessed Virgin, saying, "Fear not, Mary, thou hast
fornd grace."[8] But if Mary had never been deprived
of grace, how could the archangel say that she had then
found it? A thing may be found by a person who did
not previously possess it; but we are told by the same
archangel that the Blessed Virgin was always with God,
always in grace, nay, full of grace. "Hail, full of grace,
the Lord is with thee."[9] Since Mary, then, did not find
grace for herself, she being always full of it, for whom
did she find it? Cardinal Hugo, in his commentary on
the above text, replies that she found it for sinners who
had lost it. 'Let sinners, then,' says this devout writer,
'who by their crimes have lost grace, address themselves
to the Blessed Virgin; for with her they will surely
find it; let them humbly salute her, and say with confidence, 'Lady, that which has been found must be re-

---

[4] Audite . . . . qui ingredi cupitis regnum Dei; Virginem Mariam honorate, et invenietis vitam et salutem perpetuam.—*In Ps.* xlviii. *B. V.*
[5] Omnes libertationes et indulgentias factas in Veteri Testamento, non
ambigo Deum fecisse propter hujus benedictæ puellæ reverentiam et amorem.
—Tom. iv. *Serm.* 5, *de B. V.* c. 2.
[6] Quæramus gratiam, et per Mariam quæramus.—*Serm. de Aquæd.*
[7] Inventrix gratiæ.—*De Adv. D. Serm.* 2.
[8] Ne timeas, Maria; invenisti enim gratiam.—*Luc.* i. 30.
[9] Ave, gratia plena; Dominus tecum.—*Luc.* i. 28.

stored to him who has lost it ; restore us, therefore, our
property which thou hast found.'[10] On this subject,
Richard of St. Lawrence concludes, 'that if we hope
to recover the grace of God, we must go to Mary, who
has found it, and finds it always.'[11] And as she always
was and always will be dear to God, if we have recourse
to her, we shall certainly succeed. Again, Mary says,
in the eighth chapter of the sacred Canticles, that God
has placed her in the world to be our defence : " I am
a wall : and my breasts are as a tower." And she is
truly made a mediatress of peace between sinners and
God : " Since I am become in His presence as one finding peace."[12] On these words St. Bernard encourages
sinners, saying, ' Go to this Mother of Mercy, and show
her the wounds which thy sins have left on thy soul ;
then will she certainly entreat her Son, by the breasts
that gave him suck, to pardon thee all. And this
Divine Son, who loves her so tenderly, will most certainly grant her petition.'[13] In this sense it is that the
holy Church, in her almost daily prayer, calls upon us
to beg our Lord to grant us the powerful help of the
intercession of Mary to rise from our sins : ' Grant thy
help to our weakness, O most merciful God ; and that
we, who are mindful of the holy Mother of God, may
by the help of her intercession rise from our iniquities.[14]
With reason, then, does St. Lawrence Justinian call her
' the hope of malefactors ;'[15] since she alone is the one
who obtains them pardon from God. With reason does
St. Bernard call her ' the sinners' ladder ;'[16] since she,

[10] Currant igitur peccatores ad Virginem, qui gratiam amiserunt peccando,
et eam invenient apud eam humiliter salutando, et secure dicant, Redde nobis
rem nostram, quam invenisti.—*In cap.* i. *Luc.*

[11] Cupientes invenire gratiam, quæramus inventricem gratiæ, Mariam,
quæ, quia semper invenit, frustrari non poterit.—*De Laud. V.* l. ii. c. 5.

[12] Ego murus : et ubera mea sicut turris, ex quo facta sum coram eo
quasi pacem reperiens.—*Cant.* viii. 10.

[13] Vade ad Matrem misericordiæ, et ostende illi tuorum plagas peccatorum ; et illa ostendet pro te ubera. Exaudiet utique matrem filius. †

[14] Concede, misericors Deus, fragilitati nostræ præsidium ; ut qui sanctæ
Dei Genitricis memoriam agimus, intercessionis ejus auxilio a nostris iniqui
tatibus resurgamus.

[15] Delinquentium spes.—*Serm. de Nat. V.M.*

[16] Peccatorum scala.—*De Aquæd.*

the most compassionate Queen, extending her hand to them, draws them from an abyss of sin, and enables them to ascend to God. With reason does an ancient writer call her 'the only hope of sinners;' for by her help alone can we hope for the remission of our sins.[17] St. John Chrysostom also says 'that sinners receive pardon by the intercession of Mary alone.'[18] And therefore the Saint, in the name of all sinners, thus addresses her: 'Hail Mother' of God and of us all, 'heaven,' where God dwells, 'throne,' from which our Lord dispenses all graces, 'fair daughter, Virgin, honour, glory, and firmament of our Church, assiduously pray to Jesus that in the day of judgment we may find mercy through thee, and receive the reward prepared by God for those who love Him.'[19]

With reason, finally, is Mary called, in the words of the sacred Canticles, the Dawn; "Who is she that cometh forth as the morning rising?"[20] Yes, says Pope Innocent; 'for as the dawn is the end of night, and the beginning of day, well may the Blessed Virgin Mary, who was the end of vices, be called the dawn of day.'[21] When devotion towards Mary begins in a soul, it produces the same effect that the birth of this most Holy Virgin produced in the world. It puts an end to the night of sin, and leads the soul into the path of virtue. Therefore, St. Germanus says, 'O Mother of God, thy protection never ceases, thy intercession is life, and thy patronage never fails.'[22] And in a sermon, the same

---

[17] Tu es spes unica peccatorum, quia per te speramus veniam omnium delictorum.—*Int. op. S. Augustini, Serm.* cxciv. *de Sanctis.*

[18] Per hanc et peccatorum veniam consequimur.—*S. Joan. Chrysost. ap. Metaph. Brev. Rom. in Off. Nat. B. M. die* 5.

[19] Ave igitur, Mater, Cœlum, Puella, Virgo, Thronus, Ecclesiæ nostræ decus, gloria, et firmamentum; assidue pro nobis precare Jesum, ut per te misericordiam invenire in die judicii, et quæ reposita sunt iis, qui diligunt Deum, bona consequi possimus.—*Ib.*

[20] Quæ est ista, quæ progreditur quasi aurora consurgens?—*Cant.* vi. 9.

[21] Cum Aurora sit finis noctis, et origo diei, merito per auroram designatur Virgo Maria, quæ finis damnationis et origo salutis fuit.—*Serm.* 2. *de Ass. B.V.*

[22] Adhuc tuum viget præsidium; et vita tua est intercessio; tuumque nunquam deficit patrocinium.—*In Dorm. Dei Gen. Orat.* ii.

Saint says, that to pronounce the name of Mary with affection is a sign of life in the soul, or at least that life will soon return there.

We read in the Gospel of St. Luke, that Mary said, "Behold from henceforth all generations shall call me blessed."[23] 'Yes, my lady,' exclaims St. Bernard, 'all generations shall call thee blessed, for thou hast begotten life and glory for all generations of men.'[24] For this cause all men shall call thee blessed, for all thy servants obtain through thee the life of grace and eternal glory. 'In thee do sinners find pardon, and the just perseverance and eternal life.'[25] 'Distrust not, O sinner,' says the devout Bernardine de Busto, 'even if thou hast committed all possible sins : go with confidence to this most glorious Lady, and thou wilt find her hands filled with mercy and bounty.' And, he adds, for 'she desires more to do thee good than thou canst desire to receive favours from her.'[26]

St. Andrew of Crete calls Mary the pledge of Divine mercy ;[27] meaning that, when sinners have recourse to Mary, that they may be reconciled with God, He assures them of pardon and gives them a pledge of it ; and this pledge is Mary, whom he has bestowed upon us for our advocate, and by whose intercession (in virtue of the merits of Jesus Christ) God forgives all who have recourse to her. St. Bridget heard an angel say, that the holy Prophets rejoiced in knowing that God, by the humility and purity of Mary, was to be reconciled with sinners, and to receive those who had offended Him to favour. 'They exulted, foreknowing that our Lord Himself would be appeased by thy humility and the

---

[23] Ecce enim ex hoc beatam me dicent omnes generationes.—*Luc.* i. 48.

[24] Ex hoc beatam te dicent omnes generationes, quæ omnibus generationibus vitam et gloriam genuisti.—*Serm.* 2. *in Pentec.*

[25] In te justi gratiam, peccatores veniam, invenerunt in æternum.—*Serm.* 2. *in Pentec.*

[26] O . . . peccator, bonum novum; o peccatrix, optimum novum, non diffidas, non desperes, etiamsi commisisti omnia peccata enormia : sed confidenter et secure ad istam gloriosissimam Dominam recurras. Invenies enim eam in manibus plenam curialitate, pietate, misericordia, gratiositate, et largitate. Plus enim desiderat ipsa facere tibi bonum, et largiri aliquam gratiam, quam tu accipere concupiscas.—*Marial.* P. ii. *Serm.* 5. *de Nat. B. V.*

[27] Per eam nobis obstricta sunt salutis pignora.—·*In B. V. M. Dorm. Serm.* 2

purity of thy life, O Mary, thou super-effulgent star, and that He would be reconciled with those who had provoked His wrath.'[28]

No sinner, having recourse to the compassion of Mary, should fear being rejected; for she is the Mother of Mercy, and as such desires to save the most miserable. Mary is that happy ark, says St. Bernard, 'in which those who take refuge will never suffer the shipwreck of eternal perdition.'[29] At the time of the deluge even brutes were saved in Noah's ark. Under the mantle of Mary even sinners obtain salvation. St. Gertrude once saw Mary with her mantle extended, and under it many wild beasts—lions, bears, and tigers—had taken refuge;[30] and she remarked that Mary not only did not reject, but even welcomed and caressed them with the greatest tenderness. The Saint understood hereby that the most abandoned sinners who have recourse to Mary are not only not rejected, but that they are welcomed and saved by her from eternal death. Let us, then, enter this ark, let us take refuge under the mantle of Mary, and she most certainly will not reject us, but will secure our salvation.

EXAMPLE.

Father Bovio[31] relates that there was a wicked woman, named Ellen, who entered a church, and by chance heard a sermon on the Rosary. On leaving the church she purchased a set of beads, but wore them concealed, as she did not wish it to be known that she had them. She began to recite them, and though she did so without devotion, our most Blessed Lady poured such sweetness and consolation into her soul during the whole time, that she could not cease repeating the Hail Marys.

---

[28] Exultabant autem praenoscentes, quod ipse legum Dictator et Dominus ex tua humilitate, et tuae vitae puritate, o Maria stella praefulgida, placaretur, et quod reciperet eos in suam gratiam, qui ipsum ad iram provocaverant.—*Serm. Ang.* cap. ix.

[29] Sicut enim per illam (arcam) omnes evaserunt diluvium, sic per istam peccati naufragium.—*Serm. de B. Maria.*

[30] Insin. l. iv. c. 50.

[31] Es. e Mir. p. 1. es. 2.

At length she was filled with such a horror for her wicked life, that she no longer could find repose, and was obliged to go to confession; and she accomplished this duty with such contrition, that the priest was filled with astonishment. After her confession, she went to the foot of an altar of the most Blessed Virgin, and there, as a thanksgiving to her advocate, said the Rosary. The Divine Mother then addressed her from the Image in the following words : ' Ellen, thou hast already offended God and me too much; from this moment change thy life, and I will bestow a large share of my graces upon thee.' The poor sinner, in the deepest confusion, replied : ' Ah ! most Holy Virgin, it is true that hitherto I have been a wicked sinner; but thou canst do all, help me : on my part I abandon myself to thee, and will spend the whole remainder of my life in doing penance for my sins.' With the assistance of Mary, she distributed all her goods to the poor, and began a life of rigorous mortification. She was tormented with dreadful temptations, but constantly recommended herself to the Mother of God, and thus was always victorious. She was favoured with many extraordinary graces, with visions, revelations, and even the gift of prophecy. Finally, before her death, which was announced to her by Mary some days before it took place, the most Blessed Virgin came herself, with her Divine Son, to visit her; and when she expired, her soul was seen flying towards heaven in the form of a beautiful dove.

PRAYER.

Behold, O Mother of my God, my only hope, Mary, behold at thy feet a miserable sinner, who asks thee for mercy. Thou art proclaimed and called by the whole Church, and by all the faithful, the refuge of sinners. Thou art consequently my refuge, thou hast to save me. Thou knowest, most sweet Mother of God, how much thy Blessed Son desires our salvation.[32] **Thou** knowest all that Jesus Christ endured for this end. I present thee, O my Mother, the sufferings of Jesus; the cold He endured in the stable, His journey into Egypt, His toils, His sweat, the blood He shed; the anguish which caused His death on the cross, and of which thou wast thyself a witness. O, show that thou lovest thy beloved Son, and by this love I implore thee to assist me. Extend thy hand to a poor creature who has fallen, and asks thy help. Were I a saint, I need not seek thy mercy; but because I am a sinner, I fly to thee, who art the Mother of Mercies. I know that thy compassionate heart finds its consolation in assisting the miserable, when thou canst do so, and dost not find them obstinate. Console, then, thy compassionate heart, and console me this day; for now thou hast the opportunity of saving a poor creature condemned to hell; and thou canst do so, for I will not be obstinate. I abandon myself into thy hands, only tell me what thou wouldst have me to do, and obtain me strength to execute it, for I am resolved to do all that depends on me to recover the Divine Grace. I take refuge under thy mantle. Jesus wills that I should have recourse to thee, in order not only that His blood may save me, but also that thy prayers may assist me in this great work; for thy glory, and for His own, since thou art His Mother. He sends me to thee, that thou mayst help me. O Mary, see, I have recourse to thee; in thee do I confide. Thou prayest for so many others, pray also for me; say only a word. Tell our Lord that thou willest my salvation, and God will certainly save me. Say that I am thine, and then I have obtained all that I ask, all that I desire.

---

[32] Tu . . . scis dulcissima Dei Mater, super omnes angelos et homines nosti quantum placeat benedicto Filio tuo salus nostra.—*Guilelmus Avernus, Rhet. Div.* cap. xviii.

SECTION II. *Mary is also our Life, because she obtains us Perseverance.*

Final perseverance is so great a gift of God, that (as it was declared by the Holy Council of Trent) it is quite gratuitous on His part, and we cannot *merit* it. Yet we are told by Saint Augustine, that all who seek for it obtain it from God ; and, according to Father Suarez, they obtain it infallibly, if only they are diligent in asking for it to the end of their lives. For, as Bellarmin well remarks, 'that which is daily required must be asked for every day.'[1] Now, if it is true (and I hold it as certain, according to the now generally received opinion, and which I shall prove in the fourth chapter of this work) that all the graces that God dispenses to men pass by the hands of Mary, it will be equally true that it is only through Mary that we can hope for this greatest of all graces,—perseverance. And we shall obtain it most certainly, if we always seek it with confidence through Mary. This grace she herself promises to all who serve her faithfully during life, in the following words of Ecclesiasticus ; and which are applied to her by the Church, on the Feast of her Immaculate Conception : "They that work by me shall not sin. They that explain me shall have life everlasting."[2]

In order that we may be preserved in the life of grace, we require spiritual fortitude to resist the many enemies of our salvation. Now this fortitude can be obtained only by the means of Mary, and we are assured of it in the book of Proverbs, for the Church applies the passage to this most Blessed Virgin. "Strength is mine ; by me kings reign."[3] Meaning, by the words "strength is mine," that God has bestowed this precious

---

[1] Quotidie petenda est, ut quotidie obtineatur. †
[2] Qui operantur in me, non peccabunt. Qui elucidant me, vitam æternam abebunt.—*Eccles.* xxiv. 30, 31.
[3] Mea est fortitudo. Per me reges regnant.—*Prov.* viii. 14, 15. *In festo S. Mariæ ad Nives.*

gift on Mary, in order that she may dispense it to her faithful clients. And by the words, "By me kings reign," she signifies that by her means her servants reign over and command their senses and passions, and thus become worthy to reign eternally in heaven. O, what strength do the servants of this great Lady possess, to overcome all the assaults of hell! Mary is that tower spoken of in the sacred Canticles: "Thy neck is as the tower of David, which is built with bulwarks; a thousand bucklers hang upon it, all the armour of valiant men."[4] She is as a well-defended fortress in defence of her lovers, who in their wars have recourse to her. In her do her clients find all shields and arms, to defend themselves against hell.

And for the same reason the most Blessed Virgin is called a plane-tree in the words of Ecclesiasticus: "As a plane-tree by the waters in the streets was I exalted."[5] Cardinal Hugo explains them, and says that the 'plane-tree has leaves like shields,'[6] to show how Mary defends all who take refuge with her. Blessed Amedeus gives another explanation, and says that this holy Virgin is called a plane-tree, because, as the plane shelters travellers under its branches from the heat of the sun and from the rain, so do men find refuge under the mantle of Mary from the ardour of their passions and from the fury of temptations.[7] Truly are those souls to be pitied who abandon this defence, in ceasing their devotion to Mary, and no longer recommending themselves to her in the time of danger. If the sun ceased to rise, says St. Bernard, how could the world become other than a chaos of darkness and horror? And applying his question to Mary, he repeats it. 'Take away the sun, and

<hr>

[4] Sicut turris David collum tuum, quæ ædificata est cum propugnaculis: mille clypei pendent ex ea, omnis armatura fortium.—*Cant.* iv. 4.

[5] Quasi platanus exaltata sum juxta aquam in plateis.—*Eccl.* xxiv. 19.

[6] Platanus . . . habet mollia folia, scutis similia.—*In Eccl.* cap. xxiv.

[7] Virgo . . . ramorum suorum admirabili extensione sese ubique terrarum expandit, ut dispersos filios Adæ ab æstu, a turbine, et a pluvia umbra desiderabili protegeret.—*De Laud. Virg.* Hom. viii.

where will be the day? Take away Mary, and what
will be left but the darkest night?[8]   When a soul loses
devotion to Mary, it is immediately enveloped in darkness, and in that darkness of which the Holy Ghost
speaks in the Psalms : "Thou hast appointed darkness,
and it is night; in it shall all the beasts of the woods
go about."[9]   When the light of heaven ceases to shine
in a soul, all is darkness, and it becomes the haunt of
devils and of every sin. Saint Anselm says, that 'if anyone is disregarded and contemned by Mary, he is necessarily lost;'[10] and therefore we may with reason exclaim,
Woe to those who are in opposition with this sun!
Woe to those who despise its light! that is to say, all
who despise devotion to Mary. St. Francis Borgia always doubted the perseverance of those in whom he did
not find particular devotion to the Blessed Virgin. On
one occasion he questioned some novices as to the saints
towards whom they had special devotion, and perceiving
some who had it not towards Mary, he instantly warned
the master of novices, and desired him to keep a more
attentive watch over these unfortunate young men, who
all, as he had feared, lost their vocations and renounced
the religious state.

It was, then, not without reason that St. Germanus
called the most Blessed Virgin the breath of Christians;
for as the body cannot live without breathing, so the
soul cannot live without having recourse to and recommending itself to Mary, by whose means we certainly
acquire and preserve the life of divine grace within
our souls. But I will quote the Saint's own words:
'As breathing is not only a sign but even a cause of
life, so the name of Mary, which is constantly found on
the lips of God's servants, both proves that they are
truly alive, and at the same time causes and preserves

---

[8] Tolle corpus hoc solare, ubi dies? Tolle Mariam, quid nisi densissimæ
tenebræ relinquentur ?—*Serm. de Aquæd.*

[9] Posuisti tenebras, et facta est nox: in ipsa pertransibunt omnes bestiæ
silvæ.—*Ps.* ciii. 20.

[10] Omnis a te aversus et a te despectus necesse est ut intereat.—*Ad B.M.V.*
Orat. 51.

their life, and gives them every succour.'[11] Blessed Allan was one day assaulted by a violent temptation, and was on the point of yielding, for he had not recommended himself to Mary, when this most Blessed Virgin appeared to him; and in order that another time he might remember to invoke her aid, she gave him a blow, saying, ' If thou hadst recommended thyself to me, thou wouldst not have run into such danger.'

On the other hand, Mary says in the following words of the Book of Proverbs, which are applied to her by the Church : " Blessed is the man that heareth me, and that watcheth daily at my gates, and waiteth at the posts of my doors"[12]—as if she would say, Blessed is he that hears my voice and is constantly attentive to apply at the door of my mercy, and seeks light and help from me. For clients who do this, Mary does her part, and obtains them the light and strength they require to abandon sin and walk in the paths of virtue. For this reason Innocent III. beautifully calls her ' the moon at night, the dawn at break of day, and the sun at midday.'[13] She is a moon to enlighten those who blindly wander in the night of sin, and makes them see and understand the miserable state of damnation in which they are ; she is the dawn (that is, the forerunner of the sun) to those whom she has already enlightened, and makes them abandon sin and return to God, the true Sun of justice ; finally, she is a sun to those who are in a state of grace, and prevents them from again falling into the precipice of sin.

Learned writers apply the following words of Ecclesiasticus to Mary, " Her bands are a healthful binding."[14] ' Why bands ?' asks Saint Lawrence Justinian, ' except it be that she binds her servants, and thus prevents them

[11] Quomodo enim corpus nostrum vitalis signum operationis habet respirationem, ita etiam sanctissimum tuum nomen, quod in ore servorum tuorum versatur assidue in omni tempore, loco, et modo, vitæ, lætitiæ, et auxilii non solum est signum, sed ea etiam procurat et conciliat.—*De Zona B.V.*

[12] Beatus homo qui audit me, et qui vigilat ad fores meas quotidie, et observat ad postes ostii mei.—*Prov.* viii. 34. *In festo Conc. B.V.M.*

[13] Luna lucet in nocte, aurora in diluculo, sol in die.—*Serm.* 2, *de Ass.*

[14] Vincula illius alligatara salutaris.—*Eccl.* vi. 31.

F

from straying into the paths of vice.'[15] And truly this is the reason for which Mary binds her servants. Saint Bonaventure also, in his commentary on the words of Ecclesiasticus, frequently used in the office of Mary, " My abode is in the full assembly of saints,"[16] says that Mary not only has her abode in the full assembly of saints, but also preserves them from falling, keeps a constant watch over their virtue, that it may not fail, and restrains the evil spirits from injuring them.[17] Not only has she her abode in the full assembly of the saints, but she keeps the saints there, by preserving their merits that they may not lose them, by restraining the devils from injuring them, and by withholding the arm of her Son from falling on sinners.'

In the Book of Proverbs we are told that all Mary's clients are clothed with double garments, " For all her domestics are clothed with double garments."[18] Cornelius à Lapide explains what this double clothing is : he says that it ' consists in her adorning her faithful servants with the virtues of her Son, and with her own ;'[19] and thus clothed they persevere in virtue. And therefore St. Philip Neri, in his exhortations to his penitents, used always to say : ' My children, if you desire perseverance, be devout to our Blessed Lady.' The venerable John Berchmans, of the Society of Jesus, used also to say : ' Whoever loves Mary will have perseverance.' Truly beautiful is the reflection of the Abbot Rupert on this subject in his commentary on the parable of the prodigal son. He says, ' That if this dissolute youth had had a mother living, he would never have abandoned

---

[15] Quare vincula ? nisi quia servos ligat, ne discurrant per campos licentiæ. †

[16] In plenitudine sanctorum detentio mea.—*Eccl.* xxiv. 16.

[17] Ipsa quoque non solum in plenitudine sanctorum detinetur, sed etiam in plenitudine sanctos detinet, ne eorum plenitudo minuatur; detinet nimirum virtutes, ne fugiant : detinet merita, ne pereant : detinet dæmones, ne noceant : detinet Filium, ne peccatores percutiat.—*Spec. B. V.M.* lect. viii.

[18] Omnes enim domestici ejus vestiti sunt duplicibus.—*Prov.* xxxi. 21.

[19] Duplici veste ipsa ornat sibi devotos; eaque rursus duplex est, quia tam Christi quam B Virginis virtutibus eos vestit et induit.—*Com. in Prov. Salom.* xxxi. 21.

the paternal roof, or at least would have returned much sooner than he did ;'[20] meaning thereby that a son of Mary either never abandons God, or, if he has this misfortune, by her help he soon returns. O, did all men but love this most benign and loving Lady, had they but recourse to her always, and without delay, in their temptations, who would fall? who would ever be lost? He falls and is lost who has not recourse to Mary. St. Lawrence Justinian applies to Mary the words of Ecclesiasticus, " I have walked in the waves of the sea :"[21] and makes her say, 'I walk with my servants in the midst of the tempests to which they are constantly exposed, to assist and preserve them from falling into sin.'

Bernardine de Bustis relates that a bird was taught to say ' Hail, Mary!'[22] A hawk was on the point of seizing it, when the bird cried out ' Hail, Mary !' In an instant the hawk fell dead. God intended to show thereby, that if even an irrational creature was preserved by calling on Mary, how much more would those who are prompt in calling on her when assaulted by devils, be delivered from them. We, says St. Thomas of Villanova, need only when tempted by the devil, imitate little chickens, which, as soon as they perceive the approach of a bird of prey, run under the wings of their mother for protection. This is exactly what we should do whenever we are assaulted by temptation ; we should not stay to reason with it, but immediately fly and place ourselves under the mantle of Mary. I will, however, quote the Saint's own words addressed to Mary. ' As chickens when they see a kite soaring above, run and find refuge under the wings of the hen, so are we preserved under the shadow of thy wings.'[23] ' And thou,' he continues, ' who art our Lady and Mother, hast to defend us ; for, after God, we have no other refuge than thee, who art our only hope

[20] Si prodigus filius viventem matrem habuisset, vel a paterna domo nunquam discessisset, vel forte citius rediisset. †

[21] In fluctibus maris ambulavi.—*Eccl.* xxiv. 8.   [22] Marial. p. 12, s. 1.

[23] Sicut pulli, volitantibus desuper milvis, ad gallinæ alas occurrunt, ita nos sub velamento alarum tuarum abscondimur.—*Serm.* 3 *de Nat. Virg.*

and our protectress ; towards thee we all turn our eyes with confidence.'[24]

Let us then conclude in the words of Saint Bernard : ' O man, whoever thou art, understand that in this world thou art tossed about on a stormy and tempestuous sea, rather than walking on solid ground ; remember that if thou wouldst avoid being drowned, thou must never turn thine eyes from the brightness of this star, but keep them fixed on it, and call on Mary.   In dangers, in straits, in doubts, remember Mary, invoke Mary.'[25] Yes, in dangers of sinning, when molested by temptations, when doubtful as to how you should act, remember that Mary can help you ; and call upon her, and she will instantly succour you. ' Let not her name leave thy lips, let it be ever in thy heart.' Your hearts should never lose confidence in her holy name, nor should your lips ever cease to invoke it. ' Following her, thou wilt certainly not go astray.' O no, if we follow Mary, we shall never err from the paths of salvation. ' Imploring her, thou wilt not despair.' Each time that we invoke her aid, we shall be inspired with perfect confidence. ' If she supports thee, thou canst not fall ;' ' if she protects thee thou hast nothing to fear, for thou canst not be lost:' 'with her for thy guide, thou wilt not be weary; for thy salvation will be worked out with ease.' ' If she is propitious, thou wilt gain the port.'[26] If Mary undertakes our defence, we are certain of gaining the kingdom of heaven. " This do, and thou shalt live."[27]

[24] Nescimus aliud refugium nisi te ; tu sola es unica spes nostra, in qua confidimus; tu sola patrona nostra, ad quam omnes aspicimus.—*Serm.* 3, *de Nat. B.V.*

[25] O quisquis te intelligis in hujus seculi profluvio magis inter procellas et tempestates fluctuare, quam per terram ambulare ; ne avertas oculos a fulgore hujus sideris, si non vis obrui procellis . . . . Respice stellam, voca Mariam . . . . In periculis, in angustiis, in rebus dubiis, Mariam cogita, Mariam invoca.—*Super missus est Hom.* ii.

[26] Non recedat ab ore, non recedat a corde, et ut impetres ejus orationis suffragium non deseras conversationis exemplum: ipsam sequens, non devias : ipsam rogans, non desperas : ipsam cogitans, non erras : ipsa tenente, non corruis : ipsa protegente, non metuis : ipsa duce, non fatigaris : ipsa propitia, pervenis, et sic in temetipso experiris quam merito dictum sit, Et nomen Virginis Maria.—*Ib.*

[27] Sic fac, et vives.—*Luc.* x. 28.

EXAMPLE.

The history of St. Mary of Egypt, in the first book of the lives of the Fathers, is well known. At the age of twelve years she fled from the house of her parents, and went to Alexandria, and there led an infamous life, and was a scandal to the whole city. After living for sixteen years in sin, she took it into her head to go to Jerusalem. At the time the feast of the holy cross was being celebrated, and, moved rather by curiosity than by devotion, she determined on entering the church; but when at the door, she felt herself repelled by an invisible force. She made a second attempt, and was again unable to enter; and the same thing was repeated a third and a fourth time. Finding her efforts in vain, the unfortunate creature withdrew to a corner of the porch, and there, enlightened from above, understood that it was on account of her infamous life that God had repelled her even from the church. In that moment she fortunately raised her eyes and beheld a picture of Mary. No sooner did she perceive it, than, sobbing, she exclaimed, ' O Mother of God, pity a poor sinner! I know that on account of my sins I deserve not that thou shouldst cast thine eyes upon me. But thou art the refuge of sinners; for the love of thy Son Jesus, help me. Permit me to enter the church, and I promise to change my life and to go and do penance in whatever place thou pointest out to me.' She immediately heard an internal voice, as it were that of the Blessed Virgin, replying: ' Since thou hast recourse to me, and wishest to change thy life, go—enter the church, it is no longer closed against thee.' The sinner entered, adored the cross, and wept bitterly. She then returned to the picture, and said, ' Lady, behold I am ready, where wilt thou that I should go to do penance ?' ' Go,' the Blessed Virgin replied, ' cross the Jordan, and thou wilt find the place of thy repose.' She went to confession and communion, and then passed the river, and finding herself in the desert, she understood that it was in that place she should do penance for her sinful life. During the first seventeen years the assaults of the devil, by which he endeavoured to make the Saint again fall into sin, were terrible. And what were her means of defence? She constantly recommended herself to Mary, and this most Blessed Virgin obtained her strength to resist during the whole of the above time, after which her combats ceased. After fifty-seven years spent in the desert, and having attained the age of 87, she was by a disposition of providence met by the Abbot Zosimus; to him she related the history of her life, and entreated him to return the following year, and to bring her the holy communion. The saintly Abbot did so, and gave her the bread of angels. She then requested that he would again return to see her. This also he did, but found her dead. Her body was encompassed by a bright light, and at her head these words were written, 'Bury my body here—it is that of a poor sinner, and intercede with God for me.' A lion came and made a grave with his claws. St. Zosimus buried her, returned to his monastery, and related the wonders of God's mercy towards this happy sinner.

PRAYER.

O compassionate Mother, most sacred Virgin, behold at thy feet the traitor, who, by paying with ingratitude the graces received from God through thy means, has betrayed both thee and him. But I must tell thee, O most blessed Lady, that my misery, far from taking away my confidence, increases it; for I see that thy compassion is great in proportion to the greatness of my misery. Show thyself, O Mary, full of liberality towards me; for thus thou art towards all who invoke thy aid. All that I ask is that thou shouldst cast thine eyes of compassion on me, and pity me. If thy heart is thus far moved, it cannot do otherwise than protect me; and if thou protectest me, what can I fear? No, I fear nothing; I do not fear my sins, for thou canst provide a remedy; I do not fear devils, for thou art more powerful than the whole of hell; I do not even fear thy Son, though justly irritated against me, for at a word of thine He will be appeased. I only fear lest, in my temptations, and by my own fault, I may cease to recommend myself to thee, and thus be lost. But I now promise thee that I will always have recourse to thee; O, help me to fulfil my promise. Lose not the opportunity which now presents itself of gratifying thy ardent desire to succour such poor wretches as myself. In thee, O Mother of God, I have unbounded confidence. From thee I hope for grace to bewail my sins as I ought, and from thee I hope for strength never again to fall into them. If I am sick, thou, O heavenly physician, canst heal me. If my sins have weakened me, thy help will strengthen me. O Mary, I hope all from thee; for thou art all-powerful with God. Amen.

SECTION III. *Mary renders Death sweet to her Clients.*

"He that is a friend loveth at all times; and a brother is proved in distress,"[1] says the Book of Proverbs. We can never know our friends and relations in the time of prosperity; it is only in the time of adversity that we see them in their true colours. People of the world never abandon a friend as long as he is in prosperity; but should misfortunes overtake him, and more particularly should he be at the point of death, they immediately forsake him. Mary does not act thus with her clients. In their afflictions, and more particularly in the sorrows of death, the greatest that can be endured in this world, this good Lady and Mother not only does not abandon her faithful servants, but as, during our exile, she is our life, so also is she, at our last hour, our

---

[1] Omni tempore diligit qui amicus est : et frater in angustiis comprobatur.—*Prov.* xvii. 17.

sweetness, by obtaining us a calm and happy death.
For from the day on which Mary had the privilege and
sorrow of being present at the death of Jesus her Son,
who was the head of all the predestined, it became her
privilege to assist also at their deaths.   And for this
reason the holy Church teaches us to beg this most
Blessed Virgin to assist us, especially at the moment of
death : Pray for us sinners, now and at the hour of our
death !

O how great are the sufferings of the dying ! They
suffer from remorse of conscience on account of past sins,
from fear of the approaching judgment, and from the
uncertainty of their eternal salvation.   Then it is that
hell arms itself, and spares no efforts to gain the soul
which is on the point of entering eternity; for it knows
that only a short time remains in which to gain it, and
that if it then loses it, it has lost it for ever.   " The
devil is come down unto you, having great wrath, knowing that he hath but a short time."[2]   And for this reason the enemy of our salvation, whose charge it was to
tempt the soul during life, does not choose at death to
be alone, but calls others to his assistance, according to
the prophet Isaias : "Their houses shall be filled with
serpents."[3]   And indeed they are so ; for when a person
is at the point of death, the whole place in which he is
is filled with devils, who all unite to make him lose his
soul.

It is related of St. Andrew Avellino, that ten thousand devils came to tempt him at his death.   The con-
flict that he had in his agony with the powers of hell
was so terrible, that all the good religious who assisted
him trembled.   They saw the Saint's face swelled to
such a degree from agitation, that it became quite black;
every limb trembled and was contorted ; his eyes shed
a torrent of tears, his head shook violently : all gave

---

[2] Descendit diabolus ad vos, habens iram magnam, sciens quod modicum
tempus habet.—*Apoc.* xii. 12.
[3] Replebuntur domus eorum draconibus.—*Isaias* xiii. 21.

evidence of the terrible assault he was enduring on the part of his infernal foes. All wept with compassion, and redoubled their prayers, and at the same time trembled with fear, on seeing a Saint die thus. They were, however, consoled at seeing, that often, as if seeking for help, the Saint turned his eyes towards a devout picture of Mary; for they remembered that during life he had often said that at death Mary would be his refuge. At length God was pleased to put an end to the contest by granting him a glorious victory; for the contortions of his body ceased, his face resumed its original size and colour, and the Saint, with his eyes tranquilly fixed on the picture, made a devout inclination to Mary (who it is believed then appeared to him), as if in the act of thanking her, and with a heavenly smile on his countenance tranquilly breathed forth his blessed soul into the arms of Mary. At the same moment, a Capuchiness, who was in her agony, turning to the nuns who surrounded her, said, ' Recite a Hail Mary; for a Saint has just expired.'

Ah, how quickly do the rebellious spirits fly from the presence of this queen! . If at the hour of death we have only the protection of Mary, what need we fear from the whole of our infernal enemies? David, fearing the horrors of death, encouraged himself by placing his reliance in the death of the coming Redeemer and in the intercession of the Virgin Mother. " For though," he says, " I should walk in the midst of the shadow of death . . . . . thy rod and thy staff, they have comforted me."[4] Cardinal Hugo, explaining these words of the royal prophet, says that the staff signifies the cross, and the rod is the intercession of Mary; for she is the rod foretold by the prophet Isaias : " And there shall come forth a rod out of the root of Jesse, and a flower shall rise up out of his root."[5] 'This Divine Mother,'

[4] Et si ambulavero in medio umbræ mortis . . . . virga tua, et baculus tuus, ipsa me consolata sunt.—*Ps.* xxii. 4.

[5] Egredietur virga de radice Jesse, et flos de radice ejus ascendet.—*Isaias* xi. 1.

says Saint Peter Damian, 'is that powerful rod with which the violence of the infernal enemies is conquered.'[6]   And therefore does St. Antoninus encourage us, saying, 'If Mary is for us, who shall be against us?'[7]   When Father Emanuel Padial, of the Society of Jesus, was at the point of death, Mary appeared to him, and to console him, she said: 'See at length the hour is come when the angels congratulate with thee, and exclaim: O happy labours, O mortifications well requited!   And in the same moment an army of demons was seen taking its flight, and crying out in despair: Alas! we can do nought, for she who is without stain defends him.'[8]   In like manner, Father Gaspar Haywood was assaulted by devils at his death, and greatly tempted against faith: he immediately recommended himself to the most Blessed Virgin, and was heard to exclaim, 'I thank thee, Mary; for thou hast come to my aid.'[9]   St. Bonaventure tells us that Mary sends without delay the prince of the heavenly court, Saint Michael, with all the angels, to defend her dying servants against the temptations of the devils, and to receive the souls of all who in a special manner and perseveringly have recommended themselves to her.   The Saint, addressing our Blessed Lady, says, 'Michael, the leader and prince of the heavenly army, with all the administering spirits, obeys thy commands, O Virgin, and defends and receives the souls of the faithful who have particularly recommended themselves to thee, O Lady, day and night.'[10]

The prophet Isaias tells us that when a man is on the point of leaving the world, hell is opened and sends

6 Hæc est virga illa, qua retunduntur impetus adversantium dæmoniorum.—*Serm. de Ass. B.V.*

7 Si Maria pro nobis, quis contra nos? †

8 Menol. 28 Apr.—9 Genn.

9 Ib.

10 Michael dux et princeps militiæ cœlestis, cum omnibus administratoriis spiritibus, tuis, Virgo, paret præceptis, in defendendis in corpore et in suscipiendis de corpore animabus fidelium, specialiter tibi, Domina, die ac nocte tibi commendantium.—*Spec. B.V.* lect. 3.

forth its most terrible demons, both to tempt the soul before it leaves the body, and also to accuse it when presented before the tribunal of Jesus Christ for judgment. The prophet says, "Hell below was in an uproar to meet thee at thy coming; it stirred up the giants for thee."[11] But Richard of Saint Lawrence remarks, that when the soul is defended by Mary, the devils dare not even accuse it, knowing that the judge never condemned, and never will condemn, a soul protected by his august Mother. He asks, 'Who would dare accuse one who is patronised by the Mother of Him who is to judge?'[12] Mary not only assists her beloved servants at death and encourages them, but she herself accompanies them to the tribunal-seat of God. As St. Jerome says, writing to the virgin Eustochia, ' What a day of joy will that be for thee, when Mary, the Mother of our Lord, accompanied by choirs of virgins, will go to meet thee !'[13]

The Blessed Virgin assured Saint Bridget of this ; for, speaking of her devout clients at the point of death, she said, 'Then will I, their dear Lady and Mother, fly to them, that they may have consolation and refreshment.'[14] Saint Vincent Ferrers says, that not only does the most Blessed Virgin console and refresh them, but that ' she receives the souls of the dying.'[15] This loving Queen takes them under her mantle, and thus presents them to the Judge her Son, and most certainly obtains their salvation. This really happened to Charles the son of St. Bridget,[16] who died in the army, far from his mother. She feared much for his salvation on account of the dangers to which young men are exposed in a

[11] Infernus subter conturbatus est in occursum adventus tui, suscitavit tibi gigantes.—*Isaias* xiv. 9.
[12] Quis enim apud Filium accusare audeat, cui matrem viderit patrocinantem ?—*De Laud. V.* l. ii. c. 1.
[13] Qualis erit illa dies, quum tibi Maria Mater Domini choris occurret comitata virgineis?—*Epist. ad Eust. de Cust. Virg.*
[14] Ego carissima domina eorum et mater obviabo eis et occurram eis in morte, ut etiam in ipsa morte consolationem et refrigerium habeant.—*Rev* lib. i. c. 29.
[15] Beata Virgo animas morientium suscipit.—*Serm. de Ass.* †
[16] Rev. lib. vii. c. 13.

military career; but the Blessed Virgin revealed to her that he was saved on account of his love for her, and that in consequence she herself had assisted him at death, and had suggested to him the acts that should be made at that terrible moment.   At the same time the Saint saw Jesus on His throne, and the devil bringing two accusations against the most Blessed Virgin : the first was, that Mary had prevented him from tempting Charles at the moment of death ; and the second was, that this Blessed Virgin had herself presented his soul to the Judge, and so saved it without even giving him the opportunity of exposing the grounds on which he claimed it.   She then saw the Judge drive the devil away, and Charles's soul carried to heaven.

Ecclesiasticus says, that " her bands are a healthful binding,"[17] and that " in the latter end thou shalt find rest in her."[18]   O, you are indeed fortunate, my brother, if at death you are bound with the sweet chains of the love of the Mother of God ! These chains are chains of salvation ; they are chains that will insure your eternal salvation, and will make you enjoy in death that blessed peace which will be the beginning of your eternal peace and rest.   Father Binetti, in his book on the perfections of our blessed Lord, says, ' that having attended the deathbed of a great lover of Mary, he heard him, before expiring, utter these words : ' O my father, would that you could know the happiness that I now enjoy from having served the most holy Mother of God ; I cannot tell you the joy that I now experience.'[19]   Father Suarez (in consequence of his devotion to Mary, which was such that he used to say that he would willingly change all his learning for the merit of a single ' Hail Mary') died with such peace and joy, that in that moment he said, ' I could not have thought that death was so sweet ;' meaning, that

---

17 Vincula illius alligatura salutaris.—*Eccl.* vi. 31.
18 In novissimis enim invenies requiem in ea.—*Eccl.* vi. 29.
19 Chef-d'œuvre de D. p. 3. ch. 6.

he could never have imagined that it was possible, if he had not then experienced it, that he could have found such sweetness in death. You, devout reader, will, without doubt, experience the same joy and contentment in death, if you can then remember that you have loved this good Mother, who cannot be otherwise than faithful to her children who have been faithful in serving and honouring her, by their visits, rosaries, and fasts, and still more by frequently thanking and praising her, and often recommending themselves to her powerful protection.

Nor will this consolation be withheld, even if you have been for a time a sinner, provided that, from this day, you are careful to live well, and to serve this most gracious and benign Lady. She, in your pains, and in the temptations to despair which the devil will send you, will console you, and even come herself to assist you in your last moments. Marinus, the brother of Saint Peter Damian, who relates it,[20] had one day offended God grievously. He went before an altar of Mary, to dedicate himself to her as her slave; and for this purpose, and as a mark of servitude, put his girdle round his neck, and thus addressed her: ' My sovereign Lady, mirror of that purity which I, miserable sinner that I am, have violated, thereby outraging my God and thee, I know no better remedy for my crime than to offer myself to thee for thy slave. Behold me, then: to thee do I this day dedicate myself, that I may be thy servant; accept me, though a rebel, and reject me not.' He then left a sum of money on the step of the altar, and promised to pay a like sum every year, as a tribute which he owed as a slave of Mary. After a certain time, Marinus fell dangerously ill; but one morning, before expiring, he was heard to exclaim: ' Rise, rise, pay homage to my Queen !' and then he added : ' And whence is this favour, O Queen of Hea-

[20] Opusc. 33, cap. iv.

ven, that thou shouldst condescend to visit thy poor servant? Bless me, O Lady, and permit me not to be lost, after having honoured me with thy presence.' At this moment his brother Peter entered, and to him he related the visit of Mary; and added, that she had blest him; but at the same time complained that those who were present had remained seated in the presence of this great Queen; and shortly afterwards he sweetly expired in our Lord. Such also will be your death, beloved reader, if you are faithful to Mary. Though you may have hitherto offended God, she will procure you a sweet and happy death.

And if by chance at that moment you are greatly alarmed and lose confidence at the sight of your sins, she will come and encourage you, as she did Adolphus, Count of Alsace,[21] who abandoned the world, and embraced the order of St. Francis. In the Chronicles of that Order, we are told that he had a tender devotion to the Mother of God; and that when he was at the point of death, his former life and the rigours of Divine justice presented themselves before his mind, and caused him to tremble at the thought of death, and fear for his eternal salvation. Scarcely had these thoughts entered his mind, when Mary (who is always active when her servants are in pain), accompanied by many Saints, presented herself before the dying man, and encouraged him with words of the greatest tenderness, saying: 'My own beloved Adolph, thou art mine, thou hast given thyself to me, and now why dost thou fear death so much?' On hearing these words, the servant of Mary was instantly relieved, fear was banished from his soul, and he expired in the midst of the greatest peace and joy. Let us then be of good heart, though we be sinners, and feel certain that Mary will come and assist us at death, and comfort and console us with her presence, provided only that we serve her with love during the remainder of the time that we have to be in this world. Our Queen, one day addressing Saint Matilda, promised that she would assist all her clients at death, who, during their lives, had faithfully served her. ' I, as a most tender Mother, will faithfully be present at the death of all who piously serve me, and will console and protect them.'[22] O God, what a consolation will it be at that last moment of our lives, when our eternal lot has so soon to be decided, to see the Queen of Heaven assisting and consoling us with the assurance of her protection. For, besides the cases already given in which we have seen Mary assisting her dying servants, there are innumerable others recorded in different works. This favour was granted to Saint Clare; to Saint Felix, of the Order of Capuchins; to Saint Clare of Montefalco; to Saint Teresa; to Saint Peter of Alcantara. But, for our common consolation, I will relate the following. Father Crasset[23] tells us, that Mary of Oignes saw the Blessed Virgin at the pillow of a devout widow of Villembroe, who was ill with a violent fever. Mary stood by her side, consoling her, and cooling her with a fan. Of Saint John of God,[24] who was tenderly devoted to Mary, it is related that he fully expected that she would visit him on his deathbed; but not seeing her arrive, he was afflicted, and perhaps even complained. But when his last hour had come, the Divine Mother appeared, and gently reproving him for his little confidence, addressed him in the following tender words, which may well encourage all servants of Mary : ' John, it is not in me to forsake my clients at such a moment.' As though she had said : ' John, of what wast thou thinking? Didst thou imagine that I had abandoned thee? And dost thou not know that I never abandon

---

[22] Ego omnibus, qui mihi pie et sancte deserviunt, volo in morte fidelissime tamquam mater piissima adesse, eosque consolari ac protegere.—*Ap. Blos. Concl. an. Fid.* cap. x.

[23] *Div. alla Verg.* tom. 1. tr. 1. qu. xi.

[24] Boll. 8 Mart. v. 2. c. 8.

my clients at the hour of death? If I did not come sooner, it was that thy time was not yet come; but now that it is come, behold me here to take thee; let us go to Heaven.' Shortly afterwards the Saint expired, and fled to that blessed kingdom, there to thank his most loving Queen for all eternity.

EXAMPLE.

Let us close this subject with another example, in which we shall see how great is the tenderness of this good Mother towards her children at death. The parish priest of a country place was assisting a certain rich man who was dying, in a magnificent house, and attended upon by servants, relatives, and friends; but the good priest saw also devils, in the shape of dogs, waiting to carry off his soul, as they in fact did; for he died in sin. In the mean time, a poor woman was also ill; and desiring to receive the Holy Sacraments, sent for the parish priest; but he, being unable to leave the rich man, whose soul stood in such need of assistance, sent her another priest, who immediately went, carrying the pix which contained the Most Blessed Sacrament. On his arrival, he saw neither servants, nor attendants, nor fine furniture; for the sick woman was poor, and perhaps only lying on a little straw. But he saw a great light in the room, and near the bed of the dying person was the Mother of God, Mary, consoling her, and, with a cloth in her hand, wiping off the sweat of death. The priest, seeing Mary, feared to enter; but the Blessed Virgin made him a sign to come in. The priest entered, and Mary showed him a stool, that he might be seated, and hear the confession of her servant. This he did, and after she had communicated with great devotion, she happily breathed forth her soul in the arms of Mary.[25]

25 Bovio, Es. e Mir. p. 2. c. 4.

PRAYER.

O my most sweet Mother, how shall I die, poor sinner that I am ? Even now the thought of that important moment when I must expire, and appear before the judgment-seat of God, and the remembrance that I have myself so often written my condemnation by consenting to sins, makes me tremble. I am confounded, and fear much for my eternal salvation. O Mary, in the blood of Jesus, and in thy intercession, is all my hope. Thou art the Queen of Heaven, the mistress of the universe ; in short, thou art the Mother of God. Thou art great, but thy greatness does not prevent, nay even it inclines thee to greater compassion towards us in our miseries. Worldly friends, when raised to dignity, disdain to notice their former friends who may have fallen into distress. Thy noble and loving heart does not act thus, for the greater the miseries it beholds, the greater are its efforts to relieve. Thou, when called upon, immediately assistest ; nay more, thou anticipatest our prayers by thy favours ; thou consolest us in our afflictions ; thou dissipatest the storms by which we are tossed about ; thou overcomest all enemies ; thou, in fine, never losest an occasion to promote our welfare. May that Divine hand which has united in thee such majesty and such tenderness, such greatness and so much love, be · for ever blessed ! I thank my Lord for it, and congratulate myself in having so great an advantage ; for truly in thy felicity do I place my own, and I consider thy lot as mine. O comfortress of the afflicted, console a poor creature who recommends himself to thee. The remorse of a conscience overburdened with sins fills me with affliction. I am in doubt as to whether I have sufficiently grieved for them. I see that all my actions are soiled and defective ; hell awaits my death in order to accuse me ; the outraged justice of God demands satisfaction. My Mother, what will become of me ? If thou dost not help me, I am lost. What sayest thou, wilt thou assist me? O compassionate Virgin, console me; obtain me true sorrow for my sins; obtain me strength to amend, and to be faithful to God during the rest of my life. And finally, when I am in the last agonies of death, O Mary, my hope, abandon me not; then, more than ever, help and encourage me, that I may not despair at the sight of my sins, which the evil one will then place before me. My Lady, forgive my temerity; come thyself to comfort me with thy presence in that last struggle. This favour thou hast granted to many, grant it also to me. If my boldness is great, thy goodness is greater; for it goes in search of the most miserable to console them. On this I rely. For thy eternal glory, let it be said that thou hast snatched a wretched creature from hell, to which he was already condemned, and that thou hast led him to thy kingdom. O yes, sweet Mother, I hope to have the consolation of remaining always at thy feet in heaven, thanking and blessing and loving thee eternally. O Mary, I shall expect thee at my last hour; deprive me not of this consolation. **Fiat, fiat. Amen, amen.**

CHAPTER III.

SECTION I. *Mary is the Hope of all.*

MODERN heretics cannot endure that we should salute and call Mary our Hope : ' Hail, our Hope !' They say that God alone is our hope ; and that He curses those who put their trust in creatures in these words of the prophet Jeremias : " Cursed be the man that trusteth in man."[1] Mary, they exclaim, is a creature ; and how can a creature be our hope ? This is what the heretics say ; but in spite of it, the holy Church obliges all ecclesiastics and religious each day to raise their voices, and in the name of all the faithful, invoke and call Mary by the sweet name of ' our Hope,'—the Hope of all.

The angelical Doctor Saint Thomas says,[2] that we can place our hope in a person in two ways : as a principal cause, and as a mediate one. Those who hope for a favour from a king, hope it from him as lord ; they hope for it from his minister or favourite as an intercessor. If the favour is granted, it comes primarily from the king, but it comes through the instrumentality of the favourite ; and in this case he who seeks the favour is right in calling his intercessor his hope. The King of Heaven, being infinite goodness, desires in the highest degree to enrich us with His graces ; but, because confidence is requisite on our part, and in order to increase it in us, He has given us His own Mother

---

[1] Maledictus homo qui confidit in homine.—*Jerem.* xvii. 5.
[2] 2. 2æ q. 25, a. 1, ad 3.

to be our Mother and Advocate, and to her He has given all power to help us; and therefore He wills that we should repose our hope of salvation and of every blessing in her. Those who place their hopes in creatures alone, independently of God, as sinners do, and in order to obtain the friendship and favour of a man, fear not to outrage His Divine Majesty, are most certainly cursed by God, as the prophet Jeremias says. But those who hope in Mary, as Mother of God, who is able to obtain graces and eternal life for them, are truly blessed and acceptable to the heart of God, who desires to see that greatest of His creatures honoured; for she loved and honoured Him in this world more than all men and angels put together. And therefore we justly and reasonably call the Blessed Virgin our Hope, trusting, as Cardinal Bellarmin says, 'that we shall obtain, through her intercession, that which we should not obtain by our own unaided prayers.' 'We pray to her,' says the learned Suarez, 'in order that the dignity of the intercessor may supply for our own unworthiness; so that,'[3] he continues, 'to implore the Blessed Virgin in such a spirit, is not diffidence in the mercy of God, but fear of our own unworthiness.'[4]

It is, then, not without reason that the holy Church, in the words of Ecclesiasticus, calls Mary "the Mother of holy Hope."[5] She is the mother who gives birth to holy hope in our hearts; not to the hope of the vain and transitory goods of this life, but of the immense and eternal goods of heaven. 'Hail, then, O hope of my soul!' exclaims St. Ephrem, addressing this Divine Mother; 'hail, O certain salvation of Christians; hail, O helper of sinners; hail, fortress of the faithful and salvation of the world!'[6] Other Saints remind us, that

[3] Ut dignitas intercessoris suppleat inopiam nostram.—*De Incarnat.* p. 2, q. xxxvii. art. 4, disp. 23, sect. 3.
[4] Unde virginem interpellare, non est de divina misericordia diffidere, sed de propria indignitate et indispositione timere.—*Ib.*
[5] Ego mater . . . sanctæ spei.—*Eccles.* xxiv. 24.
[6] Ave animæ fida et optima spes. Ave firma salus universorum Chris-

after God, our only Hope is Mary; and, therefore, they call her, ' after God, their only Hope.' And St. Ephrem, reflecting on the present order of providence, by which God wills (as St. Bernard says, and as we shall prove at length) that all who are saved should be saved by the means of Mary, thus addresses her: 'O Lady, cease not to watch over us; preserve and guard us under the wings of thy compassion and mercy, for, after God, we have no hope but in thee.'[7] St. Thomas of Villanova repeats the same thing, calling her ' our only refuge, help, and asylum.'[8]

St. Bernard seems to give the reason for this when he says, ' See, O man, the designs of God,—designs by which He is able to dispense His mercy more abundantly to us; for, desiring to redeem the whole human race, He has placed the whole price of redemption in the hands of Mary, that she may dispense it at will.'[9]

In the book of Exodus we read that God commanded Moses to make a mercy-seat of the purest gold, because it was thence that He would speak to him. "Thou shalt make also a propitiatory of the purest gold. . . Thence will I give orders, and will speak to thee."[10] St. Andrew of Crete says, that ' the whole world embraces Mary as being this propitiatory.' And commenting on his words, a pious author exclaims, ' Thou, O Mary, art the propitiatory of the whole world. From thee does our most compassionate Lord speak to our hearts; from thee He speaks words of pardon and mercy; from thee He bestows His gifts; from thee all

---

tianorum ad te sincere ac vere recurrentium . . . Tu peccatorum et auxilio destitutorum unica advocata es atque adjutrix . . . Ave vallis fidelium, mundique salus.— *De Laud. Virg.*

[7] Non nobis est alia quam in te fiducia, O Virgo sincerissima . . . sub alis tuæ pietatis atque misericordiæ tuæ protege et custodi nos.—*De Laud. Virg.*

[8] Tu nostra protectio, tu nostrum refugium, tu nostrum unicum remedium, subsidium, et asylum.—*In Festo Nat. B. V.* Concio III.

[9] Intuere, O homo, consilium Dei, agnosce consilium sapientiæ, consilium pietatis . . . Redempturus humanum genus, universum pretium contulit in Mariam.—*Serm. de Nat.*

[10] Facies et propitiatorium de auro mundissimo . . . Inde præcipiam et loquar ad te.—*Exod.* xxv. 17, 22.

good flows to us.'[11] And therefore, before the **Divine**
Word took flesh in the womb of Mary, He sent an
archangel to ask her consent : because He willed that
the world should receive the Incarnate Word through
her, and that she should be the source of every good.
Hence St. Irenæus remarks, that as Eve was seduced,
by a fallen angel, to flee from God, so Mary was led to
receive God into her womb, obeying a good angel ; and
thus, by her obedience, repaired Eve's disobedience, and
became her advocate, and that of the whole human
race. 'If Eve disobeyed God, yet Mary was persuaded
to obey God, that the Virgin Mary might become the
advocate of the virgin Eve. And as the human race
was bound to death through a virgin, it is saved through
a Virgin.'[12]

And B. Raymond Jordano also says, 'that every
good, every help, every grace that men have received
and will receive from God until the end of time, came,
and will come, to them by the intercession and through
the hands of Mary.'[13] The devout Blosius, then, might
well exclaim, 'O Mary, O thou who art so loving and
gracious towards all who love thee, tell me, who can be
so infatuated and unfortunate as not to love thee? Thou,
in the midst of their doubts and difficulties, enlightenest the minds of all who, in their afflictions, have
recourse to thee. Thou encouragest those who fly to
thee in time of danger ; thou succourest those who call
upon thee ; thou, after thy Divine Son, art the certain
salvation of thy faithful servants. Hail, then, O hope

---

[11] Quocirca D. Andreas Cretensis Virginem alloquens ait, 'mundus te totus
propitiatorium commune amplectitur.'—*In Dorm. S. M.* Serm. iii. Inde
pientissimus Dominus nobis loquitur ad cor ; inde responsa dat benignitatis
et veniæ, inde se nobis propitiatum ostendit, inde delicta condonat et munera
divina largitur : inde omne nobis bonum emanat.—*Pacciuchelli Excit.* xx. *in
Salut. Ang.*

[12] Et sicut illa seducta est ut effugeret Deum, sic hæc suasa est obedire
Deo, uti virginis Evæ Virgo Maria fieret advocata. Et quemadmodum as-
trictum est morti genus humanum per virginem, solvatur per virginem.—
S. Iren. adv. Hæres. lib. v. c. 19.

[13] Per ipsam, et in ipsa, et cum ipsa, et ab ipsa, habet mundus et habiturus est omne bonum.—*De Contempl. B.M.* in Prol.

of those who are in despair; O succour of those who are abandoned. O Mary, thou art all-powerful: for thy Divine Son, to honour thee, complies instantly with all thy desires.'[14]

Saint Germanus, recognising in Mary the source of all our good, and that she delivers us from every evil, thus invokes her: ' O, my sovereign Lady, delight of my soul, heavenly dew quenching my burning thirst, liquid flowing from God into my parched heart, bright light in the midst of my soul's darkness, guide of my poor judgment, strength of my weakness, covering of my nudity, treasure of my poverty, remedy for incurable wounds, wiper away of tears, end of sighs, reverser of misfortunes, lightener of grief, loosener of my bonds, my hope of salvation, listen to my prayers, have mercy on my sighs, and reject not my lamentations; have mercy on me, and may my tears move thee; be moved by thine own feeling of compassion towards me, who art the Mother of God, the lover of men, hear and grant my prayers, fulfil my petition.'[15]

We need not, then, be surprised that Saint Antoninus applies the following verse of the Book of Wisdom to Mary: " Now all good things came to me together with her."[16] For as this blessed Virgin is the Mother and dispenser of all good things, the whole world, and more particularly each individual who lives

---

[14] Quis te non amet? Tu enim in rebus dubiis es charum lumen, in moeroribus solatium, in angustiis relevamen, in periculis et tentationibus refugium. Tu post unigenitum filium tuum certa fidelium salus ... Ave desperantium spes opportuna, et auxilia destitutorum adjutrix præsentissima Maria, cujus honori tantum tribuit filius, ut quidquid volueris mox fiat.—*Parad. An.* p. 2, cap. iv.

[15] O domina mea, voluptas mei animi, æstus quem patior divina irroratio, cordi meo exsiccato gutta manans a Deo, tenebrosæ animæ meæ lampas splendidissima, dux egenis meis consiliis, imbecillitatis robur, nuditatis operimentum, paupertatis divitiæ, insanabilium vulnerum medela, lachrymarum abstersio, suspiriorum finis, calamitatum in res secundas mutatio, dolorum levamen, meorum vinculorum solutio, salutis meæ spes; preces meas exaudi, miserere meorum gemituum, et lamentationes meas ne abjicias; miserere mei, et flectant te meæ lachrymæ; moveat te miserationis tuæ affectus erga me, quæ amantis homines Dei es Mater; respice et annue supplicationibus meis, imple petitionem meam.—*Orat.* ii. *in Præsent. B. V.*

[16] Venerunt autem mihi omnia bona pariter cum illa.— *Sap.* vii. 11.

in it as a devout client of this great Queen, may say
with truth, that with devotion to Mary, both he and
the world have obtained everything good and perfect.
The Saint thus expresses his thought: ' She is the
Mother of all good things, and the world can truly say,
that with her (that is, the most Blessed Virgin) it has
received all good things.'[17]   And hence the Blessed
Abbot of Celles expressly declares, ' that when we find
Mary, we find all.'[18]   Whoever finds Mary finds every
good thing, obtains all graces and all virtues ; for by
her powerful intercession she obtains all that is necessary to enrich him with Divine grace.   In the Book of
Proverbs Mary herself tells us that she possesses all the
riches of God, that is to say, His mercies, that she may
dispense them in favour of her lovers : " With me are
riches . . . and glorious riches . . . that I may enrich
them that love me."[19]   And therefore Saint Bonaventure says, ' That we ought all to keep our eyes constantly fixed on Mary's hands, that through them we
may receive the graces that we desire.'[20]

O, how many who were once proud have become
humble by devotion to Mary ! how many who were
passionate have become meek ! how many in the midst
of darkness have found light ! how many who were in
despair have found confidence ! how many who were
lost have found salvation by the same powerful means !
And this she clearly foretold in the house of Elizabeth,
in her own sublime canticle : " Behold, from henceforth
all generations shall call me blessed."[21]   And Saint
Bernard, interpreting her words, says, ' All generations
call thee blessed, because thou hast given life and glory

---

[17] Omnium bonorum mater est, et venerunt mihi omnia bona cum illa
scilicet virgine, potest dicere mundus.—*P.* iv. Tit. xv. cap. 20.

[18] Inventa ... Virgine Maria, invenitur omne bonum.—*De Contempl. B. M.*
in Prol.

[19] Mecum sunt divitiæ, et gloria, opes superbæ . . . ut ditem diligentes
me.—*Prov.* viii. 18, 21.

[20] Oculi omnium nostrum ad manus Mariæ semper debent respicere, ut
per manus ejus aliquid boni accipiamus.—*In Spec.* lect. iii.

[21] Ecce enim ex hoc beatam me dicent omnes . . generationes.—*Luc.* i. 48.

to all nations,[22] for in thee sinners find pardon, and the just perseverance in the grace of God.'[23]   Hence the devout Lanspergius makes our Lord thus address the world : ' Men, poor children of Adam, who live surrounded by so many enemies and in the midst of so many trials, endeavour to honour my Mother and yours in a special manner: for I have given Mary to the world, that she may be your model, and that from her you may learn to lead good lives ; and also that she may be a refuge to which you can fly in all your afflictions and trials.   I have rendered this, my Daughter, such that no one need fear or have the least repugnance to have recourse to her ; and for this purpose I have created her of so benign and compassionate a disposition, that she knows not how to despise anyone who takes refuge with her, nor can she deny her favour to anyone who seeks it.   The mantle of her mercy is open to all, and she allows no one to leave her feet without consoling him.'[24]   May the immense goodness of our God be ever praised and blessed for having given us this so great, so tender, so loving a Mother and Advocate.

O God, how tender are the sentiments of confidence expressed by the enamoured St. Bonaventure towards Jesus our most loving Redeemer, and Mary our most loving Advocate ! He says, ' Whatever God foresees to be my lot, I know that He cannot refuse Himself to anyone who loves Him and seeks for Him with his whole heart.   I will embrace Him with my love ; and if He does not bless me, I will still cling to Him so

---

[22] Ex hoc . . . beatam te dicent omnes generationes, quæ omnibus generationibus vitam et gloriam genuisti.—*Serm.* ii. *in Pentec.*

[23] In te . . . justi gratiam, peccatores veniam invenerunt in æternum.—*S. Bern. Serm.* ii. *in Pentec.*

[24] Matrem meam devotione præcipua venerare . . . Ego enim hanc mundo dedi, in sanctitatis, innocentiæ, ac puritatis exemplum, in singulare patrocinium, et in præsidium tutissimum, ut sit tribulatis ac desolatis omnibus immunitatis asylum, quam nemo horret, nemo formidet, nemo ad eam accedere trepidet.   Propterea namque adeo feci eam mitem, adeo piam, adeo misericordem; adeo denique benignam et clementem, ut neminem aspernetur, nulli se neget ; omnibus pietatis sinum apertum teneat ; neminem a se redire tristem, aut non consolatum sinat.—*Op Min.* lib. i. *Alloq. Can.* 12.

closely that He will be unable to go without me. If I can do nothing else, at least I will hide myself in his wounds, and, taking up my dwelling there, it will be in Himself alone that He will find me.' And the Saint concludes, 'If my Redeemer rejects me on account of my sins, and drives me from His sacred feet, I will cast myself at those of His beloved Mother Mary, and there I will remain prostrate until she has obtained my forgiveness; for this Mother of Mercy knows not, and has never known, how to do otherwise than compassionate the miserable, and comply with the desires of the most destitute who fly to her for succour; and therefore,' he says, 'if not by duty, at least by compassion, she will engage her Son to pardon me.'[25]

'Look down upon us, then,' let us exclaim, in the words of Euthymius, 'look down upon us, O most compassionate Mother; cast thine eyes of mercy on us, for we are thy servants, and in thee we have placed all our confidence.'[26]

EXAMPLE.

In the fourth part of the treasury of the Rosary, at the eighty-fifth miracle, it is related that there was a gentleman who was tenderly devoted to the Divine Mother. He had erected an oratory in his dwelling, and there he used often to remain in prayer before a beautiful statue of Mary, and this not only during the day, but frequently at night he rose for the purpose of honouring his beloved Lady. His wife (for he was married), who was otherwise a person of great piety,

---

[25] Quantumcumque me Deus præsciverit, scientia constat mihi, et scio, quod seipsum negare non potest. Eum ergo totis visceribus amplexabor . . . et si non mihi benedixerit, non ipsum dimittam; . . . et sine me recedere non valebit . . . In cavernis vulnerum suorum me abscondam, ibique quietus latitabo, nec extra se me invenire poterit. . . . Aut ad matris suæ pedes provolutus stabo . . . . et ut mihi veniam impetret implorabo. . . . Ipsa enim non misereri ignorat, et miseris non satisfacere nunquam sivit. . . Ideoque ex compassione maxima . . . mihi ad indulgentiam suum unicum Filium inclinabit. —P. 3, *Stim. Div. Am.* c. xiii.

[26] Respice, O Mater misericordiosissima, respice servos tuos; in te enim omnem spem nostram collocavimus.—*Ap. Sur.* 31 Aug.

perceiving that her husband rose from his bed in the silence of the night, left his room, and did not return for a considerable time, became jealous, and suspected that all was not right. One day, in order to deliver herself from her anxiety, she asked her husband if by chance he loved another. The gentleman replied, with a smile, 'You must know that I love the most delightful lady in the world. To her I have given my heart, and I could rather die than cease to love her; and did you but know her, you would tell me to love her still more.' He was, of course, speaking of the most Blessed Virgin, whom he loved thus tenderly. His wife, however, became more and more uneasy, and again questioned him, that she might assure herself of the correctness of her suspicions: she asked him if by chance it was to visit this lady that he rose every night and left his room. That gentleman, quite unaware of the troubled state of his wife's mind, answered in the affirmative. The lady then felt certain of that which she had falsely suspected, and, blinded by passion, one night that her husband, as usual, left the room, took a knife, and in despair cut her throat, and shortly expired. The gentleman, after finishing his devotions, returned to his room, but, getting into bed, he found it wet. He called his wife, but received no answer. He shook her, but in vain. He then got a light, and saw the bed saturated with blood, and his wife with her throat cut, and a corpse. In an instant the truth flashed across his mind, and he perceived that in a fit of jealousy she had destroyed herself. He instantly locked the door of the room, returned to the chapel, and there prostrate before the image of Mary, sobbing bitterly, he cried out: 'My Mother, see, see my affliction. If thou dost not relieve me, to whom can I have recourse? Consider that by coming to honour thee I have incurred the misfortune of seeing my wife dead and eternally lost. My Mother, thou canst remedy this; O do so.' And who ever invoked this Mother of mercy with confidence

without obtaining what he asked? For scarcely had
he finished his prayer when he heard a servant calling
him : 'Sir, go to your room ; for your lady wants you.'
The gentleman, in the excess of his joy, could scarcely
believe the servant. 'Return,' he said, 'and see again
if she really wants me.' The servant came back, repeating, 'Go quickly, for my mistress is waiting for
you.' He went, opened the door, and beheld his wife
alive. She immediately threw herself at his feet, and
in tears asked his pardon, saying, 'Ah, my husband, the
Mother of God, through thy prayers, has delivered me
from hell.' They then went together to the oratory,
weeping for joy, to return thanks to the most Blessed
Virgin. On the following morning the husband gave
a grand feast to all his relations, and made his wife
herself relate the whole history ; and she showed the
mark of the wound, which still remained ; and thus all
were more and more inflamed with love towards the
Divine Mother.

PRAYER.

O Mother of holy love, our life, our refuge, and our
nope, thou well knowest that thy Son Jesus Christ,
not content with being Himself our perpetual advocate
with the eternal Father, has willed that thou also
shouldst interest thyself with Him, in order to obtain
the Divine mercies for us. He has decreed that thy
prayers should aid our salvation, and has made them so
efficacious that they obtain all that they ask. To thee,
therefore, who art the hope of the miserable, do I, a
wretched sinner, turn my eyes. I trust, O Lady, that
in the first place through the merits of Jesus Christ,
and then through thy intercession, I shall be saved.
Of this I am certain ; and my confidence in thee is such,
that if my eternal salvation was in my own hands, I
should place it in thine, for I rely more on thy mercy
and protection than on all my own works. My Mother
and my hope, abandon me not, though I deserve that

thou shouldst do so. See my miseries, and, being moved thereby with compassion, help and save me. I own that I have too often closed my heart, by my sins, against the lights and helps that thou hast procured for me from our Lord. But thy compassion for the miserable, and thy power with God, far surpass the number and malice of my sins. It is well known to all, both in heaven and on earth, that whosoever is protected by thee is certainly saved. All may forget me, provided only that thou dost remember me, O Mother of an omnipotent God. Tell Him that I am thy servant; say only that thou defendest me, and I shall be saved. O Mary, I trust in thee; in this hope I live; in it I desire and hope to die, repeating always, ' Jesus is my only hope, and after Jesus the most Blessed Virgin Mary.'[27]

SECTION II. *Mary is the Hope of Sinners.*

In the first chapter of the Book of Genesis we read that " God made two great lights ; a greater light to rule the day; and a lesser light to rule the night."[1] Cardinal Hugo says that ' Christ is the greater light to rule the just, and Mary the lesser to rule sinners ;'[2] meaning that the sun is a figure of Jesus Christ, whose light is enjoyed by the just who live in the clear day of Divine grace ; and that the moon is a figure of Mary, by whose means those who are in the night of sin are enlightened. Since Mary is this auspicious luminary, and is so for the benefit of poor sinners, should anyone have been so unfortunate as to fall into the night of sin, what is he to do ? Innocent III. replies, ' Whoever is in the night of sin, let him cast his eyes on the moon, let him im-

---

[27] Unica spes mea Jesus, et post Jesum Virgo Maria.

[1] Fecitque Deus duo luminaria magna : luminare majus, ut præesset diei ; et luminare minus, ut præesset nocti.—*Gen.* i. 16.

[2] Luminare majus Christus, qui præest diei, id est justis ; luminare minus Beata Maria, quæ præest peccatoribus.—*In Lib. Gen.* cap. i.

plore Mary.'³ Since he has lost the light of the sun of justice by losing the grace of God, let him turn to the moon, and beseech Mary; and she will certainly give him light to see the misery of his state, and strength to leave it without delay. St. Methodius says 'that by the prayers of Mary, almost innumerable sinners are converted.'⁴

One of the titles which is the most encouraging to poor sinners, and under which the Church teaches us to invoke Mary in the Litany of Loretto, is that of 'Refuge of Sinners.' In Judea in ancient times there were cities of refuge, in which criminals who fled there for protection were exempt from the punishments which they had deserved. Nowadays these cities are not so numerous; there is but one, and that is Mary, of whom the Psalmist says, "Glorious things are said of thee, O city of God."⁵ But this city differs from the ancient ones in this respect—that in the latter all kinds of criminals did not find refuge, nor was the protection extended to every class of crime; but under the mantle of Mary all sinners, without exception, find refuge for every sin that they may have committed, provided only that they go there to seek for this protection. 'I am the city of refuge,' says St. John Damascene, in the name of our Queen, 'to all who fly to me.'⁶

And it is sufficient to have recourse to her, for whoever has the good fortune to enter this city need not speak to be saved. "Assemble yourselves, and let us enter into the fenced city, and let us be silent there,"⁷ to speak in the words of the prophet Jeremias. This city, says blessed Albert the Great, is the most holy Virgin fenced in with grace and glory. 'And let us be

---

³ 'qui .... jacet in nocte culpæ, respiciat lunam, deprecetur Mariam. *Serm.* ii. *de Ass. B.V.*

⁴ Mariæ virtute et precibus pene innumeræ peccatorum conversiones fiunt. —*Paciucch. in Ps.* lxxxvi. exc. 11.

⁵ Gloriosa dicta sunt de te, civitas Dei.—*Ps.* lxxxvi. 3.

⁶ Ego iis qui ad me confugiunt civitas refugii.—*Hom.* ii. *in Dorm. B.M.V.*

⁷ Convenite, et ingrediamur civitatem munitam, et sileamus ibi.—*Jerem.* viii. 14.

silent there,' that is, continues an interpreter, 'because
we dare not invoke the Lord, whom we have offended,
she will invoke and ask.'[8] For if we do not presume
to ask our Lord to forgive us, it will suffice to enter
this city and be silent, for Mary will speak and ask all
that we require. And for this reason, a devout author
exhorts all sinners to take refuge under the mantle of
Mary, exclaiming, 'Fly, O Adam and Eve, and all you
their children, who have outraged God; fly, and take
refuge in the bosom of this good Mother; know you not
that she is our only city of refuge?' 'the only hope of
sinners,'[9] as she is also called in a sermon by an ancient
writer, found in the works of Saint Augustine.[10]

Saint Ephrem, addressing this Blessed Virgin, says,
'Thou art the only advocate of sinners, and of all who
are unprotected.' And then he salutes her in the following words: 'Hail, refuge and hospital of sinners!'[11]
—true refuge, in which alone they can hope for reception and liberty. And an author remarks that this
was the meaning of David when he said, "For He hath
hidden me in His tabernacle."[12] And truly what can
this tabernacle of God be, unless it is Mary? who is
called by Saint Germanus 'A tabernacle made by God,
in which He alone entered to accomplish the great work
of the redemption of man.'[13] Saint Basil of Seleucia
remarks, 'that if God granted to some who were only
His servants such power, that not only their touch but
even their shadows healed the sick, who were placed
for this purpose in the public streets, how much greater
power must we suppose that He has granted to her,

[8] Et sileamus ibi, quia non audemus deprecari Dominum quem offendimus,
sed ipsa deprecetur et roget.—*Bib. Mar. in Jerem.* No. 3.

[9] Fugite, O Adam and Eva, fugite ipsorum liberi, et abscondite vos intra
sinum Dei Matris Mariæ: ipsa est homicidis civitas refugii, spes unica peccatorum.—*Benedictus Fernandez in Lib. Gen.* cap. iii. sect. 22.

[10] Spes unica peccatorum.—*Serm. de Sanct. int. op. St. Augustini,* i. *de
Annunc. B.M.V.*

[11] Ave peccatorum refugium atque diversorium.—*De Laud. Virg.*

[12] Protexit me in abscondito tabernaculi sui.—*Ps.* xxvi. 5.

[13] Tabernaculum non manufactum sed a Deo fabricatum, in quod solus
Deus Verbum et primus Pontifex in fine sæculorum semel ingressus est, sacris
mysticis occulte operaturus in te pro salute omnium.—*In Nat. S. Dei. Mat.*

who was not only His handmaid but His Mother?'[14] We may indeed say that our Lord has given us Mary as a public infirmary, in which all who are sick, poor, and destitute can be received. But now I ask, in hospitals erected expressly for the poor, who have the greatest claim to admission? Certainly the most infirm and those who are in the greatest need.

And for this reason should anyone find himself devoid of merit and overwhelmed with spiritual infirmities, that is to say sin, he can thus address Mary : O Lady, thou art the refuge of the sick poor ; reject me not ; for as I am the poorest and most infirm of all, I have the greatest right to be welcomed by thee. Let us then cry out with Saint Thomas of Villanova, 'O Mary, we poor sinners know no other refuge than thee, for thou art our only hope, and on thee we rely for our salvation.'[15] Thou art our only advocate with Jesus Christ ; to thee we all turn ourselves.

In the revelations of St. Bridget, Mary is called the 'Star preceding the sun ;'[16] giving us thereby to understand, that when devotion towards the Divine Mother begins to manifest itself in a soul that is in a state of sin, it is a certain mark that before long God will enrich it with His grace. The glorious Saint Bonaventure, in order to revive the confidence of sinners in the protection of Mary, places before them the picture of a tempestuous sea, into which sinners have already fallen from the ship of Divine grace ; they are already dashed about on every side by remorse of conscience and by fear of the judgments of God ; they are without light or guide, and are on the point of losing the last breath of hope and falling into despair ; then it is that our

---

[14] Siquidem enim Deus tantam servis impertitus est gratiam ut non solum tactu ægrotos sanarent, sed et umbræ ipsius projectu idem præstarent. Proponebant enim medio ipso foro ægrotos, etc. Quantam putandus Matri concessisse virtutem ? *Serm. in S. Dei Gen. M.* Orat. xxxix.

[15] Nescimus aliud refugium nisi te, tu sola es unica spes nostra, in qua confidimus, tu sola patrona nostra, ad quam omnes aspicimus.—*S.* iii. *de Nat. B.V.*

[16] Tu es quasi sidus vadens ante solem.—*Rev. Extr.* cap. i.

Lord, pointing out Mary to them, who is commonly called the 'Star of the Sea,' raises His voice and says 'O poor lost sinners, despair not; raise up your eyes, and cast them on this beautiful star; breathe again with confidence, for it will save you from this tempest, and will guide you into the port of salvation.'[17]   Saint Bernard says the same thing: 'If thou wouldst not be lost in the tempest, cast thine eyes on the Star, and invoke Mary.'[18]   And the devout Blosius declares that 'she is the only refuge of those who have offended God,[19] the asylum of all who are oppressed by temptation, calamity, or persecution.[20]   This Mother is all mercy, benignity, and sweetness, not only to the just, but also to despairing sinners;[21] so that no sooner does she perceive them coming to her, and seeking her help from their hearts, than she aids them, welcomes them, and obtains their pardon from her Son.[22]   She knows not how to despise anyone, however unworthy he may be of mercy, and therefore denies her protection to none; she consoles all, and is no sooner called upon than she helps whoever it may be that invokes her.[23] She by her sweetness often awakens and draws sinners to her devotion who are the most at enmity with God and the most deeply plunged in the lethargy of sin; and then, by the same means, she excites them effectually, and prepares them for grace, and thus renders them fit for the kingdom of heaven.[24]   God has created

[17] Respirate ad illam, perditi peccatores; et perducet vos ad indulgentiæ portum.—*S. Bonav. in Ps.* xviii.

[18] Si non vis obrui procellis . . respice stellam, voca Mariam.—*Sup. Missus est Hom.* ii.

[19] Ipsa peccantium singulare refugium.—*In Can. Vit. Sp.* cap. xviii.

[20] Ipsa omnium, quos tentatio, calamitas, aut persecutio aliqua urget tutissimum asylum.—*Ib.*

[21] Tota mitis est, tota serena, tota suavis, tota benigna, non solum justis et perfectis, verum etiam peccatoribus ac desperatis.—*Ib.*

[22] Quos, ut ad se ex corde clamare conspexerit, statim adjuvat, suscipit, fovet, et metuendo Judici materna fiducia reconciliat.—*Ib.*

[23] Nullum aspernatur, nulli se negat: omnes consolatur, omnibus sinum pietatis aperit, et vel tenuiter invocata, præsto adest.—*Ib.*

[24] Sua ingenita bonitate atque dulcedine sæpe eos, qui Deo minus affliciuntur, ad sui cultum blande allicit, potenterque excitat: ut per hujuscemodi studium præparentur ad gratiam, et tandem apti reddantur regno cœlorum. —*Ib.*

this His beloved daughter of so compassionate and sweet a disposition, that no one can fear to have recourse to her.'[25] The pious author concludes in these words : ' It is impossible for anyone to perish who attentively, and with humility, cultivates devotion towards this Divine Mother.'[26]

In Ecclesiasticus Mary is called a plane-tree : " As a plane-tree I was exalted."[27] And she is so called that sinners may understand that as the plane-tree gives shelter to travellers from the heat of the sun, so does Mary invite them to take shelter under her protection from the wrath of God, justly enkindled against them. Saint Bonaventure remarks that the prophet Isaias complained of the times in which he lived, saying, " Behold thou art angry, and we have sinned : . . . there is none . . . that riseth up and taketh hold of thee."[28] And then he makes the following commentary : ' It is true, O Lord, that at the time there was none to raise up sinners and withhold thy wrath, for Mary was not yet born ;' ' before Mary,' to quote the Saint's own words, ' there was no one who could thus dare to restrain the arm of God.'[29] But now, if God is angry with a sinner, and Mary takes him under her protection, she withholds the avenging arm of her Son, and saves him.[30] ' And so,' continues the same Saint, ' no one can be found more fit for this office than Mary, who seizes the sword of Divine justice with her own hands to prevent it from falling upon and punishing the sinner.'[31] Upon the same subject blessed Albert

[25] Talis est, talis a Deo facta est, talis nobis data est . . . ut nemo ad eam accedere trepidet.—*In Can. Vit. Sp.* cap. xviii.

[26] Fieri non potest, ut pereat, qui Mariæ sedulus et humilis cultor fuerit. —*Ib.*

[27] Quasi platanus exaltata sum.—*Eccl.* xxiv. 19.

[28] Ecce tu iratus es, et peccavimus . . . non est . . . qui consurgat, et teneat te.—*Is.* lxiv. 5, 7.

[29] Ante Mariam non fuit qui sic detinere Dominum auderet.—*In Spec.* lect. vii.

[30] Detinet Filium, ne peccatores percutiat.—*Ib.*

[31] Nemo tam idoneus Domina, qui gladio Domini pro nobis manum objiciat, ut tu Dei amantissima.—*Ib.* Lect. vi.

the Great says that 'God, before the birth of Mary, complained by the mouth of the prophet Ezechiel that there was no one to rise up and withhold Him from chastising sinners, but that He could find no one, for this office was reserved for our Blessed Lady, who withholds His arm until He is pacified.'[32] An ancient writer encourages sinners, saying, 'O sinner, be not discouraged, but have recourse to Mary in all thy necessities; call her to thine assistance, for thou wilt always find her ready to help thee; for such is the Divine will that she should help all in every kind of necessity.'[33] This Mother of mercy has so great a desire to save the most abandoned sinners, that she herself goes in search of them, in order to help them; and if they have recourse to her, she knows how to find the means to render them acceptable to God.

The patriarch Isaac, desiring to eat of some wild animal, promised his blessing to his son Esau on his procuring this food for him; but Rebecca, who was anxious that her other son Jacob should receive the blessing, called him and said, " Go thy way to the flock, bring me two kids of the best, that I may make of them meat for thy father, such as he gladly eateth."[34] Saint Antoninus says[35] 'that Rebecca was a figure of Mary, who commands the angels to bring her sinners (meant by kids), that she may adorn them in such a way (by obtaining for them sorrow and purpose of amendment) as to render them dear and acceptable to her Lord.' And here we may well apply to our Blessed Lady the words of the Abbot Franco : ' O truly sagacious woman, who so well knew how to dress these kids, that not

[32] " Quæsivi de eis virum qui interponeret sepem," id est intercessionem, " et staret oppositus contra me, pro terra," id est peccatore, " ne dissiparem eam, et non inveni," quia hoc reservatum est Virgini Mariæ.—*Bibl. Mar.* in Ezechiel. No. 6.

[33] Ne diffidas, peccator; sed in cunctis Mariam sequere et invoca, quam voluit Deus in cunctis subvenire.—*Paciucch. in Salve R.* exc. 7.

[34] Pergens ad gregem, affer mihi duos hædos optimos.—*Gen.* xxvii. 9.

[35] P. 4. t. 15. c. 2. § 2.

only they are equal to, but often superior in flavour to real venison.[36]

The Blessed Virgin herself revealed to Saint Bridget ' that there is no sinner in the world, however much he may be at enmity with God, who does not return to Him and recover His grace, if he has recourse to her and asks her assistance.'[37]   The same Saint Bridget one day heard Jesus Christ address His Mother, and say that ' she would be ready to obtain the grace of God for Lucifer himself, if only he humbled himself so far as to seek her aid.'[38]   That proud spirit will never humble himself so far as to implore the protection of Mary ; but if such a thing were possible, Mary would be suffici- ently compassionate, and her prayers would have suffi- cient power to obtain both forgiveness and salvation for him from God.   But that which cannot be verified with regard to the devil is verified in the case of sin- ners who have recourse to this compassionate Mother.

Noah's ark was a true figure of Mary ; for as in it all kinds of beasts were saved, so under the mantle of Mary all sinners, who by their vices and sensuality are already like beasts, find refuge ; but with this difference, as a pious author remarks,[39] that ' while the brutes that entered the ark remained brutes, the wolf remaining a wolf, and the tiger a tiger—under the mantle of Mary, on the other hand, the wolf becomes a lamb, and the tiger a dove.'   One day Saint Gertrude saw Mary with her mantle open, and under it there were many wild beasts of different kinds—leopards, lions, and bears ; and she saw that not only our Blessed Lady did not drive them away, but that she welcomed and caressed them with her benign hand.   The Saint understood

---

[36] Vere sapiens mulier, quæ sic novit hædos coquere, sic condire, ut gra- tiam caprearum et cervorum coæquent, aut etiam superent.—Lib. iii. *de Grat. D.*

[37] Nullus ita alienatus est de Deo . . . qui si me invocaverit, non revertatur ad Deum.—*Rev.* lib. vi. cap. 10.

[38] Etiam . . . diabolo exhiberes misericordiam si humiliter peteret.—*Rev. Extr. L.*

[39] Quod arca animalia suscepit, animalia servavit.—*Paciucch. in Sal. Ang.* exc. 4.

that these wild beasts were miserable sinners, who are welcomed by Mary with sweetness and love the moment they have recourse to her.[40]

It was, then, not without reason that Saint Bernard addressed the Blessed Virgin, saying, 'Thou, O Lady, dost not reject any sinner who approaches thee, however loathsome and repugnant he may be. If he asks thy assistance, thou dost not disdain to extend thy compassionate hand to him, to extricate him from the gulf of despair.'[41] May our God be eternally blessed and thanked, O most amiable Mary, for having created thee so sweet and benign, even towards the most miserable sinners! Truly unfortunate is he who loves thee not, and who, having it in his power to obtain thy assistance, has no confidence in thee. He who has not recourse to Mary is lost; but who was ever lost that had recourse to this most Blessed Virgin?

It is related in the sacred Scriptures that Booz allowed Ruth "to gather the ears of corn, after the reapers."[42] St. Bonaventure says, 'that as Ruth found favour with Booz, so has Mary found favour with our Lord, and is also allowed to gather the ears of corn after the reapers. The reapers followed by Mary are all evangelical labourers, missionaries, preachers, and confessors, who are constantly reaping souls for God. But there are some hardened and rebellious souls which are abandoned even by these. To Mary alone is it granted to save them by her powerful intercession.'[43] Truly unfortunate are they if they do not allow themselves to be gathered, even by this sweet Lady. They will indeed be most certainly lost and accursed. But, on the other hand, blessed is he who has recourse to this good

---

[40] Blosius, Conc. An. fid. cap. i.

[41] Tu peccatorem quantumlibet fœtidum non horres, nec despicis si ad te suspiraverit. ... Tu illum a desperationis barathro pia manu retrahis.—*Depr. ad B. V.*

[42] Colligebat spicas post terga metentium.—*Ruth* ii. 3.

[43] Ruth ergo in oculis Booz, Maria in oculis Domini hanc gratiam invenit ut ipsa spicas, id est animas a messoribus derelictas, colligere ad veniam, possit.—*In Spec. B. V. M.* lect. v.

Mother. 'There is not in the world,' says the devout Blosius, 'any sinner, however revolting and wicked who is despised or rejected by Mary; she can, she wills, and she knows how to reconcile him to her most beloved Son, if only he will seek her assistance.'[44]

With reason then, O my most sweet Queen, did St. John Damascene salute and call thee the 'hope of those who are in despair.'[45] With reason did St. Lawrence Justinian call thee 'the hope of malefactors;'[46] and another ancient writer 'the only hope of sinners.'[47] St. Ephrem calls her 'the safe harbour of all sailing on the sea of this world.'[48] This last-named Saint also calls her 'the consolation of those who are in despair.'[49] With reason, finally, does St. Bonaventure exhort even the desperate not to despair; and, full of joy and tendernesss towards his most dear Mother, he lovingly exclaims: 'And who, O Lady, can be without confidence in thee, since thou assistest even those who are in despair? And I doubt not, that whenever we have recourse to thee, we shall obtain all that we desire. Let him, then, who is without hope hope in thee.'[50] St. Antoninus relates,[51] that there was a sinner at enmity with God, who had a vision in which he found himself before the dread tribunal; the devil accused him, and Mary defended him. The enemy produced the catalogue of his sins; it was thrown into the scales of Divine justice, and weighed far more than all his good works. But then his great Advocate, extending her sweet hand, placed it on the balance, and so caused it

---

[44] Nullum tam execrabilem peccatorem orbis habet, quem ipsa abominetur, et a se repellat, quemque dilectissimo nato suo (modo suam precetur opem) non possit, sciat, et velit reconciliare.—*Sac. An. Fid.* p. iii. cap. **v**.

[45] Salve spes desperatorum. †

[46] Delinquentium spes.—*Serm. in Nat. B.V.M.*

[47] Spes unica peccatorum.—*Serm. de Sanctis int. op. S. Augustini.* 1 *de Annunc.*

[48] Ave portus tutissime in hac vita navigantium.—*Serm. de Laud. S. Dei Gen. M.*

[49] Desperantium consolatio.—*Prec. V. ad Dei Mat.*

[50] Quis enim non sperabit in te, quæ etiam adjuvas desperantes? . . . Non dubito, quod, si ad te venerimus, habebimus quod voluerimus. In te ergo speret qui desperat.—*Sup. Salv. Reg.*

[51] P. 4. t. 15. c. 5. § 1.

to turn in favour of her client; giving him thereby to understand that she would obtain his pardon if he changed his life; and this he did after the vision, and was entirely converted.

EXAMPLE.

Blessed John Herold,[52] who out of humility called himself the Disciple, relates that there was a married man who lived at enmity with God. His wife, who was a virtuous woman, being unable to engage him to give up sin, begged him, in the wretched state in which he was, to practise at least the devotion of saluting our Blessed Lady with a 'Hail Mary' each time that he might pass before her picture. He began to do so. One night this wretched man was on his way to commit a crime, when he perceived a light at a distance; he drew near to see what it was, and found that it was a lamp burning before a devout picture of Mary holding the child Jesus in her arms. He at once, according to custom, said the 'Hail Mary.' In the same moment he beheld the Divine Infant covered with wounds, from which fresh blood was streaming. Terrified, and at the same time moved to compassion at this sight, he reflected that it was he who by his sins had thus wounded his Redeemer. He burst into tears; but the Divine Infant turned His back to him. Filled with shame, he appealed to the most Blessed Virgin, saying: 'Mother of Mercy, thy Son rejects me; I can find no advocate more compassionate and more powerful than thee, for thou art His Mother; my Queen, do thou help me, and intercede for me.' The Divine Mother, speaking from the picture, replied: 'You sinners call me Mother of Mercy, but at the same time you cease not to make me a Mother of Sorrows, by crucifying my Son afresh and renewing my sorrows.' But as Mary can never let anyone leave her feet disconsolate, she began to implore her Son to pardon this miserable wretch. Jesus con-

[52] De Temp. s. 161.

tinued to show Himself unwilling to do so. The most
Blessed Virgin, seeing this, placed Him in the niche,
and prostrating herself before Him, said : ' My Son, I
will not leave Thy feet until Thou hast pardoned this
sinner.' ' My Mother,' then said Jesus, ' I can deny
thee nothing ; thou willest that he should be forgiven,
for love of thee I pardon him ; make him come and kiss
My wounds.' The sinner, sobbing and weeping, did
so ; and as he kissed them the wounds were healed.
Jesus then embraced him, as a mark of forgiveness ; and
he changed his life, which from that time was one of
holiness ; and he always preserved the most tender love
and gratitude towards this Blessed Virgin, who had obtained him so great a grace.

PRAYER.

O most pure Virgin Mary, I worship thy most holy
heart, which was the delight and resting-place of God,
thy heart overflowing with humility, purity, and divine
love. I, an unhappy sinner, approach thee with a heart
all loathsome and wounded. O compassionate Mother,
disdain me not on this account ; let such a sight rather
move thee to greater tenderness, and excite thee to
help me. Do not stay to seek virtues or merit in me
before assisting me. I am lost, and the only thing I
merit is hell. See only my confidence in thee and the
purpose I have to amend. Consider all that Jesus has
done and suffered for me, and then abandon me if thou
canst. I offer thee all the pains of His life ; the cold
that He endured in the stable ; His journey into Egypt ;
the blood which He shed ; the poverty, sweats, sorrows,
and death that He endured for me ; and this in thy
presence. For the love of Jesus, take charge of my
salvation. Ah my Mother, I will not and cannot fear
that thou wilt reject me, now that I have recourse to
thee and ask thy help. Did I fear this, I should be
offering an outrage to thy mercy, which goes in quest
of the wretched, in order to help them. O Lady, deny

not thy compassion to one to whom Jesus has not denied His blood. But the merits of this blood will not be applied to me unless thou recommendest me to God. Through thee do I hope for salvation. I ask not for riches, honours, or earthly goods. I seek only the grace of God, love towards thy Son, the accomplishment of His will, and His heavenly kingdom, that I may love Him eternally. Is it possible that thou wilt not hear me? No; for already thou hast granted my prayer, as I hope; already thou prayest for me; already thou obtainest me the graces that I ask; already thou takest me under thy protection. My Mother, abandon me not. Never, never cease to pray for me, until thou seest me safe in heaven at thy feet, blessing and thank- ing thee for ever. Amen.

CHAPTER IV.

SECTION I. *On the promptitude of Mary in assisting those who invoke her.*

TRULY unfortunate are we poor children of Eve; for, guilty before God of her fault, and condemned to the same penalty, we have to wander about in this valley of tears as exiles from our country, and to weep over our many afflictions of body and soul. But blessed is he who, in the midst of these sorrows, often turns to the comfortress of the world, to the refuge of the unfortunate, to the great Mother of God, and devoutly calls upon her and invokes her! "Blessed is the man that heareth me, and that watcheth daily at my gates."[1] Blessed, says Mary, is he who listens to my counsels, and watches continually at the gate of my mercy, and invokes my intercession and aid. The holy Church carefully teaches us her children with what attention and confidence we should unceasingly have recourse to this loving protectress; and for this purpose commands a worship peculiar to Mary. And not only this, but she has instituted so many festivals that are celebrated throughout the year in honour of this great Queen: she devotes one day in the week, in an especial manner, to her honour: in the divine office all ecclesiastics and religious are daily obliged to invoke her in the name of all Christians; and, finally, she desires that all the

---

[1] Beatus homo, qui audit me et qui vigilat ad fores meas quotidie.—*Prov.* viii. 34.

faithful should salute this most holy Mother of God three times a day, at the sound of the Angelus-bell. And that we may understand the confidence that the holy Church has in Mary, we need only remember that in all public calamities she invariably invites all to have recourse to the protection of this Divine Mother, by novenas, prayers, processions, by visiting the churches dedicated in her honour, and her images. And this is what Mary desires. She wishes us always to seek her and invoke her aid; not as if she were begging of us these honours and marks of veneration, for they are in no way proportioned to her merit; but she desires them, that by such means our confidence and devotion may be increased, and that so she may be able to give us greater succour and comfort. 'She seeks for those,' says St. Bonaventure, 'who approach her devoutly and with reverence, for such she loves, nourishes, and adopts as her children.'[2]

This last-named Saint remarks, that Ruth, whose name signifies 'seeing and hastening,' was a figure of Mary; 'for Mary, seeing our miseries, hastens in her mercy to succour us.'[3] Novarino adds, that 'Mary, in the greatness of her desire to help us, cannot admit of delay, for she is in no way an avaricious guardian of the graces she has at her disposal as Mother of mercy, and cannot do otherwise than immediately shower down the treasures of her liberality on her servants.'[4]

O how prompt is this good Mother to help those who call upon her! "Thy two breasts," says the sacred Canticle, "are like two roes that are twins."[5] Richard of Saint Lawrence explains this verse, and says, that as roes are swift in their course, so are the breasts of Mary

---

[2] Ipsa tales quærit, qui ad eam devote et reverenter accedant. Hos enim diligit, hos nutrit, hos in filios suos suscipit.—*Stim. Am.* p. iii. cap. 16.

[3] Videns etiam nostram miseriam est, et festinans ad impendendam suam misericordiam.—*Spec. B.M.V.* lect. v.

[4] Nescit nectere moras benefaciendi cupida, nec gratiarum avara custos est: tardare nescit molimina misericordiæ mater, beneficentiæ suæ thesauros in suos effusura.—*Nov. Umbr. Virg.* exc. lxxiii.

[5] Duo ubera tua sicut duo hinnuli capreæ.—*Cant.* iv. 5.

prompt to bestow the milk of mercy on all who ask it.
' By the light pressure of a devout salutation and prayer
they distil large drops.'[6]   The same author assures us
that the compassion of Mary is poured out on everyone
who asks it, even should it be sought for by no other
prayer than a simple ' Hail Mary.'   Wherefore Novarino declares that the Blessed Virgin not only runs but
flies to assist him who invokes her.   ' She,' says this
author, ' in the exercise of her mercy, knows not how
to act differently from God ; for, as He flies at once to
the assistance of those who beg His aid, faithful to His
promise, " Ask, and you shall receive,"[7] so Mary, whenever she is invoked, is at once ready to assist him who
prays to her.   ' God has wings when He assists His
own, and immediately flies to them ; Mary also takes
wing when she is about to fly to our aid.'[8]

And hence we see who the woman was, spoken of
in the following verse of the Apocalypse, to whom two
great eagle's wings were given, that she might fly to the
desert.   " And there were given to the woman two
wings of a great eagle, that she might fly into the desert."[9]   Ribeira explains these wings to mean the love
with which Mary always flew to God.   ' She has the
wings of an eagle, for she flies with the love of God.'[10]
But the blessed Amadeus, more to our purpose, remarks that these wings of an eagle signify ' the velocity, exceeding that of the Seraphim, with which Mary
always flies to the succour of her children.'[11]

This will explain a passage in the Gospel of St.
Luke, in which we are told that when Mary went to
visit and shower graces on Saint Elizabeth and her

---

[6] Compressione levissima devotæ salutationis et orationis larga distillabit
stillicidia.—Lib. i. cap. 7.

[7] Petite, et accipietis.—*Joan.* xvi. 24.

[8] Alis utitur Deus, ut suis opituletur, statim advolat : alas sumit et Virgo,
in nostri auxilium advolatura.—*Excurs.* 73.

[9] Et datæ sunt mulieri alæ duæ aquilæ magnæ, ut volaret in desertum.—
Apoc. xii. 14.

[10] Pennas habet aquilæ, quia . . . amore Dei volat.—*In Apoc.* xii. 4.

[11] Motu . . . celerrimi senas seraphim alas excedens . . . ubique suis ut
Mater jucundissima et mirificentissima occurrit.—*De Laud. Virg.* Hom. viii.

whole family, she was not slow, but went with speed. The Gospel says, " And Mary, rising up, went into the hill country with haste."[12] And this is not said of her return. For a similar reason, we are told in the sacred Canticles that the hands of Mary are used to the lathe : " her hands are skilful at the wheel,"[13] meaning, says Richard of St. Lawrence, ' that as the art of turning is the easiest and most expeditious mode of working, so also is Mary the most willing and prompt of all the Saints to assist her clients.'[14] And truly ' she has the most ardent desire to console all, and is no sooner invoked than she accepts the prayers, and helps.'[15] St. Bonaventure, then, was right in calling Mary the ' salvation of all who call upon her ;'[16] meaning, that it suffices to invoke this Divine Mother in order to be saved ; for, according to Richard of St. Lawrence, she is always ready to help those who seek her aid. '.Thou wilt always find her ready to help thee.'[17] And Bernardine de Busto adds, ' that this great Lady is more desirous to grant us graces than we are desirous to receive them.'[18]

Nor should the multitude of our sins diminish our confidence that Mary will grant our petitions when we cast ourselves at her feet. She is the Mother of mercy; but mercy would not be needed did none exist who require it. On this subject Richard of St. Lawrence remarks, ' that as a good mother does not shrink from applying a remedy to her child infected with ulcers, however nauseous and revolting they may be, so also is our good Mother unable to abandon us when we have recourse to her, that she may heal the wounds caused

---

[12] Exurgens autem Maria in diebus illis abiit in montana cum festinatione.—*Luc.* i. 39.

[13] Manus illius tornatiles.—*Cant.* v. 14.

[14] Sicut ars tornandi promptior est aliis artibus, sic Maria ad benefaciendum promptior est omnibus sanctis.—*De Laud. Virg.* lib. v. cap. 2.

[15] Omnes consolatur . . . et vel tenuiter invocata præsto adest.—*Can. Vit. Spirit.* cap. 18.

[16] Tu salus te invocantium.—*Hym. de B. V. ad inst. Te Deum.*

[17] Invenies semper paratam auxiliari. †

[18] Plus . . . desiderat ipsa facere tibi bonum . . . quam tu accipere concupiscas.—*Mar.* p. ii. *Serm.* 5 *de Nat. B. V.*

by our sins, however loathsome they may have rendered us.'[19] This is exactly what Mary gave St. Gertrude to understand, when she showed herself to her with her mantle spread out to receive all who have recourse to her. At the same time the Saint was told that 'Angels constantly guard the clients of this Blessed Virgin from the assaults of hell.'[20]

This good Mother's compassion is so great, and the love she bears us is such, that she does not even wait for our prayers in order to assist us; but, as it is expressed in the Book of Wisdom, "she preventeth them that covet her, so that she first showeth herself unto them."[21] Saint Anselm applies these words to Mary, and says that she is beforehand with those who desire her protection. By this we are to understand that she obtains us many favours from God before we have recourse to her. For this reason Richard of Saint Victor remarks, that she is called the moon, "fair as the moon,"[22] meaning, not only that she is swift as the moon in its course, by flying to the aid of those who invoke her, but that she is still more so, for her love for us is so tender, that in our wants she anticipates our prayers, and her mercy is more prompt to help us than we are to ask her aid.[23] 'And this arises,' adds the same Richard, 'from the fact, that the heart of Mary is so filled with compassion for poor sinners, that she no sooner sees our miseries than she pours her tender mercies upon us. Neither is it possible for this benign Queen to behold the want of any soul without immediately assisting it.'[24]

[19] Non enim Mater hæc dedignatur peccatores, sicut nec bona Mater filium scabiosum, quia propter peccatores factam se recolit misericordiæ genitricem. Ubi enim non est miseria, misericordia non habet locum.—*De Laud. Virg.* lib. iv. cap. 22.

[20] *Rev.* lib. iv. cap. 49.

[21] Præoccupat, qui se concupiscunt, ut illis se prior ostendat.—*Sap.* vi. 14.

[22] Pulchra ut luna.—*Cant.* vi. 9.

[23] Velocius occurrit ejus pietas, quam invocetur, et causas miserorum anticipat.—*In Cant.* cap. xxiii. 2.

[24] Adeo pietate replentur ubera tua, ut alicujus miseriæ notitia tacta, lac fundant misericordiæ : nec possis miserias scire, et non subvenire.—*In Cant.* cap. xxiii.

Mary, even when living in this world, showed at the marriage-feast of Cana the great compassion that she would afterwards exercise towards us in our necessities, and which now, as it were, forces her to have pity on and assist us, even before we ask her to do so. In the second chapter of St. Luke we read that at this feast the compassionate Mother saw the embarrassment in which the bride and bridegroom were, and that they were quite ashamed on seeing the wine fail; and therefore, without being asked, and listening only to the dictates of her compassionate heart, which could never behold the afflictions of others without feeling for them, she begged her Son to console them simply by laying their distress before Him: "they have no wine."[25] No sooner had she done so, than our Lord, in order to satisfy all present, and still more to console the compassionate heart of His Mother, who had asked the favour, worked the well-known miracle by which He changed the water, brought to Him in jars, into wine. From this Novarino argues, that 'if Mary, unasked, is thus prompt to succour the needy, how much more so will she be to succour those who invoke her and ask for her help?'[26]

Should there be anyone who doubts as to whether Mary will aid him if he has recourse to her, Innocent III. thus reproves him: 'Who is there that ever, when in the night of sin, had recourse to this sweet Lady without being relieved?'[27] 'And who ever,' exclaims the blessed Eutychian, 'faithfully implored thy all-powerful aid and was abandoned by thee?'[28] Indeed, no one; for thou canst relieve the most wretched, and save the most abandoned. Such a case certainly never did and never will occur. 'I am satisfied,' says St. Bernard,

[25] Vinum non habent.—*Joan.* ii. 3.
[26] Si tam prompta et cita ad auxilium ferendum currit non quæsita, quid requisita præstitura est ?—*Exc.* lxxii.
[27] Quis . . . de nocte invocavit eam, et non est exauditus ab ea.—*Serm.* ii. *de Assump. B. V.*
[28] Quis... Domina mea, Immaculata Virgo, speravit in te et confusus est ? aut quis hominum precatus est omnipotentiam adjutorii tui, et derelictus est. —*Bolland. Mens. Feb.* tom. i. *in Vita S. Theoph.*

' that whoever has had recourse to thee, O Blessed Virgin, in his wants, and can remember that he did so in vain, should no more speak of or praise thy mercy.'[29]

' Sooner,' says the devout Blosius, ' would heaven and earth be destroyed than would Mary fail to assist anyone who asks for her help, provided he does so with a good intention and with confidence in her.'[30]   Saint Anselm, to increase our confidence, adds, that ' when we have recourse to this Divine Mother, not only we may be sure of her protection, but that often we shall be heard more quickly, and be thus preserved, if we have recourse to Mary and call on her holy name, than we should be if we called on the name of Jesus our Saviour ;' and the reason he gives for it is, ' that to Jesus, as a Judge, it belongs also to punish ; but mercy alone belongs to the Blessed Virgin as a patroness.' Meaning, that we more easily find salvation by having recourse to the Mother than by going to the Son—not as if Mary was more powerful than her Son to save us, for we know that Jesus Christ is our only Saviour, and that He alone by His merits has obtained and obtains salvation for us ; but it is for this reason : that when we have recourse to Jesus, we consider Him at the same time as our Judge, to whom it belongs also to chastise ungrateful souls, and therefore the confidence necessary to be heard may fail us ; but when we go to Mary, who has no other office than to compassionate us as Mother of mercy, and to defend us as our advocate, our confidence is more easily established, and is often greater. ' We often obtain more promptly what we ask by calling on the name of Mary than by invoking that of Jesus. Her Son is Lord and Judge of all, and discerns the merits of each one ; and therefore if He does not immediately grant the prayers of all, He is just. When, however, the Mother's name is invoked,

---

[29] Sileat misericordiam tuam, Virgo Beata, si quis est qui invocatam te in necessitatibus suis sibi meminerit defuisse.—*Serm.* iv. *in Assump. B.V.*

[30] Citius cœlum cum terra perierint, quam tu, aliquem serio te imploran- tem, tua ope destituas.— *Consol. Pusil.* cap. xxxv.

though the merits of the suppliant are not such as to deserve that his prayer should be granted, those of the Mother supply that he may receive.'[31]

'Many things,' says Nicephorus, 'are asked from God, and are not granted : they are asked from Mary, and are obtained.' And how is this? It is 'because God has thus decreed to honour His Mother.'[32]

Saint Bridget heard our Lord make a most sweet and consoling promise; for in the 50th chapter of the first book of her Revelations, we read that Jesus addressed His Mother in the following words : 'Thou shalt present me with no petition that shall be refused. My Mother, ask what thou wilt, for never will I refuse thee anything; and know,' he added, 'that I promise graciously to hear all those who ask any favour of Me in thy name, though they may be sinners, if only they have the will to amend their lives.'[33] The same thing was revealed to Saint Gertrude, when she heard our Divine Redeemer assure His Mother, 'that in His omnipotence He granted her power to show mercy to sinners who invoke her in whatever manner she might please.'[34]

Let all, then, say, with full confidence, in the words of that beautiful prayer addressed to the Mother of mercy, and commonly attributed to St. Bernard, 'Remember, O most pious Virgin Mary, that it never was heard of in any age that any one having recourse to thy

---

[31] Velocior est nonnunquam salus memorato nomine Mariæ, quam invocato nomine Domini Jesu. . . . Filius ejus Dominus est et judex omnium discernens merita singulorum, dum igitur ipse a quovis suo nomine invocatus, non statim exaudit, profecto id juste facit. Invocato autem nomine matris, etsi merita invocantis non merentur, ut exaudiatur : merita tamen matris intercedunt ut exaudiatur.—*S. Ans. de Exc. V.* c. 6.

[32] Multa petuntur a Deo, et non obtinentur : multa petuntur a Maria, et obtinentur; non quia potentior, sed quia Deus eam decrevit sic honorare.—*Niceph. Ap.* P. Pepe, Grandez, &c. †

[33] Nulla erit petitio tua ad me, quæ non exaudiatur. Et per te omnes, qui petunt misericordiam cum voluntate emendandi, gratiam habebunt.—*Rev.* lib. i. cap. 50.

[34] Ex omnipotentia mea, Mater, tibi concessi potestatem propitiandi peccatis omnium qui devote invocant tuæ pietatis auxilium, qualicumque modo placet tibi.—*Rev.* lib. iv. cap. 53.

I

protection was abandoned.'[35] Therefore forgive me, O Mary, if I say that I will not be the first unfortunate creature who has ever had recourse to thee and was abandoned.

EXAMPLE.

We read in his Life that Saint Francis of Sales experienced the efficacy of this prayer. When he was about seventeen years of age he was residing in Paris, where he was pursuing his studies. At the same time he devoted himself to exercises of piety and to the holy love of God, in which he found the joys of paradise. Our Lord, in order to try him, and to strengthen the bands which united him to Himself, allowed the evil spirit to persuade him that all he did was in vain, as he was already condemned in the eternal decrees of God. The darkness and spiritual dryness in which God was pleased at the same time to leave him (for he was then insensible to all the sweeter thoughts of the goodness of God), caused the temptation to have greater power over the heart of the holy youth ; and, indeed, it reached such a pitch that his fears and interior desolation took away his appetite, deprived him of sleep, made him pale and melancholy ; so much so, that he excited the compassion of all who saw him.

As long as this terrible storm lasted, the Saint could only conceive thoughts and utter words of despondency and bitter grief. ' Then,' said he, ' I am to be deprived of the grace of my God, who hitherto has shown Himself so lovely and sweet to me ? O Love, O Beauty, to which I have consecrated all my affections, I am no longer to enjoy thy consolation ! O Virgin, Mother of God, the fairest amongst all the daughters of Jerusalem, then I am never to see thee in heaven ! Ah, Lady, if I am not to behold thy beautiful countenance in Paradise, at least permit me not to blaspheme thee in hell !'

[35] Memorare, O piissima Virgo Maria, non esse auditum a sæculo quemquam ad tua currentem præsidia, tua implorantem auxilia, tua petentem suffragia, esse derelictum.

Such were the tender sentiments of that afflicted, but at the same time loving heart. The temptation had lasted a month, when it pleased our Lord to deliver him by the means of that comfortress of the world, the most Blessed Mary, to whom the Saint had some time before consecrated his virginity, and in whom, as he declared, he had placed all his hopes. One evening, on returning home, he entered a church, and saw a tablet hanging to the wall. He read it, and found the following well-known prayer, commonly called ' of St. Bernard :' ' Remember, O most pious Virgin Mary, that it never has been heard of in any age, that any one having recourse to thy protection was abandoned.' Falling on his knees before the altar of the Divine Mother, he recited this prayer with tender fervour, renewed his vow of chastity, promised to say the Rosary every day, and then added : ' My Queen, be my advocate with thy Son, whom I dare not approach. My Mother, if I am so unfortunate as not to be able to love my Lord in the next world, and whom I know to be so worthy of love, at least do thou obtain that I may love Him in this world as much as possible. This is the grace that I ask and hope for from thee.' Having thus addressed the Blessed Virgin, he cast himself into the arms of divine mercy, and resigned himself entirely to the will of God. Scarcely had he finished his prayer, when in an instant he was delivered from his temptation by his most sweet Mother. He immediately regained the peace of his soul, and with it his bodily health ; and from that time forward lived most devout to Mary, whose praises and mercy he constantly extolled, both in his sermons and writings, during the remainder of his life.

PRAYER.

O Mother of God, Queen of angels and Hope of men, give ear to one who calls upon thee and has recourse to thy protection. Behold me this day prostrate at thy feet ; I, a miserable slave of hell, devote myself entirely to thee. I desire to be for ever thy servant. I offer **my-**self to serve and honour thee to the utmost of my power during the whole of my life. I know that the service of one so vile and miserable can be no honour to thee, since I have so grievously offended Jesus, thy Son and my Redeemer. But if thou wilt accept one so unworthy for thy servant, and by thy intercession change me, and thus making me worthy, this very mercy will give thee that honour which so miserable a wretch as I can never give thee. Receive me, then, and reject me not, O my Mother. The Eternal Word came from heaven on earth to seek for lost sheep, and to save them He became thy Son. And when one of them goes to thee to find Jesus, wilt thou despise it? The price of my salvation is already paid ; my Saviour has already shed His blood, which suffices to save an infinity of worlds. This blood has only to be applied even to such a one as I am. And that is thy office, O Blessed Virgin ; to thee does it belong, as I am told by Saint Bernard, to dispense the merits of this blood to whom thou pleasest. To thee does it belong, says Saint Bonaventure, to save whomsoever thou willest, 'whomsoever thou willest will be saved.'[36] O, then, help me, my Queen ; my Queen, save me. To thee do I this day consecrate my whole soul ; do thou save it. O Salvation of those who invoke thee, I conclude in the words of the same Saint, 'O Salvation of those who call upon thee, do thou save me.'

SECTION **II.** *Of the greatness of the power of Mary to defend those who invoke her when tempted by the devil.*

Not only is the most Blessed Virgin Queen of heaven and of all Saints, but she is also Queen of hell and of all evil spirits ; for she overcame them valiantly by her virtues. From the very beginning God foretold the vic-

[36] Quem vis, ipse salvus erit.—*Cant. B.M.V. inst. illius Habacuc.*

tory and empire that our Queen would one day obtain over the serpent, when He announced that a woman should come into the world to conquer him : " I will put enmities between thee and the woman—she shall crush thy head."[1]   And who could this woman, his enemy, be but Mary, who by her fair humility and holy life always conquered him and beat down his strength ?   The Mother of our Lord Jesus Christ was promised in the person of that woman, as it is remarked by an ancient writer,[2] and therefore God did not say, ' I place,' but ' I will place ;' lest he might seem to refer to Eve : meaning that God said, " I will place enmities between thee and the woman," to signify that the serpent's opponent was not to be Eve, who was then living, but would be another woman descending from her, and who, as Saint Vincent Ferrer observes, ' would bring our first parents far greater advantages than those which they had lost by their sin.'[3]   Mary, then, was this great and valiant woman, who conquered the devil and crushed his head by bringing down his pride, as it was foretold by God Himself : " she shall crush thy head."   Some doubt as to whether these words refer to Mary, or whether they do not rather refer to Jesus Christ ; for the Septuagint renders them, " HE shall crush thy head." But in the Vulgate, which alone was approved of by the sacred Council of Trent, we find " SHE," and not " HE ;" and thus it was understood by Saint Ambrose, Saint Jerome, Saint Augustin, and a great many others. However, be it as it may, it is certain that either the Son by means of the Mother, or the Mother by means of the Son, has overcome Lucifer ; so that, as Saint Bernard remarks, this proud spirit, in spite of himself, was beaten down and trampled under foot by this most Blessed

---

[1] Inimicitias ponam inter te et mulierem . . . ipsa conteret caput tuum.—*Gen.* iii. 15.

[2] De Viro p. inter op. S. Hier.

[3] Dum autem Adam et Eva essent in illa tristitia Deus revelavit eis, quod ab eis procederet Virgo sanctissima, quæ afferret majus bonum, quam ipsi perdidissent.—*Serm. in Fest. Concep. B. V.*

Virgin; so that, as a slave conquered in war, he is forced always to obey the commands of this Queen. ' Beaten down and trampled under the feet of Mary, he endures a wretched slavery.'[4]

Saint Bruno says, 'that Eve was the cause of death,' by allowing herself to be overcome by the serpent; ' but that Mary,' by conquering the devil, ' restored life to us.'[5] And she bound him in such a way that this enemy cannot stir so as to do the least injury to any of her clients.

Beautiful is the explanation given by Richard of Saint Lawrence of the following words of the Book of Proverbs: "The heart of her husband trusteth in her, and he shall have no need of spoils."[6] He says, applying them to Jesus and Mary: ' The heart of her Spouse, that is Christ, trusteth in her, and He shall have no need of spoils; for she endows Him with all those, whom, by her prayers, merits, and example, she snatches from the devil.'[7] ' God has intrusted the heart of Jesus to the hands of Mary, that she may insure it the love of men,' says Cornelius à Lapide; and thus He will not need spoils; that is, He will be abundantly supplied with souls; for she enriches Him with those whom she has snatched from hell, and saved from the devil by her powerful assistance.

It is well known that the palm is a sign of victory; and therefore our Queen is placed on a high throne, in sight of all the powers, as a palm, for a sign of the certain victory that all may promise themselves who place themselves under her protection. " I was exalted like a palm-tree in Cades," says Ecclesiasticus:[8] ' that is,

---

[4] Sub Mariæ pedibus conculcatus et contritus, miseram patitur servitutem. —*In Sign. Magn.*

[5] Hæc linea incipit ab Eva, et desinit in Mariam. In principio mors, et in fine vita consistit: mors per Evam facta est, vita per Mariam reddita est. Illa a diabolo victa est, hæc diabolum ligavit et vicit.—*De Festis Mariæ*, Serm. ii.

[6] Confidit in ea cor viri sui, et spoliis non indigebit.—*Prov.* xxxi. 11.

[7] Confidit in ea cor viri sui, et spoliis non indigebit. Quia quoscunque suis orationibus, meritis et exemplis liberat a diabolo, apponit et assignat dominio sponsi sui.—*De Laud. Virg.* lib. vi. cap. 6.

[8] Quasi palma exaltata sum in Cades.—*Eccl.* xxiv. 18.

to defend,' adds blessed Albert the Great.[9] ' My children,' Mary seems to say, ' when the enemy assails you, fly to me ; cast your eyes on me, and be of good heart ; for as I am your defender, victory is assured to you.' So that recourse to Mary is a most secure means to conquer all the assaults of hell ; for she, says Saint Bernardine of Sienna, is even the Queen of hell, and sovereign mistress of the devils : since she it is who tames and crushes them. He thus expresses his thought : ' The most Blessed Virgin rules over the infernal regions. She is therefore called the ruling mistress of the devils, because she brings them into subjection.'[10] For this reason Mary is said in the sacred Canticles to be " terrible" to the infernal powers, " as an army in battle array ;"[11] and she is called thus terrible, because she well knows how to array her power, her mercy, and her prayers, to the discomfiture of her enemies, and for the benefit of her servants, who in their temptations have recourse to her most powerful aid.

" As the vine, I have brought forth a pleasant odour."[12] Thus does the Holy Ghost make Mary speak in the book of Ecclesiasticus. ' We are told,' says Saint Bernard on this passage, that ' all venomous reptiles fly from flowering vines :'[13] for, as poisonous reptiles fly from flowering vines, so do devils fly from those fortunate souls in whom they perceive the perfume of devotion to Mary. And therefore she also calls herself, in the same book, a cedar : " I was exalted like a cedar in Libanus."[14] Not only because Mary was untainted by sin, as the cedar is incorruptible, but also, as Cardinal Hugo remarks on the

---

[9] Ad defendendum.—*Bibl. Marian.*

[10] Beata Virgo dominatur in regno inferni . . . Domina dicitur quasi domans manus, quia ipsa domat dæmonum manus et potestates.—*Serm.* iii. *de Glor. Nom. M.*

[11] Terribilis ut castrorum acies ordinata.—*Cant.* vi. 3.

[12] Ego quasi vitis fructificavi suavitatem odoris.—*Eccl.* xxiv. 23.

[13] Aiunt de florescentibus vineis omne reptile venenatum cedere loco.—*Serm.* lx. *in Cant.*

[14] Quasi cedrus exaltata sum in Libano.—*Eccl.* xxiv. 17.

above text, because, ' like the cedar, which by its odour keeps off worms, so also does Mary by her sanctity drive away the devils.'[15]

In Judea victories were gained by means of the ark. Thus it was that Moses conquered his enemies, as we learn from the book of Numbers. "And when the ark was lifted up, Moses said : Arise, O Lord, and let Thy enemies be scattered."[16] Thus was Jericho conquered ; thus also the Philistines ; "for the Ark of God was there."[17] It is well known that this ark was a figure of Mary. Cornelius à Lapide says, ' In time of danger, Christians should fly to the most Blessed Virgin, who contained Christ as manna in the ark of her womb, and brought him forth to be the food and salvation of the world.'[18] For as manna was in the ark, so is Jesus (of whom manna was a figure) in Mary ; and by means of this ark we gain the victory over our earthly and infernal enemies. ' And thus,' Saint Bernardine of Sienna well observes, ' that when Mary, the ark of the New Testament, was raised to the dignity of Queen of heaven, the power of hell over men was weakened and dissolved.'[19]

O how the infernal spirits tremble at the very thought of Mary, and of her august name! says Saint Bonaventure. ' O, how fearful is Mary to the devils !'[20] The Saint compares these enemies to those of whom Job speaks : "He diggeth through houses in the dark : if the morning suddenly appear, it is to them the shadow of death."[21] Thieves go and rob houses in the

---

[15] Cedrus odore suo fugat serpentes, et Beata Virgo dæmones.—*In lib. Eccl.* cap. xxiv.

[16] Cumque elevaretur arca, dicebat Moyses : Surge Domine, et dissipentur inimici tui.—*Num.* x. 35.

[17] Erat enim ibi arca Dei.—1 *Reg.* xiv. 18.

[18] In periculis Christiani fugiant . . . ad B. Virginem, quæ Christum quasi manna in arca ventris sui continuit, et peperit pro cibo et salute mundi.—*Comment. in lib.* 1 *Reg.* cap. xiv. 18.

[19] Quando elevata fuit Virgo gloriosa ad cœlestia regna, dæmonis potentia imminuta est et dissipata.—*Serm. in Assump. B.V.M.*

[20] O quam amara et tremenda est hæc Maria demonibus !—*Spec. B.V.M.* lect. iii.

[21] Perfodit in tenebris domos. . . . Si subito apparuerit aurora, arbitrantur umbram mortis.—*Job.* xxiv. 16, 17.

dark; but as soon as morning dawns, they fly, as if they beheld the shadow of death. ' Precisely thus,' in the words of the same Saint, ' do the devils enter a soul in the time of darkness;' meaning, when the soul is in the obscurity of ignorance. They dig through the house of our mind when it is in the darkness of ignorance. But then he adds, ' if suddenly they are overtaken by the dawn, that is, if the grace and mercy of Mary enters the soul, its brightness instantly dispels the darkness, and puts the infernal enemies to flight, as if they fled from death.'[22] O blessed is he who always invokes the beautiful name of Mary in his conflicts with hell!

In confirmation of this, it was revealed to Saint Bridget, ' that God had rendered Mary so powerful over the devils, that as often as they assault a devout client who calls on this most Blessed Virgin for help, she at a single glance instantly terrifies them, so that they fly far away, preferring to have their pains redoubled rather than see themselves thus subject to the power of Mary.'[23]

The Divine Bridegroom, when speaking of this His beloved bride, calls her a lily: " As the lily is amongst the thorns, so is my beloved amongst the daughters."[24] On these words Cornelius à Lapide makes the reflection, ' that as the lily is a remedy against serpents and venomous things, so is the invocation of Mary a specific by which we may overcome all temptations, and especially those against purity, as all find who put it in practice.'[25]

[22] Perfodiunt namque in tenebris ignorantiæ, in tenebris obscuritatis interiores domos mentium nostrarum. . . . Si enim subito apparuerit aurora, si cito nobis advenerit et supervenerit Mariæ gratia et misericordia . . . sic fugiunt, sicut homines timent et fugiunt umbram mortis.—*Spec. B. V. M.* lect. xi.

[23] Super omnes etiam malignos spiritus ipsam sic Deus potentem effecit, quod quotiescumque ipsi aliquem hominem Virginis auxilium ex charitate implorantem impugnaverint, ad ipsius Virginis nutum illico pavidi procul diffugiunt; volentes potius pœnas suas et miserias sibi multiplicari, quam ejusdem Virginis potentiam super se taliter dominari.—*Serm. Ang.* cap. xx.

[24] Sicut lilium inter spinas, sic amica mea inter filias.—*Cant.* ii. 2.

[25] Sicut lilium valet adversus serpentes et venena, sic B. Virginis invocatio singulare est remedium in omni tentatione vitiorum, et præsertim libidinis, uti experientia constat.—*Comment. in Cant.*

Saint Cosmas of Jerusalem used to say, ' While I keep my hope in thee unconquerable, O Mother of God, I shall be safe. I will fight and overcome my enemies with no other buckler than thy protection and thy all-powerful aid.'[26]   And all who are so fortunate as to be the servants of this great Queen can say the same thing. O Mother of God, if I hope in thee, I most certainly shall not be overcome ; for, defended by Thee, I will follow up my enemies, and oppose them with the shield of thy protection and thy all-powerful help ; and then without doubt I shall conquer. For, says James the monk (who was a doctor amongst the Greeks), addressing our Lord on the subject of Mary, ' Thou, O Lord, hast given us in Mary arms that no force of war can overcome, and a trophy never to be destroyed.'[27]

It is said in the Old Testament, that God guided His people from Egypt to the land of promise, " by day in a pillar of a cloud, and by night in a pillar of fire."[28]   This stupendous pillar, at times as a cloud, at others as fire, says Richard of Saint Lawrence, was a figure of Mary fulfilling the double office she constantly exercises for our good : as a cloud she protects us from the ardour of Divine justice ; and as fire she protects us from the devils. ' Behold the twofold object for which Mary is given to us ; to shelter us, as a cloud, from the heat of the sun of justice, and, as fire, to protect us all against the devil.'[29]   She protects us as a burning fire : for, Saint Bonaventure remarks : ' As wax melts before the fire, so do the devils lose their power against those souls who often remember the

[26] Invituperabilem Deipara spem tuam habens, servabor. . . . Persequar inimicos meos et fugam vertam, solam habens ut thoracem protectionem tuam et omnipotens auxilium tuum.—*Hymn* vi. *in Depr. ad Deip.*

[27] Tu arma vi omni belli potentiora, trophæumque invictum eam præstitisti.—*In Nat. S. Mariæ.*

[28] Per diem in columna nubis, et per noctem in columna ignis.—*Exod.* xiii. 21.

[29] Ecce duo officia ad quæ data est nobis Maria : scilicet, ut nos protegat a fervore solis justitiæ, tamquam nubes . . et tamquam ignis . . . nos protegat contra diabolum.—*Lib.* viii. *De Laud. Virg.* cap. 12.

name of Mary, and devoutly invoke it; and still more so, if they also endeavour to imitate her virtues.'[30]

The devils tremble even if they only hear the name of Mary. Saint Bernard declares that 'in the name of Mary every knee bows; and that the devils not only fear but tremble at the very sound of that name.'[31] And as men fall prostrate with fear if a thunderbolt falls near them, so do the devils if they hear the name of Mary. Thomas à Kempis thus expresses the same sentiment: 'The evil spirits greatly fear the Queen of heaven, and fly at the sound of her name, as if from fire. At the very sound of the word Mary, they are prostrated as by thunder.'[32] And O how many victories have the clients of Mary gained by only making use of her most holy name! It was thus that Saint Anthony of Padua was always victorious; thus the blessed Henry Suso; thus so many other lovers of this great Queen conquered. We learn from the history of the missions in Japan, that many devils appeared under the form of fierce animals to a certain Christian, to alarm and threaten him; but he thus addressed them: 'I have no arms that you can fear; and if the Most High permits it, do whatever you please with me. In the mean time, however, I take the holy names of Jesus and Mary for my defence.' At the very sound of these tremendous names, the earth opened, and the proud spirits cast themselves headlong into it.

Saint Anselm declares that he himself 'knew and had seen and heard many who had invoked the name of Mary in time of danger, and were immediately delivered from it.'[33]

---

[30] Pereunt sicut cera a facie ignis, ubicumque invenerint crebram hujus nominis recordationem, devotam invocationem, sollicitam imitationem.— *Spec. B. M. V.* lect. xi.

[31] In nomine Mariæ omne genu flectitur; et dæmones non solum pertimescunt, sed, audita hac voce, contremiscunt.—*Serm. sup. Miss.* †

[32] Expavescunt cœli Reginam spiritus maligni, et diffugiunt, audito nomine sancto ejus, velut ab igne. Tanquam tonitruum de cœlo factum, sic prosternuntur ad Sanctæ Mariæ vocabulum.—*Serm.* iv. *ad Nov.*

[33] Sæpe quippe vidimus et audivimus plurimos hominum in suis periculis recordari horum; et omnis periculi malum illico evasisse.—*De Exc. Virg.* c. vi.

'Glorious indeed, and admirable,' exclaims Saint Bonaventure, 'is thy name, O Mary; for those who pronounce it at death need not fear all the powers of hell;'[34] for the devils on hearing that name instantly fly, and leave the soul in peace.   The same Saint adds, 'that men do not fear a powerful hostile army as much as the powers of hell fear the name and protection of Mary.'[35] 'Thou, O Lady,' says Saint Germanus, 'by the simple invocation of thy most powerful name, givest security to thy servants against all the assaults of the enemy.'[36]   O were Christians but careful in their temptations to pronounce the name of Mary with confidence, never would they fall; for, as blessed Allan remarks, 'At the very sound of these words, Hail, Mary! Satan flies, and hell trembles.'[37]   Our Blessed Lady herself revealed to St. Bridget that the enemy flies even from the most abandoned sinners, and who consequently are the furthest from God, and fully possessed by the devil, if they only invoke her most powerful name with a true purpose of amendment. 'All devils, on hearing this name of Mary, filled with terror, leave the soul.'[38]   But at the same time our Blessed Lady added, 'that if the soul does not amend and obliterate its sins by sorrow, the devils almost immediately return and continue to possess it.'[39]

EXAMPLE.

In Reichersperg there was a canon regular of the name of Arnold, surnamed the Pious, on account of the

---

[34] Gloriosum et admirabile est nomen tuum : qui illud retinent, non expavescent in puncto mortis.—*In Ps.* cx.

[35] Non sic timent hostes visibiles quasi castrorum multitudinem copiosam, sicut aëreæ potestates Mariæ vocabulum, patrocinium et exemplum.—*Spec. B.M.V.* lect. iii.

[36] Tu nequissimi hostis contra servos tuos invasiones sola tui nominis invocatione sanctissima repellens, tutos atque incolumes servas.—*Serm. de Zona Virg.*

[37] Satan fugit, infernus contremiscit, cum dico Ave Maria.—*De Psalt.* p. 4. c. 30.

[38] Omnes dæmones, audito nomine meo, statim relinquunt animam quasi territi.—*Lib.* i. *Rev.* c. 9.

[39] Sed revertuntur ad eam . . . nisi aliqua emendatio subsequatur.—*Ib.*

sanctity of his life, and who had the most tender devotion to our Blessed Lady. When at the point of death, and having received the last sacraments, he summoned his religious brethren, and begged that they would not abandon him in his last passage. Scarcely had he uttered these words, when, in the presence of all, he began to tremble, to roll his eyes, and, bathed in a cold sweat, with a faltering voice said, ' Ah, do you not see the devils who are endeavouring to drag me to hell?' He then cried out, ' Brothers, implore the aid of Mary for me; in her I confide; she will give me the victory.' On hearing this, his brethren recited the Litany of our Blessed Lady, and as they said, ' Holy Mary, pray for him,' the dying man exclaimed, ' Repeat, repeat the name of Mary, for I am already before God's tribunal.' He was silent for a moment, and then added, ' It is true that I did it, but I have done penance for it.' And then turning to our Blessed Lady, he said, ' O Mary, I shall be delivered if thou helpest me.' Again the devils attacked him; but he defended himself with his crucifix and the name of Mary. Thus was the night spent; but no sooner did morning dawn than Arnold exclaimed with the greatest calmness, and full of holy joy, ' Mary, my sovereign Lady, my refuge, has obtained me pardon and salvation.' Then casting his eyes on that Blessed Virgin who was inviting him to follow her, he said, ' I come, O Lady, I come !' and making an effort to do so even with his body, his soul fled after her to the realms of eternal bliss, as we trust, for he sweetly expired.[40]

PRAYER.

Behold at thy feet, O Mary my hope, a poor sinner, who has so many times been by his own fault the slave of hell. I know that by neglecting to have recourse to thee, my refuge, I allowed myself to be over-

[40] P. Auriemma, Aff. Scamb. p. ii. cap. 8. Ludewig. Chron. Reichersp. anno 1166.

come by the devil. Had I always had recourse to thee, had I always invoked thee, I certainly should not have fallen. I trust, O Lady most worthy of all our love, that through thee I have already escaped from the hands of the devil, and that God has pardoned me. But I tremble lest at some future period I may again fall into the same bonds. I know that my enemies have not lost the hope of again overcoming me, and already they prepare new assaults and temptations for me. Ah, my Queen and refuge, do thou assist me. Place me under thy mantle; permit me not again to become their slave. I know that thou wilt help me and give me the victory, provided I invoke thee; but I dread lest in my temptations I may forget thee, and neglect to do so. The favour, then, that I seek of thee, and which thou must grant me, O most holy Virgin, is that I may never forget thee, and especially in time of temptation; grant that I may then repeatedly invoke thee, saying, ' O Mary, help me ; O Mary, help me.' And when my last struggle with hell comes, at the moment of death, ah then, my Queen, help me more than ever, and thou thyself remind me to call on thee more frequently either with my lips or in my heart; that, being thus filled with confidence, I may expire with thy sweet name and that of thy Son Jesus on my lips; that so I may be able to bless thee and praise thee, and not depart from thy feet in Paradise for all eternity. Amen.

CHAPTER V.

SECTION I. *Of the Necessity of the Intercession of Mary for our Salvation.*

THAT it is not only lawful but useful to invoke and pray to the Saints, and more especially to the Queen of Saints, the most holy and ever Blessed Virgin Mary, in order that they may obtain us the Divine grace, is an article of faith, and has been defined by general councils, against heretics who condemned it as injurious to Jesus Christ, who is our only mediator; but if a Jeremias after his death prayed for Jerusalem ;[1] if the ancients of the Apocalypse presented the prayers of the Saints to God ;[2] if a Saint Peter promises his disciples that after his death he will be mindful of them ;[3] if a holy Stephen prays for his persecutors ;[4] if a Saint Paul prays for his companions ;[5] if, in fine, the Saints can pray for us, why cannot we beseech the Saints to intercede for us ? Saint Paul recommends himself to the prayers of his disciples : " Brethren, pray for us."[6] Saint James exhorts us to pray one for another : " Pray one for another, that you may be saved."[7] Then we can do the same.

No one denies that Jesus Christ is our only mediator of justice, and that He by His merits has obtained our

---

[1] 2 Mach. xv. 14. [2] Apoc. vi. 8.
[3] 2 Pet. i. 15. [4] Act. vii. 59.
[5] Act. xxvii. 24; Eph. ii. 16; Phil. i. 4; Col. i. 3.
[6] Orate pro nobis.—1 *Thes.* v. 25.
[7] Orate pro invicem ut salvemini.—*S. Jacobi* v. 16.

reconciliation with God.   But, on the other hand, it is
impious to assert that God is not pleased to grant graces
at the intercession of His Saints, and more especially of
Mary his Mother, whom Jesus desires so much to see
loved and honoured by all.   Who can pretend that the
honour bestowed on a mother does not redound to the
honour of the son?   "The glory of children are their
fathers."[8]   Whence St. Bernard says, 'Let us not
imagine that we obscure the glory of the Son by the
great praise we lavish on the Mother; for the more she
is honoured, the greater is the glory of her Son.' 'There
can be no doubt,' says the Saint, 'that whatever we say
in praise of the Mother is equally in praise of the
Son.'[9]   And St. Ildephonsus also says, 'That which
is given to the Mother redounds to the Son; the honour
given to the Queen is honour bestowed on the King.'[10]
There can be no doubt that by the merits of Jesus
Mary was made the mediatress of our salvation; not
indeed a mediatress of justice, but of grace and intercession; as St. Bonaventure expressly calls her 'Mary
the most faithful mediatress of our salvation.'[11]   And
St. Lawrence Justinian asks, 'How can she be otherwise than full of grace, who has been made the ladder
to paradise, the gate of heaven, the most true mediatress
between God and man?'[12]

Hence the learned Suarez justly remarks, that if we
implore our Blessed Lady to obtain us a favour, it is
not because we distrust the Divine mercy, but rather
that we fear our own unworthiness and the absence
of proper dispositions; and we recommend ourselves to

---

[8] Gloria filiorum patres eorum.—*Prov.* xvii. 6.
[9] Non est dubium, quidquid in laudibus Matris proferimus, ad Filium per-
tinere.—*Hom.* iv. *sup. Miss.*
[10] Redundat ad Filium, quod impenditur Matri . . . Transit honor in regem,
qui defertur in famulatum reginæ.—*De Virg. S. M.* cap. xii.
[11] Maria . . . fidelissima mediatrix salutis fuit.—*Spec. B. V. M.* lect. ix.
[12] Quomodo non est Maria, juxta Gabrielis oraculum, plena gratia, quæ
effecta est Mater Dei, paradisi scala, cœli janua, interventrix mundi, dæmonum fuga, peccatorum spes, naufragantium portus, maris stella, confugium
periclitantium, solamen laborantium, fluctuantium robur, Dei et hominum
verissima mediatrix ?—*Serm. de Annunc.*

Mary, that her dignity may supply for our lowliness. He says that we apply to Mary 'in order that the dignity of the intercessor may supply for our misery. Hence, to invoke the aid of the most Blessed Virgin is not diffidence in the Divine mercy, but dread of our own unworthiness.'[13]

That it is most useful and holy to have recourse to the intercession of Mary can only be doubted by those who have not faith. But that which we intend to prove here is, that the intercession of Mary is even necessary to salvation; we say necessary—not absolutely, but morally. This necessity proceeds from the will itself of God, that all graces that He dispenses should pass by the hands of Mary, according to the opinion of Saint Bernard, and which we may now with safety call the general opinion of theologians and learned men. The author of the *Reign of Mary* positively asserts that such is the case. It is maintained by Vega, Mendoza, Pacciuchelli, Segneri, Poiré, Crasset, and by innumerable other learned authors. Even Father Natalis Alexander, who always uses so much reserve in his propositions, even he says that it is the will of God that we should expect all graces through the intercession of Mary. I will give his own words: 'God wills that we should obtain all good things that we hope for from Him through the powerful intercession of the Virgin Mother, and we shall obtain them whenever (as we are in duty bound) we invoke her.'[14] In confirmation of this, he quotes the following celebrated passage of St. Bernard: 'Such is His will, that we should have all by Mary.'[15] Father Contenson is also of the same opinion; for, explaining the words addressed by our Lord on the Cross to Saint John: " Behold thy

[13] Ut dignitas intercessoris suppleat inopiam nostram. Unde virginem interpellare, non est de divina misericordia diffidere, sed de propria indignitate et indispositione timere.—*De Incarnat.* p. ii. q. 37, disp. 23, § 3.

[14] Qui vult ut omnia bona ab ipso expectemus potentissima virginis macris intercessione ; cum eam, ut par est, invocamus impetranda.—Epist. lxxvi. in calce tom. iv. *Moral.*

[15] Sic est voluntas ejus, qui totum nos habere voluit per Mariam.—*Serm. le Aquæd.*

Mother,"[16] he remarks, ' That it is the same thing as if He had said : As no one can be saved except through the merits of My sufferings and death, so no one will be a partaker of the blood then shed otherwise than through the prayer of My Mother. He alone is a son of My sorrows who has Mary for his Mother. My wounds are ever-flowing fountains of grace ; but their streams will reach no one but by the channel of Mary. In vain will he invoke Me as a Father who has not venerated Mary as a Mother. And thou, my disciple John, if thou lovest Me, love her ; for thou wilt be beloved by Me in proportion to thy love for her.'[17]

This proposition (that all that we receive from our Lord comes through Mary) does not exactly please a certain modern writer, who, although in other respects he speaks of true and false devotion with much learning and piety, yet when he treats of devotion towards the Divine Mother he seems to grudge her that glory which was given her without scruple by a Saint Germanus, a Saint Anselm, a Saint John Damascen, a Saint Bonaventure, a Saint Antoninus, a Saint Bernardine, the venerable Abbot of Celles, and so many other learned men, who had no difficulty in affirming that the intercession of Mary is not only useful but necessary. The author alluded to says that the proposition that God grants no grace otherwise than through Mary, is hyperbolical and exaggerated, having dropped from the lips of some saints in the heat of fervour, but which, correctly speaking, is only to be understood as meaning that through Mary we received Jesus Christ, by whose merits we obtain all graces ; for he adds,

---

16 Ecce mater tua.—*Joan.* xix. 27.

17 Quasi aperte diceret, sicut nemo potest salvari nisi per meritum crucis et mortis meæ : ita nullus sanguinis illius particeps erit, nisi intercessione matris meæ. Ille solus filius dolorum meorum reputabitur, cui Maria mater erit. Vulnera gratiarum fontes perennes et patentes sunt : sed ad nullos derivabuntur rivi, nisi per Marianum canalem et aquæductum. Frustra me invocabit patrem, qui Mariam non fuerit veneratus ut matrem. Tu ipsemet, prædilecte discipule Joannes, si me amas, eam ama : tantum enim a me amaberis quantum eam amaveris.—*Theol. Mentis et Cord.* tom. ii. lib. 10, d. 4, c. i.

'To believe that God can grant us no graces without the intercession of Mary, would be contrary to faith and the doctrine of Saint Paul, who says that we acknowledge but " one God and one Mediator of God and men, the man Christ Jesus." '[18]

But with his leave, and going upon his own admissions, mediation of justice by way of merit is one thing, and mediation of grace by way of prayer is another. And again, it is one thing to say that God cannot, and another that He will not, grant graces without the intercession of Mary. We willingly admit that God is the source of every good, and the absolute Master of all graces ; and that Mary is only a pure creature, who receives whatever she obtains as a pure favour from God. But who can ever deny that it is most reasonable and proper to assert that God, in order to exalt this great creature, who more than all others honoured and loved Him during her life, and whom, moreover, He had chosen to be the Mother of His Son, our common Redeemer, wills that all graces that are granted to those whom He has redeemed should pass through and be dispensed by the hands of Mary ? We most readily admit that Jesus Christ is the only Mediator of justice, according to the distinction just made, and that by His merits He obtains us all graces and salvation ; but we say that Mary is the Mediatress of grace ; and that receiving all she obtains through Jesus Christ, and because she prays and asks for it in the name of Jesus Christ, yet all the same whatever graces we receive, they come to us through her intercession.

There is certainly nothing contrary to faith in this, but the reverse. It is quite in accordance with the sentiments of the Church, which, in its public and approved prayers, teaches us continually to have recourse to this Divine Mother, and to invoke her as the ' health of the weak, the refuge of sinners, the help of

---

[18] 1 Tim. ii. 5.

Christians, and as our life and hope.'[19]   In the office appointed to be said on the feasts of Mary, this same holy Church, applying the words of Ecclesiasticus to this Blessed Virgin, gives us to understand that in her we find all hope, "In me is all hope of life and of virtue;"[20] in Mary is every grace, "In me is all grace of the way and of the truth."[21]   In Mary, finally, we shall find life and eternal salvation: "Who finds me finds life, and draws salvation from the Lord."[22]   And elsewhere: "They that work by me shall not sin; they that explain me shall have everlasting life."[23]   And surely such expressions as these sufficiently prove that we require the intercession of Mary.

Moreover, we are confirmed in this opinion by so many theologians and fathers, of whom it is certainly incorrect to say, as the above-named author does, that, in exalting Mary, they spoke hyperbolically, and allowed great exaggerations to fall from their lips.   To exaggerate and speak hyperbolically is to exceed the limits of truth; and surely we cannot say that Saints who were animated by the Spirit of God, which is truth itself. spoke thus.   If I may be allowed to make a short digression, and give my own sentiment, it is, that when an opinion tends in any way to the honour of the most Blessed Virgin, when it has some foundation, and is repugnant neither to the faith, nor to the decrees of the Church, nor to truth, the refusal to hold it, or to oppose it because the reverse may be true, shows little devotion to the Mother of God.   Of the number of such as these I do not choose to be, nor do I wish my reader to be so, but rather of the number of those who fully and firmly believe all that can without error be believed of

[19] Salus infirmorum, refugium peccatorum, auxilium Christianorum, vita, spes nostra.

[20] In me omnis spes vitæ et virtutis.—*Eccl.* xxiv. 25.

[21] In me gratia omnis viæ et veritatis.—*Ib.*

[22] Qui me invenerit, inveniet vitam, et hauriet salutem a Domino.—*Prov.* viii. 35.

[23] Qui operantur in me, non peccabunt. Qui elucidant me, vitam æternam habebunt.—*Eccl* xxiv. 30, 31

the greatness of Mary, according to the Abbot Rupert, who, amongst the acts of homage most pleasing to this good Mother, places that of firmly believing all that redounds to her honour.[24] If there was nothing else to take away our fear of exceeding in the praises of Mary, St. Augustine[25] should suffice ; for he declares that whatever we may say in praise of Mary is little in comparison with that which she deserves, on account of her dignity of Mother of God ; and, moreover, the Church says, in the mass appointed for her festivals, 'Thou art happy, O sacred Virgin Mary, and most worthy of all praise.'[26]

But let us return to the point, and examine what the Saints say on the subject. Saint Bernard says 'that God has filled Mary with all graces, so that men may receive by her means, as by a channel, every good thing that comes to them.' He says, that 'she is a full aqueduct, that others may receive of her plenitude.'[27] On this the Saint makes the following significant remark : 'Before the birth of the Blessed Virgin, a constant flow of graces was wanting, because this aqueduct did not exist.'[28] But now that Mary has been given to the world, heavenly graces constantly flow through her on all.

The devil, like Holofernes, who, in order to gain possession of the city of Bethulia, ordered the aqueducts to be destroyed, exerts himself to his utmost to destroy devotion to the Mother of God in souls ; for if this channel of grace is closed, he easily gains possession of them. And here, continues the same Saint Bernard, 'See, O souls, with what tender devotion our Lord wills that we should honour our Queen, by always

---

[24] Ejus magnalia firmiter credere.—*De Laud. Virg.*

[25] Serm. 208. E.B. app.

[26] Felix namque es, sacra virgo Maria, et omni laude dignissima.

[27] Plenus equidem aquæductus, ut accipiant cæteri de ejus plenitudine.—*Serm. de Aquæd.*

[28] Propterea tanto tempore humano generi fluenta gratiæ defuerunt, quod necdum intercederet is de quo loquimur tam desiderabilis aquæductus.—*Ib.*

having recourse to and relying on her protection ; for in Mary He has placed the plenitude of every good, so that henceforward we may know and acknowledge that whatever hope, grace, or other advantage we possess, all come from the hand of Mary.'[29]   Saint Antoninus says the same thing : ' All graces that have ever been bestowed on men, all came by Mary.'[30]   And on this account she is called the Moon, according to the following remark of Saint Bonaventure : ' As the moon, which stands between the sun and the earth, transmits to this latter whatever she receives from the former, so does Mary pour out upon us who are in this world the heavenly graces that she receives from the Divine sun of justice.'[31]

Again, the holy Church calls her ' the happy gate of heaven ;'[32] for as the same Saint Bernard remarks : ' As every mandate of grace that is sent by a king passes by the palace-gates, so does every grace that comes from heaven to the world pass through the hands of Mary.'[33]   Saint Bonaventure says that Mary is called ' the gate of heaven, because no one can enter that blessed kingdom without passing by her.'[34]   An ancient author, probably Saint Sophronius, in a sermon on the Assumption, published with the works of Saint Jerome, says ' that the plenitude of grace which is in Jesus Christ came into Mary, though in a different way ;'[35] meaning that it is in our Lord, as in the head, from which the vital spirits (that is, Divine help to

---

[29] Intuemini quanto devotionis affectu a nobis eam voluerit honorari, qui totius boni plenitudinem posuit in Maria: ut proinde si quid spei in nobis est, si quid gratiæ, si quid salutis, ab ea noverimus redundare.—*Serm. de Aquæd.*

[30] Per B. Mariam exivit de cœlis ad nos quicquid unquam gratiæ creatum venit in mundum.—P. iv. tit. 15, c. 20.

[31] Quia sicut luna inter corpora cœlestia et terrena est media, et quod ab illis accipit ad inferiora refundit : sic et virgo regia inter nos et Deum est media, et gratiam ipsa nobis refundit.—*Spann. Polyanth. litt. M.* t. 6.

[32] Felix cœli porta.

[33] Nihil nos Deus habere voluit, quod per Mariæ manus non transiret.—*Serm.* iii. *in Virg. Nat. D.*

[34] Nullus potest . . . cœlum intrare, nisi per Mariam transeat tamquam per portam.—*Exposit. in cap.* i. *Luc.*

[35] In Mariam vero totius gratiæ quæ in Christo est plenitudo venit, quamquam aliter.—*Serm. de Assump. B. V.*

obtain eternal salvation) flow into us, who are the members of His mystical body; and that the same plenitude is in Mary, as in the neck, through which these vital spirits pass to the members. The same idea is confirmed by Saint Bernardine of Sienna, who explains it more clearly, saying, 'that all graces of the spiritual life that descend from Christ, their head, to the faithful, who are His mystical body, are transmitted by the means of Mary.'[36]

The same Saint Bernardine endeavours to assign a reason for this when he says, 'that as God was pleased to dwell in the womb of this holy Virgin, she acquired, so to say, a kind of jurisdiction over all graces; for when Jesus Christ issued forth from her most sacred womb, all the streams of Divine gifts flowed from her as from a celestial ocean.'[37] Elsewhere, repeating the same idea in more distinct terms, he asserts that 'from the moment that this Virgin Mother conceived the Divine Word in her womb, she acquired a special jurisdiction, so to say, over all the gifts of the Holy Ghost, so that no creature has since received any grace from God otherwise than by the hands of Mary.'[38] Another author, in a commentary on a passage of Jeremias, in which the prophet, speaking of the Incarnation of the Eternal Word, and of Mary His Mother, says that 'a woman shall compass a man,'[39] remarks, that 'as no line can be drawn from the centre of a circle without passing by the circumference, so no grace proceeds from Jesus, who is the centre of every good thing, without passing by Mary, who compassed Him when

---

[36] Per virginem a capite Christi vitales gratiæ in ejus corpus mysticum transfunduntur.—*Serm. de Nat. B.M.V.* cap. viii.

[37] Cum . . . tota natura divina . . . intra virginis uterum extiterit clausum : non timeo dicere quod omnium gratiarum effluxus quamdam jurisdictionem habuerit hæc virgo, de cujus utero, quasi de quodam divinitatis oceano, rivi et flumina emanabant omnium gratiarum.—*Ib.*

[38] A tempore . . . a quo virgo mater concepit in utero Verbum Dei, quandam (ut sic dicam) jurisdictionem seu auctoritatem obtinuit in omni Spiritus Sancti processione temporali ; ita quod nulla creatura aliquam a Deo obtinuit gratiam, nisi secundum ipsius piæ matris dispensationem.—*Ib.*

[39] Jer. xxxi. 22.

she received Him into her womb.'[40]   Saint Bernardine
says that for this reason, 'all gifts, all virtues, and all
graces are dispensed by the hands of Mary to whomsoever, when, and as she pleases.'[41]   Richard of Saint
Lawrence also asserts 'that God wills that whatever
good things He bestows on His creatures should pass
by the hands of Mary.'[42]   And therefore the venerable
Abbot of Celles exhorts all to have recourse to 'this
treasury of graces' (for so he calls her); for the world
and the whole human race has to receive every good
that can be hoped for through her alone.   'Address
yourselves to the Blessed Virgin,' he says; 'for by her,
and in her, and with her, and from her, the world
receives, and is to receive, every good.'[43]   It must be
now evident to all, that when these saints and authors
tell us in such terms that all graces come to us through
Mary, they do not simply mean to say that we 'received
Jesus Christ, the source of every good, through Mary,'
as the before-named writer pretends; but that they
assure us that God, who gave us Jesus Christ, wills
that all graces that have been, that are, and will be
dispensed to men to the end of the world through the
merits of Christ, should be dispensed by the hands and
through the intercession of Mary.

And thus Father Suarez concludes, that it is the
sentiment of the universal Church, 'that the intercession and prayers of Mary are, above those of all
others, not only useful, but necessary.[44]   Necessary,
in accordance with what we have already said, not
with an absolute necessity; for the mediation of Jesus

[40] Crasset, Ver. Dev. p. 1. tr. 1. q. 5. § 2.

[41] Ideo omnia dona, virtutes et gratiæ ipsius Spiritus Sancti, quibus vult
quando vult, quomodo vult, et quantum vult, per manus ipsius administran-
tur.—*Serm. de Nativ. B.M.V.* cap. viii.

[42] Qui quidquid boni dat creaturis suis, per manus matris virginis vult
transire.—*De Laud. Virg.* lib. ii. cap. 3.

[43] Accede ad virginem, quia per ipsam, et in ipsa, et cum ipsa, et ab ipsa
habet mundus et habiturus est omne bonum.—*De Contempl. B.V.* in prol.

[44] Sentit . . . ecclesia virginis intercessionem et orationem præ omnibus
aliis sibi esse utilem ac necessariam. — *De Incarnat.* p. ii. q. 37, disp. 23,
sect. 3.

Christ alone is absolutely necessary; but with a moral necessity; for the Church believes with Saint Bernard, that God has determined that no grace shall be granted otherwise than by the hands of Mary. 'God wills,' says the Saint, 'that we should have nothing that has not passed by the hands of Mary;'[45] and before Saint Bernard, Saint Ildephonsus asserted the same thing, addressing the Blessed Virgin in the following terms: 'O Mary, God has decided on committing all good gifts that He has provided for men to thy hands; and therefore He has intrusted all treasures and riches of grace to thee.'[46] And therefore Saint Peter Damian remarks,[47] 'that God would not become man without the consent of Mary; in the first place, that we might feel ourselves under great obligations to her; and in the second, that we might understand that the salvation of all is left to the care of this Blessed Virgin.'

Saint Bonaventure, on the words of the prophet Isaias, "And there shall come forth a rod out of the root of Jesse, and a flower shall rise up out of his root, and the spirit of the Lord shall rest upon him,"[48] makes a beautiful remark, saying: 'Whoever desires the sevenfold grace of the Holy Spirit, let him seek for the flower of the Holy Ghost in the rod.' That is, for Jesus in Mary; 'For by the rod we find the flower, and by the flower, God.' And in the twelfth chapter of the same work, he adds, 'If you desire to possess this flower, bend down the rod, which bears the flower, by prayer; and so you will obtain it.'[49] The seraphical father, in his sermon for the Epiphany, on the

---

[45] Nihil nos Deus habere voluit, quod per Mariæ manus non transiret.— *Serm.* iii. ' *Vig. Nat. Dom.*

[46] Omnia bona quæ illis summa majestas decrevit facere, tuis manibus decrevit commendare: commissi quippe sunt tibi thesauri et ornamenta gratiarum.—*In Cor. Virg.* cap. 15.

[47] Pacciuch. in Ps. lxxxvi exc. 1.

[48] Et egredietur virga de radice Jesse, et flos de radice ejus ascendet, et requiescet super eum Spiritus Domini.—*Is.* xi. 1.

[49] Quicumque septiformem Spiritus Sancti gratiam adipisci desiderat, ipse florem Spiritus Sancti in virga quærat : per virgam enim ad florem, per florem ad spiritum, in ipso requiescentem pervenimus . . . Si hunc florem habere desideras, virgam floris precibus flectas.—*Spec. B. M. V.* lect. vi. et xii.

words of St. Matthew, " They found the child, with
Mary his Mother," reminds us, that if we wish to find
Jesus we must go to Mary.[50] We may, then, conclude,
that in vain shall we seek for Jesus, unless we endeavour to find Him with Mary. And so Saint Ildephonsus says, ' I desire to be the servant of the Son ;
but because no one will ever be so without serving
the Mother, for this reason I desire the servitude of
Mary.'[51]

EXAMPLE.

Vincent of Beauvais[52] and Cæsarius[53] relate that
there was a certain noble youth who had reduced himself by his vices from a state of opulence, in which he
had been left by his father, to one of such poverty, that
he was obliged to beg his bread. He left his country, that he might be able to live with less shame in a
place where he was unknown. On his road, he one
day met a man who had formerly been his father's
servant. This man, seeing him in such affliction, on
account of the distress into which he had fallen, told
him to be of good heart, for he would take him to a
prince who was so liberal, that he would be provided
with all he could desire. This abandoned wretch was
a sorcerer ; and one day he led the poor youth to a
wood, near a lake, and began to address an invisible
person. The youth asked him to whom he was speaking. He replied, ' To the devil ;' but seeing that the
young man was alarmed, he encouraged him, and told
him to fear nothing ; and then continued to address
the evil spirit, and said : ' Master, this young man is
reduced to the greatest poverty ; he would wish to be
reinstated in his possessions.' ' If he will obey me,'
replied the fiend, ' I will make him richer than ever ;

---

[50] Invenerunt puerum cum Maria matre ejus. Si ergo hunc puerum via
invenire, ad Mariam accede.—*Serm.* iv. *Dom. infr.* 8, *Nat. D.*
[51] Ut sim devotus servus filii (generati), servitutem fideliter appeto genitricis.—*De Virginitate S. Mar.* cap. xii.
[52] Spec. Hist. l. vii. c. 105.
[53] Dial. l. 2. c. 12.

but, in the first place, he must renounce God.' This horrified the young man; but being incited to it by that cursed magician, he complied, and renounced his God. 'But that is not enough,' added the devil; 'he must also renounce Mary, for to her we are indebted for our greatest losses. O, how many does she not snatch from our hands, and lead back to God and save!' 'Ah, no,' answered the youth, 'that I will never do; deny my Mother, indeed! she is all my hope; rather would I go begging all my life long;' and so saying, he left the spot. On his return, he passed by a church dedicated to Mary. The afflicted youth entered, and cast himself on his knees before her image, and began to weep, and implore her to obtain him the pardon of his sins. He had scarcely done so, when Mary began to intercede with her Son for the poor wretch. Jesus at first replied: 'But, Mother, this ungrateful soul has denied Me.' But on seeing that His Mother did not cease to pray, He said finally, 'O Mother, I never denied thee anything; he is forgiven, since thou askest it.' The person who had purchased all the property of the young spendthrift was concealed in the chapel, and heard all that passed, and witnessed the compassion of Mary towards this sinner. He had an only daughter, and determined to give her to the young man in marriage, and make him heir of all he possessed. And thus did this youth recover both the grace of God and his temporal possessions by the means of Mary.

PRAYER.

O my soul, see what a sure hope of salvation and eternal life our Lord has given thee, by having in His mercy inspired thee with confidence in the patronage of His Mother; and this, notwithstanding that so many times by thy sins thou hast merited His displeasure and hell. Thank thy God, and thank thy protectress Mary, who has condescended to take thee under her mantle; for of this thou mayest be well convinced, after the many graces that thou hast received by her means. O yes, I do thank thee, my most loving Mother, for all thou hast done for me, who am deserving of hell. And from how many dangers hast thou not delivered me, O Queen! How many inspirations and mercies hast thou not obtained for me from God! What service, what honour, have I ever rendered thee, that thou shouldst do so much for me?

I know that it is thy sole goodness that has impelled thee. Ah, too little would it be in comparison with all that I owe thee, did I shed my blood and give my life for thee; for thou hast delivered me from eternal death; thou hast enabled me, as I hope, to recover Divine grace; to thee, in fine, I owe all I have. My most amiable Lady, I, poor wretch that I am, can make thee no return but that of always loving and praising thee. Ah, disdain not to accept the tender affection of a poor sinner, who is inflamed with love for thy goodness. If my heart is unworthy to love thee, because it is impure and filled with earthly affections, it is thou who must change it. Ah, change it, then. Bind me to my God, and bind me so that I may never more have it in my power to separate myself from His love. Thou askest of me that I should love thy God, and I ask of thee that thou shouldst obtain this love for me, to love Him always; this is all that I desire. Amen.

Section II.—*The same subject continued.*

Saint Bernard says, ' that as a man and a woman cooperated in our ruin, so it was proper that another man and another woman should coöperate in our redemption; and these two were Jesus and his Mother Mary.' ' There is no doubt,' says the Saint, ' that Jesus Christ alone was more than sufficient to redeem us; but it was more becoming that both sexes should coöperate in the repa-

ration of an evil in causing which both had shared.'[1]
Hence blessed Albert the Great calls Mary ' the helper
of redemption :'[2] and this Blessed Virgin herself revealed to Saint Bridget, that ' as Adam and Eve sold
the world for an apple, so did she with her Son redeem
it as it were with one heart.'[3] This is confirmed by
Saint Anselm, who says, ' that although God could
create the world out of nothing, yet, when it was lost
by sin, He would not repair the evil without the co-
operation of Mary.'[4]

Suarez says,[5] ' that Mary coöperated in our salvation
in three ways ; first, by having merited by a merit of
congruity the Incarnation of the Word ; secondly, by
having continually prayed for us whilst she was living
in this world ; thirdly, by having willingly sacrificed
the life of her Son to God.' For this reason our Lord
has justly decreed, that as Mary coöperated in the salvation of man with so much love, and at the same time
gave such glory to God, so all men through her intercession are to obtain their salvation.

Mary is called ' the coöperator in our justification ;
for to her God has intrusted all graces intended for us ;'[6]
and therefore Saint Bernard affirms, ' that all men, past,
present, and to come, should look upon Mary as the
means and negotiator of the salvation of all ages.'[7]

Jesus Christ says, that no one can find Him unless
the Eternal Father first draws him by the means of
Divine grace : " No one comes to me unless my Father

---

[1] Congruum magis, ut adesset nostræ reparationi sexus uterque, quorum corruptioni neuter defuisset.—*Serm. in Sign. Magn.*

[2] Adjutrix redemptionis.—*Super Miss.* q. 29. § 3.

[3] Sicut enim Adam et Eva vendiderunt mundum pro uno pomo, sic Filius meus et ego redemimus mundum quasi cum uno corde.—*Lib. i. c. 35.*

[4] Qui potuit omnia de nihilo facere, noluit ea violata sine Maria reficere. —*In Depr. li. ad B.V.*

[5] De Inc. p. 2. d. 23. § 1.

[6] Auxiliatrix nostræ justificationis, quia Deus omnes gratias faciendas Mariæ commisit.—*Bernardinus de Bustis. Marial.* p. 3. § 1.

[7] Ad illam . . . sicut ad medium, sicut ad arcam Dei, sicut ad rerum cau- sam, sicut ad negotium sæculorum respiciunt, et qui cœlo habitant, et qui in inferno, et qui nos præcesserunt, et nos qui sumus, et qui sequentur.—*Serm. ii. in Pentec.*

draws him."[8] Thus also does Jesus address His Mother, says Richard of Saint Lawrence : ' No one comes to Me unless My Mother first of all draws him by her prayers.'[9] Jesus was the fruit of Mary, as Saint Elizabeth told her : " Blessed art thou amongst women, and blessed is the fruit of thy womb."[10] Whoever, therefore, desires the fruit must go to the tree ; whoever desires Jesus must go to Mary ; and whoever finds Mary will most certainly find Jesus.

When Saint Elizabeth saw that the most Blessed Virgin had come to visit her in her own house, not knowing how to thank her, and filled with humility, she exclaimed : " And whence is this to me, that the Mother of my Lord should visit me ?"[11] But how could this be ? we may ask. Did not Saint Elizabeth already know that not only Mary, but also Jesus, had entered her house ? Why then does she say that she is un-worthy to receive the Mother, and not rather, that she is unworthy to receive the Son, who had come to visit her ? Ah, yes, it was that the Saint knew full well that when Mary comes she brings Jesus, and therefore it was sufficient to thank the Mother without naming the Son.

" She is like the merchant's ship, she bringeth her bread from afar."[12] Mary was this fortunate ship that brought us Jesus Christ from heaven, who is the living bread that comes down from heaven to give us eternal life, as He Himself says : " I am the living bread, which came down from heaven : if any man eat of this bread, he shall live for ever."[13] And hence Richard of Saint

---

[8] Nemo potest venire ad me, nisi pater, qui misit me, traxerit eum.—*Joan.* vi. 44.

[9] Nemo venit ad me, nisi mater mea suis precibus traxerit eum.—*De Laud. B.M.* l. 12. p. 2.

[10] Benedicta tu inter mulieres, et benedictus fructus ventris tui.—*Luc.* i. 42.

[11] Et unde hoc mihi, ut veniat mater Domini mei ad me ?—*Luc.* i. 43.

[12] Facta est quasi navis institoris, de longe portans panem suum.—*Prov.* xxxi. 14.

[13] Ego sum panis vivus, qui de cœlo descendi. Si quis manducaverit ex hoc pane, vivet in æternum.—*Joan.* vi. 51, 52.

Lawrence says, ' that in the sea of this world all will be lost who are not received into this ship ; that is to say, all who are not protected by Mary ;' and therefore he adds, ' As often as we see ourselves in danger of perishing in the midst of the temptations and contending passions of this life, let us have recourse to Mary, and cry out quickly, O Lady, help us, save us, if thou wilt not see us perish.'[14] And remark, by the bye, that this writer does not scruple to address these words to Mary : ' Save us, we perish ;' as does a certain author already noticed, and who says, that we cannot ask Mary to save us, as this belongs to God alone. But since a culprit condemned to death can beg a royal favourite to save him by interceding with the king that his life may be spared, why cannot we ask the Mother of God to save us by obtaining us eternal life ? Saint John Damascen scrupled not to address her in these words : ' Pure and immaculate Virgin, save me, and deliver me from eternal damnation.'[15] Saint Bonaventure called Mary ' the salvation of those who invoked her.'[16] The holy Church approves of the invocation by also calling her the ' salvation of the weak.'[17] And shall we scruple to ask her to save us, when ' the way of salvation is open to none otherwise than through Mary ?'[18] as a certain author remarks. And before him Saint Germanus had said the same thing, speaking of Mary : ' No one is saved but through thee.'[19]

But let us now see what else the Saints say of the need in which we are of the intercession of the Divine Mother. The glorious Saint Cajetan used to say, that

---

[14] In mare mundi submergentur omnes illi, quos non suscipit navis ista . . . Ideo quoties videmus insurgentes super nos fluctus ejus maris, clamare debemus ad Mariam . . . Domina, salva nos, perimus.—*De Laud. V.* lib. xi. cap. 8.

[15] A gehenna et a flamma libra me, O Virgo Immaculata . . . inexpugnabili tuo ac divino præsidio, libera et salva me.—*Paracletica in S. Deip.*

[16] Tu salus te invocantium.—*Hym. de B.M.V. ad inst. Te Deum.*

[17] Salus infirmorum.

[18] Nemini nisi per eam patet aditus ad salutem.—*Pacciuch. de B. Virg. in Ps.* lxxxvi. exc. 1.

[19] Nemo salutis compos nisi per te, Deipara.—*In Dorm. B.V.* Orat. ii.

we may seek for graces, but shall never find them without the intercession of Mary. This is confirmed by Saint Antoninus, who thus beautifully expresses himself: 'Whoever asks and expects to obtain graces without the intercession of Mary, endeavours to fly without wings;'[20] for, as Pharaoh said to Joseph, "the land of Egypt is in thy hands," and addressed all who came to him for food to Joseph, "Go to Joseph,"[21] so does God send us to Mary when we seek for grace: "Go to Mary; for 'He has decreed,' says Saint Bernard, 'that He will grant no graces otherwise than by the hands of Mary.'[22] 'And thus,' says Richard of Saint Lawrence, 'our salvation is in the hands of Mary; so that we Christians may with much greater reason say of her than the Egyptians of Joseph, "Our salvation is in thy hands." '[23] The venerable Raymond Jordano repeats the same thing: 'Our salvation is in her hands.'[24] Cassian speaks in still stronger terms. He says absolutely, 'that the salvation of all depends on their being favoured and protected by Mary.'[25] He who is protected by Mary will be saved; he who is not will be lost. Saint Bernardine of Sienna thus addresses this Blessed Virgin: 'O Lady, since thou art the dispenser of all graces, and since the grace of salvation can only come through thy hands, our salvation depends on thee.'[26] Therefore Richard of St. Lawrence had good reason for saying, that 'as we should fall into the abyss, if the ground were withdrawn from under our feet, so does a soul deprived of the succour of Mary first fall into sin, and then

---

[20] Qui petit sine ipsa duce, sine pennis seu alis tentat volare.—P. iii. tit. 15, c. 22.

[21] Ite ad Joseph.—*Gen.* xli. 55.

[22] Totum nos habere voluit per Mariam.—*Serm. de Nativ. B. Virg.*

[23] Salus nostra in manu illius est, ut ei dicere multo verius valeamus nos Christiani, quam dixerint Ægyptii Joseph: Salus nostra in manu tua est.—*De Laud. Virg.* lib. ii. cap. 1.

[24] Salus nostra in manu illius est.—*De Contempl. B. V.* in prol.

[25] Tota salus humani generis consistit in multitudine gratiæ Mariæ et favoris.—*Pelbart. Stell.* l. 12. p. 1. a. 3.

[26] Tu dispensatrix omnium gratiarum: salus nostra in manu tua est.—*Serm.* i. *de Nativ. B. Virg.*

into hell.'[27]   Saint Bonaventure says, that 'God will not save us without the intercession of Mary.'[28]   And that 'as a child cannot live without a nurse to suckle it, so no one can be saved without the protection of Mary.'[29] Therefore he exhorts us 'to thirst after devotion to her, to preserve it with care, and never to abandon it until we have received her maternal blessing in heaven.'[30] And whoever, exclaims Saint Germanus, 'could know God, were it not for thee, O most holy Mary? who could be saved? who would be preserved from dangers? who would receive any grace, were it not for thee, O Mother of God, O full of grace? The following are the beautiful words in which he expresses himself: 'There is no one, O most holy Mary, who can know God but through thee; no one who can be saved or redeemed but through thee, O Mother of God; no one who can be delivered from dangers but through thee, O Virgin Mother; no one who obtains mercy but through thee, O filled with all grace.'[31]   And in another place, addressing her, he says, 'No one would be free from the effects of the concupiscence of the flesh and from sin, unless thou didst open the way to him.'[32]

And as we have access to the Eternal Father, says Saint Bernard, only through Jesus Christ, so have we access to Jesus Christ only through Mary: 'By thee we have access to the Son, O blessed finder of grace, bearer of life, and mother of salvation, that we may receive Him by thee, Who through thee was given to

---

[27] Quia subtracta terra, statim descendimus in infernum viventes, sic subtracto nobis adjutorio Mariæ, statim labimur in peccatum, et inde in infernum.—*De Laud. Virg.* lib. viii. cap. 1.

[28] Ipse sine ea non salvabit te.—*Cant. B.M.V. inst. illius Moysi.*

[29] Quemadmodum infans sine nutrice non potest vivere; ita nec sine Domina nostra potes habere salutem.—*Ib.*

[30] Sitiat ergo anima tua ad ipsam, tene eam, nec dimitte, donec benedixerit tibi.—*Ib.*

[31] Nemo Dei cognitione repletus est, nisi per te, O Sanctissima; nemo salutis compos, nisi per te, Deipara; nemo redemptus, nisi per te, Dei Mater; nemo pericula evadit, nisi per te, Virgo Dei Mater; nemo misericordiæ consequitur gratiam, nisi per te, O Dei gratia plena.—*In Dorm. B.V.* Orat. ii.

[32] Nisi enim tu ducatum præstares, nemo spiritualis efficeretur.—*Ib.*

us.'[33] This is the reason given by the Saint why our Lord has determined that all shall be saved by the intercession of Mary; and therefore he calls her the Mother of grace and of our salvation. 'Then,' asks Saint Germanus, 'what will become of us? what hope can we have of salvation, if thou dost abandon us, O Mary, who art the life of Christians?'[34]

'But,' says the modern author already quoted, 'if all graces come through Mary, when we implore the intercession of other Saints, they must have recourse to the mediation of Mary. But that,' he says, 'no one believes or ever dreamt.' As to believing it, I reply, that in that there can be no error or difficulty. What difficulty can there be in saying that God, in order to honour His Mother, and having made her Queen of Saints, and willing that all graces shall be dispensed by her hands, should also will that the Saints should address themselves to her to obtain favours for their clients? And as to saying that no one ever dreamt of such a thing, I find that Saint Bernard, Saint Anselm, Saint Bonaventure, Suarez,[35] and others expressly declare it to be the case. 'In vain,' says Saint Bernard, 'would a person ask other Saints for a favour, if Mary did not interpose to obtain it.'[36] Some other author, explaining the words of the Psalm, "All the rich among the people shall entreat thy countenance,"[37] says, 'that the Saints are the rich of that great people of God, who, when they wish to obtain a favour from God for their clients, recommend themselves to Mary, and she immediately obtains it.' And Father Suarez correctly remarks, 'that we beg the Saints to be our intercessors with Mary, because she is their Queen and Sovereign Lady.' 'Amongst

---

[33] Per te accessum habemus ad filium, O benedicta inventrix gratiæ, genitrix vitæ, mater salutis; ut per te nos suscipiat, qui per te datus est nobis.—*De Adv. Dom.* Serm. ii.

[34] Si tu nos deserueris, quonam confugiemus? quidnam autem de nobis fiet, O sanctissima Deipara, spiritus et vita Christianorum?—*De Zona Virg.*

[35] De Incarnat. p. ii. q. 37, disp. 23, § 3.

[36] Frustra alios sanctos oraret quem ista non adjuvaret. †

[37] Vultum tuum deprecabuntur omnes divites plebis.—*Ps.* xliv. 13.

the Saints,' he says, ' we do not make use of one to intercede with the other, as all are of the same order ;
but we do ask them to intercede with Mary, because
she is their Sovereign and Queen.'[38]

And this is precisely what Saint Benedict promised
to Saint Frances of Rome, as we read in Father Marchese ;[39] for he appeared to her, and taking her under
his protection, he promised that he would be her advocate with the Divine Mother. In confirmation of this,
Saint Anselm addresses our Blessed Lady and says,
' O Lady, whatever all the Saints, united with thee, can
obtain, thou canst obtain alone.'[40] ' And why is this ?'
asks the Saint ; ' why is it that thou alone hast such
great power ? Ah, it is because thou alone art the
Mother of our common Redeemer ; thou art the spouse
of God ; thou art the universal Queen of heaven and
earth.'[41] If thou dost not speak for us, no Saint will
pray for or help us.[42] But if thou beginnest to pray for
us, then will all the Saints do the same and succour us.[43]
So that Father Segneri,[44] in his Devout Client of Mary,
applying with the Catholic Church the words of Ecclesiasticus to her, " I alone have compassed the circuit of
heaven,"[45] says, that ' as the first sphere by its motion
sets all the others in motion, so it is when Mary prays
for a soul ; immediately the whole heavenly court begins
to pray with her.' ' Nay, more,' says Saint Bonaventure,
' whenever the most sacred Virgin goes to God to intercede for us, she, as Queen, commands all the Angels and

---

[38] Inter alios sanctos non utamur uno ut intercessore ad alium, quia
omnes sunt ejusdem ordinis. Ad virginem autem tanquam ad reginam et
dominam alii adhibentur intercessores.—Tom. xvii. q. 37, art. 4, § 3.

[39] Nel diario di Maria alle 21 de Marzo.

[40] Quod possunt omnes isti tecum, tu sola potes sine illis omnibus.—Orat.
xlv. ad B. Virg.

[41] Quia mater es Salvatoris nostri, sponsa Dei, regina cœli et terræ.--
Ib.

[42] Te tacente, nullus orabit, nullus juvabit.—Ib.

[43] Te orante, omnes orabunt, omnes juvabunt.—Ib.

[44] Div. di M. p. 1. c. 7. § 4.

[45] Gyrum cœli circuivi sola.—Eccl. xxiv. 8.

Saints to accompany her, and unite their prayers with hers.'[46]

And thus, finally, do we understand why the holy Church requires that we should salute and invoke the Divine Mother under the glorious title of ' our hope.'[47] The impious Luther said, 'that he could not endure that the Roman Church should call Mary, who is only a creature, " our hope ;" for,' said he, ' God alone, and Jesus Christ as our Mediator, is our hope : and God curses those who place their hope in a creature, according to the prophet Jeremias, " Cursed be the man that trusteth in man."[48]   But the Church teaches us to invoke Mary on all occasions, and to call her ' our hope ; hail, our hope!' Whoever places his confidence in a creature independently of God, he certainly is cursed by God ; for God is the only source and dispenser of every good, and the creature without God is nothing, and can give nothing. But if our Lord has so disposed it, as we have already proved that He has done, that all graces should pass by Mary as by a channel of mercy, we not only can but ought to assert that she, by whose means we receive the divine graces, is truly our hope.   And therefore Saint Bernard says, ' that she is his greatest confidence, and the whole foundation of his hope.'[49] Saint John Damascen says the same thing ; for he thus addresses the most Blessed Virgin : ' O Lady, in thee have I placed all my hope ; and with my eyes fixed on thee, from thee do I expect salvation.'[50]   Saint Thomas says, that ' Mary is the whole hope of our salvation ;'[51] and Saint Ephrem, addressing her, says, ' O most holy Virgin, receive us under thy protection, if thou wilt see

[46] Quando virgo sanctissima procedit ad Deum pro nobis deprecandum, imperat angelis et sanctis, ut eam comitentur, et simul cum ipsa Altissimum pro nobis exorent.—*Pacciuch. super Sal. Ang.* exc. 19.

[47] Spes nostra salve.

[48] Maledictus homo qui confidit in homine.—*Jerem.* xvii. 5.

[49] Filioli, hæc peccatorum scala, hæc mea maxima fiducia est, hæc tota ratio spei meæ.—*In Nat. B.M.V.* Serm. i.

[50] In te spem meam totam ex animo collocavi, et intentis oculis abs te pendeo.—*Paracletica in S. Deip.*

[51] Omnis spes vitæ.—*Exp. in Sal. Ang.*

us saved, for we have no hope of salvation but through thy means.'[52]

Let us, then, in the words of Saint Bernard, 'endeavour to venerate this Divine Mother with the whole affection of our hearts ; for such is the will of God, who is pleased that we should receive every good thing from her hand.'[53] And therefore the Saint exhorts us, whenever we desire or ask for any grace, to recommend ourselves to Mary, and to be assured that we shall receive it by her means ;[54] for he says, if thou dost not deserve the favour from God, Mary, who will ask it for thee, will deserve to receive it ; ' because thou wast unworthy of the gift, it was bestowed on Mary, that through her thou mightest receive all that thou hast.'[55] The Saint then advises us to recommend all that we offer to God to the care of Mary, be they good works or prayers, if we wish our Lord to accept them. ' Whatever thou mayest offer to God, be sure to recommend it to Mary, in order not to meet with a repulse.'[56]

EXAMPLE.

The history of Theophilus, written by Eutychian, patriarch of Constantinople, and who was an eye-witness of the fact he relates, is well known. It is attested by Saint Peter Damian, Saint Bernard, Saint Bonaventure, Saint Antoninus, and by others quoted by Father Crasset.[57] Theophilus was archdeacon of the church of Adana, a city of Cilicia, and he was held in such veneration by the people that they wished to have him for their bishop, but he, out of humility, refused the

---

[52] Non nobis est alia quam in te fiducia, O Virgo sincerissima. Sub tua denique tutela et protectione toti sumus.—*De Laud. Virg.*

[53] Totis . . . medullis cordium, totis præcordiorum affectibus, et votis omnibus Mariam hanc veneremur ; quia sic est voluntas ejus, qui totum nos habere voluit per Mariam.—*Serm. de Aquæd.*

[54] Quæramus gratiam, et per Mariam quæramus.—*Ib.*

[55] Quia indignus eras, cui donaretur, datum est Mariæ, ut per illam acciperes quicquid haberes.—*Serm. iii. in Vig. Nat. Dom.*

[56] Modicum istud quod offerre desideras, gratissimis illis et omni acceptione dignissimis Mariæ manibus offerendum tradere cura, si non vis sustinere repulsam.—*Serm. de Aquæd.*

[57] Ver. Dev. p. 1. tr. 1. q. 10.

dignity. It happened that evil-disposed persons accused
him falsely of some crime, and for which he was deposed from his archdeaconry. He took this so much to
heart, that, blinded by passion, he went to consult a
Jewish magician, who made him consult Satan, that he
might help him in his misfortune. The devil told him
that if he desired to be helped by him, he must renounce Jesus and His Mother Mary, and consign him
the act of renunciation written in his own hand. Theophilus immediately complied with the demand. The
next day, the bishop having discovered that he had
been deceived, asked the archdeacon's pardon, and
restored him to office. No sooner was this accomplished than his conscience was torn with remorse, and
he could do nothing but weep. What could he do?
He went to a church, and there casting himself all in
tears at the feet of an image of Mary, he thus addressed
her: 'O Mother of God, I will not despair as long as
I can have access to thee, who art so compassionate,
and hast the power to help me.' He remained thus
weeping and praying to our Blessed Lady for forty
days—when, lo, one night the Mother of Mercy appeared to him, and said: 'O Theophilus, what hast
thou done? Thou hast renounced my friendship and
that of my Son, and for whom? For His and my
enemy.' 'O Lady,' answered Theophilus, 'thou must
pardon me, and obtain my forgiveness from thy Son.'
Mary seeing his confidence, replied: 'Be of good heart;
I will intercede for thee with God.' Theophilus, encouraged by these consoling words, redoubled his tears,
mortifications, and prayers, and never left the image.
At length Mary again appeared to him, and with a
cheerful countenance said: 'Theophilus, be of good
heart; I have presented thy tears and prayers to God;
He has accepted them, and has already pardoned thee;
but from this day forward be grateful to Him and
faithful.' 'But, O Lady,' replied Theophilus, 'that is
not yet enough to satisfy me entirely; the enemy still

possesses that impious writing in which I renounced thee and thy Son. Thou canst oblige him to surrender it.' Three days afterwards, Theophilus awoke in the night, and found the writing on his breast. On the following day he went to the church where the bishop was, and, in presence of an immense concourse of people, cast himself at his feet, and with bitter tears related all that had taken place, and delivered into his hands the infamous writing. The bishop committed it to the flames in the presence of the whole people, who did nothing but weep for joy, and praise the goodness of God, and the mercy of Mary shown towards this poor sinner. But he, returning to the church of our Blessed Lady, remained there for three days, and then expired, his heart filled with joy, and returning thanks to Jesus and to His most holy Mother.

PRAYER.

O Queen and Mother of mercy, who dispensest graces to all who have recourse to thee with so much liberality, because thou art a Queen, and with so much love, because thou art our most loving Mother; to thee do I, who am so devoid of merit and virtue, and so loaded with debts to the Divine justice, recommend myself this day. O Mary, thou holdest the keys of all the Divine mercies; forget not my miseries, and leave me not in my poverty. Thou art so liberal with all, and givest more than thou art asked for, O, be thus liberal with me. O Lady, protect me; this is all that I ask of thee. If thou protectest me, I fear nothing. I fear not the evil spirits; for thou art more powerful than all of them. I fear not my sins; for thou by one word canst obtain their full pardon from God. And if I have thy favour, I do not even fear an angry God; for a single prayer of thine will appease Him. In fine, if thou protectest me, I hope all; for thou art all-powerful. O Mother of mercy, I know that thou takest pleasure and dost glory in helping the most miserable, and, provided they are not obstinate, that thou canst help them. I am a sinner, but am not obstinate; I desire to change my life. Thou canst, then, help me; O, help me and save me. I now place myself entirely in thy hands. Tell me what I must do in order to please God, and I am ready for all, and hope to do all with thy help, O Mary—Mary, my Mother, my light, my consolation. my refuge, my hope. Amen, amen, amen.

CHAPTER VI.

O, GRACIOUS ADVOCATE.

SECTION I. *Mary is an Advocate who is able to save all.*

So great is the authority that mothers possess over their sons, that even if they are monarchs, and have absolute dominion over every person in their kingdom, yet never can mothers become the subjects of their sons. It is true that Jesus now in heaven sits at the right hand of the Father, that is, as Saint Thomas[1] explains it, even as man, on account of the hypostatical union with the Person of the Divine Word. He has supreme dominion over all, and also over Mary; it will nevertheless be always true that for a time, when He was living in this world, He was pleased to humble Himself and to be subject to Mary, as we are told by St. Luke: "And He was subject to them."[2] And still more, says Saint Ambrose, Jesus Christ having deigned to make Mary His Mother, inasmuch as He was her Son, He was truly obliged to obey her. And for this reason, says Richard of Saint Lawrence, ' of other Saints we say that they are with God; but of Mary alone can it be said that she was so far favoured as to be not only herself submissive to the will of God, but even that God was subject to her will.'[3] And whereas of all other virgins,

---

[1] De Human. I. C. a. 23.
[2] Et erat subditus illis.—*Luc.* ii. 51.
[3] Cum enim de omnibus cæteris sanctis dicatur et magnum sit, eis esse cum Domino ... Maria majus aliquid cæteris hominibus sanctis sortita est: nt non solum ipsa subjiceretur voluntati Domini, sed etiam Dominus volun tati ipsius.—*De Laud. V.* lib. i. cap. 5.

remarks the same author, we must say that " they follow the Lamb whithersoever he goeth,"[4] of the Blessed
Virgin Mary we can say that the Lamb followed her,
having become subject to her.[5]

And here we say, that although Mary, now in
heaven, can no longer command her Son, nevertheless
her prayers are always the prayers of a Mother, and
consequently most powerful to obtain whatever she
asks. ' Mary,' says Saint Bonaventure, ' has this great
privilege, that with her Son she above all the Saints
is most powerful to obtain whatever she wills.'[6] And
why? Precisely for the reason on which we have
already touched, and which we shall later on again examine at greater length, because they are the prayers of a
mother. And therefore, says Saint Peter Damian, the
Blessed Virgin can do whatever she pleases both in
heaven and on earth. She is able to raise even those
who are in despair to confidence; and he addresses her
in these words : ' All power is given to thee in heaven
and on earth, and nothing is impossible to thee, who
canst raise those who are in despair to the hope of
salvation.'[7] And then he adds that ' when the Mother
goes to seek a favour for us from Jesus Christ' (whom
the Saint calls the golden altar of mercy, at which
sinners obtain pardon), ' her Son esteems her prayers so
greatly, and is so desirous to satisfy her, that when she
prays, it seems as if she rather commanded than prayed,
and was rather a queen than a handmaid.'[8] Jesus is
pleased thus to honour His beloved Mother, who honoured Him so much during her life, by immediately

[4] Sequuntur agnum quocumque ierit.—*Apoc.* xiv. 4.

[5] De ista autem (Virgine Maria) potest secure dici, quod agnus sequebatur
eam, quocunque ivit unde.— *Luc.* ii. "Descendit cum eis, et venit Nazareth,
et erat subditus illis."—*De Laud. V.* lib. i. cap. 5.

[6] Grande privilegium est, quod ipsa præ omnibus sanctis apud Deum potentissima est.—*Spec. B.M.V.* lect. vi.

[7] Data est tibi omnis potestas in cœlo et in terra . . . nil tibi impossibile,
cui possibile est, desperatos in spem beatitudinis relevare.—Serm. 1, *de Nat.
B. Virg.*

[8] Accedis enim ante illud aureum humanæ reconciliationis altare, non
solum rogans, sed imperans : Domina, non ancilla . . . nam et Filius nihil
negans, honorat te.—*Ib.*

granting all that she asks or desires. This is beautifully confirmed by Saint Germanus, who addressing our Blessed Lady says: 'Thou art the Mother of God, and all-powerful to save sinners, and with God thou needest no other recommendation; for thou art the Mother of true life.'[9]

'At the command of Mary, all obey, even God.' Saint Bernardine fears not to utter this sentence; meaning, indeed, to say that God grants the prayers of Mary as if they were commands.[10] And hence Saint Anselm addressing Mary says: 'Our Lord, O most holy Virgin, has exalted thee to such a degree, that by His favour all things that are possible to Him should be possible to thee.'[11] 'For thy protection is omnipotent, O Mary,' says Cosmas of Jerusalem.[12] 'Yes, Mary is omnipotent,' repeats Richard of Saint Lawrence; 'for the queen by every law enjoys the same privileges as the king. And as,' he adds, 'the power of the son and that of the mother is the same, a mother is made omnipotent by an omnipotent son.'[13] 'And thus,' says Saint Antoninus, 'God has placed the whole Church, not only under the patronage, but even under the dominion of Mary.'[14]

Since the Mother, then, should have the same power as the Son, rightly has Jesus, who is omnipotent, made Mary also omnipotent; though, of course, it is always true that where the Son is omnipotent by nature, the Mother is only so by grace. But that she is so is evident from the fact, that whatever the Mother asks for,

---

[9] Plurimum igitur auxilium tuum pollet, O Virgo, ad salutem consequendam, nec apud Deum commendatitia alterius cujuspiam indiget ope: tu enim revera es veræ vitæ mater.—*In Dorm. B. V.* Orat. ii.

[10] Imperio virginis omnia famulantur, et Deus.—*Serm. de Nat. B.M.V.* cap. vi.

[11] Te, domina . . . pius et omnipotens Deus sic exaltavit, et omnia tibi secum possibilia esse donavit.—*De Excel. Virg.* cap. xii.

[12] Omnipotens auxilium tuum.—Hymn. vi. *in Depr. ad Deiparam.*

[13] Eisdem privilegiis secundum leges gaudent rex et regina. Cum autem eadem sit potestas et communis matris et filii, quæ ab omnipotente filio omnipotens est effecta.—Lib. iv. *de Laud. Virg.* cap. 29.

[14] Et secundum hoc tantum fuit meritum virginis, ut ecclesia sit 'sub pedibus ejus,' sub protectione; unde ipsa ait Ecclesiastici **xxiv.**: "In Jerusalem potestas mea," id est ecclesia.—Cap. **xx** *De Grat. Priv. B. Mariæ.*

the Son never denies her; and this was revealed to Saint Bridget,[15] who one day heard Jesus talking with Mary, and thus address her: 'Ask of Me what thou wilt, for no petition of thine can be void.' As if He had said, 'My Mother, thou knowest how much I love thee; therefore ask all that thou wilt of Me; for it is not possible that I should refuse thee anything.' And the reason that He gave for this was beautiful: 'Because thou never didst deny Me anything on earth, I will deny thee nothing in heaven.'[16] My Mother, when thou wast in the world, thou never didst refuse to do anything for the love of Me; and now that I am in heaven, it is right that I should deny thee nothing that thou askest. Mary, then, is called omnipotent in the sense in which it can be understood of a creature who is incapable of a divine attribute. She is omnipotent, because by her prayers she obtains whatever she wills.

With good reason, then, O great Advocate, does Saint Bernard say, 'thou willest, and all things are done.'[17] And Saint Anselm: 'Whatever thou, O Virgin, willest can never be otherwise than accomplished.'[18] Thou willest, and all is done. If thou art pleased to raise a sinner from the lowest abyss of misery to the highest degree of sanctity, thou canst do it. Blessed Albert the Great, on this subject, makes Mary say: 'I have to be asked that I may will; for if I will a thing, it is necessarily done.'[19] And thus Saint Peter Damian, reflecting on the great power of Mary, and begging her to take compassion on us, addresses her, saying: 'O, let thy nature move thee, let thy power move thee; for the more thou art powerful, the greater should thy mercy

[15] Pete ergo quod vis, non enim inanis potest esse charitas et petitio tua. —*Rev.* lib. vi. cap. 23.

[16] Quia tu mihi nihil negasti in terra, ideo ego tibi nihil negabo in cœlo. —*Rev.* lib. i. cap. 24.

[17] Velis tu, et omnia fient. †

[18] Velis salutem nostram, et vere nequaquam salvi esse non poterimus.— *Exc. Virg.* cap. xii.

[19] Roganda sum, ut velim; quia, si volo, necesse est fieri.—*De Laud. B. M.* l. 2, c. 1.

be.'[20] O Mary, our own beloved advocate, since thou hast so compassionate a heart, that thou canst not even see the wretched without being moved to pity; and since, at the same time, thou hast so great power with God, that thou canst save all whom thou dost protect,—disdain not to undertake the cause of us poor miserable creatures who place all our hope in thee. If our prayers cannot move thee, at least let thine own benign heart do so; or, at least, let thy power do so, since God has enriched thee with such great power, in order that the richer thou art in power to help us, the more merciful thou mayest be in the will to assist us. But St. Bernard reassures us on this point; for he says that Mary is as immensely rich in mercy as she is in power; and that, as her charity is most powerful, so also it is most clement and compassionate, and its effects continually prove it to be so. He thus expresses himself: 'The most powerful and merciful charity of the Mother of God abounds in tender compassion and in effectual succour: it is equally rich in both.'[21]

From the time that Mary came into the world, her only thought, after seeking the glory of God, was to succour the miserable. And even then she enjoyed the privilege of obtaining whatever she asked. This we know from what occurred at the marriage feast of Cana in Galilee. When the wine failed, the most Blessed Virgin, being moved to compassion at the sight of the affliction and shame of the bride and bridegroom, asked her Son to relieve it by a miracle, telling Him that " they had no wine." Jesus answered : "Woman, what is that to thee and Me? My hour is not yet come."[22] And here remark, that although our Lord seemed to refuse His Mother the favour she asked, and said, What is it to thee, O woman, and to Me, if the wine has failed? This

---

[20] Moveat te natura, potentia moveat; quia quanto potentior, tanto misericordior esse debebis.—Serm. i. *de Nat. B. Virg.*

[21] Potentissima et piissima charitas matris Dei et affectu compatiendi et subveniendi abundat effectu: aeque locuples in utroque.—Serm. iv. de *Assump.*

[22] Vinum non habent. Et dicit ei Jesus: Quid mihi et tibi est, mulier? nondum venit hora mea.—*Joan.* ii. 3, 4.

is not the time for Me to work a miracle; the time will
be when I begin to preach, and when miracles will be
required to confirm My doctrines. And yet Mary, as
if the favour had already been granted, desired those in
attendance to fill the jars with water, for they would
be immediately satisfied. And so it was; for Jesus, to
content His Mother, changed the water into the best
wine. But how was this? As the time for working
miracles was that of the public life of our Lord, how
could it be that, contrary to the Divine decrees, this
miracle was worked? No; in this there was nothing
contrary to the decrees of God; for though, generally
speaking, the time for miracles was not come, yet from
all eternity God had determined by another decree that
nothing that she asked should ever be refused to the
Divine Mother. And therefore Mary, who well knew
her privilege, although her Son seemed to have refused
her the favour, yet told them to fill the jars with water,
as if her request had already been granted. That is the
sense in which Saint John Chrysostom understood it;
for, explaining these words of our Lord, "Woman, what
is it to thee and Me?" he says, that 'though Jesus
answered thus, yet in honour of His Mother He obeyed
her wish.'[23] This is confirmed by Saint Thomas, who
says that by the words, "My hour is not yet come,"
Jesus Christ intended to show, that had the request
come from any other, He would not then have complied
with it; but because it was addressed to Him by His
Mother, He could not refuse it.[24] Saint Cyril and Saint
Jerome, quoted by Barradus,[25] say the same thing. Also
Gandavensis, on the above passage of Saint John, says,
that 'to honour His Mother, our Lord anticipated the
time for working miracles.'[26]

---

[23] Cum . . . id respondisset quod volebat mater effecit.—*Hom. in Joan.*

[24] Per illa verba, "nondum venit hora mea," ostendit se dilaturum fuisse
miraculum, si alius rogasset; quia tamen rogabat mater, fecit.—*S. Thom.
apud Defens. Cultus Mariani*, auctore R. P. Henr. de Cerf. p. 129. †

[25] T. 2, l. 3, c. 1.

[26] Quo matrem honoraret, prævenit tempus miracula faciendi.—*In Conc.
Ev. c. 18.*

In fine, it is certain that no creature can obtain so many mercies for us as this tender advocate, who is thus honoured by God, not only as His beloved handmaid, but also as His true Mother. And this, William of Paris says, addressing her, 'No creature can obtain so many and such great favours as thou obtainest for poor sinners; and thus without doubt God honours thee not only as a handmaid, but as His most true Mother.'[27] Mary has only to speak, and her Son executes all. Our Lord, conversing with the spouse in the sacred Canticles,—that is Mary,—says, "Thou that dwellest in the gardens, the friends hearken; make me hear thy voice."[28] The Saints are the friends, and they, when they seek a favour for their clients, wait for their Queen to ask and obtain it; for, as we said in the fifth chapter, 'no grace is granted otherwise than at the prayer of Mary.' And how does Mary obtain favours? She has only to let her voice be heard,—"make me hear thy voice." She has only to speak, and her Son immediately grants her prayer. Listen to the Abbot William explaining, in this sense, the above text. In it he introduces the Son addressing Mary: 'Thou who dwellest in the heavenly gardens, intercede with confidence for whomsoever thou wilt; for it is not possible that I should so far forget that I am thy Son as to deny anything to thee, My Mother. Only let thy voice be heard; for to be heard by a son is to be obeyed.'[29] The Abbot Godfridus says, 'that although Mary obtains favours by asking, yet she asks with a certain maternal authority, and therefore we ought to feel confident that she obtains all she desires and asks for us.'[30]

[27] Nulla . . . creatura, et tot, et tanta, et talia impetrare posset apud benedictum Filium tuum miseris, quanta tu apud ipsum impetras eisdem. In quo proculdubio non tamquam ancillam suam, quæ indubitanter es, sed tamquam matrem verissimam te honorat.—*De Rhet. Div.* cap. xviii.

[28] Quæ habitas in hortis, amici auscultant: fac me audire vocem tuam.—*Cant.* viii. 13.

[29] Quæ habitas in hortis cœlestibus, fiducialiter pro quibus volueris intercede; non enim possum me oblivisci filium tuum, ut matri quidpiam denegandum putem. Tantum in vocem proferas, quia a filio audiri, exaudiri est. †

[30] Honorabilis virgo Maria, si illum ex eo quod Deus et Dominus est, ex·

Valerius Maximus[31] relates that when Coriolanus was besieging Rome, the prayers of his friends and all the citizens were insufficient to make him desist; but as soon as he beheld his mother Veturia imploring him, he could no longer refuse, and immediately raised the siege. But the prayers of Mary with Jesus are as much more powerful than those of Veturia as the love and gratitude of this Son for His most dear Mother are greater. Father Justin Micoviensis says that 'a single sigh of the most Blessed Mary can do more than the united suffrages of all the saints.'[32] And this was acknowledged by the devil himself to Saint Dominic, who, as it is related by Father Paccinchelli,[33] obliged him to speak by the mouth of a possessed person; and he said that 'a single sigh from Mary was worth more before God than the united suffrages of all the Saints.'

Saint Antoninus says that 'the prayers of the Blessed Virgin, being the prayers of a Mother, have in them something of a command; so that it is impossible that she should not obtain what she asks.'[34] Saint Germanus, encouraging sinners who recommend themselves to this advocate, thus addresses her : ' As thou hast, O Mary, the authority of a Mother with God, thou obtainest pardon for the most enormous sinners; since that Lord in all things acknowledges thee as His true and spotless Mother, He cannot do otherwise than grant what thou askest.'[35] And so it was that Saint Bridget heard the Saints in heaven addressing our Blessed Lady : ' O most

orare merito creditur, ex eo tamen quod homo est, et natus ex ea, quasi quodam matris imperio, apud ipsum impetrare quicquid voluerit pia fide non dubitatur.—Serm. viii. *de B. V. M.*

[31] Ex mir. l. 5, c. 4.

[32] Unum Beatæ Virginis suspirium plus potest apud Filium, quam omnium sanctorum simul suffragium.— *In lit. B. V. verbo Virg. pot.*

[33] In Sal. Ang. exc. **3.**

[34] Oratio ejus erat nobilissimus modus orandi, tum quia habebat rationem jussionis et imperii, tum quia impossibile erat eam non exaudiri.—P. iv. tit. 15, c. 17.

[35] Tu vero materna qua polles apud Deum auctoritate, ad quantumvis enormia lapsis peccata, superabundantem impetras veniam : neque enim unquam datur te non exauditam dimitti, cui per omnia, et propter omnia, et in omnibus, ut veræ et intemeratæ matri suæ obsequitur Deus.— *In Dorm. B. V.* Orat. ii.

blessed Queen, what is there that thou canst not do? Thou hast only to will, and it is accomplished.'[36] And this corresponds with that celebrated saying, 'That which God can do by His power, that canst thou do by prayer, O sacred Virgin.'[37] 'And perchance,' says an ancient and pious writer, 'it is unworthy of the benignity of that Lord to be thus jealous of the honour of His Mother, who declares that He came into the world, not to break, but to observe the law; but this law commands us to honour our parents.'[38]

Saint George, Archbishop of Nicomedia, says that Jesus Christ, even as it were to satisfy an obligation under which He placed Himself towards His Mother, when she consented to give Him His human nature, grants all she asks: 'the Son, as if paying a debt, grants all thy petitions.'[39] And on this the holy martyr Saint Methodius exclaims: 'Rejoice, rejoice, O Mary, for thou hast that Son thy debtor, who gives to all and receives from none. We are all God's debtors for all that we possess, for all is His gift; but God has been pleased to become thy debtor in taking flesh from thee and becoming man.'[40] And therefore another ancient writer says, 'that Mary, having merited to give flesh to the Divine Word, and thus supply the price of our redemption, that we might be delivered from eternal death; therefore is she more powerful than all others to help us to gain eternal life.'[41] Saint Theophilus, Bishop of Alexandria, in the time of St. Jerome, left in writing

---

[36] O Domina benedicta . . . quid est quod non poteris? Quod enim tu vis, hoc factum est.—*Rev.* lib. iv. cap. 74.

[37] Quod Deus imperio, tu prece Virgo potes.

[38] Numquid non pertinet ad benignitatem Domini, Matris servare honorem, qui legem non solvere venerat, sed adimplere? *Lib. de Assump. B.V. int. op. S. August.*

[39] Eaque, tanquam Filius exaltans, postulata ceu debitor implet.—*Or. d. Ingressu B.V.*

[40] Euge, euge, Dei Mater ancillaque. Euge, is qui omnium creditor est, debitor fit. Omnes namque Deo debemus, tibique ille debitor est.—*De Simeone et Anna.*

[41] Neque enim dubium quæ meruit pro liberandis proferre pretium, posse plus sanctis omnibus liberatis impendere suffragium.—*Serm. de Sanctis, int. op. S. August. Serm. de Assump. B.M.*

the following words: 'The prayers of His Mother are a pleasure to the Son, because He desires to grant all that is granted on her account, and thus recompense her for the favour she did Him in giving Him His body.'[42] Saint John Damascen, addressing the Blessed Virgin, says, 'Thou, O Mary, being Mother of the most high God, canst save all by thy prayers, which are increased in value by the maternal authority.'[43]

Let us conclude with Saint Bonaventure, who, considering the great benefit conferred on us by our Lord in giving us Mary for our advocate, thus addresses her: 'O truly immense and admirable goodness of our God, which has been pleased to grant thee, O sovereign Mother, to us miserable sinners for our advocate, in order that thou, by thy powerful intercession, mayest obtain all that thou pleasest for us.'[44] 'O wonderful mercy of our God,' continues the same Saint, 'who, in order that we might not fly on account of the sentence that might be pronounced against us, has given us His own Mother and the patroness of graces to be our advocate.'[45]

EXAMPLE.

Father Razzi,[46] of the Camaldolese order, relates that a young man of the name of John, on the death of his father, was sent by his mother to the court of a prince. His mother, who had a tender devotion towards Mary, before bidding him farewell, made him promise that he would every day say the 'Hail Mary,' adding at the end of it these words: 'O, most Blessed

---

[42] Salazar. in Prov. viii. 18.

[43] Potes quidem omnes salvare, ut Dei altissimi Mater, precibus materna auctoritate pollentibus.—*Men. Græc.* 20 *Jan. ad Mat.*

[44] O certe Dei nostri mira benignitas, qui suis reis te dominam tribuit advocatam, ut a Filio tuo inter nos et ipsum judicem constituta, quod volueris pro nobis valeas impetrare!—*In Salv. Reg.*

[45] O mirabilis erga nos misericordia Dei nostri, qui, ne alias fugeremus pro sententia, non solum dignatus est communicare se nobis in judicem, ut esset Deus et homo Jesus Christus, a quo debet sententia promulgari, sed voluit ipse sua viscera misericordiæ matrem suam dominam gratiæ, nostram institutuere advocatam.—*In Salv. Reg.*

[46] Mir. di N.D. l. 3, m. 40.

Virgin, help me at the hour of my death.' After having been at court a short time, he became so dissolute that his master was obliged to dismiss him. No longer knowing how to obtain a living, in despair he became a highway robber and murderer; but during this time even, he never neglected to recommend himself to our Blessed Lady, according to his promise. At length he was taken and condemned to death. When in prison, and the day before his death, reflecting on his own shame, on the grief of his mother, and on the death he was about to endure, he wept bitterly; and thus the devil, seeing him disconsolate and filled with melancholy thoughts, appeared to him under the form of a handsome youth, and told him that he would deliver him from prison and death if only he would obey him. The culprit said he was ready to do all he might ask. The youth then told him that he was the devil come to aid him. In the first place, he required that he should deny Jesus Christ and the most holy sacraments. To this he consented. He then demanded that he should renounce the Blessed Virgin Mary and her protection. 'Ah, that I will never do,' answered the young man; and raising his heart to her, he repeated his accustomed prayer: 'O, Blessed Virgin, help me at the hour of my death.' At these words the devil disappeared. The young man was immediately filled with the most bitter grief for the crime he had committed in denying Jesus Christ; but having recourse to the most Blessed Virgin, she obtained him true sorrow for all his sins, and he confessed them with great sighs and contrition. On leaving the gaol to go to the scaffold, he passed on the road a statue of Mary, and saluted it with his ordinary prayer: 'O, most Blessed Virgin, help me at the hour of my death;' and the statue returned his salutation in the presence of all, by bowing its head. Moved with tenderness, he begged leave to kiss the feet of the statue. The guard refused, but at length consented on account of the acclamations of the people. The youth stooped to kiss the feet, when Mary extended her arm, took him by the hand, and held him so tight that it was impossible to remove him. At the sight of such a prodigy, all began to cry out "Mercy, pardon, forgiveness!" and it was granted. The young man returned to his own country, where he led a most exemplary life, and was always filled with the tenderest affection for Mary, who had delivered him from both temporal and eternal death.

PRAYER.

I will address thee, O great Mother of God, in the words of Saint Bernard : 'Speak, O Lady, for thy Son neareth thee ; and whatever thou askest thou wilt obtain.'[47] Speak, speak, then, O Mary, our advocate, in favour of us poor miserable creatures. Remember that it was also for our good that thou didst receive such great power and so high a dignity. A God was pleased to become thy debtor by taking humanity of thee, in order that thou mightest at will dispense the riches of divine mercy to sinners. We are thy servants, devoted in a special manner to thee ; and I am one of these, I trust, in even a higher degree. We glory in living under thy protection. Since thou doest good to all, even to those who neither know nor honour thee, nay more, to those who outrage and blaspheme thee, how much more may we not hope from thy benignity, which seeks out the wretched in order to relieve them, we who honour, love, and confide in thee ? We are great sinners, but God has enriched thee with compassion and power far exceeding our iniquities. Thou canst, and hast, the will to save us ; and the greater is our unworthiness, the greater shall be our hope in order to glorify thee the more in heaven, when, by thy intercession, we get there. O, Mother of mercy, we present thee our souls, once cleansed and rendered beautiful in

---

[47] Loquere, Domina, quia audit Filius tuus · et quæcumque petieris impetrabis.—*Ad B.V.M. depr.*

the blood of Jesus Christ, but, alas, since that time, defiled by sin. To thee do we present them; do thou purify them. Obtain for us true conversion; obtain for us the love of God, perseverance, heaven. We ask thee for much; but what is it? perhaps thou canst not obtain all? It is perhaps too much for the love God bears thee? Ah, no! for thou hast only to open thy lips and ask thy divine Son; He will deny thee nothing. Pray, then, pray, O Mary, for us; pray; thou wilt certainly obtain all: and we shall with the same certainty obtain the kingdom of heaven.

SECTION II. *Mary is so tender an Advocate, that she does not refuse to defend the cause even of the most miserable.*

So many are the reasons that we have for loving this our most loving Queen, that if Mary was praised throughout the world; if in every sermon Mary alone was spoken of; if all men gave their lives for Mary; still all would be little in comparison with the homage and gratitude that we owe her in return for the tender love she bears to men, and even to the most miserable sinners, who preserve the slightest spark of devotion for her. Blessed Raymond Jordano, who, out of humility, called himself the Idiot, used to say, 'that Mary knows not how to do otherwise than love those who love her; and that even she does not disdain to serve those who serve her; and in favour of such a one, should he be a sinner, she uses all her power in order to obtain his forgiveness from her Blessed Son.'[1] And he adds, 'that her benignity and mercy are so great, that no one, however enormous his sins may be, should fear to cast himself at her feet; for she never can reject anyone who has

[1] **Maria** . . . diligit diligentes se, imo sibi servientibus servit. Ipsa super benedicto Filio suo irato potentissime reconciliat servos et amatores suos.—*De Contempl. B. V.* in Prol.

recourse to her.'² 'Mary, as our most loving advocate, herself offers the prayers of her servants to God, and especially those who are placed in her hands; for as the Son intercedes for us with the Father, so does she intercede with the Son, and does not cease to make interest with both for the great affair of our salvation, and to obtain for us the graces we ask.'³ With good reason, then, does Denis, the Carthusian, call the Blessed Virgin 'the singular refuge of the lost, the hope of the most abandoned, and the advocate of all sinners who have recourse to her.'⁴

But should there, by chance, be a sinner who, though not doubting her power, might doubt the compassion of Mary, fearing perhaps that she might be unwilling to help him on account of the greatness of his sins, let him take courage from the words of Saint Bonaventure. 'The great, the special privilege of Mary is, that she is all-powerful with her Son.'⁵ 'But,' adds the Saint, 'to what purpose would Mary have such great power if she cared not for us?'⁶ 'No,' he concludes, 'let us not doubt, but be certain, and let us always thank our Lord and His divine Mother for it, that in proportion as her power with God exceeds that of all the Saints, so is she in the same proportion our most loving advocate, and the one who is the most solicitous for our welfare.'⁷ 'And who, O Mother of Mercy,' exclaims Saint Germanus, in the joy of his

---

² Tanta . . . est ejus benignitas, quod nulli formidandum est ad eam accedere; tantaque misericordia, ut nemo ab ea repellitur.—*De Contempl. B.V.* in Prol.

³ Ipsa preces et sacrificia servorum suorum, et maxime quæ sibi exhibentur, repræsentat in conspectu divinæ majestatis; quia est advocata nostra apud Filium, sicut Filius apud Patrem; imo apud Patrem et Filium procurat negotia et petitiones nostras.—*Ib.*

⁴ Singulare refugium perditorum, spes miserorum, advocata omnium iniquorum ad eam confugientium.—*De Laud. V.* l. 2, a. 23.

⁵ Grande privilegium est, quod ipsa præ omnibus sanctis apud Deum potentissima est.—*Spec. B.M.V.* lect. vi.

⁶ Sed quid tanta Mariæ potentia prodesset nobis, si ipsa nihil curaret de nobis?—*Ib.*

⁷ Carissimi, sciamus indubitanter, et pro hoc gratias agamus incessanter, quia sicut ipsa apud Deum omnibus sanctis est potior, ita quoque pro nobis apud Deum omnibus sanctis est sollicitior.—*Ib.*

heart, 'who, after thy Jesus, is as tenderly solicitous for our welfare as thou art?'[8] 'Who defends us in the temptations with which we are afflicted as thou defendest us? Who, like thee, undertakes to protect sinners, fighting as it were in their behalf?'[9] 'Therefore,' he adds, 'thy patronage, O Mary, is more powerful and loving than anything of which we can ever form an idea.'[10] 'For,' says the Blessed Raymond Jordano, 'whilst all the other Saints can do more for their own clients than for others, the divine Mother, as Queen of all, is the advocate of all, and has a care for the salvation of all.'[11]

Mary takes care of all, even of sinners; indeed she glories in being called in a special manner their advocate, as she herself declared to the venerable sister Mary Villani, saying: 'After the title of Mother of God, I rejoice most in that of advocate of sinners.' Blessed Amadeus says, 'that our Queen is constantly before the Divine Majesty, interceding for us with her most powerful prayers.'[12] And as in Heaven 'she well knows our miseries and wants, she cannot do otherwise than compassionate us; and thus, with the affection of a mother, moved to tenderness towards us, pitying and benign, she is always endeavouring to help and save us.'[13] And therefore does Richard of Saint Lawrence encourage each one, however bad he may be, to have recourse with confidence to this sweet advocate, being assured that he will always find her ready to help him;[14] 'for,'

---

[8] Quis, post tuum Filium, ita generis humani curam gerit sicut tu?—*De Zona B.V.M.*

[9] Quis ita nos defendit in nostris afflictionibus . . . ? Quis in supplicationibus adeo pugnat pro peccatoribus?—*Ib.*

[10] Propterea et patrocinium tuum majus est, quam ut intelligentia comprehendi possit.—*Ib.*

[11] Cæteri . . . sancti, jure quodam patrocinii pro sibi specialiter commissis, plus possunt prodesse in curia Altissimi quam pro alienis. Beatissima vero Virgo, sicut est omnium regina, sic et omnium patrona et advocata, et cura est illi de omnibus.—*De Contempl. B.V.* in Prol.

[12] Adstat . . . Beatissima singulari merito præcipua vultui Conditoris, prece potentissima, semper interpellans pro nobis.—*De Laud. Virg.* hom. viii.

[13] Cuncta nostra videt discrimina, nostrique clemens et dulcis domina materno affectu miseretur.—*Ib.*

[14] Inveniet semper paratam auxiliari.—*De Laud. B.M.* l. 2, p. 1.

says the Abbot Godfrey, 'Mary is always ready to pray for all.'[15]

'O, with what efficacy and love,' says Saint Bernard, 'does this good Advocate interest herself in the affair of our salvation !'[16] Saint Bonaventure, considering the affection and zeal with which Mary intercedes for us with the Divine Majesty, in order that our Lord may pardon us our sins, help us with His grace, free us from dangers, and relieve us in our wants, says, addressing the Blessed Virgin, in the words of an ancient writer: 'We know that we have as it were but one solicitous in Heaven for us, and thou art this one, so greatly does thy solicitude for us exceed that of all the Saints.'[17] That is, 'O Lady, it is true that all the Saints desire our salvation, and pray for us; but the love, the tenderness, that thou showest us in Heaven, in obtaining for us by thy prayers so many mercies from God, obliges us to acknowledge that in Heaven we have but one advocate, and that is thyself; and that thou alone art truly loving and solicitous for our welfare. Who can ever comprehend the solicitude with which Mary constantly stands before God in our behalf ! 'She is never weary of defending us,'[18] says Saint Germanus ; and the remark is beautiful, meaning that so great is the compassion excited in Mary by our misery, and such is the love that she bears us, that she prays constantly, and relaxes not her efforts in our behalf ; that by her prayers she may effectually defend us from evil, and obtain for us sufficient graces. 'She has never done enough.'

Truly unfortunate should we poor sinners be, had

[15] Et ipsa quidem pro universo mundo paratissima esset ad precandum, totusque mundus salvaretur, si precibus ejus se faceret dignum.—*Serm.* 8 *de B.V.M.*

[16] Advocatam præmisit peregrinatio nostra, quæ tanquam Judicis mater et mater misericordiæ, suppliciter et efficaciter salutis nostræ negotia pertractabit.—*Serm.* 1 *de Assump.*

[17] Te solam, O Maria, pro sancta Ecclesia sollicitam præ omnibus sanctis scimus, quæ impetras inducias transgressoribus, ut renuntient suis erroribus. *Spec. B.M.V.* lect. vi.

[18] Non est satietas defensionis ejus.—*De Zona B.V.M.*

we not this great Advocate, who is so powerful and compassionate, and at the same time, 'so prudent and wise, that the Judge, her Son,' says Richard of Saint Lawrence, 'cannot condemn the guilty who are defended by her.'[19]   And therefore Saint John Geometra salutes her, saying, ' Hail, O court, for putting an end to litigation.'[20]   For all causes defended by this most wise Advocate are gained.   For this reason is Mary called, by Saint Bonaventure, 'the wise Abigail.'[21] This is the woman we read of in the second Book of Kings, who knew so well how, by her beautiful supplications, to appease King David when he was indignant against Nabal; and indeed so far as to induce him to bless her, in gratitude for having prevented him, by her sweet manners, from avenging himself on Nabal with his own hands.[22]   This is exactly what Mary constantly does in heaven, in favour of innumerable sinners : she knows so well how, by her tender and unctuous prayers, to appease the Divine justice, that God Himself blesses her for it, and, as it were, thanks her for having withheld Him from abandoning and chastising them as they deserved.   ' On this account it was,' says Saint Bernard, 'that the Eternal Father, wishing to show all the mercy possible, besides giving us Jesus Christ, our principal Advocate with Him, was pleased also to give us Mary, as our Advocate with Jesus Christ.'   'There is no doubt,' the Saint adds, ' that Jesus Christ is the only mediator of justice between men and God ; that, in virtue of His own merits and promises, He will and can obtain us pardon and the Divine favours ; but because men acknowledge and fear the Divine Majesty, which is in Him as God, for this reason it was necessary to assign us another Advo-

[19] Tam prudens etiam et discreta est advocata Maria, quod non potest **Filius** vindicare in eos pro quibus ipsa allegat.—*De Laud. V.* lib. ii. cap. 1.
[20] Salve jus dirimens lites, et flumina linguæ
Oratorum obdens, oris et artis opus.—*Hymn. 4 in Virg. Deip.*
[21] Abigail sapiens.—*Laus B. M.* n. 13.
[22] Et benedicta tu, quæ prohibuisti me hodie, ne . . . ulciscerer me manu mea.--1 *Reg.* **xxv.** 33.

cate, to whom we might have recourse with less fear
and more confidence, and this Advocate is Mary, than
whom we cannot find one more powerful with His
Divine Majesty, or one more merciful towards ourselves.' The Saint says, 'Christ is a faithful and
powerful Mediator between God and men, but in
Him men fear the majesty of God. A mediator, then,
was needed with the Mediator Himself; nor could a
more fitting one be found than Mary.'[23] 'But,' continues the same Saint, 'should any one fear to go to
the feet of this most sweet Advocate, who has nothing
in her of severity, nothing terrible, but who is all courteous, amiable, and benign, he would indeed be offering an insult to the tender compassion of Mary.'[24] And
he adds, 'Read, and read again, as often as you please,
all that is said of her in the Gospels, and if you can
find any the least trait of severity recorded of her, then
fear to approach her. But no, this you can never find ;
and therefore go to her with a joyful heart, and she
will save you by her intercession.'[25]

How beautiful is the exclamation put in the mouth
of a sinner who has recourse to Mary, by William of
Paris ! 'O most glorious Mother of God, I, in the
miserable state to which I am reduced by my sins,
have recourse to thee, full of confidence, and if thou
rejectest me, I remind thee that thou art in a way
bound to help me, since the whole Church of the
faithful calls thee and proclaims thee the Mother of
Mercy.'[26] 'Thou, O Mary, art that one who, from

---

[23] Fidelis plane et potens mediator Dei et hominum, homo Christus Jesus,
sed divinam in eo reverentur homines majestatem . . . Opus est enim media-
tore ad mediatorem istum, nec alter nobis utilior quam Maria.—*Serm. in
Sign. magn.*

[24] Quid ad Mariam accedere trepidet humana fragilitas ? Nihil austerum
in ea, nihil terribile : tota suavis est.—*Ib.*

[25] Revolve diligentius evangelicæ historiæ seriem universam, et si quid
forte austerum increpatorium, si quid durum, si quod denique signum vel
tenuis indignationis occurrerit in Maria, de cætero suspectam habeas et accedere verearis.—*Ib.*

[26] Adibo te, imo etiam conveniam, gloriosissima Dei genitrix, quam matrem misericordiæ et reginam pietatis vocat, imo clamitat omnis Ecclesia
sanctorum.—*De Rhet. Div.* cap. xviii.

being so dear to God, art always listened to favourably. Thy great compassion was never wanting to
any one; thy most sweet affability never despised any
sinner that recommended himself to thee, however great
his sins.'[27] 'And what! Perhaps falsely, and for nothing, the whole Church calls thee its Advocate, and
the refuge of sinners.'[28] 'Never, O my Mother, let
my sins prevent thee from fulfilling the great office
of charity which is thine, and by which thou art, at
the same time, our Advocate and a mediatress of peace
between men and God, and who art, after thy Son,
our only hope, and the secure refuge of the miserable.'[29]
'All that thou possessest of grace and glory, and the
dignity even of Mother of God, so to speak, thou owest
to sinners, for it was on their account that the Divine
Word made thee His Mother.'[30] 'Far be it from this
Divine Mother, who brought the source itself of tender
compassion into the world, to think that she should
ever deny her mercy to any sinner who has recourse
to her.'[31] 'Since, then, O Mary, thy office is to be the
peace-maker between God and men, let thy tender compassion, which far exceeds all my sins, move thee to
succour me.'[32]

'Be comforted then, O you who fear,' will I say with
St. Thomas of Villanova; 'breathe freely and take cour-
age, O wretched sinners; this great Virgin, who is the
Mother of your God and Judge, is also the Advocate of

[27] Tu, inquam, cujus gratiositas nunquam repulsam patitur; cujus misericordia nulli unquam defuit; cujus benignissima humilitas nullum un.
quam deprecantem quantumcumque peccatorem despexit.—*De Rhet. Div.*
cap. xviii.

[28] An falso et inaniter vocat te omnis Ecclesia sanctorum advocatam
suam, et miserorum refugium?—*Ib.*

[29] Absit, ut (peccata mea) possint suspendere te a tam salubri officio pietatis tuæ, quo, et advocata es, et mediatrix hominum, post Filium tuum spes
unica et refugium tutissimum miserorum.—*Ib.*

[30] Totum siquidem quod habes gratiæ, totum quod habes gloriæ, et etiam
hoc ipsum quod es mater Dei, si fas est dicere, peccatoribus debes.—*Ib.*

[31] Absit hoc a matre Dei, quæ fontem pietatis toti mundo peperit, ut cui-
quam miserorum suæ misericordiæ subventionem unquam deneget.—*Ib.*

[32] Officium ergo tuum est mediam te interponere inter ipsum et homines
. . . Moveat ergo te, gloriosa Dei mater, benignissima misericordia tua,
quæ major incogitabiliter est omnibus vitiis meis et peccatis.—*Ib.*

the whole human race : fit for this office, for she can do what she wills with God; most wise, for she knows all the means of appeasing Him ; universal, for she welcomes all, and refuses to defend no one.'[33]

EXAMPLE.

In Rome there was a woman known by the name of ' Catherine the Fair,' who was leading a most disorderly life. She once heard Saint Dominic preaching on the devotion of the Rosary, had her name enrolled in the confraternity, and began to recite it, but without changing her life. One evening a young man of noble mien came to visit her : she received him with courtesy, but, whilst they were at supper, she remarked, that as he was cutting bread drops of blood fell from his hands, and then she saw that there was blood on all the food he took. She asked him what was the meaning of this. The young man replied, that ' the food of a Christian should be tinged with the blood of Jesus Christ, and seasoned with the remembrance of His passion.' Astonished at such an answer, Catherine asked him who he was. ' Later,' he said, ' I will tell you.' Then going into an adjoining room, the appearance of the young man changed ; he was crowned with thorns; his flesh all mangled and torn ; and he said : ' Desirest thou to know who I am ? Dost thou not recognise me ? I am thy Redeemer. O, Catherine, when wilt thou cease offending Me ? See what I have endured for thee. Thou hast now tormented Me enough ; change thy life.' Catherine burst into sobs and tears, and Jesus, encouraging her, said : ' Love Me now as much as thou hast offended Me ; and know that I have granted thee this grace on account of the Rosary thou hast recited in honour of My Mother.' He then disappeared. On the next morning Catherine went to confession to Saint

---

[33] Consolamini pusillanimes, respirate miserabiles ; Virgo deipara es' humani generis advocata idonea, sapientissima, universalis.—*In Rog. pro exp ndv. Turc. suac.* †

Dominic, distributed all she had to the poor, and ever afterwards led so holy a life that she attained a very high degree of perfection. Our Blessed Lady appeared many times to her, and our Lord Himself revealed to Saint Dominic that this penitent had become very dear to Him.[34]

PRAYER.

O great Mother of my Lord, I see full well that my ingratitude towards God and thee, and this too for so many years, has merited for me that thou shouldst justly abandon me, and no longer have a care of me, for an ungrateful soul is no longer worthy of favours. But I, O Lady, have a high idea of thy great goodness; I believe it to be far greater than my ingratitude. Continue, then, O refuge of sinners, and cease not to help a miserable sinner, who confides in thee. O Mother of Mercy, deign to extend a helping hand to a poor fallen wretch, who asks thee for pity. O Mary, either defend me thyself, or tell me to whom I can have recourse, and who is better able to defend me than thou, and where I can find with God a more clement and powerful Advocate than thou, who art His Mother. Thou, in becoming the Mother of our Saviour, wast thereby made the fitting instrument to save sinners, and wast given me for my salvation. O Mary, save him who has recourse to thee. I deserve not thy love, but it is thine own desire to save sinners that makes me hope that thou lovest me. And if thou lovest me, how can I be lost? O my own beloved Mother, if by thee I save my soul, as I hope to do, I shall no longer be ungrateful, I shall make up for my past ingratitude, and for the love thou hast shown me, by my everlasting praises, and all the affections of my soul. Happy in Heaven, where thou reignest, and wilt reign for ever, I shall always sing thy mercies, and kiss for eternity those loving hands which have delivered me from hell

[34] Diotall. tom. ii, Domen. Quinquag.

as often as I have deserved it by my sins. O Mary, my liberator, my hope, my Queen, my Advocate, my own sweet Mother, I love thee; I desire thy glory, and I will love thee for ever. Amen, amen. Thus do I hope.

SECTION III. *Mary is the Peace-maker between sinners and God.*

The grace of God is the greatest and the most desirable of treasures for every soul. It is called by the Holy Ghost an infinite treasure; for by the means of Divine grace we are raised to the honour of being the friends of God. These are the words of the Book of Wisdom: "For she is an infinite treasure to men; which they that use become the friends of God."[1] And hence Jesus, our Redeemer and God, did not hesitate to call those His friends who were in grace: "You are My friends."[2] O accursed sin, that dissolves this friendship! "But your iniquities," says the prophet Isaias, "have divided between you and your God."[3] And putting hatred between the soul and God, it is changed from a friend into an enemy of its Lord, as expressed in the Book of Wisdom: "But to God the wicked and his wickedness are hateful alike."[4] What, then, must a sinner do who has the misfortune to be the enemy of God? He must find a mediator who will obtain pardon for him, and who will enable him to recover the lost friendship of God. 'Be comforted, O unfortunate soul, who hast lost thy God,' says Saint Bernard; 'thy Lord Himself has provided thee with a mediator, and this is His Son Jesus, who can obtain for thee all that thou desirest.' 'He has given thee Jesus

---

[1] Infinitus enim thesaurus est hominibus: quo qui usi sunt, participes facti sunt amicitiæ Dei.—*Sap.* vii. 14.

[2] Vos amici mei estis.—*Joan.* xv. 14.

[3] Iniquitates vestræ diviserunt inter vos et Deum vestrum.—*Isa.* lix. 2.

[4] Odio sunt Deo impius et impietas ejus.—*Sap.* xiv. 9.

for a Mediator; and what is there that such a Son can-not obtain from the Father?[5]

But, O God, exclaims the Saint, and why should this merciful Saviour, who gave His life to save us, be ever thought severe? Why should men believe Him terrible who is all love? O distrustful sinners, what do you fear? If your fear arises from having offended God, know that Jesus has fastened all your sins on the cross with His own lacerated hands, and having satis-fied divine justice for them by His death, He has already effaced them from your souls. Here are the words of the Saint: 'They imagine Him rigorous, who is all compassion; terrible, who is all love. What do you fear, O ye of little faith? With His own hands He has fastened your sins to the cross.'[6] 'But if by chance,' adds the Saint, 'thou fearest to have recourse to Jesus Christ because the majesty of God in Him overawes thee—for though He became man, He did not cease to be God—and thou desirest another ad-vocate with this Divine Mediator, go to Mary, for she will intercede for thee with the Son, who will most certainly hear her; and then He will intercede with the Father, who can deny nothing to such a Son.'[7] Thence Saint Bernard concludes, 'this Divine Mother, O my children, is the ladder of sinners, by which they reascend to the height of Divine grace: she is my greatest confidence, she is the whole ground of my hope.'[8]

The Holy Ghost, in the sacred Canticles, makes the most Blessed Virgin use the following words: "I am a wall; and my breasts are as a tower, since I am become

---

[5] Jesum tibi dedit mediatorem. Quid non apud talem Patrem Filius talis obtineat?—*Serm. de Aquæd.*

[6] Severum imaginatur qui pius est, terribilem qui amabilis est. Quid timetis modicæ fidei? peccata afflixit cruci suis manibus.—*In Cant.* s. 38.

[7] Sed forsitan et in ipso majestatem vereare divinam, quod licet factus sit homo, manserit tamen Deus. Advocatum habere vis et ad ipsum? ad Mariam recurre . . . Exaudiet utique matrem Filius, et exaudiet Filium Pater.—*Serm. de Aquæd.*

[8] Filioli, hæc peccatorum scala, hæc mea maxima fiducia est, hæc tota ratio spei meæ.—*Ib.*

in his presence as one finding peace ;"[9] that is, I am the defender of those who have recourse to me, and my mercy towards them is like a tower of refuge, and therefore have I been appointed by my Lord the peace-maker between sinners and God. 'Mary,' says Cardinal Hugo, on the above text, 'is the great peace-maker, who finds and obtains the reconciliation of enemies with God, salvation for those who are lost, pardon for sinners, and mercy for those who are in despair.'[10] And therefore was she called by the Divine Bridegroom, "beautiful as the curtains of Solomon."[11] In the tents of David, questions of war alone were treated, but in those of Solomon, questions of peace only were entertained ; and thus does the Holy Spirit give us to understand that this Mother of Mercy never treats of war and vengeance against sinners, but only of peace and forgiveness for them.

Mary was prefigured by the dove which returned to Noah in the ark with an olive-branch in its beak,[12] as a pledge of the peace which God granted to men. And on this idea Saint Bonaventure thus addresses our Blessed Lady : 'Thou art that most faithful dove; thou wast a sure mediatress between God and the world, lost in a spiritual deluge ;'[13] thou, by presenting thyself before God, hast obtained for a lost world peace and salvation. Mary, then, was the heavenly dove which brought to a lost world the olive-branch, the sign of mercy, since she in the first place gave us Jesus Christ, who is the source of mercy, and then, by His merits, obtained all graces for us.[14] 'And as by Mary,' says Saint Epipha-

---

[9] Ego murus : et ubera mea sicut turris, ex quo facta sum coram eo quasi pacem reperiens.—*Cant.* viii. 10.

[10] Ipsa res reperit pacem inimicis, salutem perditis, indulgentiam reis, misericordiam desperatis.—*In Cant.* cap. viii.

[11] Formosa . . . sicut pelles Salomonis.—*Cant.* i. 4.

[12] Gen. viii. 11.

[13] Tu enim es illa fidelissima columba Noe, quæ inter summum Deum et mundum diluvio spirituali submersum mediatrix fidelissima extitit.—*Spec. B.M.V.* lect. ix.

[14] Nam Christum nobis detulit, fontem misericordiæ.—*P. Spinell. Mar. Devop.* c. 16.

nius, 'heavenly peace was once for all given to the world,[15] so by her are sinners still reconciled to God.' Wherefore blessed Albert the Great makes her say : ' I am that dove of Noah, which brought the olive-branch of universal peace to the Church.'[16]

Again, the rainbow seen by Saint John, which encircled the throne of God, was an express figure of Mary : "And there was a rainbow round about the throne."[17] It is thus explained by Cardinal Vitalis : The rainbow round the throne is Mary, who softens the judgment and sentence of God against sinners ;'[18] meaning, that she is always before God's tribunal, mitigating the chastisements due to sinners. Saint Bernardine of Sienna says, 'that it was of this rainbow that God spoke when He promised Noah that He would place it in the clouds as a sign of peace, that on looking at it He might remember the eternal peace which He had covenanted to man.' "I will set My bow in the clouds, and it shall be the sign of a covenant between Me and between the earth . . . . and I shall see it, and shall remember the everlasting covenant."[19] 'Mary,' says the Saint, ' is this bow of eternal peace :'[20] 'for, as God on seeing it remembers the peace promised to the earth, so does He, at the prayers of Mary, forgive the crimes of sinners, and confirm His peace with them.'[21]

For the same reason Mary is compared to the moon in the sacred Canticles : " Fair as the moon."[22] 'For,' says Saint Bonaventure, ' as the moon is between the

---

[15] Per te pax cœlestis donata est.—*Hom. in Laud. B. M.*

[16] Ego sum columba Noe, Ecclesiæ ramum olivæ et pacis deferens universalis.—*Bibl. Mar.* in lib. Cant. 16.

[17] Et iris erat in circuitu sedis.—*Apoc.* iv. 3.

[18] Iris in circuitu sedis est Maria . . . quæ mitigat Dei judicium et sententiam contra peccatores.—*Spec. S. Script. de B. V. M.*

[19] Arcum meum ponam in nubibus, et erit signum fœderis inter me et inter terram . . . Videbo illum, et recordabor fœderis sempiterni.—*Gen.* ix. 13, 16.

[20] Ipsa est arcus fœderis sempiterni.—*Serm.* 1 *de Nom. M.* cap. 3.

[21] Fructus iridis est recordatio divini fœderis, ne divino judicio disperdatur terra, et omnis anima vivens in ea : et per Virginem gloriosam offensa reis remittitur, pax restituitur, fœdus stringitur.—*Exposit. in cap.* iv. *Apoc.*

[22] Pulchra ut luna.—*Cant.* vi. 9.

heavens and the earth, so does Mary continually place
herself between God and sinners in order to appease
our Lord in their regard, and to enlighten them to return to Him.'[23]

The chief office given to Mary, on being placed in
this world, was to raise up souls that had fallen from
divine grace, and to reconcile them with God. "Feed
thy goats,"[24] was our Lord's command to her in creating
her. It is well known that sinners are understood by
goats, and that as at the last judgment, the just, under
the figure of sheep, will be on the right hand, so will
the goats be on the left. 'These goats,' says the Abbot
William, 'are intrusted to thee, O great Mother, that
thou mayest change them into sheep; and those who
by their sins deserved to be driven to the left, will by
thy intercession be placed on the right.'[25] And therefore our Lord revealed to Saint Catharine of Sienna,[26]
'that He had created this His beloved Daughter to be
as a most sweet bait by which to catch men, and especially sinners, and draw them to God.'[27] But on this
subject we must not pass over the beautiful reflection
of William the Angelical on the above text of the sacred
Canticles, in which he says, 'that God recommended
HER OWN goats to Mary;' 'for,' adds this author, 'the
Blessed Virgin does not save all sinners, but those only
who serve and honour her. So much so indeed, that
those who live in sin, and neither honour her with any
particular act of homage, nor recommend themselves to
her in order to extricate themselves from sin, they certainly are not Mary's goats, but at the last judgment

---

[23] Sicut luna est media inter corpora cœlestia et terrena, et quod ab illis
accipit ad inferiora refundit; sic et Virgo regia inter nos et Deum est media,
et gratiam ipsa nobis refundit.—*Spann. Polyanth.* litt. m. t. 6.

[24] Pasce hædos tuos.—*Cant.* i. 7.

[25] Pasce hædos tuos, quos convertis in oves, et qui a sinistris in judicio
erant collocandi, tua intercessione collocentur a dextris. †

[26] Conc. An. Fid. cap. i.

[27] Hæc enim est a me electa, parata, et posita, tanquam esca dulcissima
ad capiendos homines, et præcipue animas peccatorum.—*Ib.*

will, for their eternal misery, be driven **to** the left hand with the damned.'[28]

A certain nobleman, despairing of his salvation, on account of his many crimes, was encouraged by a monk to have recourse to the most Blessed Virgin, and, for this purpose, to visit a devout statue of Mary in a particular church. He went there, and, on seeing the image, he felt as if she invited him to cast himself at her feet and to have confidence. He hastened to prostrate and kiss her feet, when Mary extended her hand, gave it him to kiss, and on it he saw written these words : *I will deliver thee from those who oppress thee;* as though she had said, My son, despair not, for I will deliver thee from the sins and sorrows that weigh so heavily on thee. On reading these sweet words, the poor sinner was filled with such sorrow for his sins, and, at the same time, with so ardent a love for God and His tender Mother, that he instantly expired at the feet of Mary. O, how many obstinate sinners does not this loadstone of hearts draw each day to God ! For thus did she call herself one day, saying to Saint Bridget, 'As the loadstone attracts iron, so do I attract hearts.'[29] Yea, even the most hardened hearts, to reconcile them with God. We must not suppose that such prodigies are extraordinary events; they are everyday occurrences. For my own part, I could relate many cases of the kind that have occurred in our missions, where certain sinners, with hearts harder than iron, continued so through all the other sermons, but no sooner did they hear the one on the mercies of Mary, than they were filled with compunction and returned to God. Saint Gregory[30] says, that the unicorn is so

---

[28] Suos vocat, quia non omnes hædi vocantur Mariæ, sed qui Mariam colunt ac venerantur, licet sceleribus contaminati. Qui vero peccatis irretiti sunt, nec B. Virginem speciali obsequio prosequuntur, nec preces fundunt in ejus cultum, ut aliquando resipiscant, hædi profecto sunt, non Mariæ, sed ad sinistram judicis sistendi. †

[29] Sicut magnes attrahit sibi ferrum, sic ego attraho Deo dura corda.—*Rev.* lib. iii. cap. 32.

[30] Moral. l. 31, c. 13.

fierce a beast, that no hunter can take it; at the voice only of a virgin crying out, will this beast approach, and without resistance allow itself to be bound by her, O, how many sinners, more savage than the wild beasts themselves, and who fly from God, at the voice of this great Virgin Mary approach and allow themselves to be sweetly bound to God by her!

Saint John Chrysostom says, 'that another purpose for which the Blessed Virgin Mary was made the Mother of God was, that she might obtain salvation for many who, on account of their wicked lives, could not be saved according to the rigour of divine justice, but might be so with the help of her sweet mercy and powerful intercession.'[31] This is confirmed by Saint Anselm, who says, 'that Mary was raised to the dignity of Mother of God rather for sinners than for the just, since Jesus Christ declares that He came to call not the just, but sinners.'[32] For this reason, the holy Church sings, 'Thou dost not abhor sinners, without whom thou wouldst never have been worthy of such a Son.'[33] For the same reason William of Paris, invoking her, says: ' O Mary, thou art obliged to help sinners for all the gifts, the graces, and high honours which are comprised in the dignity of Mother of God, that thou hast received; thou owest all, so to say, to sinners; for on their account thou wast made worthy to have a God for thy son.'[34] ' If then, Mary,' concludes Saint Anselm, ' was made Mother of God on account of sinners, how can I, however great my sins may be, despair of pardon?'[35]

[31] Ideo mater Dei præelecta es ab æterno, ut quos justitia Filii salvare non potest, tu per tuam salvares pietatem.—*Hom. de Præs. B.V.* †

[32] Scio illam magis propter peccatores, quam propter justos, esse factam Dei matrem. Dicit enim ipse bonus Filius ejus, se non venisse vocare justos, sed peccatores.—*De Exc. B. Virg.* cap. i.

[33] Peccatores non abhorres, sine quibus nunquam fores tanto digna Filio.

[34] Totum . . . quod habes gratiæ, totum quod habes gloriæ, et etiam hoc ipsum, quod es mater Dei, si fas est dicere, peccatoribus debes : omnia enim hæc propter peccatores tibi collata sunt.—*De Rhet. Div.* c. xviii.

[35] Si . . . ipsa propter peccatores, scilicet propter me, meique similes, facta est Dei mater, quomodo immanitas peccatorum meorum cogere poterit desperare veniam eorum ?.—*De Exc. V.* c. i.

The holy Church tells us, in the prayer said in the mass of the vigil of the Assumption, 'that the Divine Mother was taken from this world that she might interpose for us with God, with certain confidence of obtaining all.'[36] Hence Saint Justin calls Mary an arbitratrix:[37] 'The eternal Word uses Mary,' he says, 'as an arbitratrix.' An arbitrator is one into whose hands contending parties confide their whole case; and so the Saint meant to say, that as Jesus is the mediator with the Eternal Father, so also is Mary our mediatress with Jesus; and that He puts all the reasons that He has for pronouncing sentence against us into her hands.

Saint Andrew of Crete calls Mary 'a pledge, a security for our reconciliation with God.'[38] That is, that God goes about seeking for reconciliation with sinners by pardoning them; and in order that they may not doubt of their forgiveness, He has given them Mary as a pledge of it, and therefore he exclaims, 'Hail, O peace of God with men!'[39] Wherefore, Saint Bonaventure encourages a sinner, saying: 'If thou fearest that on account of thy faults God in His anger will be avenged, what hast thou to do? Go, have recourse to Mary, who is the hope of sinners; and, if thou fearest that she may refuse to take thy part, know that she cannot do so, for God Himself has imposed on her the duty of succouring the miserable.'[40] The Abbot Adam also says, 'Need that sinner fear being lost to whom the Mother of the Judge offers herself to be Mother and advocate?'[41] 'And thou, O Mary,' he adds, 'who art

[36] Quam idcirco de hoc sæculo transtulisti, ut pro peccatis nostris apud te fiducialiter intercedat.

[37] Verbum usum est Virgine sequestra.—*Expos. Fid. de Trin.*

[38] Per eam nobis obstricta sunt salutis pignora.— *In B.V.M. Dorm.* Serm. iii.

[39] Ave sis divina cum hominibus reconciliatio.—*In Annunt. S.M. Serm.*

[40] Si contra te etiam, propter tuas nequitias, ipsum videris indignatum, ad spem peccatorum confugias, matrem suam . . . ab ea quod volueris impetrabis . . . sibi pro miseris satisfacere ex officio commissum est.—*Stim. Am.* p. iii. cap. xii.

[41] Timere ne debet ut pereat, cui Maria se matrem exhibet et advocatam. —*Marial.* s. 1.

the Mother of mercy, wilt thou disdain to intercede
with thy Son, who is the Judge, for another son, who
is a sinner ? Wilt thou refuse to interpose in favour of
a redeemed soul, with the Redeemer who died on a cross
to save sinners ?'[42] No, no, thou wilt not reject him,
but with all affection thou wilt pray for all who have
recourse to thee, well knowing that 'that Lord who has
appointed thy Son a mediator of peace between God
and man, has also made thee mediatress between the
Judge and the culprit.'[43] ' Then, O sinner,' says Saint
Bernard, 'whoever thou mayst be, imbedded in crime,
grown old in sin, despair not ; thank thy Lord, who,
that He might show thee mercy, has not only given
thee His Son for thy advocate, but, to encourage thee
to greater confidence, has provided thee with a mediatress who by her prayers obtains whatever she wills.[44]
Go then, have recourse to Mary, and thou wilt be saved.'

EXAMPLE.

Alan de la Roche[45] and Boniface[46] relate, that in
Florence there was a young woman of the name of
Benedicta, who was leading a most wicked and scandalous life. Fortunately for her, as it turned out,
Saint Dominic went to preach in that city, and she,
out of mere curiosity, went one day to hear him. God,
during that sermon, touched her heart, so much so that
she went and, weeping bitterly, confessed to the Saint.
Saint Dominic thereupon absolved her, and desired her
to say the Rosary for her penance. From evil habits,
the unfortunate creature again fell into her former mode
of life. The Saint heard of it, sought her out, and
again induced her to confess. God, in order to make

---

[42] **Tu** misericordiæ mater, non rogabis pro filio filium, pro redempto redemptorem ?—*Marial.* s. l.
[43] Rogabis plane, quia qui filium tuum inter Deum et hominem posuit
mediatorem, te quoque inter reum et judicem posuit mediatricem.—*Ib.*
[44] Age gratias ei, qui talem tibi mediatricem benignissima miseratione
providit.—*Serm. in Sig. Mag.*
[45] De Psalt. p. v. c. 60.   [46] Stor. Verg. lib. iv. c. 11.

her persevere, one day showed her hell, and pointed out some who were there on her account. He then opened a book, and in it made her read the frightful catalogue of her sins. The sinner was horrified at such a sight, and full of confidence, begged that Mary would assist her; and she understood that this good Mother had already obtained from God time for her to weep over so many crimes. After the vision, Benedicta led a good life; but always seeing before her eyes that terrible catalogue, she one day began to implore her comfortress in the following terms: 'My Mother,' said she, 'it is true that for my crimes I ought now to be in the lowest abyss of hell; but since thou, by obtaining me time to repent, hast delivered me from it, I ask thee this one favour more, O most compassionate Lady, that my sins may be cancelled from the book, and I will never cease all the same to weep for them.' At this prayer Mary appeared to her, and told her that, to obtain what she desired, she must always remember her sins and the mercy that God had shown her, and besides, that she should often recall to her mind the sufferings which her Divine Son had endured for her love, and consider how many were lost for less sins than she had committed; and, at the same time, revealed to her that on that day a child only eight years of age would go to hell for one mortal sin. Benedicta obeyed our Blessed Lady faithfully; and behold one day Jesus Christ appeared to her, and showing her the book, said, 'See, the book is blank,—thy sins are cancelled; now write acts of love and virtue in their stead.' Doing this, Benedicta led a holy life, and died the death of a saint.

PRAYER.

O my most sweet Lady, since thy office is, as William of Paris says, that of a mediatress between God and sinners,[47] I will address thee in the words of

---

[47] Officium tuum est, mediam te interponere inter Deum et homines.—De Rhet. Div. c. xviii.

Saint Thomas of Villanova : ' Fulfil thy office in my
behalf, O tender Advocate ; do thy work.[48] Say not
that my cause is too difficult to gain ; for I know, and
all tell me so, that every cause, no matter how desperate, if undertaken by thee, is never, and never will be,
lost. And will mine be lost ? Ah no, this I cannot
fear. The only thing that I might fear is, that, on
seeing the multitude of my sins, thou mightest not
undertake my defence. But, on seeing thy immense
mercy, and the very great desire of thy most sweet
heart to help the most abandoned sinners, even this I
cannot fear. And who was ever lost that had recourse
to thee ? Therefore I invoke thy aid, O my great Advocate, my refuge, my hope, my mother Mary. To thy
hands do I intrust the cause of my eternal salvation.
To thee do I commit my soul ; it was lost, but thou
hast to save it. I will always thank our Lord for
having given me this great confidence in thee ; and
which, notwithstanding my unworthiness, I feel is an
assurance of salvation. I have but one fear to afflict
me, O beloved Queen, and that is, that I may one day,
by my own negligence, lose this confidence in thee.
And therefore I implore thee, O Mary, by the love
thou bearest to Jesus, thyself to preserve and increase
in me more and more this sweet confidence in thy intercession, by which I hope most certainly to recover
the Divine friendship, that I have hitherto so madly
despised and lost ; and having recovered it, I hope,
through thee, to preserve it ; and preserving it by the
same means, I hope at length to thank thee for it in
heaven, and there to sing God's mercies and thine for
all eternity. Amen. This is my hope ; thus may it be,
thus it will be.

[48] Eja ergo advocata nostra . . . officium tuum imple, tuum opus exerce
—*In Nat. B.V.* concio iii.

CHAPTER VII.

*Mary is all eyes to pity and succour us in our
necessities.*

SAINT EPIPHANIUS calls the Divine Mother many-eyed,[1]
indicating thereby her vigilance in assisting us poor
creatures in this world. A possessed person was once
being exorcised, and was questioned by the exorcist as
to what Mary did. The devil replied, 'She descends
and ascends.' And he meant, that this benign Lady is
constantly descending from Heaven to bring graces to
men, and re-ascending to obtain the Divine favour on
our prayers. With reason, then, used Saint Andrew
Avellino to call the Blessed Virgin the 'Heavenly Com-
missioner,' for she is continually carrying messages of
mercy, and obtaining graces for all, for just and sinners.
'God fixes His eyes on the just,' says the royal prophet. "The eyes of the Lord are on the just."[2] 'But
the eyes of the Lady,' says Richard of Saint Lawrence,
'are on the just and on sinners.'[3] 'For,' he adds, 'the
eyes of Mary are the eyes of a mother; and a mother
not only watches her child to prevent its falling, but
when it has fallen, she picks it up.'[4]

Jesus Himself revealed this to Saint Bridget, for one
day He allowed her to hear Him thus addressing His
holy Mother: 'My Mother, ask of Me what thou wilt.'[5]

[1] Multocula.—*Hom. in Laud. S.M.*
[2] Oculi Domini super justos.—*Ps.* xxxiii. 16.
[3] Oculi Dominæ super peccatores.—*De Laud. V.* lib. v. cap. 2.
[4] Oculi Domini super justos, sicut oculi matris ad puerum ne cadat; et
si ceciderit, ut eum relevet.—*Ib.*
[5] Pete ergo quod vis.—Lib. vi. cap. 23.

And thus is her Son constantly addressing Mary in Heaven, taking pleasure in gratifying His beloved Mother in all that she asks. But what does Mary ask? Saint Bridget heard her reply : ' I ask mercy for sinners.'[6] As if she had said, ' My Son, Thou hast made me the Mother of Mercy, the refuge of sinners, the advocate of the miserable ; and now Thou tellest me to ask what I desire ; what can I ask except mercy for them?' ' I ask mercy for the miserable.' ' And so, O Mary, thou art so full of mercy,' says Saint Bonaventure, with deep feeling, ' so attentive in relieving the wretched, that it seems that thou hast no other desire, no other anxiety.'[7] And as amongst the miserable, sinners are the most miserable of all, Venerable Bede declares, ' that Mary is always praying to her Son for them.'[8]

' Even whilst living in this world,' says Saint Jerome, ' the heart of Mary was so filled with tenderness and compassion for men, that no one ever suffered so much for his own pains as Mary suffered for the pains of others.'[9] This compassion for others in affliction she well showed at the marriage-feast of Cana, spoken of in the preceding chapters, when the wine failing, without being asked, remarks Saint Bernardine of Sienna, she charged herself with the office of a tender comfortress ;[10] and moved to compassion at the sight of the embarrassment of the bride and bridegroom, she interposed with her Son, and obtained the miraculous change of water into wine.

' But perhaps,' says Saint Peter Damian, addressing Mary, ' now that thou art raised to the high dignity of

---

[6] Misericordiam et auxilium peto miseris.—*Rev.* lib. i. cap. 50.
[7] Undique sollicita de miseris, undique misericordia vallaris, solum miserari tu videris appetere.—*Super Salve Reg.*
[8] Stat Maria in conspectu filii sui, non cessans pro peccatoribus exorare.—*In cap.* i. *Luc.* †
Nullum in hac vita adeo pœnæ torserunt propriæ, sicut Mariam alienæ.—*Epist. ad Eust.* †
[10] Officium piæ auxiliatricis assumsit non rogata.—*Pro Fest. V.M.* s. 9. a. 3. c. 2.

Queen of Heaven, thou forgettest us poor creatures?
'Ah, far be such a thought from our minds,' he adds;
'for it would little become the great compassion that
reigns in the heart of Mary ever to forget such misery
as ours.'[11] The proverb, that 'honours change our manners,' does not apply to Mary. With worldlings it is
otherwise; for they, when once raised to a high dignity,
become proud, and forget their former poor friends; but
it is not so with Mary, who rejoices in her own exaltation, because she is thus better able to help the miserable. On this subject Saint Bonaventure applies to the
Blessed Virgin the words addressed to Ruth: "Blessed
art thou of the Lord, my daughter, and thy latter kindness has surpassed the former;"[12] meaning to say, 'that
if the compassion of Mary was great towards the miserable when living in this world, it is much greater now
that she reigns in Heaven.'[13] He then gives the reason
for this, saying, 'that the Divine Mother shows, by
the innumerable graces she obtains for us, her greater
mercy; for now she is better acquainted with our
miseries.'[14] Thence he adds, 'that as the splendour
of the sun surpasses that of the moon, so does the compassion of Mary, now that she is in Heaven, surpass
the compassion she had for us when in the world.'[15]
In conclusion, he asks, 'who is there living in this
world, who does not enjoy the light of the sun? and on
whom does not the mercy of Mary shine?'[16]

For this reason, in the sacred Canticles she is called
"bright as the sun."[17] 'For no one is excluded from

---

[11] Numquid, O beata Virgo, quia ita deificata, ideo nostræ humilitatis
oblita es? Nequaquam Domina . . . non enim convenit tantæ misericordiæ
tantam miseriam oblivisci.—*Serm*. i. *de Nat. B.V.*

[12] Benedicta, inquit, es a Domino filia, et priorem misericordiam poste-
riore superasti.—*Ruth* iii. 10.

[13] Magna erga miseros fuit misericordia Mariæ, adhuc exulantis in mundo,
sed multo major erga miseros est misericordia ejus, jam regnantis in cœlo.—
Spec. B.M.V. Lect. x.

[14] Majorem, per beneficia innumerabilia, nunc ostendit hominibus misericordiam, qui magis nunc videt innumerabilem hominum miseriam.—*Ib.*

[15] Nam quemadmodum sol lunam superat magnitudine splendoris, sic
priorem Mariæ misericordiam superat magnitudo posterioris.—*Ib.*

[16] Quis est super quem misericordia Mariæ non resplendeat?—*Ib.*

[17] Electa ut sol.—*Cant.* vi. 9.

the warmth of this sun,' says Saint Bonaventure ; and
the same thing was also revealed to Saint Bridget, by
Saint Agnes, who told her, 'that our Queen, now that
she is united to her Son in Heaven, cannot forget her
innate goodness ; and therefore she shows her compassion to all, even to the most impious sinners ; so
much so, that, as the celestrial and terrestial bodies are
all illumined by the sun, so there is no one in the
world, who, if he asks for it, does not, through the
tenderness of Mary, partake of the Divine mercy.[18]   A
great sinner, in the kingdom of Valencia, who, having
become desperate, and, in order not to fall into the
hands of justice, had determined on becoming a Ma-
hometan, was on the point of embarking for the purpose, when, by chance, he passed before a church, in
which Father Jerome Lopez was preaching on the mercy
of God.   On hearing the sermon he was converted, and
made his confession to the father, who asked him if he
had ever practised any devotion, on account of which
God might have shown him such great mercy ; he replied, that his only devotion was a prayer to the Blessed
Virgin, in which he daily begged her not to abandon
him.[19]   In an hospital, the same father found a sinner,
who had not been to confession for fifty-five years ; and
the only devotion he practised was, that when he saw
an image of Mary he saluted her, and begged that she
would not allow him to die in mortal sin.   He then
told him, that on an occasion, when fighting with an
enemy, his sword was broken ; and, turning to our
Blessed Lady, he cried out, ' O, I shall be killed, and
lost for eternity; Mother of sinners, help me.'   Scarcely
had he said the words when he found himself transported to a place of safety.   After making a general
confession he died, full of confidence.

[18] Nunc autem conjuncta Filio non obliviscitur innatæ bonitatis suæ, sed
ad omnes extendit misericordiam suam, etiam ad pessimos : ut sicut sole illu-
minantur et inflammentur cœlestia et terrestria, sic ex dulcedine Mariæ
nullus est, qui non per eam, si petitur, sentiat pietatem.—*Rev.* lib. iii. cap. 30.
[19] Patrign. Menol. 2 Feb.

Saint Bernard says, 'that Mary has made herself all to all, and opens her merciful heart to all, that all may receive of her fulness; the slave redemption, the sick health, those in affliction comfort, the sinner pardon, and God glory; that thus there may be no one who can hide himself from her heart.'[20] 'Who can there be in the world,' exclaims Saint Bonaventure, 'who refuses to love this most amiable Queen? She is more beautiful than the sun, and sweeter than honey. She is a treasure of goodness, amiable and courteous to all.'[21] 'I salute thee, then,' continues the enraptured Saint, ' O my Lady and Mother, nay, even my heart, my soul. Forgive me, O Mary, if I say that I love thee; for if I am not worthy to love thee, at least thou art all-worthy to be loved by me.'[22]

It was revealed to Saint Gertrude,[23] that when these words are addressed with devotion to the most Blessed Virgin, 'Turn, then, O most gracious Advocate, thine eyes of mercy towards us,' Mary cannot do otherwise than yield to the demand of whoever thus invokes her. ' Ah, truly, O great Lady,' says Saint Bernard, 'does the immensity of thy mercy fill the whole earth.'[24] 'And therefore,' says Saint Bonaventure, ' this loving Mother has so earnest a desire to do good to all, that not only is she offended by those who positively outrage her (as some are wicked enough to do), but she is offended at those who do not ask her for favours or graces.'[25] So that Saint Idelbert addresses her, saying:

[20] Maria . . . omnibus omnia facta est . . . omnibus misericordiæ sinum aperit, ut de plenitudine ejus accipiant universi : captivus redemptionem, æger curationem, tristis consolationem, peccator veniam . . . ut non sit qui se abscondat a calore ejus.—*Serm. in Sign. Magn.*

[21] Quis non te diligit, O Maria . . . pulchriorem sole, dulciorem melle ? . . . Omnibus es amabilis, omnibus es affabilis.—*Stim. Am.* p. iii. *Med. sup. Salve Reg.*

[22] Ave domina mea, mater mea, imo cor meum et anima mea . . . Mihi parce, domina, quod me amare dicam te. Etenim si non sum dignus, non es indigna amari.—*Ib.* cap. 16.

[23] Insin. l. 4. c. 53.

[24] Latitudo misericordiæ ejus replet orbem terrarum.—*Serm.* iv. *in Assump. B.M.V.*

[25] In te, domina, peccant, non solum qui tibi injuriam irrogant, sed etiam qui te non regant.—*S. Bonav. in Spec. Virg.* †

'Thou, O Lady, teachest us to hope for far greater graces than we deserve, since thou never ceasest to dispense graces far, far beyond our merits.'[26]

The prophet Isaias foretold, that, together with the great work of the redemption of the human race, a throne of Divine mercy was to be prepared for us poor creatures ; " And a throne shall be prepared in mercy."[27] What is this throne? Saint Bonaventure answers, 'Mary is this throne, at which all—just and sinners— find the consolations of mercy.' He then adds ; 'for as we have a most merciful Lord, so also we have a most merciful Lady. Our Lord is plenteous in mercy to all who call upon Him, and our Lady is plenteous in mercy to all who call upon her.'[28] As our Lord is full of mercy, so also is our Lady ; and as the Son knows not how to refuse mercy to those who call upon Him, neither does the Mother. Wherefore the Abbot Guarric thus addresses the Mother, in the name of Jesus Christ : ' My Mother, in thee will I establish the seat of My government ; through thee will I pronounce judgments, hear prayers, and grant the graces asked of Me. Thou hast given Me my human nature, and I will give thee My Divine nature,'[29] that is, omnipotence, by which thou mayest be able to help to save all whomsoever thou pleasest.

One day, when Saint Gertrude was addressing the above words, ' Turn thine eyes of mercy towards us,' to the Divine Mother, she saw the Blessed Virgin pointing to the eyes of her Son, whom she held in her arms, and then said, ' These are the most compassionate eyes

[26] Doces nos sperare majora meritis, quæ meritis majora largiri non desinis.—*Ep.* 20, *Bibl. Patr.*

[27] Præparabitur in misericordia solium.—*Is.* xvi. 5.

[28] Solium divinæ misericordiæ est Maria mater misericordiæ, in quo omnes inveniunt solatia misericordiæ. Nam sicut misericordiosissimum Dominum, ita misericordiosissimam Dominam habemus. Dominus noster multæ misericordiæ est omnibus invocantibus se, et Domina nostra multæ misericordiæ est omnibus invocantibus se.—*Spec. B.M.V.* Lect. ix.

[29] In te mihi quandam regni sedem constituam, de te judicia decernam, per te preces exaudiam . . . Communicasti mihi præter alia quod homo sum; communicabo tibi quod Deus sum.—*Serm.* ii. *de Assump. B.M.V.*

that I can turn for their salvation towards all who **call upon** me.'[30] A sinner was once weeping before an image of Mary, imploring her to obtain pardon for him from God, when he perceived that the Blessed Virgin turned towards the child that she held in her arms, and said, ' My Son, shall these tears be lost?' And he understood that Jesus Christ had already pardoned him.[31]

How, then, is it possible that anyone can perish who recommends himself to this good Mother, since her Son, as God, has promised her that for her love He will show as much mercy as she pleases to all who recommend themselves to her? This our Lord revealed to Saint Gertrude, allowing her to hear Him make the promise to His Mother in the following words : ' In My omnipotence, O revered Mother, I have granted thee the reconciliation of all sinners who devoutly invoke the aid of thy compassion, in whatever way it may please thee.'[32] On this assurance the Abbot Adam Persenius, considering the great power of Mary with God, and, at the same time, her great compassion for us, full of confidence, says, ' O Mother of mercy, thy tender compassion is as great as thy power, and thou art as compassionate in forgiving as thou art powerful in obtaining all.'[33] ' And when,' he asks, ' did the case ever occur in which thou, who art the Mother of mercy, didst not show compassion? O, when was it that thou, who art the Mother of omnipotence, couldst not aid? Ah, yes, with the same facility with which thou seest our misfortunes thou obtainest for us whatever thou willest.'[34] ' Satiate, O satiate thyself, great Queen,' says the Abbot Guarric,

[30] Isti sunt misericordiosissimi oculi mei, quos ad omnes me invocantes salubriter possum inclinare.—*Rev.* lib. iv. cap. 53.

[31] Sinisc. Il Mart. di M. ott.

[32] Ex omnipotentia mea, Mater reverenda, tibi concessi potestatem propitiandi peccatis omnium, qui devote invocant tuæ pietatis auxilium, qualicumque modo placet tibi.—*Rev.* lib. iv. cap. 53.

[33] Mater misericordiæ, tanta est pietas tua quanta potestas. Tam pia es ad petendum, quam potens ad impetrandum.—*Marial.* s. 1.

[34] Quando non compatieris miseris, mater misericordiæ? aut quando illis opem conferre non poteris, cum sis mater omnipotentiæ, eadem facilitate obtinens quodcumque vis, qua facilitate, nostra innotescit miseria.—*Ib.*

'with the glory of thy Son, and out of compassion, though not for any merit of ours, be pleased to send us, thy servants and children here below, the crumbs that fall from thy table.'[35]

Should the sight of our sins ever discourage us, let us address the Mother of mercy in the words of William of Paris: 'O Lady, do not set up my sins against me, for I oppose thy compassion to them. Let it never be said that my sins could contend in judgment against thy mercy, which is far more powerful to obtain me pardon than my sins are to obtain my condemnation.'[36]

EXAMPLE.

In the chronicles of the Capuchin fathers[37] it is related, that in Venice there was a famous lawyer, who, by fraudulent dealings and bad practices, became rich, so that he lived in a state of sin. The daily recitation of a particular prayer to the Blessed Virgin was probably the only good thing that he ever did. And yet this slight devotion obtained him, through the mercy of Mary, deliverance from eternal death. It was thus. He, happily for himself, took an affection for Father Mathew de Basso, and entreated him so often to come and dine at his house, that at length this good father complied with his request. When he got to the house the lawyer said : 'Now, father, I will show you a thing you never saw before. I have a most extraordinary monkey, who serves me as a valet, washes the glasses, lays the table, and opens the door for me.' 'Ah,' replied the father, 'take care, perhaps it is not a monkey, but something more ; bring it here.' They call again and again for the monkey, but no monkey appears ; they seek for it everywhere, but it is not to be found.

---

[35] O mater misericordiæ, saturare gloria Filii tui, et dimitte reliquias tuas parvulis tuis.—*Serm.* iv. *de Assump. B.M.V.*

[36] Ne allegaveris, dulcissima Dei mater, peccata mea contra me, qui misericordiam tuam allego contra ea. Absit, ut stent in judicio peccata mea contra misericordiam tuam, quæ omnibus vitiis et peccatis super omnem cogitatum fortior est et potentior.—*De Rhet. Div.* cap. 18.

[37] Bover. Ann. 1552, n. 69.

At length they discovered it concealed under a bed, in a lower part of the house ; but, no, the monkey would not come out. ' Well, then,' said the religious, ' let us go to it ;' and when the lawyer and he reached the place where it was, the father cried out, ' Infernal beast, come forth, and on the part of God I command thee to say what thou art.' The monkey replied, ' that he was the devil, and that he was only waiting for that sinner to omit for a single day his ordinary prayer to the Mother of God ; for, the first time he omitted it, he had permission from God to strangle him, and carry him to hell.' On hearing this the poor lawyer cast himself on his knees, to ask for help from the servant of God, who encouraged him, and commanded the devil to leave the house without doing mischief. ' Only,' said he, ' I permit thee to make a hole in the wall of the house as a sign of thy departure.' He had scarcely said the words than, with a tremendous noise, a hole was made in the wall, and which, though often closed with mortar and stone, God permitted should remain open for a long time, until, at length, the servant of God advised that it should be covered with a marble slab, with the figure of an angel on it. The lawyer was converted, and, as we hope, persevered until death in his change of life.

PRAYER.

O greatest and most sublime of all creatures, most sacred Virgin, I salute thee from this earth—I, a miserable and unfortunate rebel against my God, who deserve chastisements, not favours, justice, and not mercy. O Lady, I say not this because I doubt thy compassion. I know that the greater thou art the more thou dost glory in being benign. I know that thou rejoicest that thou art so rich, because thou art thus enabled to succour us poor miserable creatures. I know that the greater is the poverty of those who have recourse to thee, the more dost thou exert thyself to protect and save them.

O

O my Mother, it was thou who didst one day weep over thy Son who died for me. Offer, I beseech thee, thy tears to God, and by these obtain for me true sorrow for my sins. Sinners then afflicted thee so much, and I, by my crimes, have done the same. Obtain for me, O Mary, that at least from this day forward I may not continue to afflict thee and thy Son by my ingratitude. What would thy sorrow avail me if I continued to be ungrateful to thee? To what purpose would thy mercy have been shown me, if again I was unfaithful and lost? No, my Queen, permit it not; thou hast supplied for all my shortcomings. Thou obtainest from God what thou wilt. Thou grantest the prayers of all. I ask of thee two graces; I expect them from thee, and will not be satisfied with less. Obtain for me that I may be faithful to God, and no more offend Him, and love Him during the remainder of my life as much as I have offended Him.

CHAPTER VIII.

AND AFTER THIS OUR EXILE SHOW UNTO US THE BLESSED
FRUIT OF THY WOMB, JESUS.

SECTION I. *Mary delivers her Clients from Hell.*

IT is impossible for a client of Mary, who is faithful in
honouring and recommending himself to her, to be lost.
To some this proposition may appear, at first sight, exaggerated; but anyone to whom this might seem to
be the case I would beg to suspend his judgment, and,
first of all, read what I have to say on this subject.
When we say that it is impossible for a client of Mary
to be lost, we must not be understood as speaking of
those clients who take advantage of this devotion that
they may sin more freely. And therefore, those who
disapprove of the great praises bestowed on the clemency
of this most Blessed Virgin, because it causes the wicked
to take advantage of it to sin with greater freedom, do
so without foundation, for such presumptive people
deserve chastisement, and not mercy, for their rash
confidence. It is therefore to be understood of those
clients who, with a sincere desire to amend, are faithful in honouring and recommending themselves to the
Mother of God. It is, I say, morally impossible that
such as these should be lost. And I find that Father
Crasset, in his book on devotion towards the Blessed
Virgin Mary, says the same thing.[1] As did also Vega,
before him, in his Marian Theology, Mendoza, and

[1] Tom. i. q. 7.

other theologians.   And that we may see that they did
not speak at random, let us examine what other Saints
and learned men have said on this subject ; and let no
one be surprised if many of these quotations are alike,
for I have wished to give them all, in order to show
how unanimous the various writers have been on this
subject.

Saint Anselm says, ' that as it is impossible for one
who is not devout to Mary, and consequently not protected by her, to be saved, so is it impossible for one
who recommends himself to her, and consequently is
beloved by her, to be lost.'[3]   Saint Antoninus repeats
the same thing, and almost in the same words : ' As it
is impossible for those from whom Mary turns her eyes
of mercy to be saved, so also are those towards whom
she turns these eyes, and for whom she prays, necessarily saved and glorified.'[4]   Consequently the clients
of Mary will necessarily be saved.

Let us pay particular attention to the first part of
the opinions of these Saints, and let those tremble who
make but little account of, or from carelessness give up
their devotion to, this Divine Mother.   They say that
the salvation of those who are not protected by Mary
is impossible.   Many others declare the same thing ;
such as Blessed Albert, who says, that ' all those who
are not thy servants, O Mary, will perish.'[5]   And Saint
Bonaventure : ' He who neglects the service of the Blessed
Virgin will die in his sins.'[6]   Again, ' He who does not
invoke thee, O Lady, will never get to heaven.'[7]   And,
on the 99th Psalm the Saint even says, ' that not only

---

[3] Sicut enim, O Beatissima, omnis a te aversus et a te despectus necesse
est ut intereat, ita omnis ad te conversus et a te respectus impossibile est ut
pereat.—*In Depr.* li. *ad B.V.*

[4] Impossibile est, quod illi, quibus Maria oculos suæ misericordiæ avertit
salventur; ita necessarium quod hi, ad quos convertit oculos suos, pro eis
advocans, justificentur et glorificentur.—P. iv. tit. xv. cap. 14.

[5] Gens et regnum quod non servierit tibi . . . peribit.—*Bibl. Mar. in Is.*
No. 20.

[6] Qui . . . neglexerit illam, morietur in peccatis suis.—*In Ps.* cxvi. *B.V.*

[7] Qui te non invocat in hac vita, non perveniet ad regnum Dei.—*In Ps.*
lxxxvi. *B.M.V.*

those from whom Mary turns her face will not be saved,
but that there will be no hope of their salvation.'[8]
Before him, Saint Ignatius the martyr said, 'that it
was impossible for any sinner to be saved without the
help and favour of the most Blessed Virgin; because
those who are not saved by the justice of God are,
with infinite mercy, saved by the intercession of Mary.'[9]
Some doubt as to whether this passage is truly of Saint
Ignatius; but, at all events, as Father Crasset remarks,
it was adopted by Saint John Chrysostom.[10] It is also
repeated by the venerable Raymond Jordano.[11] And
in the same sense does the Church apply to Mary the
words of Proverbs, "All that hate me, love death:"[12]
that is, all who do not love me, love eternal death.
For, as Richard of Saint Lawrence says on the words
of the same book, " She is like the merchant's ship,"[13]
'All those who are out of this ship will be lost in the
sea of the world.'[14] Even the heretical Œcolampadius
looked upon little devotion to the Mother of God as a
certain mark of reprobation: and therefore he said,
'Far be it from me ever to turn from Mary.'[15]

But, on the other hand, Mary says in the words ap--
plied to her by the Church, "He that hearkeneth to me
shall not be confounded;"[16] that is to say, he that lis-
teneth to what I say shall not be lost. On which Saint
Bonaventure says, 'O Lady, he who honours thee will
be far from damnation.'[17] And this will still be the

---

[8] A quibus averteris vultum tuum non erit spes ad salutem.—*In Ps.* xcix. *B.M.V.*

[9] Impossibile est aliquem salvari peccatorem, nisi per tuum, O Virgo, auxilium et favorem. Quia quos non salvat Dei justitia, salvat sua intercessione Maria, misericordia infinita.—*Ap. Lyr. Tris. Mar.* l. ii. m. 45.

[10] In Deprec. ad Virg. †

[11] In Contempl. B. Virg. c. v.

[12] Omnes qui me oderunt, diligunt mortem.—*Prov.* viii. 36.

[13] Facta est quasi navis institoris.—*Prov.* xxxi. 14.

[14] In mare mundi submergentur omnes illi, quos non suscepit navis ista.—*De Laud. V.* lib. xi. cap. 8.

[15] Nunquam de me audietur, quasi averser Mariam, erga quam minus bene affici reprobatæ mentis certum existimem indicium.—*S. de Laud. D. in M.*

[16] Qui audit me non confundetur.—*Eccles.* xxiv. 30.

[17] Qui ... præstat in obsequio tuo procul fiat a perditione.—*In Ps.* cxviii. *B.M V.*

case, Saint Hilary observes, even should the person during the past time have greatly offended God. 'However great a sinner he may have been,' says the Saint, 'if he shows himself devout to Mary, he will never perish.'[18]

For this reason the devil does his utmost with sinners, in order that, after they have lost the grace of God, they may also lose devotion to Mary. When Sarah saw Isaac in company with Ismael, who was teaching him evil habits, she desired that Abraham would drive away both Ismael and his mother Agar : "Cast out this bond-woman and her son."[19] She was not satisfied with the son being turned out of the house, but insisted on the mother going also, thinking that otherwise the son, coming to see his mother, would continue to frequent the house. The devil, also, is not satisfied with a soul turning out Jesus Christ, unless it also turns out His Mother: "Cast out this bond-woman and her Son." Otherwise he fears that the Mother will again, by her intercession, bring back her Son. 'And his fears are well grounded,' says the learned Pacciuchelli ; 'for he who is faithful in serving the Mother of God will soon receive God Himself by the means of Mary.'[20] Saint Ephrem, then, was right in calling devotion to our Blessed Lady 'a divine charter,'[21] our safeguard from hell. The same Saint also calls the Divine Mother the only hope of those who are in despair.'[22] That which Saint Bernard says is certainly true, 'that neither the power nor the will to save us can be wanting to Mary :'[23] the power cannot be wanting, for it is impossible that her prayers should not be heard ; as Saint Antoninus says, 'It is impossible that a Mother of God

[18] Quantumcumque quis fuerit peccator, si Mariæ devotus extiterit, nunquam in æternum peribit.—*Cœn.* xii. *in Matt.* †
[19] Ejice ancillam hanc et filium ejus.—*Gen.* xxi. 10.
[20] Qui Dei Genitrici perseveranter obsequitur, non multa mora et Deum ipsum in se recipiet.—*In Salv. Reg.* exc. 5.
[21] Charta divinissima.—*Or. de Laud.* V.
[22] Unica spes desperantium.—*Ib.*
[23] Nec facultas ei deesse poterit nec voluntas.—*Serm.* i. *de Assump. B. V. al.*

should pray in vain ;'[24] and Saint Bernard says the same
thing : ' that her requests can never be refused, but
that she obtains whatever she wills.'[25]   The will to save
us cannot be wanting, for Mary is our Mother, and desires our salvation more than we can desire it ourselves.
Since, then, this is the case, how can it be possible for a
client of Mary to be lost ?   He may be a sinner, but if
he recommends himself to this good Mother with perseverance and purpose of amendment, she will undertake to obtain him light to abandon his wicked state,
sorrow for his sins, perseverance in virtue, and, finally,
a good death.   And what mother would not deliver
her son from death if it only depended on her asking
the favour to obtain it from the judge ?   And can we
think that Mary, who loves her clients with a mother's
most tender love, will not deliver her child from eternal
death when she can do it so easily ?

Ah ! devout reader, let us thank our Lord if we see
that He has given us affection for, and confidence in,
the Queen of Heaven : ' for,' says Saint John Damascen, ' God only grants this favour to those whom He is
determined to save.'   The following are the beautiful
words of the Saint, and with which he rekindles his
own and our hope : ' O Mother of God, if I place my
confidence in thee, I shall be saved.   If I am under
thy protection, I have nothing to fear, for the fact of
being thy client is the possession of a certainty of salvation, and which God only grants to those whom
He intends to save.'[26]   Therefore Erasmus salutes the
Blessed Virgin in these words : ' Hail ! O terror of
hell ; O hope of Christians ; confidence in thee is a
pledge of salvation.'[27]

O, how enraged is the devil when he sees a soul per--
severing in devotion to the Divine Mother !   We read

[24] Impossibile erat eam non exaudiri.—P. iv. tit. xv. c. 17.
[25] Quod quærit, invenit, et frustrari non potest.—Serm. de Aquæd.
[26] Ap. Crasset, Vér. Dév. p. 1. tr. 1. q. 6.
[27] Salve inferorum formido, Christianorum spes ; quo major est tua præ-
cellentia, hoc certior est nostra fiducia.—Pœan. ad Virg.

in the Life of Blessed Alphonsus Rodriguez, who was very devout to Mary, that once when in prayer, finding himself much troubled by the devil with impure thoughts, this enemy said, ' Give up thy devotion to Mary, and I will cease to tempt thee.'

We read in Blosius that God revealed to Saint Catherine of Sienna, 'that in His goodness, and on account of the Incarnate Word, He had granted to Mary, who was His Mother, that no one, not even a sinner, who devoutly recommends himself to her should ever become the prey of hell.'[28] Even the Prophet David prayed to be delivered from hell, for the sake of the love he bore to Mary. " I have loved, O Lord, the beauty of Thy house . . . take not away my soul, O God, with the wicked."[29] He says of ' Thy house,' for Mary was the house that God Himself constructed for His dwelling on earth, and in which He could find repose on becoming man, as it is written in the book of Proverbs, " Wisdom hath built herself a house."[30] ' No,' says Saint Ignatius the martyr; ' he who is devout to the Virgin Mother will certainly never be lost.'[31] And Saint Bonaventure confirms this, saying, ' Thy lovers, O Lady, enjoy peace in this life, and will never see eternal death.'[32] The devout Blosius assures us, ' that the case never did and never will occur in which a humble and attentive servant of Mary was lost.'[33]

' O, how many would have remained obstinate in sin, and have been eternally lost,' says Thomas à Kempis,

---

[28] Mariæ unigeniti Filii mei gloriosæ genitrici a bonitate mea concessum est propter incarnati Verbi reverentiam, ut quicumque etiam peccator ad eam cum devota veneratione recurrit, nullo modo diripiatur a dæmone infernali. —*Conc. An. Fid.* p. ii. cap. i.

[29] Domine, dilexi decorem domus tuæ . . . Ne perdas cum impiis, Deus, animam meam.—*Ps.* xxv. 8, 9.

[30] Sapientia ædificavit sibi domum.—*Prov.* ix. 1.

[31] Numquid peribit, qui genitrici Virgini devotus, sedulusque extiterit.— *Lohner. Bibl.* t. 70. § 3.

[32] Pax multa diligentibus te, Domina : anima eorum non videbit mortem in æternum.—*Ps.* lxvii. *B.M.V.*

[33] Fieri non potest, ut pereat qui Mariæ sedulus et humilis cultor fuerit.— *In Can. Vit. Spir.* cap. xviii.

'if Mary had not interposed with her Son, that He might show them mercy !'[34] It is also the opinion of many theologians, and of Saint Thomas[35] in particular, that for many who have died in mortal sin the Divine Mother has obtained from God a suspension of their sentence, and a return to life to do penance. Trustworthy authors give us many instances in which this has occurred. Amongst others, Flodoardus, who lived about the ninth century, relates in his Chronicles,[36] that a certain deacon named Adelman, who was apparently dead, and was being buried, returned to life, and said 'that he had seen hell, to which he was condemned, but that, at the prayers of the Blessed Virgin, he had been sent back to this world to do penance.'

Surius relates a similar case[37] of a Roman citizen named Andrew, who had died impenitent, and for whom Mary obtained that he should come to life again, that he might be pardoned. Pelbertus[38] says, 'that in his time, when the Emperor Sigismund was crossing the Alps with his army, a voice was heard coming from a skeleton, asking for a confessor, and declaring that the Mother of God, for whom he had had a tender devotion when a soldier, had obtained that he should thus live until he had been able to make his confession; and, having done so, the soul departed.' These, and other such examples, however, must not encourage rash persons to live in sin, with the hope that Mary will deliver them from hell even should they die in this state; for as it would be the height of folly for anyone to throw himself into a well with a hope that Mary would preserve his life because she has occasionally preserved some under similar circumstances, still greater folly would it be to run the

---

[34] Quot fuissent æternaliter condemnati, vel in desperatione permansissent obstinati, nisi benignissima Virgo Maria pro eis interpellasset ad Filium!— P. iii. *Serm. ad Nov.* iv.

[35] Suppl. q. 71. a. 5.

[36] Chron. Eccl. Rem. anno 934.

[37] 4 Dec. S. Ann. l. 1. c. 35.

[38] Stellar. Cor. B.V. lib. xii. p. 2, a. 1.

risk of dying in sin, in the hope that the Blessed Virgin would save him from hell. But these examples serve to revive our confidence with the reflection, that if the Divine Mother has been able to deliver from hell even some who have died in sin, how much more will she be able to preserve from a similar lot those who, during life, have recourse to her with a purpose of amendment, and who serve her faithfully!

'What, then, will be our lot, O tender Mother,' let us ask with Saint Germanus, 'who are sinners, but desire to change, and have recourse to thee, who art the life of Christians?'[39] Saint Anselm says, 'that he will not be lost for whom thou once prayest.'[40] O, pray, then, for us, and we shall be preserved from hell. 'Who,' exclaims Richard of Saint Victor, 'will presume to say, if I have thee to defend me, O Mother of mercy, that the Judge will be unfavourable to me when I am presented before the Divine tribunal?'[41] Blessed Henry Suso used to say, 'that he had placed his soul in the hands of Mary, and that if he was condemned, the sentence must pass through her hands;'[42] being confident that if it was in such hands, this tender Virgin would certainly prevent its execution. The same do I hope for myself, O my own most holy Queen; and therefore I will always repeat the words of Saint Bonaventure : 'In thee, O Lady, have I placed all my hopes; and thus I confidently trust that I shall never be lost, but praise and love thee for ever in heaven.'[43]

EXAMPLE.

In the year 1604, in a city of Flanders, there were

---

[39] Quidnam autem de nobis fiet, O sanctissima Deipara, spiritus et vita Christianorum ?—*De Zona Virg.*

[40] Æternum væ non sentiet ille pro quo semel oraverit Maria. †

[41] Si . . . accedam ad judicium, et matrem misericordiæ in causa mea habuero mecum, quis judicem denegabit propitium ?—*In Cant.* cap. xxxix.

[42] Si judex servum suum damnare voluerit, per manus tuas piissimas, O Maria, hoc faciat.—*Hor. Sap.* l. i. c. 16.

[43] In te, Domina, speravi ; non confundar in æternum.—*Ps.* xxx. *B.M.V.*

two young men, students, but who, instead of attending to their studies, gave themselves up to a life of debauchery. One night they were both in a house with an evil companion, when one of them, named Richard, returned home, leaving his companion there. After he got home, and had begun to undress, he remembered he had not that day said some 'Hail Marys' that he was in the habit of reciting. Feeling very sleepy he was loth to say them; he did himself violence, and repeated them, though without devotion, and half asleep. He then lay down, and had fallen into a sound slumber, when he was suddenly roused by a violent knocking at the door, and without its opening he saw his companion, deformed and hideous, standing before him. 'Who art thou?' he cried out. 'What! dost thou not know me?' 'Ah, yes! but how thou art changed; thou seemest to me a devil.' 'Truly,' he exclaimed, 'poor unfortunate creature that I am, I am damned; and how? When I was leaving that wicked house, a devil came and strangled me: my body is in the street, and my soul in hell; and thou must know,' added he, 'that the same fate awaited thee, had not the Blessed Virgin preserved thee in consideration of that little act of homage of the 'Hail, Mary.' Fortunate art thou if only thou knowest how to take advantage of this warning sent thee by the Mother of God.' With these words he opened his mantle, and, showing the flames and serpents by which he was tormented, he disappeared. Richard immediately burst into sobs and tears, and, casting himself prostrate on the ground, he returned thanks to Mary, his protectress; and, whilst thinking how to change his life, he heard the bell of the Franciscan monastery ringing for matins. 'Ah! it is there,' says he, 'that God calls me to do penance.' He went straight off to the convent, and implored the fathers to admit him. But they were hardly willing to do so, knowing his wicked life; but he, sobbing bitterly, told all that had taken place; and two fathers being sent to the street, and having found the strangled body, which was as black as a coal, they admitted him.   From that time forward Richard led a most exemplary life, and at length went to preach the gospel in the Indies, and thence to Japan, where he had the happiness of giving his life for Jesus Christ, being burnt alive for the Faith.[44]

PRAYER.

O Mary, my most dear Mother, in what an abyss of evils should I not now be, if thou hadst not so many times delivered me with thy compassionate hand !   How many years ago should I not have been in hell, hadst thou not saved me by thy powerful prayers !   My grievous sins already drove me there ; Divine justice had already condemned me ; the devils already longed to execute the sentence ; and thou didst fly to my aid, and save me without being even called or asked.   And what return can I make to thee, O my beloved protectress, for so many favours and for such love ?   Thou also didst overcome the hardness of my heart, and didst draw me to thy love and to confidence in thee.   And into how many other evils should I not have fallen, if with thy compassionate hand thou hadst not so often helped me in the dangers into which I was on the point of falling !   Continue, O my hope, to preserve me from hell, and from the sins into which I may still fall. Never allow me to have this misfortune—to curse thee in hell.   My beloved Lady, I love thee.   Can thy goodness ever endure to see a servant of thine that loves thee lost ?   Ah ! then, obtain that I may never more be ungrateful to thee and to my God, who for the love of thee has granted me so many graces.   O Mary, tell

[44] Appresso il P. Alf. And. de Bapt. Virg. †   In the church of Ham-sur-Heure, in Hainault, there is a picture of the martyrdom of F. Richard of St. Anne with the following inscription : " The Bl. F. Richard of St. Anne, born at Ham-sur-Heure in 1585, made his religious profession as a Recollect at Nivelles, April 13, 1605, and having been ordained Priest in the Philippine Isles, was martyred at Nagasaki, September 10, 1622, being put to death by slow fire."   Note from F. Dujardin's translation.—ED.

me, shall I be lost? Yes, if I abandon thee. But is this possible? Can I ever forget the love thou hast borne me? Thou, after God, art the love of my soul. I can no longer trust myself to live without loving thee. O most beautiful, most holy, most amiable, sweetest creature in the world, I rejoice in thy happiness, I love thee, and I hope always to love thee both in time and in eternity. Amen.

SECTION II. *Mary succours her Clients in Purgatory.*

Fortunate, indeed, are the clients of this most compassionate Mother ; for not only does she succour them in this world, but even in purgatory they are helped and comforted by her protection. And as in that prison poor souls are in the greatest need of assistance, since in their torments they cannot help themselves, our Mother of mercy does proportionately more to relieve them. Saint Bernardine of Sienna says, ' that in that prison, where souls which are spouses of Jesus Christ are detained, Mary has a certain dominion and plenitude of power, not only to relieve them, but even to deliver them from their pains.'[1]

And, first, with respect to the relief she gives. The same Saint, in applying those words of Ecclesiasticus, "I have walked in the waves of the sea,"[2] adds, ' that it is by visiting and relieving the necessities and torments of her clients, who are her children.'[3] He then says, ' that the pains of purgatory are called waves, because they are transitory, unlike the pains of hell, which never end ; and they are called waves of the sea, because they are so bitter. The clients of Mary, thus suffering, are often visited and relieved by her.' ' See,

---

[1] Beata Virgo in regno purgatorii dominium tenet.—*Serm.* iii. *de Nom. Mar.* art. 2, cap. 3.

[2] In fluctibus maris ambulavi.—*Eccles.* xxiv. 8.

[3] Scilicet, visitans et subveniens necessitatibus et tormentis devotorum meorum : immo et omnium qui ibi existunt, quia filii ejus sunt.—*Serm.* iii. *de Nom. M.* art. 2, cap.

therefore,' says Novarinus, 'of what consequence it is to
be the servant of this good Lady, for her servants she
never forgets when they are suffering in those flames;
for though Mary relieves all suffering souls in purgatory, yet she always obtains far greater indulgence and
relief for her own clients.'[4]

The Divine Mother once addressed these words to
Saint Bridget: 'I am the Mother of all souls in purgatory; for all the pains that they have deserved for
their sins are every hour, as long as they remain there,
in some way mitigated by my prayers.'[5] The compassionate Mother even condescends to go herself occasionally into that holy prison, to visit and comfort
her suffering children. Saint Bonaventure, applying to
Mary the words of Ecclesiasticus, "I have penetrated
into the bottom of the deep,"[6] says, 'the deep, that is,
purgatory, to relieve by my presence the holy souls
detained there.'[7] 'O, how courteous and benign is the
most Blessed Virgin,' says Saint Vincent Ferrer, 'to
those who suffer in purgatory! through her they constantly receive comfort and refreshment.'[8]

And what other consolation have they in their
sufferings than Mary, and the relief they receive from
this Mother of mercy? Saint Bridget once heard Jesus
say to His holy Mother, 'Thou art My Mother, the
Mother of mercy, and the consolation of souls in purgatory.'[9] The Blessed Virgin herself told the Saint,
'that as a poor sick person, bedridden, suffering, and
abandoned, is relieved by words of encouragement and

---

[4] Vides quantum referat hic Virginem colere ac venerari, cum cultorum
suorum, in purgatoriis flammis existentium, non obliviscatur; et licet omnibus opem ac refrigerium ferat, id tamen præcipue erga suos præstat.—*Virg.
Umb.* exc. lxxxvi.

[5] Ego sum etiam mater omnium qui sunt in purgatorio : quia omnes
pœnæ, quæ debentur purgandis pro peccatis suis, in qualibet hora propter
preces meas quodammodo mitigantur.—*Rev.* lib. iv. cap. 138.

[6] Profundum abyssi penetravi.—*Eccles.* xxiv. 8.

[7] Abyssi, id est, purgatorii, adjuvans illas sanctas animas. †

[8] Maria . . . bona animabus purgatorii; quia per eam habent suffragium.
—*Serm.* ii. *in Nat. B.V.*

[9] Tu es mater mea . . . tu mater misericordiæ, tu consolatio eorum qui
sunt in purgatorio.—*Lib.* i. cap. 16.

consolation, so are the souls in purgatory consoled and relieved by only hearing her name.'[10] The mere name of Mary, that name of hope and salvation, and which is frequently invoked by her beloved children in their prison, is a great source of comfort to them ; ' for,' says Novarinus, ' that loving Mother no sooner hears them call upon her than she offers her prayers to God, and these prayers, as a heavenly dew, immediately refresh them in their burning pains.'[11]

Mary not only consoles and relieves her clients in purgatory, but she delivers them by her prayers. Gerson says, ' that on the day of her assumption into heaven purgatory was entirely emptied.'[12] Novarinus confirms this, saying, ' that it is maintained by many grave authors, that when Mary was going to heaven, she asked, as a favour from her Son, to take all the souls then in purgatory with her.'[13] ' And from that time forward,' says Gerson, ' Mary had the privilege of delivering her servants.' Saint Bernardine of Sienna also positively asserts, ' that the Blessed Virgin has the power of delivering souls from purgatory, but particularly those of her clients, by her prayers, and by applying her merits for them.'[14] Novarinus says, ' that by the merits of Mary, not only are the pains of those souls lessened, but the time of their sufferings is shortened through her intercession.'[15] She has only to ask, and all is done.

[10] Hoc nomen cum audiunt . . . illi, qui in purgatorio sunt, ultra modum gaudent, tanquam æger in lecto jacens, si audierit ab aliquibus verbum solatii.—Lib. i. cap. 9.

[11] Virginis nomen illarum pœnarum refrigerium est. Addit eadem Virgo preces, quibus veluti supero quodam rore, cruciatus illi magni mitigantur.—Virg. Umbr. exc. lxxxvi.

[12] Super. Magn. tr. 4.

[13] Ferunt quippe bonæ notæ auctores, Virginem morituram, in cœlumque ituram, a Filio hoc petiisse, ut omnes animas quæ in purgatorio detinebantur, secum ad gloriam ducere posset.—Umbr. Virg. exc. lxxxvi.

[14] Ab iis tormentis liberat Beata Virgo maxime devotos suos.—Serm. iii. de Nom. Mar. a. 2, c. 3.

[15] Crediderim . . . omnibus, qui in purgatricibus illis flammis purgarunt, Mariæ meritis, non solum leviores fuisse reditas illas pœnas . . . sed et breviores contractioresque, adeo ut, cruciatuum tempus contractum Virginis ope illis sit.—Umbr. Virg. exc. lxxxvi.

Saint Peter Damian relates, 'that a lady named Marozia appeared after her death to her godmother, and told her that on the feast of the Assumption she, together with a multitude exceeding the population of Rome, had been delivered by Mary from purgatory.'[16] Denis the Carthusian says, 'that on the feasts of the Nativity and Resurrection of Jesus Christ Mary does the same thing; for on those days, accompanied by choirs of angels, she visits that prison, and delivers very many souls from their torments.'[17] Novarinus says, 'that he can easily believe that on all her own solemn feasts she delivers many souls from their sufferings.'[18]

The promise made by our Blessed Lady to Pope John XXII. is well known. She appeared to him, and ordered him to make known to all that on the Saturday after their death she would deliver from purgatory all who wore the Carmelite scapular. This, as Father Crasset[19] relates, was proclaimed by the same Pontiff in a Bull, which was afterwards confirmed by Alexander V., Clement VII., Pius V., Gregory XIII., and Paul V.; and this latter, in a Bull of the year 1612, says, 'that Christian people may piously believe that the Blessed Virgin will help them after death by her continual intercession, her merits, and special protection; and that on Saturdays, the day consecrated by the Church to her, she will, in a more particular manner, help the souls of the brethren of the Confraternity of our Blessed Lady of Mount Carmel who have departed this life in a state of grace, provided they have worn the habit, observed the chastity of their state, and recited her office: or, if they could

---

[16] Tom. iii. opusc. 34; Disp. de Var. App. et Mirac. cap. iii.

[17] Beatissima Virgo singulis annis, in festivitate Nativitatis Christi, ad purgatorii loca cum multitudine angelorum descendit, et multas inde animas eripit. Etiam in nocte Dominicæ Resurrectionis solet descendere ad purgatorium, pro eductione animarum.—*S. Dion. Cart. Serm.* ii. *de Assump.*

[18] Facile autem crediderim, in Virginis honorem gaudiique cumulum, in quocumque Virginis festo plures animas ab illis pœnis eximi.—*Exc.* lxxxvi.

[19] Tom. ii. div. d. B. Virg. tr. 6, prat. 4.

not recite it, if they have observed the fasts of the Church, and abstained from meat on all Wednesdays except Christmas-day.' In the solemn office of our Blessed Lady of Mount Carmel we read, that it is piously believed that the Blessed Virgin comforts the brethren of this confraternity in purgatory with maternal love, and that by her intercession she soon delivers them, and takes them to heaven.[20]

Why should we not hope for the same graces and favours, if we are devout clients of this good Mother? And if we serve her with more special love, why can we not hope to go to heaven immediately after death, without even going to purgatory? This really took place in the case of Blessed Godfrey, to whom Mary sent the following message, by Brother Abondo: 'Tell Brother Godfrey to endeavour to advance rapidly in virtue, and thus he will belong to my Son and to me: and when his soul departs, I will not allow it to go to purgatory, but will take it and offer it to my Son.'[21] And if we wish to relieve the holy souls in purgatory, let us do so by imploring the aid of our Blessed Lady in all our prayers, and especially by offering the Rosary for them, as that relieves them greatly, as we shall see in the following example.

EXAMPLE.

Father Eusebius Nieremberg[22] says, that in a city of Aragon there was a beautiful young lady of noble birth named Alexandra, who was courted by two young men. Out of jealousy, they one day fought, and both were killed. Their enraged relatives, considering the young lady as the cause of this sad event, murdered her, cut off her head, and threw it into a

---

[20] Materno plane affectu, dum igne purgatorii expiantur, solari, ac in cœlestem patriam obtentu suo quantocius pie creditur efferre.—*In festo S. Mar. de Mont. Carm.* xvi. Jul.

[21] Men. Cist. 2 Oct.

[22] Troph. Marian. l. iv. c. 29.

well. Some days afterwards, Saint Dominic passing by the spot, and inspired by God, went to the well, and cried out, ' Alexandra, come forth !' In an instant the head of the murdered woman came up, and remained on the edge of the well, and entreated the Saint to hear her confession. The Saint did so, and in the presence of an immense concourse of people, drawn there by the wonderful event, gave her communion. He then commanded her to say for what reason she had received so great a grace. Alexandra replied, that when her head was cut off, she was in mortal sin ; but that, on account of the Rosary she was in the habit of saying in her honour, the most Blessed Virgin had kept her alive. The animated head remained for two days on the edge of the well, so as to be seen by all, and after that the soul went to purgatory. A fortnight afterwards Alexandra appeared, beautiful and shining like a star, to Saint Dominic, and said, that the Rosary recited for the souls in purgatory is one of the greatest reliefs that they meet with in their torments ; and that, as soon as ever they get to heaven, they pray earnestly for those who have performed this devotion for them. Hardly had she said this, when Saint Dominic saw her happy soul ascend with the greatest joy to the kingdom of the blessed.

PRAYER.

O Queen of heaven and earth ! O Mother of the Lord of the world ! O Mary, of all creatures the greatest, the most exalted, and the most amiable ! it is true that there are many in this world who neither know thee nor love thee ; but in heaven there are many millions of angels, and blessed spirits, who love and praise thee continually. Even in this world, how many happy souls are there not who burn with thy love, and live enamoured of thy goodness ! O, that I also could love thee, O Lady worthy of all love ! O that I could always remember to serve thee, to praise thee, to honour thee, and engage all to love thee! Thou hast attracted the love of God, whom, by thy beauty, thou hast, so to say, torn from the bosom of His Eternal Father, and engaged to become man, and be thy Son. And shall I, a poor worm of the earth, not be enamoured of thee? No, my most sweet Mother, I also will love thee much, and will do all that I can to make others love thee also. Accept, then, O Mary, the desire that I have to love thee, and help me to execute it. I know how favourably thy lovers are looked upon by God. He, after His own glory, desires nothing more than thine, and to see thee honoured and loved by all. From thee, O Lady, do I expect all; through thee the remission of my sins, through thee perseverance. Thou must assist me at death, and deliver me from purgatory; and, finally, thou must lead me to heaven. All this thy lovers hope from thee, and are not deceived. I, who love thee with so much affection, and above all other things, after God, hope for the same favours.

SECTION III. *Mary leads her Servants to Heaven.*

O, what an evident mark of predestination have the servants of Mary! The holy Church, for the consolation of her clients, puts into her mouth the words of Ecclesiasticus, "In all these I sought rest, and I shall abide in the inheritance of the Lord."[1] Cardinal Hugo explains these words, and says, ' Blessed is he in whose house the most Holy Virgin finds repose.'[2] Mary, out of the love she bears to all, endeavours to excite in all devotion towards herself; many either do not admit it into their souls, or do not preserve it. But blessed is he that receives and preserves it. "And

---

[1] In his omnibus requiem quæsivi, et in hæreditate Domini morabor.—*Eccles.* xxiv. 11.
[2] Beatus in cujus domo requiem invenerit.—*In Lib. Eccles.* cap. xxiv.

I shall abide in the inheritance of the Lord." 'That is,' adds the Cardinal, 'in those who are the inheritance of our Lord.' Devotion towards the Blessed Virgin remains in all who are the inheritance of our Lord; that is to say, in all, who will praise Him eternally in heaven. Mary continues, speaking in the words of Ecclesiasticus : " He that made me rested in my tabernacle, and He said to me: Let thy dwelling be in Jacob, and thy inheritance in Israel, and take root in My elect."[3] That is, my Creator has condescended to come and repose in my bosom, and His will is, that I should dwell in the hearts of all the elect (of whom Jacob was a figure, and who are the inheritance of the Blessed Virgin), and that devotion and confidence in me should take root in all the predestined. O, how many blessed souls are there now in heaven, who would never have been there, had not Mary, by her powerful intercession, led them thither : " I made that in the heavens there should rise light that never faileth."[4] Cardinal Hugo, in his commentary on the above text of Ecclesiasticus, says, in the name of Mary, 'I have caused as many lights to shine eternally in heaven as I have clients;' and then he adds, 'There are many saints in heaven through her intercession, who would never have been there but through her.'[5] Saint Bonaventure says, 'that the gates of heaven will open to all who confide in the protection of Mary.'[6] Hence, Saint Ephrem calls devotion to the Divine Mother 'the unlocking of the gates of the heavenly Jerusalem.'[7] The devout Blosius also, addressing our Blessed Lady, says, 'To thee, O Lady, are committed

[3] Qui creavit me requievit in tabernaculo meo ; et dixit mihi : In Jacob inhabita, et in Israel hæreditare, et in electis meis mitte radices.—*Eccles.* xxiv. 12, 13.

[4] Ego feci in cœlis ut oriretur lumen indeficiens.—*Ib.* 6.

[5] Multi . . . sancti sunt in cœlis intercessione ejus, qui nunquam ibi fuissent nisi per eam.—*In Lib. Eccles.* cap. xxiv.

[6] Qui speraverit in illa, porta paradisi reserabitur ei.—*In Ps.* xc. *de B.M.V.*

[7] Portarum cœlestis paradisi reseramentum.—*Orat. de Laud. Virg.*

the keys and the treasures of the kingdom of heaven.'[8]
And therefore we ought constantly to pray to her, in
the words of Saint Ambrose, ' Open to us, O Mary, the
gates of paradise, since thou hast its keys.'[9] Nay more,
the Church says, that ' thou art its gate.'

For the same reason, again, is this great Mother
called by the Church the Star of the Sea, ' Hail, Star
of the Sea !' ' For,' says the angelical Saint Thomas,
' as sailors are guided by a star to the port, so are
Christians guided to heaven by Mary.'[10]

For the same reason, finally, is she called, by Saint
Peter Damian, ' the heavenly ladder.'   ' For,' says the
Saint, ' by Mary God descended from heaven into the
world, that by her men might ascend from earth to
heaven.'[11] ' And thou, O Lady,' says Saint Athanasius,
' wast filled with grace, that thou mightest be the way
of our salvation, and the means of ascent to the heavenly kingdom.'[12]   Saint Bernard calls our Blessed
Lady ' the heavenly chariot.'[13]   And Saint John Geometra salutes her, saying, ' Hail, resplendent car !'[14]
signifying that she is the car in which her clients
mount to heaven. ' Blessed are they who know thee,
O Mother of God,' says Saint Bonaventure ; ' for the
knowledge of thee is the high road to everlasting life,
and the publication of thy virtues is the way of eternal
salvation.'[15]

In the Franciscan chronicles it is related, that
Brother Leo once saw a red ladder, on the summit of

---

[8] Tibi regni cœlestis claves thesaurique commissi sunt.—*Parad. An.* p. ii.
cap. 4.

[9] Aperi nobis, O Virgo, cœlum, cujus claves habes. †

[10] Convenit ei nomen Maria, quæ interpretatur Stella maris : quia sicut
per stellam maris navigantes diriguntur ad portum, ita Christiani diriguntur
per Mariam ad gloriam.—*Opusc.* viii.

[11] Scala cœlestis, per quam Supernus Rex humiliatus ad ima descendit, et
homo, qui prostratus jacebat, ad superna exaltatus, ascendit.—*Hom. in Nat.
B.M.V.*

[12] Ave gratiosa, Dominus tecum : quod facta sis nobis salutis via ; ascen-
susque ad superos.—*Serm.* i. *in Annunc. B.M.V.*

[13] Tibi vehiculum voluit providere.—*Serm. de Aquæd.*

[14] Gaude . . . clarissime currus.—*Hymn.* i. *in Deip. Virg.*

[15] Scire et cognoscere te est radix immortalitatis : et enarrare virtutes
tuas est via salutis.—*Ps.* lxxxv. *B.M.V.*

which was Jesus Christ; and a white one, on the top
of which was His most holy Mother; and he saw some
who tried to ascend the red ladder, and they mounted
a few steps, and fell—they tried again, and again fell.
They were then advised to go and try the white ladder,
and by that one they easily ascended, for our Blessed
Lady stretched out her hand and helped them, and
so they got safely to heaven.[16]   Denis the Carthusian
asks, 'Who is there that is saved? who is there that
reigns in heaven?'   And he answers, 'They are certainly saved and reign in heaven for whom this Queen
of mercy intercedes.'[17]   And this Mary herself confirms
in the book of Proverbs, "By me kings reign;"[18] through
my intercession souls reign, first in this mortal life by
ruling their passions, and so come to reign eternally in
heaven, where, says Saint Augustine, 'all are kings.'[19]
'Mary, in fine,' says Richard of Saint Lawrence, 'is
the mistress of heaven; for there she commands as she
wills, and admits whom she wills.'   And applying to
her the words of Ecclesiasticus, "And my power was
in Jerusalem,"[20] he makes her say, 'I command what I
will, and introduce whom I will.'[21]   Our Blessed Lady,
being Mother of the Lord of Heaven, it is reasonable
that she also should be sovereign Lady of that kingdom, according to Rupert, who says, 'that by right she
possesses the whole kingdom of her Son.'[22]   Saint Antoninus tells us 'that this Divine Mother has already,
by her assistance and prayers, obtained heaven for us,
provided we put no obstacle in the way.'[23]   Hence,
says the Abbot Guarric, 'he who serves Mary, and for

---

[16] Wadding. ann. 1232. n. 28.

[17] Quis salvatur? quis regnat in cœlo? Illi sane pro quibus Regina misericordiæ interpellat. †

[18] Per me reges regnant.—*Prov.* viii. 15.

[19] Quot cives, tot reges. †

[20] In Jerusalem potestas mea.—*Eccles.* xxiv. 15.

[21] Imperando scilicet, quidquid volo . . . et quos volo introducendo.—*De
Laud. Virg.* lib. iv. cap. 4.

[22] Regina cœlorum totum jure possidens Filii regnum.—Lib. iii. *in Cant.*

[23] Cœleste nobis regnum suo interventu, auxiliis et precibus impetravit.—
S. Ant. p. iv. tit. 15. c. 2. § 1. †

whom she intercedes, is as certain of heaven as if he was already there.'[24] Saint John Damascen also says, 'that to serve Mary and be her courtier is the greatest honour we can possibly possess; for to serve the Queen of Heaven is already to reign there, and to live under her commands is more than to govern.'[25] On the other hand, he adds, 'that those who do not serve Mary will not be saved; for those who are deprived of the help of this great Mother are also deprived of that of her Son and of the whole court of heaven.'[26] 'May the infinite goodness of our Lord be ever praised,' says Saint Bernard, 'for having been pleased to give us Mary as our advocate in heaven, that she, being at the same time the Mother of our Judge and a Mother of mercy, may be able, by her intercession, to conduct to a prosperous issue the great affair of our eternal salvation.'[27] Saint James, a doctor of the Greek Church, says, 'that God destined Mary as a bridge of salvation, by using which we might with safety pass over the stormy sea of this world, and reach the happy haven of paradise.'[28] Therefore Saint Bonaventure exclaims, 'Give ear, O ye nations; and all you who desire heaven, serve, honour Mary, and certainly you will find eternal life.'[29]

Nor should those even who have deserved hell be in the least doubtful as to obtaining heaven, provided they are faithful in serving this Queen. 'O, how many sinners,' says Saint Germanus, 'have found God and

[24] Qui Virgini famulatur, ita securus est de paradiso, ac si esset in paradiso.—*Guerricus abbas.* †

[25] Summus honor servire Mariæ, et de ejus esse familia. Etenim ei servire regnare est, et ejus agi frænis plusquam regium.—*Damasc. de Exc. V.* c. ix. †

[26] Gens quæ non servierit illi, peribit. Gentes destitutæ tantæ Matris auxilio destituuntur auxilio Filii et totius curiæ cœlestis.—*Ib.* †

[27] Advocatam præmisit peregrinatio nostra: quæ tamquam Judicis Mater et mater misericordiæ, suppliciter et efficaciter salutis nostræ negotia pertractabit.—*Serm.* i. *de Ass.*

[28] Eam tu pontem fecisti, quo a mundi fluctibus trajicientes, ad tranquillum portum tuum perveniamus.—*In Nat. Deip.*

[29] Audite hæc, omnes gentes . . . qui ingredi cupitis regnum Dei. Virginem Mariam honorate: et invenietis vitam et salutem perpetuam.—*Ps* xlviii. *B.M.V.*

have been saved by thy means, O Mary!"[30] Richard
of Saint Lawrence remarks, that Saint John in the
Apocalypse says that Mary was crowned with stars:
"And on her head a crown of twelve stars."[31] On the
other hand, in the sacred Canticles, she is said to be
crowned with wild beasts, lions, and leopards: "Come
from Libanus, my spouse, come from Libanus, come;
thou shalt be crowned . . . from the dens of the lions,
from the mountains of the leopards."[32] How is this?
He answers, that 'these wild beasts are sinners, who
by the favour and intercession of Mary have become
stars of paradise, better adapted to the head of this
Queen of mercy than all the material stars of heaven.'[33]
We read in the life of the servant of God, Sister Sera-
phina of Capri, that once during the novena of the
Assumption of Mary she asked our Blessed Lady for
the conversion of a thousand sinners, but afterwards
thought that she had asked too much; and then the
Blessed Virgin appeared to her, and corrected her for
her ungrounded anxiety, saying, 'Why dost thou fear?
Is it that I am not sufficiently powerful to obtain from
my Son the conversion of a thousand sinners? See, I
have already obtained the favour.' With these words,
she took her in spirit to heaven, and there showed her
innumerable souls which had deserved hell, but had
been saved through her intercession, and were already
enjoying eternal happiness.

It is true that in this world no one can be certain
of his salvation: "Man knoweth not whether he be
worthy of love or hatred," says Ecclesiastes.[34] But
Saint Bonaventure, on the words of King David, "Lord,

---

[30] Per te peccatores exquisierunt Deum, et salvi facti sunt.—*In Dorm. B.V.* orat. ii.

[31] Et in capite ejus corona stellarum duodecim.—*Apoc.* xii. 1.

[32] Veni de Libano, sponsa mea, veni de Libano, veni: coronaberis de cubilibus leonum, de montibus pardorum.—*Cant.* iv. 8.

[33] Et quid est hoc? nisi quod feræ per gratiam et orationes Mariæ fiunt stellæ, ut conveniant capiti tantæ reginæ.—*De Laud. V.* lib. iii. cap. 13.

[34] Nescit homo, utrum amore an odio dignus sit. Sed omnia in futurum servantur incerta.—*Eccl.* ix. 1, 2.

who shall dwell in Thy tabernacle ?"[35] and on the preceding quotation, answers, 'Sinners, let us follow Mary
closely, and casting ourselves at her feet, let us not leave
them until she has blessed us ; for her blessing will insure our salvation.'[36]   'It suffices, O Lady,' says Saint
Anselm, 'that thou willest it, and our salvation is certain.'[37]   And Saint Antoninus says that, 'souls protected
by Mary, and on which she casts her eyes, are necessarily justified and saved.'[38]

'With reason, therefore,' observes Saint Ildephonsus,
'did the most Holy Virgin predict that all generations
would call her blessed ;'[39] 'for all the elect obtain eternal
salvation through the means of Mary.'[40]   'And thou,
O great Mother,' says Saint Methodius, 'art the beginning, the middle, and the end of our happiness ;'[41]—the
beginning, for Mary obtains us the pardon of our sins ;
the middle, for she obtains us perseverance in divine
grace ; and the end, for she finally obtains us heaven.
'By thee, O Mary, was heaven opened,' says St. Bernard ; 'by thee was hell emptied ; by thee was paradise
restored ; and through thee, in fine, is eternal life given
to so many miserable creatures who deserved eternal
death.'[42]

But that which above all should encourage us to
hope with confidence for heaven, is the beautiful promise made by Mary herself to all who honour her, and
especially to those who, by word and example, endea-

[35] Domine, quis habitabit in tabernaculo tuo ?—*Ps.* xiv. 1.

[36] Amplectamur Mariæ vestigia peccatores : et ejus beatis pedibus provolvamur. Teneamus eam fortiter, nec dimittamus, donec ab ea meruimus
benedici.—*Ps.* xiv. *B.M.V.*

[37] Tantummodo . . . velis salutem nostram, et vere nequaquam salvi esse
non poterimus.—*De Exc. Virg.* cap. vi.

[38] Necessarium est, quod hi, ad quos (Maria) convertit oculos suos, pro eis
advocans, justificentur et glorificentur.—P. iv. tit. xv. c. 17.

[39] Beatam me dicent omnes generationes.—*Luc.* i. 48.

[40] Beata jure dicitur, quia omnes ex ea beatificantur.—*Serm.* iii. *de
Assump.*

[41] Tu solemnitatis nostræ exordium, tu medium, tu finis.—*De Simeone et
Anna.*

[42] Per te . . . cœlum repletum, infernus evacuatus est : instauratæ ruinæ
cœlestis Jerusalem : expectantibus miseris vita perdita data.—*Serm.* iv. *de
Assump. B. Virg.*

vour to make her known and honoured by others:
"They that work by me shall not sin; they that explain me shall have life everlasting."[43]   ' O, happy they
who obtain the favour of Mary !' exclaims Saint Bonaventure ; 'they will be recognised by the blessed as
their companions, and whoever bears the stamp of a
servant of Mary is already enrolled in the Book of Life.'[44]
Why, then, should we trouble ourselves about the opinions of scholastics as to whether predestination to glory
precedes or follows the prevision of merits ?   If we are
true servants of Mary, and obtain her protection, we
most certainly shall be inscribed in the Book of Life ;
for, says Saint John Damascen, ' God only grants devotion towards His most Holy Mother to those whom
He will save.'   This is also clearly expressed by our
Lord in Saint John : " He that shall overcome . . . I
will write upon him the name of My God, and the name
of the city of My God."[45]   And who but Mary is this
city of God ? observes Saint Gregory, on the words of
David : " Glorious things are said of thee, O city of
God."[46]

Correctly, then, can we here say with Saint Paul,
"Having this seal, the Lord knoweth who are His ;"[47]
that is to say, whoever carries with him the mark of
devotion to Mary is recognised by God as His.   Hence
Saint Bernard writes, that 'devotion to the Mother of
God is a most certain mark of eternal salvation.'[48]   Blessed
Alan, speaking of the 'Hail Mary,' also says, that 'whoever often honours our Blessed Lady with this angelical salutation has a very great mark of predestination.'[49]

---

[43] Qui operantur in me, non peccabunt; qui elucidant me, vitam æternam habebunt.—*Eccl.* xxiv. 30, 31.

[44] Qui acquirit gratiam Mariæ, agnoscetur a civibus paradisi ; et qui habuerit characterem nominis ejus, adnotabitur in libro vitæ.—*Ps.* xci. *de
B. V. M.*

[45] Qui vicerit . . . scribam super eum nomen Dei mei, et nomen civitatis
Dei mei.—*Apoc.* iii. 12.

[46] Gloriosa dicta sunt de te, civitas Dei.—*Ps.* lxxxvi. 3.

[47] Habens signaculum hoc, cognovit Dominus qui sunt ejus.—2 *Tim.* ii. 19.

[48] Certissimum est signum salutis æternæ consequendæ. †

[49] Habentibus devotionem ad hanc, signum est prædestinationis permag-
num ad gloriam.—*De Psalt.* p. 2. c. 11.

He says the same thing of perseverance in the daily recital of the Rosary, 'that those who do so have a very great assurance of salvation.'[50]   Father Nieremberg says, in the tenth chapter of his book on *Affection for Mary*, that 'the servants of the Mother of God are not only privileged and favoured in this world, but even in heaven they are more particularly honoured.'   He then adds : 'that in heaven they will be recognised as servants of its Queen, and as belonging to her court, by a distinguishing and richer garment,' according to the words of the Proverbs, "All her domestics are clothed with double garments."[51]

Saint Mary Magdalen of Pazzi saw a vessel in the midst of the sea : in it were all the clients of Mary, and this Blessed Mother herself steered it safely into the port.   By this the Saint understood, that those who live under the protection of Mary are secure, in the midst of the dangers of this life, from the shipwreck of sin, and from eternal damnation ; for she guides them safely into the haven of salvation.   Let us then enter this blessed ship of the mantle of Mary, and there we can be certain of the kingdom of heaven ; for the Church says : 'O holy Mother of God, all those who will be partakers of eternal happiness dwell in thee, living under thy protection.'[52]

EXAMPLE.

Cæsarius[53] relates, that a Cistercian who was very devout to the Blessed Virgin desired to receive a visit from this dear Lady, and continually asked for it in his prayers.   Being one night in the garden, as he was looking up to heaven and sighing with the desire of seeing her, he beheld a beautiful virgin coming down from heaven surrounded with light, who said to him,

---

[50] Signum sit tibi probabilissimum æternæ salutis, si perseveranter in dies eam in suo psalterio salutaveris.—*De Psal.* p. 2, c. 11, p. 4, c. 24.

[51] Omnes enim domestici ejus vestiti sunt duplicibus.—*Prov.* xxxi. 21.

[52] Sicut lætantium omnium habitatio est in te, sancta Dei Genitrix.

[53] Dial. l. 7, c. 22.

'Thomas, would you hear me sing?' 'Certainly,' he replied. And forthwith the virgin sang with such sweetness, that the monk believed himself to be in paradise. As soon as she had ceased to sing, she disappeared, leaving him full of desire to know who she was. But, behold, another most beautiful virgin appeared to him, who also let him hear her sing. Upon this he could no longer restrain himself from asking who she might be. She replied, ' She whom you saw just now was Catherine, and I am Agnes, both martyrs of Jesus Christ; and we are sent by our Lady to console you. Give thanks to Mary, and prepare yourself to receive a greater favour.' And saying this she disappeared. But the monk had now greater hopes to see at last his Queen. He was not deceived; for he presently saw a bright light, and felt his heart filled with a new joy; and, behold, the Mother of God appeared in the midst of that light, surrounded by angels, and of a beauty incomparably greater than that of the two other Saints, and said to him, ' My dear servant and son, I have accepted your devotion to me, and have heard your prayers : you have desired to see me ; behold me, and I will allow you to hear me also sing.' The most Holy Virgin began to sing ; and so great was the sweetness, that the pious monk lost his senses, and fell with his face to the ground. The bell for matins rang ; the monks assembled in choir, and not seeing Thomas, sought for him in his cell and in other places. At last they found him in the garden, as it were dead. The Superior ordered him to relate what had happened to him ; and then coming to himself, through virtue of obedience he related all the favours he had received from the Divine Mother.

PRAYER.

O Queen of Heaven, Mother of holy love ! since thou art the most amiable of creatures, the most beloved of God, and His greatest lover, be pleased to allow the most miserable sinner living in this world, who, having by thy means been delivered from hell, and without any merit on his part been so benefited by thee, and who is filled with love for thee, to love thee. I would desire, were it in my power, to let all men who know thee not know how worthy thou art of love, that all might love and honour thee. I would desire to die for the love of thee, in defence of thy virginity, of thy dignity of Mother of God, of thy Immaculate Conception, should this be necessary, to uphold these thy great privileges. Ah! my most beloved Mother, accept this my ardent desire, and never allow a servant of thine, who loves thee, to become the enemy of thy God, whom thou lovest so much. Alas! poor me, I was so for a time, when I offended my Lord. But then, O Mary, I loved thee but little, and strove but little to be beloved by thee. But now there is nothing that I so much desire, after the grace of God, as to love and be beloved by thee. I am not discouraged on account of my past sins, for I know that thou, O most benign and gracious Lady, dost not disdain to love even the most wretched sinners who love thee; nay more, that thou never allowest thyself to be surpassed by any in love. Ah! Queen most worthy of love, I desire to love thee in heaven. There, at thy feet, I shall better know how worthy thou art of love, how much thou hast done to save me; and thus I shall love thee with greater love, and love thee eternally, without fear of ever ceasing to love thee. O Mary, I hope most certainly to be saved by thy means. Pray to Jesus for me. Nothing else is needed; thou hast to save me; thou art my hope. I will therefore always sing, O Mary, my hope, thou hast to save me.

CHAPTER IX.

*Of the greatness of the Clemency and Compassion
of Mary.*

SAINT BERNARD, speaking of the great compassion of
Mary towards us poor creatures, says, 'that she is the
land overflowing with milk and honey promised by
God.'[1] Hence Saint Leo observes, 'that the Blessed
Virgin has so merciful a heart, that she deserves not
only to be called merciful, but mercy itself.'[2] Saint
Bonaventure also, considering that Mary was made
Mother of God on account of the miserable, and that
to her is committed the charge of dispensing mercy;
considering, moreover, the tender care she takes of all,
and that her compassion is so great that she seems to
have no other desire than that of relieving the needy;
says, that when he looks at her, he seems no longer to
see the justice of God, but only the divine mercy, of
which Mary is full. 'O Lady, when I behold thee, I
can only discern mercy, for thou wast made Mother of
God for the wretched, and then thou wast intrusted
with their charge : thou art all solicitude for them ;
thou art walled in with mercy ; thy only wish is to
show it.'[3] In fine, the compassion of Mary is so great
towards us, that the Abbot Guarric says, ' that her

[1] Terra repromissionis Maria, lacte et melle manans.—*Serm. sup. Salv.
Reg.*
[2] Maria adeo prædita est misericordiæ visceribus, ut non tantum misericors, sed ipsa misericordia dici promereatur.—*Serm.* i. *de Nat. Dom.* †
[3] Certe, Domina, cum te aspicio, nihil nisi misericordiam cerno. Nam
pro miseris Mater Dei facta es, misericordiam insuper genuisti, et demum
tibi miserendi est officium commissum. Undique sollicita de miseris, undique misericordia vallaris ; solum misereri tu videris appetere.—*Stim. Am.*
p. iii. cap. 19.

loving heart can never remain a moment without bringing forth its fruits of tenderness.'[4] 'And what,' exclaims Saint Bernard, 'can ever flow from a source of compassion but compassion itself?'[5] Mary is also called an olive-tree: "As a fair olive-tree on the plains."[6] For as from the olive oil (a symbol of mercy) alone is extracted, so from the hands of Mary graces and mercy alone proceed. Hence the venerable Father Louis de Ponte says, 'that Mary may properly be called the Mother of oil, since she is the Mother of mercy.'[7] And thus, when we go to this good Mother for the oil of her mercy, we cannot fear that she will deny it to us, as the wise virgins in the Gospel did to the foolish ones: "lest perhaps there be not enough for us and for you."[8] O no! for she is indeed rich in this oil of mercy, as Saint Bonaventure assures us, 'Mary is filled with the oil of compassion.'[9] She is called by the Church not only a prudent Virgin, but most prudent, that we may understand, says Hugo of Saint Victor, that she is so full of grace and compassion, that she can supply all, without losing any herself. 'Thou, O Blessed Virgin, art full of grace, and indeed so full, that the whole world may draw of this overflowing oil.' 'For if the prudent virgins provided oil in vessels with their lamps, thou, O most prudent Virgin, hast borne an overflowing and inexhaustible vessel, from which, the oil of mercy streaming, thou replenishest the lamps of all.'[10]

---

[4] Cujus viscera . . . nunquam desinunt fructum parturire pietatis.—*Serm.* i. *de Ass.*

[5] Quid de fonte pietatis procederet, nisi pietas?—*Serm.* i. *in D. post Ep.*

[6] Quasi oliva speciosa in campis.—*Eccl.* xxiv. 19.

[7] Optime dici potest Mater olei, nam est Mater misericordiæ.—*In Cant.* l. 1. exh. 21.

[8] Ne forte non sufficiat nobis et vobis.—*Matt.* xx. 9.

[9] Maria plena est . . . oleo pietatis.—*Spec. B.M.V.* lect. vii.

[10] Gratia plena, in tantum plena, ut ex tuo redundante totus hauriat mundus. Si enim "prudentes virgines oleum acceperunt in vasis suis cum lampadibus," tu prudentissima Virgo et Virgo virginum, non unum tantum vas nabuisti oleo gratiæ repletum, quo lampadem tuam inextinguibiliter ardentem nutrires, sed aliud gestasti vas redundans et indeficiens, ex quo effuso oleo misericordiæ omnium lampades illuminares.—*De Verb. Inc.* Coll. iii.

But why, I ask, is this beautiful olive-tree said to stand in the midst of the plains, and not rather in the midst of a garden, surrounded by a wall and hedges? The same Hugo of St. Victor tells us, that it is 'that all may see her, that all may go to her for refuge;'[11] that all may see her easily, and as easily have recourse to her, to obtain remedies for all their ills. This beautiful explanation is confirmed by Saint Antoninus, who says, 'that all can go to, and gather the fruit of, an olive-tree that is exposed in the midst of a plain; and thus all, both just and sinners, can have recourse to Mary, to obtain her mercy.'[12] He then adds, 'O, how many sentences of condemnation has not this most Blessed Virgin revoked by her compassionate prayers, in favour of sinners who have had recourse to her!'[13] 'And what safer refuge,' says the devout Thomas à Kempis, 'can we ever find than the compassionate heart of Mary? there the poor find a home, the infirm a remedy, the afflicted relief, the doubtful counsel, and the abandoned succour.'[14]

Wretched indeed should we be, had we not this Mother of mercy always attentive and solicitous to relieve us in our wants! "Where there is no woman, he mourneth that is in want,"[15] says the Holy Ghost. 'This woman,' says Saint John Damascen, 'is precisely the most Blessed Virgin Mary; and wherever this most holy woman is not, the sick man groans.'[16] And surely it cannot be otherwise, since all graces are dispensed at

[11] Fuit Beata Maria oliva per misericordiam . . . Et bene in campis . . . ut omnes peccatores ad ipsam libere et absque impedimento respiciant, ad ipsam confugiant.—*Serm.* iv. *de Ass. B.V.*

[12] Ad olivam, quæ est speciosa in campis, omnes possunt accedere, et accipere fructum ejus, sic ad Mariam et justi et peccatores accedere possunt, ut inde misericordiam accipiant.—P. iii. tit. xxxi. cap. 4.

[13] O quot sententias terribilium flagellorum, quæ meruit mundus propter peccata sua, hæc sanctissima Virgo misericorditer revocavit!—*Ib.*

[14] Non est tutior locus ad latendum quam sinus Mariæ . . . Ibi pauper habet domicilium, ibi infirmus invenit remedium, ibi tristis accipit solatium, ibi turbatus meretur consilium, ibi destitutus acquirit juvamen.—*Serm.* v. *ad Nov.*

[15] Ubi non est mulier, ingemiscit egens.—*Eccl.* xxxvi. 27.

[16] Ingemiscit infirmus, ubi non fuerit hæc sanctissima mulier. †

the prayer of Mary; and where this is wanting, there can be no hope of mercy, as our Lord gave Saint Bridget to understand in these words: 'Unless the prayers of Mary interposed, there could be no hope of mercy.'[17]

But perhaps we fear that Mary does not see, or does not feel for, our necessities? O no, she sees and feels them far better than we do ourselves. 'There is not one amongst all the Saints,' says Saint Antoninus, 'who can ever feel for us in our miseries, both corporal and spiritual, like this woman, the most Blessed Virgin Mary.'[18] So much so, that there where she sees misery, she cannot do otherwise than instantly fly and relieve it with her tender compassion.[19] Richard of Saint Victor repeats the same thing; and Mendoza says, 'Therefore, O most Blessed Virgin, thou dispensest thy mercies with a generous hand, wherever thou seest necessities.'[20] Our good Mother herself protests that she will never cease to fulfil this office of mercy: "And unto the world to come I shall not cease to be, and in the holy dwelling-place I have ministered before him;"[21] that is, as Cardinal Hugo explains, 'I will never cease until the end of the world relieving the miseries of men, and praying for sinners,'[22] that they may be delivered from eternal misery, and be saved.

Suetonius relates,[23] that the Emperor Titus was so desirous of rendering service to those who applied to him, that, when a day passed without his being able

---

[17] Nisi preces Matris meæ intervenirent, non esset spes misericordiæ.—*Rev.* lib. vi. cap. 26.

[18] Non reperitur aliquem sanctorum ita compati et adjuvare in infirmitatibus spiritualibus et corporalibus ægris personis, sicut mulier hæc beata Virgo Maria.—P. iv. tit. xv. cap. 2.

[19] Ubicumque fuerit miseria, tua et currit et succurrit misericordia.—*In Cant. Exp.* cap. 23.

[20] Itaque, O Virgo Mater, ubi nostras miserias invenis, ibi tuas misericordias effundis.—*In Lib.* i. *Reg.* cap. 4, No. 11.

[21] Et usque ad futurum sæculum non desinam; et in habitatione sancta coram ipso ministravi.—*Eccl.* xxiv. 14.

[22] Usque ad futurum sæculum, quod est sæculum beatorum, non desinam miseris subvenire, humiles introducere, et pro peccatoribus orare.—*In* cap. xxiv. *Eccl.*

[23] In Tit. c. 8.

to grant a favour, he used to say with sorrow, '**I have**
lost a day ; for I have spent it without benefiting anyone.' It is probable that Titus spoke thus more from
vanity, and the desire of being esteemed, than from
true charity. But should such a thing happen to our
Empress Mary, as to have to pass a day without granting a grace, she would speak as Titus did, but from a
true desire to serve us, and because she is full of charity.
'So much so, indeed,' says Bernardine de Bustis, 'that
she is more anxious to grant us graces than we are to
receive them.'[24] 'And therefore,' says the same author,
'whenever we go to her, we always find her hands
filled with mercy and liberality.'[25]

Rebecca was a figure of Mary ; and she, when asked
by Abraham's servant for a little water to drink, replied, that not only would she give him plenty for
himself, but also for his camels, saying, " I will draw
water for thy camels also, till they all drink."[26] On
these words Saint Bernard addresses our Blessed Lady,
saying : 'O Mary, thou art far more liberal and compassionate than Rebecca ; and therefore thou art not
satisfied with distributing the treasures of thy immense
mercy only to the just, of whom Abraham's servants
were types, but also thou bestowest them on sinners,
who are signified by the camels.'[27] 'The liberality of
Mary,' says Richard of Saint Lawrence, 'is like that
of her Son, who always gives more than He is asked
for.'[28] " He is," says Saint Paul, " rich unto all that
call upon Him." 'And the liberality of Mary is like
His : she bestows more than is sought.'[29] Hear how

[24] Plus enim desiderat ipsa facere tibi bonum, et largiri aliquam gratiam,
quam tu accipere concupiscas.—*Mar.* pars ii. *Serm.* v. *de Nat. M.*
[25] Invenies enim eam in manibus plenam, pietate, misericordia, gratiositate, et largitate.—*Ib.*
[26] Quin et camelis tuis hauriam aquam, donec cuncti bibant.—*Gen.* xxiv.
19.
[27] Domina . . . nec puero Abrahæ tantum, sed et camelis potum tribuas
de supereffluenti hydria tua.—*Serm. Sign. Mag.*
[28] Largitas Mariæ imitatur et assimilat largitatem Filii sui, qui dat
amplius quam petatur.—*De Laud. Virg.* l. iv. cap. 22.
[29] Dives in omnes qui invocant illum.—*Rom.* x, 12.

a devout writer thus addresses the Blessed Virgin : 'O Lady, do thou pray for me, for thou wilt ask for the graces I require with greater devotion than I can dare to ask for them ; and thou wilt obtain far greater graces from God for me than I can presume to seek.'[30]

When the Samaritans refused to receive Jesus Christ and His doctrines, Saint James and Saint John asked Him whether they should command fire to fall from heaven and devour them ; our Lord replied, "You know not of what spirit you are."[31] As if He had said, 'I am of so tender and compassionate a spirit that I came from heaven to save and not to chastise sinners, and you wish to see them lost. Fire, indeed ! and punishment !—speak no more of chastisements, for such a spirit is not mine.' But of Mary, whose spirit is the same as that of her Son, we can never doubt but that she is all-inclined to mercy ; for, as she said to Saint Bridget, she is called the Mother of mercy, and it was by God's own mercy that she was made thus compassionate and sweet towards all : 'I am called the Mother of mercy, and truly God's mercy made me thus merciful.'[32] For this reason Mary was seen by Saint John clothed with the sun : "And a great sign appeared in heaven, a woman clothed with the sun."[33] On which words Saint Bernard, turning towards the Blessed Virgin, says, 'Thou, O Lady, hast clothed the sun, that is the Eternal Word, with human flesh ; but He has clothed thee with His power and mercy.'[34]

'This Queen,' continues the same Saint Bernard, 'is so compassionate and benign, that when a sinner, whoever he may be, recommends himself to her charity, she does not question his merits, or whether he is

[30] Majori devotione orabis pro me, quam ego auderem petere; et majora mihi impetrabis, quam petere præsumam.—*De Rhet. div.* c. 18.

[31] Nescitis cujus spiritus estis.—*Luc.* ix. 55.

[32] Ego vocor ab omnibus Mater misericordiæ, vere, filia, misericordia Filii mei fecit me misericordem.—*Rev.* l. ii. c. 23.

[33] Et signum magnum apparuit in cœlo : mulier amicta sole.—*Apoc.* xii. 1.

[34] Vestis solem nube. et sole ipsa vestiris.—*Serm. in Sign. Magn.*

worthy or unworthy to be attended to, but she hears
and succours all.'[35]   'And therefore,' remarks Saint
Idelbert, 'Mary is said to be "fair as the moon."[36]
For as the moon enlightens and benefits the lowest
creatures on earth, so does Mary enlighten and succour
the most unworthy sinners.'[37]   And though the moon,
says another writer, receives all its light from the sun,
yet it works quicker than the sun ; 'for what this latter
does in a year the moon does in a month.'[38]   For this
reason Saint Anselm says, 'that we often more quickly
obtain what we ask by calling on the name of Mary
than by invoking that of Jesus.'[39]   On this subject
Hugo of Saint Victor remarks, that 'though our sins
may cause us to fear to approach the Almighty, because it is His infinite majesty that we have offended,
we must never fear to go to Mary, for in her we shall
find nothing to terrify us.   True it is that she is holy,
immaculate, and the Queen of the world ; but she is
also of our flesh, and, like us, a child of Adam.'[40]

'In fine,' says Saint Bernard, 'all that belongs to
Mary is filled with grace and mercy, for she, as a
Mother of mercy, has made herself all to all, and out
of her most abundant charity she has made herself a
debtor to the wise and the foolish, to the just and
sinners, and opens to all her compassionate heart, that
all may receive of the fulness of its treasures.'[41]   So
much so, that as "the devil," according to Saint Peter,

[35] Non discutit merita, sed omnibus sese exorabilem, omnibus clementis-
simam præbet.—*Serm. in Sign. Magn.*

[36] Pulchra ut luna.—*Cant.* vi. 9.

[37] Pulchra ut luna, quia pulchrum est benefacere indignis.—*Epist.* xxvi. †

[38] Quod sol facit in anno, luna facit in mense.—*Joann. a. S. Gem. Summ.*
l. i. c. 3.

[39] Velocior est nonnunquam nostra salus, memorato nomine ejus, quam
invocato nomine Domini Jesu.—*De Excel. Virg.* cap. vi.

[40] Si pertimescis ad Deum accedere, respice ad Mariam ; non illic invenis
quod timeas ; genus tuum vides.—*Spinelli, M. Deip.* c. 30. n. 12.

[41] Plena omnia pietatis et gratiæ . . . quæ ad eam pertinent . . . Deni
que omnibus omnia facta est, sapientibus et insipientibus copiosissima cha
ritate debitricem se fecit : omnibus misericordiæ sinum aperit, ut de plenitudine ejus accipiant universi.—*Serm. in Sign. Magn.*

" goes about seeking whom he may devour ;"[42] ' so,' on the other hand, says Bernardine de Bustis, ' does Mary go about seeking whom she may save, and to whom she may give life.'[43]

We should fully understand and always bear in mind a remark of Saint Germanus, who says, ' that the protection of Mary is greater and more powerful than anything of which we can form an idea.'[44] ' How is it,' asks another writer, ' that that Lord who under the old dispensation was so rigorous in his punishments, now shows such mercy to persons guilty of far greater crimes ?' And he answers, ' that it is all for the love of Mary, and on account of her merits.'[45] ' O, how long since,' exclaims Saint Fulgentius, ' would the world have been destroyed, had not Mary sustained it by her powerful intercession !'[46] ' But now,' says Arnold of Chartres, ' that we have the Son as our mediator with the Eternal Father, and the Mother as a mediatress with the Son, we have full access, and can go to God with entire confidence and hope for every good thing. How,' he goes on to say, ' can the Father refuse to hear the Son who shows Him His side and wounds, the marks of His sufferings endured for sinners ; and how can the Son refuse to hear His Mother when she shows Him her bosom and the breasts that gave him suck ?'[47] Saint Peter Chrysologus says, ' that a gentle maiden having lodged a God in her womb, asks as its price peace for the world, salvation for those who are lost, and life for

[42] Circuit quærens quem devoret.—*Ep.* 1 *S. Petri Ap.* v. 8.
[43] Ipsa semper circuit, quærens quem salvet.—*Marial.* p. iii. *Serm.* 1.
[44] Patrocinium tuum majus est quam ut intelligentia comprehendi possit. —*De Zona Virg.*
[45] Quare parcit nunc mundo ipse Deus, qui olim multo his minora peccata acrius punivit ? Totum hoc facit propter B. Virginem et ejus merita.— *Pelbart. Stell.* l. 11, p. 2, c. 2.
[46] Cœlum et terra jamdudum ruissent, si Maria suis precibus non sustentasset.—*Ib.*
[47] Securum accessum jam habet homo ad Deum, ubi mediatorem causæ suæ Filium habet ante Patrem, et ante Filium Matrem. Christus nudato latere, Patri ostendit latus et vulnera, Maria Christo pectus et ubera.—*De Laud. Virg.*

the dead.'[48] 'O, how many,' exclaims the Abbot of
Celles, 'who deserved to be condemned by the justice
of the Son are saved by the mercy of the Mother! for
she is God's treasure, and the treasurer of all graces;
and thus our salvation is in her hands, and depends
on her.'[49]   Let us, then, always have recourse to this
compassionate Mother, and confidently hope for salvation through her intercession; for she, according to
the encouraging assurance of Bernardine de Bustis, 'is
our salvation, our life, our hope, our counsel, our refuge, our help.'[50]   'Mary,' says Saint Antoninus,[51] 'is
that throne of grace to which the Apostle Saint Paul,
in his epistle to the Hebrews, exhorts us to fly with
confidence, that we may obtain the Divine mercy, and
all the help we need for our salvation:' "Let us therefore go with confidence to the throne of grace: that
we may obtain mercy, and find grace in seasonable
aid."[52]   'To the throne of grace, that is to Mary,' says
Saint Antoninus; and for this reason Saint Catharine
of Sienna called Mary 'the dispenser of Divine mercy.'[53]

Let us conclude with the beautiful and tender exclamation of Saint Bonaventure on these words, 'O
clement, O pious, O sweet Virgin Mary!' 'O Mary,
thou art clement with the miserable, compassionate towards those who pray to thee, sweet towards those who
love thee; clement with the penitent, compassionate to
those who advance, sweet to the perfect.   Thou showest
thyself clement in delivering us from chastisement, com-

---

[48] Una puella sic Deum sui pectoris capit, recipit, oblectat hospitio, ut
pacem terris, cœlis gloriam, salutem perditis, vitam mortuis . . . pro ipsa
domus exigat pensione.—*Serm.* clx.

[49] Sæpe quos justitia Filii potest damnare, Matris misericordia liberat,
quia thesaurus Domini est, et thesauraria gratiarum ipsius . . . quia salus
nostra in manibus illius est.—*Prol. in Contempl. Virg.*

[50] Hæc est nostra salus, vita, spes, consilium, refugium, auxilium nostrum.
—P. 1. *Serm.* 6 *de Com. Mar.*

[51] P. 4, t. 15, c. 14, § 7.

[52] Adeamus ergo cum fiducia ad thronum gratiæ, ut misericordiam consequamur, et gratiam inveniamus in auxilio opportuno.—*Hebr.* iv. 16.

[53] Administratrix misericordiæ.—*Or. in Annunt.*

passionate in bestowing graces, and sweet in giving thyself to those who seek thee.'[54]

EXAMPLE.

Father Charles Bovio[55] relates, that in the principality of Dombes, in France, there was a married man whose wife was jealous of another woman, and did nothing but call down both on her husband and the woman the judgments of God; and this she did especially one day that she went before an altar of the Blessed Virgin to pray for justice against this woman. The woman, however, was in the habit of going every day to recite a "Hail Mary," before the same image. One night the Divine Mother appeared in a dream to the wife, who, on seeing her, began as usual to exclaim, 'Justice, O Mother of God, justice!' But our Blessed Lady replied: 'Justice! chastisements! dost thou seek them of me? No, go to others, for I will not grant what thou askest; for know,' she added, 'that that sinner recites every day a salutation in my honour, and by whomsoever it is recited, it deprives me of the power of allowing him to suffer or to be chastised for his sins.' In the morning the wife went to hear Mass in the above-named church of our Blessed Lady, and on returning home met this woman, and immediately began to abuse her, and then declared that she was a witch, and that she had succeeded even in enchanting the Blessed Virgin herself. The people who were present told her to hold her tongue. 'Be silent! indeed, I will not, for what I say is true; for last night our Blessed Lady appeared to me, and when I demanded justice, she told me that she could not grant it on account of a salutation offered her every day by this wretch.' The woman was then asked what salutation it was that she

---

[54] O clemens indigentibus! O pia exorantibus! O dulcis diligentibus! O clemens pænitentibus! O pia proficientibus! O dulcis contemplantibus! O clemens laborando! O pia largiendo! O dulcis te donando!—*Sup. Salv. Reg.*
[55] Es. e mir. p. 5, es. 32.

offered every day to the Mother of God, and she replied that it was the 'Hail Mary.' On hearing that for that trifling devotion the Blessed Virgin had shown her such mercy, she went and cast herself before the holy image, and there, in the presence of all, she asked pardon for the scandal she had given, and made a vow of perpetual chastity. She then clothed herself with the habit of a nun, built herself a little room near the church, and there remained until her death, leading a life of continual mortification and penance.

PRAYER.

O Mother of mercy, since thou art so compassionate, and hast so great a desire to render service to us poor creatures and to grant our requests, behold I, the most miserable of all men, have now recourse to thy compassion, in order that thou mayest grant me that which I ask. Others may ask what they please of thee,—bodily health, and earthly goods and advantages; but I come, O Lady, to ask thee for that which thou desirest of me, and which is most in conformity with and agreeable to thy most sacred heart. Thou art so humble; obtain for me humility and love of contempt. Thou wast so patient under the sufferings of this life; obtain for me patience in trials. Thou wast all filled with the love of God; obtain for me the gift of His pure and holy love. Thou wast all love towards thy neighbour; obtain for me charity towards all, and particularly towards those who are in any way my enemies. Thou wast entirely united to the Divine will; obtain for me entire conformity with the will of God in whatever way He may be pleased to dispose of me. Thou, in fine, art the most holy of all creatures; O Mary, make me a saint. Love for me is not wanting on thy part; thou canst do all, and thou hast the will to obtain me all. The only thing, then, that can prevent me from receiving thy graces is, either neglect on my part in having recourse to thee, or little confidence in thy intercession; but these two things thou must obtain for me. These two greatest graces I ask from thee ; from thee I must obtain them ; from thee I hope for them with the greatest confidence, O Mary, my Mother Mary, my hope, my love, my life, my refuge, my help, and my consolation. Amen.

CHAPTER X.

O SWEET VIRGIN MARY.

Of the sweetness of the name of Mary during life and at death.

THE great name of Mary, which was given to the Divine Mother, did not come to her from her parents, nor was it given to her by the mind or will of man, as is the case with all other names that are imposed in this world; but it came from heaven, and was given her by a divine ordinance. This is attested by Saint Jerome,[1] Saint Epiphanius,[2] Saint Antoninus,[3] and others. 'The name of Mary came from the treasury of the Divinity,'[4] says Saint Peter Damian. Ah, yes, O Mary, it was from that treasury that thy high and admirable name came forth; for the most Blessed Trinity, says Richard of Saint Lawrence, bestowed on thee a name above every other name after that of thy Son, and ennobled it with such majesty and power, that He willed that all heaven, earth, and hell, on only hearing it, should fall down and venerate it; but I will give the author's own words: 'The whole Trinity, O Mary, gave thee a name after that of thy Son above every other name, that in thy name every knee should bow, of things in heaven, on earth, and under the earth.'[5] But amongst the other privileges of the name of Mary, and which were given

---

[1] De Nat. S.M.
[2] Oratio de Præs. Deip.
[3] P. i. Hist. tit. 4, c. 6. § 10.
[4] De thesauro divinitatis Mariæ nomen evolvitur.—Tom. ii. *Serm.* 11 *de Annunt. B.V.*
[5] Dedit enim ei tota Trinitas nomen quod est super omne nomen, post nomen Filii sui; ut in nomine ejus omne genu flcctatur . . . cœlestium, terrestrium, et infernorum.—*De Laud. Virg.* lib. i. cap. ii.

to it by God, we will now examine that of the peculiar sweetness found in it by the servants of this most holy Lady during life and in death.

And in the first place, speaking of the course of our life, the holy anchoret Honorius used to say, that 'this name of Mary is filled with every sweetness and divine savour;'[6] so much so, that the glorious Saint Anthony of Padua found the same sweetness in the name of Mary that Saint Bernard found in that of Jesus. 'Name of Jesus!' exclaimed the one. 'O name of Mary!' replied the other; 'joy in the heart, honey in the mouth, melody to the ear of her devout clients.'[7] It is narrated in the life of the Ven. Father Juvenal Ancina, Bishop of Saluzzo, that in pronouncing the name of Mary he tasted so great and sensible a sweetness, that, after doing so, he licked his lips. We read also that a lady at Cologne told the Bishop Massilius, that as often as she uttered the name of Mary she experienced a taste far sweeter than honey. The Bishop imitated her, and experienced the same thing.[8] We gather from the sacred Canticles, that on the Assumption of our Blessed Lady, the angels asked her name three times. "Who is she that goeth up by the desert as a pillar of smoke?"[9] again, "Who is she that cometh forth as the morning rising?"[10] and again, "Who is this that cometh up from the desert, flowing with delights?"[11] 'And why,' says Richard of Saint Lawrence, 'do the angels so often ask the name of their Queen?' He answers, 'that it was so sweet even to the angels to hear it pronounced, that they desired to hear that sweet name in reply.'[12]

---

[6] Hoc nomen Mariæ plenum est omni dulcedine ac suavitate divine.—*Ap. Lyr. Tris. Mar.* l. 2, m. 13.

[7] Nomen Mariæ jubilus in corde, mel in ore, in aure melos.—*Dom. 3 Quadr.* § 2.

[8] Cæsarius, Dial. l. 7. c. 50.

[9] Quæ est ista, quæ ascendit per desertum, sicut virgula fumi?—*Cant.* iii. 6.

[10] Quæ est ista, quæ progreditur quasi aurora consurgens?—*Ib.* vi. 9.

[11] Quæ est ista, quæ ascendit de deserto, deliciis affluens?—*Ib.* viii. 5.

[12] Forsitan quia dulce nomen sibi desiderant responderi.—*De Laud. Virg.* lib. i. cap. 2.

But here I do not intend to speak of that sensible sweetness, for it is not granted to all; I speak of that salutary sweetness of consolation, of love, of joy, of confidence, of strength, which the name of Mary ordinarily brings to those who pronounce it with devotion. The Abbot Francone, speaking on this subject, says, 'there is no other name after that of the Son, in heaven or on earth, whence pious minds derive so much grace, hope, and sweetness.'[13] After the most sacred name of Jesus, the name of Mary is so rich in every good thing, that on earth and in heaven there is no other from which devout souls receive so much grace, hope, and sweetness. 'For,' he continues, 'there is something so admirable, sweet, and divine in this name of Mary, that when it meets with friendly hearts it breathes into them an odour of delightful sweetness.' And he adds, in conclusion, 'that the wonder of this great name is, that if heard by the lovers of Mary a thousand times, it is always heard again with renewed pleasure, for they always experience the same sweetness each time it is pronounced.'[14]

The blessed Henry Suso,[15] also speaking of this sweetness, says, 'that when he named Mary, he felt himself so excited to confidence, and inflamed with such love and joy, that between the tears and joy with which he pronounced the beloved name, he desired that his heart might leave his breast; for he declared that this most sweet name was like a honeycomb dissolving in the inmost recess of his soul;' and then he would exclaim: 'O most sweet name! O Mary, what must thou thyself be, since thy name alone is thus amiable and gracious!'

---

[13] Neque enim, post illud singulare dilecti Filii sui nomen, quod est super omne nomen, aliud nomen cœlum aut terra nominat, unde tantum gratiæ, tantum spei, tantum suavitatis, tantum consolationis piæ mentes concipiant. —*De Grat. Nov. Test.* lib. vi.

[14] Nomen namque Mariæ, mirum quid suave atque divinum in se continet, ut cum sonuerit amicis cordibus, amicæ suavitatis odorem spiret. Et mirum illud est de nomine Mariæ, et valde mirum: ut millies auditum, semper audiatur quasi novum.—*Ib.*

[15] Dial. c. 16.

The enamoured Saint Bernard, raising his heart to his good Mother, says, with tenderness, 'O great! O pious! O thou, who art worthy of all praise! O most Holy Virgin Mary! Thy name is so sweet and amiable, that it cannot be pronounced without inflaming those who do so with love towards thee and God. It only need occur to the thought of thy lovers to move them to love thee more, and to console them.' 'Thou canst not be named without inflaming; thou canst not be thought of by those who love thee without filling their minds with joy.'[16] 'And if riches comfort the poor, because they relieve them in their distress, O how much more does thy name, O Mary,' says Richard of Saint Lawrence, 'comfort us than any earthly riches! It comforts us in the anguishes of this life.' 'Thy name, O Mary, is far better than riches, because it can better relieve poverty.'[17] In fine, 'thy name, O Mother of God, is filled with divine graces and blessings,'[18] as Saint Methodius says. So much so, that Saint Bonaventure declares 'that thy name, O Mary, cannot be pronounced without bringing some grace to him who does so devoutly.'[19] The blessed Raymond Jordano says, 'that however hardened and diffident a heart may be, the name of this most Blessed Virgin has such efficacy, that if it is only pronounced, that heart will be wonderfully softened.' I will, however, give his own words. 'The power of thy most holy name, O ever-blessed Virgin Mary, is such that it softens the hardness of the human heart in a wonderful manner.' He then tells us that it is she who leads sinners to the hope of pardon and grace: 'By thee does the sinner

---

[16] O pia, O magna, O multum laudabilis Maria ; tu nec nominari quidem potes quin accendas, nec cogitari quin recrees affectus diligentium te.— *Depr. et Laus ad B.V.M.*

[17] Mariæ nomen longe melius quam divitiæ corporales, quia melius angustiam relevat paupertatis.—*De Laud. Virg.* lib. i. cap. 2.

[18] Tuum, Dei genitrix, nomen divinis benedictionibus et gratiis ex omni parte refertum.—*Or. de Sim. et Anna.*

[19] Nomen tuum . . . devote nominari non potest sine nominantis utilitate.—*Spec. B.M.V.* lect. ix.

recover the hope of forgiveness and of grace.'[20] 'Thy
most sweet name, O Mary,' according to St. Ambrose,
'is a precious ointment, which breathes forth the odour
of divine grace.' The Saint then prays to the Divine
Mother, saying: 'Let this ointment of salvation enter
the inmost recesses of our souls:'[21] that is, grant, O
Lady, that we may often remember to name thee with
love and confidence; for this practice either shows the
possession of divine grace, or else is a pledge that we
shall soon recover it.

'And truly it is so, O Mary; for the remembrance
of thy name comforts the afflicted, recalls those who
have erred to the way of salvation, and encourages
sinners, that they may not abandon themselves to despair.' It is thus that Landolph of Saxony addresses
her.[22] And Father Pelbart says, 'that as Jesus Christ,
by His five wounds, gave a remedy for the evils of the
world, so also does Mary, by her most holy name,
which is composed of five letters, daily bring pardon
to sinners.'[23]

For this reason is the holy name of Mary likened
in the sacred Canticles to oil: "Thy name is as oil
poured out."[24] On these words blessed Alan says,
'that the glory of her name is compared to oil poured
out; because oil heals the sick, sends out a sweet
odour, and nourishes flames.'[25] Thus also does the
name of Mary heal sinners, rejoice hearts, and inflame
them with divine love. Hence Richard of Saint Law-

[20] Tanta est virtus tui sacratissimi nominis, O semper benedicta Virgo
Maria, quod mirabiliter emollit et penetrat duritiam cordis humani . . . peccator per te respirat in spe veniæ et gratiæ.—*In Contemp. B. V.* cap. v.

[21] Unguentum . . . nomen tuum; descendat istud unguentum in ima
præcordia viscerumque secreta, quo non deliciarum odores sancta Maria, sed
divinæ gratiæ spiramenta redolebat.—*De Instit. Virg.* c. 13.

[22] O Maria, tui recordatio nominis melle dulcior, nectare suavior, fessos
recreat, mœstos lætificat, oppressos relevat, errantes ad viam salutis revocat,
et peccatores, ne desperent, suæ suavitatis odore confortat.—*In vita Christi*,
p. ii. cap. 86.

[23] Sic Maria suo sanctissimo nomine, quod quinque litteris constat, con-
fert quotidie veniam peccatoribus.—*Stellar.* l. 6, p. 1, a. 2.

[24] Oleum effusum nomen tuum.—*Cant.* i. 2.

[25] Gloria nominis ejus oleo effuso comparatur. Oleum ægrotantem sanat,
odorem parat, flammam nutrit.—*In Cant.* i.

rence 'encourages sinners to have recourse to this great name,' because it alone will suffice to cure them of all their evils; and 'there is no disorder, however malignant, that does not immediately yield to the power of the name of Mary.'[26]

On the other hand, Thomas à Kempis affirms, 'that the devils fear the Queen of Heaven to such a degree, that on only hearing her great name pronounced, they fly from him who does so as from a burning fire.'[27] The Blessed Virgin herself revealed to Saint Bridget 'that there is not on earth a sinner, however devoid he may be of the love of God, from whom the devil is not obliged immediately to fly, if he invokes her holy name with a determination to repent.'[28] On another occasion she repeated the same thing to the Saint, saying, 'that all the devils venerate and fear her name to such a degree, that on hearing it they immediately loosen the claws with which they hold the soul captive.'[29]

Our Blessed Lady also told Saint Bridget, 'that in the same way as the rebel angels fly from sinners who invoke the name of Mary, so also do the good angels approach nearer to just souls who pronounce her name with devotion.'[30] Saint Germanus declares, 'that as breathing is a sign of life, so also is the frequent pronunciation of the name of Mary a sign either of the life of divine grace, or that it will soon come; for this powerful name has in it the virtue of obtaining help and life for him who invokes it devoutly.' Addressing the Blessed Virgin, he says, 'As breathing is a sign of

[26] Peccator es, ad Mariæ nomen confugias. Ipsum solum sufficit ad medendum: nam pestis tam efficax nulla sic hæret, quæ ad nomen Mariæ non cedat continuo.—*De Laud. Virg.* lib. i. cap. 2.

[27] Expavescunt cœli reginam spiritus maligni, et diffugiunt audito nomine ejus, velut ab igne.—*Serm.* iv. *ad Nor.*

[28] Nullus etiam tam frigidus ab amore Dei est, nisi sit damnatus, si invocaverit hoc nomen, hac intentione, ut nunquam reverti velit ad opus solitum, quod non discedat ab eo statim diabolus.—*Rev.* lib. i. cap. 9.

[29] Omnes dæmones verentur hoc nomen, et timent. Qui audientes hoc nomen Mariæ, statim relinquunt animam de unguibus, quibus tenebant eam. —*Ib.*

[30] Angeli etiam boni, audito hoc nomine, statim appropinquant magis justis.—*Ib.*

life in the body, so is the frequent repetition of thy most holy name, O Virgin, by thy servants, not only a sign of life and of strength, but also it procures and conciliates both.'[31]   In fine, 'This admirable name of our Sovereign Lady,' says Richard of Saint Lawrence, 'is like a fortified tower, in which, if a sinner takes refuge, he will be delivered from death; for it defends and saves even the most abandoned.'[32] But it is a tower of strength, which not only delivers sinners from chastisement, but also defends the just from the assaults of hell. Thus the same Richard says, 'that after the name of Jesus, there is no other in which men find such powerful assistance and salvation as in the great name of Mary.'[33]   He says, 'there is not such powerful help in any name, nor is there any other name given to men, after that of Jesus, from which so much salvation is poured forth upon men as from the name of Mary.' Moreover, it is well known, and is daily experienced by the clients of Mary, that her powerful name gives the particular strength necessary to overcome temptations against purity.   The same author in his commentary on the words of St. Luke, " and the Virgin's name was Mary,"[34] remarks that these two words, Mary and Virgin, are joined together by the Evangelist, to denote that the name of this most pure Virgin should always be coupled with the virtue of chastity.'[35] Hence Saint Peter Chrysologus says, 'that the name of Mary is an indication of chastity;'[36] meaning, that when we

[31] Quomodo enim corpus nostrum vitalis signum operationis habet respirationem, ita etiam sanctissimum tuum nomen, quod in ore servorum tuorum versatur assidue, in omni tempore, loco, et modo, vitæ, lætitiæ, et auxilii non solum est signum, sed ea etiam procurat et conciliat.—*De Zona Virg.*

[32] Turris fortissima nomen Dominæ: ad ipsam confugiet peccator in tentatione, et etiam qui peccavit, et salvabitur.   Hæc defendit quoslibet, et quantumlibet peccatores.—*De Laud. Virg.* lib. i. cap. 2.

[33] Non est . . . in aliquo alio nomine, post nomen Filii, tam potens adjutorium, nec est aliquod nomen sub cœlo datum hominibus, post dulce nomen Jesu, ex quo tanta salus refundatur hominibus.—*Ib.*

[34] Et nomen Virginis Maria.—*Luc.* i. 27.

[35] Nomini Mariæ virginitas et sanctitas inseparabiliter sunt adjuncta.—*De Laud. V.* lib. i. cap. ii.

[36] Nomen hoc . . . judicium castitatis.—*Serm.* cxlvi.

doubt as to whether we have consented to thoughts against this virtue, if we remember having invoked the name of Mary, we have a certain proof that we have not sinned.

Let us, therefore, always take advantage of the beautiful advice given us by Saint Bernard, in these words : ' In dangers, in perplexities, in doubtful cases, think of Mary, call on Mary; let her not leave thy lips; let her not depart from thy heart.'[37]   In every danger of forfeiting divine grace, we should think of Mary, and invoke her name, together with that of Jesus ; for these two names always go together. O, then, never let us permit these two most sweet names to leave our hearts, or be off our lips ; for they will give us strength not only not to yield, but to conquer all our temptations. Consoling indeed are the promises of help made by Jesus Christ to those who have devotion to the name of Mary; for one day, in the hearing of Saint Bridget, He promised His most holy Mother that He would grant three special graces to those who invoke that holy name with confidence : first, that He would grant them perfect sorrow for their sins; second, that their crimes should be atoned for ; and, thirdly, strength to attain perfection, and at length the glory of paradise.[38] And then our Divine Saviour added : ' For thy words, O my Mother, are so sweet and agreeable to Me, that I cannot deny what thou askest.'[39]

Saint Ephrem goes so far as to say, ' that the name of Mary is the key of the gates of heaven,'[40] in the hands of those who devoutly invoke it.   And thus it is not without reason that Saint Bonaventure says

[37] In periculis, in angustiis, in rebus dubiis, Mariam cogita, Mariam invoca.   Non recedat ab ore, non recedat a corde.—*Hom.* ii. *sup. Miss.*
[38] Habitatores mundi indigent tribus : primo, contritione pro peccatis; secundo, satisfactione ; tertio, fortitudine ad faciendum bona . . . Omnis quicumque invocaverit nomen tuum, et spem habet in te, cum proposito emendandi commissa, ista tria dabuntur ei, insuper et regnum cœleste.— Lib. i. *Rev.* cap. 50.
[39] Tanta enim est mihi dulcedo in verbis tuis, ut non possim negare quæ petis.—*Ib.*
[40] Ave portarum cœlestis paradisi reseramentum.—*Serm. de Laud. B.V.M*

'that Mary is the salvation of all who call upon her;
for he addresses her, saying: 'O salvation of all who
invoke thee!'[41] meaning, that to obtain eternal salvation and invoke her name are synonymous; and Richard
of Saint Lawrence affirms, 'that the devout invocation
of this sweet and holy name leads to the acquisition of
superabundant graces in this life, and a very high degree of glory in the next.'[42] 'If then, O brethren,'
concludes Thomas à Kempis, 'you desire consolation
in every labour, have recourse to Mary; invoke the
name of Mary, honour Mary, recommend yourselves to
Mary, rejoice with Mary, weep with Mary, pray with
Mary, walk with Mary, seek Jesus with Mary; in fine,
desire to live and die with Jesus and Mary. By act-
ing thus you will always advance in the ways of God,
for Mary will most willingly pray for you, and the
Son will most certainly grant all that His Mother
asks.'[43]

Thus we see that the most holy name of Mary is
sweet indeed to her clients during life, on account of
the very great graces she obtains for them. But sweeter
still will it be to them in death, on account of the
tranquil and holy end that it will insure them. Father
Sertorius Caputo exhorted all who assist the dying,
frequently to pronounce the name of Mary; for this
name of life and hope, when repeated at the hour of
death, suffices to put the devils to flight, and to comfort such persons in their sufferings. Saint Camillus of
Lellis also recommended his religious, in the strongest
terms, to remind the dying frequently to invoke the

---

[41] O salus te invocantium!

[42] Devota . . . invocatio et recordatio nominis ejus ducit ad virorem
gratiæ in præsenti, ad virorem cælestium in futuro.—*De Laud. V.* lib. i.
cap. 2.

[43] Si consolari in omni tribulatione quæritis, accedite ad Mariam . . .
Mariam invocate, Mariam salutate, Mariam cogitate, Mariam nominate,
Mariam honorate, Mariam semper glorificate, Mariæ inclinate, Mariæ vos
commendate . . . cum Maria gaudete, cum Maria dolete . . . cum Maria
orate . . . cum Maria ambulate . . . cum Maria Jesum quærite . . . cum
Maria et Jesu vivere et mori desiderate. Fratres, si ista bene cogitatis et
exercetis . . . proficietis. Maria libenter pro vobis orabit . . . et Jesus libenter Matrem suam exaudiet.—*Serm.* ii. *ad Nov.*

names of Jesus and Mary. This was his own custom when attending others ; but O, how sweetly did he practise it himself on his death-bed, for then he pronounced the beloved names of Jesus and Mary with such tenderness, that he inflamed even those who heard him with love, and at length, with his eyes fixed on their venerated images, and his arms in the form of a cross, the Saint breathed forth his soul with an air of holiness and in the midst of heavenly peace, and in the very moment that he was pronouncing those sweet names. 'The invocation of the sacred names of Jesus and Mary,' says Thomas à Kempis, 'is a short prayer, which is as sweet to the mind, and as powerful to protect those who use it against the enemies of their salvation, as it is easy to remember.'[44]

'Blessed is the man who loves thy name, O Mary,'[45] exclaims Saint Bonaventure. 'Yes, truly blessed is he who loves thy sweet name, O Mother of God ! for,' he continues, 'thy name is so glorious and admirable, that no one who remembers it has any fears at the hour of death.'[46] Such is its power, that none of those who invoke it at the hour of death fear the assaults of their enemies.

O, that we may end our lives as did the Capuchin father, Fulgentius of Ascoli, who expired singing, 'O Mary, O Mary, the most beautiful of creatures ! let us depart together ;' or like blessed Henry the Cistercian, who expired in the very moment that he was pronouncing the most sweet name of Mary. Let us then, O devout reader, beg God to grant us, that at death the name of Mary may be the last word on our lips. This was the prayer of Saint Germanus : ' May the last movement of my tongue be to pronounce the name of the Mother of

[44] Hæc sancta oratio, Jesus et Maria, brevis est ad legendum . . . facilis ad tenendum, dulcis ad cogitandum, fortis ad protegendum.—*Vall. Lil.* cap. xiii.

[45] Beatus vir qui diligit nomen tuum, Maria Virgo.—*In Ps.* i. *B.V.M.*

[46] Gloriosum et admirabile est nomen tuum; qui illud retinent, non expavescent in puncto mortis.—*Ps.* cx. *B.M.V.*

God !'[47]　O sweet, O safe is that death which is accom·
panied and protected by such a saving name ; for God
only grants the grace of invoking it to those whom He
is about to save.

O my sweet Lady and Mother, I love thee much,
and because I love thee I also love thy holy name.　I
purpose and hope, with thy assistance, always to invoke
it during life and at death.　And to conclude with the
tender prayer of Saint Bonaventure : ' I ask thee, O
Mary, for the glory of thy name, to come and meet my
soul when it is departing from this world, and to take
it in thine arms.'[48]　' Disdain not, O Mary,' the Saint
continues, ' to come then and comfort me with thy presence.　Be thyself my soul's ladder and way to heaven.
Do thou thyself obtain for it the grace of forgiveness
and eternal repose.'[49]　He then concludes, saying, ' O
Mary, our advocate, it is for thee to defend thy clients,
and to undertake their cause before the tribunal of
Jesus Christ.'[50]

EXAMPLE.

Father Rho,[51] and also Father Lyræus[52] relate, that
in Gelderland, about the year 1465, there was a young
woman, named Mary, who was one day sent by her
uncle to the city of Nymegen to market.　He desired
her to purchase different things, and to spend the night
with an aunt who dwelt there.　The girl executed the
commissions ; but in the evening, on presenting herself
at her aunt's house, she was refused admittance, and

---

[47] Idem Dei Matris nomen sit mihi ultimus linguæ loquentis motus.—*In
Aunant. S. Dei Gen. Orat.*

[48] In exitu animæ meæ de hoc mundo, occurre illi Domina, et suscipe
eam.—*Ps. cxiii. B.M.V.*

[49] Consolare eat: vultu sancto tuo ; aspectus dæmonis non turbet illam ;
esto illi scala ad regnum cœlorum, et iter rectum ad paradisum Dei.　Im-
petra ei a Patre indulgentiam pacis, et sedem lucis inter servos Dei.—*Ib.*

[50] Sustine devotos ante tribunal Christi ; suscipe causam eorum in manibus
tuis.—*Ib.*

[51] Ne' suoi Sabbati. †

[52] Tris. Mar. l. 3, t. 8.

obliged to make the best of her way home. Night came on whilst she was on the road, and in a great passion she called on the devil with a loud voice to assist her. She had scarcely done so when he appeared to her under the form of a man, and promised to help her, provided she would do one thing. 'I will do anything,' replied the unfortunate creature. 'All that I require,' said the enemy, 'is, that you should no longer make the sign of the cross, and that you should change your name.' 'As to the sign of the cross,' said the girl, 'I will no more make it; but my name of Mary is too dear to me, I will never change it.' 'Then I will not help you,' said the devil. At length, after much disputing, it was agreed that she should be called by the first letter of the name of Mary, that is Emme. On this arrangement they started for Antwerp, and there the poor wretch remained with this wicked companion for seven years, leading a most shameful life, and a scandal to all. One day she told the devil she wished to see her country once more; the enemy opposed it, but was at length obliged to yield. On entering Nymegen, they found that a theatrical piece was being performed, representing the life of the Blessed Virgin. On seeing it, the poor Emme began to weep, having still preserved a spark of devotion towards the Mother of God. 'What are we doing here?' exclaimed her companion. 'Are we also to act a comedy?' And, at the same time, he endeavoured to drive her from the place. She resisted; but he, seeing that he was already losing her, in a passion, raised her in the air, and cast her to the ground in the midst of the theatre. The poor creature then related all that had happened. She went to confession to the parish priest, but he sent her to the Bishop of Cologne; and the Bishop referred her to the Pope, who, after having heard her confession, imposed upon her as a penance, that she should always wear three circlets of iron, one round her neck and two round her arms. The penitent obeyed, and on reaching Maestricht she shut herself up in a convent of penitents, and lived there for fourteen years in the exercise of the most rigorous mortification. One morning, on rising from her bed, she found that the three circlets had broken of their own accord; and two years afterwards she died in the odour of sanctity, and desired to be buried with those three circlets of iron, which, from being a slave of hell, had transformed her into a happy captive of her benefactress.

PRAYER.

O great Mother of God and my Mother Mary, it is true that I am unworthy to name thee; but thou, who lovest me and desirest my salvation, must, notwithstanding the impurity of my tongue, grant that I may always invoke thy most holy and powerful name in my aid, for thy name is the succour of the living, and the salvation of the dying. Ah, most pure Mary, most sweet Mary, grant that from henceforth thy name may be the breath of my life. O Lady, delay not to help me when I invoke thee, for in all the temptations which assail me, and in all my wants, I will never cease calling upon thee, and repeating again and again, Mary, Mary. Thus it is that I hope to act during my life, and more particularly at death, that after that last struggle I may eternally praise thy beloved name in heaven, O clement, O pious, O sweet Virgin Mary. Ah, Mary, most amiable Mary, with what consolation, what sweetness, what confidence, what tenderness, is my soul penetrated in only naming, in only thinking of thee! I thank my Lord and God, who, for my good, has given thee a name so sweet and deserving of love, and at the same time so powerful.

But, my sovereign Lady, I am not satisfied with only naming thee, I wish to name thee with love: I desire that my love may every hour remind me to call on thee, so that I may be able to exclaim with Saint

Bonaventure, 'O name of the Mother of God, thou art my love.'[53]

My own dear Mary, O my beloved Jesus, may your most sweet names reign in my heart, and in all hearts. Grant that I may forget all others to remember, and always invoke, your adorable names alone. Ah! Jesus my Redeemer, and my Mother Mary, when the moment of death comes, in which I must breathe forth my soul and leave this world, deign, through your merits, to grant that I may then pronounce my last words, and that they may be, '*I love thee, O Jesus; I love thee, O Mary;* to you do I give my heart and my soul.'

[53] O amor mei, nomen Matris Dei.—*Stim. Am.* p. 3, cap. 16.

DEVOUT PRAYERS

ADDRESSED BY VARIOUS SAINTS TO THE DIVINE MOTHER.

———

The following Prayers are put here, not only that they may be used, but also that they may show the high idea that the Saints had of the power and mercy of Mary, and the great confidence they had in her patronage.

———

PRAYER OF SAINT EPHREM.

O immaculate and entirely-pure Virgin Mary, Mother of God, Queen of the Universe, our own good Lady; thou art above all the Saints, the only hope of the Patriarchs, and the joy of the Saints. Through thee we have been reconciled with our God. Thou art the only advocate of sinners, and the secure haven of those who are sailing on the sea of this life. Thou art the consolation of the world, the ransom of captives, the joy of the sick, the comfort of the afflicted, the refuge, the salvation of the whole world. O great Princess, Mother of God, cover us with the wings of thy mercy, and pity us. No other hope but thee is given us, O most pure Virgin. We are given to thee, and consecrated to thy service; we bear the name of thy servants. O, then, permit not that Lucifer should drag us to hell. O immaculate Virgin, we are under thy protection, and therefore we have recourse to thee alone; and we beseech thee to prevent thy beloved Son, who is irritated by our sins, from abandoning us to the power of the devil.

O thou who art full of grace, enlighten my understanding, loosen my tongue, that it may sing thy praises; and more particularly the angelic Salutation, so worthy of thee. I salute thee, O peace, O joy, O consolation of the whole world. I salute thee, O greatest of miracles, O paradise of delights, secure haven of those who are in danger, fountain of graces, mediatress between God and men.[1]

PRAYER OF SAINT BERNARD.

We raise our eyes to thee, O Queen of the world. We must appear before our Judge after so many sins; who will appease Him? No one can do it better than thou canst, O holy Lady, who hast loved Him so much, and by whom thou art so tenderly beloved. Open, then, O Mother of mercy, the ears of thy heart to our sighs and prayers. We fly to thy protection; appease the wrath of thy Son, and restore us to His grace. Thou dost not abhor a sinner, however loathsome he may be. Thou dost not despise him, if he sighs to thee, and, repentant, asks thy intercession. Thou, with thy compassionate hand, deliverest him from despair. Thou animatest him to hope, and dost not leave him until thou hast reconciled him with his Judge. Thou art that chosen Lady in whom our Lord found repose, and in whom He has deposited all His treasures without measure. Hence the whole world, O my most holy Lady, honours thy chaste womb as the temple of God, in which the salvation of the world began. In thee was effected the reconciliation between God and man. Thou, O great Mother of God, art the enclosed garden, into which the hand of a sinner never entered to gather

---

[1] De Laud. Dei Gen.

its flowers. Thou art the beautiful garden in which God has planted all the flowers that adorn the Church, and amongst others the violet of thy humility, the lily of thy purity, the rose of thy charity. With whom can we compare thee, O Mother of grace and beauty? Thou art the paradise of God; from thee issued forth the fountain of living water that irrigates the whole earth. O, how many benefits thou hast bestowed on the world by meriting to be so salutary a channel!

Of thee it is that the question is asked, " Who is sne that cometh forth like the morning rising, fair as the moon, bright as the sun?"[2] Thou camest, then, into the world, O Mary, as a resplendent dawn, preceding with the light of thy sanctity the coming of the Sun of Justice. The day on which thou camest into the world can indeed be called a day of salvation, a day of grace. Thou art fair as the moon; for as amongst all planets the moon it is which is most like the sun, so amongst all creatures thou art the nearest in resemblance to God. The moon illumines the night with the light it receives from the sun, and thou enlightenest our darkness with the splendour of thy virtues. But thou art fairer than the moon, for in thee there is neither spot nor shadow. Thou art bright as the sun; I mean as that Sun which created the sun; He was chosen amongst all men, and thou wast chosen amongst all women. O sweet, O great, O all-amiable Mary, no heart can pronounce thy name but thou inflamest it with thy love; nor can they who love thee think of thee without feeling themselves strengthened to love thee more.

O holy Lady, help our weakness. And who is more fit to address our Lord Jesus Christ than thou, who enjoyest in such close vicinity His most sweet converse? Speak then, speak, O Lady; for thy Son listens to thee, and thou wilt obtain all that thou askest of Him.[3]

---

[2] Cant. vi. 9.   [3] Depr· ad gl. V.

PRAYER OF SAINT GERMANUS.

O my only and sovereign Lady, who art the sole consolation that I receive from God, thou who art the only celestial dew that gives me refreshment in my pains, thou who art the light of my soul when it is surrounded with darkness, thou who art my guide in journeyings, my strength in weakness, my treasure in poverty, the balm of my wounds, my consolation in sorrow, thou who art my refuge in miseries and the hope of my salvation; listen to my prayers, have pity on me as it becomes the Mother of a God who has such love for men.[4] O thou who art our defence and joy, grant me all that I ask; make me worthy to enjoy with thee that great happiness which thou enjoyest in heaven. Yes, my Lady, my refuge, my life, my help, my defence, my strength, my joy, my hope, grant that I may one day be with thee in heaven. I know that, being the Mother of God, thou canst, if thou wilt, obtain it for me. O Mary, thou art omnipotent to save sinners, nor needest thou any other recommendation; for thou art the Mother of true life.[5]

PRAYER OF BLESSED RAYMOND JOURDAIN, ABBOT OF CELLES.[6]

Draw me after thee, O Virgin Mary, that I may run to the odour of thy ointments. Draw me, for I am held back by the weight of my sins and by the malice of my enemies. As no one goes to thy Son unless the heavenly Father draws him, so do I presume to say, in a certain manner, that no one goes to Him unless thou drawest him by thy holy prayers. It is thou who teachest true wisdom, thou who obtainest grace for sinners, for thou art their advocate; it is thou who promisest glory to him who honours thee, for thou art the treasurer of graces.[7]

[4] Encom. in S. Deip.   [5] In Dorm. V.M. §. 2.
[6] Out of humility he surnamed himself the Idiot.
[7] Cont. de V.M. in prol.

Thou, O most sweet Virgin, hast found grace with God, for thou wast preserved from the stain of original sin, wast filled with the Holy Ghost, and didst conceive the Son of God. Thou, O most humble Virgin, didst receive all these graces not for thyself only, but also for us, that thou mightest assist us in all our necessities. And this thou dost indeed; thou succourest the good, preserving them in grace, and the wicked thou preparest to receive divine mercy. Thou assistest the dying, protecting them against the snares of the devil; and thou helpest them also after death, receiving their souls and conducting them to the kingdom of the blessed.[8]

PRAYER OF SAINT METHODIUS.

Thy name, O Mother of God, is filled with all graces and divine blessings. Thou hast contained Him who cannot be contained, and nourished Him who nourishes all creatures. He who fills heaven and earth, and is Lord of all, was pleased to stand in need of thee, for it was thou who didst clothe Him with that flesh which He had not before. Rejoice then, O Mother and handmaid of God; be glad then, with exceeding great joy, for thou hast Him for thy debtor who gives their being to all creatures. We are all God's debtors, but He is a debtor to thee. Hence it is, O most holy Mother of God, that thou hast greater goodness and greater charity than all the other Saints, and hast freer access to God than any of them, for thou art His Mother. Ah, deign, we beseech thee, to remember us in our miseries, who celebrate thy glories, and know how great is thy goodness.[9]

PRAYER OF SAINT JOHN DAMASCEN.

I salute thee, O Mary; thou art the hope of Christians; receive the supplication of a sinner who loves thee tenderly, honours thee in a special manner, and places in thee the whole hope of his salvation. From

---

[8] Cont. de V.M. c. 6.　　　　　[9] De Sim. et Anna.

thee I have my life. Thou reinstatest me in the grace
of thy Son; thou art the certain pledge of my salvation. I implore thee, then, deliver me from the burden
of my sins, dispel the darkness of my mind, banish
earthly affections from my heart, repress the temptations of my enemies, and so rule my whole life that by
thy means and under thy guidance I may attain the
eternal happiness of heaven.[10]

PRAYER OF SAINT ANDREW OF CANDIA.[11]

I salute thee, O full of grace, our Lord is with
thee; I salute thee, O cause of our joy, through whom
the sentence of our condemnation was revoked and
changed into one of blessing. I salute thee, O temple
of the glory of God, sacred dwelling of the King of
heaven. Thou art the reconciliation of God with men.
I salute thee, O Mother of our joy. Truly thou art
blessed, for thou alone amongst all women wast found
worthy to be the Mother of thy Creator. All nations
call thee Blessed.[12]

O Mary, if I place my confidence in thee, I shall
be saved; if I am under thy protection, I have nothing
to fear, for the fact of being thy client is the possession
of a certainty of salvation, which God only grants to
those whom He will save.

O Mother of Mercy, appease thy beloved Son.
Whilst thou wast on earth thou didst only occupy a
small part of it, but now that thou art raised above the
highest heavens, the whole world considers thee as the
propitiatory of all nations. I implore thee, then, O
Holy Virgin, to grant me the help of thy prayers with
God; prayers which are dearer and more precious to
us than all the treasures of the earth: prayers which
render God propitious to us in our sins, and obtain us
a great abundance of graces, both for the pardon of our

10 In Nat. V.M. §. 1.
11 Or of Jerusalem; for it is not known whether it was one person under
the two titles, or two different persons.
12 In S. Deip. Ann.

offences and the practice of virtue : prayers which check our enemies, confound their designs, and triumph over their strength.[13]

PRAYER OF SAINT ILDEPHONSUS.

I come to thee, O Mother of God, and implore thee to obtain me the pardon of my sins, and that I may be cleansed from those of my whole life. I beseech thee to grant me the grace to unite myself in affection with thy Son and with thyself: with thy Son as my God, and with thee as the Mother of my God.[14]

PRAYER OF SAINT ATHANASIUS.

Give ear to our prayers, O most Holy Virgin, and be mindful of us. Dispense unto us the gifts of thy riches, and the abundance of the graces with which thou art filled. The archangel saluted thee, and called thee full of grace. All nations call thee blessed. The whole hierarchy of heaven blesses thee ; and we, who are of the terrestrial hierarchy, also address thee, saying, Hail, O full of grace, our Lord is with thee ; pray for us, O holy Mother of God, our Lady and our Queen.[15]

PRAYER OF ST. ANSELM.

We beseech thee, O most holy Lady, by the favour that God did thee, in raising thee so high as to make all things possible to thee with Him, so to act that the plenitude of grace, which thou didst merit, may render us partakers of thy glory. Strive, O most merciful Lady, to obtain us that for which God was pleased to become man in thy chaste womb. O, lend us a willing ear. If thou deignest to pray to thy Son for this, He will immediately grant it. It suffices that thou willest our salvation, and then we are sure to obtain it. But who can restrain thy great mercy? If thou, who art our Mother, and the Mother of mercy, dost not pity

---

[13] In Dorm. S. M. ₰. 3.   [14] De Virg. p. S. M. c. 12.
[15] In Annunt. Deip.

us, what will become of us when thy Son comes to judge us?

Help us, then, O most compassionate Lady, and consider not the multitude of our sins. Remember always that our Creator took human flesh of thee, not to condemn sinners, but to save them. If thou hadst become Mother of God only for thine own advantage, we might say that it signified little to thee whether we were lost or saved; but God clothed Himself with thy flesh for thy salvation, and for that of all men. What would thy great power and glory avail us, if thou dost not make us partakers of thy happiness? O, help us, then, and protect us: thou knowest how greatly we stand in need of thy assistance. We recommend ourselves to thee; O, let us not lose our souls, but make us eternally serve and love thy beloved Son, Jesus Christ.[16]

PRAYER OF SAINT PETER DAMIAN.

Holy Virgin, Mother of God, succour those who implore thy aid. O, turn towards us. Hast thou, perhaps, forgotten men, because thou hast been raised to so close a union with God? Ah no, most certainly. Thou knowest well in what danger thou didst leave us, and the wretched condition of thy servants; ah no, it would not become so great a mercy as thine to forget such great misery as ours is. Turn towards us, then, with thy power; for He who is powerful has made thee omnipotent in heaven and on earth. Nothing is impossible to thee, for thou canst raise even those who are in despair to the hope of salvation. The more powerful thou art, the greater should be thy mercy.

Turn also to us in thy love. I know, O my Lady, that thou art all benign, and that thou lovest us with a love that can be surpassed by no other love. How often dost thou not appease the wrath of our Judge, when He is on the point of chastising us! All the

treasures of the mercies of God are in thy hands.   **Ah,**
never cease to benefit us; thou only seekest occasion
to save all the wretched, and to shower thy mercies
upon them; for thy glory is increased when, by thy
means, penitents are forgiven, and thus reach heaven.
Turn, then, towards us, that we also may be able to go
and see thee in heaven; for the greatest glory we can
have will be, after seeing God, to see thee, to love thee,
and be under thy protection.   Be pleased, then, to
grant our prayer; for thy beloved Son desires to honour
thee, by denying thee nothing that thou askest.[17]

PRAYER OF WILLIAM OF PARIS.

O Mother of God, I have recourse to thee, and I
call upon thee not to reject me; for the whole congregation of the faithful calls and proclaims thee the
Mother of mercy.   Thou art that one who, from being
so dear to God, art always graciously heard; thy clemency was never wanting to anyone; thy most benign
affability never despised any sinner who had recourse
to thee, however enormous his crimes.   Can it be
falsely or in vain that the Church calls thee her advocate, and the refuge of sinners?   Never let it be said
that my sins could prevent thee from fulfilling the
great office of mercy, which is peculiarly thine own, by
which thou art the advocate and mediatress of peace,
the only hope and most secure refuge of the miserable.
Never shall it be said that the Mother of God, who
for the benefit of the world brought forth the Fountain
of Mercy, denied her mercy to any sinner who had recourse to her.   Thine office is that of peacemaker between God and men: let, then, the greatness of thy
compassion, and which far exceeds my sins, move thee
to help me.[18]

[17] In Nat. B. M. §. 1.   [18] De Rhet. div. §. 18.

THE GLORIES OF MARY.

PART THE SECOND.

TREATING OF

HER PRINCIPAL FEASTS AND HER DOLOURS:

ALSO

OF EACH OF HER DOLOURS IN PARTICULAR,

AND OF HER VIRTUES.

FOLLOWED BY THE DEVOTIONS USUALLY PRACTISED IN HER HONOUR

Discourses on the principal Feasts of Mary and on her Sorrows.

DISCOURSE I.

ON MARY'S IMMACULATE CONCEPTION.

How becoming it was that each of the Three Divine Persons should preserve Mary from Original Sin.

GREAT indeed was the injury entailed on Adam and all his posterity by his accursed sin; for at the same time that he thereby, for his own great misfortune, lost grace, he also forfeited all the other precious gifts with which he had originally been enriched, and drew down upon himself and all his descendants the hatred of God and an accumulation of evils. But from this general misfortune God was pleased to exempt that Blessed Virgin whom He had destined to be the Mother of the

S

Second Adam—Jesus Christ—who was to repair the
evil done by the first. Now, let us see how becoming
it was that God, and all the three Divine Persons,
should thus preserve her from it; that the Father
should preserve her as His Daughter, the Son as His
Mother, and the Holy Ghost as His Spouse.

First point.—In the first place it was becoming that
the Eternal Father should preserve Mary from the stain
of original sin, because she was His Daughter, and His
first-born daughter, as she herself declares : " I came
out of the mouth of the Most High, the first-born before
all creatures."[1]   For this text is applied to Mary by
sacred interpreters, the holy Fathers, and by the Church
on the solemnity of her Conception.   For be she the
first-born inasmuch as she was predestined in the Divine
decrees, together with the Son, before all creatures, according to the Scotists ; or be she the first-born of
grace as the predestined Mother of the Redeemer, after
the prevision of sin, according to the Thomists ; nevertheless all agree in calling her the first-born of God.
This being the case, it was quite becoming that Mary
should never have been the slave of Lucifer, but only
and always possessed by her Creator ; and this she in
reality was, as we are assured by herself : " The Lord
possessed me in the beginning of His ways."[2]   Hence
Denis of Alexandria rightly calls Mary ' the one and
only daughter of life.'[3]   She is the one and only daughter of life, in contradistinction to others who, being born
in sin, are daughters of death.

Besides this, it was quite becoming that the Eternal
Father should create her in His grace, since He destined
her to be the repairer of the lost world, and the mediatress of peace between men and God; and, as such, she
is looked upon and spoken of by the holy Fathers, and
in particular by Saint John Damascen, who thus ad-

---

[1] Ego ex ore Altissimi prodivi, primogenita ante omnem creaturam.—
Eccl. xxiv. 5.
[2] Dominus possedit me in initio viarum suarum.—*Prov.* viii. 22.
[3] Una . . . et sola virgo, filia vitæ.—*Epist. contra Paul. Sam.*

dresses her : 'O Blessed Virgin, thou wast born that thou mightest minister to the salvation of the whole world.'[4] For this reason Saint Bernard says, 'that Noah's ark was a type of Mary; for as, by its means, men were preserved from the deluge, so are we all saved by Mary from the shipwreck of sin : but with the difference, that in the ark few were saved, and by Mary the whole human race was rescued from death.'[5] Therefore, in a sermon found amongst the works of Saint Athanasius, she is called 'the new Eve, and the Mother of life ;'[6] and not without reason, for the first was the Mother of death, but the most Blessed Virgin was the Mother of true life. Saint Theophanius of Nice, addressing Mary, says, 'Hail, thou who hast taken away Eve's sorrow !'[7] Saint Basil of Seleucia calls her the peacemaker between men and God : 'Hail, thou who art appointed umpire between God and men !'[8] and Saint Ephrem, the pacificator of the whole world : 'Hail, reconciler of the whole world !'[9]

But now, it certainly would not be becoming to choose an enemy to treat of peace with the offended person, and still less an accomplice in the crime itself. Saint Gregory[10] says, 'that an enemy cannot undertake to appease his judge, who is at the same time the injured party; for if he did, instead of appeasing him, he would provoke him to greater wrath.' And therefore, as Mary was to be the mediatress of peace between men and God, it was of the utmost importance that she

---

[4] O desiderabilissima femina, ac terque beata! . . . in mundum prodiisti, ut orbis universi saluti obsequaris.—*Serm.* i. *in Nat. B. V.*

[5] Sicut . . . per illam omnes evaserunt diluvium, sic per istam peccati naufragium . . . Per illam paucorum facta est liberatio : per istam humani generis salvatio.—*Serm. de B. Maria.*

[6] Nova Heva, Mater vitæ nuncupata.—*Int. op. S. Athan. Serm. de Annunt. Deip.*

[7] Ave Domina Virgo, ave purissima, ave receptaculum Dei, ave candelabrum luminis, Adæ revocatio, Evæ redemptio, mons sanctus, manifestum sanctuarium, et sponsarium immortalitatis.—*In Annunt. B M. V. Hymn.*

[8] Ave gratia plena, Dei ac hominum mediatrix, quo medius paries inimicitiæ tollatur, ac cœlestibus terrena coeant ac uniantur.—*Orat. in S. M. et de Inc. D.N.J.C.*

[9] Av totius terrarum orbis conciliatrix efficacissima.—*Serm. de Laud. Virg.* [10] *Past.* p. 1, c. 11.

should not herself appear as a sinner and as an enemy of God, but that she should appear in all things as a friend, and free from every stain.

Still more was it becoming that God should preserve her from original sin, for He destined her to crush the head of that infernal serpent, which, by seducing our first parents, entailed death upon all men; and this our Lord foretold : " I will put enmities between thee and the woman, and thy seed and her seed : she shall crush thy head."[11] But if Mary was to be that valiant woman brought into the world to conquer Lucifer, certainly it was not becoming that he should first conquer her, and make her his slave; but it was reasonable that she should be preserved from all stain, and even momentary subjection to her opponent. The proud spirit endeavoured to infect the most pure soul of this Virgin with his venom, as he had already infected the whole human race. But praised and ever blessed be God, who, in His infinite goodness, preëndowed her for this purpose with such great grace, that, remaining always free from any guilt of sin, she was ever able to beat down and confound his pride, as Saint Augustine, or whoever may be the author of the commentary on Genesis, says : ' Since the devil is the head of original sin, this head it was that Mary crushed : for sin never had any entry into the soul of this Blessed Virgin, which was consequently free from all stain.'[12] And Saint Bonaventure more expressly says, ' It was becoming that the Blessed Virgin Mary, by whom our shame was to be blotted out, and by whom the devil was to be conquered, should never, even for a moment, have been under his dominion.'[13]

---

[11] Inimicitias ponam inter te et mulierem, et semen tuum et semen illius; ipsa conteret caput tuum.—*Gen.* iii. 15.

[12] Cum peccati originalis caput sit diabolus, tale caput Maria contrivit, quia nulla peccati subjectio ingressum habuit in animam Virginis, et ideo ab omni macula immunis fuit.—*Ib.* †

[13] Congruum erat ut beata Virgo Maria, per quam aufertur nobis opprobrium, vinceret diabolum, ut nec ei succumberet ad modicum.—**Lib. iii. dist.** 3, art. 2, q. 1

But, above all, it principally became the Eternal
Father to preserve this His daughter unspotted by
Adam's sin, as Saint Bernardine of Sienna remarks,
because He destined her to be the Mother of His only-
begotten Son : ' Thou wast preordained in the mind of
God, before all creatures, that thou mightest beget God
Himself as man.'[14]   If, then, for no other end, at least
for the honour of His Son, who was God, it was reasonable that the Father should create Mary free from every
stain.   The angelic Saint Thomas says, that all things
that are ordained for God should be holy and free from
stain : ' Holiness is to be attributed to those things
which are ordained for God.'[15]   Hence when David
was planning the temple of Jerusalem, on a scale of
magnificence becoming a God, he said, " For a house
is prepared not for man, but for God."[16]   How much
more reasonable, then, is it not, to suppose that the
Sovereign Architect, who destined Mary to be the Mother of His own Son, adorned her soul with all most
precious gifts, that she might be a dwelling worthy of a
God !   Denis the Carthusian says, ' that God, the arti-
ficer of all things, when constructing a worthy dwelling
for His Son, adorned it with all attractive graces.'[17]
And the Holy Church herself, in the following prayer,
assures us that God prepared the body and soul of the
Blessed Virgin, so as to be a worthy dwelling on earth
for His only-begotten Son.   ' Almighty and Eternal
God, who, by the coöperation of the Holy Ghost, didst
prepare the body and soul of the glorious Virgin and

[14] Tu ante omnem creaturam in mente Dei præordinata fuisti, ut, omnium feminarum castissima, Deum ipsum hominem verum ex tua carne
procreares.—*Serm. de Concep. B.M.V.* art. iii. cap. 3.

[15] Sanctitas illis rebus attribuitur, quæ in Deum ordinantur.—1 p. q. xxxvi.
art. 1, concl.

[16] Neque enim homini præparatur habitatio, sed Deo.—1 *Paralipom.*
xxix. 1.

[17] Omnium artifex Deus, ad ipsius formationem in utero supernaturaliter
concurrens, Filio suo dignum habitaculum fabricaturus, eam intrinsecus
omnium gratificantium charismatum et dignificantium habituum plenitr-
dine adornavit.—*De Laud. V.* lib. ii. art. 2.

Mother Mary, that she might become a worthy habitation for thy Son,' &c.[18]

We know that a man's highest honour is to be born of noble parents : " And the glory of children are their fathers."[19] Hence in the world the reputation of being possessed of only a small fortune, and little learning, is more easily tolerated than that of being of low birth ; for, whilst a poor man may become rich by his industry, an ignorant man learned by study, it is very difficult for a person of humble origin to attain the rank of nobility ; but, even should he attain it, his birth can always be made a subject of reproach to him. How, then, can we suppose that God, who could cause His Son to be born of a noble mother by preserving her from sin, would on the contrary permit Him to be born of one infected by it, and thus enable Lucifer always to reproach Him with the shame of having a mother who had once been his slave and the enemy of God ? No, certainly, the Eternal Father did not permit this ; but He well provided for the honour of His Son by preserving His Mother always Immaculate, that she might be a Mother becoming such a Son. The Greek Church bears witness to this, saying, ' that God, by a singular providence, caused the most Blessed Virgin to be as perfectly pure from the very first moment of her existence, as it was fitting that she should be, who was to be the worthy Mother of Christ.'[20]

It is a common axiom amongst theologians that no gift was ever bestowed on any creature with which the Blessed Virgin was not also enriched. Saint Bernard says on this subject, ' It is certainly not wrong to suppose that that which has evidently been bestowed, even

---

[18] Omnipotens sempiterne Deus, qui gloriosæ Virginis Matris Mariæ corpus et animam, ut dignum Filii tui habitaculum effici mereretur, Spiritu Sancto cooperante, præparasti, &c.

[19] Gloria filiorum patres eorum.—*Prov.* xvii. 6.

[20] Providentia singulari perfecit, ut ss. Virgo, ab ipso vitæ suæ principio tam omnino existeret pura, quam decebat illam, quæ Christo digna mater existeret.—*In Men. die* xxv. *Martii.*

on only a few, was not denied to so great a Virgin.'[21] Saint Thomas of Villanova says, 'Nothing was ever granted to any Saint which did not shine in a much higher degree in Mary from the very first moment of her existence.'[22] And as it is true that 'there is an infinite difference between the Mother of God and the servants of God,'[23] according to the celebrated saying of Saint John Damascen, we must certainly suppose, according to the doctrine of Saint Thomas, that 'God conferred privileges of grace in every way greater on His Mother than on His servants.'[24] And now admitting this, Saint Anselm, the great defender of the Immaculate Mary, takes up the question and says, 'Was the wisdom of God unable to form a pure dwelling, and to remove every stain of human nature from it?'[25] Perhaps God could not prepare a clean habitation for His Son by preserving it from the common contagion? 'God,' continues the same Saint, 'could preserve angels in heaven spotless, in the midst of the devastation that surrounded them; was He, then, unable to preserve the Mother of His Son and the Queen of angels from the common fall of men?'[26] And I may here add, that as God could grant Eve the grace to come immaculate into the world, could He not, then, grant the same favour to Mary?

Yes, indeed! God could do it, and did it; for on every account 'it was becoming,' as the same Saint

---

[21] Quod . . . vel paucis mortalium constat fuisse collatum, fas certe non est suspicari tantæ Virgini esse negatum.—*Ep.* clxxiv. *ad Can. Lugd.*

[22] Nihil . . . usquam sanctorum speciali privilegio concessum est, quod non a principio vitæ accumulatius præfulgeat in Maria.—*In fest. Assump. B.V.* conc. i.

[23] Infinitum Dei servorum ac Matris discrimen est.—*Hom.* i. *in Dorm. B.V.M.*

[24] Rationabiliter . . . creditur, quod illa, quæ genuit Unigenitum, a Patre plenum gratiæ et veritatis præ omnibus aliis, majora privilegia gratiæ acceperit.—3 p. q. xxvii. art. 1, concl.

[25] Inscia ne fuit et impotens sapientia Dei et virtus mundum sibi habitaculum condere, remota omni labe conditionis humanæ?—*De Concept. B.M.V.*

[26] Angelis aliis peccantibus, bonos a peccatis servavit; et feminam, matrem suam mox futuram, ab aliorum peccatis exsortem servare non potuit?—*Ib.*

Anselm says, 'that that Virgin, on whom the Eternal Father intended to bestow His only-begotten Son, should be adorned with such purity as not only to exceed that of all men and angels, but exceeding any purity that can be conceived after that of God.'[27] And Saint John Damascen speaks in still clearer terms; for he says, 'that our Lord had preserved the soul, to gether with the body of the Blessed Virgin, in that purity which became her who was to receive a God into her womb; for, as He is holy, He only rep ses in holy places.'[28] And thus the Eternal Father could well say to His beloved daughter, 'As the lily among thorns; so is my love among the daughters.'[29] My daughter, amongst all my other daughters, thou art as a lily in the midst of thorns; for they are all stained with sin, but thou wast always Immaculate, and always my beloved.

Second point.—In the second place it was becoming that the Son should preserve Mary from sin, as being His Mother. No man can choose his mother; but should such a thing ever be granted to anyone, who is there who, if able to choose a queen, would wish for a slave? If able to choose a noble lady, would he wish for a servant? Or if able to choose a friend of God, would he wish for His enemy? If, then, the Son of God alone could choose a Mother according to His own heart, His liking, we must consider, as a matter of course, that He chose one becoming a God. Saint Bernard says, 'that the Creator of men becoming Man, must have selected Himself a Mother whom He knew became Him.'[30] And as it was becoming that a most

[27] Decens erat, ut ea puritate, qua major sub Deo nequit intelligi, Virgo illa niteret, cui Deus Pater unicum Filium suum . . . ita dare disponebat. —*De Concep. Virg.* cap. xviii.

[28] . . . Animum una cum corpore Virginem conservasset, veluti decebat illam, quæ sinu suo conceptura Deum erat, qui, cum ipse sanctus sit, in sanctis requiescit.—*De Fide Orth.* lib. iv. cap. 14.

[29] Sicut lilium inter spinas, sic amica mea inter filias.—*Cant.* ii. 2.

[30] Factor hominum, ut homo fieret, nasciturus de homine, talem sibi ex omnibus debuit deligere, imo condere matrem, qualem et se decere sciebat, et sibi noverat placituram.—*Sup. Miss.* Hom. ii.

pure God should have a Mother pure from all sin, He created her spotless. Saint Bernardine of Sienna, speaking of the different degrees of sanctification, says, that 'the third is that obtained by becoming the Mother of God ; and that this sanctification consists in the entire removal of original sin. This is what took place in the Blessed Virgin : truly God created Mary such, both as to the eminence of her nature and the perfection of grace with which He endowed her, as became Him who was to be born of her.'[31] Here we may apply the words of the Apostle to the Hebrews : "For it was fitting that we should have such a high priest ; holy, innocent, undefiled, separated from sinners."[32] A learned author observes that, according to Saint Paul, it was fitting that our Blessed Redeemer should not only be separated from sin, but also from sinners ; according to the explanation of Saint Thomas, who says, 'that it was necessary that He, who came to take away sins, should be separated from sinners, as to the fault under which Adam lay.'[33] But how could Jesus Christ be said to be separated from sinners if He had a Mother who was a sinner ?

Saint Ambrose says, 'that Christ chose this vessel into which He was about to descend, not of earth, but from heaven ; and He consecrated it a temple of purity.'[34] The Saint alludes to the text of Saint Paul : "The first man was of the earth, earthly : the second man from heaven, heavenly."[35] The Saint calls the

---

[31] Tertia fuit sanctificatio maternalis, et hæc removet culpam originalem. . . . Hæc fuit in B. Virgine Maria matre Dei. Sane Deus . . . talem, tam nobilitate naturæ, quam perfectione gratiæ, condidit matrem, qualem eam decebat habere suam gloriosissimam majestatem.—*Pro Concep. Im. V.* art. i. cap. 1.

[32] Talis enim decebat, ut nobis esset pontifex, sanctus, innocens, impollutus, segregatus a peccatoribus, et excelsior cœlis factus.—*Heb.* vii. 26.

[33] Oportuit eum, qui peccata venerat tollere, esse a peccatoribus segregatum, quantum ad culpam cui Adam subjacuit.—3 p. q. iv. art. 6, ad 2.

[34] Non de terra utique, sed de cœlo, vas sibi hoc per quod descenderet, Christus elegit, et sacravit templum pudoris.—*De Inst. V.* cap. v.

[35] Primus homo de terra, terrenus ; secundus homo de cœlo, cœlestis.— 1 *Cor.* xv. 47.

Divine Mother 'a heavenly vessel,' not because **Mary**
was not earthly by nature, as heretics have dreamt, but
because she was heavenly by grace ; she was as superior
to the angels of heaven in sanctity and purity, as it
was becoming that she should be, in whose womb a
King of Glory was to dwell.   This agrees with that
which Saint John the Baptist revealed to St. Bridget,
saying, 'It was not becoming that the King of Glory
should repose otherwise than in a chosen vessel, exceeding all men and angels in purity.'[36]   And to this
we may add that which the Eternal Father Himself
said to the same Saint : 'Mary was a clean and an unclean vessel : clean, for she was all fair ; but unclean,
because she was born of sinners ; though she was conceived without sin, that My Son might be born of her
without sin.'[37]   And remark these last words, 'Mary
was conceived without sin, that the Divine Son might
be born of her without sin.'   Not that Jesus Christ
could have contracted sin ; but that He might not be
reproached with even having a Mother infected with
it, who would consequently have been the slave of the
devil.

The Holy Ghost says that " the glory of a man is
from the honour of his father, and a father without
honour is the disgrace of the son."[38]   'Therefore it
was,' says an ancient writer, 'that Jesus preserved the
body of Mary from corruption after death ; for it would
have redounded to His dishonour, had that virginal flesh
with which He had clothed Himself become the food of
worms.'   'For,' he adds, ' corruption is a disgrace of human nature ; and as Jesus was not subject to it, Mary
was also exempted ; for the flesh of Jesus is the flesh of

---

[36] Non decuit Regem gloriæ jacere, nisi in vase purissimo et mundissimo
et electissimo, præ omnibus angelis et hominibus.—*Rev.* lib. i. cap. 31.
[37] Maria fuit vas mundum, et non mundum.   Mundum vero fuit, quia
tota pulchra . . . sed non mundum fuit, quia . . . de peccatoribus nata est,
licet sine peccato concepta, ut Filius meus de ea sine peccato nasceretur.—
Rev. lib. v. *Exp. Rev.* xiii.
[38] Gloria enim hominis ex honore patris sui, et dedecus filii pater sine
honore.—*Eccles.* iii. 13.

Mary.'[39] But since the corruption of her body would
have been a disgrace for Jesus Christ, because He was
born of her, how much greater would the disgrace have
been, had He been born of a mother whose soul was
once infected with the corruption of sin? For not only
is it true that the flesh of Jesus is the same as that of
Mary, 'but,' adds the same author, 'the flesh of our
Saviour, even after His resurrection, remained the same
that He had taken from His Mother.' 'The flesh of
Christ is the flesh of Mary; and though it was glorified
by the glory of His resurrection, yet it remains the same
that was taken from Mary.'[40] Hence the Abbot Arnold
of Chartres says, 'The flesh of Mary and that of Christ
are one; and therefore I consider the glory of the Son
as being not so much common to, as one with that of
His Mother.'[41] And now if this is true, supposing that
the Blessed Virgin was conceived in sin, though the
Son could not have contracted its stain, nevertheless
His having united flesh to Himself which was once infected with sin, a vessel of uncleanness and subject to
Lucifer, would always have been a blot.

Mary was not only the Mother, but the worthy Mother of our Saviour. She is called so by all the holy
Fathers. Saint Bernard says, 'Thou alone wast found
worthy to be chosen as the one in whose virginal womb
the King of kings should have His first abode.'[42] Saint
Thomas of Villanova says, 'Before she conceived, she
was already fit to be the Mother of God.'[43] The holy
Church herself attests that Mary merited to be the
Mother of Jesus Christ, saying, 'the Blessed Virgin,

[39] Putredo namque et vermis humanæ est opprobrium conditionis, a quo
opprobrio cum Jesus sit alienus, natura Mariæ excipitur . . . caro enim
Jesu caro est Mariæ.—*De Assump. B.M.V.* lib. c. 5.

[40] Caro enim Christi, quamvis gloria resurrectionis fuerit magnificata
. . . eadem tamen carnis mansit et manet natura, quæ suscepta est de Maria.
—*Ib.*

[41] Una est Mariæ et Christi caro . . . Filii gloriam cum matre non tam
communem judico, quam eandem.—*De Laud. B.M.*

[42] Tu sola inventa es digna, ut in tua virginali aula Rex regum . . .
primam sibi mansionem . . . elegit.—*Depr. ad B.V.*

[43] Antequam conciperet Filium Dei, jam idonea erat, ut esset Mater Dei
—*Serm.* iii. *de Nat. B.V.*

who merited to bear in her womb Christ our Lord;[44] and Saint Thomas Aquinas, explaining these words, says, that 'the Blessed Virgin is said to have merited to bear the Lord of all; not that she merited His Incarnation, but that she merited, by the graces she had received, such a degree of purity and sanctity, that she could becomingly be the Mother of God;'[45] that is to say, Mary could not merit the Incarnation of the Eternal Word, but by Divine grace she merited such a degree of perfection as to render her worthy to be the Mother of a God; according to what Saint Peter Damian also writes: 'Her singular sanctity, the effect of grace, merited that she alone should be judged worthy to receive a God.'[46]

And now, supposing that Mary was worthy to be the Mother of God, 'what excellency and what perfection was there that did not become her?'[47] asks Saint Thomas of Villanova. The angelic Doctor says, 'that when God chooses anyone for a particular dignity, He renders him fit for it;' whence he adds, 'that God, having chosen Mary for His Mother, He also by His grace rendered her worthy of this highest of all dignities.' 'The Blessed Virgin was divinely chosen to be the Mother of God, and therefore we cannot doubt that God had fitted her by His grace for this dignity; and we are assured of it by the angel: "For thou hast found grace with God; behold, thou shalt conceive," &c.[48] And thence the Saint argues that 'the Blessed Virgin never committed any actual sin, not even a

[44] Regina cœli, lætare . . . quia quem meruisti portare . . . resurrexit, sicut dixit.—*Antiph. temp. Pasch.*

[45] Beata Virgo dicitur meruisse portare Dominum omnium: non quia meruit ipsum incarnari, sed quia meruit, ex gratia sibi data, illum puritatis et sanctitatis gradum, ut congrue posset esse Mater Dei.—3 p. q. 2, art. xi. ad 3.

[46] Venerabilis Mater Domini, septem Sancti Spiritus donis . . . dotata fuit. Quam utique æterna sapientia . . . talem construxit, quæ digna fieret illum suscipere.—*Serm.* ii. *de Nat. B.M.V.*

[47] Quæ autem excellentia, quæ perfectio, quæ magnitudo decuit eam, ut esset idonea Mater Dei.—*Serm.* iii. *de Nat. B.M.V.*

[48] Beata autem Virgo fuit electa divinitus, ut esset mater Dei; et ideo non est dubitandum quin Deus per suam gratiam eam ad hoc idoneam reddidit, secundum quod angelus ad eam dicit, "Invenisti gratiam apud Deum: ecce, concipies," &c.—3 p. q. xxvii. art. 4, concl.

venial one. Otherwise,' he says, 'she would not have been a Mother worthy of Jesus Christ; for the ignominy of the Mother would also have been that of the Son, for He would have had a sinner for His Mother.'[49] And now if Mary, on account of a single venial sin, which does not deprive a soul of Divine grace, would not have been a Mother worthy of God, how much more unworthy would she have been, had she contracted the guilt of original sin, which would have made her an enemy of God and a slave of the devil? And this reflection it was that made Saint Augustine utter those memorable words, that, 'when speaking of Mary for the honour of our Lord,' whom she merited to have for her Son, he would not entertain even the question of sin in her; 'for we know,' he says, 'that through Him, who it is evident was without sin, and whom she merited to conceive and bring forth, she received grace to conquer all sin.'[50]

Therefore, as Saint Peter Damian observes, we must consider it as certain 'that the Incarnate Word chose Himself a becoming Mother, and one of whom He would not have to be ashamed.'[51] Saint Proclus also says, 'that He dwelt in a womb which He had created free from all that might be to His dishonour.'[52] It was no shame to Jesus Christ, when He heard Himself contemptuously called by the Jews the Son of Mary, meaning that He was the Son of a poor woman: " Is not His Mother called Mary?"[53] for He came into this world to give us an example of humility and patience. But, on

---

[49] Non . . . fuisset idonea Mater Dei, si peccasset aliquando . . . quia . . . ignominia Matris ad Filium redundasset.—3 p. q. xxvii. art. 4, concl.

[50] Excepta itaque sancta virgine Maria, de qua, propter honorem Domini, nullam prorsus cum de peccatis agitur haberi volo quæstionem : unde enim scimus, quod ei plus gratiæ collatum fuerit ad vincendum omni ex parte peccatum, quæ concipere ac parere meruit, quem constat nullum habuisse peccatum.—De Nat. et Gratia, contra Pelag. cap. xxxvi.

[51] Quam utique æterna Sapientia . . . talem construxit, quæ digna fieret illum suscipere, et de intemeratæ carnis suæ visceribus procreare.—Serm. ii. in Nat. B.M.V.

[52] Intra viscera, quæ citra omnem dedecoris notam condiderat, inhabitat. — Hom. de Nat. D.N.J.C.

[53] Nonne mater ejus dicitur Maria?—Matt. xiii. 55.

the other hand, it would undoubtedly have been a disgrace, could He have heard the devil say, 'Was not His
Mother a sinner? was He not born of a wicked Mother,
who was once our slave?' It would even have been unbecoming had Jesus Christ been born of a woman whose
body was deformed, or crippled, or possessed by devils:
but how much more would it have been so, had He
been born of a woman whose soul had been once deformed by sin, and in the possession of Lucifer!

Ah! indeed, God, who is Wisdom itself, well knew
how to prepare Himself a becoming dwelling, in which
to reside on earth: "Wisdom hath built herself a
house."[54] "The Most High hath sanctified His own
tabernacle . . . . God will help it in the morning
early."[55]   David says that our Lord sanctified this
His dwelling "in the morning early;" that is to say,
from the beginning of her life, to render her worthy
of Himself; for it was not becoming that a holy God
should choose Himself a dwelling that was not holy:
"Holiness becometh Thy house."[56]   And if God declares that He will never enter a malicious soul, or
dwell in a body subject to sin, "for wisdom will not
enter into a malicious soul, nor dwell in a body subject
to sins,"[57] how can we ever think that the Son of God
chose to dwell in the soul and body of Mary, without
having previously sanctified and preserved it from
every stain of sin? for, according to the doctrine of
Saint Thomas, 'the Eternal Word dwelt not only in
the soul of Mary, but even in her womb.'[58]   The holy
Church sings, 'Thou, O Lord, hast not disdained to
dwell in the Virgin's womb.'[59]   Yes, for He would

---

[54] Sapientia ædificavit sibi domum.—*Prov.* ix. 1.
[55] Sanctificavit tabernaculum suum Altissimus . . . adjuvabit eam Deus
mane diluculo.—*Ps.* xlv. 5, 6.
[56] Domum tuam decet sanctitudo.—*Ps.* xcii. 5.
[57] In malevolam animam non introibit sapientia, nec habitabit in corpore
subdito peccatis.—*Sap.* i. 4.
[58] Singulari modo Dei Filius, qui est Dei sapientia, in ipsa habitavit; non
solum in anima, sed etiam in utero.—3 p. q. xxvii. art. 4, concl.
[59] Non horruisti Virginis uterum.

have disdained to have taken flesh in the womb of an Agnes, a Gertrude, a Teresa, because these virgins, though holy, were nevertheless for a time stained with original sin ; but He did not disdain to become man in the womb of Mary, because this beloved Virgin was always pure and free from the least shadow of sin, and was never possessed by the infernal serpent. And therefore Saint Augustine says, 'that the Son of God never made Himself a more worthy dwelling than Mary, who was never possessed by the enemy, or despoiled of her ornaments.'[60]

On the other hand, Saint Cyril of Alexandria asks, 'Who ever heard of an architect who built himself a temple, and yielded up the first possession of it to his greatest enemy ?'[61]

Yes, says Saint Methodius, speaking on the same subject, that Lord who commanded us to honour our parents would not do otherwise, when He became man, than observe it, by giving His Mother every grace and honour : 'He who said, Honour thy father and thy mother, that He might observe His own decree, gave all grace and honour to His Mother.'[62] Therefore the author of the book already quoted from the works of Saint Augustine says, 'that we must certainly believe that Jesus Christ preserved the body of Mary from corruption after death ; for if He had not done so, He would not have observed the law,' which, 'at the same time that it commands us to honour our mother, forbids us to show her disrespect.'[63] But how little would Jesus have guarded His Mother's honour, had He not preserved her from Adam's sin ! 'Certainly that son

[60] Nullam digniorem domum sibi Filius Dei ædificavit quam Mariam, quæ nunquam fuit ab hostibus capta, neque suis ornamentis spoliata. †

[61] Quis unquam de architecto audivit, qui suum ipsius templum construxerit, et in eo habitare prohibitus sit ?—*Hom.* vi.

[62] Qui dixit, "Honora patrem tuum et matrem," longe potius id ipse præstare volens gratiam servaverit, ac quod ita statuit, ei, quæ ministravit, ut sic sponte nasceretur, divinisque laudibus decoraverit, quam sine patre, velut innuptam sibi matrem ascivit.—*Serm. de Simeone et Anna.*

[63] Lex enim, sicut honorem matris præcipit, ita inhonorationem damnat —*Lib. de Assump. B. V. int. op. S. Augustini*

would sin,' says the Augustinian father Thomas of Strasburg, 'who, having it in his power to preserve his mother from original sin, did not do so;' 'but that which would be a sin in us,' continues the same author, 'must certainly be considered unbecoming in the Son of God, who, whilst He could make His Mother immaculate, did it not.' 'Ah, no!' exclaims Gerson, 'since thou, the supreme Prince, choosest to have a Mother, certainly Thou owest her honour. But now if Thou didst permit her, who was to be the dwelling of all purity, to be in the abomination of original sin, certainly it would appear that that law was not well fulfilled.'[64]

'Moreover, we know,' says Saint Bernardine of Sienna, 'that the Divine Son came into the world more to redeem Mary than all other creatures.'[65] There are two means by which a person may be redeemed, as Saint Augustine teaches us; the one by raising him up after having fallen, and the other by preventing him from falling;[66] and this last means is doubtless the most honourable. 'He is more honourably redeemed,' says the learned Suarez, 'who is prevented from falling, than he who after falling is raised up;'[67] for thus the injury or stain is avoided which the soul always contracts by falling. This being the case, we ought certainly to believe that Mary was redeemed in the more honourable way, and the one which became the Mother of God, as Saint Bonaventure remarks; 'for it is to be believed that the Holy Ghost, as a

---

[64] Cum tu summus Princeps, vis habere Matrem carnaliter in terra, illi debebis honorem, &c. Nunc autem appareret illam legem non bene adimpleri, si in hujusmodi abominatione, immunditia, et subjectione peccati aliquo tempore permitteres illam, quæ esse debet habitaculum, templum, et palatium totius puritatis.—*Serm. de Concep. B.M.V.*

[65] Christus plus pro ipsa redimenda venit, quam pro omni alia creatura. —*Pro Fest. V.M.* s. 4. a. 3. c. 3. art. iii. cap. 3.

[66] Enarratio in Ps. lxxxv. versic. 3.

[67] Duplex est redimendi modus; unus erigendo lapsum, alter præveniendo jamjam lapsurum ne cadat: juxta illud Psalm. 143, "Redemisti servum tuum de gladio maligno;" id est, custodisti, ne interficeretur. Ex his autem posterior modus est sine dubio opus majoris gratiæ et benevolentiæ, et, cæteris paribus, majoris efficaciæ ac potestatis; ergo decuit, ut Christus Matrem suam nobilissimo modo redimeret. — *De Incarnat.* p. 2, q. xxvii. art. 2, disp. 3, sect. 5.

very special favour, redeemed and preserved her from original sin by a new kind of sanctification, and this in the very moment of her conception; not that sin was in her, but that it otherwise would have been.'[68] The sermon from which this passage is taken is proved by Frassen[69] to be really the work of the holy Doctor above named. On the same subject Cardinal Cusano elegantly remarks, that ' others had Jesus as a liberator, but to the most Blessed Virgin He was a pre-libera tor ;'[70] meaning, that all others had a Redeemer who delivered them from sin with which they were already defiled, but that the most Blessed Virgin had a Redeemer who, because He was her Son, preserved her from ever being defiled by it.

In fine, to conclude this point in the words of Hugo of Saint Victor, the tree is known by its fruits. If the Lamb was always immaculate, the Mother must also have been always immaculate: ' Such the Lamb, such the Mother of the Lamb; for the tree is known by its fruit.'[71] Hence this same Doctor salutes Mary, saying, 'O worthy Mother of a worthy Son;' meaning, that no other than Mary was worthy to be the Mother of such a Son, and no other than Jesus was a worthy Son of such a Mother: and then he adds these words, ' O fair Mother of beauty itself, O high Mother of the Most High, O Mother of God !'[72] Let us then address this most Blessed Mother in the words of Saint Ildephonsus, ' Suckle, O Mary, thy Creator, give milk to

---

[68] Credendum est enim, quod novo sanctificationis genere, in ejus conceptionis primordio, Spiritus Sanctus eam a peccato originali (non quod infuit, sed quod infuisset) redemit, atque singulari gratia præservavit.—*Serm.* ii. *de B.V.M.*

[69] Scot. Acad. de Inc. d. 3, a. 3, ⅔ 3, q. 1, § 5.

[70] Præliberatorem enim Virgo sancta habuit, cæteri liberatorem et postliberatorem. Christus enim sic omnium liberator, quod et Virginis liberator et præliberator, cæterorum vero liberator et postliberator. Ipsa sola post Adæ lapsum, non indiga, sed plena originali justitia, ut Eva, et multo magis, creata fuit.—*Excitat.* lib. viii. *Serm.* Sicut lil. int. sp.

[71] Talis . . . Agnus, qualis Mater Agni . . . quoniam omnis arbor ex fructu suo cognoscitur.—*De Verbo Inc.* coll. iii.

[72] O digna digni, formosa pulchri, munda incorrupti, excelsa altissimi, Mater Dei, Sponsa Regis æterni.—*Serm.* iii. *de Assump. B.M.V.*

Him who made thee, and who made thee such that He could be made of thee.'[73]

Third point.—Since, then, it was becoming that the Father should preserve Mary from sin as His daughter, and the Son as His Mother, it was also becoming that the Holy Ghost should preserve her as His spouse. Saint Augustine says that ' Mary was that only one who merited to be called the Mother and Spouse of God.'[74] For Saint Anselm asserts that ' the Divine Spirit, the love itself of the Father and the Son, came corporally into Mary, and enriching her with graces above all creatures, reposed in her and made her His Spouse, the Queen of heaven and earth.'[75] He says that He came into her corporally, that is, as to the effect : for He came to form of her immaculate body the immaculate body of Jesus Christ, as the Archangel had already predicted to her : " The Holy Ghost shall come upon thee."[76] And therefore it is, says Saint Thomas, ' that Mary is called the temple of the Lord, and the sacred resting-place of the Holy Ghost ; for by the operation of the Holy Ghost she became the Mother of the Incarnate Word.'[77]

And now, had an excellent artist the power to make his bride such as he could represent her, what pains would he not take to render her as beautiful as possible ! Who, then, can say that the Holy Ghost did otherwise with Mary, when He could make her who was to be His spouse as beautiful as it became Him that she should be ?

Ah no! He acted as it became Him to act ; for this

---

[73] Lacta, Maria, Creatorem tuum, lacta panem cœli, lacta præmium mundi . . . lacta ergo eum qui fecit te, qui talem fecit te, ut ipse fieret ex te.—*Serm. de Nat. B.M.V.*

[74] Hæc est quæ sola meruit Mater et Sponsa vocari.—*Serm.* 208. ed.B. app.

[75] Ipse . . . Spiritus Dei, ipse amor omnipotentis Patris et Filii . . . ipse, inquam, corporaliter, ut bene dicam, venit in eam, singularique gratia præ omnibus quæ creata sunt, sive in cœlo, sive in terra, requievit in ea, et reginam ac imperatricem cœli et terræ, et omnium quæ in eis sunt, fecit eam.— *De Excel. Virg.* cap. iv.

[76] Spiritus Sanctus superveniet in te.—*Luc.* i. 35.

[77] Unde dicitur templum Domini, sacrarium Spiritus Sancti, quia concepit ex Spiritu Sancto.—*Opusc.* vi i.

same Lord Himself declares : " Thou art all fair, O my
love, and there is not a spot in thee."[78]   These words,
say Saint Ildephonsus and Saint Thomas, are properly
to be understood of Mary, as Cornelius à Lapide remarks ; and Saint Bernardine of Sienna,[79] and Saint
Lawrence Justinian,[80] assert that they are to be understood precisely as applying to her Immaculate Conception ; whence Blessed Raymond Jordano addresses her,
saying, ' Thou art all fair, O most glorious Virgin, not
in part, but wholly ; and no stain of mortal, venial, or
original sin, is in thee.'[81]

The Holy Ghost signified the same thing when He
called this His spouse an enclosed garden and a sealed
fountain : " My sister, my spouse, is a garden enclosed,
a fountain sealed up."[82]   ' Mary,' says Saint Sophronius, ' was this enclosed garden and sealed fountain,
into which no guile could enter, against which no fraud
of the enemy could prevail, and who always was holy
in mind and body.'[83]   Saint Bernard likewise says, addressing the Blessed Virgin, ' Thou art an enclosed
garden, into which the sinner's hand has never entered
to pluck its flowers.'[84]

We know that this Divine Spouse loved Mary more
than all the other Saints and Angels put together, as
Father Suarez,[85] with Saint Lawrence Justinian, and
others, assert.   He loved her from the very beginning,
and exalted her in sanctity above all others, as it is
expressed by David in the Psalms : " The foundations

---

[78] Tota pulchra es, amica mea, et macula non est in te.—*Cant.* **iv. 7.**

[79] Serm. de Concep. B.M.V. art. ii. c. 2.

[80] Serm. de Nat. B.M V.

[81] Tota . . . pulchra es, Virgo gloriosissima, non in parte, sed in toto : et macula peccati, sive mortalis, sive venialis, sive originalis, non est in te.— *Contempl. B. V.* cap. ii.

[82] Hortus conclusus soror mea sponsa, hortus conclusus, fons signatus.— *Cant.* iv. 12.

[83] Hæc est hortus conclusus, fons signatus, puteus aquarum viventium, ad quam nulli potuerunt doli irrumpere, nec prævaluit fraus inimici ; sed permansit sancta mente et corpore.—*Serm. de Assump. B.M.V. int. op. S. Hieron.*

[84] Hortus conclusus tu es, Dei genitrix, ad quem deflorandum manus peccatoris nunquam introivit.—*Depr. ad B. V.M.*

[85] De Inc. p. 2. d. 18, § 4.

thereof are in the holy mountains : the Lord loveth the
gates of Sion above all the tabernacles of Jacob . . . a
man is born in her, and the Highest Himself hath
founded her."[86] Words which all signify that Mary
was holy from her conception. The same thing is
signified by other passages addressed to her by the
Holy Ghost. In Proverbs we read, " Many daughters
have gathered together riches : thou hast surpassed
them all."[87] If Mary has surpassed all others in the
riches of grace, she must have had original justice, as
Adam and the Angels had it. In the Canticles we
read, " There are . . . young maidens without number.
One is my dove, my perfect one" (in the Hebrew it is
"my entire, my immaculate one") "is but one, she is the
only one of her mother."[88] All just souls are daughters
of divine grace ; but amongst these Mary was the *dove*
without the gall of sin, the *perfect* one without spot in
her origin, the *one* conceived in grace.

Hence it is that the angel, before she became the
Mother of God, already found her full of grace, and thus
saluted her, " Hail, full of grace;" on which words
Saint Sophronius writes, that ' grace is given partially
to other Saints, but to the Blessed Virgin all was
given.'[89] So much so, says Saint Thomas, that ' grace
not only rendered the soul, but even the flesh of Mary
holy, so that this Blessed Virgin might be able to clothe
the Eternal Word with it.'[90] Now all this leads us to
the conclusion, that Mary, from the moment of her conception, was enriched and filled with Divine grace by
the Holy Ghost, as Peter of Celles remarks, ' the pleni-

[86] Fundamenta ejus in montibus sanctis. Diligit Dominus portas Sion
super omnia tabernacula Jacob . . . Homo natus est in ea : et ipse fundavit
eam Altissimus.—*Ps.* lxxxvi. 1, 5.

[87] Multæ filiæ congregaverunt divitias : tu supergressa es universas.—
Prov. xxxi. 29.

[88] Adolescentularum non est numerus. Una est columba mea ; perfecta
mea, una est matris suæ.—*Cant.* vi. 7, 8.

[89] Gratia plena : et bene plena, quia cæteris per partes præstatur : Mariæ
vero simul se tota infudit plenitudo gratiæ.—*Serm. de Assump. B.M.V. int.
op. S. Hieron.*

[90] Anima B. Virginis ita fuit plena, quod ex ea refundit gratia in carnem,
ut de ipsa conciperet Deum.—*Opusc.* viii.

tude of grace was in her; for from the very moment of her conception the whole grace of the Divinity overflowed upon her, by the outpouring of the Holy Ghost.'[91] Hence Saint Peter Damian says, ' that the Holy Spirit was about to bear her off entirely to Himself, who was chosen and preëlected by God.'[92] The Saint says 'to bear her off,' to denote the holy velocity of the Divine Spirit, in being beforehand in making this Spouse His own, before Lucifer should take possession of her.

Finally, I wish to conclude this discourse, which I have prolonged beyond the limits of the others, because our Congregation has this Blessed Virgin Mary, precisely under the title of her Immaculate Conception, for its principal Patroness : I say that I wish to conclude by giving, in as few words as possible, the reasons which make me feel certain, and which, in my opinion, ought to convince every one, of the truth of so pious a belief, and which is so glorious for the Divine Mother: that is, that she was free from original sin.

There are many doctors who maintain that Mary was exempted from contracting even the debt of sin ; for instance, Cardinal Galatino,[93] Cardinal Cusano,[94] De Ponte,[95] Salazar,[96] Catharinus,[97] Novarino,[98] Viva,[99] De Lugo,[1] Egidio,[2] Richelio, and others. And this opinion is also probable; for if it is true that the wills of all men were included in that of Adam, as being the head of all, and this opinion is maintained as probable by Gonet,[3] Habert,[4] and others, founded on the doctrine of Saint Paul, contained in the fifth chapter to the

---

[91] Simul collecta gratiæ plenitudo, nullatenus creaturæ humanæ capacitate potest apprehendi . . . privilegio . . . Filii sui, supra totius creaturæ meritum Mater Dei, aspersione Spiritus Sancti, tota Deitatis gratia est perfusa. —*Lib. de Panib.* cap. xii.

[92] A Deo electam et præelectam, totam eam rapturus erat sibi Spiritus Sanctus.—*Serm. de Annunt. B.M.V.*

[93] De Arca, lib. vii. passim.

[94] Lib. viii. Excit. ex Serm. Sicut lil. int. sp.

[95] Lib. ii. Cant. ex. 10. [96] Pro Imm. Conc. c. 7.

[97] De Pecc. orig. c. ult. [98] Umbr. Virg. Excursus xviii.

[99] P. viii. disp. i. q. 2, art. 2. [1] De Inc. d. 7, § 3, 4.

[2] De Imm. Conc. l. 2, q. 4, a. 5. [3] Clyp. p. 2, tr. 5, d. 7, a. 2.

[4] Tr. de Vit. et Pecc. c. 7, § 1.

Romans.[5] If this opinion, I say, is probable, it is also probable that Mary did not contract the debt of sin ; for whilst God distinguished her from the common of men by so many graces, it ought to be piously believed that He did not include her will in that of Adam.

This opinion is only probable, and I adhere to it as being more glorious for my sovereign Lady. But I consider the opinion that Mary did not contract the sin of Adam as certain ; and it is considered so, and even as proximately definable as an article of faith (as they express it), by Cardinal Everard, Duval,[6] Raynauld,[7] Lossada,[8] Viva,[9] and many others. I omit, however, the revelations which confirm this belief, particularly those of Saint Bridget, which were approved of by Cardinal Turrecremata, and by four sovereign Pontiffs, and which are found in various parts of the sixth book of her Revelations.[10] But on no account can I omit the opinions of the holy Fathers on this subject, whereby to show their unanimity in conceding this privilege to the Divine Mother. Saint Ambrose says, 'Receive me not from Sarah, but from Mary; that it may be an uncorrupted Virgin, a Virgin free by grace from every stain of sin.'[11] Origen, speaking of Mary, asserts that 'she was not infected by the venomous breath of the serpent.'[12] Saint Ephrem, that 'she was immaculate, and remote from all stain of sin.'[13] An ancient writer, in a sermon, found amongst the works of Saint Augustine, on the words "Hail, full of grace," says, 'By these words the angel shows that she was altogether [remark the word 'altoge-

---

[5] Per unum hominem peccatum in hunc mundum intravit . . in quo (Ada) omnes peccaverunt.—*Rom.* v. 12.

[6] De Pecc. q. ult. a 7.   [7] Piet. Lugd. erga V.M. n. 29.

[8] Disc. Thomist. de Imm. Conc.   [9] P. 8, d. 1, q. 2, a. 2.

[10] Lib. vi. cap. 12, 49, 55.

[11] Suscipe me non ex Sara, sed ex Maria ; ut incorrupta sit Virgo, sed Virgo per gratiam ab omni integra labe peccati.—*Serm.* xxii. *in Ps.* cxviii. No. 30.

[12] Nec serpentis venenosis afflatibus infecta est.—*In Div.* Hom. 1.

[13] Immaculata et intemerata, incorrupta et prorsus pudica, atque ab omni sorde ac labe peccati alienissima.—*Ad S. Dei Gen. Orat.*

ther'] excluded from the wrath of the first sentence, and restored to the full grace of blessing.'[14] The author of an old work, called the Breviary of Saint Jerome, affirms that ' that cloud was never in darkness, but always in light.'[15] Saint Cyprian, or whoever may be the author of the work on the 77th Psalm, says, ' Nor did justice endure that that vessel of election should be open to common injuries ; for being far exalted above others, she partook of their nature, not of their sin.'[16] Saint Amphilochius, that ' He who formed the first Virgin without deformity, also made the second one without spot or sin.'[17] Saint Sophronius, that ' the Virgin is therefore called immaculate, for in nothing was she corrupt.'[18] Saint Ildephonsus argues, that ' it is evident that she was free from original sin.'[19] Saint John Damascen says, that ' the serpent never had any access to this paradise.'[20] Saint Peter Damian, that ' the flesh of the Virgin, taken from Adam, did not admit of the stain of Adam.'[21] Saint Bruno affirms, ' that Mary is that uncorrupted earth which God blessed, and was therefore free from all contagion of sin.'[22] Saint Bonaventure, ' that our Sovereign Lady was

[14] Cum dixit "gratia plena," ostendit ex integro iram exclusam primæ sententiæ, et plenam benedictionis gratiam restitutam.—*Int. op. S. Augustini, Serm.* xxiii. ed. B. app.

[15] Nubem levem debemus sanctam Mariam accipere . . . Et deduxit eos in nube diei. Pulchre dixit, diei : nubes enim illa non fuit in tenebris, sed semper in luce.—*Brev. S. Hieron. in Ps.* lxxvii.

[16] Nec sustinebat justitia, ut illud vas electionis communibus lassaretur injuriis ; quoniam, plurimum a cæteris differens, natura communicabat, non culpa.—*De Car. Christi.*

[17] Qui antiquam illam virginem sine probro condidit ; ipse et secundam sine nota et crimine fabricatus est.—*Orat. in S. Deip. et Simeon.*

[18] Virgo sancta accipitur, et anima corpusque sanctificatur ; atque ita ministravit in incarnatione Creatoris, ut munda et casta atque incontaminata . . . Ex inviolabili namque et virginali sanguine atque immaculatæ Virginis Mariæ Verbum vere factum est incarnatum.—*Harduin.* tom. iii. Conc. Œcumen. 6, act. 11.

[19] Constat, eam ab omni originali peccato immunem fuisse.—*Cont. disp. de Virginit. B.V.M.*

[20] In hunc paradisum serpenti aditum non patuit.—*Or.* ii. *de Nat. B.M.V.*

[21] Caro . . . Virginis ex Adam assumpta, maculas Adæ non admisit.—*Serm. de Assump. B.M.V.*

[22] Maria . . . incorrupta terra illa, cui benedixit Dominus, ab omni propterea peccati contagione libera, per quam vitæ viam agnovimus, et promissam veritatem accepimus.—*In Ps.* ci.

full of preventing grace for her sanctification; that is, preservative grace against the corruption of original sin.[23] Saint Bernardine of Sienna argues, that ' it is not to be believed that He, the Son of God, would be born of a Virgin, and take her flesh, were she in the slightest degree stained with original sin.'[24]   Saint Lawrence Justinian affirms, ' that she was prevented in blessings from her very conception.'[25]   And the blessed Raymond Jordano, on the words " Thou hast found grace," says, ' thou hast found a singular grace, O most sweet Virgin, that of preservation from original sin,' &c.[26] And many other Doctors speak in the same sense.

But finally, there are two arguments that conclusively prove the truth of this pious belief.   The first of these is the universal concurrence of the faithful. Father Egidius, of the Presentation,[27] assures us that all the religious orders follow this opinion ; and a modern author tells us that though there are ninety-two writers of the order of Saint Dominic against it, nevertheless there are a hundred and thirty-six in favour of it, even in that religious body.   But that which above all should persuade us that our pious belief is in accordance with the general sentiment of Catholics is, that we are assured of it in the celebrated bull of Alexander VII., ' Sollicitudo omnium ecclesiarum,' published in 1661, in which he says, ' This devotion and homage towards the Mother of God was again increased and propagated. . . . so that the universities having adopted this opinion' (that is, the pious one) ' already nearly all

---

[23] Domina nostra fuit plena gratia præveniente in sua sanctificatione, gratia scilicet præservativa contra fœditatem originalis culpæ.—*Serm.* ii. *de B.M.V.*

[24] Non est credendum, quod ipse Filius Dei voluerit nasci ex virgine, et sumere ejus carnem, quæ esset maculata ex aliquo peccato originali.—*Serm.* xlix. *in Feria* iii. *post Pascha.*

[25] Ab ipsa namque sui conceptione, in benedictionibus est prævcnta.— *Serm. in Annunt. B.M.V.*

[26] Invenisti, Virgo Maria, gratiam cœlestem ; quia fuerunt in te ab originis labe præservatio, &c.—*Contempl. de B.V.M.* cap. vi.

[27] De Imm. Conc. l. 3, q. 6, a. 3.

Catholics have embraced it.'[28] And in fact this opinion is defended in the universities of the Sorbonne, Alcala, Salamanca, Coimbra, Cologne, Mentz, Naples, and many others, in which all who take their degrees are obliged to swear that they will defend the doctrine of Mary's Immaculate Conception. The learned Petavius mainly rests his proofs of the truth of this doctrine on the argument taken from the general sentiment of the faithful.[29] An argument, writes the most learned bishop Julius Torni,[30] which cannot do otherwise than convince ; for, in fact, if nothing else does, the general consent of the faithful makes us certain of the sanctification of Mary in her mother's womb, and of her Assumption, in body and soul, into heaven. Why, then, should not the same general feeling and belief, on the part of the faithful, also make us certain of her Immaculate Conception?

The second reason, and which is stronger than the first, that convinces us that Mary was exempt from original sin, is the celebration of her Immaculate Conception commanded by the universal Church. And on this subject I see, on the one hand, that the Church celebrates the first moment in which her soul was created and infused into her body ; for this was declared by Alexander VII., in the above-named bull, in which he says that the Church gives the same worship to Mary in her Conception, which is given to her by those who hold the pious belief that she was conceived without original sin. On the other hand, I hold it as certain, that the Church cannot celebrate anything which is not holy, according to the doctrine of the holy Pope Saint Leo,[31] and that of the Sovereign Pontiff Saint Eusebius : ' In the Apostolic See the

---

[28] Aucta rursus et propagata fuit pietas hæc et cultus erga Deiparam ... ita ut accedentibus quoque plerisque celebrioribus academiis ad hanc sententiam, jam fere omnes Catholici eam amplectantur.
[29] Tom. v. lib. 14, cap. 2, no. 10.
[30] In Adn. ad Æst. l. ii. dist. 3, no. 2. †
[31] Ep. Decret. iv. c 2.

Catholic religion was always preserved spotless.'[32]   All
theologians, with Saint Augustine,[33] Saint Bernard,[34]
and Saint Thomas, agree on this point ; and the latter,
to prove that Mary was sanctified before her birth,
makes use of this very argument : ' The Church celebrates the nativity of the Blessed Virgin ; but a feast
is celebrated only for a Saint : therefore the Blessed
Virgin was sanctified in her mother's womb.[35]   But
if it is certain, as the angelic Doctor says, that Mary
was sanctified in her mother's womb, because it is only
on that supposition that the Church can celebrate her
nativity, why are we not to consider it as equally certain that Mary was preserved from original sin from
the first moment of her conception, knowing as we do,
that it is in this sense that the Church herself celebrates the feast ?   And finally, in confirmation of this
great privilege of Mary, we may be allowed to add the
well-known innumerable and prodigious graces that our
Lord is daily pleased to dispense throughout the kingdom of Naples, by means of the pictures of her Immaculate Conception.   I could refer to many which passed,
so to say, through the hands of fathers of our own Congregation ; but I will content myself with two which
are truly admirable.

EXAMPLE.

A woman came to a house of our little Congregation in this kingdom to let one of the fathers know
that her husband had not been to confession for many
years, and the poor creature could no longer tell by
what means to bring him to his duty; for if she named
confession to him, he beat her.   The father told her to
give him a picture of Mary Immaculate.   In the even-

---

[32] In Sede Apostolica extra maculam semper est Catholica servata religio.
—*Decr.* xxiv. no. 1, c. *in sede.* †
[33] S. 310-314 ed. B.   [34] Ep. ad Can. Ludg.
[35] Ecclesia celebrat nativitatem Beatæ Virginis : non autem celebratur
festum in Ecclesia nisi pro aliquo sancto : ergo Beata Virgo in ipsa sua nati-
vitate fuit sancta ; fuit ergo in utero sanctificata.—3 p. q. xxvii. art. 1.

ing the woman once more begged her husband to go to confession ; but as he as usual turned a deaf ear to her entreaties, she gave him the picture. Behold ! he had scarcely received it, when he said, 'Well, when will you take me to confession, for I am willing to go ' The wife, on seeing this instantaneous change, began to weep for joy. In the morning he really came to our church, and when the father asked him how long it was since he had been to confession, he answered twenty-eight years. The father again asked him what had induced him to come that morning. 'Father,' he replied, ' I was obstinate; but last night my wife gave me a picture of our Blessed Lady, and in the same moment I felt my heart changed, so much so, that during the whole night every moment seemed a thousand years, so great was my desire to go to confession.' He then confessed his sins with great contrition, changed his life, and continued for a long time to go frequently to confession to the same father.

In another place, in the diocese of Salerno, in which we were giving a mission, there was a man who bore a great hatred to another who had offended him. One of our fathers spoke to him that he might be reconciled; but he answered: 'Father, did you ever see me at the sermons ? No, and for this very reason, I do not go. I know that I am damned; but nothing else will satisfy me, I must have revenge.' The father did all that he could to convert him ; but seeing that he lost his time, he said, ' Here, take this picture of our Blessed Lady.' The man at first replied, ' But what is the use of this picture ?' But no sooner had he taken it, than, as if he had never refused to be reconciled, he said to the missionary, ' Father, is anything else required besides reconciliation ? — I am willing.' The following morning was fixed for it. When, however, the time came, he had again changed, and would do nothing. The father offered him another picture, but he refused it ; but at length, with great reluctance,

took it, when, behold ! he scarcely had possession of it
than he immediately said, 'Now let us be quick; where
is Mastrodati ?' and he was instantly reconciled with
him, and then went to confession.

PRAYER.

Ah, my Immaculate Lady ! I rejoice with thee on
seeing thee enriched with so great purity. I thank,
and resolve always to thank, our common Creator for
having preserved thee from every stain of sin ; and
I firmly believe this doctrine, and am prepared and
swear even to lay down my life, should this be necessary, in defence of this thy so great and singular privilege of being conceived immaculate. I would that the
whole world knew thee and acknowledged thee as
being that beautiful 'Dawn' which was always illumined with Divine light ; as that chosen 'Ark' of salvation, free from the common shipwreck of sin ; that perfect and immaculate 'Dove' which thy Divine Spouse
declared thee to be : that 'enclosed Garden' which
was the delight of God ; that 'sealed Fountain' whose
waters were never troubled by an enemy ; and finally,
as that 'white Lily,' which thou art, and who though
born in the midst of the thorns of the children of Adam,
all of whom are conceived in sin, and the enemies of
God, wast alone conceived pure and spotless, and in
all things the beloved of thy Creator.

Permit me, then, to praise thee also as thy God Himself has praised thee : "Thou art all fair, and there is
not a spot in thee."[36]   O most pure Dove, all fair, all
beautiful, always the friend of God. "O how beautiful
art thou, my beloved ! how beautiful art thou !"[37]   Ah,
most sweet, most amiable, immaculate Mary, thou who
art so beautiful in the eyes of thy Lord,—ah, disdain
not to cast thy compassionate eyes on the wounds of
my soul, loathsome as they are.   Behold me, pity me,

[36] Tota pulchra es, amica mea, et macula non est in te.—*Cant.* **iv.** 7.
[37] Quam pulchra es, amica mea, quam pulchra es !—*Ib.* 1.

heal me. O beautiful loadstone of hearts, draw also my miserable heart to thyself. O thou, who from the first moment of thy life didst appear pure and beautiful before God, pity me, who not only was born in sin, but have again since baptism stained my soul with crimes. What grace will God ever refuse thee, who chose thee for His daughter, His Mother, and Spouse, and therefore preserved thee from every stain, and in His love preferred thee to all other creatures? I will say, in the words of Saint Philip Neri, 'Immaculate Virgin, thou hast to save me.' Grant that I may always remember thee; and thou, do thou never forget me. The happy day, when I shall go to behold thy beauty in Paradise, seems a thousand years off; so much do I long to praise and love thee more than I can now do, my Mother, my Queen, my beloved, most beautiful, most sweet, most pure, Immaculate Mary. Amen.

DISCOURSE II.

Mary was born a Saint, and a great Saint ; for the grace with which God enriched her from the beginning was great, and the fidelity with which she immediately corresponded with it was great.

MEN usually celebrate the birth of their children with great feasts and rejoicings ; but they should rather pity them, and show signs of mourning and grief on reflecting that they are born, not only deprived of grace and reason, but worse than this—they are infected with sin and children of wrath, and therefore condemned to misery and death. It is indeed right, however, to celebrate with festivity and universal joy the birth of our infant Mary ; for she first saw the light of this world a baby, it is true, in point of age, but great in merit and virtue. Mary was born a Saint, and a great Saint. But to form an idea of the greatness of her sanctity, even at this early period, we must consider, first, the greatness of the first grace with which God enriched her ; and secondly, the greatness of her fidelity in immediately corresponding with it.

First point.—To begin with the first point, it is certain that Mary's soul was the most beautiful that God had ever created ; nay more, after the work of the Incarnation of the Eternal Word, this was the greatest and most worthy of Himself that an omnipotent God ever did in the world. Saint Peter Damian calls it ʻa work only surpassed by God.ʼ[1] Hence it follows that

---

[1] Videbis quidquid majus est, minus Virgine, solumque opificem opus istud supergredi.—*Serm.* i. *de Nat. B.M.V.*

Divine grace did not come into Mary by drops as in other Saints, "but like rain on the fleece,"[2] as it was foretold by David. The soul of Mary was like fleece, and imbibed the whole shower of grace, without losing a drop. Saint Basil of Seleucia says, 'that the holy Virgin was full of grace, because she was elected and preëlected by God, and the Holy Spirit was about to take full possession of her.'[3] Hence she said, by the lips of Ecclesiasticus, "My abode is in the full assembly of saints ;"[4] that is, as Saint Bonaventure explains it, 'I hold in plenitude all that other Saints have held in part.'[5] And Saint Vincent Ferrer, speaking particularly of the sanctity of Mary before her birth, says 'that the Blessed Virgin was sanctified' (surpassed in sanctity) 'in her mother's womb above all Saints and angels.'[6]

The grace that the Blessed Virgin received exceeded not only that of each particular Saint, but of all the angels and saints put together, as the most learned Father Francis Pepe, of the Society of Jesus, proves in his beautiful work on the greatness of Jesus and Mary.[7] And he asserts that this opinion, so glorious for our Queen, is now generally admitted, and considered as beyond doubt by modern theologians (such as Carthagena, Suarez, Spinelli, Recupito, and Guerra, who have professedly examined the question, and this was never done by the more ancient theologians). And besides this he relates, that the Divine Mother sent Father Martin Guttierez to thank Father Suarez, on her part, for having so courageously defended this most probable opinion, and which, according to Father

---

[2] Descendet sicut pluvia in vellus.—*Ps.* lxxi. 6.
[3] Gratia plena, quia a Deo electam et præelectam, totam eam rapturus erat Spiritus Sanctus, et cœlestibus insigniturus ornamentis.—*De Annunt. B.M.V.*
[4] In plenitudine sanctorum detentio mea.—*Eccl.* xxiv, 16.
[5] Totum teneo in plenitudine, quod alii sancti tenent in parte.—*Serm.* iii. *de B.M.V.*
[6] Super alios omnes est sanctificatio Virginis Mariæ.—*Serm. in Fest. Concep. B.M.V.*
[7] Tom. iii. lect. 136. †

Segneri, in his 'Client of Mary,' was afterwards believed and defended by the University of Salamanca.

But if this opinion is general and certain, the other is also very probable; namely, that Mary received this grace, exceeding that of all men and angels together, in the first instant of her Immaculate Conception. Father Suarez[8] strongly maintains this opinion, as do also Father Spinelli,[9] Father Recupito,[10] and Father la Colombiere.[11] But besides the authority of theologians, there are two great and convincing arguments, which sufficiently prove the correctness of the above opinion. The first is, that Mary was chosen by God to be the Mother of the Divine Word. Hence Denis the Carthusian says,[12] 'that as she was chosen to an order superior to that of all other creatures (for in a certain sense the dignity of Mother of God, as Father Suarez asserts,[13] belongs to the order of hypostatic union), it is reasonable to suppose that from the very beginning of her life gifts of a superior order were conferred upon her, and such gifts, that they must have incomparably surpassed those granted to all other creatures. And indeed it cannot be doubted that when the Person of the Eternal Word was, in the Divine decrees, predestined to make Himself man, a Mother was also destined for Him, from whom He was to take His human nature; and this Mother was our infant Mary. Now Saint Thomas teaches that 'God gives everyone grace proportioned to the dignity for which He destines him.'[14] And Saint Paul teaches us the same thing when he says, " Who also hath made us fit ministers of the New Testament;"[15] that is, the apostles received gifts from God, proportioned to the greatness of the office with which they were charged.

[8] De Inc. p. 2, d. 4, ⸹ 1.   [9] M. Deip. c. 4.
[10] Sign. Præd. 3.   [11] Imm. Conc. s. 1.
[12] De Laud. V. l. 1-3, passim.   [13] De Inc. p. 2, d. 1, ⸹ 2.
[14] Unicuique a Deo datur gratia, secundum hoc ad quod eligitur.—3 p. ⸹ xxvii. art. 5, ad 1.
[15] Qui et idoneos nos fecit ministros Novi Testamenti.—2 Cor. iii. 6.

Saint Bernardine of Sienna adds, 'that it is an axiom in theology, that when a person is chosen by God for any state, he receives not only the dispositions necessary for it, but even the gifts which he needs to sustain that state with decorum.'[16] But as Mary was chosen to be the Mother of God, it was quite becoming that God should adorn her, in the first moment of her existence, with an immense grace, and one of a superior order to that of all other men and angels, since it had to correspond with the immense and most high dignity to which God exalted her. And all theologians come to this conclusion with Saint Thomas, who says, 'the Blessed Virgin was chosen to be the Mother of God ; and therefore it is not to be doubted but that God fitted her for it by His grace ;'[17] so much so, that Mary, before becoming Mother of God, was adorned with a sanctity so perfect that it rendered her fit for this great dignity. The holy Doctor says, 'that in the Blessed Virgin there was a preparatory perfection, which rendered her fit to be the Mother of Christ, and this was the perfection of sanctification.'[18]

And before making this last remark the Saint had said,[19] 'that Mary was called full of grace, not on the part of grace itself, for she had it not in the highest possible degree, since even the habitual grace of Jesus Christ (according to the same holy Doctor) was not such, that the absolute power of God could not have made it greater, although it was a grace sufficient for the end for which His humanity was ordained by the Divine Wisdom, that is, for its union with the Person of the Eternal Word : 'Although the Divine power

[16] Regula firma est in sacra theologia, quod quandocunque Deus per gratiam aliquem eligit ad aliquem statum, omnia dona illi dispensat atque largitur, quæ illi statui necessaria sunt, et illum copiose decorant.—*In Purific. B.M.V.* Serm. i.

[17] Beata Virgo fuit electa divinitus, ut esset Mater Dei : et ideo non est dubitandum quin Deus per suam gratiam eam ad hoc idoneam reddidit.— P. 3, q. xxvii. art. 4, concl.

[18] In Beata Virgine fuit . . . perfectio . . . quasi dispositiva, per quam reddebatur idonea ad hoc, quod esset Mater Christi ; et hæc fuit perfectio sanctificationis.—*Ib.* art. 5, ad 2.

[19] *Ib.* art. 10, ad 1.

could make something greater and better than the
habitual grace of Christ, it could not fit it for anything greater than the personal union with the only-
begotten Son of the Father, and with which union
that measure of grace sufficiently corresponds, according to the limit placed by Divine Wisdom.'[20]   For the
same angelic Doctor teaches that the Divine power is
so great, that, however much it gives, it can always
give more; and although the natural capacity of creatures is in itself limited as to receiving, so that it can
be entirely filled, nevertheless its power to obey the
Divine will is illimited, and God can always fill it
more by increasing its capacity to receive.   'As far as
its natural capacity goes, it can be filled; but it cannot
be filled as far as its power of obeying goes.'[21]   But
now to return to our proposition, Saint Thomas says,
'that the Blessed Virgin was not filled with grace, as
to grace itself; nevertheless she is called full of grace
as to herself, for she had an immense grace, one which
was sufficient, and corresponded with her immense
dignity, so much so that it fitted her to be the Mother
of God : ' The Blessed Virgin is full of grace, not with
the fulness of grace itself, for she had not grace in the
highest degree of excellence in which it can be had,
nor had she it as to all its effects ; but she was said to
be full of grace as to herself, because she had sufficient
grace for that state to which she was chosen by God,
that is, to be the Mother of His only-begotten Son.'[22]

[20] Virtus divina licet possit facere aliquid majus et melius quam sit
habitualis gratia Christi, non tamen posset facere, quod ordinaretur ad
aliquid majus quam sit unio personalis ad Filium unigenitum a Patre ; cui
unioni sufficienter correspondet talis mensura gratiæ, secundum definitionem
Divinæ Sapientiæ.—P. 3, q. vii. art. 12, ad 2.
[21] Est duplex potentia creaturæ ad recipiendum.   Una naturalis, quæ
potest tota impleri, quia hæc non se extendit nisi ad perfectiones naturales.
Alia est potentia obedientiæ, secundum quod potest recipere aliquid a Deo ;
et talis capacitas non potest impleri, quia quidquid Deus de creatura faciat,
adhuc remanet in potentia recipiendi a Deo.—De Verit. q. xxix. (de Grat. C.)
art. 3, ad 3.
[22] Beata Virgo dicta est plena gratia, non ex parte ipsius gratiæ, quia
non habuit gratiam in summa excellentia qua potest haberi, nec ad omnes
effectus gratiæ ; sed dicitur fuisse plena gratia per comparationem ad ipsam,
quia scilicet habebat gratiam sufficientem ad statum illum ad quem erat
electa a Deo, ut esset scilicet Mater Unigeniti ejus.—3 p. q. vii. art. 10, ad 1

Hence Benedict Fernandez says, 'that the measure whereby we may know the greatness of the grace communicated to Mary is her dignity of Mother of God.'[23]

It was not without reason, then, that David said that the foundations of this city of God, that is, Mary, are planted above the summits of the mountains: "The foundations thereof are in the holy mountains."[24] Whereby we are to understand that Mary, in the very beginning of her life, was to be more perfect than the united perfections of the entire lives of the Saints could have made her. And the Prophet continues: "The Lord loveth the gates of Sion above all the tabernacles of Jacob."[25] And the same King David tells us why God thus loved her; it was because He was to become man in her virginal womb: "A man is born in her."[26] Hence it was becoming that God should give this Blessed Virgin, in the very moment that He created her, a grace corresponding with the dignity of Mother of God.

Isaias signified the same thing, when he said that, in a time to come, a mountain of the house of the Lord (which was the Blessed Virgin) was to be prepared on the top of all other mountains; and that, in consequence, all nations would run to this mountain to receive the Divine mercies. "And in the last days the mountain of the house of the Lord shall be prepared on the top of mountains, and it shall be exalted above the hills, and all nations shall flow unto it."[27] Saint Gregory, explaining this passage, says, 'It is a mountain on the top of mountains; for the perfection of Mary is resplendent above that of all the Saints.'[28]

---

[23] Secundum dignitatem Filii, Matris illius sanctitas requirebatur.—*In Gen.* cap. xxvii. sect. 3, No. 10.

[24] Fundamenta ejus in montibus sanctis.—*Ps.* lxxxvi. 1.

[25] Diligit Dominus portas Sion super omnia tabernacula Jacob.—*Ib.* 2.

[26] Homo natus est in ea.—*Ib.* 5.

[27] Et erit in novissimis diebus præparatus mons domus Domini in vertice montium, et elevabitur super colles, et fluent ad eum omnes gentes.—*Is.* ii. 2.

[28] Mons quippe in vertice montium fuit, quia altitudo Mariæ supra omnes sanctos refulsit.—Lib. **i.** *in* 1 *Reg.* cap. 1.

And Saint John Damascen, that it is 'a mountain in which God was well pleased to dwell.'[29]   Therefore Mary was called a cypress, but a cypress of Mount Sion : she was called a cedar, but a cedar of Libanus : an olive-tree, but a fair olive-tree ;[30] beautiful, but beautiful as the sun ;[31] for as Saint Peter Damian says, 'As the light of the sun so greatly surpasses that of the stars, that in it they are no longer visible ; it so over-whelms them, that they are as if they were not ;'[32] 'so does the great Virgin Mother surpass in sanctity the whole court of heaven.'[33]   So much so that Saint Bernard elegantly remarks, that the sanctity of Mary was so sublime, that 'no other mother than Mary became a God, and no other Son than God became Mary.'[34]

The second argument by which it is proved that Mary was more holy in the first moment of her exist-ence than all the Saints together, is founded on the great office of mediatress of men, with which she was charged from the beginning ; and which made it neces-sary that she should possess a greater treasure of grace from the beginning than all other men together.   It is well known with what unanimity theologians and holy fathers give Mary this title of Mediatress, on account of her having obtained salvation for all, by her powerful intercession and merit, so called of congruity, thereby procuring the great benefit of redemption for the lost world.   By her merit of congruity, I say ; for Jesus Christ alone is our Mediator by way of justice and by merit, 'de condigno,' as the scholastics say, He having offered His merits to the Eternal Father, who accepted them for our salvation.   Mary, on the other hand, is a

---

[29] Mons in quo beneplacitum est Deo habitare in eo.—Hom. i. in *Nat. B.M.V.*
[30] Eccl. xxiv. 17-19.   [31] Cant. vi. 9.
[32] Sibi siderum et lunæ rapit positionem, ut sint quasi non sint, et viden non possunt.—*Serm. de Assump. B.M.V.*
[33] Sic et Virgo inter animas sanctorum et angelorum choros supereminens et evecta, merita singulorum et omnium titulos antecedit.—*Ib.*
[34] Neque enim Filius alius Virginem, nec Deum decuit partus alter.—Serm. iv. in *Assump. B.M.V.*

mediatress of grace, by way of simple intercession and merit of congruity, she having offered to God, as theologians say, with Saint Bonaventure, her merits, for the salvation of all men; and God, as a favour, accepted them with the merits of Jesus Christ. On this account Arnold of Chartres says that ' she effected our salvation in common with Christ.'[35] And Richard of Saint Victor says that ' Mary desired, sought, and obtained the salvation of all ; nay, even she effected the salvation of all.'[36] So that everything good, and every gift in the order of grace, which each of the Saints received from God, Mary obtained for them.

And the holy Church wishes us to understand this, when she honours the Divine Mother by applying the following verses of Ecclesiasticus to her : " In me is all grace of the way and the truth."[37] ' Of the way,' because by Mary all graces are dispensed to wayfarers. ' Of the truth,' because the light of truth is imparted by her. " In me is all hope of life and of virtue."[38] ' Of life,' for by Mary we hope to obtain the life of grace in this world, and that of glory in heaven. ' And of virtue,' for through her we acquire virtues, and especially the theological virtues, which are the principal virtues of the Saints. " I am the Mother of fair love, and of fear, and of knowledge, and of holy hope."[39] Mary, by her intercession, obtains for her servants the gifts of Divine love, holy fear, heavenly light, and holy perseverance. From which Saint Bernard concludes that it is a doctrine of the Church, that Mary is the universal mediatress of our salvation. He says : ' Magnify the finder of grace, the mediatress of salvation, the restorer of ages. This I am taught by

[35] Ad hunc beatitudinis cumulum Virgo sancta devenerit, ut cum Christo communem in salute mundi effectum obtineat.—*De Laud. B.M.V.*

[36] Omnium salutem desideravit, quæsivit, et obtinuit : imo salus omnium per ipsam facta est, unde et mundi salus dicta est.—*In Cant.* cap. xxvi.

[37] In me gratia omnis viæ et veritatis.—*Eccl.* xxiv. 25.

[38] In me omnis spes vitæ et virtutis.—*Ib.*

[39] Ego mater pulchræ dilectionis, et timoris, et agnitionis, et sanctæ spei. —*Ib.* 24.

the Church proclaiming it ; and thus also she teaches me to proclaim the same thing to others.'[40]

Saint Sophronius, Patriarch of Jerusalem, asserts that the reason for which the Archangel Gabriel called her full of grace, "Hail, full of grace !" was because only limited grace was given to others, but it was given to Mary in all its plenitude : 'Truly was she full; for grace is given to other Saints partially, but the whole plenitude of grace poured itself into Mary.'[41] Saint Basil of Seleucia declares that she received this plenitude, that she might thus be a worthy mediatress between men and God : 'Hail, full of grace, mediatress between God and men, and by whom heaven and earth are brought together and united.'[42] 'Otherwise,' says Saint Lawrence Justinian, 'had not the Blessed Virgin been full of Divine grace, how could she have become the ladder to heaven, the advocate of the world, and the most true mediatress between men and God ?'[43]

The second argument has now become clear and evident. If Mary, as the already-destined Mother of our common Redeemer, received from the very beginning the office of mediatress of all men, and consequently even of the Saints, it was also requisite from the very beginning she should have a grace exceeding that of all the Saints for whom she was to intercede. I will explain myself more clearly. If, by the means of Mary, all men were to render themselves dear to God, necessarily Mary was more holy and more dear to Him than all men together. Otherwise, how

[40] Magnifica gratiæ inventricem, mediatricem salutis, restauratricem sæculorum . . . Hæc mihi de illa cantat ecclesia, et me eadem docuit decantare. —*Epist.* clxxiv. *ad Can. Lugd.*

[41] Ave, inquit, gratia plena : et bene plena, quia cæteris per partes præstatur : Mariæ vero simul se tota infudit plenitudo gratiæ.—*Int. op. S. Hier. Serm. de Assump. B.M.V.*

[42] Ave gratia plena, Dei ac hominum mediatrix, quo . . . cœlestibus terrena coeant ac uniantur.—*Orat. in S. Dei Gen.* &c.

[43] Quomodo non est Maria, juxta Gabrielis oraculum, plena gratia, quæ effecta est Mater Dei, paradisi scala, cœli janua, interventrix mundi, dæmonum fuga, peccatorum spes, naufragantium portus, maris stella, confugium periclitantium, solamen laborantium, fluctuantium rober, Dei et hominum verissima mediatrix ?—*Serm. de Annunt. B.M.V.*

could she have interceded for all others? That an intercessor may obtain the favour of a prince for all his vassals, it is absolutely necessary that he should be more dear to his prince than all the other vassals. And therefore Saint Anselm concludes, that Mary deserved to be made the worthy repairer of the lost world, because she was the most holy and the most pure of all creatures. 'The pure sanctity of her heart, surpassing the purity and sanctity of all other creatures, merited for her that she should be made the repairer of the lost world.'[44]

Mary, then, was the mediatress of men; it may be asked, but how can she be called also the mediatress of angels? Many theologians maintain that Jesus Christ merited the grace of perseverance for the angels also; so that as Jesus was their mediator '*de condigno*,' so also Mary may be said to be the mediatress even of the angels '*de congruo*,' she having hastened the coming of the Redeemer by her prayers. At least meriting '*de congruo*' to become the Mother of the Messiah, she merited for the angels that the thrones lost by the devils should be filled up. Thus she at least merited this accidental glory for them; and therefore Richard of Saint Victor says, 'By her every creature is repaired; by her the ruin of the angels is remedied; and by her human nature is reconciled.'[45] And before him Saint Anselm said, 'All things are recalled and reinstated in their primitive state by this Blessed Virgin.'[46]

So that our heavenly child, because she was appointed mediatress of the world, as also because she was destined to be the Mother of the Redeemer, received, at the very beginning of her existence, grace

44 Pura enim sanctitas et sanctissima puritas piissimi pectoris ejus, omnem omnis creaturæ puritatem sive sanctitatem transcendens, incomparabili sublimitate hoc promeruit, ut reparatrix perditi orbis dignissime fieret.—*De Excell. Virg.* cap. ix.

45 Utraque creatura per hanc reparatur : angelorum ruina per hanc restaurata est, et humana natura reconciliata.—*Exp. in Cant.* cap. xxiii.

46 Cuncta per hanc beatissimam Virginem in statum pristinum revocata sunt et restituta.—*De Excell. Virg.* cap. xi.

exceeding in greatness that of all the Saints together.
Hence, how delightful a sight must the beautiful soul
of this happy child have been to heaven and earth,
although still enclosed in her mother's womb! She
was the most amiable creature in the eyes of God, because she was already loaded with grace and merit, and
could say, ' When I was a little one I pleased the Most
High.'[47]   And she was at the same time the creature
of all others that had ever appeared in the world up to
that moment, who loved God the most; so much so,
that had Mary been born immediately after her most
pure conception, she would have come into the world
richer in merits, and more holy, than all the Saints
united.   Then let us only reflect how much greater her
sanctity must have been at her nativity; coming into
the world after acquiring all the merits that she did
acquire during the whole of the nine months that she
remained in the womb of her mother.   And now let
us pass to the consideration of the second point, that is
to say, the greatness of the fidelity with which Mary
immediately corresponded with Divine grace.

Second point.—It is not a private opinion only,
says a learned author,[48] but it is the opinion of all, that
the holy child, when she received sanctifying grace in
the womb of Saint Anne, received also the perfect use
of her reason, and was also divinely enlightened, in a
degree corresponding with the grace with which she was
enriched.   So that we may well believe, that from the
first moment that her beautiful soul was united to her
most pure body, she, by the light she had received from
the Wisdom of God, knew well the eternal truths, the
beauty of virtue, and above all, the infinite goodness of
God; and how much He deserved to be loved by all,
and particularly by herself, on account of the singular
gifts with which He had adorned and distinguished her

---

[47] Cum essem parvula placui Altissimo.—*In Fest. B.M. Resp. ad ii. Lect.*
[48] P. La Colombière. Imm. Conc. s. 2.

above all creatures, by preserving her from the stain of original sin, by bestowing on her such immense grace, and destining her to be the Mother of the Eternal Word, and Queen of the Universe.

Hence from that first moment Mary, grateful to God, began to do all that she could do, by immediately and faithfully trafficking with that great capital of grace which had been bestowed upon her; and applying herself entirely to please and love the Divine goodness, from that moment she loved Him with all her strength, and continued thus to love Him always, during the whole of the nine months preceding her birth, during which she never ceased for a moment to unite herself more and more closely with God by fervent acts of love. She was already free from original sin, and hence was exempt from every earthly affection, from every irregular movement, from every distraction, from every opposition on the part of the senses, which could in any way have hindered her from always advancing more and more in Divine love : her senses also concurred with her blessed spirit in tending towards God. Hence her beautiful soul, free from every impediment, never lingered, but always flew towards God, always loved Him, and always increased in love towards Him. It was for this reason that she called herself a plane-tree, planted by flowing waters : " As a plane-tree by the waters . . . was I exalted."[49] For she was that noble plant of God which always grew by the streams of Divine grace. And therefore she also calls herself a vine : " As a vine I have brought forth a pleasant odour."[50] Not only because she was so humble in the eyes of the world, but because she was like the vine, which, according to the common proverb, 'never ceases to grow.' Other trees—the orange-tree, the mulberry, the pear-tree—have a determined height, which they attain; but the vine always grows, and grows to the

[49] Quasi platanus exaltata sum juxta aquam in plateis.—*Eccles.* xxiv. 19.
[50] Ego quasi vitis fructifio—' suavitatem odoris.—*Ib.* v. 23.

height of the tree to which it is attached. And thus did the most Blessed Virgin always grow in perfection. ' Hail, then, O vine, always growing!'[51] says Saint Gregory Thaumaturgus; for she was always united to God, on whom alone she depended. Hence it was of her that the Holy Ghost spoke, saying, "Who is this that cometh up from the desert, flowing with delights, leaning upon her beloved?"[52] which Saint Ambrose thus paraphrases : 'She it is that cometh up, clinging to the Eternal Word, as a vine to a vine-stock.'[53] Who is this accompanied by the Divine Word, that grows as a vine planted against a great tree?

Many learned theologians say that a soul which possesses a habit of virtue, as long as she corresponds faithfully with the actual grace which she receives from God, always produces an act equal in intensity to the habit she possesses; so much so that she acquires each time a new and double merit, equal to the sum of all the merits previously acquired. This kind of augmentation was, it is said, granted to the angels in the time of their probation; and if it was granted to the angels, who can ever deny that it was granted to the Divine Mother when living in this world, and especially during the time of which I speak, that she was in the womb of her mother, in which she was certainly more faithful than the angels in corresponding with Divine grace? Mary, then, during the whole of that time, in each moment, doubled that sublime grace which she possessed from the first instant; for, corresponding with her whole strength, and in the most perfect manner in her every act, she subsequently doubled her merits in every instant. So that supposing she had a thousand degrees of grace in the first instant, in the second she had two thousand, in

---

[51] Ave gratia plena, vitis semper vigens.—*In Annunt. B.M.V.* Serm. i.

[52] Quæ est ista, quæ ascendit de deserto, deliciis affluens, innixa super dilectum suum?—*Cant.* viii. 5.

[53] Hæc est quæ ascendit ita ut inhæreat Dei Verbo sicut vitis propago.—*De Isaac. et An.* c. 5.

the third four thousand, in the fourth eight thousand, in the fifth sixteen thousand, in the sixth thirty-two thousand. And we are as yet only at the sixth instant ; but multiplied thus for an entire day, multiplied for nine months, consider what treasures of grace, merit, and sanctity Mary had already acquired at the moment of her birth !

Let us, then, rejoice with our beloved infant, who was born so holy, so dear to God, and so full of grace. And let us rejoice, not only on her account, but also on our own ; for she came into the world full of grace, not only for her own glory, but also for our good. Saint Thomas remarks, in his eighth treatise, that the most Blessed Virgin was full of grace in three ways : first, she was filled with grace as to her soul, so that from the beginning her beautiful soul belonged all to God. Secondly, she was filled with grace as to her body, so that she merited to clothe the Eternal Word with her most pure flesh. Thirdly, she was filled with grace for the benefit of all, so that all men might partake of it : 'She was also full of grace as to its overflowing for the benefit of all men.'[54] The angelical Doctor adds, that some Saints have so much grace that it is not only sufficient for themselves, but also for the salvation of many, though not for all men ; only to Jesus Christ and to Mary was such a grace given as sufficed to save all : 'should anyone have as much as would suffice for the salvation of all, this would be the greatest ; and this was in Christ and in the Blessed Virgin.'[55] Thus far Saint Thomas. So that what Saint John says of Jesus, " And of His fulness we all have received,"[56] the Saints say of Mary. Saint Thomas of Villanova calls her 'full of grace, of whose

[54] Dicitur . . . gratia plena . . . quantum ad refusionem in omnes homines. —*Exp. sup. Salut. Ang. Opusc.* viii.

[55] . . . Sed quando haberet tantum de gratia, quod sufficeret ad salutem omnium hominum de mundo, hoc esset maximum, et hoc est in Christo et in Beata Virgine.—*Ib.*

[56] Et de plenitudine ejus nos omnes accepimus.—*Joan.* i. 16.

plenitude all receive ;'[57] so much so that Saint Anselm says, 'that there is no one who does not partake of the grace of Mary.'[58] And who is there in the world to whom Mary is not benign, and does not dispense some mercy? 'Who was ever found to whom the Blessed Virgin was not propitious? who is there whom her mercy does not reach?'[59] From Jesus, however, it is (we must understand) that we receive grace as the author of grace, from Mary as a mediatress; from Jesus as a Saviour, from Mary as an advocate; from Jesus as a source, from Mary as a channel.

Hence Saint Bernard says, that God established Mary as the channel of the mercies that He wished to dispense to men; therefore He filled her with grace, that each one's part might be communicated to him from her fulness: 'A full aqueduct, that others may receive of her fulness, but not fulness itself.'[60] Therefore the Saint exhorts all to consider, with how much love God wills that we should honour this great Virgin, since He has deposited the whole treasure of His graces in her: so that whatever we possess of hope, grace, and salvation, we may thank our most loving Queen for all, since all comes to us from her hands and by her powerful intercession. He thus beautifully expresses himself: 'Behold with what tender feelings of devotion He wills that we should honour her! He who has placed the plenitude of all good in Mary; that thus, if we have any hope, or anything salutary in us, we may know that it was from her that it overflowed.'[61] Miserable is that soul which closes this channel of grace against itself, by neglect-

---

[57] "Gratia plena," de cujus plenitudine accipiunt universi.—*In Fest. Annunt. B.M.V.* conc. i.

[58] Ita ut nullus sit, qui de plenitudine gratiæ Virginis non sit particeps. †

[59] Quis unquam reperiatur, cui Virgo propitia non sit? quis ad quem ejus misericordia non se extendat? †

[60] Plenus equidem aquæductus, ut accipiant cæteri de plenitudine, sed non plenitudinem ipsam.—*Serm. de Aquæd.*

[61] Altius ergo intuemini, quanto devotionis affectu a nobis eam voluerit honorari, qui totius boni plenitudinem posuit in Maria: ut proinde si quid spei in nobis est, si quid gratiæ, si quid salutis, ab ea noverimus redundare quæ ascendit deliciis affluens.—*Ib.*

ing to recommend itself to Mary! When Holofernes wished to gain possession of the city of Bethulia, he took care to destroy the aqueducts : " He commanded their aqueduct to be cut off."[62] And this the devil does when he wishes to become master of a soul ; he causes her to give up devotion to the most Blessed Virgin Mary ; and when once this channel is closed, she easily loses supernatural light, the fear of God, and finally eternal salvation. Read the following example, in which may be seen how great ' is the compassion of the heart of Mary, and the destruction that he brings on himself who closes this channel against himself, by giving up devotion to the Queen of Heaven.

EXAMPLE.

Trithemius,[63] Canisius, and others, relate that in Magdeburg, a city of Saxony, there was a man called Udo, who from his youth was so destitute of talent, that he was the laughing-stock of all his companions. One day, more afflicted than usual at his own incapacity, he went to recommend himself to the most Blessed Virgin, and for this purpose was kneeling before her statue. Mary appeared to him in a vision, and said, ' Udo, I will console thee, and not only will I obtain thee from God sufficient capacity to free thee from the scoffs of others, but, moreover, such talents as to render thee an object of wonder ; and besides this, I promise thee, that after the death of the bishop, thou shalt be chosen to fill his place.' All that Mary said was verified. Udo made rapid progress in the sciences, and obtained the bishopric of that city. But Udo was to such a degree ungrateful to God and his benefactress, as to give up every devotion, and became a scandal to all. One night, when in bed, he heard a voice which said, ' Udo, cease thy wickedness ; thou hast sinned

---

[62] Incidi præcepit aquæductum illorum.—*Judith.* **vii. 6.**

[63] Chron. Hist 1101. Bovio Es. e Mir. p. 3. **es. 35, 36.**

enough.'[64] The first time he was enraged at these
words, thinking it was some one who had concealed
himself, and thus addressed him for his correction.
Hearing the same voice a second and a third night,
he began to fear that it was a voice from heaven. Yet
with all this he continued his wicked life. After three
months which God gave him to repent, chastisement
came, and it was this : a devout canon named Frederic
was one night in the church of Saint Maurice, praying
that God would apply a remedy to the scandal given
by the prelate, when a violent wind threw open the
doors of the church, and two young men entered with
lighted torches in their hands, stationing themselves
on either side of the high altar. Two others followed,
and extended a carpet before the altar, and placed two
golden chairs on it. After this another young man
came dressed as a soldier, with a sword in his hand,
and standing in the midst of the church, cried out : 'O
ye Saints of heaven, whose sacred relics are in this
church, come and witness the great act of justice about
to be executed by the Sovereign Judge.' At this cry
many Saints appeared, and also the twelve Apostles as
assessors of this judgment ; and finally Jesus Christ
entered, and seated Himself on one of the chairs that
had been prepared. Mary then appeared, accompanied
by many holy virgins, and her Son seated her on the
other chair. The Judge now commanded the criminal
to be brought, and it was the miserable Udo. Saint
Maurice spoke, and on the part of the scandalised
people asked that justice should be executed on the
prelate for his infamous life. All raised their voices
and exclaimed, ' Lord, he deserves death.' ' Let him
die immediately,' answered the Eternal Judge. But
before the execution of the sentence (see how great is
the compassion of Mary!) the compassionate Mother,
that she might not assist at that tremendous act of
justice, left the church ; and then the heavenly minis-

ter, who entered with a sword amongst the first, approached Udo, and with one stroke cut off his head, and all disappeared. All remained in darkness. The canon trembling went to get a light from a lamp which was burning under the church, and found the decapitated body of Udo and the pavement all covered with blood. On the following morning, when the people had assembled in the church, the canon related the vision, and the whole history of the horrible tragedy he had witnessed. On the same day the miserable Udo appeared, in the flames of hell, to one of his chaplains. who knew notning of what had taken place in the church. Udo's dead body was thrown into a marsh, and his blood remained on the pavement as a perpetual memorial, and was always kept covered with a carpet. From that time forward it became the custom to uncover it when a new bishop took possession of his see, that at the sight of such a chastisement he might learn how to regulate his life, and not be ungrateful for the graces of our Lord, and those of His most Holy Mother.

PRAYER.

O holy and heavenly Infant, Thou who art the destined Mother of my Redeemer and the great Mediatress of miserable sinners, pity me. Behold at thy feet another ungrateful sinner who has recourse to thee and asks thy compassion. It is true, that for my ingratitude to God and to thee, I deserve that God and thou should abandon me; but I have heard, and believe it to be so (knowing the greatness of thy mercy), that thou dost not refuse to help any one who recommends himself to thee with confidence. O most exalted creature in the world! since this is the case, and since there is no one but God above thee, so that compared with thee the greatest Saints of heaven are little; O Saint of Saints, O Mary! abyss of charity, and full of grace, succour a miserable creature who by his own fault has lost the divine favour. I know that thou art so dear to God that He denies thee nothing. I know also that thy pleasure is to use thy greatness for the relief of miserable sinners. Ah, then, show how great is the favour that thou enjoyest with God, by obtaining me a divine light and flame so powerful that I may be changed from a sinner into a Saint; and detaching myself from every earthly affection, divine love may be enkindled in me. Do this, O Lady, for thou canst do it. Do it for the love of God, who has made thee so great, so powerful, and so compassionate. This is my hope. Amen.

DISCOURSE III.

OF THE PRESENTATION OF MARY.

The Offering that Mary made of herself to God was prompt without delay, and entire without reserve.

THERE never was, and never will be, an offering on the part of a pure creature greater or more perfect than that which Mary made to God when, at the age of three years, she presented herself in the temple to offer Him, not aromatical spices, nor calves, nor gold, but her entire self, consecrating herself as a perpetual victim in His honour. She well understood the voice of God, calling her to devote herself entirely to His love, when He said, "Arise, make haste, my love, my dove, my beautiful one, and come !"[1] Therefore her Lord willed that from that time she should forget her country, and all, to think only of loving and pleasing Him: " Hearken, O daughter, and see, and incline thine ear; and forget thy people, and thy father's house."[2] She with promptitude and at once obeyed the divine call. Let us, then, consider how acceptable was this offering which Mary made of herself to God; for it was prompt and entire. Hence the two points for our consideration are, first, Mary's offering was prompt and without delay; secondly, it was entire and without reserve.

First point.—Mary's offering was prompt. From the first moment that this heavenly child was sanctified in her mother's womb, which was in the instant of her Immaculate Conception, she received the perfect

---

[1] Surge, propera, amica mea . . . et veni.—*Cant.* ii. 10.
[2] Audi filia, et vide, et inclina aurem tuam : et obliviscere populum tuum et domum patris tui.—*Ps.* xliv. 11.

use of reason, that she might begin to merit. This is in accordance with the general opinion of theologians, and with that of Father Suarez in particular, who says, that as the most perfect way in which God sanctifies a soul is by its own merit, as Saint Thomas also teaches,[3] it is thus we must believe that the Blessed Virgin was sanctified : 'To be sanctified by one's own act is the more perfect way. Therefore it is to be believed that the Blessed Virgin was thus sanctified.'[4] And if this privilege was granted to the angels, and to Adam, as the angelic Doctor says,[5] much more ought we to believe that it was granted to the Divine Mother, on whom, certainly, we must suppose that God, having condescended to make her His Mother, also conferred greater gifts than on all other creatures. 'From her,' says the same holy Doctor, 'He received His human nature, and therefore she must have obtained a greater plenitude of grace from Christ than all others.'[6] 'For being a mother,' Father Suarez says, 'she has a sort of special right to all the gifts of her Son;'[7] and as, on account of the hypostatic union, it was right that Jesus should receive the plenitude of all graces, so, on account of the divine maternity, it was becoming that Jesus should confer, as a natural debt, greater graces on Mary than He granted to all other Saints and angels.

Thus, from the beginning of her life, Mary knew God, and knew Him so that 'no tongue' (as the angel declared to Saint Bridget) 'will ever express how clearly this Blessed Virgin understood His greatness in that very first moment of her existence.'[8] And thus enlightened, she instantly offered her entire self to her

---

[3] 3 p. q. xix. art. 3. concl.

[4] Sanctificari per proprium actum est perfectior modus. Ergo credendum est hoc modo fuisse sanctificatam Virginem.—*De Incarn.* p. ii. q. xxvii. art. 6, disp. 4, § 8.

[5] 1 p. q. lxiii. art. 5.

[6] Ex ea accepit humanam naturam : et ideo præ cæteris majorem debuit a Christo gratiæ plenitudinem obtinere.—3 p. q. xxvi. art. 5.

[7] Unde fit ut singulare jus habeat ad bona Dei Filii sui.—*De Incarn.* p. ii. q. xxvii. art. 1, disp. 1, § 2.   [8] Serm. Ang. cap. xiv.

Lord, dedicating herself, without reserve, to His love and glory. 'Immediately,' the angel went on to say, 'our Queen determined to sacrifice her will to God, and to give Him all her love for the whole of her life. No one can understand how entire was the subjection in which she then placed her will, and how fully she was determined to do all according to His pleasure.'[9]

But the Immaculate Child, afterwards understanding that her holy parents, Joachim and Anne, had promised God, even by vow, as many authors relate, that if He granted them issue, they would consecrate it to His service in the temple; as it was, moreover, an ancient custom amongst the Jews to take their daughters to the temple, and there to leave them for their education (for which purpose there were cells contiguous), as it is recorded by Baronius,[10] Nicephorus, Cedrenus, and Suarez, with Josephus, the Jewish historian, and also on the authority of Saint John Damascen,[11] Saint George of Nicomedia, Saint Anselm,[12] and Saint Ambrose,[13] and, as we may easily gather from the Second Book of Machabees, where, speaking of Heliodorus, who besieged the temple, that he might gain possession of the treasure there deposited, says, "Because the place was like to come into contempt . . . and the virgins also that were shut up came forth, some to Onias."[14] Mary hearing this, I say, having scarcely attained the age of three years, as Saint Germanus[15] and Saint Epiphanius attest — the latter of whom says, 'In her third year she was brought to the temple'[16]—an age at which children are the most desirous and stand in the greatest need of their parents' care, she desired to offer and solemnly to consecrate herself to God, by presenting herself in the temple.

[9] Loc. cit.
[10] Appar. ad Ann. n. 47.
[11] De Fide Orth. l. 4, c. 15.
[12] De Form. et Mor. B.M.
[13] De Virg. lib. i. cap. 3.
[14] Pro eo quod in contemptum locus esset venturus . . . Virgines, quæ conclusæ erant, procurrebant ad Oniam.—2 Machab. iii. 18, 19.
[15] Enc. in S. Deip.
[16] Tertio anno oblata est in templo.

Hence, of her own accord, she requested her parents, with earnestness, to take her there, that they might thus accomplish their promise.   And her holy mother, says Saint Gregory of Nyssa, 'did not long delay leading her to the temple, and offering her to God.'[17]

Behold now Joachim and Anne, generously sacrificing to God the most precious treasure that they possessed in the world, and the one which was dearest to their hearts, setting out from Nazareth, carrying their well-beloved little daughter in turns, for she could not otherwise have undertaken so long a journey as that from Nazareth to Jerusalem, it being a distance of eighty miles, as several authors say.   They were accompanied by few relatives, but choirs of angels, according to Saint George of Nicomedia,[18] escorted and served the Immaculate little Virgin, who was about to consecrate herself to the Divine Majesty.   " How beautiful are thy steps, O prince's daughter !"[19]   O, how beautiful (must the angels have sung), how acceptable to God is thy every step, taken on thy way to present and offer thyself to Him !   O noble daughter, most beloved of our common Lord !   'God Himself, with the whole heavenly court,' says Bernardine de Bustis, 'made great rejoicings on that day, beholding His spouse coming to the temple.'[20]   ' For He never saw a more holy creature, or one whom He so tenderly loved, come to offer herself to Him.'[21]   ' Go then' (says Saint Germanus, archbishop of Constantinople), 'go, O Queen of the world, O Mother of God, go joyfully to the house of God, there to await the coming of the Divine Spirit, who will make thee the Mother of the Eternal Word.'   ' Enter with exultation the courts of the Lord, in ex-

[17] Illam igitur, cum jam grandiuscula esset, nec ubere matris amplius indigeret, ducens ad templum Deo reddidit.—*Or. in Nat. D.N.J.C.*
[18] De Oblat. Deip.
[19] Quam pulchri sunt gressus tui in calceamentis, filia principis!—*Cant.* vii. 1.
[20] Magnam quoque festivitatem fecit Deus cum angelis, in deductione suæ sponsæ ad templum.—*Maria!.* p. iv. Serm. i.
[21] Quia nullus unquam Deo gratior usque ad illud tempus templum subivit.—*Ib.*

pectation of the coming of the Holy Ghost, and the Conception of the only-begotten Son of God.'[22]

When the holy company had reached the temple the fair child turned to her parents, and on her knees kissed their hands, and asked their blessing; and then, without again turning back, she ascended the fifteen steps of the temple (according to Arius Montano, quoting Josephus), and as we are told by Saint Germanus, presented herself to the priest, Saint Zachary. Having done this, she bade farewell to the world, and renouncing all the pleasures which it promises to its votaries, she offered and consecrated herself to her Creator.

At the time of the deluge a raven sent out of the ark by Noah, remained to feed on the dead bodies; but the dove, without resting her foot, quickly "returned to him into the ark."[23] Many who are sent by God into this world unfortunately remain to feed on earthly goods. It was not thus that Mary, our heavenly dove, acted; she knew full well that God should be our only good, our only hope, our only love; she knew that the world is full of dangers, and that he who leaves it the soonest is freest from its snares : hence she sought to do this in her tenderest years, and as soon as possible shut herself up in the sacred retirement of the temple, where she could better hear His voice, and honour and love Him more. Thus did the Blessed Virgin in her very first actions render herself entirely dear and agreeable to her Lord, as the holy Church says in her name : ' Rejoice with me, all ye who love God; for when I was a little one I pleased the Most High.'[24] For this reason she was likened to the moon; for as the moon completes her course with

[22] Abi igitur, Domina Dei Genitrix, abi et perambula Domini aulas, exultans et gaudens, educatione virens, deque die in diem expectans Sancti Spiritus in te adventum, virtutis Altissimi obumbrationem, et Filii tui conceptionem.—*In Praesent. Dei Mat.* Orat. ii.

[23] Quae cum non invenisset ubi requiesceret pes ejus, reversa est ad eum in arca.—*Gen.* viii. 9.

[24] Congratulamini mihi, omnes qui diligitis Dominum, quia, cum essem parvula placui Altissimo.—*In* 2 *Resp.* 1 *Noct. in Fest. S.M. ad Niv.*

greater velocity than the other planets, so did Mary attain perfection sooner than all the Saints, by giving herself to God promptly and without delay, and making herself all His without reserve. Let us now pass to the second point, on which we shall have much to say.

Second point.—The enlightened child well knew that God does not accept a divided heart, but wills that, as He has commanded, it should be consecrated to His love without the least reserve: "Thou shalt love the Lord thy God with thy whole heart."[25] Hence from the first moment of her life she began to love God with all her strength, and gave herself entirely to Him. But still her most holy soul awaited with the most ardent desire the moment when she might consecrate herself to Him in a more solemn and public way. Let us, then, consider with what fervour this loving and tender Virgin, on finding herself actually enclosed in the holy place, first prostrate, kissed that ground as the house of her Lord; and then adored His Infinite Majesty, thanked Him for the favour she had received in being thus brought to dwell for a time in His house, and then offered her entire self to her God, wholly, without reserving anything—all her powers and all her senses, her whole mind and her whole heart, her whole soul and her whole body; for then it was, according to many authors, that to please God 'she vowed Him her virginity,' a vow which, according to the Abbot Rupert, 'Mary was the first to make.'[26] And the offering she then made of her entire self was without any reserve as to time, as Bernardine de Bustis declares : 'Mary offered and dedicated herself to the perpetual service of God ;'[27] for her intention was to dedicate herself to the service of His Divine Majesty in the

---

[25] Diliges Dominum Deum tuum ex toto corde tuo.—*Deut.* vi. 5.
[26] Votum egregium Deo prima vovisti, votum virginitatis.—Lib. iii. in *Cant.* c. 4.
[27] Maria . . . seipsam perpetuis Deo obsequiis obtulit et dedicavit.—*Marial.* p. iv. Serm. i.

temple for her whole life, should such be the good pleasure of God, and never to leave that sacred place.   O,
with what effusion of soul must she then have exclaimed,
" My beloved to me, and I to Him !"[28]   Cardinal Hugo
paraphrases these words, saying, ' I will live all His,
and die all His.'[29]   ' My Lord and my God,' she said,
' I am come here to please Thee alone, and to give Thee
all the honour that is in my power ; here will I live all
Thine, and die all Thine, should such be Thy pleasure ;
accept the sacrifice which Thy poor servant offers Thee
and enable me to be faithful to Thee.'

Here let us consider how holy was the life which
Mary led in the temple, where, as " the morning
rising,"[30] which rapidly bursts out into the full brightness of mid-day, she progressed in perfection.   Who
can ever tell the alway-increasing brightness with
which her resplendent virtues shone forth from day
to day : charity, modesty, humility, silence, mortification, meekness.   This fair olive-tree, says Saint John
Damascen, planted in the house of God, and nurtured
by the Holy Ghost, became the dwelling-place of all
virtues ; ' led to the temple, and thenceforward planted
in the house of God, and cultivated by the Spirit, she
as a fruitful olive-tree became the abode of all virtues.'[31]   The same Saint says elsewhere, ' that the
countenance of the Blessed Virgin was modest, her
mind humble, her words proceeding from a composed
interior were engaging.'[32]   In another place he asserts
that she turned her thoughts far from earthly things,
embracing all virtues ; and thus exercising herself in
perfection, she made such rapid progress in a short
time, that she merited to become a temple worthy of
God.[33]

---

[28] Dilectus meus mihi, et ego illi !—*Cant.* **ii. 16.**
[29] Ego illi . . . tota vivam, et tota moriar.—*In Cant.* cap. ii.
[30] Quæ est ista, quæ progreditur quasi aurora consurgens ?—*Cant.* **vi. 9.**
[31] . . . Ad templum adducitur. Tum deinde in domo Dei plantata, et
per Spiritum saginata, instar olivæ fructiferæ virtutum omnium domicilium
instruitur.—*De Fide Orth.* lib. **iv.** cap. 14.
[32] Hom. i. in Nat. B.M.V.   [33] De Fide Orth. lib. **iv.** cap. 14

St. Anselm also speaks of the life of the Blessed Virgin in the temple, and says that ' Mary was docile, spoke little, was always composed, did not laugh, and that her mind was never disturbed. She also persevered in prayer, in the study of the sacred Scriptures, in fastings, and all virtuous works.'[34] Saint Jerome enters more into detail. He says that Mary thus regulated her life : In the morning until the third hour she remained in prayer ; from the third hour until the ninth she employed herself with work ; and from the ninth hour she again prayed until the angel brought her her food, as he was wont to do. She was always the first in watchings, the most exact in the observance of the Divine law, the most profoundly humble, and the most perfect in every virtue. No one ever saw her angry : her every word carried such sweetness with it that it was a witness to all that God was with her.[35]

We read in St. Bonaventure's *Life of Christ*, that the Divine Mother herself revealed to Saint Elizabeth of Hungary that ' when her father and mother left her in the temple, she determined to have God alone for her Father, and often thought how she could please Him most.'[36] Moreover, as we learn from the Revelations of Saint Bridget, ' she determined to consecrate her virginity to Him, and to possess nothing in the world, and to give Him her entire will.'[37] Besides this, she told Saint Elizabeth that of all the commandments to be observed she especially kept this one before her eyes : " Thou shalt love the Lord thy God ;"[38] and that at midnight she went before the altar of the temple to beg that He would grant her the grace to observe them all, and also that she might live to see the birth of the

[34] De Form. et. Mor. B.M.V.   [35] De Nat. S. Mariæ.

[36] Cum pater meus et mater mea me dimiserunt in templo, statui in corde meo habere Deum in patrem ; et devote ac frequenter cogitabam, quid possem facere Deo gratum.—*S. Bonav. Vita Christi*, cap. iii.

[37] Vovi etiam in corde meo, si esset ei acceptabile observare virginitatem, nihil unquam possidere in mundo . . . ei omnem voluntatem meam commisi.—*Rev.* lib. i. cap. 10.

[38] Diliges Dominum Deum tuum.—*Deut.* vi 5

Mother of the Redeemer, entreating Him at the same time to preserve her eyes to behold her, her tongue to praise her, her hands and feet to serve her, and her knees to adore her Divine Son in her womb.   Saint Elizabeth, on hearing this, said, 'But, Lady, wast thou not full of grace and virtue?'   Mary replied, 'Know that I considered myself most vile and unworthy of Divine grace, and therefore thus earnestly prayed for grace and virtue.'   And finally, that we might be convinced of the absolute necessity under which we all are of asking the graces that we require from God, she added: 'Dost thou think that I possessed grace and virtue without effort?   Know that I obtained no grace from God without great effort, constant prayer, ardent desire, and many tears and mortifications.'

But above all we should consider the revelation made to Saint Bridget of the virtues and practices of the Blessed Virgin in her childhood, in the following words: 'From her childhood Mary was full of the Holy Ghost, and as she advanced in age she advanced also in grace.   Thenceforward she determined to love God with her whole heart, so that she might never offend Him, either by her words or actions; and therefore she despised all earthly goods.   She gave all that she could to the poor.   In her food she was so temperate, that she only took as much as was barely necessary to sustain her body.   Afterwards, on discovering in the sacred Scriptures that God was to be born of a Virgin, that He might redeem the world, her soul was to such a degree inflamed with Divine love, that she could desire and think of nothing but God; and finding pleasure in Him alone, she avoided all company, even that of her parents, lest their presence might deprive her of His remembrance.   She desired, with the greatest ardour, to live until the time of the coming of the Messiah, that she might be the servant of that happy Virgin, who merited to be His Mother.'   Thus far the Revelations of Saint Bridget.[39]

[39] Lib. i. cap. 10.

Ah, yes, for the love of this exalted child the Re-deemer did indeed hasten His coming into the world; for whilst she, in her humility, looked upon herself as unworthy to be the servant of the Divine Mother, she was herself chosen to be this Mother; and by the sweet odour of her virtues and her powerful prayers she drew the Divine Son into her virginal womb. For this rea-son Mary was called a turtle-dove by her Divine Spouse: " The voice of the turtle is heard in our land."[40] Not only because as a turtle-dove she always loved solitude, living in this world as in a desert, but also because, like a turtle-dove, which always sighs for its companions, Mary always sighed in the temple, compassionating the miseries of the lost world, and seeking from God the redemption of all. O, with how much greater feeling and fervour than the prophets did she repeat their prayers and sighs, that God would send the promised Redeemer ! " Send forth, O Lord, the Lamb, the ruler of the earth."[41] " Drop down dew, ye heavens, from above, and let the clouds rain the Just."[42] " O that thou wouldst rend the heavens, and wouldst come down !"[43]

In a word, it was a subject of delight to God to behold this tender Virgin always ascending towards the highest perfection, like a pillar of smoke, rich in the sweet odour of all virtues, as the Holy Ghost Him-self clearly describes her in the sacred Canticles: " Who is she that goeth up by the desert as a pillar of smoke, of aromatical spices, of myrrh and frankincense, and of all the powders of the perfumer?"[44] ' This child,' says Saint Sophronius, ' was truly God's garden of delights; for He there found every kind of flower, and all the sweet odours of virtues.'[45]   Hence Saint John Chryso-

[40] Vox turturis audita est in terra nostra.—*Cant.* ii. 12.
[41] Emitte agnum, Domine, dominatorem terræ.—*Is.* xvi. 1.
[42] Rorate cœli desuper, et nubes pluant Justum.—*Ib.* xlv. 8.
[43] Utinam disrumperes cœlos, et descenderes.—*Ib.* lxiv. 1.
[44] Quæ est ista, quæ ascendit per desertum, sicut virgula fumi, ex aro-matibus myrrhæ, et thuris, et universi pulveris pigmentarii ?—*Cant.* iii. 6.
[45] Vere hortus deliciarum, in quo consita sunt universa florum genera et odoramenta virtutum.— *Serm. de Assump. int. op. S. Hieron.*

stom affirms,[46] that God chose Mary for His Mother in this world because He did not find on earth a Virgin more holy and more perfect than she was, nor any dwelling more worthy than her most sacred womb. Saint Bernard also says, 'that there was not on earth a more worthy place than the virginal womb.'[47] This also agrees with the assertion of Saint Antoninus, that the Blessed Virgin, to be chosen for, and destined to the dignity of Mother of God, was necessarily so great and consummate in perfection as to surpass all other creatures : 'The last grace of perfection is that which prepared her for the conception of the Son of God.'[48]

As, then, the holy child Mary presented and offered herself to God in the temple with promptitude and without reserve, so let us also present ourselves this day to Mary without delay and without reserve ; and let us entreat her to offer us to God, who will not reject us when He sees us presented by the hand of that blessed creature, who was the living temple of the Holy Ghost, the delight of her Lord, and the chosen Mother of the Eternal Word. Let us also have unbounded confidence in this high and gracious Lady, who rewards, indeed, with the greatest love the homage that she receives from her clients, as we may gather from the following example.

EXAMPLE.

We read in the life of Sister Domenica del Paradiso, written by the Dominican Father Ignatius del Niente, that she was born of poor parents, in the village of Paradiso, near Florence. From her very infancy she began to serve the Divine Mother. She fasted every day in her honour, and on Saturdays gave her food, of which she deprived herself, to the poor. Every

---

[46] Ap. Canis. lib. i. de B.V. c. 13.
[47] Nec in terris locus dignior uteri virginalis templo.—*In Assump. B.M.* Serm. i.
[48] Ultima gratia perfectionis est præparatio ad Filium Dei concipiendum ; quæ præparatio fuit per profundam humilitatem.—P. iv. tit. 15, c. 6, No. 2.

Saturday she went into the garden and into the neighbouring fields, and gathered all the flowers that she
could find, and presented them before an image of the
Blessed Virgin with the Child in her arms, which she
kept in the house.   But let us now see with how many
favours this most gracious Lady recompensed the homage of her servant.   One day, when Domenica was ten
years of age, standing at the window, she saw in the
street a lady of noble mien, accompanied by a little
child, and they both extended their hands, asking for
alms.   She went to get some bread, when in a moment,
without the door being opened, she saw them by her
side, and perceived that the child's hands and feet and
side were wounded.   She therefore asked the Lady
who had wounded the child.   The mother answered,
' It was love.'   Domenica, inflamed with love at the
sight of the beauty and modesty of the child, asked him
if the wounds pained him ?   His only answer was a
smile.   But, as they were standing near the statue of
Jesus and Mary, the lady said to Domenica : ' Tell me,
my child, what is it that makes thee crown these images
with flowers ?'   She replied, ' It is the love that I bear
to Jesus and Mary.'   ' And how much dost thou love
them ?'   ' I love them as much as I can.'   ' And how
much canst thou love them ?'   'As much as they enable
me.'   ' Continue, then,' added the lady, ' continue to
love them ;   for they will amply repay thy love in
heaven.'

The little girl then perceiving that a heavenly odour
came forth from those wounds, asked the mother with
what ointment she anointed them, and if it could be
bought.   The lady answered, ' It is bought with faith
and good works.'   Domenica then offered the bread.
The Mother said, ' Love is the food of my Son; tell
Him that thou lovest Jesus, and He will be satisfied.'
The child at the word love seemed filled with joy, and
turning towards the little girl, asked her how much she
loved Jesus.   She answered that she loved Him so

much, that night and day she always thought of Him, and sought for nothing else but to give Him as much pleasure as she possibly could. ' It is well,' He replied; ' love Him, for love will teach thee what to do to please Him.' The sweet odour which exhaled from those wounds then increasing, Domenica cried out, ' O God! this odour makes me die of love.' If the odour of a child is so sweet, what must that of heaven be? But behold the scene now changed; the Mother appeared clothed as a Queen, and the child resplendent with beauty like the sun. He took the flowers and scattered them on the head of Domenica, who recognising Jesus and Mary in those personages, was already prostrate adoring them. Thus the vision ended. Domenica afterwards took the habit of a Dominicaness, and died in the odour of sanctity in the year 1553.

PRAYER.

O beloved Mother of God, most amiable child Mary, O that, as thou didst present thyself in the temple, and with promptitude and without reserve, didst consecrate thyself to the glory and love of God, I could offer thee, this day, the first years of my life, to devote myself without reserve to thy service, my holy and most sweet Lady! But it is now too late to do this; for, unfortunate creature that I am, I have lost so many years in the service of the world and my own caprices, and have lived in almost entire forgetfulness of thee and of God: " Woe to that time in which I did not love thee !"[49] But it is better to begin late than not at all. Behold, O Mary, I this day present myself to thee, and I offer myself without reserve to thy service for the long or short time that I still have to live in this world; and in union with thee I renounce all creatures, and devote myself entirely to the love of my Creator. I consecrate my mind to thee, O Queen, that it may always think of

---

[9] Væ tempori illi, ik ꝗuo non amavi te.

the love that thou deservest, my tongue to praise thee, my heart to love thee.   Do thou accept, O most holy Virgin, the offering which this miserable sinner now makes thee : accept it, I beseech thee, by the consolation that thy heart experienced when thou gavest thyself to God in the temple.   But since I enter thy service late, it is reasonable that I should redouble my acts of homage and love, thereby to compensate for lost time. Do thou help my weakness with thy powerful intercession, O Mother of Mercy, by obtaining me perseverance from thy Jesus, and strength to be always faithful to thee until death ; that thus always serving thee in life, I may praise thee in Paradise for all eternity.   Amen.

DISCOURSE IV.

OF THE ANNUNCIATION OF MARY.

In the Incarnation of the Eternal Word, Mary could not have humbled herself more than she did humble herself: God, on the other hand, could not have exalted her more than He did exalt her.

"Whosoever shall exalt himself shall be humbled; and he that shall humble himself shall be exalted."[1] These are the words of our Lord, and cannot fail. Therefore, God having determined to become man, that He might redeem lost man, and thus show the world His infinite goodness, and having to choose a Mother on earth, He sought amongst women for the one who was the most holy and the most humble. But amongst all, one there was whom He admired, and this one was the tender Virgin Mary, who, the more exalted were her virtues, so much the more dove-like was her simplicity and humility, and the more lowly was she in her own estimation. "There are young maidens without number: one is my dove, my perfect one."[2] Therefore God said: This one shall be my chosen Mother. Let us now see how great was Mary's humility, and consequently how greatly God exalted her. Mary could not have humbled herself more than she did humble herself in the Incarnation of the Word; this will be the first point. That God could not have exalted Mary more than He did exalt her; this will be the second.

First point.—Our Lord in the sacred Canticles,

---

[1] Qui autem se exaltaverit, humiliabitur: et qui se humiliaverit, exaltabitur.—*Matt.* xxiii. 12.

[2] Adolescentularum non est numerus. Una est columba mea, perfecta mea.—*Cant.* vi. 8.

speaking precisely of the humility of the most humble Virgin, says : "While the king was at his repose, my spikenard sent forth the odour thereof."[3]   Saint Antoninus, explaining these words, says that 'spikenard, from its being a small and lowly herb, was a type of Mary, the sweet odour of whose humility, ascending to heaven so to say, awakened the Divine Word, reposing in the bosom of the Eternal Father, and drew Him into her virginal womb.'[4]   So that our Lord, drawn as it were by the sweet odour of this humble Virgin, chose her for His Mother, when He was pleased to become man to redeem the world.   But He, for the greater glory and merit of this Mother, would not become her Son without her previous consent.   The Abbot William says, ' He would not take flesh from her unless she gave it.'[5]   Hence, when this humble Virgin (for so it was revealed to Saint Elizabeth of Hungary) was in her poor little cottage, sighing and beseeching God more fervently than ever, and with desires more than ever ardent, that He would send the Redeemer ; behold, the Archangel Gabriel arrives, the bearer of the great message.   He enters and salutes her, saying : "Hail, full of grace ; the Lord is with thee ; blessed art thou amongst women."[6]   Hail, O Virgin full of grace ; for thou wast always full of grace above all other saints The Lord is with thee, because thou art so humble Thou art blessed amongst women, for all others fell under the curse of sin ; but thou, because thou art the Mother of the Blessed One, art, and always wilt be blessed, and free from every stain.

But what does the humble Mary reply to a salutation so full of praises ?   Nothing ; she remains silent,

---

[3] Dum esset rex in accubitu suo nardus mea dedit odorem suum.—*Cant.* i. 11.
[4] Nardus est herba parva, sed multum medicinalis, et significat beatam Virginem humilem, quæ permaxime dedit odorem suæ humilitatis.—P. iv. tit. 15, c. 21, No. 2.
[5] Noluit carnem sumere ex ipsa, non dante ipsa.—*Delrio in Cant.* i. 2.
[6] Ave, gratia plena : Dominus tecum : benedicta tu in mulieribus.—*Luc.* i. 28.

but reflecting upon it, is troubled : "Who having heard
was troubled at his saying, and thought with herself
what manner of salutation this should be."[7]   Why was
she troubled ?   Did she fear an illusion, or was it her
virginal modesty which caused her to be disturbed at
the sight of a man, as some suppose, in the belief that
the Angel appeared under a human form ?   No, the
text is clear : "She was troubled at his saying."   'Not
at his appearance, but at what he said,'[8] remarks Eusebius Emissenus.   Her trouble, then, arose entirely from
her humility, which was disturbed at the sound of
praises so far exceeding her own lowly estimate of herself.   Hence, the more the angel exalted her, the more
she humbled herself, and entered into the consideration
of her own nothingness.   Here Saint Bernardine remarks, that 'had the angel said, O Mary, thou art the
greatest sinner in the world, her astonishment would
not have been so great ; the sound of such high praises
filled her with fear.'[9]   She was troubled ; for, being so
full of humility, she abhorred every praise of herself,
and her only desire was that her Creator, the giver of
every good thing, should be praised and blessed.   This
Mary herself revealed to Saint Bridget, when speaking
of the time in which she became Mother of God :
'I desired not my own praise, but only that my Creator,
the giver of all, should be glorified.'[10]   The Blessed
Virgin was already well aware, from the sacred Scriptures, that the time foretold by the prophets for the
coming of the Messiah had arrived ; that the weeks of
Daniel were completed ; that already, according to the
prophecy of Jacob, the sceptre of Juda had passed into
the hands of Herod, a strange king : she already knew

---

[7] Quæ, cum audisset, turbata est in sermone ejus, et cogitabat qualis esset
ista salutatio.—*Luc.* i. 29.

[8] Turbata est, inquit, non in vultu ejus, sed in sermone ejus. – *Serm. in
Fer.* iv. *post Dom.* 4, *Advent.*

[9] Si ipse dixisset, Tu, O Maria, es lascivior quæ sit in mundo, non ita ad-
mirata fuisset . . . unde . . . turbata fuit de tantis . . . laudibus.—*Serm.
de Amore incarnante,* p. iii.

[10] Nolui laudem meam, sed solius datoris et Creatoris.—*Rev.* l. **2. c. 23.**

Y

that a Virgin was to be the Mother of the Messiah. She then heard the angel give her praises which, it was evident, could apply to no other than to the Mother of God. Hence, may not the thought, or at least some vague impression, have entered her mind, that perhaps she was this chosen Mother of God? No, her profound humility did not even admit such an idea. Those praises only caused great fear in her: 'so much so,' as Saint Peter Chrysologus remarks, 'that as Christ was pleased to be comforted by an angel, so was it necessary that the Blessed Virgin should be encouraged by one.'[11] Saint Gabriel, seeing Mary so troubled and almost stupefied by the salutation, was obliged to encourage her, saying, "Fear not, Mary; for thou hast found grace with God."[12] Fear not, O Mary, and be not surprised at the great titles by which I have saluted thee; for if thou in thine own eyes art so little and lowly, God, who exalts the humble, has made thee worthy to find the grace lost by men; and therefore He has preserved thee from the common stain of the children of Adam. Hence, from the moment of thy conception, He has honoured thee with a grace greater than that of all the Saints; and therefore He now finally exalts thee even to the dignity of being His Mother. "Behold, thou shalt conceive in thy womb, and shalt bring forth a Son: and thou shalt call His name Jesus."[13]

And now, why this delay, O Mary? 'The angel awaits thy reply' (says Saint Bernard); 'and we also, O Lady, on whom the sentence of condemnation weighs so heavily, await the word of mercy;'[14] we, who are already condemned to death. 'Behold, the price of our salvation is offered thee; we shall be instantly delivered

---

[11] Sicut Christus per angelum confortari voluit, ita decuit Virginem per angelum animari.—*Ap. Suarez. de Inc.* q. 30, a. 2.

[12] Ne timeas, Maria; invenisti enim gratiam apud Deum.—*Luc.* i. 30.

[13] Ecce concipies in utero, et paries filium, et vocabis nomen ejus Jesum. —*Luc.* i. 31.

[14] Expectat angelus responsum . . . . expectamus et nos, O Domina, verbum miserationis, quos miserabiliter premit sententia damnationis.— *Hom.* iv. *sup. Miss.*

if thou consentest,'[15] continues the same Saint Bernard. Behold, O Mother of us all, the price of our salvation is already offered thee; that price will be the Divine Word, made man in thee; in that moment in which thou acceptest Him for thy Son we shall be delivered from death. 'For thy Lord Himself desires thy consent, by which He has determined to save the world, with an ardour equal to the love with which He has loved thy beauty.'[16] 'Answer then, O sacred Virgin,' says Saint Augustine, or some other ancient author; 'why delayest thou giving life to the world?'[17] Reply quickly, O Lady; no longer delay the salvation of the world, which now depends upon thy consent.

But see, Mary already answers; she replies to the angel and says: "Behold the handmaid of the Lord; be it done to me according to thy word."[18] O, what more beautiful, more humble, or more prudent answer could all the wisdom of men and angels together have invented, had they reflected for a million years? O powerful answer, which rejoiced heaven, and brought an immense sea of graces and blessings into the world!—answer which had scarcely fallen from the lips of Mary, before it drew the only-begotten Son of God from the bosom of His Eternal Father, to become man in her most pure womb! Yes indeed; for scarcely had she uttered these words, "Behold the handmaid of the Lord; be it done to me according to thy word," than instantly "the Word was made flesh;"[19] the Son of God became also the Son of Mary. 'O powerful Fiat!' exclaims Saint Thomas of Villanova; 'O efficacious Fiat! O

---

[15] Et ecce offertur tibi pretium salutis nostræ; statim liberabimur, si consentis.—*Hom.* iv. *sup. Miss.*

[16] Ipse quoque omnium Rex et Dominus, quantum concupivit decorem tuum, tantum desiderat et responsionis assensum, in qua nimirum proposuit salvare mundum.—*Ib.*

[17] Responde nunc verbum ... O Beata Maria, sæculum omne captivum tuum deprecatur assensum ... Noli morari, Virgo: nuntio festinanter responde verbum, et suscipe Filium.—*Int. op. S. Augustini, Serm.* ii. *de Annunt.*

[18] Ecce ancilla Domini, fiat mihi secundum verbum tuum.—*Luc.* i. 38

[19] Et Verbum caro factum est, et habitavit in nobis.—*Joan.* i. 14.

Fiat to be venerated above every other Fiat ! For with a
fiat God created light, heaven, earth ; but with Mary's
fiat,' says the Saint, ' God became man, like us.'[20]

Let us, however, not wander from our point, but
consider the great humility of the Blessed Virgin in
this answer. She was fully enlightened as to the greatness of the dignity of a Mother of God. She had already been assured by the angel that she was this happy
Mother chosen by our Lord. But with all this, she in
no way rises in her own estimation, she does not stop
to rejoice in her exultation ; but seeing, on the one side,
her own nothingness, and on the other the infinite
majesty of God, who chose her for His Mother, she acknowledges how unworthy she is of so great an honour,
but will not oppose His will in the least thing. Hence,
when her consent is asked, what does she do ? what
does she say ? Wholly annihilated within herself, yet
all inflamed at the same time by the ardour of her desire to unite herself thus still more closely with God,
and abandoning herself entirely to the Divine will, she
replies, " Behold the handmaid of the Lord." Behold
the slave of the Lord, obliged to do that which her Lord
commands. As if she meant to say : Since God chooses
me for His Mother, who have nothing of my own, and
since all that I have is His gift, who can ever think
that He has done so on account of my own merits ?
" Behold the handmaid of the Lord." What merit can
a slave ever have, that she should become the Mother
of her Lord ? " Behold the handmaid of the Lord."
May the goodness of God alone be praised, and not
His slave : since it is all His goodness, that he fixes
His eyes on so lowly a creature as I am, to make her so
great.

'O humility !' here exclaims the Abbot Guarric ;
'as nothing in its own eyes, yet sufficiently great for

---

[20] O *fiat* potens! O *fiat* efficax ! O *fiat* super omne *fiat,* perpetuo honore
venerandum ! Hoc verbo *fiat* factus est mundus, *Gen.* i. : hoc verbo cœlestia
terrestriaque Altissimus condidit : sed tale *fiat* non sonuit in orbe, quale tu
nunc Beata dixisti.—*Conc.* i. *in Annunt. B.M.V.*

the Divinity ! Insufficient for itself, sufficient for Him whom the heavens cannot contain.'[21] O great humility of Mary ! which makes her little to herself, but great before God. Unworthy in her own eyes, but worthy in the eyes of that immense Lord whom the world cannot contain. But the exclamation of Saint Bernard on this subject is still more beautiful, in his fourth sermon on the Assumption of Mary, in which, admiring her humility, he says: ' And how, O Lady, couldst thou unite in thy heart so humble an opinion of thyself with such great purity, with such innocence, and so great a plenitude of grace as thou didst possess ?'[22] 'And how, O Blessed Virgin,' continues the Saint, 'did this humility, and so great humility, ever take such deep root in thy heart, seeing thyself thus honoured and exalted by God ?' ' Whence thy humility, and so great humility, O blessed one ?'[23] Lucifer, seeing himself endowed with great beauty, aspired to exalt his throne above the stars, and to make himself like God : " I will exalt my throne above the stars of God . . . . I will be like the Most High."[24] O, what would that proud spirit have said, and to what would he have aspired, had he ever been adorned with the gifts of Mary ! The humble Mary did not act thus ; the higher she saw herself raised, the more she humbled herself. Ah, Lady ! concludes Saint Bernard, by this admirable humility thou didst indeed render thyself worthy to be regarded by God with singular love ; worthy to captivate thy King with thy beauty ; worthy to draw, by the sweet odour of thy humility, the Eternal Son from His repose, from the bosom of God, into thy most pure womb. ' She was indeed worthy

---

[21] O humilitas angusta sibi, ampla Divinitati ! Insufficiens sibi, sufficiens ei quem non capit orbis!—*In Assumpt.* § 3.

[22] Quanta vero et quam pretiosa humilitatis virtus, cum tanta puritate, cum innocentia tanta, cum conscientia prorsus absque delicto, uno cum tantæ gratiæ plenitudine?—*Serm.* iv. *in Assump. B.M.V.*

[23] Unde tibi humilitas et tanta humilitas, O Beata?—*Ib.*

[24] Super astra Dei exaltabo solium meum . . . similis ero Altissimo.-*Is.* xiv. 13, 14.

to be looked upon by the Lord, whose beauty the King
so greatly desired, and by whose most sweet odour He
was drawn from the eternal repose of His Father's
bosom.'[25] Hence Bernardine de Bustis says that 'Mary
merited more by saying with humility, "Behold the
handmaid of the Lord!" than all pure creatures could
merit together by all their good works.'[26]

Thus, says Saint Bernard, this innocent Virgin,
although she made herself dear to God by her virginity, yet it was by her humility that she rendered
herself worthy, as far as a creature can be worthy, to
become the Mother of her Creator. 'Though she
pleased by her virginity, she conceived by her humility.'[27] Saint Jerome confirms this, saying that
'God chose her to be His Mother more on account of
her humility than all her other sublime virtues.'[28]
Mary herself also assured Saint Bridget of the same
thing, saying: 'How was it that I merited so great
a grace as to be made the Mother of my Lord, if it
was not that I knew my own nothingness, and that
I had nothing, and humbled myself?'[29] This she had
already declared in her canticle, breathing forth the
most profound humility, when she said: "Because He
hath regarded the humility of His handmaid . . . .
He that is mighty hath done great things to me."[30]
On these words Saint Lawrence Justinian remarks, that
the Blessed Virgin 'did not say, He hath regarded the

[25] Digna plane quam respiceret Dominus, cujus decorem concupisceret
Rex, cujus odore suavissimo ab æterno illo paterni sinus attraheretur
accubitu.—*In Assump.* iv. 13, 14.

[26] Benedicta Virgo plus meruit sola, quam omnes aliæ creaturæ, unde S.
Bonav. 'Ipsa plus meruit intensive post annunciationem, quam omnes
Sancti et Sanctæ Dei simul.'—P. xi. *Marial. Serm.* ii. p. 7, z.

[27] Etsi placuit ex virginitate, tamen ex humilitate concepit.—*Hom.* i.
sup. Missus est.

[28] Maluit Deus de Beata Maria incarnari propter humilitatem, quam
propter aliam quamcumque virtutem.—*Euseb. de Morte Hier.*

[29] Unde promerui tantam gratiam, nisi quia cogitavi, et scivi, me nihil a
me esse vel habere ?—*Rev.* lib. ii. cap. 23.

[30] Quia respexit humilitatem ancillæ suæ . . . fecit mihi magna qui potens
est.—*Luc.* i. 48, 49.

virginity, or the innocence, but only the humility:'[31] and by this humility, as Saint Francis of Sales observes, Mary did not mean to praise the virtue of her own humility, but she meant to declare that God had regarded her nothingness (humility, that is nothingness),[32] and that, out of His pure goodness, He had been pleased thus to exalt her.

In fine, the author of a sermon found amongst the works of Saint Augustine says, that Mary's humility was a ladder by which our Lord deigned to descend from heaven to earth, to become man in her womb: ' Mary's humility,' he says, ' became a heavenly ladder, by which God came into the world.'[33] This is confirmed by Saint Antoninus, who says, that the humility of Mary was her most perfect virtue, and the one which immediately prepared her to become the Mother of God. ' The last grace of perfection is preparation for the conception of the Son of God, which preparation is made by profound humility.'[34] The prophet Isaias foretold the same thing: " And there shall come forth a rod out of the root of Jesse, and a flower shall rise up out of his root."[35] Blessed Albert the Great remarks on these words, that the Divine flower, that is to say the only-begotten Son of God, was to be born, not from the summit, nor from the trunk, of the tree of Jesse, but from the root, precisely to denote the humility of the Mother: ' By the root humility of heart is understood.'[36] The Abbot of Celles explains it more clearly still, saying: ' Remark that the flower rises, not from the summit, but out of the root.'[37] For this

---

[31] Non ait, respexit Viginitatem, non innocentiam, non virtutes cæteras, sed humilitatem tantum.—*De Vita solit.* cap. xiv.

[32] Humilitatem, id est nihilitatem.

[33] Facta est certe Mariæ humilitas scala cœlestis, per quam descendit Deus ad terras.—*Serm. de Assump. int. op. S. August.*

[34] Ultima gratia perfectionis est, præparatio ad Filium Dei concipiendum; quæ præparatio fuit per profundam humilitatem.—P. iv. tit. 15, c. 6, no. 2.

[35] Et egredietur virga de radice Jesse, et flos de radice ejus ascendet.—*Is.* xi. 1.

[36] In radice humilitas cordis.—*Serm.* lvi. *de B.V.M.*

[37] Nota quod non ex summitate sed de radice ascendit flos. ✝

reason God said to His beloved daughter, " Turn away
thy eyes from Me, for they have made Me flee away." [38]
Saint Augustine asks, ' Whence have they made Thee
flee, unless it be from the bosom of Thy Father into
the womb of Thy Mother ?' [39]   On this same thought
the learned interpreter Fernandez says, that the most
humble eyes of Mary, which she always kept fixed on
the Divine greatness, never losing sight of her own
nothingness, did such violence to God Himself, that
they drew Him into her womb : ' Her most humble
eyes held God in such a way captive, that this Blessed
Virgin, with a kind of most sweet violence, drew the
Word Himself of God the Father into her womb.' [40]
' Thus it is that we can understand,' says the Abbot
Franco, ' why the Holy Ghost praised the beauty of this
His Spouse, so greatly, on account of her dove's eyes :'
" How beautiful art thou, my love ! how beautiful art
thou ! thine eyes are dove's eyes." [41]   For Mary, looking at God with the eyes of a simple and humble dove,
enamoured Him to such a degree by her beauty, that
with the bands of love she made Him a prisoner in
her chaste womb.   The Abbot thus speaks : ' Where
on earth could so beautiful a Virgin be found, who
could allure the King of heaven by her eyes, and by a
holy violence lead Him captive, bound in the chains of
love ?' [42]   So that, to conclude this point, we will remark, that in the Incarnation of the Eternal Word, as
we have already seen at the commencement of our discourse, Mary could not have humbled herself more
than she did humble herself.   Let us now see how it

---

[38] Averte oculos tuos a me, quia ipsi me avolare fecerunt.—*Cant.* **vi. 4.**

[39] Unde avolare, nisi a sinu Patris in uterum Matris ? †

[40] Ita illius oculi humillimi ac modestissimi Deum tenuerunt, ut suavis-
sima quadam violentia, non modo divinos thesauros diripuerit, sed ipsummet
Dei Patris Verbum ac Filium unigenitum in uterum suum, atque in materna ubera et brachia sua, hominem et infantulum natum pulcherrima
Virgo attraxerit.—*In cap.* xxiv. *Gen.* sect. 1, no. 8.

[41] Quam pulchra es, amica mea, quam pulchra es !   Oculi tui columbarum.
—*Cant.* iv. 1.

[42] Ubinam terrarum tam speciosa, quæ Filium Dei de sinu Patris alli-
ceret ; et in amplexus suos vinculis charitatis pia violentia captivum tra-
heret ?—*De Grat. Dei*, lib. vi.

was that God, having made her His Mother, could **not** **have** exalted her more than He did exalt her.

Second point. To understand the greatness to which Mary was exalted, it would be necessary to understand the sublimity and greatness of God. It is sufficient, then, to say simply, that God made this Blessed Virgin His Mother, to understand that God could not have exalted her more than He did exalt her. Arnold of Chartres, then, rightly asserts that God, by becoming the Son of the Blessed Virgin, 'established her in a rank far above that of all the Saints and angels.'[43] So that, with the exception of God Himself, there is no one who is so greatly exalted; as Saint Ephrem also asserts : 'Her glory is incomparably greater than that of all the other celestial spirits.'[44] This is confirmed by Saint Andrew of Crete, saying, 'God excepted, she is higher than all.'[45] Saint Anselm also says, 'No one is equal to thee, O Lady ; for all are either above or beneath thee : God alone is above thee, and all that is not God is inferior to thee.'[46] In fine, says St. Bernardine, 'the greatness and dignity of this Blessed Virgin are such, that God alone does, and can, comprehend it.'[47]

In this reflection we have more than sufficient, remarks Saint Thomas of Villanova, to take away the surprise which might be caused on seeing that the sacred Evangelists, who have so fully recorded the praises of a John the Baptist and of a Magdalen, say so little of the precious gifts of Mary : 'It was sufficient

[43] Constituta quippe est (Maria) super omnem creaturam : et quicumque Jesu curvat genu, Matri quoque pronus supplicat et acclivis.—*De Laud. B.M.V.*

[44] Incomparabiliter reliquis omnibus supernis exercitibus gloriosior.—*Ib.*

[45] Quæ, uno excepto Deo, rebus omnibus excelsior es.—*In Dorm. S.M. Serm.* iii.

[46] Nihil tibi, Domina, æquale, nihil comparabile est ; omne enim quod est, aut supra te est, aut subtus te est : quod supra te est solus Deus est; quod infra te, omne quod Deus non est.—*De Concept. B.M.V.*

[47] Perfectiones gratiarum quas Virgo suscepit in conceptione Filii Dei, solo intellectu Divino, Christo, et sibi comprehensibiles extiterunt.—*Serm. de Nat. B.M.V.* cap. xii

to say of her, "Of whom was born Jesus."' 'What more could you wish the Evangelists to have said of the greatness of this Blessed Virgin?' continues the Saint. 'Is it not enough that they declare that she was the Mother of God? In these few words they recorded the greatest, the whole, of her precious gifts; and since the whole was therein contained, it was unnecessary to enter into details.'[48] And why not? Saint Anselm replies, 'that when we say of Mary she is the Mother of God, this alone transcends every greatness that can be named or imagined after that of God.'[49] Peter of Celles, on the same subject, adds: 'Address her as Queen of Heaven, Sovereign Mistress of the angels, or any other title of honour you may please, but never can you honour her so much as by simply calling her the Mother of God.'[50]

The reason of this is evident; for, as the angelic Doctor teaches, the nearer a thing approaches its author, the greater is the perfection it receives from him; and therefore Mary being of all creatures the nearest to God, she, more than all others, has partaken of His graces, perfections, and greatness. He says, 'The Blessed Virgin Mary was the nearest possible to Christ; for from her it was that He received His human nature, and therefore she must have obtained a greater plenitude of grace from Him than all others.'[51] To this Father Suarez traces the reason for which 'the dignity of Mo-

---

[48] Sufficit ad ejus plenam historiam quod scriptum est in themate; quia de illa natus est Jesus. Quid amplius quæris? Quid ultra requiris in Virgine? Sufficit tibi quod Mater Dei est . . Ubi ergo totum erat, pars scribenda non fuit.—*Conc. II. de Nat. B.M.V.*

[49] Hoc solum de Sancta Virgine prædicari, quod Dei Mater est, excedit omnem altitudinem quæ post Deum dici vel cogitari potest.—*De Excel. Virg.* cap. ii.

[50] Si cœli Reginam, si angelorum Dominam, vel quodlibet aliud excellentissimum, tam ab humano corde, quam ore excogitatum protuleris, non adsurget ad hunc superindicibilem honorem, quo creditur et prædicatur Dei Genitrix.—*De Panibus*, cap. xxi.

[51] Quanto aliquid magis appropinquat principio in quolibet genere, tanto magis participat effectum illius principii, &c. Beata autem Virgo Maria propinquissima Christo fuit secundum humanitatem, quia ex ea accepit humanam naturam: et ideo præ cæteris majorem debuit a Christo gratiæ plenitudinem obtinere.—p. 3, q. xxvii. art. 5, concl.

ther of God is above every other created dignity;' for he says, ' It belongs in a certain way to the order of hypostatic union; for it intrinsically appertains to it, and has a necessary conjunction with it.'[52] Hence Denis the Carthusian asserts, that ' after the hypostatic union, there is none more intimate than that of the Mother of God with her Son.'[53] This, Saint Thomas teaches, is the supreme, the highest degree of union that a pure creature can have with God : ' It is a sort of supreme union with an Infinite Person.'[54] Blessed Albert the Great also asserts, that ' to be the Mother of God is the highest dignity after that of being God.'[55] Hence he adds, that ' Mary could not have been more closely united to God than she was without becoming God.'

Saint Bernardine says, that ' to become Mother of God, the Blessed Virgin had to be raised to a sort of equality with the Divine Persons by an almost infinity of graces.'[56] And as children are, morally speaking, considered one with their parents, so that their properties and honours are in common, it follows, says Saint Peter Damian, that God who dwells in creatures in different ways dwelt in Mary in an especial way, and was singularly identified with her, making Himself one and the same thing with her. ' The fourth mode,' he says, ' in which God is in a creature is that of identity; and this He is in the Blessed Virgin Mary, for He is one

[52] Dignitas matris est altioris ordinis, pertinet enim quodammodo ad ordinem unionis hypostaticæ, illam enim intrinsice respicit, et cum illa necessariam conjunctionem habet,—*De Incarnat.* p. 2, q. xxvii. art. 1, disp. 1, sect. 2.

[53] Post hypostaticam conjunctionem non est alia tam vicina, ut unio Matris Dei cum Filio suo.—*De Laud. V.M.* l. i. c. 35.

[54] Humanitas Christi ex hoc quod est unita Deo, et beatitudo creata ex hoc quod est fruitio Dei, et beata Virgo ex hoc quod est Mater Dei, habent quandam dignitatem infinitam ex bono infinito, quod est Deus : et ex hac parte non potest aliquid fieri melius eis, sicut non potest aliquid melius esse Deo.—p. 1. q. xxv. art. 6. ad 4.

[55] Immediate post esse Deum, est esse Matrem Dei . . . Non potest intelligi puræ creaturæ major participari gratia, quam esse Matrem Dei.—*Sup. Missus. Resp.* 3, 15, ad q. cxl.

[56] Quod fœmina conciperet, et pareret Deum est, et fuit, miraculum miraculorum. Oportuit enim, ut sic dicam, fœminam elevari ad quamdam æqualitatem Divinam, per quamdam quasi infinitatem perfectionum et gratiarum.—*Serm. de Nat. B.M.V.* cap. xii.

with her.' Thence he exclaims in those celebrated words, 'Let every creature be silent and tremble, and scarcely dare glance at the immensity of so great a dignity. God dwells in the Blessed Virgin, with whom He has the identity of one nature.'[57]

Therefore Saint Thomas asserts that when Mary became Mother of God, by reason of so close a union with an infinite good, she received a dignity which Father Suarez calls 'infinite in its kind.'[58] The dignity of Mother of God is the greatest dignity that can be conferred on a pure creature. For although the angelic Doctor teaches that 'even the humanity of Jesus Christ could have received greater habitual grace from God,—since grace is a created gift, and therefore its essence is finite; for all creatures have a determined measure of capacity, so that it is yet in God's power to make another creature whose determined measure is greater,'[59]—yet since His humanity was destined to a personal union with a Divine Person, it could not have for its object anything greater; or, as the Saint expresses himself in another place, 'though the Divine power could create something greater and better than the habitual grace of Christ, nevertheless it could not destine it to anything greater than the personal union of the only-begotten Son of the Father.'[60] Thus, on the other hand, the Blessed

[57] Quarto modo inest (Deus) uni creaturæ, videlicet Mariæ Virgini, identitate, quia idem est, quod illa. Hic taceat et contremiscat omnis creatura, et vix audeat aspicere tantæ dignitatis, et dignationis immensitatem . . . Habitat Deus in Virgine, habitat cum illa, cum qua unius naturæ habet identitatem.—*Serm.* i. *de Nat. B.M.V.*

[58] Et illi favet etiam D. Th. dicens hanc dignitatem esse suo genere infinitam.—*De Incarnat.* p. 2, q. xxvii. art. 1, disp. 1, sect. 2.

[59] De gratia habituali dubium esse potest an sit infinita. Cum enim hujusmodi gratia fit etiam donum creatum, confiteri oportet quod habeat essentiam finitam. Potest tamen dici infinita triplici ratione. Primo quidem ex parte recipientis. Manifestum est enim uniuscujusque naturæ creatæ capacitatem esse finitam, quia et si infinitum bonum recipere possit cognoscendo et fruendo, non tamen ipsam recipit infinite, est igitur cujuslibet creaturæ, secundum suam speciem et naturam, capacitatis determinata mensura, quæ tamen Divinæ potestati non præjudicat, quin posset aliam creaturam majoris capacitatis facere.—*Opusc.* ii. *Compend. Theol.* cap. 215.

[60] Virtus Divina, licet possit facere aliquid majus et melius, quam sit habitualis gratia Christi: non tamen posset facere, quod ordinaretur ad aliquid majus, quam sit unio personalis ad Filium unigenitum a Patre —p. 3. q. vii. art. 12, ad 2.

Virgin could not have been raised to a greater dignity than that of Mother of God. ' Which dignity is in a certain manner infinite, inasmuch as God is an infinite good ; in this respect, then, she could not have been made greater.'[61]   Saint Thomas of Villanova says the same thing : ' There is something infinite in being the Mother of Him who is Infinite.'[62]   Saint Bernardine also says, that ' the state to which God exalted Mary in making her His Mother was the highest state which could be conferred on a pure creature ; so that He could not have exalted her more.'[63]   This opinion is confirmed by Blessed Albert the Great, who says, that ' in bestowing on Mary the maternity of God, God gave her the highest gift of which a pure creature is capable.'[64]

Hence that celebrated saying of Saint Bonaventure, that ' to be the Mother of God is the greatest grace that can be conferred on a creature.'   It is such that God could make a greater world, a greater heaven, but that He cannot exalt a creature more than by making her His Mother.'[65]   But no one has so well expressed the greatness of the dignity to which God had raised her as the Divine Mother herself when she said, " He that is mighty hath done great things in me."[66]   And why did not the Blessed Virgin make known what were the great things conferred on her by God ?   Saint Thomas of Villanova answers, that Mary did not explain them

[61] Beata Virgo, ex hoc quod est Mater Dei, habet quandam dignitatem infinitam ex bono infinito, quod est Deus : et ex hac parte non potest aliquid fieri melius.—p. 1, q. xxv. art. 6, ad 4.

[62] Utique habet quandam infinitatem, esse matrem Infiniti et Omnipotentis.—*Conc.* iii. *de Nat. B.M.V.*

[63] Status maternitatis Dei, ad quem Deus Virginem eligebat, erat summus status, qui puræ creaturæ dari posset.—*De Consensu Virg. Serm.* ii. art. 3, c. 1.

[64] Dominus B. Virgini summum donavit cujus capax fuit pura creatura, scilicet Dei maternitatem.—*Sup. M.* q. 138.

[65] Ipsa est qua majorem Deus facere non posset. Majorem mundum posset facere Deus, majus cœlum posset facere Deus : majorem matrem quam matrem Dei non posset facere Deus.—*Spec. B.M.V.* Lect. x.

[66] Fecit mihi magna qui potens est.—*Luc.* i. 49.

because they could not be expressed : ' She did not explain them, because they were inexplicable.'[67]

Hence Saint Bernard with reason says, ' that for
this Blessed Virgin, who was to be His Mother, God
created the whole world.'[68] And Saint Bonaventure,
that its existence depends on her will.   He says, addressing her, ' The world which thou with God didst
form from the beginning continues to exist at thy will,
O most holy Virgin ;'[69] the Saint adhering in this to
the words of Proverbs applied by the Church to Mary :
" I was with Him forming all things."[70]   Saint Bernardine adds, that it was for the love of Mary that God
did not destroy man after Adam's sin : ' He preserved
it on account of His most singular love for this Blessed
Virgin.'[71]   Hence the Holy Ghost with reason sings of
Mary : ' She has chosen the best part ;'[72] for this Virgin Mother not only chose the best things, but she
chose the best part of the best things ; ' God endowing
her in the highest degree,' as Blessed Albert the Great
asserts, ' with all the general and particular graces and
gifts conferred on all other creatures, in consequence
of the dignity granted her of the Divine maternity.'[73]
Thus Mary was a child, but of this state she had only
the innocence, not the defect of incapacity ; for from
the very first moment of her existence she had always
the perfect use of reason.   She was a Virgin without
the reproach of sterility.   She was a Mother, but at
the same time possessed the precious treasure of virginity.   She was beautiful, even most beautiful, as

[67] Excedit . . . enim intellectum et loquelam Virginis magnitudo, non
modo nostram, imo forte et suam. Fecit, inquit, mihi magna qui potens est.
Sed quam magna ?   Nescio an ipsamet valuit comprehendere suam magnitudinem.—*Conc.* iii. *de Nat. B.M.V.*

[68] Propter hanc totus mundus factus est.—*Serm.* iii. *sup. Salve Reg.*

[69] Dispositione tua perseverat mundus, quem et tu cum Deo fundasti ab
initio.—*Ps.* cxviii. *de B.V.M.*

[70] Cum eo eram cuncta componens.—*Prov.* viii. 30.

[71] Propter præcipuam reverentiam et singularissimam dilectionem, quam
habebat ad Virginem præservavit.—*Serm. de Nat. B.M.V.* cap. ii.

[72] Optimam partem elegit.

[73] Fuit gratia plena, quia omnes gratias generales et speciales in summa
habuit a quibus omnis alia creatura vacua fuit.—*Bibl. Mar. in Luc.*

Richard of Saint Victor asserts,[74] with Saint George of Nicomedia,[75] and Saint Denis the Areopagite, who (as it is believed) had the happiness of once beholding her beauty ; and he declared that had not faith taught him that she was only a creature, he should have adored her as God. Our Lord Himself also revealed to Saint Bridget that the beauty of His Mother surpassed that of all men and angels. Allowing the Saint to hear Him addressing Mary, He said : ' Thy beauty exceeds that of all angels, and of all created things.'[76] She was most beautiful, I say ; but without prejudice to those who looked upon her, for her beauty banished all evil thoughts, and even enkindled pure ones, as Saint Ambrose attests : ' So great was her grace, that not only it preserved her own virginity, but conferred that admirable gift of purity on those who beheld her.'[77] This is confirmed by Saint Thomas, who says, ' that sanctifying grace not only repressed all irregular motions in the Blessed Virgin herself, but was also efficacious for others ; so that, notwithstanding the greatness of her beauty, she was never coveted by others.'[78] For this reason she was called myrrh, which prevents corruption, in the words of Ecclesiasticus, applied to her by the Church : " I yielded a sweet odour like the best myrrh."[79] The labours of active life, when engaged in them, did not interrupt her union with God. In her contemplative life she was wrapped in Him, but not so as to cause her to neglect her temporal affairs, and the charity due to her neighbour. She had to die, but her

---

[74] In Cant. s. 26.

[75] Or. de Ingr. B.V.

[76] Omnes angelos, et omnia quæ creata sunt, excessit pulchritudo tua.— *Rev.* lib. i. cap. 51.

[77] Tanta erat ejus gratia, ut non solum in se virginitatis gratiam reservaret, sed etiam his, quos viseret, integritatis insigne conferret.—*De Inst. Virg.* cap. vii.

[78] Gratia sanctificationis non tantum repressit in ipsa (B.V.) motus illicitos, sed etiam in aliis efficaciam habuit ; ita ut, quamvis esset pulchro corpore, a nullo unquam concupisci poterat.— *In* 3 lib. *Sent.* dist. 3, q. i art. 2, quæstiuncula 1, ad 4.

[79] Qvasi myrrha electa dedi suavitatem odoris.—*Eccles.* xxiv. 20.

death was unaccompanied by its usual sorrows, and not followed by the corruption of the body.

In conclusion, then, this Divine Mother is infinitely inferior to God, but immensely superior to all creatures; and as it is impossible to find a Son more noble than Jesus, so is it also impossible to find a Mother more noble than Mary. This reflection should cause the clients of so great a Queen not only to rejoice in her greatness, but should also increase their confidence in her powerful patronage; for, says Father Suarez, as she is the Mother of God, ' she has a certain peculiar right to His gifts,'[80] to dispense them to those for whom she prays. Saint Germanus, on the other hand, says, ' that God cannot do otherwise than grant the petitions of this Mother; for He cannot but acknowledge her for His true and immaculate Mother.' Here are his words addressed to this Blessed Virgin : ' For thou, who by thy maternal authority hast great power with God, obtainest the very great grace of reconciliation even for those who have been guilty of grievous crimes. It is impossible that thou shouldst not be graciously heard; for God in all things complies with thy wishes as being those of His true and spotless Mother.'[81] Therefore power to succour us is not wanting to thee, O Mother of God, and Mother of us all. The will is not wanting : ' neither the power nor the will can fail her.'[82] For thou well knowest (will I say, addressing thee in the words of thy servant the Abbot of Celles) that ' God did not create thee for Himself only; He gave thee to the angels as their restorer, to men as their repairer, to the devils as their vanquisher; for through

[80] Unde fit, ut singulare jus habeat ad bona Dei Filii sui.—*De Incarnat.* p. 2, q. xxvii. art. 1, disp. i. sect. 2.

[81] Tu vero materna, qua polles, apud Deum auctoritate, ad quantumvis enormia lapsis peccata superabundantem impetras veniam. Neque enim unquam datur te non exauditam dimitti, cui per omnia, propter omnia, et in omnibus, ut veræ et intemeratæ Matri suæ obsequitur Deus.—*In Dorm. B.M.V.* Orat. ii.

[82] Nec facultas ei deesse poterit, nec voluntas.—S. Bern. *Serm. i. de Assump. B.M.V.*

thy means we recover Divine grace, and by thee the enemy is conquered and crushed.'[83]

If we really desire to please the Divine Mother, let us often salute her with the 'Hail Mary.' She once appeared to Saint Matilda,[84] and assured her that she was honoured by nothing more than by this salutation. By its means we shall certainly obtain even special graces from this Mother of mercy, as will be seen in the following example.

EXAMPLE.

The event recorded by Father Paul Segneri, in his Christian Instructed,'[85] is justly celebrated. A young man of vicious habits and laden with sins, went to confession to Father Nicholas Zucchi in Rome. The confessor received him with charity, and, filled with compassion for his unfortunate state, assured him that devotion to our Blessed Lady could deliver him from the accursed vice to which he was addicted; he therefore imposed on him as his penance, that he should say a 'Hail Mary' to the Blessed Virgin every morning and evening, on getting up and on going to bed, until his next confession; and, at the same time, that he should offer her his eyes, his hands, and his whole body, beseeching her to preserve them as something belonging to herself, and that he should kiss the ground three times. The young man performed the penance, but at first there was only slight amendment. The father, however, continued to inculcate the same practice on him, desiring him never to abandon it, and at the same time encouraged him to confide in the patron-

---

[83] Non solum sibi ipsi te fecit ; sed te angelis dedit instaurationem, hominibus et nostræ naturæ in reparationem, inferiori creaturæ in liberationem, sibi in matrem, dæmonibus in hostem, detentis in Limbo in ereptionem. Nam in principio cum ceciderunt angeli, natura erat corrupta, Deus offensus, et diabolus victor. Sed per te, O superbenedicta Virgo Maria, innocentia reparatur, vita angelica reducitur, Deus homini pacificatur et unitur, diabolus vincitur et conteritur.—*Contempl. Virg.* cap. iv.

[84] Spir. Grat. l. i. c. 67.

[85] P. 3, r. 34, § 2.

age of Mary. In the mean time the penitent left Rome with other companions, and during several years travelled in different parts of the world. On his return he again sought out his confessor, who, to his great joy and admiration, found that he was entirely changed, and free from his former evil habits. 'My son,' said he, 'how hast thou obtained so wonderful a change from God?' The young man replied, 'Father, our Blessed Lady obtained me this grace on account of that little devotion which thou taughtest me.' Wonders did not cease here. The same confessor related the above fact from the pulpit: a captain heard it who for many years had carried on improper intercourse with a certain woman, and determined that he also would practise the same devotion, that he too might be delivered from the horrible chains which bound him a slave of the devil (for it is necessary that sinners should have this intention, in order that the Blessed Virgin may be able to help them), and he also gave up his wickedness and changed his life.

But still more. After six months he foolishly, and relying too much on his own strength, went to pay a visit to the woman, to see if she also was converted. But on coming up to the door of the house, where he was in manifest danger of relapsing into sin, he was driven back by an invisible power, and found himself as far from the house as the whole length of the street, and standing before his own door. He was then clearly given to understand that Mary had thus delivered him from perdition. From this we may learn how solicitous our good Mother is, not only to withdraw us from a state of sin, if we recommend ourselves to her for this purpose, but also to deliver us from the danger of relapsing into it.

PRAYER.

O immaculate and holy Virgin! O creature the most humble and the most exalted before God! Thou wast so lowly in thine own eyes, but so great in the eyes of thy Lord, that He exalted thee to such a degree as to choose thee for His Mother, and then made thee Queen of heaven and earth. I therefore thank God who so greatly has exalted thee, and rejoice in seeing thee so closely united with Him, that more cannot be granted to a pure creature. Before thee, who art so humble, though endowed with such precious gifts, I am ashamed to appear, I who am so proud in the midst of so many sins. But miserable as I am, I will also salute thee, "Hail, Mary, full of grace." Thou art already full of grace; impart a portion of it to me. "Our Lord is with thee." That Lord who was always with thee from the first moment of thy creation, has now united Himself more closely to thee by becoming thy son. "Blessed art thou amongst women." O Lady, blessed amongst all women, obtain the Divine blessing for us also. "And blessed is the fruit of thy womb." O blessed plant which hath given to the world so noble and holy a fruit! 'Holy Mary, Mother of God!' O Mary, I acknowledge that thou art the true Mother of God, and in defence of this truth I am ready to give my life a thousand times. 'Pray for us sinners.' But if thou art the Mother of God, thou art also the Mother of our salvation, and of us poor sinners; since God became man to save sinners, and made thee His Mother, that thy prayers might have power to save any sinner. Hasten, then, O Mary, and pray for us, 'now, and at the hour of our death.' Pray always: pray now, that we live in the midst of so many temptations and dangers of losing God; but still more, pray for us at the hour of our death, when we are on the point of leaving this world, and being presented before God's tribunal; that being saved by the merits of Jesus Christ and by thy intercession, we may come one day, without further danger of being lost, to salute thee and praise thee with thy Son in heaven for all eternity. Amen.

DISCOURSE V.

OF THE VISITATION OF MARY.

Mary is the Treasurer of all Divine Graces; therefore, whoever desires Graces must have recourse to Mary; and he who has recourse to Mary may be certain of obtaining the Graces he desires.

FORTUNATE does that family consider itself which is visited by a royal personage, both on account of the honour that redounds from such a visit, and the advantages that may be hoped to accrue from it. But still more fortunate should that soul consider itself which is visited by the Queen of the world, the most holy Virgin Mary, who cannot but fill with riches and graces those blessed souls whom she deigns to visit by her favours. The house of Obededom was blessed when visited by the ark of God: "And the Lord blessed his house."[1] But with how much greater blessings are those persons enriched who receive a loving visit from this living ark of God, for such was the Divine Mother ! ' Happy is that house which the Mother of God visits,'[2] says Engelgrave. This was abundantly experienced by the house of Saint John the Baptist; for Mary had scarcely entered it when she heaped graces and heavenly benedictions on the whole family ; and for this reason the present feast of the Visitation is commonly called that of ' our Blessed Lady of Graces.' Hence we shall see in the present discourse that the Divine Mother is the treasurer of all graces. We shall divide

---

[1] Et benedixit Dominus domui ejus, et omnibus quæ habebat.—1 *Paralip.* xiii. 14.

[2] Felix illa domus quam Mater Dei visitat.—*Cœl. Panth. in Vis.* § 2.

it into two parts. In the first we shall see that who-ever desires graces must have recourse to Mary. In the second, that he who has recourse to Mary should be confident of receiving the graces he desires.

First point. After the Blessed Virgin had heard from the archangel Gabriel that her cousin Saint Eli-zabeth had been six months pregnant, she was inter-nally enlightened by the Holy Ghost to know that the Incarnate Word, who had become her Son, was pleased then to manifest to the world the riches of His mercy in the first graces that He desired to impart to all that family. Therefore, without interposing any delay, ac-cording to Saint Luke, "Mary, rising up, . . . went into the hill-country with haste."[3] Rising from the quiet of contemplation to which she was always devoted, and quitting her beloved solitude, she immediately set out for the dwelling of Saint Elizabeth; and because "cha-rity beareth all things,"[4] and cannot support delay, as Saint Ambrose remarks on this Gospel, 'the Holy Ghost knows not slow undertakings;'[5] without even reflecting on the arduousness of the journey, this tender Virgin, I say, immediately undertook it. On reaching the house, she salutes her cousin: "And she entered into the house of Zachary, and saluted Elizabeth."[6] Saint Ambrose here remarks that Mary was 'the first to salute'[7] Elizabeth. The visit of Mary, however, had no resemblance with those of worldlings, which, for the greater part, consist in ceremony and outward demon-strations, devoid of all sincerity; for it brought with it an accumulation of graces. The moment she entered that dwelling, on her first salutation, Elizabeth was filled with the Holy Ghost; and Saint John was cleansed from original sin, and sanctified; and therefore gave

[3] Exsurgens autem Maria in diebus illis abiit in montana cum festina-tione.—*Luc.* i. 39.

[4] Charitas omnia suffert.—1 *Cor.* xiii. 7.

[5] Nescit tarda molimina Sancti Spiritus gratia.—*Exp. Evang. sec. Luc.* lib. ii. no. 19.

[6] Et intravit in domum Zachariæ, et salutavit Elizabeth.—*Luc.* i. 40.

[7] Nec solum venit, sed etiam prior salutavit.—*Loc. cit.* no. 22.

that mark of joy by leaping in his mother's **womb,**
wishing thereby to manifest the grace that he had received by the means of the Blessed Virgin, as Saint
Elizabeth herself declared : "As soon as the voice of
thy salutation sounded in my ears, the infant in my
womb leaped for joy."[8] Thus, as Bernardine de Bustis
remarks, in virtue of Mary's salutation Saint John received the grace of the Divine Spirit which sanctified
him : 'When the Blessed Virgin saluted Elizabeth, the
voice of the salutation, entering her ears, descended
to the child, and by its virtue he received the Holy
Ghost.'[9]

And now, if all these first-fruits of Redemption
passed by Mary as the channel through which grace
was communicated to the Baptist, the Holy Ghost to
Elizabeth, the gift of prophecy to Zachary, and so many
other blessings to the whole house, the first graces
which to our knowledge the Eternal Word had granted
on earth after His Incarnation, it is quite correct to
believe that from thenceforward God made Mary the
universal channel, as she is called by Saint Bernard,
through which all the other graces which our Lord is
pleased to dispense to us should pass, as we have already declared in the fifth chapter of the first part of
this work.

With reason, then, is this Divine Mother called
the treasure, the treasurer, and the dispenser of Divine
graces. She is thus called by the venerable Abbot of
Celles, ' the Treasure of God, and the Treasurer of
graces ;'[10] by Saint Peter Damian, ' the Treasure of
Divine graces ;'[11] by Blessed Albert the Great, 'the
Treasurer of Jesus Christ ;'[12] by Saint Bernardine, 'the

---

[8] Ecce enim ut facta est vox salutationis tuæ in auribus meis, exsultavit
in gaudio infans in utero meo.— *Luc.* i. 44.
[9] Christus fecit Mariam salutare Elizabeth, ut sermo procedens de utero
Matris ubi habitabat Dominus, per aures Elizabeth ingressus descenderet ad
Joannem : ut illic eum ungeret in prophetam.— *Marial.* P. vi. Serm. 1, p. 3.
[10] Thesaurus Domini est, et thesauraria gratiarum ipsius.— *Contempl. de
B.V.M.* in Prol.
[11] Gazophylacium thesauri.— *Serm. ii. de Nat. B.M.V.*
[12] Thesauraria Jesu Christi. †

Dispenser of graces ;'[13] by a learned Greek, quoted by Petavius, 'the Storehouse of all good things.'[14] So also by Saint Gregory Thaumaturgus, who observes that 'Mary is said to be thus full of grace, for in her all the treasures of grace were hidden.'[15] Richard of St. Lawrence also says that 'Mary is a treasure, because God has placed all gifts of graces in her as in a treasury; and from thence He bestows great stipends on His soldiers and labourers.'[16] She is a treasury of mercies, whence our Lord enriches His servants.

Saint Bonaventure, speaking of the field in the gospel, in which a treasure is hidden, and which should be purchased at however great a price, "the kingdom of heaven is like unto a treasure hidden in a field, which a man having found hid it, and for joy thereof goeth and selleth all that he hath and buyeth that field,"[17] says that 'our Queen Mary is this field, in which Jesus Christ, the treasure of God the Father, is hid,'[18] and with Jesus Christ the source and flowing fountain of all graces. Saint Bernard affirms that our Lord 'has deposited the plenitude of every grace in Mary, that we may thus know that if we possess hope, grace, or anything salutary, that it is from her that it came.'[19] Of this we are also assured by Mary herself, saying, "In me is all grace of the way and of the truth ;"[20] in me are all the graces of real blessings that you men can desire in life. Yes, sweet Mother and our Hope, we

[13] Dispensatrix omnium gratiarum.—*Serm. de Exalt. B.M.V.* art. ii. cap. 3.
[14] Tu promtuarium omnium bonorum. †
[15] Cum ipsa, totus gratiæ thesaurus reconditus erat.—*Serm.* i. *in Annunt. B.M.V.*
[16] Maria est thesaurus : quia in ea, ut in gazophylacio, reposuit Dominus omnia dona gratiarum, meritorum, virtutum et prærogativarum, donorum et charismatum : et de thesauro largitur ipse larga stipendia suis militibus et operariis.—*De Laud. V.* l. iv. c. 21.
[17] Simile est regnum cœlorum thesauro abscondito in agro : quem qui invenit homo, abscondit, et præ gaudio illius vadit et vendit universa quæ habet, et emit agrum illum.—*Matt.* xiii. 44.
[18] Ager iste est Maria, in qua thesaurus angelorum, imo totus Dei Patris absconditus est.—*Spec. B.M.V.* lect. vii.
[19] Totius boni plenitudinem posuit in Maria ; ut proinde si quid spei in nobis est, si quid gratiæ, si quid salutis, ab ea noverimus redundare.—*Serm. de Aquæd.*
[20] In me gratia omnis viæ et veritatis.—*Eccles.* xxiv. 25.

know full well, says Saint Peter Damian, 'that all the treasures of Divine mercies are in thy hands.'[21] Before Saint Peter Damian, Saint Ildephonsus asserted the same thing in even stronger terms, when, speaking to the Blessed Virgin, he said, 'O Lady, all the graces that God has decreed for men He has determined to grant through thy hands; and therefore to thee has He committed all the treasures and ornaments of grace;'[22] so that, O Mary, concludes Saint Germanus, no grace is dispensed to anyone otherwise than through thy hands: 'there is no one saved but by thee; no one who receives a gift of God but through thee.'[23] Blessed Albert the Great makes a beautiful paraphrase of the words of the angel addressed to the most Blessed Virgin, " Fear not, Mary, for thou hast found grace with God :"[24] 'Fear not, O Mary, for thou hast found, not taken grace, as Lucifer tried to take it; thou hast not lost it as Adam lost it; thou hast not bought it as Simon Magus would have bought it; but thou hast found it because thou hast desired and sought it.'[25] Thou hast found increated grace; that is, God Himself become thy Son; and with that grace thou hast found and obtained every created good. Saint Peter Chrysologus confirms this thought, saying, 'This great Virgin and Mother found grace to restore thereby salvation to all men.'[26] And elsewhere he says that Mary found a grace so full that it sufficed to save all: ' Thou hast found grace, but how great a grace ! It was such that

---

[21] In manibus tuis sunt thesauri miserationum Domini.—*Serm.* ii. *in Nat. B.M.V.*

[22] Omnia bona, quæ illis summa majestas decrevit facere, tuis manibus decrevit commendare; commissi quippe tibi sunt thesauri et ornamenta gratiarum.—*In Cor. Virg.* cap. xv.

[23] Nullus enim est, qui salvus fiat, O Sanctissima, nisi per te . . . nemo est, cui donum concedatur, nisi per te, O Castissima.—*De Zon. V.*

[24] Ne timeas, Maria, invenisti enim gratiam apud Deum.—*Luc.* i. 30.

[25] Ne timeas, quia invenisti gratiam apud Deum, non creasti ut Deus . . . non rapuisti ut primus angelus, non perdidisti ut primus parens, non emisti ut Simon Magus: sed invenisti, quia quæsivisti ut Virgo prudentissima, docuisti ut fidelissima, reddidisti ut Mater misericordissima. Invenisti quid ? dico, Dei miserantis charitatem, Dei promittentis veritatem, tui ad hoc idoneitatem.—*Bibl. Mar. in Lu .*

[26] Hanc gratiam detulit angelus, accepit Virgo salutem sæculis redditura. —*Serm.* iii *de Annunt*

it filled thee; and so great was its plenitude, that it could be poured down as a torrent on every creature.'[27] So much so indeed, says Richard of Saint Lawrence, 'that as God made the sun, that by its means light might be diffused on the whole earth, so has He made Mary, that by her all Divine mercies may be dispensed to the world.'[28]   Saint Bernardine adds, that 'from the time that the Virgin Mother conceived the Divine Word in her womb, she obtained a kind of jurisdiction, so to say, over all the temporal manifestations of the Holy Ghost; so that no creature can obtain any grace from God that is not dispensed by this tender and compassionate Mother.'[29]

Hence let us conclude this point in the words of Richard of Saint Lawrence, who says, 'that if we wish to obtain any grace, we must have recourse to Mary, the finder of grace, who cannot but obtain all that she asks for her servants; for she has recovered the Divine grace which was lost, and always finds it.'[30]   This thought he borrowed from Saint Bernard, who says, 'Let us seek for grace, and seek it by Mary; for that which she seeks she finds, and cannot be frustrated.'[31] If we, then, desire graces, we must go to this treasurer and dispenser of graces; for it is the sovereign will of the Giver of every good thing; and we are assured of it by the same Saint Bernard, that all graces should be dispensed by the hands of Mary: 'for such is His will, who is pleased that we should have all by Mary.'[32] *All, all;* and he who says all excludes nothing.   But

[27] Invenisti gratiam. Quantam! quantam superius dixerat. Plenam, et vere plenam, quæ largo imbre totam funderet et infunderet creaturam. —*Serm.* ii. *de Annunt.*

[28] Sicut sol ad hoc factus est, ut illuminet totum mundum, sic Maria ad hoc facta est a Deo Trinitate, ut misericordiam, veniam, gratiam, et gloriam, quasi lumen a Deo impetret toti mundo.—*De Laud.* V. l. vii. c. 3.

[29] Pro Fest. V.M. s. 5. c. 8.

[30] Cupientes invenire gratiam, quæramus inventricem gratiæ, Mariam, quæ quia semper invenit, frustrari non poterit.—*De Laud.* V. lib. ii. cap. 5.

[31] Quæramus gratiam, et per Mariam quæramus: quia quod quærit, invenit, et frustrari non potest.—*Serm. de Aquæd.*

[32] Quia sic est voluntas ejus, qui TOTUM nos habere voluit per Mariam.— *Ib.*

because confidence is necessary to obtain graces, we will now consider how certain we ought to feel of obtaining them when we have recourse to Mary.

Second point. Why did Jesus Christ deposit all the riches of mercy which He intends for us in the hands of His Mother, unless it was that she might therewith enrich all her clients who love her, who honour her, and who have recourse to her with confidence? "With me are riches... that I may enrich them that love me."[33] Thus the Blessed Virgin herself assures us that it is so in this passage, which the Holy Church applies to her on so many of her festivals. Therefore for no other purpose than to serve us, says the Abbot Adam, are those riches of eternal life kept by Mary, in whose breast our Lord has deposited the treasure of the miserable, and that the poor being supplied from it may become rich : 'The riches of salvation are in custody of the Blessed Virgin for our use. Christ has made Mary's womb the treasury of the poor ; thence the poor are enriched.'[34] And Saint Bernard says, 'that she is a full aqueduct, that others may receive of her plenitude.'[35] Mary was therefore given to the world that by her graces might continually descend from heaven upon men.

Hence the same holy father goes on to ask, 'But why did Saint Gabriel, having found the Divine Mother already full of grace, according to his salutation, "Hail, full of grace!" afterwards say, that the Holy Ghost would come upon her to fill her still more with grace? If she was already full of grace, what more could the coming of the Divine Spirit effect?' The Saint answers, 'Mary was already full of grace ; but the Holy Ghost

---

[33] Mecum sunt divitiæ et gloria ... ut ditem diligentes me.—*Prov.* viii. 18, 21.

[34] Divitiæ salutis penes Virginem nostris usibus reservantur. Christus in Virginis utero pauperum gazophylacium collocavit; inde pauperes spiritu locupletati sunt.—Titelman, *Alleg. utr. Test.*

[35] Plenus aquæductus, ut accipiant cæteri de plenitudine ... propterea tanto tempore humano generi fluenta gratiæ defuerunt, quod necdum intercederet is de quo loquimur tam desiderabilis aquæductus.—*Serm. de Aquæd.*

filled her to overflowing, for our good, that from her superabundance we miserable creatures might be provided.'[36] For this same reason Mary was called the moon, of which it is said, 'She is full for herself and others.'[37]

"He that shall find me shall find life, and shall have salvation from the Lord."[38] Blessed is he who finds me by having recourse to me, says our Mother. He will find life, and will find it easily; for as it is easy to find and draw as much water as we please from a great fountain, so it is easy to find graces and eternal salvation by having recourse to Mary. A holy soul once said, 'We have only to seek graces from our Blessed Lady to receive them.' Saint Bernard also says, 'That it was because the Blessed Virgin was not yet born that in ancient times the great abundance of graces which we now see flow on the world was wanting; for Mary, this desirable channel, did not exist.' But now that we have this Mother of mercy, what graces are there that we need fear not to obtain when we cast ourselves at her feet? 'I am the city of refuge' (thus Saint John Damascen makes her speak) 'for all those who have recourse to me.' 'Come, then, to me, my children; for from me you will obtain graces, and these in greater abundance than you can possibly imagine.'[39]

It is true that that which the Venerable Sister Mary Villani saw in a celestial vision is experienced by many. This servant of God once saw the Divine Mother as a great fountain, to which many went, and from it they carried off the waters of grace in great abundance. But what then happened? Those who had sound jars preserved the graces they received; but those who brought broken vessels, that is to say,

---

[36] Ad quid, nisi ut adveniente jam spiritu plena, sibi eodem superveniente, nobis quoque superplena et supereffluens fiat?—*Serm.* ii. *de Assump. B.M.V.*
[37] Luna plena sibi et aliis.
[38] Qui me invenerit, inveniet vitam, et hauriet salutem a Domino.—*Prov.* viii. 35.
[39] Ego iis qui ad me confugiunt, civitas refugii. Accedite populi cum fide, et gratiarum dona affluentissime haurite.—*Hom.* ii. *in Dormit. B.M.V.*

those whose souls were burdened with sin, received
graces, but did not long preserve them.   It is, however, certain that men, even those who are ungrateful
sinners and the most miserable, daily obtain innumerable graces from Mary. Saint Augustine, addressing the
Blessed Virgin, says, ' Through thee do the miserable
obtain mercy, the ungracious grace, sinners pardon, the
weak strength, the worldly heavenly things, mortals
life, and pilgrims their country.'[40]

Let us, then, O devout clients of Mary, rouse ourselves to greater and greater confidence each time that
we have recourse to her for graces.   That we may do
so, let us always remember two great prerogatives of
this good Mother ; her great desire to do us good, and
the power she has with her Son to obtain whatever she
asks. To be convinced of the desire that Mary has to be
of service to all, we need only consider the mystery of the
present festival, that is, Mary's visit to Saint Elizabeth.
The journey from Nazareth, where the most Blessed Virgin lived, to the city of Judea, in which Saint Elizabeth
resided, was one of at least sixty-nine miles, as we learn
from Brother Joseph of Jesus Mary, the author of a life
of the Blessed Virgin,[41] Bede, and Brocardus; but, notwithstanding the arduousness of the undertaking, the
Blessed Virgin, tender and delicate as she then was,
and unaccustomed to such fatigue, did not delay her
departure. And what was it that impelled her ? It
was that great charity with which her most tender
heart was ever filled that drove her, so to say, to go
and at once commence her great office of dispenser of
graces.   Precisely thus does Saint Ambrose speak of
her journey : ' She did not go in incredulity of the
prophecy, but glad to do what she had undertaken ;
it was joy that hastened her steps, in the fulfilment
of a religious office ;'[42] the Saint thereby meaning, that

---

[40] Per te hæreditamus misericordiam miseri, ingrati gratiam, veniam
peccatores, sublimia infirmi, cœlestia terreni, mortales vitam, et patriam
peregrini.—*Serm. de Assump. B.M.V.* †

[41] Lib. iii. c. 22.

[42] Ubi audivit hoc Maria, non quasi incredula de oraculo, nec quasi in-

she did not undertake the journey to inquire into the truth of what the angel had pronounced to her of the pregnancy of St. Elizabeth, but exulting in the greatness of her desire to be of service to that family, and hastening for the joy she felt in doing good to others, and wholly intent on that work of charity : " Rising, she went with haste." Here, let it be observed, the Evangelist, in speaking of Mary's departure for the house of Elizabeth, says, that she went with haste ; but when he speaks of her return, he no longer says anything of haste, but simply that " Mary abode with her about three months ; and she returned to her own house."[43] What other object, then, asks Saint Bonaventure, could the Mother of God have had in view, when she hastened to visit the house of Saint John the Baptist, if it was not the desire to render service to that family? ' What caused her to hasten in the performance of that act of charity but the charity which burnt in her heart?'[44] This charity of Mary towards men certainly did not cease when she went to heaven ; nay more, it greatly increased there, for there she better knows our wants, and has still greater compassion for our miseries. Bernardine de Bustis writes, ' that Mary desires more earnestly to do us good and grant us graces than we desire to receive them.'[45] So much so, that Saint Bonaventure says, that she considers herself offended by those who do not ask her for graces : ' Not only those, O Lady, offend thee who outrage thee, but thou art also offended by those who neglect to ask thy favours.'[46] For Mary's desire to enrich all with graces is, so to say, a

[43] certa de nuntio, nec quasi dubitans de exemplo : sed quasi læta pro voto, religiosa pro officio, festina pro gaudio, in montana perrexit.—*Exp. Ev. sec. Luc.* lib. ii. no. 19.

[43] Mansit autem Maria cum illa quasi mensibus tribus : et reversa est in domum suam.— *Luc.* i. 56.

[44] Quid eam ad officium charitatis festinare cogebat, nisi charitas, quæ in corde ejus fervebat.—*Spec. B.M.V.* lect. iv.

[45] Plus enim desiderat ipsa facere tibi bonum, et largiri aliquam gratiam, quam tu accipere concupiscas.—*Marial.* P. ii. *Serm.* v. *de Nat. B.M.V.*

[46] In te, Domina, peccant non solum qui tibi injuriam irrogant, sed etiam qui te non rogant.—*Spec. B.M.V.* †

part of her nature, and she superabundantly enriches her servants, as blessed Raymond Jordano affirms : 'Mary is God's treasure, and the treasurer of His graces; she plentifully endows her servants with choice gifts.'[47]

Hence the same author says, that ' he who finds Mary finds every good.'[48] And he adds, that everyone can find her, even the most miserable sinner in the world ; for she is so benign that she rejects none who have recourse to her : ' Her benignity is such, that no one need fear to approach her. And her mercy is so great, that no one meets with a repulse.'[49] Thomas à Kempis makes her say : ' I invite all to have recourse to me ; I expect all, I desire all, and I never despise any sinner, however unworthy he may be, who comes to seek my aid.'[50] Richard of St. Lawrence says, that whoever goes to ask graces from Mary 'finds her always prepared to help ;'[51] that is, she is always ready and inclined to help us, and to obtain us every grace of eternal salvation by her powerful prayers.

I say, by her powerful prayers ; for another reflection, which should increase our confidence, is, that we know and are certain that she obtains of God all that she asks for her clients. Observe especially, says Saint Bonaventure, in this visit of Mary to Saint Elizabeth, the great power of her words. According to the Evangelist, at the sound of her voice the grace of the Holy Ghost was conferred on Saint Elizabeth, as well as on her son Saint John the Baptist : "And it came to pass, that when Elizabeth heard the salutation of Mary, the infant leaped in her womb, and she was filled with the Holy Ghost."[52] On this text Saint Bonaventure says,

---

[47] Maria thesaurus Domini est, et thesauraria gratiarum ipsius. Donis specialibus ditat copiossisime servientes sibi.—*Contempl. B.M.V.* in prol.

[48] Inventa . . . Virgine Maria, invenitur omne bonum.—*Ib.*

[49] Tanta quoque est ejus benignitas, quod nulli formidandum est ad eam accedere ; tantaque misericordia, quod ab ea nemo repellitur.—*Ib.*

[50] Omnes invito, omnes expecto, omnes venire desidero, nullum peccatorem despicio.—*Soliloq. An.* cap. xxiv.

[51] Inveniet semper paratam auxiliari.—*De Laud. B.M.* l. 2. p. 1.

[52] Et factum est, ut audivit salutationem Mariæ Elizabeth, exsultavit infans in utero ejus ; et repleta est Spiritu Sancto Elizabeth.—*Luc.* i. 41.

'See how great is the power of the words of our Lady; for no sooner has she pronounced them, than the Holy Ghost is given.'[53] Theophilus of Alexandria says, 'that Jesus is greatly pleased when Mary intercedes with Him for us; for all the graces which He is, so to say, forced to grant through her prayers, He considers as granted not so much to us as to herself.'[54] And remark the words, 'forced by the prayers of His Mother.' Yes, for, as Saint Germanus attests, Jesus cannot do otherwise than graciously accede to all that Mary asks; wishing, as it were, in this to obey her as His true Mother. Hence the Saint says, that 'the prayers of this Mother have a certain maternal authority with Jesus Christ; so that she obtains the grace of pardon even for those who have been guilty of grievous crimes, and commend themselves to her;' and then he concludes: 'for it is not possible that thou shouldst not be graciously heard; for God in all things acts towards thee as His true and spotless Mother.'[55] This is fully confirmed, as Saint John Chrysostom observes, by what took place at the marriage-feast of Cana, when Mary asked her Son for wine, which had failed: "They have no wine." Jesus answered: "Woman, what is that to Me and to thee? My hour is not yet come."[56] But though the time for miracles was not yet come, as Saint Chrysostom and Theophylact explain it; yet, says Saint Chrysostom, 'the Saviour, notwithstanding His answer, and to obey His Mother, worked the miracle she asked for,'[57] and converted the water into wine.

"Let us go, therefore, with confidence to the throne of grace," says the Apostle, exhorting us, "that we may

53 Vide quanta virtus sit in verbis Dominæ, quia ad eorum pronuntiationem confertur Spiritus Sanctus.—*Med. Vit. Christi*, cap. v.

54 Gaudet Filius orante Matre, quia omnia quæ nobis precibus suæ genitricis evictus donat, ipsi Matri se donasse putat.—*Salazar. in Prov.* viii. 18.

55 In Dorm. B.M.V. Orat. ii. See page 336, note 81.

56 Dicit Mater Jesu ad eum: Vinum non habent. Et dicit ei Jesus Quid mihi et tibi est, mulier? nondum venit hora mea.—*Joan.* ii. 3, 4.

57 Cum id, inquam, respondisset, quod volebat Mater effecit.—*In Joan. Homil.* xxii.

obtain mercy, and find grace in seasonable aid."[58]   'The throne of grace is the Blessed Virgin Mary,'[59] says blessed Albert the Great.   If, then, we wish for graces, let us go to the Throne of Grace, which is Mary; and let us go with the certain hope of being heard; for we have Mary's intercession, and she obtains from her Son all whatever she asks.   'Let us seek for grace,' I repeat with Saint Bernard, 'and let us seek it through Mary,[60] trusting to what the Blessed Virgin Mother herself said to Saint Matilda, that the Holy Ghost, filling her with all His sweetness, has rendered her so dear to God, that whoever seeks graces through her intercession is certain to obtain them.'[61]

And if we credit that celebrated saying of Saint Anselm, 'that salvation is occasionally more easily obtained by calling on the name of Mary than by invoking that of Jesus;'[62] we shall sometimes sooner obtain graces by having recourse to Mary than by having directly recourse to our Saviour Jesus Himself; not that He is not the source and Lord of all graces, but because, when we have recourse to the Mother, and she prays for us, her prayers have greater efficacy than ours, as being those of a mother.   Let us then never leave the feet of this treasurer of graces; but ever address her in the words of Saint John Damascen: 'O Blessed Mother of God, open to us the gate of mercy; for thou art the salvation of the human race.'[63]   O Mother of God, open to us the door of thy compassion, by always praying for us; for thy prayers are the salvation of all men. When we have recourse to Mary, it would be advisable

---

[58] Adeamus ergo cum fiducia ad thronum gratiæ, ut misericordiam consequamur, et gratiam inveniamus in auxilio opportuno.—Heb. iv. 16.

[59] Thronus gratiæ est B. Virgo Maria.—Serm. liii. de Dedic. Eccl.

[60] Quæramus gratiam, et per Mariam quæramus.—Serm. de Aquæd.

[61] Spiritus Sanctus tota sua dulcedine me penetrando, tam gratiosam effecit, ut omnis qui per me gratiam quærit, ipsam inveniet.—Spir. Grat. l. l. c. 67.

[62] Velocior est nonnunquam salus memorato nomine ejus (Mariæ), quam invocato nomine Domini Jesu.—De Excel. B.M.V. cap. vi.

[63] Misericordiæ januam aper inobis, benedicta Deipara; tu enim es salus generis humani.—In Annunt.

to entreat her to ask and obtain us the graces which she knows to be the most expedient for our salvation; this is precisely what the Dominican Brother Reginald did, as it is related in the chronicles of the order.[64] This servant of Mary was ill, and he asked her to obtain him the recovery of his health. His sovereign Lady appeared to him, accompanied by Saint Cecily and Saint Catherine, and said with the greatest sweetness, 'My son, what dost thou desire of me?' The religious was confused at so gracious an offer on the part of Mary, and knew not what to answer. Then one of the saints gave him this advice: Reginald, I will tell thee what to do; ask for nothing, but place thyself entirely in her hands, for Mary will know how to grant thee a greater grace than thou canst possibly ask. The sick man followed this advice, and the Divine Mother obtained the reëstablishment of his health.

But if we also desire the happiness of receiving the visits of this Queen of Heaven, we should often visit her by going before her image, or praying to her in churches dedicated in her honour. Read the following example, in which you will see with what special favours she rewards the devout visits of her clients.

EXAMPLE.

In the Franciscan chronicles it is related, that two religious of that order, who were going to visit a sanctuary of the Blessed Virgin, were overtaken by night in a great forest, where they became so bewildered and troubled, that they knew not what to do. But, advancing a little further, dark as it was, they thought they discovered a house. They went towards it, and felt the wall with their hands; they sought the door, knocked, and immediately heard some one within asking who they were. They replied that they were two poor religious, who had lost their way in the forest, and that they begged at least for shelter, that they might

[64] Lib. i. p. i. cap. 33.

not be devoured by the wolves. In an instant the doors were thrown open, and two pages richly dressed stood before them, and received them with the greatest courtesy. The religious asked them who resided in that palace. The pages replied that it was a most compassionate Lady. We should be glad to present her our respects, and thank her for her charity. 'She also,' the pages answered, 'wishes to see you; and we are now going to conduct you into her presence.' They ascended the staircase, and found all the apartments illuminated, richly furnished, and scented with an odour of Paradise. Finally, they entered the apartment of the Lady, who was majestic and most beautiful in her appearance. She received them with the greatest affability, and then asked them where they were going. They answered, that they were going to visit a certain church of the Blessed Virgin. 'O, since that is the case,' she replied, 'I will give you before you go a letter, which will be of great service to you.' Whilst the Lady was addressing them, they felt their hearts inflamed with the love of God, and an internal joy which they had never before experienced. They then retired to sleep, if, indeed, they could do so, overcome as they were by the happiness they experienced; and in the morning they again went to take leave of the Lady and thank her, and also to receive the letter, which she gave them, and they then departed. But when they got a short distance from the house, they perceived that the letter had no direction; they turned about, and sought first on one side, then on another, but in vain; they could no longer find the house. Finally, they opened the letter to see for whom it was meant, and what it contained; and they found that it was from the most Blessed Virgin Mary, and addressed to themselves. In it she told them that she was the Lady whom they had seen the night before, and that on account of their devotion for her she had provided a lodging and refreshment for them in that wood. She exhorted them to continue to serve and love her, for she always would amply reward their devotion, and would succour them in life and at death. At the foot of the page they read her signature: 'I, Mary the Virgin.' Let each one here imagine the gratitude of these good religious, and how they thanked the Divine Mother, and how greatly they were inflamed with the desire to love and serve her for their whole lives.[65]

PRAYER.

Immaculate and Blessed Virgin, since thou art the universal dispenser of all divine graces, thou art the hope of all, and my hope. I will ever thank my Lord for having granted me the grace to know thee, and for having shown me the means by which I may obtain graces and be saved. Thou art this means, O great Mother of God; for I now understand that it is principally through the merits of Jesus Christ, and then through thy intercession, that my soul must be saved. Ah! my Queen, thou didst hasten so greatly to visit, and by that means didst sanctify the dwelling of Saint Elizabeth; deign, then, to visit, and visit quickly, the poor house of my soul. Ah! hasten, then; for thou well knowest, and far better than I do, how poor it is, and with how many maladies it is afflicted; with disordered affections, evil habits, and sins committed, all of which are pestiferous diseases, which would lead it to eternal death. Thou canst enrich it, O Treasurer of God; and thou canst heal all its infirmities. Visit me, then, in life, and visit me especially at the moment of death, for then I shall more than ever require thy aid. I do not indeed expect, neither am I worthy, that thou shouldst visit me on this earth with thy visible presence, as thou hast visited so many of thy servants; but they were not unworthy and ungrateful as I am. I am satisfied to see thee in thy kingdom of heaven, there to be able to love thee more, and thank thee for all

65 Lyræus, Tris. Mar. l. 2. m. 26.

that thou hast done for me. At present I am satisfied that thou shouldst visit me with thy mercy; thy prayers are all that I desire.

Pray, then, O Mary, for me, and commend me to thy Son. Thou, far better than I do, knowest my miseries and my wants. What more can I say? Pity me; I am so miserable and ignorant, that I neither know, nor can I seek for, the graces that I stand the most in need of. My most sweet Queen and Mother, do thou seek and obtain for me from thy Son those graces which thou knowest to be the most expedient and necessary for my soul. I abandon myself entirely into thy hands, and only beg the Divine Majesty, that by the merits of my Saviour Jesus He will grant me the graces which thou askest Him for me. Ask, ask, then, O most Holy Virgin, that which thou seest is best for me; thy prayers are never rejected; they are the prayers of a Mother addressed to a Son, who loves thee, His Mother, so much, and rejoices in doing all that thou desirest, that He may honour thee more, and at the same time show thee the great love He bears thee. Let us make an agreement, O Lady, that while I live confiding in thee, thou on thy part wilt charge thyself with my salvation. Amen.

DISCOURSE VI.

The great Sacrifice which Mary made on this day to
God in offering Him the Life of her Son.

In the old law there were two precepts concerning the
birth of first-born sons : one was, that the mother
should remain as unclean, retired in her house for forty
days ; after which she was to go to purify herself in the
temple. The other was, that the parents of the first-
born son should take him to the temple, and there offer
him to God. On this day the most Blessed Virgin
obeyed both these precepts. Although Mary was not
bound by the law of purification, since she was always
a Virgin and always pure, yet her humility and obedience made her wish to go like other mothers to purify
herself. She at the same time obeyed the second precept, to present and offer her Son to the Eternal Father.
" And after the days of her purification, according to
the law of Moses, were accomplished, they carried Him
to Jerusalem to present Him to the Lord."[1] But the
Blessed Virgin did not offer Him as other mothers
offered their sons. Others offered them to God ; but
they knew that this oblation was simply a legal ceremony, and that by redeeming them they made them
their own, without fear of having again to offer them
to death. Mary really offered her Son to death, and
knew for certain that the sacrifice of the life of Jesus
which she then made was one day to be actually consummated on the altar of the cross ; so that Mary, by

---

[1] Et postquam impleti sunt dies purgationis ejus secundum legem Moysi,
tulerunt illum in Jerusalem, ut sisterent eum Domino.—*Luc.* ii. 22.

offering the life of her Son, came, in consequence of the love she bore this Son, really to sacrifice her own entire self to God. Leaving, then, aside all other considerations into which we might enter on the many mysteries of this festival, we will only consider the greatness of the sacrifice which Mary made of herself to God in offering Him on this day the life of her Son. And this will be the whole subject of the following discourse.

The Eternal Father had already determined to save man, who was lost by sin, and to deliver him from eternal death. But because He willed at the same time that His Divine justice should not be defrauded of a worthy and due satisfaction, He spared not the life of His Son already become man to redeem man, but willed that He should pay with the utmost rigour the penalty which men had deserved. " He that spared not even His own Son, but delivered Him up for us all."[2] He sent Him, therefore, on earth to become man. He destined Him a mother, and willed that this mother should be the Blessed Virgin Mary. But as He willed not that His Divine Word should become her Son before she by an express consent had accepted Him, so also He willed not that Jesus should sacrifice His life for the salvation of men without the concurrent assent of Mary ; that, together with the sacrifice of the life of the Son, the Mother's heart might also be sacrificed. Saint Thomas teaches that the quality of mother gives her a special right over her children ; hence, Jesus being in Himself innocent and undeserving of punishment, it seemed fitting that He should not be condemned to the cross as a victim for the sins of the world without the consent of His Mother, by which she should spontaneously offer Him to death.

But although, from the moment she became the Mother of Jesus, Mary consented to His death, yet God willed that on this day she should make a solemn sa-

---

[2] Qui etiam proprio Filio suo non pepercit, sed pro nobis omnibus tradidit illum.—*Rom.* viii. 32.

crifice of herself, by offering her Son to Him in the Temple, sacrificing His precious life to Divine justice. Hence Saint Epiphanius calls her 'a priest.'[3] And now we begin to see how much this sacrifice cost her, and what heroic virtue she had to practise when she herself subscribed the sentence by which her beloved Jesus was condemned to death.   Behold Mary is actually on her road to Jerusalem to offer her Son; she hastens her steps towards the place of sacrifice, and she herself bears the beloved victim in her arms.   She enters the Temple, approaches the altar, and there, beaming with modesty, devotion, and humility, presents her Son to the Most High.   In the mean time the holy Simeon, who had received a promise from God that he should not die without having first seen the expected Messiah, takes the Divine child from the hands of the Blessed Virgin, and, enlightened by the Holy Ghost, announces to her how much the sacrifice which she then made of her Son would cost her, and that with Him her own blessed soul would also be sacrificed.   Here St. Thomas of Villanova contemplates the holy old man becoming troubled and silent at the thought of having to give utterance to a prophecy so fatal to this poor Mother. The saint then considers Mary, who asks him, 'Why, O Simeon, art thou thus troubled in the midst of such great consolations?' 'O royal Virgin,' he replies, ' I would desire not to announce thee such bitter tidings; but since God thus wills it for thy greater merit, listen to what I have to say.[4]   This child, which is now such a source of joy to thee—and, O God, with how much reason !—this child, I say, will one day be a source of such bitter grief to thee that no creature in the world has ever experienced the like ; and this will be when thou seest Him persecuted by men of every class, and

---

[3] Virginem appello velut sacerdotem.—*Hom. in Laud. S.M.*

[4] Unde tibi tanta turbatio? . . . O Virgo regia . . . nollem tibi talia nuntiare ; sed audi : Nimium nunc pro isto infante lætaris, et merito lætaris . . . Ecce enim . . . positus est hic infans in signum, cui contradicetur a multis . . . O quot millia hominum pro isto puero laniabuntur, jugulabuntur ! . . . Et si omnes patientur in corpore, tu Virgo amplius in animo patieris.—*In Festo Purific. B.M.V.* Conc. i.

made a butt upon earth for their scoffs and outrages; they will even go so far as to put Him to death as a malefactor before thine own eyes. Thou so greatly rejoicest in this infant; but, behold, He is placed for a sign which shall be contradicted. Know that after His death there will be many martyrs, who for the love of this Son of thine will be tormented and put to death; their martyrdom, however, will be endured in their bodies; but thine, O Divine Mother, will be endured in thy heart. O, how many thousands of men will be torn to pieces and put to death for the love of this child! and although they will all suffer much in their bodies, thou, O Virgin, wilt suffer much more in thy heart.'

Yes, in her heart; for compassion alone for the sufferings of this most beloved Son was the sword of sorrow which was to pierce the heart of the Mother, as Saint Simeon exactly foretold: " And thy own soul a sword shall pierce."[5] Already the most Blessed Virgin, as Saint Jerome says, was enlightened by the sacred Scriptures, and knew the sufferings that the Redeemer was to endure in His life, and still more at the time of His death. She fully understood from the Prophets that He was to be betrayed by one of His disciples: " For even the man of my peace, in whom I trusted, who ate my bread, hath greatly supplanted me,"[6] as David foretold: that He was to be abandoned by them: " Strike the shepherd, and the sheep shall be scattered."[7] She well knew the contempt, the spitting, the blows, the derisions He was to suffer from the people: " I have given my body to the strikers, and my cheeks to them that plucked them: I have not turned away my face from them that rebuked me and spit upon me."[8] She knew that He was to become the reproach

---

[5] Et tuam ipsius animam pertransibit gladius.—*Luc.* ii. 35.

[6] Qui edebat panes meos, magnificavit super me supplantationem.—*Ps.* xl. 10.

[7] Percute pastorem, et dispergentur oves.—*Zach.* xiii. 7.

[8] Corpus meum dedi percutientibus, et genas meas vellentibus: faciem meam non averti ab increpantibus et conspuentibus in me.—*Is.* l. 6.

of men, and the outcast of the most degraded of the people, so as to be saturated with insults and injuries : " But I am a worm, and no man : the reproach of men, and the outcast of the people."[9] " He shall be filled with reproaches."[10] She knew that at the end of His life His most sacred flesh would be torn and mangled by scourges : " But He was wounded for our iniquities ; He was bruised for our sins."[11] And this to such a degree that His whole body was to be disfigured, and become like that of a leper—all wounds, and the bones appearing. " There is no beauty in Him nor comeliness . . . and we have thought Him, as it were, a leper."[12] " They have numbered all my bones."[13] She knew that He was to be pierced by nails : " They have dug my hands and feet."[14] To be ranked with malefactors : " And was reputed with the wicked."[15] And that finally, hanging on a cross, He was to die for the salvation of men : " And they shall look upon Me, whom they have pierced."[16]

Mary, I say, already knew all these torments which her Son was to endure ; but, in the words addressed to her by Simeon, " And thy own soul a sword shall pierce," all the minute circumstances of the sufferings, internal and external, which were to torment her Jesus in His Passion, were made known to her, as our Lord revealed to Saint Teresa.[17] She consented to all with a constancy which filled even the angels with astonishment ; she pronounced the sentence that her Son should die, and die by so ignominious and painful a death, saying, ' Eternal Father, since Thou willest that it

---

[9] Ego autem sum vermis, et non homo : opprobrium hominum, et abjectio plebis.—*Ps.* xxi. 7.

[10] Dabit percutienti se maxillam, saturabitur opprobriis.—*Thren.* iii. 30.

[11] Ipse autem vulneratus est propter iniquitates nostras, attritus est propter scelera nostra.—*Is.* liii. 5.

[12] Non est species ei, neque decor . . . et nos putavimus eum quasi leprosum.—*Ib.* 2, 4.

[13] Dinumeraverunt omnia ossa mea.—*Ps.* xxi. 18.

[14] Foderunt manus meas et pedes meos.—*Ib.* 17.

[15] Et cum sceleratis reputatus est.—*Is.* liii. 12.

[16] Et aspicient ad me, quem confixerunt.—*Zach.* xii. 10.

[17] Vita, addit.

should be so, " not my will, but Thine be done."[18]   I
unite my will to Thy most holy will, and I sacrifice
this my Son to Thee.   I am satisfied that He should
lose His life for Thy glory and the salvation of the
world.   At the same time I sacrifice my heart to Thee,
that it may be transpierced with sorrow, and this as
much as Thou pleasest : it suffices me, my God, that
Thou art glorified and satisfied with my offering : " Not
my will, but Thine be done." '   O charity without
measure !   O constancy without parallel !   O victory
which deserves the eternal admiration of heaven and
earth !

Hence it was that Mary was silent during the Passion of Jesus, when He was unjustly accused.   She
said nothing to Pilate, who was somewhat inclined to
set Him at liberty, knowing, as he did, His innocence ;
she only appeared in public to assist at the great sacrifice, which was to be accomplished on Calvary ; she
accompanied her beloved Son to the place of execution ;
she was with Him from the first moment, when He was
nailed on the cross : " There stood by the cross of Jesus
His Mother,"[19] until she saw Him expire, and the sacrifice was consummated.   And all this she did to complete the offering which she had made of Him to God in
the Temple.

To understand the violence which Mary had to offer
herself in this sacrifice, it would be necessary to understand the love that this Mother bore to Jesus.   Generally speaking, the love of mothers is so tender towards
their children, that, when these are at the point of
death, and there is fear of losing them, it causes them
to forget all their faults and defects, and even the injuries they may have received from them, and makes
them suffer an inexpressible grief.   And yet the love
of these mothers is a love divided amongst other children, or at least amongst other creatures.   Mary had

---

[18] Non mea voluntas, sed tua fiat.—*Luc.* xxii. 42.
[19] Stabant autem juxta crucem Jesu Mater ejus, &c.—*Joan.* xix. 25.

an only Son, and He was the most beautiful of all the sons of Adam—most amiable, for He had everything to make Him so : He was obedient, virtuous, innocent, holy ; suffice it to say, He was God. Again, this Mother's love was not divided amongst other objects ; she had concentrated all her love in this only Son ; nor did she fear to exceed in loving Him ; for this Son was God, who merits infinite love. This Son it was who was the victim which she of her own free will had to sacrifice to death.

Let each one, then, consider how much it must have cost Mary, and what strength of mind she had to exercise in this act, by which she sacrificed the life of so amiable a Son to the cross. Behold, therefore, the most fortunate of Mothers, because the Mother of a God ; but who was at the same time, of all mothers, the most worthy of compassion, being the most afflicted, inasmuch as she saw her Son destined to the cross from the day on which He was given to her. What mother would accept of a child, knowing that she would afterwards miserably lose him by an ignominious death, and that moreover she herself would be present and see him thus die ? Mary willingly accepts this Son on so hard a condition ; and not only does she accept Him, but she herself on this day offers Him, with her own hand, to death, sacrificing him to Divine justice. Saint Bonaventure says that the Blessed Virgin would have accepted the pains and death of her Son far more willingly for herself ; but, to obey God, she made the great offering of the Divine life of her beloved Jesus ; conquering, but with an excess of grief, the tender love which she bore Him. 'Could it have been so, she would willingly have endured all the torments of her Son ; but it pleased God that His only-begotten Son should be offered for the salvation of the human race.'[20]

[20] Et in hoc miro modo debet laudari et amari, quod placuit ei, quod Unigenitus suus pro salute generis humani offerretur. Et tantum etiam compassa est, ut si fieri potuisset, omnia tormenta quæ Filius pertulit, ipsa multo libentius sustinuisset.—*Lib.* i. *Sent.* dist. xlviii. art. 2, q. 2, concl.

Hence it is that, in this offering, Mary had to do her-self more violence, and was more generous, than if she had offered herself to suffer all that her Son was to endure. Therefore she surpassed all the Martyrs in generosity; for the Martyrs offered their own lives, but the Blessed Virgin offered the life of her Son, whom she loved and esteemed infinitely more than her own life.

Nor did the sufferings of this painful offering end here; nay, even, they only began; for from that time forward, during the whole life of her Son, Mary had constantly before her eyes the death and all the tor-ments which He was to endure. Hence, the more this Son showed Himself beautiful, gracious, and amiable, the more did the anguish of her heart increase. Ah, most sorrowful Mother, hadst thou loved thy Son less, or had He been less amiable, or had He loved thee less, thy sufferings, in offering Him to death, would certainly have been diminished. But there never was, and never will be, a mother who loved her son more than thou didst love thine; for there never was, and never will be, a son more amiable, or one who loved his mother more than thy Jesus loved thee. O God, had we beheld the beauty, the majesty of the countenance of that Divine Child, could we have ever had courage to sacrifice His life for our salvation? And thou, O Mary, who wast His Mother, and a Mother loving Him with so tender a love, thou couldst offer thy innocent Son, for the salvation of men, to a death more painful and cruel than ever was endured by the greatest male-factor on earth!

Ah, how sad a scene from that day forward must love have continually placed before the eyes of Mary, —a scene representing all the outrages and mockeries which her poor Son was to endure! See, love already represents Him agonised with sorrow in the garden, mangled with scourges, crowned with thorns in the prætorium, and finally hanging on the ignominious cross on Calvary! 'Behold, O Mother,' says love, 'what an amiable and innocent Son thou offerest to so many torments and to so horrible a death!' And to what purpose save Him from the hands of Herod, since it is only to reserve Him for a far more sorrowful end?

Thus Mary not only offered her Son to death in the Temple, but she renewed that offering every moment of her life; for she revealed to Saint Bridget 'that the sorrow announced to her by the holy Simeon never left her heart until her assumption into heaven.'[21] Hence Saint Anselm thus addresses her: 'O compassionate Lady, I cannot believe that thou couldst have endured for a moment so excruciating a torment without expiring under it, had not God Himself, the Spirit of Life, sustained thee.'[22] But Saint Bernard affirms, speaking of the great sorrow which Mary experienced on this day, that from that time forward 'she died living, enduring a sorrow more cruel than death.'[23] In every moment she lived dying; for in every moment she was assailed by the sorrow of the death of her beloved Jesus, which was a torment more cruel than any death.

Hence the Divine Mother, on account of the great merit she acquired by this great sacrifice which she made to God for the salvation of the world, was justly called by Saint Augustine 'the repairer of the human race;'[24] by Saint Epiphanius, 'the redeemer of captives;'[25] by Saint Anselm, 'the repairer of a lost world;'[26] by Saint Germanus, 'our liberator from our calamities;'[27] by Saint Ambrose, 'the Mother of all the

[21] Dolor iste, usquedum assumpta fui corpore et anima in cœlum, nunquam defuit a corde meo.—*Rev.* lib. vi. cap. 57.

[22] Pia Domina, non crediderim te potuisse ullo pacto stimulos tanti cruciatus, quin vitam amitteres sustinere, nisi ipse Spiritus vitæ . . . te confortaret.—*De Excel. V.* cap. v.

[23] Quasi mortua vivens vivebat moriens, moriebatur vivens; nec mori poterat quæ vivens mortua erat. In illius anima dolor sæve sæviebat.—*Tr de Lament. B.M.V.*

[24] Reparatrix generis humani. †

[25] Redemtrix captivorum. †

[26] Reparatrix perditi orbis.—*De Excel. V.* cap. ix.

[27] Prima primi lapsus primorum parentum revocatio; lapsi generis in rectum statum restitutio.—*In Dei Mat. Nat.*

faithful ;'[28] by Saint Augustine, 'the Mother of the
living ;'[29] and by Saint Andrew of Crete, 'the Mother
of life.'[30]   For Arnold of Chartres says, 'The wills of
Christ and of Mary were then united, so that both
offered the same holocaust ; she thereby producing with
Him the one effect, the salvation of the world.'[31]   At
the death of Jesus Mary united her will to that of her
Son ; so much so, that both offered one and the same
sacrifice ; and therefore the holy abbot says that both
the Son and the Mother effected human redemption,
and obtained salvation for men—Jesus by satisfying for
our sins, Mary by obtaining the application of this
satisfaction to us.   Hence Denis the Carthusian also
asserts 'that the Divine Mother can be called the saviour of the world, since by the pain she endured in
commiserating her Son (willingly sacrificed by her to
Divine justice) she merited that through her prayers
the merits of the Passion of the Redeemer should be
communicated to men.'[32]

Mary, then, having by the merit of her sorrows, and
by sacrificing her Son, become the Mother of all the
redeemed, it is right to believe that through her hands
Divine graces, and the means to obtain eternal life,
which are the fruits of the merits of Jesus Christ, are
given to men.   To this it is that Saint Bernard alludes
when he says, that 'when God was about to redeem the
human race, He deposited the whole price in Mary's
hands ;'[33] by which words the Saint gives us to under-

---

[28] Mater omnium credentium. †
[29] Mater viventium. †
[30] Te enim grato animi affectu ac devote lingua omnis vitæ Matrem
glorificans prædicat.—*In Dormit. S.M.* iii.
[31] Omnino tunc erat una Christi et Mariæ voluntas, unumque holocaustum
ambo pariter offerebant Deo : hæc in sanguine cordis, hic in sanguine carnis
... cum Christo communem in salute mundi effectum obtinuit.—*De Laud.
B.M.V.*
[32] Amantissima Dei Virgo Christifera dici potest mundi salvatrix propter
eminentiam, virtuositatem, et meritum suæ compassionis, qua patienti Filio
fidelissime ac acerbissime condolendo, excellenter promeruit, ut per ipsam,
hoc est, per preces ejus ac merita, virtus ac meritum passionis Christi com-
municetur hominibus.—*Ib.* lib. ii. art. 23.
[33] Redempturus humanum genus, pretium universum contulit in Mariam
—*Serm. de Aquæd.*

stand that the merits of the Redeemer are applied to our souls by the intercession of the Blessed Virgin ; for all graces, which are the fruits of Jesus Christ, were comprised in that price of which she had charge.

If the sacrifice of Abraham by which he offered his son Isaac to God was so pleasing to the Divine Majesty, that as a reward He promised to multiply his descendants as the stars of heaven—" Because thou hast done this thing, and hast not spared thy only-begotten son for My sake, I will bless thee, and I will multiply thy seed as the stars of heaven,"[34]—we must certainly believe that the more noble sacrifice which the great Mother of God made to Him of her Jesus, was far more agreeable to Him, and therefore that He has granted that through her prayers the number of the elect should be multiplied, that is to say, increased by the number of her fortunate children ; for she considers and protects all her devout clients as such.

Saint Simeon received a promise from God that he should not die until he had seen the Messiah born : " And he had received an answer from the Holy Ghost, that he should not see death before he had seen the Christ of the Lord."[35] But this grace he only received through Mary, for it was in her arms that he found the Saviour. Hence, he who desires to find Jesus, will not find Him otherwise than by Mary. Let us, then, go to this Divine Mother if we wish to find Jesus, and let us go with great confidence. Mary told her servant Prudenziana Zagnoni that every year, on this day of her purification, a great grace would be bestowed upon some sinner. Who knows but one of us may be the favoured sinner of this day ? If our sins are great, the power of Mary is greater. ' The Son can deny nothing to such a Mother,' says Saint Bernard.[36] If Jesus

[34] Quia fecisti hanc rem, et non pepercisti filio tuo unigenito propter me, benedicam tibi, et multiplicabo semen tuum sicut stellas cœli.—*Gen.* xxii. 16, 17.

[35] Et responsum acceperat a Spiritu Sancto, non visurum se mortem, nisi prius videret Christum Domini.—*Luc.* ii. 26.

[36] Exaudiet utique Matrem Filius.—*Serm. de Aquæd.*

is irritated against us, Mary immediately appeases Him.
Plutarch relates that Antipater wrote a long letter to
Alexander the Great, filled with accusations against
his mother Olympia.   Having read the letter, Alexander said, ' Antipater does not know that a single tear
of my mother suffices to cancel six hundred letters of
accusation.'[37]   We also may imagine that Jesus thus
answers the accusations presented against us by the
devil, when Mary prays for us : ' Does not Lucifer know
that a prayer of My Mother in favour of a sinner suffices
to make Me forget all accusations of offences committed
against Me ?'   The following example is a proof of this.

EXAMPLE.

This example is not recorded in any book, but was
told me by a priest, a friend of mine, as having happened to himself.   This priest was hearing confessions
in a church (to compromise no one, I do not mention
the name of the place, though the penitent gave him
leave to publish the fact), when a young man stood before him, who seemed to wish, but at the same time to
fear, to go to confession.   The father, after looking at
him several times, at length called him, and asked him
if he wished to confess.   He replied that he did ; but
as his confession was likely to be very long, he begged
to be taken to a private room.   The penitent there began by saying that he was a foreigner, and of noble
birth, but who had led such a life that he did not believe it possible that God would pardon him.   Besides
the other innumerable shameful crimes and murders he
had committed, he said that, having entirely despaired
of salvation, he committed sins, no longer from inclination, but expressly to outrage God, out of the hatred
he bore Him.   He said, amongst other things, that he
wore a crucifix, and that he beat it out of disrespect ;
and that that very morning, only a short time before,

---

[37] Ignorare Antipatrum sexcentas epistolas una deleri matris lacrymula.
—*Plut. in Alex.*

he had communicated sacrilegiously; and for what purpose? It was that he might trample the sacred particle under his feet. And he had indeed already received it, and had only been prevented from executing his horrible design by the people who would have seen him. He then consigned the sacred particle in a piece of paper to the confessor. Having done this, he said that, passing before the church, he had felt himself strongly impelled to enter it; that, unable to resist, he had done so. After entering, he was seized with great remorse of conscience, and at the same time a sort of confused and irresolute desire to confess his sins; and hence the reason for which he stood before the confessional; but while standing there his confusion and diffidence were so great that he endeavoured to go away, but it seemed to him as if some one held him there by force. ' In the mean time,' he said, ' Father, you called me, and now I am here making my confession, and I know not how.' The father then asked him if he ever practised any devotion during the time, meaning towards the Blessed Virgin; for such conversions only come through the powerful hands of Mary. ' None, father. Devotions, indeed! I looked on myself as damned.' ' But reflect again,' said the father. ' Father, I did nothing,' he repeated. But, putting his hand to his breast to uncover it, he remembered that he wore the scapular of Mary's dolours. ' Ah, my son,' said the confessor, ' dost thou not see it is our Blessed Lady who has obtained thee so extraordinary a grace? And know,' he added, ' that to her this church is dedicated.' On hearing this the young man was moved, and began to grieve, and at the same time to weep; then, continuing the confession of his sins, his compunction increased to such a degree that with a loud sob he fell fainting at the father's feet. When he had been restored to consciousness, he finished his confession; and the father with the greatest consolation absolved him, and sent him back to his own country entirely contrite, and resolved to change his life, giving the father full permission to preach and publish everywhere the great mercy that Mary had shown him.

PRAYER.

O holy Mother of God, and my Mother Mary, thou wast so deeply interested in my salvation as to offer to death the dearest object of thy heart, thy beloved Jesus ! Since, then, thou didst so much desire to see me saved, it is right that, after God, I should place all my hopes in thee. O yes, most Blessed Virgin, I do indeed entirely confide in thee. Ah, by the merit of the great sacrifice which thou didst offer this day to God, the sacrifice of the life of thy Son, entreat Him to have pity on my poor soul, for which this Immaculate Lamb did not refuse to die on the cross.

I could desire, O my Queen, to offer my poor heart to God on this day, in imitation of thee ; but I fear that, seeing it so sordid and loathsome, He may refuse it. But if thou offerest it to Him, He will not reject it. He is always pleased with and accepts the offerings presented to Him by your most pure hands. To thee, then, O Mary, do I this day present myself, miserable as I am ; to thee do I give myself without reserve. Do thou offer me as thy servant, together with Jesus, to the Eternal Father ; and beseech Him, by the merits of thy Son and for thy sake, to accept me and take me as His own. Ah, my sweetest Mother, for the love of thy sacrificed Son, help me always and at all times, and abandon me not. Never permit me to lose by my sins this most amiable Redeemer, whom on this day thou didst offer with such bitter grief to the cruel death of the cross. Remind Him that I am thy servant, that in thee I have placed all my hope ; say, in fine, that thou willest my salvation, and He will certainly graciously hear thee.

DISCOURSE VII.

OF THE ASSUMPTION OF MARY.

On this day the Church celebrates, in honour of Mary, two solemn festivals; the first is that of her happy passage from this world; the second, that of her glorious Assumption into Heaven.

IN the present discourse we shall speak of her happy passage from this world; and in the next of her glorious Assumption.

How precious was the death of Mary!
1. On account of the special graces that attended it.
2. On account of the manner in which it took place.

Death being the punishment of sin, it would seem that the Divine Mother—all holy, and exempt as she was from its slightest stain — should also have been exempt from death, and from encountering the misfortunes to which the children of Adam, infected by the poison of sin, are subject. But God was pleased that Mary should in all things resemble Jesus; and as the Son died, it was becoming that the Mother should also die; because, moreover, He wished to give the just an example of the precious death prepared for them, He willed that even the most Blessed Virgin should die, but by a sweet and happy death. Let us, therefore, now consider how precious was Mary's death: first, on account of the special favours by which it was accompanied; secondly, on account of the manner in which it took place.

First point. There are three things which render death bitter : attachment to the world, remorse for sins, and the uncertainty of salvation. The death of Mary was entirely free from these causes of bitterness, and was accompanied by three special graces, which rendered it precious and joyful. She died as she had lived, entirely detached from the things of the world ; she died in the most perfect peace ; she died in the certainty of eternal glory.

And in the first place, there can be no doubt that attachment to earthly things renders the death of the worldly bitter and miserable, as the Holy Ghost says : " O death, how bitter is the remembrance of thee to a man who hath peace in his possessions !"[1] But because the Saints die detached from the things of the world, their death is not bitter, but sweet, lovely, and precious ; that is to say, as Saint Bernard remarks, worth purchasing at any price, however great. " Blessed are the dead who die in the Lord."[2] Who are they who, being already dead, die ? They are those happy souls who pass into eternity already detached, and, so to say, dead to all affection for terrestrial things ; and who, like Saint Francis of Assisium, found in God alone all their happiness, and with him could say, 'My God and my all.'[3] But what soul was ever more detached from earthly goods, and more united to God, than the beautiful soul of Mary? She was detached from her parents; for at the age of three years, when children are most attached to them, and stand in the greatest need of their assistance, Mary, with the greatest intrepidity, left them, and went to shut herself up in the temple to attend to God alone. She was detached from riches, contenting herself to live always poor, and supporting herself with the labour of her own hands. She was detached from honours, loving an humble and abject

---

[1] O mors, quam amara est memoria tua homini pacem habenti in substantiis suis!—*Eccl.* xli. 1.

[2] Beati mortui qui Domino moriuntur.—*Apoc.* xiv. 13.

[3] Deus meus et omnia.

life, though the honours due to a queen were hers, as she was descended from the kings of Israel. The Blessed Virgin herself revealed to Saint Elizabeth of Hungary, that when her parents left her in the temple, she resolved in her heart to have no father, and to love no other good than God.

Saint John saw Mary represented in that woman, clothed with the sun, who held the moon under her feet. "And a great sign appeared in heaven: a woman clothed with the sun, and the moon under her feet."[4] Interpreters explain the moon to signify the goods of this world, which, like her, are uncertain and changeable. Mary never had these goods in her heart, but always despised them and trampled them under her feet; living in this world as a solitary turtle-dove in a desert, never allowing her affection to centre itself on any earthly thing; so that of her it was said : "The voice of the turtle is heard in our land."[5] And elsewhere : "Who is she that goeth up by the desert ?"[6] Whence the Abbot Rupert says, ' Thus didst thou go up by the desert; that is, having a solitary soul.'[7] Mary, then, having lived always and in all things detached from the earth, and united to God alone, death was not bitter, but, on the contrary, very sweet and dear to her; since it united her more closely to God in heaven, by an eternal bond.

Secondly. Peace of mind renders the death of the just precious. Sins committed during life are the worms which so cruelly torment and gnaw the hearts of poor dying sinners, who, about to appear before the Divine tribunal, see themselves at that moment surrounded by their sins, which terrify them, and cry out, according to Saint Bernard, ' We are thy works; we will not abandon

[4] Et signum magnum apparuit in cœlo : Mulier amicta sole, et luna sub pedibus ejus. ~ *Apoc.* xii. 1.

[5] Vox turturis audita est in terra nostra.—*Cant.* ii. 12.

[6] Quæ est ista quæ ascendit per desertum, &c.—*Ib.* iii. 6.

[7] Talis ascendisti per desertum, id est, animam habens valde solitariam.~ *Lib.* iii. *in Cant.* cap. iii.

thee.'[8] Mary certainly could not be tormented at death by any remorse of conscience, for she was always pure, and always free from the least shade of actual or original sin; so much so, that of her it was said: "Thou art all fair, O my love, and there is not a spot in thee."[9] From the moment that she had the use of reason, that is, from the first moment of her Immaculate Conception in the womb of Saint Anne, she began to love God with all her strength, and continued to do so, always advancing more and more throughout her whole life in love and perfection. All her thoughts, desires, and affections were of and for God alone; she never uttered a word, made a movement, cast a glance, or breathed, but for God and His glory; and never departed a step or detached herself for a single moment from the Divine love. Ah, how did all the lovely virtues she had practised during life surround her blessed bed in the happy hour of her death! That faith so constant; that loving confidence in God; that unconquerable patience in the midst of so many sufferings; that humility in the midst of so many privileges; that modesty; that meekness; that tender compassion for souls; that insatiable zeal for the glory of God; and, above all, that most perfect love towards Him, with that entire uniformity to the Divine will: all, in a word, surrounded her, and consoling her, said: 'We are thy works; we will not abandon thee.' Our Lady and Mother, we are all daughters of thy beautiful heart; now that thou art leaving this miserable life, we will not leave thee, we also will go, and be thy eternal accompaniment and honour in Paradise, where, by our means, thou wilt reign as Queen of all men and of all angels.

In the third place, the certainty of eternal salvation renders death sweet. Death is called a passage; for by death we pass from a short to an eternal life. And as

---

[8] Opera tua sumus, non te deseremus.—*Medit.* c. 2.

[9] Tota pulchra es, amica mea, et macula non est in te —*Cant.* iv. 7.

the dread of those is indeed great who die in doubt of their salvation, and who approach the solemn moment with well-grounded fear of passing into eternal death; thus, on the other hand, the joy of the Saints is indeed great at the close of life, hoping with some security to go and possess God in heaven. A nun of the order of Saint Teresa, when the doctor announced to her her approaching death, was so filled with joy that she exclaimed, ' O, how is it, sir, that you announce to me such welcome news, and demand no fee?' Saint Lawrence Justinian, being at the point of death, and perceiving his servants weeping round him, said : ' Away, away with your tears ; this is no time to mourn.'[10] Go elsewhere to weep ; if you would remain with me, rejoice, as I rejoice, in seeing the gates of heaven open to me, that I may be united to my God. Thus also a Saint Peter of Alcantara, a Saint Aloysius Gonzaga, and so many other Saints, on hearing that death was at hand, burst forth into exclamations of joy and gladness. And yet they were not certain of being in possession of Divine grace, nor were they secure of their own sanctity, as Mary was. But what joy must the Divine Mother have felt in receiving the news of her approaching death ! she who had the fullest certainty of the possession of Divine grace, especially after the Angel Gabriel had assured her that she was full of it, and that she already possessed God. " Hail, full of grace, the Lord is with thee . . . thou hast found grace."[11] And well did she herself know that her heart was continually burning with Divine love ; so that, as Bernardine de Bustis says,[12] ' Mary, by a singular privilege granted to no other Saint, loved, and was always actually loving God, in every moment of her life, with such ardour, that Saint Bernard declares, it required a

---

[10] Abite hinc cum vestris lacrymis ; tempus lætitiæ est, non lacrymarum. —*Bern. Just. Vit.* c. 10.

[11] Ave gratia plena : Dominus tecum . . . invenisti enim gratiam apud Deum.—*Luc.* i. 28, 30.

[12] Marial. p. 2. § 5.

continued miracle to preserve her life in the midst of
such flames.

Of Mary it had already been asked in the sacred
Canticles, " Who is she that goeth up by the desert,
as a pillar of smoke, of aromatical spices, of myrrh,
and frankincense, and all the powders of the perfumer ?"[13]   Her entire mortification typified by the
myrrh, her fervent prayers signified by the incense,
and all her holy virtues, united to her perfect love
for God, kindled in her a flame so great that her beautiful soul, wholly devoted to and consumed by Divine
love, arose continually to God as a pillar of smoke,
breathing forth on every side a most sweet odour.
' Such smoke, nay even such a pillar of smoke,' says the
Abbot Rupert, ' hast thou, O Blessed Mary, breathed
forth a sweet odour to the Most High.'[14]   Eustachius
expresses it in still stronger terms : 'A pillar of smoke,
because burning interiorly as a holocaust with the
flame of Divine love, she sent forth a most sweet
odour.'[15]   As the loving Virgin lived, so did she die.
As Divine love gave her life, so did it cause her death ;
for the Doctors and holy Fathers of the Church generally say she died of no other infirmity than pure love ;
Saint Ildephonsus says that Mary either ought not to
die, or only die of love.

Second point. But now let us see how her blessed
death took place.   After the ascension of Jesus Christ,
Mary remained on earth to attend to the propagation
of the faith.   Hence the disciples of our Lord had recourse to her, and she solved their doubts, comforted
them in their persecutions, and encouraged them to
labour for the Divine glory and the salvation of redeemed souls.   She willingly remained on earth, knowing that such was the will of God, for the good of the

13 Quæ est ista quæ ascendit per desertum, sicut virgula fumi ex aroma-
tibus myrrhæ, et thuris, et universi pulveris pigmentarii ?— *Cant.* iii. 6.
14 Talis fumus, imo talis fumi virgula, tu, O beata Maria, suavem odorem
spirasti Altissimo.—Lib. iii. *in Cant.* c. iii.
15 Virgula fumi, quia concremata intus in holocaustum incendio Divini
amoris, ex ea flagrabat suavissimus odor. †.

Church; but she could not but feel the pain of being far from the presence and sight of her beloved Son, who had ascended to heaven. "Where your treasure is, there will your heart be also,"[16] said the Redeemer. Where anyone believes his treasure and his happiness to be, there he always holds the love and desires of his heart fixed. If Mary, then, loved no other good than Jesus, He being in heaven, all her desires were in heaven. Taulerus says, that 'Heaven was the cell of the heavenly and most Blessed Virgin Mary; for, being there with all her desires and affections, she made it her continual abode. Her school was eternity; for she was always detached and free from temporal possessions. Her teacher was Divine truth; for her whole life was guided by this alone. Her book was the purity of her own conscience, in which she always found occasion to rejoice in the Lord. Her mirror was the Divinity; for she never admitted any representations into her soul but such as were transformed into and clothed with God, that so she might always conform herself to His will. Her ornament was devotion; for she attended solely to her interior sanctification, and was always ready to fulfil the Divine commands. Her repose was union with God; for He alone was her treasure and the resting-place of her heart.'[17] The most holy Virgin consoled her loving heart during this painful separation by visiting, as it is related, the holy places of Palestine, where her Son had been during His life. She frequently visited—at one time the stable at Bethlehem, where her Son was born; at

---

[16] Ubi enim thesaurus vester est, ibi et cor vestrum erit.—*Luc.* xii. 34.

[17] Cœlestis . . . hujus ac Beatissimæ Virginis Mariæ cella fuit cœlum : in quo cum universis desideriis suis tota inclusa fuit. Schola illius fuit æternitas : enimvero a rebus temporalibus prorsus remota et libera erat. Pædagogus ejus Divina veritas fuit : cuncta namque ipsius vita juxta hanc solam dirigebat. Liber ejus, conscientiæ ipsius fuit puritas, in qua nunquam non inveniebat unde delectaret in Domino. Speculum illius Divinitas fuit : nullas namque imagines, nisi in Deum transformatas et Deum indutas, in se recepit. Ornatus ejus devotio illius fuit : soli quippe interiori vacabat homini. Quies ejus unitas ipsius cum Deo fuit : quamquidem cordis illius locus et thesaurus solus Deus erat.—*Serm. de Nat. B.M.V.*

another the workshop of Nazareth, where her Son had
lived so many years poor and despised; now the
Garden of Gethsemani, where her Son commenced
His Passion; then the Prætorium of Pilate, where He
was scourged, and the spot on which He was crowned
with thorns; but she visited most frequently the Mount
of Calvary, where her Son expired; and the Holy Sepulchre, in which she had finally left Him: thus did
the most loving Mother soothe the pains of her cruel
exile. But this could not be enough to satisfy her
heart, which was unable to find perfect repose in this
world. Hence she was continually sending up sighs to
her Lord, exclaiming with David: "Who will give me
wings like a dove, and I will fly and be at rest ?"[18]
Who will give me wings like a dove, that I may fly
to my God, and there find my repose? "As the hart
panteth after the fountains of water: so my soul panteth after Thee, my God."[19] As the wounded stag pants
for the fountain, so does my soul, wounded by Thy
love, O my God, desire and sigh after Thee. Yes,
indeed, the sighs of this holy turtle-dove could not but
deeply penetrate the heart of her God, who indeed so
tenderly loved her. "The voice of the turtle is heard
in our land."[20] Wherefore being unwilling to defer
any longer the so-much-desired consolation of His beloved, behold, He graciously hears her desire, and calls
her to His kingdom.

Cedrenus,[21] Nicephorus,[22] and Metaphrastes,[23] relate
that, some days before her death, our Lord sent her
the Archangel Gabriel, the same who announced to
her that she was that blessed woman chosen to be
the Mother of God: 'My Lady and Queen,' said the

---

[18] Quis dabit mihi pennas sicut columbæ, et volabo, et requiescam ?—*Ps*
liv. 7.

[19] Quemadmodum desiderat cervus ad fontes aquarum, ita desider
anima mea ad te, Deus.—*Ps.* xli. 1.

[20] Vox turturis audita est in terra nostra.—*Cant.* ii. 12.

[21] Comp. Histor. n. 86.

[22] Lib. ii. c. 21.

[23] Orat. de Dorm. B.M.V.

angel, 'God has already graciously heard thy holy desires, and has sent me to tell thee to prepare thyself to leave the earth; for He wills thee in heaven. Come, then, to take possession of thy kingdom; for I and all its holy inhabitants await and desire thee.' On this happy annunciation, what else could our most humble and most holy Virgin do, but, with the most profound humility, reply in the same words in which she had answered Saint Gabriel when he announced to her that she was to become the Mother of God: "Behold the handmaid of the Lord." Behold, she answered again, the slave of the Lord. He in His pure goodness chose me and made me His Mother; He now calls me to Paradise. I did not deserve that honour, neither do I deserve this. But since He is pleased to show in my person His infinite liberality, behold, I am ready to go where He pleases. "Behold the handmaid of the Lord." May the will of my God and Lord be ever accomplished in me!

After receiving this welcome intelligence she imparted it to Saint John: we may well imagine with what grief and tender feelings he heard the news; he who for so many years had attended upon her as a son, and had enjoyed the heavenly conversation of this most holy Mother. She then once more visited the holy places of Jerusalem, tenderly taking leave of them, and especially of Mount Calvary, where her beloved Son had died. She then retired into her poor cottage, there to prepare for death. During this time the angels did not cease their visits to their beloved Queen, consoling themselves with the thought that they would soon see her crowned in heaven. Many authors assert[24] that, before her death, the Apostles, and also many disciples who were scattered in different parts of the world, were miraculously assembled in Mary's room, and that when she saw all these her

---

[24] S. Andr. Cret. Or. de Dorm. Deip.; S. J. Damasc. de Dorm. Deip.; Euthim. Hist. l. iii. c. 40.

dear children in her presence, she thus addressed them : ' My beloved children, through love for you and to help you my Son left me on this earth. The holy Faith is now spread throughout the world, already the fruit of the Divine seed is grown up; hence my Lord, seeing that my assistance on earth is no longer necessary, and compassionating my grief in being separated from Him, has graciously listened to my desire to quit this life and to go and see Him in heaven. Do you remain, then, to labour for His glory. If I leave you, my heart remains with you ; the great love I bear you I shall carry with me and always preserve. I go to Paradise to pray for you.' Who can form an idea of the tears and lamentations of the holy disciples at this sad announcement, and at the thought that soon they were to be separated from their Mother? All then, weeping, exclaimed, ' Then, O Mary, thou art already about to leave us. It is true that this world is not a place worthy of or fit for thee ; and as for us, we are unworthy to enjoy the society of a Mother of God ; but, remember, thou art our Mother ; hitherto thou hast enlightened us in our doubts ; thou hast consoled us in our afflictions ; thou hast been our strength in persecutions ; and now, how canst thou abandon us, leaving us alone in the midst of so many enemies and so many conflicts, deprived of thy consolation? We have already lost on earth Jesus, our Master and Father, who has ascended into heaven ; until now we have found consolation in thee, our Mother ; and now, how canst thou also leave us orphans without father or mother? Our own sweet Lady, either remain with us, or take us with thee.' Thus Saint John Damascen writes :[25] ' No, my children' (thus sweetly the loving Queen began to speak), ' this is not according to the will of God ; be satisfied to do that which He has decreed for me and for you. To you it yet remains to labour on earth for the glory of

[25] Orat. in Dorm. B.M.V.

your Redeemer, and to make up your eternal crown. I do not leave you to abandon you, but to help you still more in heaven by my intercession with God. Be satisfied. I commend the holy Church to you; I commend redeemed souls to you; let this be my last farewell, and the only remembrance I leave you: execute it if you love me, labour for the good of souls and for the glory of my Son; for one day we shall meet again in Paradise, never more for all eternity to be separated.'

She then begged them to give burial to her body after death; blessed them, and desired Saint John, as Saint John Damascen relates, to give after her death two of her gowns to two virgins who had served her for some time.[26] She then decently composed herself on her poor little bed, where she laid herself to await death, and with it the meeting with the Divine Spouse, who shortly was to come and take her with Him to the kingdom of the blessed. Behold, she already feels in her heart a great joy, the forerunner of the coming of the Bridegroom, which inundates her with an unaccustomed and novel sweetness. The holy Apostles seeing that Mary was already on the point of leaving this world, renewing their tears, all threw themselves on their knees around her bed; some kissed her holy feet, some sought a special blessing from her, some recommended a particular want, and all wept bitterly; for their hearts were pierced with grief at being obliged to separate themselves for the rest of their lives from their beloved Lady. And she, the most loving Mother, compassionated all, and consoled each one; to some promising her patronage, blessing others with particular affection, and encouraging others to the work of the conversion of the world; especially she called Saint Peter to her, and as head of the Church and Vicar of her Son, recommended to him in a particular man-

---

[26] Niceph. et Metaphr., quoted by Father Joseph and Mary in his Life of Mary, lib. v. c. 13. †

ner the propagation of the Faith, promising him at the same time her especial protection in heaven. But more particularly did she call Saint John to her, who more than any other was grieved at this moment when he had to part with his holy Mother; and the most gracious Lady, remembering the affection and attention with which this holy disciple had served her during all the years she had remained on earth since the death of her Son, said: 'My own John' (speaking with the greatest tenderness)—'my own John, I thank thee for all the assistance thou hast afforded me; my son, be assured of it, I shall not be ungrateful. If I now leave thee, I go to pray for thee. Remain in peace in this life until we meet again in heaven, where I await thee. Never forget me. In all thy wants call me to thy aid; for I will never forget thee, my beloved son. Son, I bless thee. I leave thee my blessing. Remain in peace. Farewell!'

But already the death of Mary is at hand; divine love, with its vehement and blessed flames, had already almost entirely consumed the vital spirits; the heavenly phœnix is already losing her life in the midst of this fire. Then the host of angels come in choirs to meet her, as if to be ready for the great triumph with which they were to accompany her to Paradise. Mary was indeed consoled at the sight of these holy spirits, but was not fully consoled; for she did not yet see her beloved Jesus, who was the whole love of her heart. Hence she often repeated to the angels who descended to salute her: "I adjure you, O daughters of Jerusalem, if you find my Beloved, that you tell Him that I languish with love."[27] Holy angels, O fair citizens of the heavenly Jerusalem, you come in choirs kindly to console me; and you all console me with your sweet presence. I thank you; but you do not fully satisfy me, for as yet I do not see my Son coming to console me : go, if you love me, return to Paradise, and on my part tell my Beloved that "I languish with love." Tell Him to come, and to come quickly, for I am dying with the vehemence of my desire to see Him.

But, behold, Jesus is now come to take His Mother to the kingdom of the blessed. It was revealed to Saint Elizabeth that her Son appeared to Mary before she expired with His cross in His hands, to show the special glory He had obtained by the redemption ; having, by His death, made acquisition of that great creature, who for all eternity was to honour Him more than all men and angels. Saint John Damascen relates that our Lord Himself gave her the viaticum, saying with tender love, 'Receive, O My Mother, from My hands that same body which thou gavest to Me.' And the Mother, having received with the greatest love that last communion, with her last breath said, ' My Son, into Thy hands do I commend my spirit. I commend to Thee this soul, which from the beginning Thou didst create rich in so many graces, and by a singular privilege didst preserve from the stain of original sin. I commend to Thee my body, from which Thou didst deign to take Thy flesh and blood. I also commend to Thee these my beloved children (speaking of the holy disciples, who surrounded her) ; they are grieved at my departure. Do Thou, who lovest them more than I do, console them ; bless them, and give them strength to do great things for Thy glory.'[28]

The life of Mary being now at its close, the most delicious music, as Saint Jerome relates, was heard in the apartment where she lay ; and, according to a revelation of Saint Bridget, the room was also filled with a brilliant light. This sweet music, and the unaccustomed splendour, warned the holy Apostles that Mary was then departing. This caused them again to burst forth in tears and prayers ; and raising their hands, with one voice they exclaimed, ' O, Mother, thou already

[28] S. J. Damasc. Orat. de Dorm. B.M.V.

goest to heaven ; thou leavest us ; give us thy **last bless-ing,** and never forget us miserable creatures.' Mary, turning her eyes around upon all, as if to bid them a last farewell, said, ' Adieu, my children ; I bless you ; fear not, I will never forget you.' And now death came ; not indeed clothed in mourning and grief, as it does to others, but adorned with light and gladness. But what do we say ? Why speak of death ? Let us rather say that Divine love came, and cut the thread of that noble life. And as a light, before going out, gives a last and brighter flash than ever, so did this beautiful creature, on hearing her Son's invitation to follow Him, wrapped in the flames of love, and in the midst of her amorous sighs, give a last sigh of still more ardent love, and breathing forth her soul, expired. Thus was that great soul, that beautiful dove of the Lord, loosened from the bands of this life ; thus did she enter into the glory of the blessed, where she is now seated, and will be seated, Queen of Paradise, for all eternity.

Mary, then, has left this world ; she is now in heaven. Thence does this compassionate Mother look down upon us who are still in this valley of tears. She pities us, and, if we wish it, promises to help us. Let us always beseech her, by the merits of her blessed death, to obtain us a happy death ; and should such be the good pleasure of God, let us beg her to obtain us the grace to die on a Saturday, which is a day dedicated in her honour, or on a day of a novena, or within the octave of one of her feasts ; for this she has obtained for so many of her clients, and especially for Saint Sta-nislaus Kostka, for whom she obtained that he should lie on the feast of her Assumption, as Father Bartoli relates in his life.[29]

EXAMPLE.

During his lifetime this holy youth, who was wholly dedicated to the love of Mary, happened, on the first of

[29] Lib. i. ch. 12.

August, to hear a sermon preached by Father Peter Canisius, in which, exhorting the novices of the society, he urged them all, with the greatest fervour, to live each day as if it was the last of their lives, and the one on which they were to be presented before God's tribunal. After the sermon Saint Stanislaus told his companions that that advice had been for him, in an especial manner, the voice of God; for that he was to die in the course of that very month. It is evident, from what followed, that he said this either because God had expressly revealed it to him, or at least because He gave him a certain internal presentiment of it. Four days afterwards the blessed youth went with Father Emanuel to Saint Mary Major's. The conversation fell on the approaching feast of the Assumption, and the Saint said, ' Father, I believe that on that day a new Paradise is seen in Paradise, as the glory of the Mother of God, crowned Queen of heaven, and seated so near to our Lord, above all the choirs of angels, is seen. And if— as I firmly believe it to be—this festival is renewed every year, I hope to see the next.' The glorious martyr St. Lawrence had fallen by lot to Saint Stanislaus as his patron for that month, it being customary in the society thus to draw them. It is said that he wrote a letter to his Mother Mary, in which he begged her to obtain him the favour to be present at her next festival in heaven. On the feast of Saint Lawrence he received the holy Communion, and afterwards entreated the Saint to present his letter to the Divine Mother, and to support his petition with his intercession, that the most Blessed Virgin might graciously accept and grant it. Towards the close of that very day he was seized with fever; and though the attack was slight, he considered that certainly he had obtained the favour asked for. This indeed he joyfully expressed, and with a smiling countenance, on going to bed, said, ' From this bed I shall never rise again.' And speaking to Father Claudius Aquaviva, he added, ' Father, I believe that Saint

Lawrence has already obtained me the favour from Mary to be in heaven on the feast of her Assumption.' No one, however, took much notice of his words. On the vigil of the feast his illness still seemed of little consequence, but the Saint assured a brother that he should die that night. 'O brother,' the other answered, 'it would be a greater miracle to die of so slight an illness than to be cured.' Nevertheless in the afternoon he fell into a deathlike swoon; a cold sweat came over him, and he lost all his strength. The Superior hastened to him, and Stanislaus entreated him to have him laid on the bare floor, that he might die as a penitent. To satisfy him, this was granted: he was laid on a thin mattress on the ground. He then made his confession, and in the midst of the tears of all present received the Viaticum: I say, of the tears of all present, for when the Divine Sacrament was brought into the room his eyes brightened up with celestial joy, and his whole countenance was inflamed with holy love, so that he seemed like a seraph. He also received extreme unction, and in the mean while did nothing but constantly raise his eyes to heaven and lovingly press to his heart an image of Mary. A father asked him to what purpose he kept a rosary in his hand, since he could not use it? He replied, 'It is a consolation to me, for it is something belonging to my Mother.' 'O, how much greater will your consolation be,' added the father, 'when you shortly see her and kiss her hands in heaven!' On hearing this, the Saint, with his countenance all on fire, raised his hands to express his desire soon to be in her presence. ' His dear Mother then appeared to him, as he himself told those who surrounded him; and shortly afterwards, at the dawn of day on the fifteenth of August, with his eyes fixed on heaven, he expired like a saint, without the slightest struggle; so much so, that it was only on presenting him the image of the Blessed Virgin, and seeing that he made no movement towards it, that it was perceived that he was already gone to kiss the feet of his beloved Queen in Paradise.

PRAYER.

O most sweet Lady and our Mother, thou hast already left the earth and reached thy kingdom, where, as Queen, thou art enthroned above all the choirs of angels, as the Church sings : "She is exalted above the choirs of angels in the celestial kingdom.'[30] We well know that we sinners are not worthy to possess thee in this valley of darkness ; but we also know that thou, in thy greatness, hast never forgotten us miserable creatures, and that by being exalted to such great glory thou hast never lost compassion for us poor children of Adam ; nay, even that it is increased in thee. From the high throne, then, to which thou art exalted, turn, O Mary, thy compassionate eyes upon us, and pity us. Remember, also, that in leaving this world thou didst promise not to forget us. Look at us and succour us. See in the midst of what tempests and dangers we constantly are, and shall be until the end of our lives. By the merits of thy happy death obtain us holy perseverance in the Divine friendship, that we may finally quit this life in God's grace ; and thus we also shall one day come to kiss thy feet in Paradise, and unite with the blessed spirits in praising thee and singing thy glories as thou deservest. Amen.

[30] Exaltata est super choros angelorum ad cœlestia regna.—*Is Fest. Assump. B.M.V.*

DISCOURSE VIII.

1st. How glorious was the Triumph of Mary when she ascended to Heaven. 2d. How exalted was the Throne to which she was elevated in Heaven.

It would seem right that on this day of the Assumption of Mary to heaven the holy Church should rather invite us to mourn than to rejoice, since our sweet Mother has quitted this world and left us deprived of her sweet presence, as Saint Bernard says : 'It seems that we should rather weep than rejoice.'[1] But no ; the holy Church invites us to rejoice : ' Let us all rejoice in the Lord, celebrating a festival in honour of the Blessed Virgin Mary.'[2] And justly ; for, if we love our Mother, we ought to congratulate ourselves more upon her glory than on our own private consolation. What son does not rejoice, though on account of it he has to be separated from his mother, if he knows that she is going to take possession of a kingdom ? Mary, on this day, is crowned Queen of Heaven ; and shall we not keep it a festival and rejoice if we truly love her ? ' Let us rejoice, then ; let us all rejoice.' And that we may rejoice, and be consoled the more by her exaltation, let us consider, first, how glorious was the triumph of Mary when she ascended to heaven ; and, secondly, how glorious was the throne to which she was there exalted.

---

[1] Plangendum nobis quam plaudendum magis esse videatur.—*In Assump B.M.V.* Serm. i.

[2] Gaudeamus omnes in Domino, diem festum celebrantes sub honore F Mariæ Virginis.—*Intro. Missæ in Assump. B.M.V.*

First point. After Jesus Christ our Saviour had completed, by His death, the work of redemption, the angels ardently desired to possess Him in their heavenly country ; hence they were continually supplicating Him in the words of David : " Arise, O Lord, into Thy rest ing-place, Thou and the ark which Thou hast sancti- fied."[3] Come, O Lord, come quickly, now that Thou hast redeemed men ; come to Thy kingdom and dwell with us, and bring with Thee the living ark of Thy sanctification, Thy Mother, who was the ark which Thou didst sanctify by dwelling in her womb. Pre- cisely thus does Saint Bernardine make the angels say : Let Thy most holy Mother Mary, sanctified by Thy conception, also ascend.'[4] Our Lord was, therefore, at length pleased to satisfy the desire of these heavenly citizens by calling Mary to Paradise. But if it was His will that the ark of the old dispensation should be brought with great pomp into the city of David — " And David and all the house of Israel brought the ark of the covenant of the Lord with joyful shouting, and with sound of trumpet"[5]—with how much greater and more glorious pomp did He ordain that His Mother should enter heaven ! The prophet Elias was carried to heaven in a fiery chariot, which, according to inter- preters, was no other than a group of angels who bore him off from the earth. ' But to conduct thee to hea- ven, O Mother of God,' says the Abbot Rupert, ' a fiery chariot was not enough ; the whole court of heaven, headed by its King thy Son, went forth to meet and accompany thee.'[6]

Saint Bernardine of Sienna is of the same opinion. He says, that ' Jesus,' to honour the triumph of Hi:

[3] Surge, Domine, in requiem tuam, tu et arca sanctificationis tuæ.—*Ps.* cxxxi. 8.

[4] Ascendat etiam Maria, tua sanctissima Mater, tui conceptione sanctifi- cata. †

[5] Et David et omnis domus Israel ducebant arcam testamenti Domini, in jubilo et in clangore buccinæ.—2 *Reg.* vi. 15.

[6] Ad transferendum te in cœlum, non unus tantum currus igneus, sed totus cum rege suo, Filio tuo, venit atque occurrit exercitus angelorum.— *In Cant.* l. 5.

most sweet Mother, ' went forth in His glory to meet
and accompany her.'[7]   Saint Anselm also says, ' that
it was precisely for this purpose that the Redeemer
was pleased to ascend to heaven before His Mother;
that is, He did so not only to prepare a throne for her
in that kingdom, but also that He might Himself accompany her with all the blessed spirits, and thus
render her entry into heaven more glorious and such
as became one who was His Mother.'[8]   Hence Saint
Peter Damian, contemplating the splendour of this
assumption of Mary into heaven, says, ' that we shall
find it more glorious than the ascension of Jesus
Christ; for, to meet the Redeemer, angels only went
forth ; but when the Blessed Virgin was assumed to
glory, she was met and accompanied by the Lord Himself of glory, and by the whole blessed company of
saints and angels.'[9]   For this reason the Abbot Guarric
supposes the Divine Word thus speaking : ' To honour
the Father, I descended from heaven ; to honour My
Mother, I reascended there :'[10] that thus I might be enabled to go forth to meet her, and myself accompany
her to Paradise.

Let us now consider how our Saviour went forth
from heaven to meet His Mother.   On first meeting
her, and to console her, He said : " Arise, make haste,
My love, My dove, My beautiful one, and come ; for
winter is now past and gone."[11]   Come, My own dear

[7] Surrexit gloriosus Jesus in occursum suæ dulcissimæ Matris.—*Serm. in Assump. B.M.V.* art. ii.

[8] Prudentiori et digniori consilio usus præcedere illam volebas, quatenus ei locum immortalitatis in regno tuo præparares, ac sic comitatus tota curia tua festivius ei occurreres, eamque sublimius, sicut decebat, tuam Matrem ad teipsum exaltares.—*De Excel. V.* cap. vii.

[9] Attolle jam oculos ad assumptionem Virginis, et salva Filii majestate, invenies occursum hujus pompæ non mediocriter digniorem.   Soli quippe angeli Redemptori occurrere potuerunt, Matri vero cœlorum palatia pene-tranti Filius ipse, cum tota curia, tam angelorum, quam justorum, solem-niter occurrens, evexit ad beatæ consistorium sessionis.—*Serm. in Assump. B.M.V.*

[10] Ego sum qui patrem et matrem filiis honorandos commendavi ; ego, ut facerem quod docui, et exemplo essem aliis, ut Patrem honorarem, in terram descendi : nihilominus ut Matrem honorarem, in cœlum reascendi.—*Serm. ii. in Assump. B.M.V.*

[11] Surge, propera, amica mea, columba mea, formosa mea, et veni.   Jam enim hiems transiit, imber abiit et recessit.—*Cant.* ii. 10, 11.

Mother, My pure and beautiful dove; leave that valley of tears, in which, for My love, thou hast suffered so much. "Come from Libanus, My Spouse, come from Libanus, come: thou shalt be crowned."[12] Come in soul and body, to enjoy the recompense of thy holy life. If thy sufferings have been great on earth, far greater is the glory which I have prepared for thee in heaven. Enter, then, that kingdom, and take thy seat near Me; come to receive that crown which I will bestow upon thee as Queen of the universe. Behold, Mary already leaves the earth, at which she looks with affection and compassion; with affection, remembering the many graces she had there received from her Lord; and with affection and compassion, because in it she leaves so many poor children surrounded with miseries and dangers. But see, Jesus offers her His hand, and the Blessed Mother already ascends; already she has passed beyond the clouds, beyond the spheres. Behold her already at the gates of heaven. When monarchs make their solemn entry into their kingdoms, they do not pass through the gates of the capital, for they are removed to make way for them on this occasion. Hence, when Jesus Christ entered Paradise, the angels cried out: "Lift up your gates, O ye princes, and be ye lifted up, O eternal gates; and the King of Glory shall enter in."[13] Thus also, now that Mary goes to take possession of the kingdom of heaven, the angels who accompany her cry out to those within: 'Lift up your gates, O ye princes, and be ye lifted up, O eternal gates; and the Queen of Glory shall enter in.'

Behold, Mary already enters that blessed country. But on her entrance the celestial spirits, seeing her so beautiful and glorious, ask the angels without, as Origen supposes it, with united voices of exultation, "Who is this that cometh up from the desert, flowing

---

[12] Veni de Libano, sponsa mea veni de Libano, veni, coronaberis.—*Cant.* iv. 8.

[13] Attollite portas, principes vestras, et elevamini, portæ æternales; et introibit rex gloriæ.—*Ps.* xxiii. 7.

with delights, leaning upon her Beloved ?"[14] And who can this creature so beautiful be, that comes from the desert of the earth—a place of thorns and tribulation? But this one comes pure and rich in virtue, leaning on her beloved Lord, who is graciously pleased Himself to accompany her with so great honour. Who is she? The angels accompanying her answer: 'She is the Mother of our King; she is our Queen, and the blessed one among women; full of grace, the Saint of saints, the beloved of God, the immaculate one, the dove, the fairest of all creatures.' Then all the blessed spirits begin to bless and praise her; singing with far more reason than the Hebrews did to Judith: "Thou art the glory of Jerusalem; thou art the joy of Israel; thou art the honour of our people."[15] Ah, our Lady and our Queen, thou, then, art the glory of Paradise, the joy of our country, thou art the honour of us all; be thou ever welcome, be thou ever blessed! Behold thy kingdom; behold us also, who are thy servants, ever ready to obey thy commands.

All the Saints who were in Paradise then came to welcome her and salute her as their Queen. All the holy virgins came: "The daughters saw her, and declared her most blessed; and they praised her."[16] 'We,' they said, 'O most Blessed Lady, are also queens in this kingdom, but thou art our Queen; for thou wast the first to give us the great example of consecrating our virginity to God; we all bless and thank thee for it.' Then came the holy confessors to salute her as their mistress; who, by her holy life, had taught them so many beautiful virtues. The holy martyrs also came to salute her as their Queen; for she, by her great constancy in the sorrows of her Son's Passion,

---

[14] Una omnium in cœlo erat lætantium (vox): "Quæ est ista, quæ ascendit de deserto, deliciis affluens, innixa super dilectum suum?"—*Cant.* viii 5. †

[15] Tu gloria Jerusalem, tu lætitia Israel, tu honorificentia populi nostri.—*Judith* xv. 10.

[16] Viderunt eam filiæ, et beatissimam prædicaverunt. . . et laudaverunt eam.—*Cant.* vi. 8.

had taught them, and also by her merits had obtained them strength, to lay down their lives for the faith. Saint James, the only one of the apostles who was yet in heaven, also came to thank her in the name of all the other Apostles for all the comfort and help she had afforded them while she was on earth. The prophets next came to salute her, and said: 'Ah, Lady, thou wast the one foreshadowed in our prophecies.' The holy patriarchs then came, and said: 'O Mary, it is thou who wast our hope; for thee it was that we sighed with such ardour and for so long a time.' But amongst these latter came our first parents, Adam and Eve, to thank her with still greater affection. 'Ah, beloved daughter,' they said, 'thou hast repaired the injury which we inflicted on the human race; thou hast obtained for the world that blessing which we lost by our crime; by thee we are saved, and for it be ever blessed.'

Saint Simeon then came to kiss her feet, and with joy reminded her of the day when he received the infant Jesus from her hands. Saint Zachary and Saint Elizabeth also came, and again thanked her for that loving visit which, with such great humility and charity, she had paid them in their dwelling, and by which they had received such treasures of grace. Saint John the Baptist came with still greater affection to thank her for having sanctified him by her voice. But how must her holy parents, Saint Joachim and Saint Anne, have spoken when they came to salute her? O God, with what tenderness must they have blessed her, saying: 'Ah, beloved daughter, what a favour it was for us to have such a child! Be thou now our Queen; for thou art the Mother of our God, and as such we salute and adore thee.' But who can ever form an idea of the affection with which her dear spouse, Saint Joseph, came to salute her? Who can ever describe the joy which the holy patriarch felt at seeing his spouse so triumphantly enter heaven and made Queen of Paradise? With what tenderness must he have addressed her: 'Ah, my Lady and Spouse, how can I ever thank our God as I ought, for having made me thy spouse, thou who art His true Mother! Through thee I merited to assist on earth the childhood of the Eternal Word, to carry Him so often in my arms, and to receive so many special graces. Ever blessed be those moments which I spent in life in serving Jesus and thee, my holy spouse. Behold our Jesus! let us rejoice that now He no longer lies on straw in a manger, as we saw Him at His birth in Bethlehem. He no longer lives poor and despised in a shop, as He once lived with us in Nazareth; He is no longer nailed to an infamous gibbet, as when He died in Jerusalem for the salvation of the world; but He is seated at the right hand of His Father, as King and Lord of heaven and earth. And now, O my Queen, we shall never more be separated from His feet; we shall there bless Him and love Him for all eternity.'

All the angels then came to salute her; and she, the great Queen, thanked all for the assistance they had given her on earth, and more especially she thanked the archangel Gabriel, who was the happy ambassador, the bearer of all her glories, when he came to announce to her that she was the chosen Mother of God. The humble and holy Virgin, then kneeling, adored the Divine Majesty, and, all absorbed in the consciousness of her own nothingness, thanked Him for all the graces bestowed upon her by His pure goodness, and especially for having made her the Mother of the Eternal Word. And then, let him who can, comprehend with what love the Most Holy Trinity blessed her. Let him comprehend the welcome given to His Daughter by the Eternal Father, to His Mother by the Son, to His Spouse by the Holy Ghost. The Father crowned her by imparting His power to her; the Son, His wisdom; the Holy Ghost, His love. And the three Divine Persons, placing her throne at the right of that of Jesus, declared her Sovereign of heaven and earth; and commanded the angels and all creatures to acknowledge her as their Queen, and as such to serve and obey her. Let us now consider how exalted was the throne to which Mary was raised in heaven!

Second point. 'If the mind of man,' says Saint Bernard,[17] 'can never comprehend the immense glory prepared in heaven by God for those who on earth have loved Him, as the Apostle tells us,[18] who can ever comprehend the glory He has prepared for His beloved Mother, who, more than all men, loved Him on earth; nay, even from the very first moment of her creation, loved Him more than all men and angels united?' Rightly, then, does the Church sing, that Mary having loved God more than all the angels, 'the Mother of God has been exalted above them all in the heavenly kingdom.'[19] Yes, 'she was exalted,' says the abbot Guarric, 'above the angels; so that she sees none above her but her Son,'[20] who is the only-begotten of the Father.

Hence it is that the learned Gerson asserts that, as all the orders of angels and saints are divided into three hierarchies (according to the Angelic Doctor[21] and St. Denis), so does Mary of herself constitute a hierarchy apart, the sublimest of all, and next to that of God.[22] And as (adds St. Antoninus) the mistress is, without comparison, above her servants, so is 'Mary, who is the sovereign Lady of the angels, exalted incomparably above the angelic hierarchies.'[23] To understand this, we need only know what David said: "The Queen

---

[17] In Assumpt. § 1.
[18] 1 Cor. ii. 9.
[19] Exaltata est sancta Dei genitrix super choros angelorum ad coelestia regna.—*In Festo Assump.*
[20] Matrem dico exaltatam super choros angelorum, ut nihil contempletur supra se Mater nisi Filium solum.—*Serm. i. de Assump.*
[21] P. 1. q. 108.
[22] Virgo sola constituit hierarchiam secundam sub Deo hierarchia primo. —*Sup. Magn.* tr. 4.
[23] Beata Maria est domina angelorum . . . ergo improportionabiliter est . . . super omnem hierarchiam exaltata —P. iv. tit. 15, c. 20, no. 15.

stood on Thy right hand."[24] And in a sermon by an ancient author, among the works of St. Athanasius, these words are explained as meaning that 'Mary is placed at the right hand of God.'

It is certain, as St. Ildephonsus says, that Mary's good works incomparably surpassed in merit those of all the saints, and therefore her reward must have surpassed theirs in the same proportion; for, 'as that which she bore was incomprehensible, so is the reward which she merited and received incomprehensibly greater than that of all the saints.'[25] And, since it is certain that God rewards according to merit, as the Apostle writes, "who will render to every man according to his works,"[26] it is also certain, as St. Thomas teaches, that the Blessed Virgin, 'who was equal to and even superior in merit to all men and angels, was exalted above all the celestial orders.'[27] 'In fine,' adds Saint Bernard, 'let us measure the singular grace that she acquired on earth, and then we may measure the singular glory which she obtained in heaven;' for 'according to the measure of her grace on earth is the measure of her glory in the kingdom of the blessed.'[28]

A learned author[29] remarks that the glory of Mary, which is a full, a complete glory, differs in that from the glory of other saints in heaven. It is true that in heaven all the blessed enjoy perfect peace and full contentment; yet it will always be true that no one of them enjoys as great glory as he could have merited had he loved and served God with greater fidelity. Hence, though the saints in heaven desire nothing more than they possess, yet in fact there is something

---

[24] Astitit regina a dextris tuis.—*Ps.* xliv. 10.
[25] Sicut incomparabile est quod gessit, et ineffabile donum quod percepit, et inæstimabile atque incomprehensibile præmium et gloria . . . inter omnes sanctos, quam promeruit.—*Serm.* ii. *de Assump. B.M.V.*
[26] Qui reddet unicuique secundum opera ejus.—*Rom.* ii. 6.
[27] Sicut habuit meritum omnium et amplius, ita congruum fuit, ut super omnes ponatur hic sermo, "Quæ est ista quæ progeditur," &c.—*S. de Ass. ex Ep.*
[28] Quantum enim gratiæ in terris adepta est, tantum et in cœlis obtinet gloriæ singularis.—*Serm.* i. *in Assump.*
[29] P. la Colombière. Serm i. Assomp.

that they could desire. It is also true that the sins which they have committed, and the time which they have lost, do not bring suffering; still it cannot be denied that a greater amount of good done in life, innocence preserved, and time well employed, give the greatest happiness. Mary desires nothing in heaven, and has nothing to desire. Who amongst the saints in heaven, except Mary, says Saint Augustine,[30] if asked whether he has committed sins, could say no? It is certain, as the holy Council of Trent[31] has defined, that Mary never committed any sin or the slightest imperfection. Not only she never lost Divine grace, and never even obscured it, but she never kept it idle; she never performed an action which was not meritorious; she never pronounced a word, never had a thought, never drew a breath, that was not directed to the greater glory of God. In fine, she never cooled in her ardour or stopped a single moment in her onward course towards God; she never lost anything by negligence, but always corresponded with grace with her whole strength, and loved God as much as she could love Him. 'O Lord,' she now says to Him in heaven, 'if I loved Thee not as much as Thou didst deserve, at least I loved Thee as much as I could.'

In each of the saints there were different graces, as Saint Paul says, "there are diversities of graces."[32] So that each of them, by corresponding with the grace he had received, excelled in some particular virtue — the one in saving souls, the other in leading a penitential life; one in enduring torments, another in a life of prayer: and this is the reason for which the holy Church, in celebrating their festivals, says of each, 'there was not found one like him.'[33] And as in their merits they differ, so do they differ in celestial glory: "for star

---

[30] De Nat. et Gratia, contra Pelag. cap. **xxxvi.**

[31] Sess. vi. can. 23.

[32] Divisiones vero gratiarum sunt, idem autem spiritus.—1 *Cor.* **xii.** 4.

[33] Non est inventus similis illi.

differeth from star."[34]   Apostles differ from martyrs,
confessors from virgins, the innocent from penitents.
The Blessed Virgin, being full of all graces, excelled each
saint in every particular virtue : she was the Apostle
of the apostles ; she was the Queen of martyrs, for she
suffered more than all of them ; she was the standard-
bearer of virgins, the model of married people ; she
united in herself perfect innocence and perfect mortification : in fine, she united in her heart all the most
heroic virtues that any saint ever practised.   Hence of
her it was said that "the Queen stood on Thy right
hand in gilded clothing, surrounded with variety."[35]
For all the graces, privileges, and merits of the other
saints were all united in Mary, as the Abbot of Celles
says : ' The prerogatives of all the saints, O Virgin, thou
hast united in thyself.'[36]

   She possessed them in such a degree that, as ' the
splendour of the sun exceeds that of all the stars united,'
so, says Saint Basil of Seleucia, ' does Mary's glory exceed that of all the blessed.'[37]   Saint Peter Damian
adds, that ' as the light of the moon and stars is so en
tirely eclipsed on the appearance of the sun, that it is
as if it was not, so also does Mary's glory so far exceed
the splendour of all men and angels, that, so to say,
they do not appear in heaven.'[38]   Hence St. Bernardine
of Sienna asserts, with Saint Bernard, that the blessed
participate in part in the Divine glory; but that the
Blessed Virgin has been, in a certain way, so greatly enriched with it, that it would seem that no creature could
be more closely united with God than Mary is : ' She

---

[34] Stella enim a stella differt in claritate.—1 *Cor.* xv. 41.

[35] Astitit regina a dextris tuis in vestitu deaurato, circumdata varietate.
—*Ps.* xliv. 10.

[36] Omnium sanctorum privilegia omnia habes in te congesta.—*Contempl.*
B.V. cap. ii.

[37] Tanto supra martyres omnes splendore enituit, quantis sol stellarum
micantes radios fulgoribus vincit.—*Orat. in B.V. et Incarnat. D.N.J.C.*

[38] Claritas solis . . . ita sibi siderum, et lunæ rapit positionem, ut sint
quasi non sint, et videri non possint. Similiter et Virga Jesse, viri prævia
luminis, in illa inaccessibili luce perlucens, sic utrorumque spirituum hebetat
dignitatem, ut in comparatione Virginis nec possint, nec debeant apparere.
—*Serm. de Assump. B.M.V.*

has penetrated into the bottom of the deep, and seems immersed as deeply as it is possible for a creature in that inaccessible light.'[39] Blessed Albert the Great confirms this, saying that our Queen ' contemplates the majesty of God in incomparably closer proximity than all other creatures.'[40] The above-named Saint Bernardine more-over says, ' that as the other planets are illumined by the sun, so do all the blessed receive light and an in-crease of happiness from the sight of Mary.'[41] And in another place he also asserts, that ' when the glorious Virgin Mother of God ascended to heaven, she aug-mented the joy of all its inhabitants.'[42]

For the same reason Saint Peter Damian says, that ' the greatest glory of the blessed in heaven is, after seeing God, the presence of this most beautiful Queen.'[43] And Saint Bonaventure, that, ' after God, our greatest glory and our greatest joy is Mary.'[44]

Let us, then, rejoice with Mary that God has ex-alted her to so high a throne in heaven. Let us also rejoice on our own account; for though our Mother is no longer present with us on earth, having ascended in glory to heaven, yet in affection she is always with us. Nay, even being there nearer to God, she better knows our miseries; and her pity for us is greater, while she is better able to help us. ' Is it possible, O Blessed Virgin,' says Saint Peter Damian, ' because thou art so greatly exalted, thou hast forgotten us in our miseries? Ah no, God forbid that we should have such a thought! So compassionate a heart cannot but pity our so great

---

[39] In paradiso divinæ gloriæ participatio, cæteris quodammodo per partes datur. Sed secundum Bernardum beata Virgo Maria divinæ sapientiæ pro-fundissimam, ultra quam credi valeat, penetravit abyssum : ut quantum sine personali unione creaturæ conditio patitur, illi luci inaccessibili videatur immersa.—*De Exalt. B. V.* art. i. cap. 10.

[40] Visio gloriosæ Virginis Matris Dei, quæ super omnes creaturas impro-portionabiliter . . . contemplatur majestatem Dei.—*Sup. Missus*, q. lxii.

[41] Quodammodo sicut cætera luminaria irradiantur a sole, sic tota cœlestis curia a gloriosa Virgine lætificatur et decoratur.—*Loc. cit.* art. i. cap. 3.

[42] Gloriosa Virgo dum cœlos ascendit, etiam supernorum gaudia civium copiosis augmentis cumulavit.—*Serm. de Exalt. B.M.V.* art. i. cap. 3.

[43] Summa gloria est post Deum te videre.—*Serm.* i. *de Nat. B.M.V.*

[44] Post Deum, major nostra gloria et majus nostrum gaudium ex Maria est.—*Spec. B V.* lect. 6.

miseries.'[45] ' If Mary's compassion for the miserable,'
says Saint Bonaventure, ' was great when she lived
upon earth, it is far greater now that she reigns in
heaven.'[46]

Let us, in the mean time, dedicate ourselves to the
service of this Queen, to honour and love her as much
as we can; for, as Richard of St. Lawrence remarks,
' she is not like other rulers, who oppress their vassals
with burdens and taxes ; but she enriches her servants
with graces, merits, and rewards.'[47] Let us also entreat
her in the words of the Abbot Guarric : ' O Mother of
mercy, thou who sittest on so lofty a throne and in such
close proximity to God, satiate thyself with the glory of
thy Jesus, and send us, thy servants, the fragments that
are left.'[48] Thou dost now enjoy the heavenly banquet
of thy Lord ; and we, who are still on earth, as dogs
under the table, ask thy mercy.

EXAMPLE.

Father Silvano Razzi[49] relates that a devout ecclesiastic and tender lover of our Queen Mary, having
heard her beauty greatly extolled, had a most ardent
desire once to see his Lady ; and therefore, with humble prayers, begged this favour. The clement Mother
sent him word by an angel that she would gratify him,
by allowing him to see her ; but on this condition, that
after seeing her he should remain blind. He accepted
the condition. Behold, one day the Blessed Virgin
appeared to him ; but that he might not remain quite
blind, he at first wished to look at her with one eye
only ; but afterwards, overcome by the great beauty of

---

45 Numquid quia ita deificata, ideo nostræ humanitatis oblita es ? Nequaquam domina . . . non convenit tantæ misericordiæ tantam miseriam
oblivisci.—Serm. i. in Nat. B.M.V.

46 Magna erga miseros fuit misericordia Mariæ adhuc exulantis in mundo,
sed multo major erga miseros est misericordia ejus jam regnantis in cœlo.—
Spec. B.M.V. lect. x.

47 Regina Maria largitur servis suis dona gratiarum, vestes virtutum,
thesauros meritorum, et magnitudinem præmiorum.—De Laud. V. l. vi, c. 12.

48 Serm. iv. in Assump. B.M.V. Vid. page 192, note 35.

49 Lib. iii. Mir. B.V. m. 5.

Mary, he wished to contemplate her with both; whereupon the Mother of God disappeared. Grieved at having lost the presence of his Queen, he could not cease weeping, not indeed for his lost eye, but because he had not seen her with both. He then began to entreat her again that she would once more appear to him, being quite willing, for this purpose, to lose the other eye and become blind. 'Happy and contented shall I be, O my Lady,' he said, 'to become wholly blind for so good a cause, which will leave me more than ever enamoured of thee and of thy beauty.' Mary was graciously pleased once more to satisfy him, and again consoled him with her presence; but because this loving Queen can never injure any one, she not only did not deprive him of the sight of the other eye, but even restored him the one he had lost.

PRAYER.

O great, exalted, and most glorious Lady, prostrate at the foot of thy throne we adore thee from this valley of tears. We rejoice at thy immense glory, with which our Lord has enriched thee; and now that thou art enthroned as Queen of heaven and earth, ah forget us not, thy poor servants. Disdain not, from the high throne on which thou reignest, to cast thine eyes of mercy on us miserable creatures. The nearer thou art to the source of graces, in the greater abundance canst thou procure those graces for us. In heaven thou seest more plainly our miseries; hence thou must compassionate and succour us the more. Make us thy faithful servants on earth, that thus we may one day bless thee in heaven. On this day, on which thou wast made Queen of the universe, we also consecrate ourselves to thy service. In the midst of thy so great joy, console us also by accepting us as thy servants. Thou art, then, our mother. Ah, most sweet Mother, most amiable Mother, thine altars are surrounded by many people: some ask to be cured of a disorder, some to be relieved in their necessities, some for an abundant harvest, and some for success in litigation. We ask thee for graces more pleasing to thy heart: obtain for us that we may be humble, detached from the world, resigned to the Divine will; obtain us the holy fear of God, a good death, and Paradise. O Lady, change us from sinners into saints; work this miracle, which will redound more to thy honour than if thou didst restore sight to a thousand blind persons, or didst raise a thousand from the dead. Thou art so powerful with God, we need only say that thou art His Mother, His beloved one, His most dear one, filled with His grace. What can He ever deny thee? O most beautiful Queen, we have no pretensions to see thee on earth, but we do desire to go to see thee in Paradise; and it is thou who must obtain us this grace. For it we hope with confidence. Amen, amen.

DISCOURSE IX.

OF THE DOLOURS OF MARY.

Mary was the Queen of Martyrs, for her martyrdom was longer and greater than that of all the Martyrs.

WHO can ever have a heart so hard that it will not melt on hearing the most lamentable event which once occurred in the world? There was a noble and holy Mother who had an only Son. This Son was the most amiable that can be imagined—innocent, virtuous, beautiful, who loved His Mother most tenderly; so much so that He had never caused her the least displeasure, but had ever shown her all respect, obedience, and affection: hence this Mother had placed all her affections on earth in this Son. Hear, then, what happened. This Son, through envy, was falsely accused by His enemies; and though the judge knew, and himself confessed, that He was innocent, yet, that he might not offend His enemies, he condemned Him to the ignominious death that they had demanded. This poor Mother had to suffer the grief of seeing that amiable and beloved Son unjustly snatched from her in the flower of His age by a barbarous death; for, by dint of torments and drained of all His blood, He was made to die on an infamous gibbet in a public place of execution, and this before her own eyes.

Devout souls, what say you? Is not this event, and is not this unhappy Mother worthy of compassion? You already understand of whom I speak. This Son, so cruelly executed, was our loving Redeemer Jesus; and this Mother was the Blessed Virgin Mary; who, for the love she bore us, was willing to see Him sacri-

ficed to Divine Justice by the barbarity of men. This
great torment, then, which Mary endured for us—a
torment which was more than a thousand deaths—
deserves both our compassion and our gratitude. If
we can make no other return for so much love, at
least let us give a few moments this day to consider
the greatness of the sufferings by which Mary became
the Queen of martyrs ; for the sufferings of her great
martyrdom exceeded those of all the martyrs ; being,
in the first place, the longest in point of duration ;
and, in the second place, the greatest in point of intensity.

First point. As Jesus is called the King of sorrows and the King of martyrs, because He suffered
during His life more than all other martyrs ; so also
is Mary with reason called the Queen of martyrs,
having merited this title by suffering the most cruel
martyrdom possible after that of her Son. Hence,
with reason, was she called by Richard of Saint
Lawrence, ' the Martyr of martyrs ;'[1] and of her can
the words of Isaias with all truth be said, " He will
crown thee with a crown of tribulation ;"[2] that is to
say, that that suffering itself, which exceeded the suffering of all the other martyrs united, was the crown
by which she was shown to be the Queen of martyrs.
That Mary was a true martyr cannot be doubted, as
Denis the Carthusian,[3] Pelbart,[4] Catharinus, and others
prove ; for it is an undoubted opinion that suffering
sufficient to cause death is martyrdom, even though
death does not ensue from it. Saint John the Evangelist is revered as a martyr, though he did not die in
the caldron of boiling oil, but ' came out more vigorous
than he went in.'[5] Saint Thomas says, ' that to have
the glory of martyrdom, it is sufficient to exercise obedience in its highest degree, that is to say, to be

[1] Martyr martyrum.—*De Laud. B.M.* l. 3.
[2] Coronans coronabit te tribulatione.—*Is.* xxii. 18.
[3] De Laud. V.M. l. 3. a. 24.   [4] Stell. B.V. l. 3. p. 2, 3.
[5] Vegetior exiverit, quam intraverit.—*Brev. Rom.* vi. Maii.

obedient unto death.'[6] 'Mary was a martyr,' says
Saint Bernard, 'not by the sword of the executioner,
but by bitter sorrow of heart.'[7] If her body was not
wounded by the hand of the executioner, her blessed
heart was transfixed by a sword of grief at the passion
of her Son ; grief which was sufficient to have caused
her death, not once, but a thousand times. From this
we shall see that Mary was not only a real martyr, but
that her martyrdom surpassed all others ; for it was
longer than that of all others, and her whole life may
be said to have been a prolonged death.

'The passion of Jesus,' as Saint Bernard says, 'commenced with His birth.'[8] So also did Mary, in all things
like unto her Son, endure her martyrdom throughout
her life. Amongst other significations of the name of
Mary, as Blessed Albert the Great asserts, is that of
'a bitter sea.'[9] Hence to her is applicable the text of
Jeremias : "great as the sea is thy destruction."[10] For
as the sea is all bitter and salt, so also was the life of
Mary always full of bitterness at the sight of the passion of the Redeemer, which was ever present to her
mind. 'There can be no doubt, that, enlightened by
the Holy Ghost in a far higher degree than all the prophets, she, far better than they, understood the predic-
tions recorded by them in the sacred Scriptures concerning the Messias.' This is precisely what the angel
revealed to St. Bridget ;[11] and he also added, 'that the
Blessed Virgin, even before she became His Mother,
knowing how much the Incarnate Word was to suffer
for the salvation of men, and compassionating this innocent Saviour, who was to be so cruelly put to death

---

[6] Martyrium complectitur id quod summum in obedientia esse potest, ut
scilicet aliquis sit obediens usque ad mortem.—2, 2 q. cxxiv. art. 3, ad 2.
[7] Non ferro carnificis, sed acerbo dolore cordis.—*De Serm. Dom. in Cœna,*
§ 4.
[8] A nativitatis exordio, passio crucis simul exorta.—*Serm.* ii. *de Pass.* †
[9] Mare amarum.—*De Laud. B.M.* l. 1. c. 3.
[10] Magna est enim velut mare contritio tua.—*Thren.* ii. 13.
[11] Proculdubio est credendum, quod ex inspiratione Spiritus Sancti ipsa
perfectius intellexit quicquid prophetarum eloquia figurabant.—*Serm. Ang.*
cap. xvii

for crimes not His own, even then began her great martyrdom.'[12]

Her grief was immeasurably increased when she became the Mother of this Saviour; so that at the sad sight of the many torments which were to be endured by her poor Son, she indeed suffered a long martyrdom,[13] a martyrdom which lasted her whole life. This was signified with great exactitude to Saint Bridget in a vision which she had in Rome, in the church of Saint Mary Major, where the Blessed Virgin with Saint Simeon, and an angel bearing a very long sword, reddened with blood, appeared to her, denoting thereby the long and bitter grief which transpierced the heart of Mary during her whole life.[14] Whence the above-named Rupert supposes Mary thus speaking: 'Redeemed souls, and my beloved children, do not pity me only for the hour in which I beheld my dear Jesus expiring before my eyes; for the sword of sorrow predicted by Simeon pierced my soul during the whole of my life: when I was giving suck to my Son, when I was warming Him in my arms, I already foresaw the bitter death that awaited Him. Consider, then, what long and bitter sorrows I must have endured.'[15]

Wherefore Mary might well say, in the words of David, "My life is wasted with grief, and my years in sighs."[16] "My sorrow is continually before me."[17] 'My whole life was spent in sorrow and in tears; for my sorrow, which was compassion for my beloved Son,

[12] Ex prophetarum scripturis Deum incarnari velle intelligens, et quod tam diversis pœnis in carne assumpta deberet cruciari, tribulationem protinus non modicam . . . in corde suo sustinuit.—*Serm. Ang.* cap. xvi.

[13] Tu quoque longum in cogitationibus tuis præscia futuræ passionis Filii tui pertulisti martyrium.—Rupert. lib. iii. *in Cant.* c. 4.

[14] Rev. lib. vii. cap. 1.

[15] Nolite solam attendere horam vel diem illam, qua vidi talem dilectum ab impiis comprehensum male tractari . . . mori et sepeliri. Nam tunc quidem gladius animam meam pertransivit; sed antequam sic pertransiret, longum per me transitum fecit . . . Cum igitur carne mea alitur progenitum, talem Filium sinu meo foverem, ulnis gestarem, uberibus lactarem, et talem ejus futuram mortem semper præ oculis haberem . . . qualem, quantam, quam prolixam me putatis materni doloris pertulisse passionem ?—Lib. i. *in Cant.* 1.

[16] Defecit in dolore vita mea, et anni mei in gemitibus.—*Ps.* xxx. 11.

[17] Et dolor meus in conspectu meo semper.—*Ps.* xxxvii. 18

never departed from before my eyes, as I always foresaw the sufferings and death which He was one day to endure.' The Divine Mother herself revealed to Saint Bridget, that ' even after the death and ascension of her Son, whether she ate, or worked, the remembrance of His passion was ever deeply impressed on her mind, and fresh in her tender heart.'[18] Hence Tauler says, ' that the most Blessed Virgin spent her whole life in continual sorrow ;'[19] for her heart was always occupied with sadness and with suffering.

Therefore time, which usually mitigates the sorrows of the afflicted, did not relieve Mary ; nay, even it increased her sorrow ; for, as Jesus, on the one hand, advanced in age, and always appeared more and more beautiful and amiable ; so also, on the other hand, the time of His death always drew nearer, and grief always increased in the heart of Mary, at the thought of having to lose Him on earth. So that, in the words addressed by the angel to Saint Bridget : ' As the rose grows up amongst thorns, so the Mother of God advanced in years in the midst of sufferings ; and as the thorns increase with the growth of the rose, so also did the thorns of her sorrows increase in Mary, the chosen rose of the Lord, as she advanced in age ; and so much the more deeply did they pierce her heart.'[20] Having now considered the length of this sorrow in point of duration, let us pass to the second point—its greatness in point of intensity.

Second point. Ah, Mary was not only Queen of martyrs because her martyrdom was longer than that of all others, but also because it was the greatest of all

[18] Omni tempore quod post ascensionem Filii mei vixi . . . passio sua in corde meo fixa erat, quod sive comedebam, sive laborabam, quasi recens erat in memoria mea.—*Rev.* lib. vi. c. 61.

[19] Beatissima Virgo pro tota vita fecit professionem doloris.—*Vit. Chr.* c. 18. †

[20] Sicut rosa crescere solet inter spinas, ita hæc venerabilis Virgo in hoc mundo crevit inter tribulationes. Et quemadmodum quanto rosa in crescendo se plus dilatat, tanto fortior et auctior spina efficitur, ita et hæc electissima rosa **Maria** quanto plus ætate crescebat, tanto fortiorum tribulationum spinis acutius pungebatur.—*Serm. Ang.* cap. xvi

martyrdoms. Who, however, can measure its greatness? Jeremias seems unable to find any one with whom he can compare this Mother of Sorrows, when he considers her great sufferings at the death of her Son. "To what shall I compare thee? or to what shall I liken thee, O daughter of Jerusalem? . . . for great as the sea is thy destruction: who shall heal thee?"[21] Wherefore Cardinal Hugo, in a commentary on these words, says, 'O Blessed Virgin, as the sea in bitterness exceeds all other bitterness, so does thy grief exceed all other grief.'[22]   Hence Saint Anselm asserts, that 'had not God by a special miracle preserved the life of Mary in each moment of her life, her grief was such that it would have caused her death.'[23]   Saint Bernardine of Sienna goes so far as to say, 'that the grief of Mary was so great that, were it divided amongst all men, it would suffice to cause their immediate death.'[24]

But let us consider the reasons for which Mary's martyrdom was greater than that of all martyrs. In the first place, we must remember that the martyrs endured their torments, which were the effect of fire and other material agencies, in their bodies; Mary suffered hers in her soul, as Saint Simeon foretold: "And thy own soul a sword shall pierce."[25] As if the holy old man had said: 'O most sacred Virgin, the bodies of other martyrs will be torn with iron, but thou wilt be transfixed, and martyred in thy soul by the Passion of thine own Son.' Now, as the soul is more noble than the body, so much greater were Mary's sufferings

[21] Cui comparabo te? vel cui assimilabo te, filia Jerusalem? cui exæquabo te . . . magna est enim velut mare contritio tua: quis medebitur tui?—*Thren.* ii. 13.

[22] Quemadmodum mare est in amaritudine excellens, ita tuæ contritioni nulla calamitas æquari potest.

[23] Utique, pia domina, non crediderim te potuisse ullo pacto, stimulos tanti cruciatus, quin vitam amitteres, sustinere, nisi ipse Spiritus vitæ, Spiritus consolationis, Spiritus scilicet dulcissimi tui Filii . . . te confortaret.— *De Excel.* V. cap. v.

[24] Virginis dolor erat major et plus quam omnes creaturæ mundi possent portare, in tantum, quod si ille dolor foret partitus et divisus inter omnes creaturas mundi vitales, caderent mortuæ.—*Serm. in die Veneris S.* p. ii.

[25] Et tuam ipsius animam pertransibit gladius.—*Luc.* ii. 35.

than those of all the martyrs, as Jesus Christ Himself
said to Saint Catherine of Sienna : ' Between the sufferings of the soul and those of the body there is no
comparison.'   Whence the holy Abbot Arnold of
Chartres says, ' that whoever had been present on
Mount Calvary, to witness the great sacrifice of the
Immaculate Lamb, would there have beheld two great
altars, the one in the body of Jesus, the other in the
heart of Mary ; for, on that mount, at the same time
that the Son sacrificed His body by death, Mary sacrificed her soul by compassion.'[26]

Moreover, says Saint Antoninus,[27] while other
martyrs suffered by sacrificing their own lives, the
Blessed Virgin suffered by sacrificing her Son's life—
a life that she loved far more than her own ; so that
she not only suffered in her soul all that her Son endured in His body, but moreover the sight of her Son's
torments brought more grief to her heart than if she
had endured them all in her own person.   No one can
doubt that Mary suffered in her heart all the outrages
which she saw inflicted on her beloved Jesus.   Any
one can understand that the sufferings of children are
also those of their mothers who witness them.   Saint
Augustine, considering the anguish endured by the
mother of the Macchabees in witnessing the tortures
of her sons, says, ' she, seeing their sufferings, suffered
in each one ; because she loved them all, she endured
in her soul what they endured in their flesh.'[28]   Thus
also did Mary suffer all those torments, scourges, thorns,
nails, and the cross, which tortured the innocent flesh
of Jesus, all entered at the same time into the heart of
this Blessed Virgin, to complete her martyrdom.   ' He
suffered in the flesh, and she in her heart,'[29] writes the

[26] Nimirum in tabernaculo illo duo videres altaria ; aliud in pectore Mariæ,
aliud in corpore Christi : Christus carnem, Maria immolabat animam.—*Tr.
de* vii. *Verb. D. in Cruce*, 3.
[27] P. 4. t. 15. 24. § 1.
[28] Illa videndo in omnibus passa est ; amabat omnes, ferebat in oculis quo.
in carne omnes.—*Serm*. 300, ed. B.
[29] Ille carne, illa corde passa est.—*Hom*. v.

Blessed Amadeus. 'So much so,' says Saint Lawrence Justinian, 'that the heart of Mary became, as it were, a mirror of the Passion of the Son, in which might be seen, faithfully reflected, the spitting, the blows and wounds, and all that Jesus suffered.'[30] Saint Bonaventure also remarks that 'those wounds which were scattered over the body of our Lord were all united in the single heart of Mary.'[31]

Thus was our Blessed Lady, through the compassion of her loving heart for her Son, scourged, crowned with thorns, insulted, and nailed to the cross. Whence the same Saint, considering Mary on Mount Calvary, present at the death of her Son, questions her in these words: 'O Lady, tell me where didst thou stand? Was it only at the foot of the cross? Ah, much more than this, thou wast on the cross itself, crucified with thy Son.'[32] Richard of Saint Lawrence, on the words of the Redeemer, spoken by Isaias the prophet, "I have trodden the wine-press alone, and of the Gentiles there is not a man with me,"[33] says, 'It is true, O Lord, that in the work of human redemption Thou didst suffer alone, and that there was not a man who sufficiently pitied Thee; but there was a woman with Thee, and she was Thine own Mother; she suffered in her heart all that Thou didst endure in Thy body.'[34]

But all this is saying too little of Mary's sorrows, since, as I have already observed, she suffered more in witnessing the sufferings of her beloved Jesus than if she had herself endured all the outrages and death of her Son. Erasmus, speaking of parents in general,

[30] Clarissimum passionis Christi speculum effectum erat cor Virginis, necnon et perfecta mortis imago. In illo agnoscebantur sputa, convitia, verbera, et Redemptoris vulnera.—*De triumphali Chr. Agone*, cap. xxi.

[31] Ejus vulnera, per corpus ejus dispersa, sunt in corde tuo unita.—*Stim. Am.* p. i. c. 3.

[32] O domina mea, ubi stabas? Numquid tantum juxta crucem? Imo certe in cruce cum Filio ibi crucifixa eras secum.—*Ib.*

[33] Torcular calcavi solus, et de gentibus non est vir mecum.—*Is.* lxiii. 3.

[34] Verum est, Domine, quod non est vir tecum : sed mulier una tecum est, quæ omnia vulnera quæ tu suscepisti in corpore suscepit in corde.—*De Laud. V.* l. i. c. 5.

says, that 'they are more cruelly tormented by their children's sufferings than by their own.'[35] This is not always true, but in Mary it evidently was so; for it is certain that she loved her Son and His life beyond all comparison more than herself or a thousand lives of her own. Therefore Blessed Amadeus rightly affirms, that 'the afflicted Mother, at the sorrowful sight of the torments of her beloved Jesus, suffered far more than she would have done had she herself endured His whole Passion.'[36] The reason is evident, for, as Saint Bernard says, 'the soul is more where it loves than where it lives.'[37] Our Lord Himself had already said the same thing: "where our treasure is, there also is our heart."[38] If Mary, then, by love, lived more in her Son than in herself, she must have endured far greater torments in the sufferings and death of her Son than she would have done, had the most cruel death in the world been inflicted upon her.

Here we must reflect on another circumstance which rendered the martyrdom of Mary beyond all comparison greater than the torments of all the martyrs: it is, that in the Passion of Jesus she suffered much, and she suffered, moreover, without the least alleviation. The martyrs suffered under the torments inflicted on them by tyrants; but the love of Jesus rendered their pains sweet and agreeable. A Saint Vincent was tortured on a rack, torn with pincers, burnt with red-hot iron plates; but, as Saint Augustine remarks, 'it seemed as if it was one who suffered, and another who spoke.'[39] The Saint addressed the tyrant with such energy and contempt for his torments, that it seemed as if one Vincent suffered and another spoke; so greatly did God strengthen him with the sweetness of His love in the midst of all

---

[35] Parentes atrocius torquentur in liberis, quam in seipsis.—*Lib. de Ma-chab.* †

[36] Torquebatur (Maria) magis, quasi torqueretur ex se, quoniam supra s? incomparabiliter diligebat id unde dolebat.—*Hom.* v. *de Laud. V.*

[37] Anima magis est ubi amat, quam ubi animat. †

[38] Ubi enim thesaurus vester est, ibi et cor vestrum erit.—*Luc.* xii. 34.

[39] Tanquam alius torqueretur, alius loqueretur.—*Serm.* 275, ed. B.

he endured. A Saint Boniface had his body torn with iron hooks; sharp-pointed reeds were thrust between his nails and flesh; melted lead was poured into his mouth; and in the midst of all he could not tire saying, 'I give Thee thanks. O Lord Jesus Christ.'[40] A Saint Mark and a Saint Marcellinus were bound to a stake, their feet pierced with nails; and when the tyrant addressed them, saying, 'Wretches, see to what a state you are reduced; save yourselves from these torments,' they answered: 'Of what pains, of what torments dost thou speak? We never enjoyed so luxurious a banquet as in the present moment, in which we joyfully suffer for the love of Jesus Christ.'[41] A Saint Lawrence suffered; but when roasting on the gridiron, 'the interior flame of love,' says Saint Leo, 'was more powerful in consoling his soul than the flame without in torturing his body.'[42] Hence love rendered him so courageous that he mocked the tyrant, saying, 'If thou desirest to feed on my flesh, a part is sufficiently roasted; turn it, and eat.'[43] But how, in the midst of so many torments, in that prolonged death, could the Saint thus rejoice? 'Ah!' replies Saint Augustine, 'inebriated with the wine of Divine love, he felt neither torments nor death.'[44]

So that the more the holy martyrs loved Jesus, the less did they feel their torments and death; and the sight alone of the sufferings of a crucified God was sufficient to console them. But was our suffering Mother also consoled by love for her Son, and the sight of His torments? Ah, no; for this very Son who suffered was the whole cause of them, and the love she bore Him was her only and most cruel executioner; for Mary's

[40] Gratias tibi ago, Domine Jesu Christe.—*Offic.* lect. 2.

[41] Nunquam tam jucunde epulati sumus, quam cum hæc libenter Jesu Christi amore perferimus.—*Ib.* lect. 3.

[42] Segnior fuit ignis qui foris ussit, quam qui intus accendit.—*In Festo S. Laur.*

[43] Assatum est jam, versa et manduca.—*Offic. Ant. ad Magn.*

[44] In illa . . . longa morte, in illis tormentis, quia bene manducaverat et bene biberat, tamquam illa esca saginatus et illo calice ebrius, tormenta non sensit.—*Tract.* xxvii. *in Joan. Ev.*

whole martyrdom consisted in beholding and pitying her innocent and beloved Son, who suffered so much. Hence, the greater was her love for Him, the more bitter and inconsolable was her grief. "Great as the sea is thy destruction; who shall heal thee?"[45] Ah, Queen of Heaven, love hath mitigated the sufferings of other martyrs, and healed their wounds; but who hath ever soothed thy bitter grief? Who hath ever healed the too cruel wounds of thy heart? "Who shall heal thee," since that very Son who could give thee consolation was, by His sufferings, the only cause of thine, and the love which thou didst bear Him was the whole ingredient of thy martyrdom. So that, as other martyrs, as Diez remarks, are all represented with the instruments of their sufferings—a Saint Paul with a sword, a Saint Andrew with a cross, a Saint Lawrence with a gridiron—Mary is represented with her dead Son in her arms; for Jesus Himself, and He alone, was the instrument of her martyrdom, by reason of the love she bore Him. Richard of Saint Victor confirms in a few words all that I have now said : ' In other martyrs, the greatness of their love soothed the pains of their martyrdom ; but in the Blessed Virgin, the greater was her love, the greater were her sufferings, the more cruel was her martyrdom.'[46]

It is certain that the more we love a thing, the greater is the pain we feel in losing it. We are more afflicted at the loss of a brother than at that of a beast of burden ; we are more grieved at the loss of a son than at that of a friend. Now, Cornelius à Lapide says, ' that to understand the greatness of Mary's grief at the death of her Son, we must understand the greatness of the love she bore Him.'[47] But who can ever measure

[45] Magna est enim velut mare contritio **tua: quis** medebit.. tui ?—*Thren.* ii. 13.

[46] In martyribus magnitudo amoris dolorem lenivit passionis ; sed Beata Virgo, quanto plus amavit, tanto plus doluit, tantoque ipsius martyrium gravius fuit.—*In Cant.* cap. xxvi.

[47] Ut scies quantus fuerit **dolor B. Virginis, cogita** quantus fuerit amor —*In Thren.* i. 12.

that **love**? Blessed Amadeus says that 'in the heart of Mary were united two kinds of love for her Jesus—supernatural love, by which she loved Him as her God, and natural love, by which she loved Him as her Son.'[48] So that these two loves became one ; but so immense a love, that William of Paris even says that the Blessed Virgin 'loved Him as much as it was possible for a pure creature to love Him.'[49]   Hence Richard of Saint Victor affirms that ' as there was no love like her love, so there was no sorrow like her sorrow.'[50]   And if the love of Mary towards her Son was immense, immense also must have been her grief in losing Him by death.   'Where there is the greatest love,' says Blessed Albert the Great, 'there also is the greatest grief.'[51]

Let us now imagine to ourselves the Divine Mother standing near her Son expiring on the cross, and justly applying to herself the words of Jeremias, thus addressing us : "O all ye that pass by the way attend, and see if there be any sorrow like to my sorrow."[52]   O you who spend your lives upon earth, and pity me not, stop awhile to look at me, now that I behold this beloved Son dying before my eyes; and then see if, amongst all those who are afflicted and tormented, a sorrow is to be found like unto my sorrow.   ' No, O most suffering of all mothers,' replies Saint Bonaventure, ' no more bitter grief than thine can be found ; for no son more dear than thine can be found.'[53]   Ah, ' there never was a more amiable son in the world than Jesus,' says Richard of Saint Lawrence ; ' nor has there ever been a mother who more tenderly loved her son than

---

[48] Duæ dilectiones in unam convenerant, et ex duobus amoribus factus est amor unus, cum Virgo Mater Filio divinitatis amorem impenderet, et in Deo amorem nato exhiberet.—*Hom.* v. *de Laud. V.*

[49] Quantum capere potuit puri hominis modus.

[50] Unde sicut non fuit amor sicut amor ejus, ita nec fuit dolor similis dolori ejus.—*In Cant.* cap. **xxvi.**

[51] Ubi summus amor, ibi summus dolor.—*Super Miss.* q. 78.

[52] O vos omnes qui transitis per viam, attendite, et videte si est dolor sicut dolor meus.—*Thren.* i. 12.

[53] Nullus dolor amarior,
    Nam nulla proles carior.—*Hymn. de Compass. B.M.*

Mary! But since there never has been in the world a love like unto Mary's love, how can any sorrow be found like unto Mary's sorrow ?'[54]

Therefore Saint Ildephonsus did not hesitate to assert, 'to say that Mary's sorrows were greater than all the torments of the martyrs united, was to say too little.'[55] And Saint Anselm adds, that 'the most cruel tortures inflicted on the holy martyrs were trifling, or as nothing in comparison with the martyrdom of Mary.'[56] Saint Basil of Seleucia also writes, 'that as the sun exceeds all the other planets in splendour, so did Mary's sufferings exceed those of all the other martyrs.'[57] A learned author[58] concludes with a beautiful sentiment. He says that so great was the sorrow of this tender Mother in the Passion of Jesus, that she alone compassionated in a degree by any means adequate to its merits the death of a God made man.

But here Saint Bonaventure, addressing this Blessed Virgin, says, 'And why, O Lady, didst thou also go to sacrifice thyself on Calvary? Was not a crucified God sufficient to redeem us, that thou, His Mother, wouldst also go to be crucified with Him?'[59] Indeed, the death of Jesus was more than enough to save the world, and an infinity of worlds; but this good Mother, for the love she bore us, wished also to help the cause of our salvation with the merits of her sufferings, which she offered for us on Calvary. Therefore, Blessed Albert the Great says, 'that as we are under great obligations to Jesus for His Passion endured for our love, so

---

[54] Non fuit talis Filius, non fuit talis Mater; non fuit tanta charitas sicut inter matrem et filium, non fuit tam indigna mors, non fuit dolor tantus ... Ideo quanto dilexit tenerius, tanto vulnerata est profundius.—*De Laud. V. l.* iii. c. 12.

[55] Parum est Mariam in passione Filii tam acerbos pertulisse dolores, ut omnium martyrum collective tormenta superaret.—*Ap. Sinisc. Mart. di Mar. Cons.* xxxvi.

[56] Quidquid enim crudelitatis inflictum est corporibus martyrum leve fuit aut potius nihil comparatione tuæ passionis.—*De Excel. V.* cap. v.

[57] Orat. in S. Dei Gen. see page 398, note 37.

[58] Father Pinamonti, Cuore di M. cons. 6.

[59] O domina, cur ivisti immolari pro nobis? numquid non sufficiebat Filii passio nobis, nisi crucifigeretur et Mater?—*Stim. Am.* p. i. cap. 3.

also are we under great obligations to Mary for the martyrdom which she voluntarily suffered for our salvation in the death of her Son.'[60]   I say voluntarily, since, as Saint Agnes revealed to Saint Bridget, 'our compassionate and benign Mother was satisfied rather to endure any torment than that our souls should not be redeemed, and be left in their former state of perdition.'[61]   And, indeed, we may say that Mary's only relief in the midst of her great sorrow in the Passion of her Son, was to see the lost world redeemed by His death, and men who were His enemies reconciled with God.   'While grieving she rejoiced,' says Simon of Cassia, 'that a sacrifice was offered for the redemption of all, by which He who was angry was appeased.'[62]

So great a love on the part of Mary deserves our gratitude, and that gratitude should be shown by at least meditating upon and pitying her in her sorrows. But she complained to Saint Bridget that very few did so, and that the greater part of the world lived in forgetfulness of them: 'I look around at all who are on earth, to see if by chance there are any who pity me, and meditate upon my sorrows; and I find that there are very few.   Therefore, my daughter, though I am forgotten by many, at least do thou not forget me; consider my anguish, and imitate, as far as thou canst, my grief.'[63]   To understand how pleasing it is to the Blessed Virgin that we should remember her dolours, we need only know that, in the year 1239, she appeared to seven devout clients of hers (who were afterwards founders of the religious order of the Servants of Mary), with a black garment in her hand, and desired them, if they

---

[60] Sicut totus mundus obligatur Deo per suam passionem, ita et dominæ omnium per compassionem.—*Sup. Miss.* q. cl. Resp. ad q. cxlviii.

[61] Sic pia et misericors fuit et est, ut maluit omnes tribulationes sufferre, quam quod animæ non redimerentur.—*Rev.* lib. iii. c. 30.

[62] Lætabatur dolens, quod offerebatur sacrificium in redemptionem omnium, quo placabatur iratus —*De Gest. D.* l. ii. c. 27.

[63] Respicio ad omnes qui in mundo sunt, si forte sint aliqui qui compatiantur mihi, et recogitent dolorem meum, et valde paucos invenio . . . Ideo, filia mea, licet a multis oblita et neglecta sim, tu tamen non obliviscaris me; vide dolorem meum, et imitare quantum potes.—*Rev.* lib. ii. c. 24.

wished to please her, often to meditate on her sorrows: for this purpose, and to remind them of her sorrows, she expressed her desire that in future they should wear that mourning dress.[64] Jesus Christ Himself revealed to the Blessed Veronica da Binasco, that He is, as it were, more pleased in seeing His Mother compassionated than Himself; for thus He addressed her: 'My daughter, tears shed for My Passion are dear to Me; but as I love My Mother Mary with an immense love, the meditation of the torments which she endured at My death is even more agreeable to Me.'[65]

Wherefore the graces promised by Jesus to those who are devoted to the dolours of Mary are very great. Pelbert[66] relates that it was revealed to Saint Elizabeth, that after the assumption of the Blessed Virgin into heaven, Saint John the Evangelist desired to see her again. The favour was granted him; his dear Mother appeared to him, and with her Jesus Christ also appeared; the Saint then heard Mary ask her Son to grant some special grace to all those who are devoted to her dolours. Jesus promised her four principal ones: 1st, that those who before death invoke the Divine Mother in the name of her sorrows should obtain true repentance of all their sins. 2d, that He would protect all who have this devotion in their tribulations, and that He would protect them especially at the hour of death. 3d, that He would impress upon their minds the remembrance of His Passion, and that they should have their reward for it in heaven. 4th, that He would commit such devout clients to the hands of Mary, with the power to dispose of them in whatever manner she might please, and to obtain for them all the graces she might desire. In proof of this, let us see, in the following example, how greatly devotion to the dolours of Mary aids in obtaining eternal salvation.

[64] Gian. Ann. Serv. cent. i. l. i. o. 14.
[65] Ap. Bolland. xiii. Jan. Vit. l. 1. c. 9.
[66] Stellar. lib. iii. p. 3, a. 3.

EXAMPLE.

In the revelations of Saint Bridget[67] we read that there was a rich man, as noble by birth as he was vile and sinful in his habits. He had given himself, by an express compact, as a slave to the devil; and for sixty successive years had served him, leading such a life as may be imagined, and never approaching the sacraments. Now this prince was dying; and Jesus Christ, to show him mercy, commanded Saint Bridget to tell her confessor to go and visit him, and exhort him to confess his sins. The confessor went, and the sick man said that he did not require confession, as he had often approached the sacrament of penance. The priest went a second time; but this poor slave of hell persevered in his obstinate determination not to confess. Jesus again told the Saint to desire the confessor to return. He did so; and on this third occasion told the sick man the revelation made to the Saint, and that he had returned so many times because our Lord, who wished to show him mercy, had so ordered. On hearing this the dying man was touched, and began to weep: 'But how,' he exclaimed, 'can I be saved; I, who for sixty years have served the devil as his slave, and have my soul burdened with innumerable sins?' 'My son,' answered the father, encouraging him, 'doubt not; if you repent of them, on the part of God I promise you pardon.' Then, gaining confidence, he said to the confessor, 'Father, I looked upon myself as lost, and already despaired of salvation; but now I feel a sorrow for my sins, which gives me confidence; and since God has not yet abandoned me, I will make my confession.' In fact, he made his confession four times on that day, with the greatest marks of sorrow, and on the following morning received the holy communion. On the sixth day, contrite and resigned, he died. After his death, Jesus Christ again spoke to Saint Bridget, and told her that

[67] Rev. lib. vi. c. 97.

that sinner was saved; that he was then in purgatory, and that he owed his salvation to the intercession of the Blessed Virgin His Mother; for the deceased, although he had led so wicked a life, had nevertheless always preserved devotion to her dolours, and whenever he thought of them, pitied her.

PRAYER.

O my afflicted Mother! Queen of martyrs and of sorrows, thou didst so bitterly weep over thy Son, who died for my salvation; but what will thy tears avail me if I am lost? By the merit, then, of thy sorrows, obtain me true contrition for my sins, and a real amendment of life, together with constant and tender compassion for the sufferings of Jesus and thy dolours. And if Jesus and thou, being so innocent, have suffered so much for love of me, obtain that at least I, who am deserving of hell, may suffer something for your love. 'O Lady,' will I say with St. Bonaventure, 'if I have offended thee, in justice wound my heart; if I have served thee, I now ask wounds for my reward. It is shameful to me to see my Lord Jesus wounded, and thee wounded with Him, and myself without a wound.'[68] In fine, O my Mother, by the grief thou didst experience in seeing thy Son bow down His head and expire on the cross in the midst of so many torments, I beseech thee to obtain me a good death. Ah, cease not, O advocate of sinners, to assist my afflicted soul in the midst of the combats in which it will have to engage on its great passage from time to eternity. And as it is probable that I may then have lost my speech, and strength to invoke thy name and that of Jesus, who are all my hope, I do so now; I invoke thy Son and thee to succour me in that last moment; and I say, Jesus and Mary, to you I commend my soul. Amen.

[68] O domina .... si te offendi, pro justitia cor meum vulnera. Si tibi servivi, nunc pro mercede peto vulnera . . . Verecundum enim et opprobriosum est mihi videre Dominum meum Jesum vulneratum et te convulneratam dominam, et me servum vilissimum pertransire illæsum *—Stim. Am.* p. i. cap. 3.

REFLECTIONS

ON EACH OF THE SEVEN DOLOURS OF MARY IN PARTICULAR.

ON THE FIRST DOLOUR.

Of Saint Simeon's Prophecy.

In this valley of tears every man is born to weep, and all must suffer, by enduring the evils which are of daily occurrence. But how much greater would the misery of life be, did we also know the future evils which await us! 'Unfortunate, indeed, would his lot be,' says Seneca, 'who, knowing the future, would have to suffer all by anticipation.'[1] Our Lord shows us this mercy. He conceals the trials which await us, that, whatever they may be, we may endure them but once. He did not show Mary this compassion; for she, whom God willed to be the Queen of Sorrows, and in all things like His Son, had to see always before her eyes and continually to suffer all the torments that awaited her; and these were the sufferings of the Passion and death of her beloved Jesus; for in the temple Saint Simeon, having received the Divine Child in his arms, foretold to her that that Son would be a mark for all the persecutions and oppositions of men. "Behold, this Child is set . . . for a sign which shall be contradicted." And therefore, that a sword of sorrow should pierce her soul: "And thy own soul a sword shall pierce."[2]

---

[1] Calamitosus esset animus futuri præscius, et ante miserias miser.—*Ep.* xcviii.

[2] Ecce positus est hic . . . in signum cui contradicetur: Et tuam ipsius animam pertransibit gladius.—*Luc.* ii. 34, 35.

The Blessed Virgin herself told Saint Matilda, that, on this announcement of Saint Simeon, 'all her joy was changed into sorrow.'[3] For, as it was revealed to Saint Teresa,[4] though the Blessed Mother already knew that the life of her Son would be sacrificed for the salvation of the world, yet she then learnt more distinctly and in greater detail the sufferings and cruel death that awaited her poor Son. She knew that He would be contradicted, and this in everything : contradicted in His doctrines ; for, instead of being believed, He would be esteemed a blasphemer for teaching that He was the Son of God ; this He was declared to be by the impious Caiphas, saying, " He hath blasphemed, He is guilty of death."[5] Contradicted in His reputation ; for He was of noble, even of royal descent, and was despised as a peasant : " Is not this the carpenter's son ?"[6] " Is not this the carpenter, the son of Mary ?"[7] He was wisdom itself, and was treated as ignorant : " How doth this man know letters, having never learned ?"[8] As a false prophet : "And they blindfolded Him, and smote His face . . . saying : Prophesy, who is it that struck Thee ?"[9] He was treated as a madman : " He is mad, why hear you Him ?"[10] As a drunkard, a glutton, and a friend of sinners : " Behold a man that is a glutton, and a drinker of wine, a friend of publicans and sinners."[11] As a sorcerer : " By the prince of devils He casteth out devils."[12] As a heretic, and possessed by the evil spirit : " Do we not say well of Thee that Thou art a Samari-

---

[3] Omnis lætitia mea, ad verba Simeonis, versa est mihi in mœrorem.—*Spir. Grat.* l. i. c. 16.

[4] Vita, addit.

[5] Blasphemavit . . . reus est mortis.—*Matt.* xxvi. 65, 66.

[6] Nonne hic est fabri filius ?—*Ib.* xiii. 55.

[7] Nonne hic est faber, filius Mariæ ?—*Marc.* vi. 3.

[8] Quomodo hic litteras scit, cum non didicerit ?—*Joan.* vii. 15.

[9] Et velaverunt eum, et percutiebant faciem ejus . . . dicentes : Prophetiza, quis est, qui te percussit ?—*Luc.* xxii. 64.

[10] Insanit : quid eum auditis ?—*Joan.* x. 20.

[11] Ecce homo devorator, et bibens vinum, amicus publicanorum et peccatorum.—*Luc.* vii. 34.

[12] In principe dæmoniorum ejicit dæmones.—*Matt.* ix. 34.

tan, and hast a devil?"[13] In a word, Jesus was considered so notoriously wicked, that, as the Jews said to Pilate, no trial was necessary to condemn Him. "If He were not a malefactor, we would not have delivered Him up to thee."[14] He was contradicted in His very soul; for even His Eternal Father, to give place to Divine Justice, contradicted Him, by refusing to hear His prayer, when He said. "Father, if it be possible, let this chalice pass from Me;"[15] and abandoned Him to fear, weariness, and sadness; so that our afflicted Lord exclaimed, "My soul is sorrowful unto death!"[16] and His interior sufferings even caused Him to sweat blood. Contradicted and persecuted, in fine, in His body and in His life; for He was tortured in all His sacred members, in His hands, His feet, His face, His head, and in His whole body; so that, drained of His blood, and an object of scorn, He died of torments on an ignominious cross.

When David, in the midst of all his pleasures and regal grandeur, heard, from the Prophet Nathan, that his son should die—"The child that is born to thee shall surely die,"[17] he could find no peace, but wept, fasted, and slept on the ground. Mary with the greatest calmness received the announcement that her Son should die, and always peacefully submitted to it; but what grief must she continually have suffered, seeing this amiable Son always near her, hearing from Him words of eternal life, and witnessing His holy demeanour! Abraham suffered much during the three days he passed with his beloved Isaac, after knowing that he was to lose him. O God, not for three days, but for three and thirty years had Mary to endure a like sorrow! But do I say a like sorrow? It was as much greater as the Son of

---

[13] Nonne bene dicimus nos, quia Samaritanus es tu, et dæmonium habes? —*Joan.* viii. 48.

[14] Si non esset hic malefactor, non tibi tradidissemus eum.—*Ib.* xviii. 30.

[15] Pater mi, si possibile est, transeat a me calix iste.—*Matt.* xxvi. 39.

[16] Tristis est anima mea usque ad mortem.—*Ib.* 38.

[17] Filius, qui natus est tibi, morte morietur.—*2 Reg.* xii. 14.

Mary was more lovely than the son of Abraham. The Blessed Virgin herself revealed to Saint Bridget, that, while on earth, there was not an hour in which this grief did not pierce her soul : 'As often,' she continued, ' as I looked at my Son, as often as I wrapped Him in His swaddling-clothes, as often as I saw His hands and feet, so often was my soul absorbed, so to say, in fresh grief; for I thought how He would be crucified.'[18] The Abbot Rupert contemplates Mary suckling her Son, and thus addressing Him : "A bundle of myrrh is my Beloved to me ; He shall abide between my breasts."[19] Ah, Son, I clasp Thee in my arms, because Thou art so dear to me; but the dearer Thou art to me, the more dost Thou become a bundle of myrrh and sorrow to me when I think of Thy sufferings. ' Mary,' says Saint Bernardine of Sienna, ' reflected that the strength of the Saints was to be reduced to agony; the beauty of Paradise to be disfigured; the Lord of the world to be bound as a criminal; the Creator of all things to be made livid with blows; the Judge of all to be condemned; the Glory of heaven despised; the King of kings to be crowned with thorns, and treated as a mock king.'[20]

Father Engelgrave says, that it was revealed to the same Saint Bridget, that the afflicted Mother, already knowing what her Son was to suffer, ' when suckling Him, thought of the gall and vinegar; when swathing Him, of the cords with which He was to be bound; when bearing Him in her arms, of the cross to which He was to be nailed; when sleeping, of His death.'[21] As often as she put Him on His garment, she reflected that it would one day be torn from Him, that He might

[18] Quoties aspiciebam Filium meum, quoties involvebam pannis, quoties videbam ejus manus et pedes, toties animus meus quasi novo dolore absorptus est, quia cogitabam quomodo crucifigeretur.—*Rev.* lib. vi. cap. 57.

[19] Fasciculus myrrhæ dilectus meus mihi ; inter ubera mea commorabitur. —*Cant.* i. 12.

[20] Serm. ii. de Glor. Nom. B.M.V. art. 3, cap. 1.

[21] Eum lactans, cogitabat de elle et aceto ; quando fasciis involvebat, funes cogitabat quibus ligandus erat ; quando gestabat, cogitabat in cruce confixum ; quando dormiebat, cogitabat mortuum.—*Lux Ev. s. infra Oct. Nat.*

be crucified; and when she beheld His sacred hands and feet, she thought of the nails which would one day pierce them; and then, as Mary said to Saint Bridget, 'my eyes filled with tears, and my heart was tortured with grief.'[22]

The Evangelist says, that as Jesus Christ advanced in years, so also did "He advance in wisdom and in grace with God and men."[23] This is to be understood as Saint Thomas[24] explains it, that He advanced in wisdom and grace in the estimation of men and before God, inasmuch as all His works would continually have availed to increase His merit, had not grace been conferred upon Him from the beginning, in its complete fulness, in virtue of the hypostatic union. But since Jesus advanced in the love and esteem of others, how much more must He have advanced in that of Mary! But, O God, as love increased in her, so much the more did her grief increase at the thought of having to lose Him by so cruel a death; and the nearer the time of the Passion of her Son approached, so much the deeper did that sword of sorrow, foretold by Saint Simeon, pierce the heart of His Mother. This was precisely revealed by the angel to Saint Bridget, saying: 'That sword of sorrow was every hour approaching nearer to the Blessed Virgin, as the time for the Passion of her Son drew near.'[25]

Since, then, Jesus, our King, and His most holy Mother, did not refuse, for love of us, to suffer such cruel pains throughout their lives, it is reasonable that we, at least, should not complain if we have to suffer something. Jesus, crucified, once appeared to Sister Magdalen Orsini, a Dominicaness, who had been long

---

[22] Oculi mei replebantur lacrymis, et cor meum quasi scindebatur præ tristitia.—*Rev.* lib. i. cap. x.

[23] Et Jesus proficiebat sapientia et ætate, et gratia apud Deum et homines.—*Luc.* ii. 52.

[24] 3 p. q. vii. art. 12.

[25] Ille doloris gladius cordi Virginis omni hora, tanto se propius approximabat, quanto suus dilectus Filius passionis tempori magis appropinquabat.—*Serm. Ang.* cap. xvii.

suffering under a great trial, and encouraged her to remain, by means of that affliction, with Him on the cross. Sister Magdalen complainingly answered: 'O Lord, Thou wast tortured on the cross only for three hours, and I have endured my pain for many years.' The Redeemer then replied: 'Ah, ignorant soul, what dost thou say? from the first moment of My conception I suffered in heart all that I afterwards endured dying on the cross.' If, then, we also suffer and complain, let us imagine Jesus, and His Mother Mary, addressing the same words to ourselves.

EXAMPLE.

Father Roviglione, of the Society of Jesus,[26] relates, that a young man had the devotion of every day visiting a statue of our Lady of Sorrows, in which she was represented with seven swords piercing her heart. The unfortunate youth one night committed a mortal sin. The next morning, going as usual to visit the image, he perceived that there were no longer only seven, but eight swords in the heart of Mary. Wondering at this, he heard a voice telling him that his crime had added the eighth. This moved his heart; and, penetrated with sorrow, he immediately went to confession, and by the intercession of his advocate recovered divine grace.

PRAYER.

Ah, my Blessed Mother, it is not one sword only with which I have pierced thy heart, but I have done so with as many as are the sins which I have committed. Ah, Lady, it is not to thee, who art innocent, that sufferings are due, but to me, who am guilty of so many crimes. But since thou hast been pleased to suffer so much for me, ah, by thy merits, obtain me great sorrow for my sins, and patience under the trials of this life, which will always be light in comparison

[26] Fasc. di Rose, p. 2, c. 2. †

with my demerits; for I have often deserved hell.
Amen.

ON THE SECOND DOLOUR.

Of the Flight of Jesus into Egypt.

As the stag, wounded by an arrow, carries the pain
with him wherever he goes, because he carries with him
the arrow which has wounded him, so did the Divine
Mother, after the sad prophecy of Saint Simeon, as we
have already seen in the consideration of the first dolour,
always carry her sorrow with her in the continual remembrance of the Passion of her Son.   Hailgrino, explaining this passage of the Canticles, " The hairs of
thy head, as the purple of the king, bound in the channel,"[1] says that these purple hairs were Mary's continual
thoughts of the Passion of Jesus, which kept the blood
which was one day to flow from His wounds always
before her eyes : ' Thy mind, O Mary, and thy thoughts,
steeped in the blood of our Lord's Passion, were always
filled with sorrow, as if they actually beheld the blood
flowing from His wounds.'[2]   Thus her Son Himself was
that arrow in the heart of Mary ; and the more amiable
He appeared to her, so much the more deeply did the
thought of losing Him by so cruel a death wound her
heart.   Let us now consider the second sword of sorrow which wounded Mary, in the flight of her Infant
Jesus into Egypt from the persecution of Herod.

Herod, having heard that the expected Messias was
born, foolishly feared that He would deprive him of
his kingdom.   Hence Saint Fulgentius, reproving him
for his folly, thus addresses him : ' Why art thou troubled, O Herod ?   This King who is born comes not to
conquer kings by the sword, but to subjugate them

---

[1] Et comæ capitis tui, sicut purpura regis, vincta canalibus.—*Cant.* vii. 5.

[2] Mens tua, O Maria, et cogitationes tuæ tinctæ in sanguine dominicæ
passionis, sic affectæ semper fuere, quasi recenter viderent sanguinem de
vulneribus profluentem.—*In Cant.* l. cit. †

wonderfully by His death.'[3] The impious Herod, therefore, waited to hear from the holy Magi where the King was born, that he might take His life; but finding himself deceived, he ordered all the infants who could be found in the neighbourhood of Bethlehem to be put to death. Then it was that the angel appeared in a dream to Saint Joseph, and desired him to " Arise, and take the Child and His Mother, and fly into Egypt."[4] According to Gerson,[5] Saint Joseph immediately, on that very night, made the order known to Mary; and taking the Infant Jesus, they set out on their journey, as it is sufficiently evident from the Gospel itself : " Who arose and took the Child and His Mother, by night, and retired into Egypt."[6] O God, says Blessed Albert the Great, in the name of Mary, ' must He then fly from men, who came to save men ?'[7] Then the afflicted Mother knew that already the prophecy of Simeon concerning her Son began to be verified : " He is set for a sign that shall be contradicted."[8] Seeing that He was no sooner born than He was persecuted unto death, what anguish, writes Saint John Chrysostom, must the intimation of that cruel exile of herself and her Son have caused in her heart : ' Flee from thy friends to strangers, from God's temple to the temples of devils. What greater tribulation than that a new-born child, hanging from its mother's breast, and she too in poverty, should with Him be forced to fly ?'[9]

Any one may imagine what Mary must have suffered on this journey. To Egypt the distance was

---

[3] Quid est quod sic turbaris, Herodes ? . . . Rex iste, qui natus est, non venit reges pugnando superare, sed moriendo mirabiliter subjugare.—*Serm. de Epiph. et Innoc. nece.*

[4] Surge, et accipe puerum et matrem ejus, et fuge in Ægyptum.—*Matt.* ii. 13.

[5] Joseph. dist. 1.

[6] Qui consurgens, accepit puerum et matrem ejus nocte, et secessit in Ægyptum.—*Matt.* ii. 14.

[7] Debet fugere, qui Salvator est mundi ? †

[8] Ecce positus est hic . . . in signum cui contradicetur.—*Luc.* ii. 34.

[9] Fuge a tuis ad extraneos, a templo ad dæmonum fana. Quæ major tribulatio, quam quod recens natus, a collo matris pendens, cum ipsa matre paupercula fugere cogatur ? †

great. Most authors agree that it was three hundred
miles; so that it was a journey of upwards of thirty
days. The road was, according to Saint Bonaventure's
description of it, 'rough, unknown, and little frequented.'[10] It was in the winter season; so that they
had to travel in snow, rain, and wind, through rough
and dirty roads. Mary was then fifteen years of age—
a delicate young woman, unaccustomed to such jour-
neys. They had no one to attend upon them. Saint
Peter Chrysologus says, 'Joseph and Mary have no
male or female servants; they were themselves both
masters and servants.'[11] O God, what a touching sight
must it have been to have beheld that tender Virgin,
with her new-born Babe in her arms, wandering through
the world! 'But how,' asks Saint Bonaventure, 'did
they obtain their food? Where did they repose at
night? How were they lodged?'[12] What can they have
eaten but a piece of hard bread, either brought by Saint
Joseph or begged as an alms? Where can they have
slept on such a road (especially on the two hundred
miles of desert, where there were neither houses nor
inns, as authors relate), unless on the sand or under a
tree in a wood, exposed to the air and the dangers of
robbers and wild beasts, with which Egypt abounded?
Ah, had any one met these three greatest personages in
the world, for whom could he have taken them but for
three poor wandering beggars?

They resided in Egypt, according to Brocard and
Jansenius,[13] in a district called Maturea; though Saint
Anselm says[14] that they lived in the city of Heliopolis,
or at Memphis, now called old Cairo. Here let us consider the great poverty they must have suffered during
the seven years which, according to Saint Antoninus,[15]

[10] Portabat eum mater . . . per viam silvestrem, obscuram, nemorosam,
asperam, et inhabitatam.—*De Vita Christi*, cap. xii.

[11] Joseph et Maria non habent famulum, non ancillam; ipsi domini et
famuli. †

[12] Quomodo faciebant de victu secum portando? Ubi etiam, et quomodo
te nocte quiescebant et hospitabantur?—*De Vit. C.* cap. xii.

[13] In Conc. c. 11.   [14] Enarr. in Matt. ii.   [15] P. 4. tit. 15. c. 36.

Saint Thomas, and others, they spent there. They were foreigners unknown, without revenues, money, or relations, barely able to support themselves by their humble efforts. 'As they were destitute,' says Saint Basil, 'it is evident that they must have laboured much to provide themselves with the necessaries of life.'[16] Landolph of Saxony has, moreover, written (and let this be a consolation for the poor), that 'Mary lived there in the midst of such poverty that at times she had not even a bit of bread to give to her Son, when, urged by hunger, He asked for it.'[17]

After the death of Herod, Saint Matthew relates, the angel again appeared to Saint Joseph in a dream, and directed him to return to Judea. Saint Bonaventure, speaking of this return, considers how much greater the Blessed Virgin's sufferings must have been on account of the pains of Jesus being so much increased, as He was then about seven years of age—an age, re marks the Saint, at which 'He was too big to be carried, and not strong enough to walk without assistance.'[18]

The sight, then, of Jesus and Mary wandering as fugitives through the world teaches us that we also must live as pilgrims here below, detached from the goods which the world offers us, and which we must soon leave to enter eternity : " We have not here a lasting city, but seek one that is to come."[19] To which Saint Augustine adds : 'Thou art a guest ; thou givest a look, and passest on.'[20] It also teaches us to embrace crosses, for without them we cannot live in this world. Blessed Veronica da Binasco, an Augustinian nun, was carried in spirit to accompany Mary with the Infant

[16] Cum enim essent egeni, manifestum est quod sudores frequentabant, necessaria vitæ inde sibi quærentes.—*Const. Mon.* c. .

[17] Aliquando filius famem patiens panem petit, nec unde dare mater habuit.—*Vit. Christi*, p. 1. cap. xiii.

[18] Nunc sic magnus est quod portari non prævalet, et sic parvus quod per se ire non potest.—*In Vita C.* cap. xiii.

[19] Non enim habemus hic manentem civitatem, sed futuram inquirimus. *Heb.* xiii. 14.

[20] Hospes es, vides, et transis.

Jesus on their journey into Egypt; and after it the
Divine Mother said, 'Daughter, thou hast seen with
how much difficulty we have reached this country;
now learn that no one receives graces without suffering.'[21]   Whoever wishes to feel less the sufferings of
this life must go in company with Jesus and Mary:
"Take the Child and His Mother."[22]   All sufferings
become light, and even sweet and desirable, to him
who by his love bears this Son and this Mother in his
heart.   Let us, then, love them; let us console Mary
by welcoming in our hearts her Son, whom men even
now continue to persecute by their sins.

EXAMPLE.

The most holy Virgin one day appeared to Blessed
Collette, a Franciscan nun, and showed her the Infant
Jesus in a basin, torn to pieces, and then said: 'Thus
it is that sinners continually treat my Son, renewing
His death and my sorrows.   My daughter, pray for
them, that they may be converted.'[23]   To this we may
add another vision, which the venerable sister Joanna
of Jesus and Mary, also a Franciscan nun, had.   She
was cne day meditating on the Infant Jesus persecuted
by Herod, when she heard a great noise, as of armed
men pursuing some one; and immediately she saw before her a most beautiful child, who, all out of breath
and running, exclaimed: 'O my Joanna, help Me, conceal Me!   I am Jesus of Nazareth; I am flying from
sinners, who wish to kill Me, and persecute Me as
Herod did.   Do thou save Me.'[24]

PRAYER.

Then, O Mary, even after thy Son hath died by the
hands of men, who persecuted Him unto death, these

---

[21] Boll. 13 Jan. Vit. l. 4. c. 6.
[22] Accipe puerum et matrem ejus.—*Matt.* ii. 13.
[23] Boll. 6 Mart. Summ. Virt. c. 3.
[24] Ap. p. Genov. Serv. Dol. di Mar. †

ungrateful men have not yet ceased persecuting Him by their sins, and continue to afflict thee, O sorrowful Mother! And, O God, I also have been one of these. Ah, my most sweet Mother, obtain me tears to weep over such ingratitude. By the sufferings thou didst endure in thy journey to Egypt, assist me in the journey in which I am now engaged towards eternity; that thus I may at length be united with thee in loving my persecuted Saviour in the kingdom of the blessed. Amen.

ON THE THIRD DOLOUR.

Of the Loss of Jesus in the Temple.

The Apostle Saint James says that our perfection consists in the virtue of patience. "And patience hath a perfect work, that you may be perfect and entire, failing in nothing."[1] Our Lord having, then, given us the blessed Virgin Mary as a model of perfection, it was necessary that she should be laden with sorrows, that in her we might admire heroic patience, and endeavour to imitate it. The sorrow which we have this day to consider was one of the greatest that Mary had to endure in her life,—the loss of her Son in the temple. He who is born blind feels but little the privation of the light of day; but he who has once enjoyed it, and loses it by becoming blind, indeed suffers much. Thus it is also with those unhappy souls who, blinded by the mire of this world, have but little knowledge of God— they suffer but little at not finding Him; but, on the other hand, he who, illumined by celestial light, has become worthy to find by love the sweet presence of the supreme good, O God, how bitterly does he grieve

[1] Patientia autem opus perfectum habet: ut sitis perfecti et integri, in nullo deficientes.—*Jac.* i. 4.

when he finds himself deprived of it! Hence, let us
see how much Mary must have suffered from this third
sword of sorrow which pierced her heart, when, having
lost her Jesus in Jerusalem for three days, she was deprived of His most sweet presence, accustomed as she
was constantly to enjoy it.

St. Luke relates, in the second chapter of his Gospel,
that the Blessed Virgin, with her spouse St. Joseph,
and Jesus, was accustomed every year at the paschal
solemnity to visit the temple. When her Son was
twelve years of age, she went as usual, and Jesus remained in Jerusalem. Mary did not at once perceive
it, thinking He was in company with others. When
she reached Nazareth, she inquired for her Son; but
not finding Him, she immediately returned to Jerusalem to seek for Him, and only found Him after three
days. Now let us imagine what anxiety this afflicted
Mother must have experienced in those three days during which she was seeking everywhere for her Son,
and inquiring for Him with the spouse in the Canticles: " Have you seen him whom my soul loveth ?"[2]
But she could have no tidings of Him. O, with how
far greater tenderness must Mary, overcome by fatigue,
and having not yet found her beloved Son, have repeated those words of Ruben, concerning his brother
Joseph : " The boy doth not appear; and whither shall
I go ?"[3] ' My Jesus doth not appear, and I no longer
know what to do to find Him; but where shall I go
without my treasure ?' Weeping continually, with how
much truth did she repeat with David, during those
three days, " My tears have been my bread day and
night, whilst it is said to me daily : Where is thy
God ?"[4] Wherefore Pelbart, with reason, says, that
' during those nights the afflicted Mary did not sleep ;
she was constantly weeping, and entreating God that

<hr />

[2] Num quem diligit anima mea, vidistis ?—*Cant.* iii. 3.
[3] Puer non comparet, et ego quo ibo ?—*Gen.* xxxvii. 30.
[4] Fuerunt mihi lacrymæ meæ panes die ac nocte, dum dicitur mihi quotidie : Ubi est Deus tuus ?—*Ps.* xli. 4.

He would enable her to find her Son.'[5] Frequently, during that time, according to St. Bernard, she addressed her Son in the words of the spouse in the Canticles: "Show me where thou feedest, where thou liest in the mid-day, lest I begin to wander."[6] My Son, tell me where Thou art, that I may no longer wander, seeking Thee in vain.

There are some who assert, and not without reason, that this dolour was not only one of the greatest, but the greatest and most painful of all. For, in the first place, Mary, in her other dolours, had Jesus with her: she suffered when Saint Simeon prophesied to her in the temple; she suffered in the flight into Egypt; but still in company with Jesus; but in this dolour she suffered far from Jesus, not knowing where He was: "And the light of my eyes itself is not with me."[7] Thus weeping she then said, ' Ah, the light of my eyes, my dear Jesus, is no longer with me; He is far from me, and I know not whither He is gone.' Origen says that through the love which this holy Mother bore her Son, ' she suffered more in this loss of Jesus than any martyr ever suffered in the separation of his soul from his body.'[8] Ah, too long indeed were those three days for Mary; they seemed three ages; they were all bitterness, for there was none to comfort her. And who can ever comfort me, she said with Jeremias, who can console me, since He who alone could do so is far from me? and therefore my eyes can never weep enough: "Therefore do I weep, and my eyes run down with water: because the Comforter . . . is far from me."[9] And with Tobias she repeated, "What manner of joy shall be

<hr />

[5] Illas noctes insomnes duxit in lacrymosis orationibus, Deum deprecando, ut daret sibi reperire Filium.—*Stell.* l. 3, p. 4, a. 3.

[6] Indica mihi, quem diligit anima mea, ubi pascas, ubi cubes in meridie, ne vagari incipiam.— *Cant.* i. 6.

[7] Lumen oculorum meorum, et ipsum non est mecum.—*Ps.* xxxvii. 11.

[8] Vehementer doluit, quia vehementer amabat. Plus doluit de ejus amissione, quam aliquis martyr dolorem sentiat de animæ a corpore separatione.—*Hom. infr. Oct. Ep.* †

[9] Idcirco ego plorans, et oculus meus deducens aquas: quia longe factus est a me consolator.—*Thren.* i. 16.

to me who sit in darkness, and see not the light of heaven ?"[10]

In the second place, Mary, in all her other sorrows, well understood their cause — the redemption of the world, the Divine will ; but in this she knew not the cause of the absence of her Son. 'The sorrowful Mother,' says Lanspergius, 'was grieved at the absence of Jesus, because, in her humility, she considered herself unworthy to remain longer with or to attend upon Him on earth, and have the charge of so great a treasure.'[11] 'And who knows,' perhaps she thought within herself, 'maybe I have not served Him as I ought ; perhaps I have been guilty of some negligence, for which He has left me.' 'They sought Him,' says Origen, 'lest perchance He had entirely left them.'[12] It is certain that, to a soul which loves God, there can be no greater pain than the fear of having displeased Him. Therefore in this sorrow alone did Mary complain, lovingly expostulating with Jesus, after she had found Him : "Son, why hast Thou done so to us ? Thy father and I have sought Thee sorrowing."[13] By these words she had no idea of reproving Jesus, as heretics blasphemously assert, but only meant to express to Him the grief proceeding from the great love she bore Him, which she had experienced during His absence : 'It was not a rebuke,' says Denis the Carthusian, 'but a loving complaint.'[14] In fine, this sword so cruelly pierced the heart of the most holy Virgin, that the blessd Benvenuta, desiring one day to share the holy Mother's pain in this dolour, and entreating her for this favour, Mary appeared to her with the Infant

---

[10] Quale gaudium mihi erit, qui in tenebris sedeo, et lumen cœli non video. —*Tob.* v. 12.

[11] Tristabatur ex humilitate, quia arbitrabatur se indignam cui tam pretiosus commissus fuerat thesaurus.—*Dom.* 2, *post Nat. exeg. Ev.*

[12] Quærebant eum, ne forte recessisset ab eis, ne relinquens eos ad alia transmigrasset, ad quod magis puto, ne revertisset ad cœlos.—*In Luc. Hom.* xix.

[13] Fili, quid fecisti nobis sic ? ecce pater tuus et ego dolentes quærebamus te.—*Luc.* ii. 48.

[14] Et est verbum hoc non quasi increpatio, sed quasi pia et amorosa conquæstio.—*In Luc.* ii.

Jesus in her arms; but while Benvenuta was enjoying the sight of this most beautiful child, in a moment she was deprived of it. So great was her grief, that she had recourse to Mary, entreating her to mitigate it, that it might not cause her death. In three days the holy Virgin again appeared, and said : ' Know, my daughter, that thy sorrow is only a small part of that which I endured when I lost my Son.'[15]

This sorrow of Mary ought, in the first place, to serve as a consolation to those souls who are desolate, and no longer enjoy, as they once enjoyed, the sweet presence of their Lord. They may weep, but they should weep in peace, as Mary wept the absence of her Son; and let them take courage, and not fear that on this account they have lost the Divine favour; for God Himself assured Saint Teresa, that ' no one is lost without knowing it ; and that no one is deceived without wishing to be deceived.' If our Lord withdraws Himself from the sight of a soul which loves Him, He does not, therefore, depart from the heart; He often conceals Himself from a soul, that she may seek Him with a more ardent desire and greater love. But whoever wishes to find Jesus, must seek Him, not amidst delights and the pleasures of the world, but amidst crosses and mortifications, as Mary sought Him : " we sought Thee sorrowing," as Mary said to her Son. ' Learn, then, from Mary,' says Origen, ' to seek Jesus.'[16]

Moreover, in this world she would seek no other good than Jesus. Job was not unhappy when he lost all that he possessed on earth ; riches, children, health, and honours, and even descended from a throne to a dunghill ; but because he had God with him, he was even then happy. Saint Augustine says, ' he had lost what God had given him, but he still had God Him-

---

[15] Marchese Diar. 30 Ott.
[16] Disce ubi eum quærentes reperiant, ut et tu quærens cum Joseph Mariaque reperias.—*Hom.* xviii. *in Luc.*

self.'[17]　Truly miserable and unhappy are those souls which have lost God. If Mary wept the absence of her Son for three days, how should sinners weep, who have lost divine grace, and to whom God says: "You are not my people, and I will not be yours."[18]　For this is the effect of sin; it separates the soul from God: "Your iniquities have divided between you and your God."[19]　Hence, if sinners possess all the riches of the earth, but have lost God, all, even in this world, becomes vanity and affliction to them, as Solomon confessed: "Behold, all is vanity and vexation of spirit."[20] But the greatest misfortune of these poor blind souls is, as St. Augustine observes, that 'if they lose an ox, they do not fail to go in search of it; if they lose a sheep, they use all diligence to find it; if they lose a beast of burden, they cannot rest; but when they lose their God, who is the supreme good, they eat, drink, and repose.'[21]

EXAMPLE.

In the Annual Letters of the Society of Jesus, it is related that in India a young man was leaving his room with the intention of committing a sin, when he heard a voice saying: 'Stop! where art thou going?' He turned round, and saw an image in relief, representing our Lady of Sorrows, who, drawing out the sword which was in her breast, said: 'Take this dagger and pierce my heart, rather than wound my Son by committing such a sin.' On hearing these words, the youth prostrated himself on the ground, and bursting into tears, with deep sorrow, asked and obtained pardon from God and our Blessed Lady.

---

[17] Amissis omnibus talis est, quia illum qui dederat omnia non amisit.—*Enarr. in Ps.* lv.

[18] Vos non populus meus, et ego non ero vester.—*Os.* i. 9.

[19] Iniquitates vestræ diviserunt inter vos et Deum vestrum.—*Is.* lix. 2.

[20] Ecce universa vanitas et afflictio spiritus.—*Eccl.* i. 14.

[21] Perdit homo bovem, et post eum vadit: perdit ovem, et solicite eam quærit: perdit asinum, et non quiescit. Perdit homo Deum, et comedit, et bibit, et quiescit. †

PRAYER.

O Blessed Virgin, why dost thou afflict thyself, seeking for thy lost Son? Is it that thou knowest not where He is? Knowest thou not that He is in thy heart? Art thou ignorant that He feeds amongst lilies? Thou thyself hast said it: "My Beloved to me, and I to Him, who feedeth among the lilies."[22] These, thy thoughts and affections, which are all humble, pure, and holy, are all lilies which invite thy Divine Spouse to dwell in thee. Ah, Mary, dost thou sigh after Jesus, thou who lovest none but Jesus? Leave sighs to me, and to so many sinners who love Him not, and who have lost Him by offending Him. My most amiable Mother, if through my fault thy Son is not yet returned to my soul, do thou obtain for me that I may find Him. I well know that He is found by those who seek Him: "The Lord is good to the soul that seeketh Him."[23] But do thou make me seek Him as I ought. Thou art the gate through which all find Jesus; through thee I also hope to find Him. Amen.

ON THE FOURTH DOLOUR.

On the Meeting of Mary with Jesus, when He was going to Death.

Saint Bernardine says,[1] that to form an idea of the greatness of Mary's grief in losing her Jesus by death, we must consider the love that this Mother bore to her Son. All mothers feel the sufferings of their children as their own. Hence, when the Canaanitish woman

---

[22] Dilectus meus mihi, et ego illi, qui pascitur inter lilia.—*Cant.* ii. 16.
[23] Bonus est Dominus . . . animæ quærenti illum.—*Thren.* iii. 25.
[1] T. iii. s. 45, p. 2.

entreated our Saviour to deliver her daughter from the devil that tormented her, she asked Him rather to pity her, the mother, than her daughter : " Have mercy on me, O Lord, Thou Son of David, my daughter is griev-ously troubled by a devil."[2] But what mother ever loved her son as Mary loved Jesus ? He was her only Son, reared amidst so many troubles ; a most amiable Son, and tenderly loving His Mother ; a Son who, at the same time that He was her Son, was also her God, who had come on earth to enkindle in the hearts of all the fire of Divine love, as He Himself declared : " I am come to cast fire on the earth, and what will I but that it be kindled ?"[3] Let us only imagine what a flame He must have enkindled in that pure heart of His holy Mother, void as it was of every earthly affection. In fine, the Blessed Virgin herself told Saint Bridget, 'that love had rendered her heart and that of her Son but one.'[4] That blending together of Servant and Mother, of Son and God, created in the heart of Mary a fire com-posed of a thousand flames. But the whole of this flame of love was afterwards, at the time of the Passion, changed into a sea of grief, when Saint Bernardine de-clares, ' that if all the sorrows of the world were united, they would not equal that of the glorious Virgin Mary.'[5] Yes, because, as Richard of St. Lawrence writes, ' the more tenderly this Mother loved, so much the more deeply was she wounded.'[6] The greater was her love for Him, the greater was her grief at the sight of His sufferings ; and especially when she met her Son, al-ready condemned to death, and bearing His cross to the place of punishment. This is the fourth sword of sorrow which we have this day to consider.

[2] Miserere mei, Domine, fili David : filia mea male a dæmonio vexatur.— *Matt.* xv. 22.
[3] Ignem veni mittere in terram, et quid volo nisi ut accendatur ?—*Luc.* xii. 49.
[4] Unum erat cor meum et cor Filii mei.
[5] Omnes dolores mundi . . . si essent simul conjuncti, non essent tot et tanti, quantus fuit dolor gloriosæ Virginis Mariæ.—*Serm. in die Ven. Sanct.*
[6] Quanto dilexit tenerius, tanto est vulnerata profundius.—*De Laud. Virg.* lib. iii. cap. 12.

The Blessed Virgin revealed to Saint Bridget, that when the time of the Passion of our Lord was approaching, her eyes were always filled with tears, as she thought of her beloved Son, whom she was about to lose on earth, and that the prospect of that approaching suffering caused her to be seized with fear, and a cold sweat to cover her whole body.[7] Behold, the appointed day at length came, and Jesus, in tears, went to take leave of His Mother, before going to death. Saint Bonaventure, contemplating Mary on that night, says : ' Thou didst spend it without sleep, and whilst others slept thou didst remain watching.'[8] In the morning the disciples of Jesus Christ came to this afflicted Mother, the one to bring her one account, the other another; but all were tidings of sorrow, verifying in her the prophecy of Jeremias : " Weeping, she hath wept in the night, and her tears are on her cheeks ; there is none to comfort her of all them that were dear to her."[9] Some then came to relate to her the cruel treatment of her Son in the house of Caiphas ; and others, the insults He had received from Herod. Finally—to come to our point, I omit all the rest—Saint John came, and announced to Mary, that the most unjust Pilate had already condemned Him to die on the cross. I say the most unjust Pilate ; for, as Saint Leo remarks, ' This unjust judge condemned Him to death with the same lips with which he had declared Him innocent.'[10] ' Ah, afflicted Mother,' said Saint John, ' thy Son is already condemned to death ; He is already gone forth, bearing Himself His cross, on His way to Calvary,' as the Saint afterwards related in his Gospel: " and bearing His own cross, He went forth to that place which is called

[7] Imminente passione Filii mei, lacrymæ erant in oculis ejus, et sudor in corpore præ timore.—*Rev.* lib. iv. cap. 70.

[8] Sine somno duxisti, et soporatis cæteris vigil permansisti.—*Off. de Comp. B.M.V.*

[9] Plorans ploravit in nocte, et lacrymæ ejus in maxillis ejus: non est qui consoletur eam ex omnibus caris ejus.—*Thren.* i. 2.

[10] Iisdem labiis misit ad crucem, quibus eum pronuntiaverat innocentem.—*De Pass.* s. 3.

Calvary."[11] 'Come, if thou desirest to see Him, and bid Him a last farewell, in some street through which He must pass.'

Mary goes with Saint John, and by the blood with which the way is sprinkled, she perceives that her Son has already passed. This she revealed to Saint Bridget: 'By the footsteps of my Son, I knew where He had passed : for along the way the ground was marked with blood.'[12] Saint Bonaventure[13] represents the afflicted Mother taking a shorter way, and placing herself at the corner of a street, to meet her afflicted Son as He was passing by. 'The most sorrowful Mother,' says Saint Bernard, 'met her most sorrowful Son.'[14] While Mary was waiting in that place, how much must she have heard said by the Jews, who soon recognised her, against her beloved Son, and perhaps even words of mocking against herself. Alas, what a scene of sorrows then presented itself before her!—the nails, the hammers, the cords, the fatal instruments of the death of her Son, all of which were borne before Him. And what a sword must the sound of that trumpet have been to her heart, which proclaimed the sentence pronounced against her Jesus ! But behold, the instruments, the trumpeter, and the executioners, have already passed ; she raised her eyes, and saw, O God ! a young man covered with blood and wounds from head to foot, a wreath of thorns on His head, and two heavy beams on His shoulders. She looked at Him, and hardly recognised Him, saying, with Isaias, " and we have seen Him, and there was no sightliness."[15] Yes, for the wounds, the bruises, and the clotted blood, gave Him the appearance of a leper: "we have thought

[11] Et bajulans sibi crucem, exivit in eum, qui dicitur Calvariæ, locum.—*Joan.* xix. 17.

[12] Ex vestigiis Filii mei cognoscebam incessum ejus : quo enim procedebat, apparebat terra infusa sanguine.—*Rev.* lib. i. cap. 10.

[13] De Vita C. cap. lxxvi.

[14] Mœstissima Mater mœstissimo Filio occurrit.

[15] Et vidimus eum, et non erat aspectus.—*Is.* liii. 2.

Him as it were a leper,"[16] so that He could no longer
be known: "and His look was, as it were, hidden and
despised; whereupon we esteemed Him not."[17]   But at
length love revealed Him to her, and as soon as she
knew that it indeed was He, ah what love and fear
must then have filled her heart! as Saint Peter of Alcantara says in his meditations.[18]   On the one hand
she desired to behold Him, and on the other she dreaded
so heart-rending a sight.   At length they looked at each
other.   The Son wiped from His eyes the clotted blood,
which, as it was revealed to Saint Bridget,[19] prevented
Him from seeing, and looked at His Mother, and the
Mother looked at her Son.   Ah, looks of bitter grief,
which, as so many arrows, pierced through and through
those two beautiful and loving souls.   When Margaret,
the daughter of Sir Thomas More, met her father on
his way to death, she could only exclaim, ' O father!
father!' and fell fainting at his feet.   Mary, at the
sight of her Son, on His way to Calvary, did not faint,
no, for it was not becoming, as Father Suarez remarks,[20]
that this Mother should lose the use of her reason; nor
did she die, for God reserved her for greater grief: but
though she did not die, her sorrow was enough to have
caused her a thousand deaths.

The Mother would have embraced Him, as Saint
Anselm says, but the guards thrust her aside with insults, and urged forward the suffering Lord; and Mary
followed Him.   Ah, holy Virgin, whither goest thou?
To Calvary.   And canst thou trust thyself to behold
Him, who is thy life, hanging on a cross?   "And thy
life shall be, as it were, hanging before thee."[21]   ' Ah,
stop, my Mother' (says Saint Lawrence Justinian, in
the name of the Son), 'where goest thou?   Where

---

[16] Et nos putavimus eum quasi leprosum.—*Is.* liii. 4.
[17] Et quasi absconditus vultus ejus et despectus, unde nec reputavimus
eum.—*Ib.* 3.
[18] P. i. c. iv. fer. 5.
[19] Rev. l. i. c. 10.; l. iv. c. 70.
[20] De Inc. q. 51, a. 3, § 2.
[21] Et erit vita tua quasi pendens ante te.— *Deut.* xxviii. 66.

wouldst thou come? If thou comest whither I go, thou
wilt be tortured with my sufferings, and I with thine.'[22]
But although the sight of her dying Jesus was to cost
her such bitter sorrow, the loving Mary will not leave
Him : the Son advanced, and the Mother followed, to
be also crucified with her Son, as the Abbot William
says : 'the Mother also took up her cross and followed,
to be crucified with Him.'[23] 'We even pity wild
beasts,'[24] as Saint John Chrysostom writes ; and did
we see a lioness following her cub to death, the sight
would move us to compassion. And shall we not also
be moved to compassion on seeing Mary follow her
immaculate Lamb to death? Let us, then, pity her, and
let us also accompany her Son and herself, by bearing
with patience the cross which our Lord imposes on us.
Saint John Chrysostom asks why Jesus Christ, in His
other sufferings, was pleased to endure them alone, but
in carrying His cross was assisted by the Cyrenean?
He replies, that it was 'that thou mayest understand that
the cross of Christ is not sufficient without thine.'[25]

EXAMPLE.

Our Saviour one day appeared to Sister Diomira, a
nun in Florence, and said, 'Think of Me, and love Me,
and I will think of thee and love thee.' At the same
time He presented her with a bunch of flowers and a
cross, signifying thereby that the consolations of the
Saints in this world are always to be accompanied by
the cross. The cross unites souls to God. Blessed
Jerome Emilian, when a soldier, and loaded with sins,
was shut up by his enemies in a tower. There, moved
by his misfortunes, and enlightened by God to change
his life, he had recourse to the ever-blessed Virgin ;

[22] Ut quid venisti, mater mea ? Dolor tuus meum auget, cruciatus tuus
transfigit me.—*De Triumph. Chr. Agone*, cap. xi.
[23] Tollebat et mater crucem suam, et sequebatur eum, crucifigenda cum
ipso.—*Delrio in Cant.* vii. 7.
[24] Ferarum etiam miseremur.—*In Phil. Hom.* 4.
[25] Ut intelligas, Christi crucem non sufficere sine tua.

and from that time, by the help of this Divine Mother, he began to lead the life of a saint, so much so that he merited once to see the very high place which God had prepared for him in heaven. He became the founder of the religious order of the Somaschi, died as a saint, and has lately been canonized by the holy Church.

PRAYER.

My sorrowful Mother, by the merit of that grief which thou didst feel in seeing thy beloved Jesus led to death, obtain me the grace, that I also may bear with patience the crosses which God sends me. Happy indeed shall I be, if I only know how to accompany thee with my cross until death. Thou with thy Jesus— and you were both innocent—hast carried a far heavier cross; and shall I, a sinner, who have deserved hell, refuse to carry mine? Ah, immaculate Virgin, from thee do I hope for help to bear all crosses with patience. Amen.

ON THE FIFTH DOLOUR.

Of the Death of Jesus.

WE have now to witness a new kind of martyrdom —a Mother condemned to see an innocent Son, and one whom she loves with the whole affection of her soul, cruelly tormented and put to death before her own eyes: "There stood by the cross of Jesus His Mother."[1] Saint John believed that in these words he had said enough of Mary's martyrdom. Consider her at the foot of the cross in the presence of her dying Son, and then see if there be sorrow like unto her sorrow. Let us remain for a while this day on Calvary,

---

[1] Stabant autem juxta crucem Jesu mater ejus, &c.—*Joan.* xix. 25.

and consider the fifth sword which, in the death of Jesus, transfixed the heart of Mary.

As soon as our agonized Redeemer had reached the Mount of Calvary, the executioners stripped Him of His clothes, and piercing His hands and feet 'not with sharp but with blunt nails,' as Saint Bernard says, to torment Him more,[2] they fastened Him on the cross. Having crucified Him, they planted the cross, and thus left Him to die. The executioners left Him; but not so Mary. She then drew nearer to the cross, to be present at His death : 'I did not leave Him' (thus the Blessed Virgin revealed to Saint Bridget), 'but stood nearer to the cross.'[3] 'But what did it avail thee, O Lady,' says Saint Bonaventure, 'to go to Calvary, and see this Son expire? Shame should have prevented thee ; for His disgrace was thine, since thou wert His Mother. At least, horror of witnessing such a crime as the crucifixion of a God by His own creatures, should have prevented thee from going there.' But the same Saint answers, 'Ah, thy heart did not then think of its own sorrows, but of the sufferings and death of thy dear Son,'[4] and therefore thou wouldst thyself be present, at least to compassionate Him. 'Ah, true Mother,' says the Abbot William, 'most loving Mother, whom not even the fear of death could separate from thy beloved Son.'[5] But, O God, what a cruel sight was it there to behold this Son in agony on the cross, and at its foot this Mother in agony, suffering all the torments endured by her Son! Listen to the words in which Mary revealed to Saint Bridget the sorrowful state in which she saw her dying Son on the cross : 'My dear Jesus was breathless, exhausted, and in His last agony on the cross ; His eyes were sunk, half-

---

[2] *Serm.* ii. *de Pass.*

[3] Ego non separabar ab eo, et stabam vicinior cruci ejus.—*Rev.* l. i. c. 35.

[4] O domina . . . quare ivisti ad Calvariæ locum ? . . . Cur te non retinuit pudor mulieris, cur te non retinuit horror facinoris? Non considerabat cor tuum . . . horrorem sed dolorem.—*Stim. Am.* P. i. cap. 3.

[5] Plane mater, quæ nec in terrore mortis Filium deserebat.—*Serm.* iv. *de assump.*

closed, and lifeless; His lips hanging, and His mouth open; His cheeks hollow and drawn in; His face elongated, His nose sharp, His countenance sad: His head had fallen on His breast, His hair was black with blood, His stomach collapsed, His arms and legs stiff, and His whole body covered with wounds and blood.'[6]

All these sufferings of Jesus were also those of Mary: 'Every torture inflicted on the body of Jesus,' says Saint Jerome, 'was a wound in the heart of the Mother.'[7] 'Whoever then was present on the Mount of Calvary,' says Saint John Chrysostom, 'might see two altars, on which two great sacrifices were consummated; the one in the body of Jesus, the other in the heart of Mary.' Nay, better still may we say with Saint Bonaventure, 'there was but one altar—that of the cross of the Son, on which, together with this Divine Lamb, the victim, the Mother was also sacrificed;' therefore the Saint asks this Mother, 'O Lady, where art thou? near the cross? Nay, rather, thou art on the cross, crucified, sacrificing thyself with thy Son.'[8] Saint Augustine assures us of the same thing: 'The cross and nails of the Son were also those of His Mother; with Christ crucified the Mother was also crucified.'[9] Yes; for, as Saint Bernard says, 'Love inflicted on the heart of Mary the tortures caused by the nails in the body of Jesus.'[10] So much so, that, as Saint Bernardine writes, 'At the same time that the Son sacrificed His body, the Mother sacrificed her soul.'[11]

Mothers ordinarily fly from the presence of their dying children; but when a mother is obliged to witness such a scene, she procures all possible relief for

---

[6] Rev. lib. i. cap. 10; lib. iv. cap. 70.

[7] Quot læsiones in corpore Christi, tot vulnera in corde matris.

[8] O domina mea, ubi stabas? Numquid tantum juxta crucem? Imo certe in cruce cum Filio ibi crucifixa eras secum.—*Stim. Am.* P. i. cap. 3.

[9] Crux et clavi Filii fuerunt et Matris; Christo crucifixo crucifigebatur et Mater. †

[10] Quod in carne Christi agebant clavi, in Virginis mente affectus erga Filium.

[11] Dum ille corpus, ista spiritum immolabat.—*Serm. in Fer.* vi. *post Dom. Oliv.*

her child; she arranges his bed, that he may be more at ease; she administers refreshments to him; and thus the poor mother soothes her own grief. Ah, most afflicted of all Mothers! O Mary, thou hast to witness the agony of thy dying Jesus; but thou canst administer Him no relief. Mary heard her Son exclaim, 'I thirst,' but she could not even give Him a drop of water to refresh Him in that great thirst. She could only say, as Saint Vincent Ferrer remarks, ' My Son, I have only the water of tears.'[12] She saw that on that bed of torture her Son, suspended by three nails, could find no repose; she would have clasped Him in her arms to give Him relief, or that at least He might there have expired; but she could not. ' In vain,' says Saint Bernard, ' did she extend her arms; they sank back empty on her breast.'[13] She beheld that poor Son, who in His sea of grief sought consolation, as it was foretold by the prophet, but in vain: "I have trodden the winepress alone; I looked about, and there was none to help; I sought, and there was none to give aid."[14] But who amongst men would console Him, since all were enemies? Even on the cross He was taunted and blasphemed on all sides: "and they that passed by, blasphemed Him, wagging their heads."[15] Some said in His face, " If thou be the Son of God, come down from the cross."[16] Others, " He saved others, Himself He cannot save."[17] Again, " If He be the King of Israel, let Him now come down from the cross."[18] Our Blessed Lady herself said to St. Bridget,[19] ' I heard some say that my Son was a

---

12 O Fili, non habeo nisi aquam lacrymarum.—*Serm. in Fer.* vi. *Parasc.*

13 Volebat amplecti Christum in alto pendentem, sed manus frustra protensæ in se complexæ redibant.—*De Lament. B.M.V.*

14 Torcular calcavi solus . . . Circumspexi, et non erat auxiliator: quæsivi, et non fuit qui adjuvaret.—*Is.* lxiii. 3, 5.

15 Prætereuntes autem blasphemabant eum, moventes capita sua.—*Matt.* xxvii. 39.

16 Si Filius Dei es, descende de cruce.—*Ib.* 40.

17 Alios salvos fecit, seipsum non potest salvum facere.—*Ib.* **42**

18 Si Rex Israel est, descendat nunc de cruce.—*Ib.* 42.

19 Rev. lib. iv. cap. 70.

thief; others, that He was an impostor; others, that no one deserved death more than He did; and every word was a new sword of grief to my heart.'

But that which the most increased the sorrows which Mary endured through compassion for her Son, was hearing Him complain on the cross that even His Eternal Father had abandoned Him: " My God, My God, why hast Thou forsaken Me?"[20] Words which the Divine Mother told the same Saint Bridget, could never, during her whole life, depart from her mind.[21] So that the afflicted Mother saw her Jesus suffering on every side; she desired to comfort Him, but could not. And that which grieved her the most was to see that she herself, by her presence and sorrow, increased the sufferings of her Son. 'The grief,' says Saint Bernard, ' which filled Mary's heart, as a torrent flowed into and embittered the heart of Jesus.'[22] ' So much so,' says the same Saint, ' that Jesus on the cross suffered more from compassion for His Mother than from His own torments.' He thus speaks in the name of our Blessed Lady: ' I stood with my eyes fixed on Him, and His on me, and He grieved more for me than for Himself.'[23] And then, speaking of Mary beside her dying Son, he says, 'that she lived dying without being able to die:' ' Near the cross of Christ His Mother stood half-dead; she spoke not; dying she lived, and living she died; nor could she die, for death was her very life.'[24] Passino writes that Jesus Christ Himself one day, speaking to blessed Baptista Varani of Camerino, assured her that when on the cross, so great was His affliction at seeing His Mother at His feet in such bitter anguish, that compassion for her caused Him to die without con-

---

[20] Deus meus, Deus meus, ut quid dereliquisti me?—*Matt.* xxvii. 46.
[21] Rev. lib. iv. cap. 70.
[22] Repleta Matre, ad Filium redundaret inundatio amaritudinis.
[23] Stabam et ego videns eum: et ipse videns me, plus dolebat de me quam de se.—*De Lament. B.V.M.*
[24] Juxta crucem Christi stabat emortua mater . . . vox illi non erat . . . quasi mortua vivens vivebat moriens, moriebatur vivens, nec mori poterat quæ vivens mortua erat.—*Ib.*

solation; so much so, that the blessed Baptista, being supernaturally enlightened as to the greatness of this suffering of Jesus, exclaimed, 'O Lord, tell me no more of this Thy sorrow, for I can no longer bear it.'[25]

'All,' says Simon of Cassia, 'who then saw this Mother silent, and not uttering a complaint in the midst of such great suffering, were filled with astonishment.'[26] But if Mary's lips were silent, her heart was not so, for she incessantly offered the life of her Son to the Divine Justice for our salvation. Therefore we know that by the merits of her dolours she coöperated in our birth to the life of grace; and hence we are the children of her sorrows. 'Christ,' says Lanspergius, 'was pleased that she, the coöperatress in our redemption, and whom He had determined to give us for our Mother, should be there present; for it was at the foot of the cross that she was to bring us, her children, forth.'[27] If any consolation entered that sea of bitterness, the heart of Mary, the only one was this, that she knew that by her sorrows she was leading us to eternal salvation, as Jesus Himself revealed to Saint Bridget: 'My Mother Mary, on account of her compassion and love, was made the Mother of all in heaven and on earth.'[28] And indeed these were the last words with which Jesus bid her farewell before His death: this was His last recommendation, leaving us to her for her children in the person of Saint John: "Woman, behold thy son."[29] From that time Mary began to perform this good office of a Mother for us; for Saint Peter Damian attests, 'that by the prayers of Mary, who stood between the cross of the good thief and that of her Son, the thief was converted and saved, and thereby she re-

[25] Boll. 31 Maii, Vit. rev. § 2.

[26] Stupebant omnes qui noverant hujus hominis matrem, quod etiam in tantæ angustiæ pressura silentium servabat. †

[27] Voluit eam Christus cooperatricem nostræ redemptionis adstare, quam nobis constituerat dare matrem: debebat enim ipsa sub cruce nos parere filios. —*Hom.* xliv. *de Pass. D.*

[28] Maria, mater mea, propter compassionem et charitatem, facta est mater omnium in cœlis et in terra.—*Rev.* l. viii. c. 12.

[29] Mulier, ecce filius tuus.—*Joan.* xix. 26.

paid a former service.'[30]   For, as other authors also relate, this thief had been kind to Jesus and Mary on
their journey to Egypt; and this same office the Blessed
Virgin has ever continued, and still continues, to perform.

EXAMPLE.

A young man in Perugia promised the devil, that
if he would enable him to attain a sinful object he had
in view, he would give him his soul; and he gave him
a written contract to this effect, signed in his own blood.
When the crime had been committed, the devil demanded the performance of the promise; and for this
purpose led him to the brink of a well, at the same
time threatening, that if he did not throw himself in, he
would drag him, body and soul, to hell. The wretched
youth, thinking that it would be impossible to escape
from his hands, got on the little parapet to cast himself
in; but terrified at the idea of death, he told the devil
that he had not courage to take the leap, but that if he
was determined on his death, he must push him in.
The young man wore a scapular of the *Dolours of Mary;*
the devil therefore said, ' Take off that scapular, and then
I will push thee in.' But the youth, discovering in the
scapular the protection still vouchsafed to him by the Divine Mother, refused to do so, and at length, after much
altercation, the devil, filled with confusion, departed; and
the sinner, grateful to his sorrowful Mother, went to
thank her, and, penitent for his sins, presented as a votive
offering to her altar, in the church of Santa Maria la
Nuova in Perugia, a picture of what had taken place.[31]

PRAYER.

Ah, Mother, the most sorrowful of all mothers, thy
Son is, then, dead; that Son so amiable, and who loved

<hr>

[30] Idcirco resipuit bonus latro, quia B. Virgo inter cruces Filii et latronis
posita, Filium pro latrone deprecabatur, hoc suo beneficio antiquum latronis
obsequium recompensans.—*Ap. Silveira Com.* l. 8, c. 14, q. 8.
[31] Siniscalchi, Marav. di M. cons. 16.

thee so much! Weep, then, for thou hast reason to weep. Who can ever console thee? The thought alone, that Jesus by His death conquered hell, opened heaven until then closed to men, and gained so many souls, can console thee. From that throne of the cross He will reign in so many hearts, which, conquered by His love, will serve Him with love. Disdain not, in the mean time, O my Mother, to keep me near thee, to weep with thee, since I have so much reason to weep for the crimes by which I have offended Him. Ah, Mother of Mercy, I hope, first, through the death of my Redeemer, and then through thy sorrows, to obtain pardon and eternal salvation. Amen.

ON THE SIXTH DOLOUR.

The Piercing of the Side of Jesus, and His descent from the Cross.

"O, all ye that pass by the way, attend, and see if there be any sorrow like to my sorrow."[1] Devout souls, listen to what the sorrowful Mary says this day: ' My beloved children, I do not wish you to console me ; no, for my soul is no longer susceptible of consolation in this world after the death of my dear Jesus. If you wish to please me, this is what I ask of you ; behold me, and see if there ever has been in the world a grief like mine, in seeing Him who was all my love torn from me with such cruelty.' But, my sovereign Lady, since thou wilt not be consoled, and hast so great a thirst for sufferings, I must tell thee that, even with the death of thy Son, thy sorrows have not ended. On this day thou wilt be wounded by another sword of sorrow, a

---

[1] O vos omnes qui transitis per viam, attendite, et videte si est dolor sicut dolor meus.—*Thren.* i. 12.

cruel lance will pierce the side of thy Son already dead, and thou hast to receive Him in thine arms after He is taken down from the cross. And now we are to consider the Sixth Dolour which afflicted this poor Mother. Attend and weep. Hitherto the dolours of Mary tortured her one by one; on this day they are all, as it were, united to assail her.

It is enough to tell a mother that her son is dead, to excite all her love towards her lost child. Some persons, that they may lessen a mother's grief, remind her of the displeasure at one time caused by her departed child. But I, my Queen, did I thus wish to lighten thy grief for the death of Jesus, of what displeasure that He ever caused thee could I remind thee? No, indeed. He always loved thee, always obeyed thee, and always respected thee. Now thou hast lost Him, who can ever tell thy grief? Do thou explain it, thou who hast experienced it. A devout author says, that when our beloved Redeemer was dead, the first care of the great Mother was to accompany in spirit the most holy soul of her Son, and present it to the Eternal Father. 'I present Thee, O my God,' Mary must then have said, 'the Immaculate soul of Thine and my Son; He has now obeyed Thee unto death; do Thou, then, receive it in Thine arms. Thy justice is now satisfied, Thy will is accomplished; behold, the great sacrifice to Thy eternal glory is consummated.' Then, turning towards the lifeless members of her Jesus, 'O wounds,' she said, 'O wounds of love, I adore you, and in you do I rejoice; for by your means salvation is given to the world. You will remain open in the body of my Son, and be the refuge of those who have recourse to you. O, how many, through you, will receive the pardon of their sins, and by you be inflamed with love for the supreme good!'

That the joy of the following Paschal Sabbath might not be disturbed, the Jews desired that the body of Jesus should be taken down from the cross; but as

this could not be done unless the criminals were dead,
men came with iron bars to break our Lord's legs,
as they had already done those of the two thieves
who were crucified with Him.   Mary was still weeping over the death of her Son, when she saw these
armed men advancing towards her Jesus.   At this
sight she first trembled with fear, and then exclaimed:
'Ah, my Son is already dead; cease to outrage Him;
torment me no more, who am His poor Mother.'   She
implored them, writes Saint Bonaventure, 'not to break
His legs.'[2]   But while she thus spoke, O God! she saw
a soldier brandish a lance, and pierce the side of Jesus:
"One of the soldiers with a spear opened His side, and
immediately there came out blood and water."[3]   At the
stroke of the spear the cross shook, and, as it was afterwards revealed to Saint Bridget, the heart of Jesus was
divided in two.[4]   There came out blood and water; for
only those few drops of blood remained, and even those
our Saviour was pleased to shed, that we might understand that He had no more blood to give us.   The injury of that stroke was inflicted on Jesus, but Mary
suffered its pain.   'Christ,' says the devout Lanspergius,
'shared this wound with His Mother; He received the
insult, His Mother endured its agony.'[5]   The holy fathers maintain that this was literally the sword foretold
to the Blessed Virgin by Saint Simeon: a sword, not a
material one, but one of grief, which transpierced her
blessed soul in the heart of Jesus, where it always dwelt.
Thus, amongst others, Saint Bernard says: "The lance
which opened His side passed through the soul of the
Blessed Virgin, which could never leave her Son's heart.'[6]

  [2] Hanc misericordiam mecum facite, ne ipsum confringatis, ut saltem in-
tegrum valeam tradere sepulturæ.   Non expedit, ut ejus crura frangantur:
videtis enim quod jam mortuus est et migravit.—*De Vit. Chr.* cap. lxxx.
  [3] Unus militum lancea latus ejus aperuit, et continuo exivit sanguis et
aqua.—*Joan.* xix. 34.
  [4] Ita ut ambæ partes essent in lancea.—*Rev.* lib. ii. c. 21.
  [5] Ipse quidem vulnus in corpore, sed beata Maria vulneris dolorem accepit
in mente.—*In Pass. Dom.* hom. lxv.
  [6] Lancea quæ ipsius aperuit latus, animam Virginis penetravit, quæ inde
nequebat avelli.—*In Sign. Magn.*

The divine Mother herself revealed the same thing to
Saint Bridget: 'When the spear was drawn out, the
point appeared red with blood : then, seeing the heart
of my most dear Son pierced, it seemed to me as if
my own heart was also pierced.'[7]   An angel told the
same Saint, 'that such were the sufferings of Mary, that
it was only by a miraculous interposition on the part of
God, that she did not die.'[8]   In her other dolours she
at least had her Son to compassionate her; but now she
has not even Him to pity her.

The afflicted Mother, fearing that other injuries
might still be inflicted on her Son, entreated Joseph of
Arimathea to obtain the body of her Jesus from Pilate,
that at least in death she might guard and protect it
from further outrage.   Joseph went, and represented to
Pilate the grief and desires of this afflicted Mother.
Saint Anselm[9] believes that compassion for the Mother
softened the heart of Pilate, and moved him to grant
her the body of the Saviour.   Jesus was then taken
down from the cross.   O most sacred Virgin, after thou
hast given thy Son to the world, with so great love, for
our salvation, behold the world now restores Him to
thee ; but, O God, in what state dost thou receive Him?
O world, said Mary, how dost thou return Him to me?
"My Son was white and ruddy;"[10] but thou returnest
Him to me blackened with bruises, and red—yes ! but
with the wounds which thou hast inflicted upon Him.
He was all fair and beautiful; but now there is no more
beauty in Him ; He is all disfigured.   His aspect enamoured all ; now He excites horror in all who behold
Him.   'O, how many swords,' says Saint Bonaventure,
'pierced the poor Mother's soul'[11] when she received the

[7] Cum extraheretur hasta, apparuit cuspis rubea sanguine. Tunc mihi
videbatur, quod quasi cor meum perforaretur, cum vidissem cor Filii mei
carissimi perforatum.—*Rev.* lib. i. cap. 10.

[8] Non parvum miraculum in hoc Deus tunc fecisse dignoscitur, cum Virgo
Mater tot et tantis doloribus intrinsecus sauciata, suum spiritum non emisit.
—*Serm. Ang.* c. 18.

[9] Dial. de Pass. c. 16.

[10] Dilectus meus candidus et rubicundus.—*Cant.* v. 10.

[11] O quot gladii animam matris pertransierunt!

body of her Son from the cross! Let us only consider
the anguish it would cause any mother to receive into
her arms the body of her lifeless son. It was revealed
to Saint Bridget,[12] that three ladders were placed against
the cross to take down the Sacred Body; the holy disciples first drew out the nails from the hands and feet,
and, according to Metaphrastes,[13] gave them to Mary.
Then one supported the upper part of the body of Jesus,
and the other the lower, and thus descended it from the
cross. Bernardine de Bustis describes the afflicted
Mother as standing, and extending her arms to meet her
dear Son; she embraced Him, and then sat at the foot
of the cross. His mouth was open, His eyes were dim;
she then examined his mangled flesh and uncovered
bones; she took off the crown, and saw the sad injuries
which the thorns had inflicted on that sacred head; she
saw the holes in His hands and feet, and thus addressed
Him: 'Ah, Son, to what has Thy love for men brought
Thee; and what evil hadst Thou done them, that they
should thus cruelly have tormented Thee? Thou wast
my father' (continues Bernardine de Bustis, in Mary's
name), 'Thou wast my brother, my spouse, my delight,
my glory; Thou wast my all.'[14] My Son, see my affliction, look at me, console me; but no, Thou no longer
lookest at me. Speak, say but a word, and console me;
but Thou speakest no more, for Thou art dead. Then,
turning to those barbarous instruments of torture, she
said, O cruel thorns, O cruel nails, O merciless spear,
how, how could you thus torture your Creator? But
why do I speak of thorns or nails? Alas! sinners, she
exclaimed, it is you who have thus cruelly treated my
Son.

Thus did Mary speak and complain of us. But what
would she now say, were she still susceptible of suffering? What would be her grief to see that men, notwith-

---

[12] Rev. l. 2, c. 21.   [13] Ap. Sur. 15 Aug.
[14] O Jesu, tu mihi Pater, tu mihi Sponsus, tu mihi Filius, tu mihi omnia
eras.—*Marial.* p. x. *Serm.* 1.

standing that her Son has died for them, still continue to torment and crucify Him by their sins ! Let us, at least, cease to torment this afflicted Mother; and if we have hitherto grieved her by our sins, let us now do all that she desires. She says, " Return, ye transgressors, to the heart."[15] Sinners, return to the wounded heart of my Jesus ; return as penitents, and He will welcome you. 'Flee from Him to Him,' she continues to say with the Abbot Guarric ; 'from the Judge to the Redeemer, from the tribunal to the cross.'[16] Our Blessed Lady herself revealed to St. Bridget,[17] that 'she closed the eyes of her Son, when He was taken down from the cross, but she could not close His arms;' Jesus Christ giving us thereby to understand that He desired to remain with His arms extended to receive all penitent sinners who return to Him. ' O world,' continues Mary, " behold, then, thy time is the time of lovers."[18] 'Now that my Son has died to save thee, it is no longer for thee a time of fear, but one of love—a time to love Him, who to show thee the love He bore thee was pleased to suffer so much.' 'The heart of Jesus,' says St. Bernard, ' was wounded, that through the visible wound, the invisible wound of love might be seen.'[19] 'If, then,' concludes Mary, in the words of Blessed Raymond Jordano, ' my Son by excess of love was pleased that His side should be opened, that He might give thee His heart, it is right, O man, that thou in return shouldst also give Him thine.'[20] And if you desire, O children of Mary, to find a place in the heart of Jesus, without fear of being rejected, 'go,' says Ubertino da Casale, 'go with Mary; for she will obtain the grace for

---

[15] Redite, prævaricatores, ad cor.—*Is.* xlvi. 8.

[16] Ab ipso fuge ad ipsum, a judice ad redemptorem, a tribunali ad crucem.—*In Dom. Palm.* §. 4.

[17] Rev. l. 4, c. 70.

[18] Et ecce tempus tuum, tempus amantium.—*Ezech.* xvi. 8.

[19] Vulneratum est cor Christi, ut per vulnus visibile, vulnus amoris invisibile videamus.—*Lib. de Pass.* c. 3.

[20] Præ nimio amore aperuit sibi latus, ut præberet cor suum. †

you.'[21] Of this you have a proof in the following bea‐
tiful example.

EXAMPLE.

The disciple relates,[22] that there was a poor sinner
who, among other crimes which he had committed, had
killed his father and a brother, and therefore was a
fugitive. One day in Lent, hearing a sermon on the
Divine mercy, he went to confess his sins to the preacher
himself. The confessor, on hearing the enormous crimes
which he had committed, sent him to an altar of Mary
in Sorrow, that she might obtain him contrition, and
the pardon of his sins. The sinner obeyed, and began
to pray; when, behold, he suddenly dropped down dead
from excess of grief. On the following day, when the
priest recommended the deceased to the prayers of the
people, a white dove appeared in the church, and let a
card drop at his feet. The priest took it up, and found
the following words written upon it : ' The soul of the
deceased, on leaving his body, went straight to heaven.
Continue thou to preach the infinite mercy of God.'

PRAYER.

O afflicted Virgin ! O soul great in virtue but great
also in sorrow, for the one and the other took their rise
in that immense love with which thy heart was inflamed
towards God, for thou couldst love Him alone ; ah,
Mother, pity me, for instead of loving God I have greatly
offended Him. Thy sorrows encourage me to hope for
pardon. But this is not enough ; I wish to love my
Lord ; and who can better obtain me this love than thou,
who art the Mother of fair love ? Ah, Mary, thou com‐
fortest all ; console me also. Amen.

[21] Fili hujus matris, ingredere cum ipsa intra penetralia cordis Jesu.—
Arb. Vit. l. 4, c. 24.
[22] Promt. ex Litt. M. 21.

ON THE SEVENTH DOLOUR.

The Burial of Jesus.

WHEN a mother is by the side of her suffering and dying child, she undoubtedly feels and suffers all his pains ; but after he is actually dead, when, before the body is carried to the grave, the afflicted mother must bid her child a last farewell ; then, indeed, the thought that she is to see him no more is a grief which exceeds all other griefs. Behold the last sword of Mary's sorrow, which we have now to consider ; for after witnessing the death of her Son on the cross, and embracing for a last time His lifeless body, this blessed Mother had to leave Him in the sepulchre, never more to enjoy His beloved presence on earth.

That we may better understand this last dolour, we will return to Calvary and consider the afflicted Mother, who still holds the lifeless body of her Son clasped in her arms. O my Son, she seemed to say in the words of Job, my Son, " Thou art changed to be cruel towards me."[1] Yes, for all Thy noble qualities, Thy beauty, grace, and virtues, Thy engaging manners, all the marks of special love which Thou hast bestowed upon me, the peculiar favours Thou hast granted me,—all are now changed into grief, and as so many arrows pierce my heart, and the more they have excited me to love Thee, so much the more cruelly do they now make me feel Thy loss. Ah, my own beloved Son, in losing Thee I have lost all. Thus does St. Bernard speak in her name : ' O truly-begotten of God, Thou wast to me a father, a son, a spouse : Thou wast my very soul ! Now I am

---

[1] Mutatus es mihi in crudelem.—*Job.* xxx. 21.

deprived of my father, widowed of my spouse, a deso·
late, childless Mother; having lost my only Son, I have
lost all.'[2]

Thus was Mary, with her Son locked in her arms,
absorbed in grief. The holy disciples, fearful that the
poor Mother might die of grief, approached her to take
the body of her Son from her arms, to bear it away for
burial. This they did with gentle and respectful violence, and having embalmed it, they wrapped it in a
linen cloth which was already prepared. On this cloth,
which is still preserved at Turin, our Lord was pleased
to leave to the world an impression of His sacred body.
The disciples then bore Him to the tomb. To do this,
they first of all raised the sacred body on their shoulders, and then the mournful train set forth; choirs of
angels from heaven accompanied it; the holy women
followed, and with them the afflicted Mother also followed her Son to the place of burial. When they had
reached the appointed place, ' O, how willingly would
Mary have there buried herself alive with her Son, had
such been His will!' for this she herself revealed to
St. Bridget.[3] But such not being the Divine will, there
are many authors who say that she accompanied the
sacred body of Jesus into the sepulchre, where, according to Baronius,[4] the disciples also deposited the nails
and the crown of thorns. In raising the stone to close
up the entrance, the holy disciples of the Saviour had to
approach our Blessed Lady, and say: Now, O Lady, we
must close the sepulchre: forgive us, look once more at
thy Son, and bid Him a last farewell. Then my beloved Son (for thus must the afflicted Mother have
spoken); then I shall see Thee no more? Receive,
therefore, on this last occasion that I behold Thee, re-

---

[2] O vere Dei Nate, tu mihi Pater, tu mihi Filius, tu mihi Sponsus, tu mihi
anima eras. Nunc orbor Patre, viduor Sponso, desolor Filio, omnia perdo.—
De Lament. B.M.V.

[3] O quam libenter tunc posita fuissem viva cum Filio meo, si fuisset voluntas ejus!—Rev. lib. i. cap. 10.

[4] Anno Chr. 34, n. 131.

ceive my last farewell, the farewell of Thy dear Mother, and receive also my heart, which I leave buried with Thee. 'The Blessed Virgin,' writes St. Fulgentius, 'would ardently have desired to have buried her soul with the body of Christ.'[5] And this Mary herself revealed to St. Bridget, saying: 'I can truly say that at the burial of my Son one tomb contained as it were two hearts.'[6]

Finally, the disciples raised the stone and closed up the holy sepulchre, and in it the body of Jesus, that great treasure—a treasure so great that neither earth nor heaven had a greater. Here I may be permitted to make a short digression, and remark that Mary's heart was buried with Jesus, because Jesus was all her treasure: "Where your treasure is, there will your heart be also."[7] And where, may we ask, are our hearts buried? In creatures—perchance in mire. And why not in Jesus, who, although He has ascended to heaven, is still pleased to remain on earth, not dead indeed, but living in the most holy sacrament of the altar, precisely that our hearts may be with Him, and that He may possess them? But let us return to Mary. Before leaving the sepulchre, according to St. Bonaventure, she blessed the sacred stone which closed it, saying, 'O happy stone, that doth now enclose that sacred body, which for nine months was contained in my womb; I bless thee and envy thee; I leave thee the guardian of my Son, of that Son who is all my treasure and all my love.' Then raising her heart to the Eternal Father, she said, 'O Father, to Thee do I recommend Him—Him who is Thy Son at the same time that He is mine.' Thus bidding her last farewell to her beloved Jesus and to the sepulchre, she left it, and returned to her own house. 'This Mother,' says St. Bernard, 'went away so afflicted and sad, that she moved many to tears

---

[5] Animam cum corpore Christi contumulari Virgo vehementer exoptavit.

[6] Vere dicere possum, quod sepulto Filio meo, quasi duo corda in uno sepulchro fuerunt.—*Rev.* lib. ii. cap. 21.

[7] Ubi enim thesaurus vester est, ibi et cor vestrum erit.—*Luc.* xii. 34.

in spite of themselves; and wherever she passed, all who met her wept,'[8] and could not restrain their tears. And he adds that the holy disciples and women who accompanied her 'mourned even more for her than for their Lord.'[9]

Saint Bonaventure says, that her sisters covered her with a mourning cloak: 'The sisters of our Lady veiled her as a widow, almost covering her whole face.'[10] He also says that, passing, on her return, before the cross still wet with the blood of her Jesus, she was the first to adore it. 'O holy cross,' she then said, 'I kiss thee, I adore thee; for thou art no longer an infamous gibbet, but a throne of love and an altar of mercy, consecrated by the blood of the Divine Lamb, which on thee has been sacrificed for the salvation of the world.' She then left the cross, and returned home. When there, the afflicted Mother cast her eyes around, and no longer saw her Jesus; but, instead of the sweet presence of her dear Son, the remembrance of His beautiful life and cruel death presented itself before her eyes. She remembered how she had pressed that Son to her bosom in the crib of Bethlehem; the conversations she had held with Him during the many years they had dwelt in the house of Nazareth; she remembered their mutual affection, their loving looks, the words of eternal life which fell from those Divine lips; and then the sad scene which she had that day witnessed, again presented itself before her. The nails, the thorns, the lacerated flesh of her Son, those deep wounds, those uncovered bones, that open mouth, those dimmed eyes, all presented themselves before her. Ah, what a night of sorrow was that night for Mary! The afflicted Mother, turning to Saint John, mournfully said: 'Ah, John, tell me where is thy Master?' She then asked

---

[8] Sui ploratus pietate, multos etiam invitos ad lacrymas provocabat . . . Omnes plorabant qui obviabant ei.—*De Lament. B.M.V.*

[9] Major illis incrat dolor de dolore Matris, quam de morte Domini sui,—*Ib.*

[10] Sorores Dominæ velaverunt eam tanquam viduam, cooperientes quasi totum vultum.—*De Vita C.* cap. lxxxiii.

the Magdalen : ' Daughter, tell me, where is thy beloved ? O God, who has taken Him from us ?' Mary wept, and all who were present wept with her. And thou, my soul, weepest not ! Ah, turn to Mary, and address her with Saint Bonaventure, saying : ' O my own sweet Lady, let me weep ; thou art innocent, I am guilty.'[11] Entreat her at least to let thee weep with her : ' Grant that with thee I may weep.'[12] She weeps for love ; do thou weep through sorrow for thy sins. Thus weeping, thou mayest have the happy lot of him of whom we read in the following example.

EXAMPLE.

Father Engelgrave relates[13] that a certain religious was so tormented with scruples, that he was sometimes almost driven to despair ; but as he had the greatest devotion to Mary in Sorrow, he always had recourse to her in his interior agonies, and felt himself consoled whilst meditating on her dolours. Death came, and the devil then tormented him more than ever with scruples, and tempted him to despair. When, behold, the compassionate Mother seeing her poor son in such anguish, appeared to him, saying : ' And thou, my son, why art thou so overcome with sorrow? why fearest thou so much? thou who hast so often consoled me by pitying me in my sorrows. But now,' she added, ' Jesus sends me to console thee ; be comforted, then ; rejoice, and come with me to heaven.' On hearing these consoling words, the devout religious, filled with joy and confidence, tranquilly expired.

PRAYER.

My afflicted Mother, I will not leave thee alone to weep ; no, I will accompany thee with my tears. This

---

[11] Sine, Domina mea, sine me flere ; tu innocens es, ego sum reus.—*Stim. Div. Am.* p. i. c. 3.
[12] Fac ut tecum lugeam.   [13] Dom. infr. Oct. Nat. Lux Ev.

grace I now ask of thee: obtain that I may always bear in mind and always have a tender devotion towards the Passion of Jesus and thy sorrows, that the remainder of my days may thus be spent in weeping over thy sufferings, my own sweet Mother, and those of my Redeemer.   These sorrows, I trust, will give me the confidence and strength which I shall require at the hour of death, that I may not despair at the sight of the many sins by which I have offended my Lord. They must obtain me pardon, perseverance, and heaven, where I hope to rejoice with thee, and to sing the infinite mercies of my God for all eternity.   Thus do I hope ; thus may it be.   Amen. Amen.

Should any of my readers wish to practise the devotion of reciting the little Rosary of the Dolours of Mary, they will find it at the end of the Third Part of this book.   I composed it many years since, and now insert it for the convenience of all devout clients of Mary in Sorrow ; to whom I beg that, as an act of charity, they will recommend me when they meditate on her Dolours.

PRAYER OF SAINT BONAVENTURE.

O Lady, who by thy sweetness dost ravish the hearts of men, hast thou not ravished mine ?   O ravisher of hearts, when wilt thou restore me mine ?   Rule and govern it like thine own ; preserve it in the Blood of the Lamb, and place it in thy Son's side.   Then shall I obtain what I desire, and possess what I hope for; for thou art our hope.[1]

----

[1] O Domina, quæ rapis corda dulcedine; nonne cor meum, Domina, rapuisti . . . O raptrix cordium, quando mihi restitues cor meum ? . . . Guberna illud cum tuo, et in sanguine agni conserva, et in latere Filii colloca. Tunc assequar quod intendo, tunc possidebo quod spero, quia tu es spes nostra.—*S Bern. Med. in Salv. Reg. ap. S. Bo.. Stim. Amor.* P. iii. cap. 19.

OF THE VIRTUES OF THE MOST BLESSED VIRGIN MARY.

SAINT AUGUSTINE says,[1] that to obtain with more certainty, and in greater abundance the favour of the Saints, we must imitate them; for when they see us practise their virtues, they are more excited to pray for us. The Queen of Saints and our principal Advocate, Mary, has no sooner delivered a soul from Lucifer's grasp, and united it to God, than she desires that it should begin to imitate her, otherwise she cannot enrich it with the graces she would wish, seeing it so opposed to her in conduct. Therefore Mary calls those blessed who with diligence imitate her life : " Now, therefore, children, hear me ; blessed are they that keep my ways."[2] Whosoever loves, resembles the person loved, or endeavours to become like that person; according to the well-known proverb, 'Love either finds or makes its like.'[3] Hence Saint Sophronius exhorts us to endeavour to imitate Mary, if we love her, because this is the greatest act of homage which we can offer her : ' My beloved children,' the Saint says, ' serve Mary, whom you love; for you then truly love her, if you endeavour to imitate her whom you love.'[4] Richard of Saint Lawrence says, ' that those are and can call themselves true children of Mary, who strive to imitate her life.'[5] ' Let the child,

[1] S. 225, e. B. app.
[2] Nunc ergo, filii, audite me : beati qui custodiunt vias meas.—*Prov.* viii. 32.
[3] Amor aut pares invenit aut facit.
[4] Dilectissimæ, amate quam colitis, et colite quam amatis : quia tunc eam vere colitis et amatis, si imitari velitis de toto corde quam laudatis.—*Serm. de Assump. int. op. S. Hieron.*   [5] See note 6, page 45.

then,' concludes Saint Bernard, 'endeavour to imitate his Mother, if he desires her favour; for Mary, seeing herself treated as a Mother, will treat him as her child.'[6]

Although there is little recorded in the Gospels of Mary's virtues in detail, yet when we learn from them that she was full of grace, this alone gives us to understand that she possessed all virtues in an heroic degree. 'So much so,' says Saint Thomas, 'that whereas other Saints excelled, each in some particular virtue, the one in chastity, another in humility, another in mercy; the Blessed Virgin excelled in all, and is given as a model of all.'[7] Saint Ambrose also says, 'Mary was such, that her life alone was a model for all.'[8] And then he concludes in the following words: 'Let the virginity and life of Mary be to you as a faithful image, in which the form of virtue is resplendent. Thence learn how to live, what to correct, what to avoid, and what to retain.[9] Humility being the foundation of all virtues, as the holy fathers teach, let us in the first place consider how great was the humility of the Mother of God.

SECTION I. *Of the Humility of Mary.*

'Humility,' says Saint Bernard, 'is the foundation and guardian of virtues;'[1] and with reason, for without it no other virtue can exist in a soul. Should she possess all virtues, all will depart when humility is gone. But, on the other hand, as Saint Francis of Sales wrote

---

[6] In Salve Reg. s. 1.

[7] Ipsa enim omnium virtutum opera exercuit; alii autem sancti specialia quædam: quia alius fuit humilis, alius castus, alius misericors, et ideo dantur in exemplum specialium virtutum; sed beata Virgo in exemplum omnium virtutum.—*Opusc.* viii.

[8] Talis fuit Maria, ut ejus unius vita omnium sit disciplina.—*De Virginibus*, lib. ii. c. 2.

[9] Sit igitur vobis tamquam in imagine descripta, virginitas, vita Mariæ, de qua velut speculo refulgeat species castitatis et forma virtutis. Hinc sumatis licet exempla vivendi ... quid corrigere, quid effugere, quid tenere debeatis ostendunt.—*Ib.*

[1] Humilitas est fundamentum custosque virtutum.—*In Nat. D. s.* 1.

to Saint Jane de Chantal, 'God so loves humility, that
wherever He sees it, He is immediately drawn thither.'
This beautiful and so necessary virtue was unknown
in the world; but the Son of God Himself came on
earth to teach it by His own example, and willed that
in that virtue in particular we should endeavour to
imitate Him: "Learn of Me, because I am meek and
humble of heart."[2] Mary, being the first and most perfect disciple of Jesus Christ in the practice of all virtues, was the first also in that of humility, and by it
merited to be exalted above all creatures. It was revealed to Saint Matilda that the first virtue in which
the Blessed Mother particularly exercised herself, from
her very childhood, was that of humility.[3]

The first effect of humility of heart is a lowly opinion
of ourselves : 'Mary had always so humble an opinion
of herself, that, as it was revealed to the same Saint
Matilda, although she saw herself enriched with greater
graces than all other creatures, she never preferred herself to any one.'[4] The Abbot Rupert, explaining the
passage of the sacred Canticles, "Thou hast wounded
my heart, my sister, my spouse, . . . with one hair of
thy neck,"[5] says, that the humble opinion which Mary
had of herself was precisely that hair of the Spouse's
neck with which she wounded the heart of God.[6] Not
indeed that Mary considered herself a sinner : for humility is truth, as Saint Teresa remarks; and Mary knew
that she had never offended God : neither was it that
she did not acknowledge that she had received greater
graces from God than all other creatures; for an humble
heart always acknowledges the special favours of the

---

[2] Et discite a me, quia mitis sum et humilis corde.—*Matt.* xi. 29.
[3] Prima virtus, in qua Virgo nata, et infans se singulariter exercuit, fuit
humilitas.—*Spir. Grat.* l. i. c. 52.
[4] Ita modeste de se sentiebat, ut cum tot gratias haberet, nulli se prætulit.
—*Ib.* c. 5.
[5] Vulnerasti cor meum, soror mea, sponsa . . . in uno crine colli tui.—
Cant. iv. 9.
[6] In uno crine colli tui, id est, in nimia humilitate cordis tui. . . . Quid
uno crine gracilius, et quid humilitate subtilius? . . . Iste est crinis colli,
humilis cogitatus mulieris.—Lib. iii. *in Cant.* cap. 4.

2 H

Lord, to humble herself the more : but the Divine Mother, by the greater light wherewith she knew the infinite greatness and goodness of God, also knew her own nothingness, and therefore, more than all others, humbled herself, saying with the sacred Spouse : " Do not consider that I am brown, because the sun hath altered my colour."[7] That is, as Saint Bernard explains it, ' When I approach Him, I find myself black.'[8]   Yes, says Saint Bernardine, for ' the Blessed Virgin had always the majesty of God, and her own nothingness, present to her mind.'[9]   As a beggar, when clothed with a rich garment, which has been bestowed upon her, does not pride herself on it in the presence of the giver, but is rather humbled, being reminded thereby of her own poverty ; so also the more Mary saw herself enriched, the more did she humble herself, remembering that all was God's gift ; whence she herself told Saint Elizabeth of Hungary, that ' she might rest assured that she looked upon herself as most vile, and unworthy of God's grace.'[10]   Therefore Saint Bernardine says, that ' after the Son of God, no creature in the world was so exalted as Mary, because no creature in the world ever humbled itself so much as she did.'[11]

Moreover, it is an act of humility to conceal heavenly gifts. Mary wished to conceal from Saint Joseph the great favour whereby she had become the Mother of God, although it seemed necessary to make it known to him, if only to remove from the mind of her poor spouse any suspicions as to her virtue, which he might have entertained on seeing her pregnant: or at least the perplexity in which it indeed threw him : for Saint Joseph, on the one hand unwilling to doubt Mary's

---

[7] Nolite me considerare quod fusca sim, quia decoloravit me sol.—*Cant.* i. 5.

[8] Appropinquans illi ex eo me nigram invenio.—*In Cant.* § 28.

[9] Virgo continue habebat actualem relationem ad Divinam majestatem et ad suam nihilitatem.—*Serm. de Concep. B.M.V.* art. iii. cap. 2.

[10] Pro firmo scias, quod me reputabam vilissimam, et gratia Dei indignam.—*S. Bonav. de Vita C.* cap. iii.

[11] Sicut nulla post Filium Dei creatura tantum ascendit in gratiæ dignitatem, sic nec tantum descendit in abyssum humilitatis profundæ.—*Serm. de Concep. B.M.V.* art. i. cap. 3.

chastity and on the other ignorant of the mystery, "was minded to put her away privately."[12] This he would have done, had not the angel revealed to him that his Spouse was pregnant by the operation of the Holy Ghost. Again, a soul which is truly humble refuses her own praise; and should praises be bestowed on her, she refers them all to God. Behold, Mary is disturbed at hearing herself praised by Saint Gabriel; and when Saint Elizabeth said, "Blessed art thou among women . . . and whence is this to me, that the Mother of my Lord should come to me? . . . blessed art thou that hast believed, &c."[13] Mary referred all to God, and answered in that humble Canticle, "My soul doth magnify the Lord," as if she had said: 'Thou dost praise me, Elizabeth; but I praise the Lord, to whom alone honour is due: thou wonderest that I should come to thee, and I wonder at the Divine goodness, in which alone my spirit exults: "and my spirit hath rejoiced in God my Saviour." Thou praisest me because I have believed; I praise my God, because He hath been pleased to exalt my nothingness: "because He hath regarded the humility of His handmaid." '[14] Hence Mary said to Saint Bridget: 'I humbled myself so much, and thereby merited such great grace, because I thought, and knew, that of myself I possessed nothing. For this same reason I did not desire to be praised; I only desired that praises should be given to the Creator and Giver of all.'[15] Wherefore an ancient author, speaking of the humility of Mary, says: 'O truly blessed humility, which hath given God to men, opened heaven, and delivered souls from hell!'[16]

[12] Voluit occulte dimittere eam.—*Matt.* i. 19.

[13] Benedicta tu inter mulieres . . . Et unde hoc mihi, ut veniat Mater Domini mei ad me? . . . Et beata quæ credidisti, &c.—*Luc.* i. 42-44.

[14] Magnificat anima mea Dominum, et exsultavit spiritus meus in Deo salutari meo; quia respexit humilitatem ancillæ suæ.—*Ib.* 46, 47.

[15] Ut quid enim ego me tantum humiliabam, aut unde promerui tantam gratiam, nisi quia cogitavi, et scivi, me nihil a me esse vel habere? Ideo et nolui laudem meam, sed solius Datoris et Creatoris.—*Rev.* lib. ii. c. 23.

[16] O vere beata humilitas, quæ Deum hominibus peperit, vitam mortalibus edidit, cœlos innovavit, mundum purificavit, paradisum aperuit, et hominum animas ab inferis liberavit.—*Serm. de Assump. int. Op. S. Augustini.*

It is also a part of humility to serve others. Mary did not refuse to go and serve Elizabeth for three months. Hence Saint Bernard says, ' Elizabeth wondered that Mary should have come to visit her ; but that which is still more admirable is, that she came not to be ministered to, but to minister.'[17] Those who are humble are retiring, and choose the last places ; and therefore Mary, remarks Saint Bernard, when her Son was preaching in a house, as it is related by Saint Matthew,[18] wishing to speak to Him, would not of her own accord enter, but ' remained outside, and did not avail herself of her maternal authority to interrupt Him.'[19] For the same reason also when she was with the Apostles awaiting the coming of the Holy Ghost, she took the lowest place, as Saint Luke relates, " All these were persevering with one mind in prayer, with the women and Mary the Mother of Jesus."[20] Not that Saint Luke was ignorant of the Divine Mother's merits, on account of which he should have named her in the first place, but because she had taken the last place amongst the Apostles and women ; and therefore he described them all, as an author remarks, in the order in which they were. Hence Saint Bernard says, ' Justly has the last become the first, who being the first of all became the last.'[21] In fine, those who are humble love to be contemned ; therefore we do not read that Mary showed herself in Jerusalem on Palm Sunday, when her Son was received by the people with so much honour ; but on the other hand, at the death of her Son she did not shrink from appearing on Calvary, through fear of the dishonour which would accrue to her when it was known that she was the Mother of Him who was condemned

---

[17] Venisse Mariam mirabatur Elisabeth . . . sed jam magis miretur, quod instar utique Filii, et ipsa non ministrari venerit, sed ministrare.—*Serm. de Aquæd.* [18] Matt. xii.

[19] Foris stabat . . . nec materna auctoritate aut sermonem interrupit, aut in habitationem irruit in qua Filius loquebatur.—*Serm. Sign. Magn.*

[20] Hi omnes erant perseverantes unanimiter in oratione cum mulieribus et Maria matre Jesu.—*Act.* i. 14.

[21] Merito facta est novissima prima, quæ cum prima esset omnium, sese novissimam faciebat.—*In Sign. Magn.*

to die an infamous death as a criminal. Therefore she said to Saint Bridget, 'What is more humbling than to be called a fool, to be in want of all things, and to believe oneself the most unworthy of all? Such, O daughter, was my humility; this was my joy; this was all my desire, with which I thought how to please my Son alone.'[22]

The venerable sister Paula of Foligno was given to understand in an ecstasy, how great was the humility of our blessed Lady; and giving an account of it to her confessor, she was so filled with astonishment at its greatness that she could only exclaim, 'O the humility of the Blessed Virgin! O father, the humility of the Blessed Virgin, how great was the humility of the Blessed Virgin! In the world there is no such thing as humility, not even in its lowest degree, when you see the humility of Mary.' On another occasion our Lord showed Saint Bridget two ladies. The one was all pomp and vanity: 'She,' He said, 'is Pride; but the other one whom thou seest with her head bent down, courteous towards all, having God alone in her mind, and considering herself as no one, is Humility, her name is Mary.'[23] Hereby God was pleased to make known to us that the humility of His blessed Mother was such that she was humility itself.

There can be no doubt, as Saint Gregory of Nyassa remarks,[24] that of all virtues there is perhaps none the practice of which is more difficult to our nature, corrupted as it is by sin, than that of humility. But there is no escape; we can never be true children of Mary if we are not humble. 'If,' says Saint Bernard, 'thou canst not imitate the virginity of this humble Virgin,

---

[22] Quid enim contemptibilius est quam vocari fatua, et non irasci, vel verba reddere? Quid despectius quam omnia relinquere, et omnibus indigere? Quid dolorosius apud mundiales quam injuriam suam dissimulare, et omnibus se credere et tenere indigniorem et humiliorem? Talis, O filia, erat humilitas mea, hoc gaudium meum, hæc voluntas tota, quæ nulli nisi Filio meo placere cogitabam.—*Rev.* lib. ii. cap. 23.

[23] Rev. lib. i. cap. 29.

[24] De Beatit. Hom. 1.

imitate her humility.'[25]   She detests the proud, and
only invites the humble to come to her : " Whosoever
is a little one, let him come to me."[26]   ' Mary,' says
Richard of Saint Lawrence, ' protects us under the
mantle of humility.'[27]   The Mother of God herself
explained what her mantle was to Saint Bridget, saying, ' Come, my daughter, and hide thyself under my
mantle ; this mantle is my humility.'[28] She then added,
that the consideration of her humility was a good mantle
with which we could warm ourselves : but that as a
mantle only renders this service to those who wear it,
not in thought but in deed, ' so also would her humility
be of no avail except to those who endeavoured to
imitate it.'   She then concluded in these words, ' Therefore, my daughter, clothe thyself with this humility.'[29]
' O, how dear are humble souls to Mary !' says Saint Bernard ; ' this blessed Virgin recognises and loves those
who love her, and is near to all who call upon her ;
and especially to those whom she sees like unto herself
in chastity and humility.'[30]   Hence the Saint exhorts
all who love Mary to be humble : ' Emulate this virtue of Mary, if thou lovest her.'[31]   Marinus, or Martin
d'Alberto, of the Society of Jesus, used to sweep the
house, and collect the filth, through love for this Blessed
Virgin.   The Divine Mother one day appeared to him,
as Father Nieremberg relates in his life, and thanking
him, as it were, said, ' O, how pleasing to me is this
humble action, done for my love !' Then, O my Queen,

---

[25] Si non potes virginitatem humilis, imitare humilitatem Virginis.—
Hom. i. *sup. Missus.*
[26] Si quis est parvulus, veniat ad me.—*Prov.* ix. 4.
[27] Maria protegit nos . . . sub pallio humilitatis.—*De Laud. Virg.* lib. ii.
cap. 1.
[28] Ergo tu, filia mea, veni, et absconde te sub mantello meo . . . Hic man-
tellus humilitas mea est.—*Rev.* lib. ii. cap. 23.
[29] Nec humilitas mea proficit eam cogitantibus, nisi et pro modulo suo
unusquisque studuerit eam imitari. Ergo, filia mea, indue te hac humilitate.—*Ib.*
[30] Agnoscit certe, et diligit diligentes se, et prope est in veritate invocantibus se : præsertim his quos videt sibi conformes factos in castitate et
humilitate.—*In Salv. Reg.*
[31] Æmulamini hanc virtutem, si Mariam diligitis.—*Serm. in Sign. Magn.*

I can never be really thy child unless I am humble ; but dost thou not see that my sins, after having rendered me ungrateful to my Lord, have also made me proud ? O my Mother, do thou supply a remedy. By the merit of thy humility obtain that I may be truly humble, and thus become thy child. Amen.

Section II. *Of Mary's Charity towards God.*

Saint Anselm says, that 'wherever there is the greatest purity, there is also the greatest charity.'[1] The more a heart is pure, and empty of itself, the greater is the fulness of its love towards God. The most holy Mary, because she was all humility, and had nothing of self in her, was filled with divine love, so that 'her love towards God surpassed that of all men and angels,'[2] as Saint Bernardine writes. Therefore Saint Francis of Sales with reason called her 'the Queen of love.' God has indeed given men the precept to love Him with their whole hearts, " Thou shalt love the Lord thy God with thy whole heart ;"[3] but, as Saint Thomas declares, 'this commandment will be fully and perfectly fulfilled by men in heaven alone, and not on earth, where it is only fulfilled imperfectly.'[4] On this subject, blessed Albert the Great remarks, that, in a certain sense, it would have been unbecoming had God given a precept which was never to have been perfectly fulfilled. But this would have been the case, had not the Divine Mother perfectly fulfilled it. The Saint says, ' Either some one fulfilled this precept, or no one; if any one, it must have been the most Blessed Virgin.'[5] Richard of Saint Victor confirms this opinion,

[1] Ubi major puritas, ibi major charitas. †
[2] Superat . . . omnium creaturarum amores . . . in Filium suum.—*Serm. de Glor. Nom. M.* art. i. cap. 2.
[3] Diliges Dominum Deum tuum ex toto corde tuo.—*Matt.* xxii. 37.
[4] 2. 2. q. xxiv. art. 8.
[5] Aut aliquis implet hoc præceptum, aut nullus ; si aliquis, ergo Beatissima Virgo.—*Sup. Missus.* q. 135.

saying, 'The Mother of our Emmanuel practised virtues in their very highest perfection. Who has ever fulfilled as she did that first commandment, "Thou shalt love the Lord thy God with thy whole heart"? In her Divine love was so ardent, that no defect of any kind could have access to her.'[6] 'Divine love,' says Saint Bernard, 'so penetrated and filled the soul of Mary, that no part of her was left untouched; so that she loved with her whole heart, with her whole soul, with her whole strength, and was full of grace.'[7] Therefore Mary could well say, My Beloved has given Himself all to me, and I have given myself all to Him : " My Beloved to me, and I to Him."[8] 'Ah! well might even the Seraphim,' says Richard, 'have descended from heaven to learn, in the heart of Mary, how to love God.'[9]

God, who is love,[10] came on earth to enkindle in the hearts of all the flame of His Divine love; but in no heart did He enkindle it so much as in that of His Mother; for her heart was entirely pure from all earthly affections, and fully prepared to burn with this blessed flame. Thus Saint Sophronius says, that 'Divine love so inflamed her, that nothing earthly could enter her affections; she was always burning with this heavenly flame, and, so to say, inebriated with it.'[11] Hence the heart of Mary became all fire and flames, as we read of her in the sacred Canticles: "The lamps thereof are

---

[6] Emanuelis nostri puerpera, in omni fuit virtutum consummatione perfecta. Quis illud primum et maximum mandatum sic unquam implevit? Quis sic unquam implere poterit? Diliges Dominum Deum tuum ex toto corde tuo, et ex tota anima tua . . . Divinus amor in ea adeo convaluit, adeo eam ipsam in omni bono solidavit, ut de cætero, spiritualis qualiscunque defectus, in eam incidere omnino non posset.—Lib. ii. *de Emanuele,* cap. 29, 30.

[7] Amor Christi, Mariæ animam non modo confixit, sed etiam pertransivit, ut nullam in pectore virginali particulam vacuam amore relinqueret, sed toto corde, tota anima, tota virtute diligeret, et esset gratia plena.—*Serm.* xxix. *in Cant.*

[8] Dilectus meus mihi, et ego illi.—*Cant.* ii. 16.

[9] Seraphim de cœlo descendere poterant, ut amorem discerent in corde Virginis. †

[10] Deus charitas est.—1 *Joan.* iv. 8.

[11] Mariam totam incanduerat divinus amor. ita ut in ea nihil esset mundanum, quod violaret affectus, sed ardor continuus, et ebrietas perfusi amoris.—*Serm. de Assump. int. op. S. Hieron.*

fire and flames ;[12] fire burning within through love, as
Saint Anselm explains it ;[13] and flames shining without,
by the example she gave to all in the practice of virtues.
When Mary, then, was in this world, and bore Jesus
in her arms, she could well be called, 'fire carrying
fire ;' and with far more reason than a woman spoken
of by Hippocrates, who was thus called because she
carried fire in her hand. Yes, for Saint Ildephonsus
said, that 'the Holy Ghost heated, inflamed, and
melted Mary with love, as fire does iron ; so that the
flame of this Holy Spirit was seen, and nothing was
felt but the fire of the love of God.'[14] Saint Thomas
of Villanova says,[15] that the bush seen by Moses,[16]
which burnt without being consumed, was a real symbol of Mary's heart. Therefore with reason, says Saint
Bernard, was she seen by Saint John clothed with the
sun : "and there appeared a great wonder in heaven,
a woman clothed with the sun ;"[17] 'for,' continues the
Saint, 'she was so closely united to God by love, and
penetrated so deeply the abyss of divine wisdom, that,
without a personal union with God, it would seem impossible for a creature to have a closer union with
Him.'[18]

Hence Saint Bernardine of Sienna asserts that the
most holy Virgin was never tempted by hell; for, he
says : 'As flies are driven away by a great fire, so were
the evil spirits driven away by her ardent love; so much
so, that they did not even dare approach her.'[19] Richard

---

[12] Lampades ejus, lampades ignis atque flammarum.—*Cant.* viii. 6.

[13] Ap. Corn. á Lap.

[14] Beatam Mariam . . . velut ignis ferrum, Spiritus Sanctus totam de-
coxit, incanduit, et ignivit : ita ut in ea Spiritus Sancti flamma videatur, nec
sentiatur nisi tantum ignis amoris Dei.—*Orat.* i. *de Assump. B.M.V.*

[15] In Nat. D. Conc. 2. [16] Exod. iii. 2.

[17] Et signum magnum apparuit in cœlo : mulier amicta sole.—*Apoc.* xii. 1.

[18] Jure ergo Maria sole perhibetur amicta, quæ profundissimam divinæ
sapientiæ ultra quam credi valeat, penetravit abyssum ; ut quantum sine
personali unione creaturæ conditio patitur, luci illi inaccessibili videatur immersa.—*In Sign. Magn.*

[19] Sicut magnus ignis effugat muscas, sic a sua ardentissima mente et
inflammatissima charitate dæmones effugabantur et pellebantur, in tantum
quod solum in modico non erant ausi respicere mentem ejus, nec de magno
spatio illi appropinquare.—*Serm. de Concep. B.M.V.* art. iii. cap. 2.

of Saint Victor also says, that 'the Blessed Virgin was terrible to the princes of darkness, so that they did not presume to tempt or approach her ; for the fire of her charity deterred them.'[20] Mary herself revealed to Saint Bridget, that in this world she never had any thought, desire, or joy, but in and for God : 'I thought,' she said, 'of nothing but God, nothing pleased me but God;'[21] so that her blessed soul being in the almost continual contemplation of God whilst on earth, the acts of love which she formed were innumerable, as Father Suarez writes : 'The acts of perfect charity formed by the Blessed Virgin in this life, were without number ; for nearly the whole of her life was spent in contemplation, and in that state she constantly repeated acts of love.'[22] But a remark of Bernardine de Bustis pleases me still more : he says that Mary did not so much repeat acts of love as other saints do, but that her whole life was one continued act of it; for, by a special privilege, she always actually loved God.[23] As a royal eagle, she always kept her eyes fixed on the Divine Sun of Justice : 'so that,' as Saint Peter Damian says, 'the duties of active life did not prevent her from loving, and love did not prevent her from attending to those duties.'[24] Therefore Saint Germanus says, that the altar of propitiation, on which the fire was never extinguished day or night, was a type of Mary.[25]

Neither was sleep an obstacle to Mary's love for God ; since, as Saint Augustine asserts, 'the dreams,

---

[20] Virgo . . . principibus tenebrarum terribilis fuit, ut ad eam accedere, eamque tentare non præsumpserint. Deterrebat enim eos flamma charitatis.—*In Cant.* cap. xxvi.

[21] Nihil nisi Deum cogitabam, nihil volebam nisi ipsum.—*Rev.* lib. i. cap. 10.

[22] Actus perfectæ charitatis, quos B. Virgo habuit in hac vita innumerabiles fuerunt, ita ut eorum multitudo possit fortasse cum numero sanctorum omnium conferri, quia fere totam vitam in perpetua contemplatione transegit, in qua ferventissime Deum amabat, et hunc amoris actum frequentissime repetebat.—*De Incarnat.* p. ii. q. 37, art. 4, disp. 18, § iv.

[23] Tamen ipsa gloriosissima Virgo de privilegio singulari continue et semper Deum amabat actualiter.— *Marial.* p. 2, Serm. v. p. 7.

[24] Adeo ut nec actio contemplationem minueret, et contemplatio non de sereret actionem.—*Serm.* i. *in Nat. B.M.V.*

[25] In Annunt.

when sleeping, of our first parents, in their state of innocence, were as happy as their lives when waking;'[26] and if such a privilege were granted them, it certainly cannot be denied that it was also granted to the Divine Mother, as Suarez, the Abbot Rupert, and Saint Bernardine fully admit. Saint Ambrose is also of this opinion; for speaking of Mary, he says, 'while her body rested, her soul watched,'[27] verifying in herself the words of the wise man: "Her lamp shall not be put out in the night."[28] Yes, for while her blessed body took its necessary repose in gentle sleep, 'her soul,' says Saint Bernardine, 'freely tended towards God; so much so, that she was then wrapped in more perfect contemplation than any other person ever was when awake.'[29] Therefore could she well say with the Spouse in the Canticles, "I sleep, and my heart watcheth."[30] 'As happy in sleep as awaking,'[31] as Suarez says. In fine, Saint Bernardine asserts, that as long as Mary lived in this world she was continually loving God: 'The mind of the Blessed Virgin was always wrapped in the ardour of love.'[32] The Saint moreover adds, 'that she never did anything which the Divine Wisdom did not show her to be pleasing to Him; and that she loved God as much as she thought He was to be loved by her;'[33] so much so, indeed, that, according to blessed Albert the Great, we can well say that Mary was filled with so great charity, that greater was not

[26] Tam felicia erant somnia dormentium, quam vita vigilantium.—*In Jul.* lib. v. cap. 2.

[27] Cum quiesceret corpus, vigilaret animus.—*De Virg.* lib. ii. cap. 2.

[28] Non extinguetur in nocte lucerna ejus.—*Prov.* xxxi. 18.

[29] Anima sua libere ac meritorio actu tunc tendebat in Deum. Unde illo tempore erat perfectior contemplatrix, quam unquam fuerit aliquis alius dum vigilavit.—*Serm. de Concep. B.M.V.* art. i. cap. 2.

[30] Ego dormio, et cor meum vigilat.—*Cant.* v. 2.

[31] Tam felix dormiendo, quam vigilando.—*De Inc.* p. 2. d. 18. § 2.

[32] Mens illius in ardore dilectionis continue tenebatur.—*Serm. de Concep. B.M.V.* art. iii. cap. 2.

[33] Tertius Virginis splendor fuit charitas, scilicet quantum ad voluntatem, in quam tanta plenitudine divinus amor infusus est, quod nihil elicere vellet, nisi quod Dei sapientia præmonstrabat. Proinde hac sapientia illustrata, tantum Deum diligebat, quantum a se diligendum illum intelligebat.—*Ib.* art. i. cap. 3.

possible in any pure creature on earth.[34] Hence Saint
Thomas of Villanova affirms, that by her ardent charity
the Blessed Virgin became so beautiful, and so enamoured her God, that, captivated as it were by her
love, He descended into her womb and became man.[35]
Wherefore Saint Bernardine exclaims, 'Behold the
power of the Virgin Mother: she wounded and took
captive the heart of God.'[36]

But since Mary loves God so much, there can be
nothing which she so much requires of her clients as
that they also should love Him to their utmost. This
precisely she one day told blessed Angela of Foligno
after communion, saying, ' Angela, be thou blessed by
my Son, and endeavour to love Him as much as thou
canst.'[37] She also said to Saint Bridget, ' Daughter, if
thou desirest to bind me to thee, love my Son.' Mary
desires nothing more than to see her beloved, who is
God, loved. Novarinus asks why the Blessed Virgin,
with the Spouse in the Canticles, begged the angels to
make the great love she bore Him known to our Lord,
saying, " I adjure you, O daughters of Jerusalem, if you
find my Beloved, that you tell Him that I languish
with love."[38] Did not God know how much she loved
Him? ' Why did she seek to show the wound to her
Beloved, since He it was who had inflicted it?' The
same author answers, that the Divine Mother thereby
wished to make her love known to us, not to God; that
as she was herself wounded, so might she also be enabled to wound us with Divine love.[39] And ' because

---

[34] Credimus etiam, sine præjudicio melioris sententiæ, Beatam Virginem
in conceptione Filii Dei, charitatem Filii talem et tantam accepisse, qualis et
quanta percipi poterat a pura creatura in statu viæ.—*Sup. Missus Resp.* ad q.
xlvi.

[35] Hæc Virgo beata nobis Deum protulit et hominem : hæc sua eum pul-
chritudine et decore a cœlis allexit : amore illius captus est, humanitatis
nostræ nexibus irretitus.—*Conc.* viii. *in Nat. Dom.*

[36] O incogitabilis virtus Virginis matris . . . . una puella, nescio quibus
blanditiis, nescio quibus violentiis decepit, et ut ita dicam, vulneravit et ra-
puit divinum cor.—*Serm. de Nat. B.M.V.* cap. iv.

[37] Boll. 4 Jan. Vit. c. 7.

[38] Adjuro vos, filiæ Jerusalem, si inveneritis dilectum meum, ut nuntietis
ei quia amore langueo.—*Cant.* v. 8.

[39] Ut vulnerata vulneret.—*Umbra Virg.* exc. 28.

Mary was all on fire with the love of God, all who love and approach her are inflamed by her with this same love ; for she renders them like unto herself.'[40] For this reason Saint Catherine of Sienna called Mary ' the bearer of fire,'[41] the bearer of the flame of Divine love. If we also desire to burn with these blessed flames, let us endeavour always to draw nearer to our Mother by our prayers and the affections of our souls. Ah, Mary, thou Queen of love, of all creatures the most amiable, the most beloved, and the most loving, as Saint Francis of Sales addressed thee,—my own sweet Mother, thou wast always and in all things inflamed with love towards God ; deign, then, to bestow at least a spark of it on me. Thou didst pray thy Son for the spouses whose wine had failed : " They have no wine."[42] And wilt thou not pray for us, in whom the love of God, whom we are under such obligations to love, is wanting ? Say also, 'They have no love,' and obtain us this love. This is the only grace for which we ask. O Mother, by the love thou bearest to Jesus, graciously hear and pray for us. Amen.

Section III. *Of Mary's Charity towards her Neighbour.*

Love towards God and love towards our neighbour are commanded by the same precept : " And this commandment we have from God, that he who loveth God love also his brother."[1] Saint Thomas[2] says that the reason for this is, that he who loves God loves all that God loves. Saint Catherine of Genoa one day said, ' Lord, Thou willest that I should love my neighbour,

---

[40] Quia tota ardens fuit, omnes se amantes, eamque tangentes incendit, et sibi assimilat.

[41] Portatrix ignis.—*Or. in Annunt.*

[42] Joan. ii. 3.

[1] Et hoc mandatum habemus a Deo ut oui diligit **Deum, diligat et fra**trem suum.—1 *Joan.* iv. 21.

[2] 2. 2æ ɑ. 25. a. 1.

and I can love none but Thee.' God answered her in
these words: 'All who love Me love what I love.'[3]
But as there never was, and never will be, any one who
loved God as much as Mary loved Him, so there never
was, and never will be, any one who loved her neighbour as much as she did. Father Cornelius à Lapide,
on these words of the Canticles, "King Solomon hath
made him a litter of the wood of Libanus . . . the midst
he covered with charity for the daughters of Jerusalem,"[4] says, that 'this litter was Mary's womb, in which
the Incarnate Word dwelt, filling it with charity for the
daughters of Jerusalem ; for Christ, who is love itself,
inspired the Blessed Virgin with charity in its highest
degree, that she might succour all who had recourse to
her.'[5] So great was Mary's charity when on earth, that
she succoured the needy without even being asked; as
was the case at the marriage-feast of Cana, when she
told her Son that family's distress: "They have no
wine,"[6] and asked Him to work a miracle. O, with
what speed did she fly when there was question of
relieving her neighbour ! When she went to the house
of Elizabeth to fulfil an office of charity, "she went
into the hill-country with haste."[7] She could not, however, more fully display the greatness of her charity
than she did in the offering which she made of her Son
to death for our salvation. On this subject Saint Bonaventure says, 'Mary so loved the world as to give
her only-begotten Son.' Hence Saint Anselm exclaims,
' O blessed amongst women, thy purity surpasses that
of the angels, and thy compassion that of the Saints !'[8]

---

[3] Boll. 15 Sept. Vit. c. 4.

[4] Ferculum fecit sibi rex Salomon de lignis Libani.—*Cant.* iii. 9.

[5] Beatæ Virginis . . . . . sinus fuit ferculum augustissimum, **ferens et**
bajulans Verbum incarnatum, ideoque media charitate constratum propter
filias Jerusalem ; quia Christus, qui est ipsa charitas, maximam gratiam et
charitatem B. Virgini aspiravit, ut ipsa filiabus Jerusalem, id est, animabus
devotis, ad illam in quavis difficultate recurrentibus, opem ferret.—*In Cant.*
cap. iii.

[6] Joan. ii. 3.   [7] Luc. i. 39.

[8] O tu benedicta super mulieres, quæ angelos vincis puritate, sanctos superat pietate.—*Invoc. B.V. et Filii.*

'Nor has this love of Mary for us,' says Saint Bonaventure, 'diminished now that she is in heaven, but
it has increased; for now she better sees the miseries
of men.' And therefore the Saint goes on to say:
'Great was the mercy of Mary towards the wretched
when she was still in exile on earth; but far greater
is it now that she reigns in heaven.'[9] Saint Agnes assured Saint Bridget that 'there was no one who prayed
without receiving graces through the charity of the
Blessed Virgin.'[10] Unfortunate, indeed, should we be,
did not Mary intercede for us! Jesus Himself, addressing the same Saint, said, 'Were it not for the
prayers of My Mother, there would be no hope of
mercy.'[11]

Blessed is he, says the Divine Mother, who listens
to my instructions, pays attention to my charity, and,
in imitation of me, exercises it himself towards others:
"Blessed is the man that heareth me, and that watcheth daily at my gates, and waiteth at the posts of my
doors."[12] Saint Gregory Nazianzen assures us that
'there is nothing by which we can with greater certainty gain the affection of Mary than by charity towards our neighbour.'[13] Therefore, as God exhorts us,
saying, "Be ye merciful, as your Father also is merciful,"[14] so also does Mary seem to say to all her children,
'Be ye merciful, as your Mother also is merciful.' It
is certain that our charity towards our neighbour will
be the measure of that which God and Mary will show
us: "Give, and it shall be given to you. For with the
same measure that you shall mete withal, it shall be mea-
sured to you again."[15] Saint Methodius used to say,

---

[9] Spec. B.M.V. lect. x.—See page 187, note 13.
[10] Ex dulcedine Mariæ, nullus est, qui non per eam, si petitur, sentiat pietatem.—*Rev.* lib. iii. c. 30.
[11] Nisi preces matris meæ intervenirent, non esset spes misericordiæ.—*Ib.*
lib. vi. c. 26.
[12] Beatus homo qui audit me, et qui vigilat ad fores meas quotidie, et observat ad postes ostii mei.—*Prov.* viii. 34.
[13] Nulla res est, quæ Virginis benevolentiam conciliat ac misericordia. †
[14] Estote ergo misericordes, sicut et Pater vester misericors est.—*Luc.* vi.
36.
[15] Eadem quippe mensura qua mensi fueritis, remetietur vobis.—*Ib.* 38.

'Give to the poor, and receive paradise.'[16] For the apostle writes, that charity towards our neighbour renders us happy both in this world and in the next : " But piety is profitable to all things, having promise of the life that now is, and of that which is to come."[17] Saint John Chrysostom, on the words of Proverbs, " He that hath mercy on the poor lendeth to the Lord,"[18] makes a remark to the same effect, saying, ' He who assists the needy makes God his debtor.'[19] O Mother of Mercy, thou art full of charity for all ; forget not my miseries ; thou seest them full well. Recommend me to God, who denies thee nothing. Obtain me the grace to imitate thee in holy charity, as well towards God as towards my neighbour. Amen.

Section IV. *Of Mary's Faith.*

As the Blessed Virgin is the mother of holy love and hope, so also is she the mother of faith : " I am the mother of fair love, and of fear, and of knowledge, and of holy hope."[20] And with reason is she so, says Saint Ireneus ; for ' the evil done by Eve's incredulity was remedied by Mary's faith.'[21] This is confirmed by Tertullian, who says that because Eve, contrary to the assurance she had received from God, believed the serpent, she brought death into the world ; but our Queen, because she believed the angel when he said that she, remaining a virgin, would become the mother of God, brought salvation into the world.[22] For Saint Augus-

---

[16] Da pauperi, et accipe paradisum. †
[17] Pietas autem ad omnia utilis est, promissionem habens vitæ, quæ nunc est et futuræ.—1 *Tim.* iv. 8.
[18] Fœneratur Domino qui miseretur pauperis.—*Prov.* xix. 17.
[19] Si Deo fœneramur, is ergo nobis debitor est.—*De Pœnit.* hom. 5.
[20] Ego mater pulchræ dilectionis, et timoris, et agnitionis, et sanctæ spei. —*Eccles.* xxiv. 24.
[21] Quod alligavit virgo Eva per incredulitatem, hoc virgo Maria solvit per fidem.—*Adv. Hæres.* lib. iii. cap. 33.
[22] Crediderat Heva serpenti, Maria Gabrieli : quod illa credendo deliquit, hæc credendo delevit.—*De Carne Chr.*

tine says, that 'when Mary consented to the incarnation of the Eternal Word, by means of her faith she opened heaven to men.'[23]   Richard, on the words of Saint Paul, "for the unbelieving husband is sanctified by the believing wife,"[24] also says, that 'Mary is the believing woman by whose faith the unbelieving Adam and all his posterity are saved.'[25]   Hence, on account of her faith, Elizabeth called the holy Virgin blessed: "Blessed art thou that hast believed, because those things shall be accomplished in thee that were spoken by the Lord."[26] And Saint Augustine adds, that 'Mary was rather blessed by receiving the faith of Christ than by conceiving the flesh of Christ.'[27]

Father Suarez says,[28] that the most holy Virgin had more faith than all men and angels.   She saw her Son in the crib of Bethlehem, and believed Him the Creator of the world.   She saw Him fly from Herod, and yet believed Him the King of kings.   She saw Him born, and believed Him eternal.   She saw Him poor and in need of food, and believed Him the Lord of the universe.   She saw Him lying on straw, and believed Him omnipotent.   She observed that He did not speak, and she believed Him infinite wisdom.   She heard Him weep, and believed Him the joy of Paradise.   In fine, she saw Him in death, despised and crucified, and, although faith wavered in others, Mary remained firm in the belief that He was God.   On these words of the Gospel, "there stood by the cross of Jesus His Mother,"[29] Saint Antoninus says, 'Mary stood, supported by her faith, which she retained firm in the divinity of Christ.'[30]

---

[23] Fides Mariæ cœlum aperu i, cum angelo nuntianti consensit.—*Spinelli, M. Deip.* c. 21. n. 7.

[24] Sanctificatus est enim vir infidelis per mulierem fidelem.—1 *Cor.* vii. 14.

[25] Hæc est mulier fidelis, p ŗr cujus fidem salvatus est Adam vir infidelis, et tota posteritas.—*De L. B.*) l. l. 6.

[26] Et beata, quæ credidisti, quoniam perficientur ea, quæ dicta sunt tibi a Domino.—*Luc.* i. 45.

[27] Beatior Maria percip endo fidem Christi, quam concipiendo carnem Christi.—*De S. Virginitate,* ap. iii.

[28] De Inc. p. 2. d. 19. s. 1.

[29] Stabant autem juxtἀ crucem Jesu mater ejus, &c.—*Joan.* xix. 25.

[30] Stabat Maria fide el ʋata, quam de Christi divinitate fixam retinuit.

2 I

And for this reason it is, the Saint adds, that in the office of Tenebræ only one candle is left lighted. Saint Leo, on this subject, applies to our Blessed Lady the words of Proverbs, " Her lamp shall not be put out in the night."[31]   And on the words of Isaias, " I have trodden the wine-press alone,"[32] Saint Thomas remarks that the prophet says a man, on account of the Blessed Virgin, in whom faith never failed.   Hence blessed Albert the Great assures us that ' Mary then exercised perfect faith ; for even when the disciples were doubting she did not doubt.'[33]   Therefore Mary merited by her great faith to become ' the light of all the faithful,'[34] as Saint Methodius calls her ; and the ' Queen of the true faith,'[35] as she is called by Saint Cyril of Alexandria.   The holy Church herself attributes to the merits of Mary's faith the destruction of all heresies : ' Rejoice, O Virgin Mary, for thou alone hast destroyed all heresies throughout the world.'[36]   Saint Thomas of Villanova, explaining the words of the Holy Ghost, " Thou hast wounded my heart, my sister, my spouse . . . with one of thy eyes,"[37] says that ' these eyes denoted Mary's faith, by which she greatly pleased the Son of God.'[38]

Here Saint Ildephonsus exhorts us to imitate Mary's faith.[39]   But how can we do so ?   Faith, at the same time that it is a gift, is also a virtue.   It is a gift of God, inasmuch as it is a light infused by Him into our souls ; and a virtue, inasmuch as the soul has to exercise itself in the practice of it.   Hence faith is not only to be the rule of our belief, but also that of our actions ;

---

[31] Non extinguetur in nocte lucerna ejus.—*Prov.* xxxi. 18.

[32] Torcular calcavi solus, et de gentibus non est vir mecum.—*Is.* lxiii. 3.

[33] Fidem habuit in excellentissimo gradu, quæ, etiam discipulis dubitantibus non dubitavit.—*In Luc.* i.

[34] Fidelium fax.—*De Sim. et Anna.*

[35] Sceptrum orthodoxæ fidei.—*Hom.* 4. int. div.

[36] Gaude, Maria Virgo, cunctas hæreses sola interemisti in universo mundo.

[37] Vulnerasti cor meum, soror mea, spousa . . . in uno oculorum tuorum.—*Cant.* v. 9.

[38] Oculus fidem, capillus humilitatem designat : quibus potentis Dei filio Virgo maxime complacuit.—*De Nat. Dom. Conc.* viii.

[39] Imitamini signaculum fidei vestræ beatam Mariam.—*De Assump. B M.* Serm. 1.

therefore Saint Gregory says, ' He truly believes who puts what he believes in practice ;'[40] and Saint Augustine, ' Thou sayest, I believe ; do what thou sayest, and it is faith.'[41] This is to have a lively faith, to live according to our belief : " My just man liveth by faith."[42] Thus did the Blessed Virgin live very differently from those who do not live in accordance with what they believe, and whose faith is dead, as Saint James declares, " Faith without works is dead."[43] Diogenes sought for a man on earth ; but God, amongst the many faithful, seems to seek for a Christian, for few there are who have good works ; the greater part have only the name of Christian. To such as these should be applied the words once addressed by Alexander to a cowardly soldier who was also named Alexander : ' Either change thy name or change thy conduct.' But as Father Avila used to say, ' It would be better to shut up these poor creatures as madmen, believing, as they do, that an eternity of happiness is prepared for those who lead good lives, and an eternity of misery for those who lead bad ones, and who yet live as if they believed nothing. Saint Augustine therefore exhorts us to see things with the eyes of Christians, that is to say, with eyes which look at all in the light of faith ;[44] for, as Saint Teresa often said, all sins come from a want of faith. Let us therefore entreat the most holy Virgin, by the merit of her faith, to obtain us a lively faith : ' O Lady, increase our faith.'

SECTION V. *Of Mary's Hope.*

Hope takes its rise in faith ; for God enlightens us by faith to know His goodness and the promises He has

---

[40] Ille vere credit, qui exercet operando quod credit.—*In Evang.* hom. 26.
[41] Dicis, credo : fac quod dicis, et fides est.—*Serm.* xlix. ed. B.
[42] Justus autem meus ex fide vivit.—*Heb.* x. 38.
[43] Fides sine operibus mortua est.—*Jac.* ii. 26.
[44] Christianos oculos habete.—*In Ps.* lvi.

made, that by this knowledge we may rise by hope to the desire of possessing Him. Mary, then, having had the virtue of faith in its highest degree, had also hope in the same degree of excellence; and this made her say with David, "But it is good for me to adhere to my God, to put my hope in the Lord God."[1] Mary was indeed that faithful spouse of the Holy Ghost, of whom it was said, "Who is this that cometh up from the desert, flowing with delights, leaning on her beloved?"[2] For she was always perfectly detached from earthly affections, looking upon the world as a desert, and therefore, in no way relying either on creatures or on her own merits, but relying only on Divine grace, in which was all her confidence, she always advanced in the love of God. Thus Ailgrino said of her: 'She ascended from the desert, that is, from the world, which she so fully renounced, and so truly considered as a desert, that she turned all her affection from it. She leant upon her Beloved, for she trusted not in her own merits, but in His graces who bestows graces.'[3]

The most holy Virgin gave a clear indication of the greatness of her confidence in God, in the first place, when she saw the anxiety of her holy spouse Saint Joseph. Unable to account for her wonderful pregnancy, he was troubled at the thought of leaving her: "but Joseph . . . minded to put her away privately."[4] It appeared then necessary, as we have elsewhere remarked, that she should discover the hidden mystery to Saint Joseph; but no, she would not herself manifest the grace she had received; she thought it better to abandon herself to Divine Providence, in the full

---

[1] Mihi autem adhærere Deo bonum est: ponere in Domino Deo spem meam.—*Ps.* lxxii. 28.

[2] Quæ est ista, quæ ascendit de deserto, deliciis affluens, innixa super dilectum suum?—*Cant.* viii. 5.

[3] Ascendit de deserto, scilicet de mundo, quem sic deseruit, et tamquam desertum reputavit, quod ab ipso omnem suum avertit affectum. Affluere autem dicitur gratiarum deliciis et virtutum, et innixa super dilectum. Nam ne perderet delicias affluentes, non suis meritis, sed ipsius innitebatur gratiæ, qui gratiam tribuit, et meritum præmium superaddit.—*Ap. Corn. a Lap.* in loc. cit.

[4] Joseph autem . . . voluit occulte dimittere eam.—*Matt.* i. 19.

confidence that God Himself would defend her innocence and reputation. This is precisely what Cornelius
à Lapide says, in his commentary on the words of the
Gospel quoted above : ' The Blessed Virgin was unwilling to reveal this secret to Joseph, lest she might seem
to boast of her gifts ; she therefore resigned herself to
the care of God, in the fullest confidence that He would
guard her innocence and reputation.'[5]   She again
showed her confidence in God when she knew that the
time for the birth of our Lord approached, and was yet
driven even from the lodgings of the poor in Bethlehem, and obliged to bring forth in a stable : " and she
laid Him in a manger, because there was no room for
Him in the inn."[6]   She did not then let drop a single
word of complaint, but, abandoning herself to God, she
trusted that He would there assist her.   The Divine
Mother also showed how great was her confidence in
Divine Providence when she received notice from Saint
Joseph that they must fly into Egypt.   On that very
night she undertook so long a journey to a strange and
unknown country without provisions, without money,
accompanied only by her Infant Jesus and her poor
spouse, " who arose and took the Child and His Mother by night, and retired into Egypt."[7]   But much
more did she show her confidence when she asked her
Son for wine at the marriage-feast of Cana ; for when
she had said, " They have no wine," Jesus answered
her, " Woman, what is it to thee and to me ? My hour
is not yet come."[8]   After this answer, which seemed an
evident refusal, her confidence in the Divine goodness
was such that she desired the servants to do whatever

[5] B. Virgo autem ex modestia noluit ultro secretum hoc divinum Josepho
pandere, ne sua dona tanta et tam divina jactare videretur, sed Deo Deique
providentiæ et curæ, cujus totum hoc opus erat, idipsum resignavit, certis-
sime confidens Deum suam innocentiam et famam tutaturum.—*Comment.* in
loc. cit.

[6] Et reclinavit eum in præsepio : quia non erat eis locum in diversorio.—
Luc. ii. 7.

[7] Qui consurgens, accepit puerum et matrem ejus nocte, et secessit in
Ægyptum.—*Matt.* ii. 14.

[8] Vinum non habent . . . . Quid mihi et tibi est, mulier ? nondum venit
hora mea.—*Joan.* ii. 3, 4.

her Son told them; for the favour was certain to be granted: "whatsoever He shall say to you, do ye."[9] It indeed was so: Jesus Christ ordered the vessels to be filled with water, and changed it into wine.

Let us, then, learn from Mary to have that confidence in God which we ought always to have, but principally in the great affair of our eternal salvation—an affair in which it is true that we must coöperate; yet it is from God alone that we must hope for the grace necessary to obtain it. We must distrust our own strength, and say with the Apostle, "I can do all things in Him who strengtheneth me."[10]

Ah, my most holy Lady, the Ecclesiasticus tells me that thou art "the Mother of holy hope;"[11] and the holy Church, that thou art our hope.[12] For what other hope, then, need I seek? Thou, after Jesus, art all my hope. Thus did Saint Bernard call thee; thus will I also call thee: 'Thou art the whole ground of my hope;'[13] and, with Saint Bonaventure, I will repeat again and again, 'O, salvation of all who call upon thee, save me!'[14]

SECTION VI. *Of Mary's Chastity.*

Since the fall of Adam, the senses being rebellious to reason, chastity is of all virtues the one which is the most difficult to practise. Saint Augustine says: 'Of all the combats in which we are engaged, the most severe are those of chastity; its battles are of daily occurrence, but victory is rare.'[1] May God be ever praised, however, who in Mary has given us a great example of

9 Quodcumque dixerit vobis, facite.—*Joan.* ii. 5.
10 Omnia possum in eo qui me confortat.—*Philipp.* iv. 13.
11 Ego mater ... sanctæ spei.—*Eccl.* xxiv. 24.
12 Spes nostra salve.
13 Tota ratio spei meæ.—*Serm. de Aquæd.*
14 O salus te invocantium, salva me.
1 Inter omnia enim Christianorum certamina, soia duriora sunt prælia castitatis; ubi quotidiana est pugna, et rara victoria.—*Int. Op. S. August.* Serm. 293, cap. ii ~d. B. App.

this virtue. ' With reason,' says Richard of Saint Lawrence, ' is Mary called the Virgin of virgins; for she,
without the counsel or example of others, was the first
who offered her virginity to God.'[2]   Thus did she bring
all virgins who imitate her to God, as David had already
foretold : " After her shall virgins be brought . . . into
the temple of the King."[3]   Without counsel and without example. Yes; for Saint Bernard says : ' O Virgin,
who taught thee to please God by virginity, and to lead
an angel's life on earth ?'[4]   ' Ah,' replies Saint Sophronius, ' God chose this most pure virgin for His Mother,
that she might be an example of chastity to all.'[5]   Therefore does Saint Ambrose call Mary ' the standard-bearer
of virginity.'[6]

By reason of her purity the Blessed Virgin was also
declared by the Holy Ghost to be beautiful as the turtle-
dove : " Thy cheeks are beautiful as the turtle-dove's."[7]
' Mary,' says Aponius, ' was a most pure turtle-dove.'[8]
For the same reason she was also called a lily : " As
the lily among the thorns, so is my love among the
daughters."[9]   On this passage Denis the Carthusian
remarks, that ' Mary was compared to a lily amongst
thorns, because all other virgins were thorns, either to
themselves or to others; but that the Blessed Virgin
was so neither to herself nor to others ;'[10] for she in-

---

[2] Merito dicitur Virgo virginum, quæ primo consecravit et vovit virginitatem absque omni præcepto, consilio, et exemplo.—*De Laud. V.* lib. i. cap. 5.
[3] Adducentur regi virgines post eam . . . in templum regis.—*Ps.* xliv. 15,
10.
[4] O Virgo prudens, O Virgo devota, quis te docuit Deo placere virginitatem . . . et in terris angelicam ducere vitam ?—*Hom.* iii. *sup. Missus.*
[5] Christus matrem virginem ideo elegit, ut ipsa omnibus esset exemplum
castitatis.—*Serm. de Assump. int. Op. S. Hieron.*
[6] Egregia Maria, quæ signum sacræ virginitatis extulit.—*De Inst. Virg.*
cap. v.
[7] Pulchræ sunt genæ tuæ sicut turturis.—*Cant.* i. 9.
[8] Justa ratione turturi, castissimæ avi, virginitas comparatur : quæ in B.
Maria obtinet principatum.—*In Cant.* lib. iv.
[9] Sicut lilium inter spinas, sic amica mea inter filias.—*Cant.* ii. 2.
[10] Quamvis enim fuerint multæ virgines sanctæ . : . tamen respectu hujus
unicæ Virginis . . . quasi spinæ fuisse videntur, in quantum aliquid culpæ
habebant, et quamvis in se fuerint mundæ, non tamen fuit in eis fomes prorsus extinctus, fuerunt et aliis spinæ, qui ex earum intuitu mucrone concupis-
centiæ pungebantur . . . Porro hæc unica Dei delectabilissima Virgo, totius
Superbeatissimæ Trinitatis media, et amica, ac socia, ab omni culpa fuit

spired all who looked at her with chaste thoughts.
This is confirmed by Saint Thomas,[11] who says, that
the beauty of the Blessed Virgin was an incentive to
chastity in all who beheld her. Saint Jerome declared
that it was his opinion that Saint Joseph remained a
virgin by living with Mary; for, writing against the
heretic Helvidius, who denied Mary's virginity, he says,
'Thou sayest that Mary did not remain a virgin. I
say, that not only she remained a virgin, but even that
Joseph preserved his virginity through Mary.'[12] An
author says, that so much did the Blessed Virgin love
this virtue, that, to preserve it, she would have been
willing to have renounced even the dignity of Mother
of God. This we may conclude from her answer to the
archangel, " How shall this be done, because I know
not man ?"[13] and from the words she afterwards added
" Be it done to me according to thy word,"[14] signifying
that she gave her consent on the condition that, as the
angel had assured her, she should become a Mother
only by the overshadowing of the Holy Ghost.

Saint Ambrose says, that ' whoever has preserved
chastity is an angel, and that he who has lost it is
a devil.'[15] Our Lord assures us that those who are
chaste become angels, " They shall be as the angels of
God in heaven."[16] But the impure become as devils,
hateful in the sight of God. Saint Remigius used to
say that the greater part of adults are lost by this vice.
Seldom, as we have already said with St. Augustine, is a

---

prorsus immunis: fuit in ea fomes plene extinctus, et tam intensissima ca*-
titate erat repleta, quod intuentium corda sic penetravit sua inestimabili
castitate virginea, quod a nullo potuit concupisci, imo potius extinxit ad
horam illorum libidinem.—*Exp. in Cant.* cap. ii. art. 8.

[11] Pulchritudo Beatæ Virginis intuentes ad castitatem excitabat.—*Spinelli,
M. Deip.* c. 14. n. 6.

[12] Tu dicis Mariam Virginem non permansisse; ego mihi plus vindico,
teiam ipsum Joseph virginem fuisse per Mariam.—*Adv. Helvid. de Virginitate
Mariæ.*

[13] Quomodo fiet istud, quoniam virum non cognosco ?—*Luc.* i. 34.

[14] Fiat mihi secundum verbum tuum.—*Ib.* 38.

[15] Castitas angelos fecit. Qui eam servavit, angelus est; qui perdidit,
diabolus.—*De Virginibus,* lib. i. cap. 9.

[16] Erunt sicut angeli Dei in cœlo.—*Matt.* xxii. 30.

victory gained over this vice. But why? It is because the means by which it may be gained are seldom made use of. These means are three, according to Bellarmine and the masters of a spiritual life : fasting, the avoidance of dangerous occasions, and prayer. By fasting, is to be understood especially mortification of the eyes and of the appetite. Although our Blessed Lady was full of Divine grace, yet she was so mortified in her eyes, that, according to Saint Epiphanius and Saint John Damascen, she always kept them cast down, and never fixed them on any one ; and they say that from her very childhood her modesty was such, that it filled every one who saw her with astonishment. Hence Saint Luke remarks, that, in going to visit Saint Elizabeth, " she went with haste," that she might be less seen in public. Philibert relates, that, as to her food, it was revealed to a hermit named Felix, that when a baby she only took milk once a day. Saint Gregory of Tours affirms, that throughout her life she fasted;[17] and Saint Bonaventure adds, 'that Mary would never have found so much grace, had she not been most moderate in her food ; for grace and gluttony cannot subsist together.'[18] In fine, Mary was mortified in all, so that of her it was said, "my hands dropped with myrrh."[19]

The second means is to fly the occasions of sin : " He that is aware of the snares shall be secure."[20] Hence Saint Philip Neri says, that, 'in the war of the senses, cowards conquer :' that is to say, those who fly from dangerous occasions. Mary fled as much as possible from the sight of men ; and therefore Saint Luke remarks, that in going to visit Saint Elizabeth, " she went with haste into the hill country." An author observes, that the Blessed Virgin left Saint Elizabeth before Saint John was born, as we learn from the same

---

[17] Nullo tempore Maria non jejunavit.—*Novarin. Umbra Virg.* exc. 38.
[18] Nunquam Maria tantam gratiam invenisset, nisi gratia Mariam in cibo et potu temperatissimam invenisset ; non enim se compatiuntur gratia et gula.—*Spec. B.V.M.* lect. iv.
[19] Manus meæ stillaverunt myrrham.—*Cant.* v. 5.
[20] Qui autem cavet laqueos, securus erit.—*Prov.* xi. 15.

Gospel, where it is said, that "Mary abode with her about three months, and she returned to her own house. Now Elizabeth's full time of being delivered was come, and she brought forth a son." And why did she not wait for this event? It was that she might avoid the conversations and visits which would accompany it.

The third means is prayer. "And as I knew," said the wise man, "that I could not otherwise be continent except God gave it . . . I went to the Lord and besought Him."[21] The Blessed Virgin revealed to Saint Elizabeth of Hungary, that she acquired no virtue without effort and continual prayer.[22] Saint John Damascen says, that Mary 'is pure, and a lover of purity.'[23] Hence she cannot endure those who are unchaste. But whoever has recourse to her will certainly be delivered from this vice, if he only pronounces her name with confidence. The venerable John d'Avila[24] used to say, 'that many have conquered impure temptations by only having devotion to her immaculate conception.' O Mary, O most pure Dove, how many are now in hell on account of this vice! Sovereign Lady, obtain us the grace always to have recourse to thee in our temptations, and always to invoke thee, saying, 'Mary, Mary, help us.' Amen.

Section VII. *Of Mary's Poverty.*

Our most loving Redeemer, that we might learn from Him to despise the things of the world, was pleased to be poor on earth: "Being rich," says Saint Paul, "He became poor for your sake, that through His poverty you might be rich."[1] Therefore doth Jesus Christ exhort each one who desires to be His disciple,

---

[21] Et ut scivi quoniam aliter non possem esse continens, nisi Deus det . . . adii Dominum, et deprecatus sum illum.—*Sap.* viii. 21.

[22] S. Bonav. Med. Vit. Chr. c. 3.

[23] Pura est et puritatem amans.—*De Dorm. B.M.* § 2.

[24] Audi fil. c. 14.

[1] Propter vos egenus factus est, cum esset dives, ut illius inopia vos divites essetis.—*2 Cor.* viii. 9.

"If thou wilt be perfect, go sell what thou hast, and give to the poor . . . and come, follow Me."[2] Behold Mary, His most perfect disciple, who indeed imitated His example. Father Canisius[3] proves that Mary could have lived in comfort on the property she inherited from her parents, but she preferred to remain poor, and reserving only a small portion for herself, distributed the rest in alms to the temple and the poor. Many authors[4] are of opinion that Mary even made a vow of poverty; and we know that she herself said to Saint Bridget, ' from the beginning I vowed in my own heart that I would never possess anything on earth.'[5] The gifts received from the holy Magi cannot certainly have been of small value; but we are assured by Saint Bernard[6] that she distributed them to the poor through the hands of Saint Joseph. That the divine Mother immediately disposed of these gifts is also evident from the fact, that at her purification in the temple she did not offer a lamb, which was the offering prescribed in Leviticus for those who could afford it, " for a son she shall bring a lamb;"[7] but she offered two turtle-doves, or two pigeons, which was the oblation prescribed for the poor : "And to offer a sacrifice, according as it is written in the law of the Lord, a pair of turtle-doves, or two young pigeons."[8] Mary herself said to Saint Bridget, ' All that I could get I gave to the poor, and only reserved a little food and clothing for myself.'[9]

Out of love for poverty she did not disdain to marry

---

[2] Si vis perfectus esse, vade, vende quæ habes, et da pauperibus . . . et veni, sequere me.—*Matt.* xix. 21.

[3] De V.M. l. 1. c. 4. l. 4. c. 7.

[4] Ap. Parav. p. 2, cap. 2. †

[5] Vovi in corde meo . . . nihil unquam possidere in mundo.—*Rev.* lib. i, cap. 10.

[6] Aurum sibi oblatis a Magis non modicum, prout decebat eorum regiam majestatem, non sibi reservavit, sed pauperibus per Joseph distribuit. †

[7] Pro filio . . . deferet agnum anniculum.—*Lev.* xii. 6.

[8] Et ut darent hostiam secundum quod dictum est in lege Domini, par turturum, aut duos pullos columbarum.—*Luc.* ii. 24.

[9] Omnia quæ habere potui, dedi indigentibus. Nihilque, nisi victum tenuem et vestitum reservavi.—*Rev.* lib. cap. 10.

Saint Joseph, who was only a poor carpenter, and afterwards to maintain herself by the work of her hands, by
spinning or sewing, as we are assured by Saint Bonaventure.[10]   The angel, speaking of Mary, told Saint
Bridget that ' worldly riches were of no more value in
her eyes than dirt.'[11]   In a word, she always lived poor,
and she died poor ; for at her death we do not know
that she left anything but two poor gowns, to two women who had served her during her life, as it is recorded
by Metaphrastes[12] and Nicephorus.[13]

Saint Philip Neri used to say that ' he who loves
the things of the world will never become a Saint.' We
may add what Saint Teresa said on the same subject,
that 'it justly follows that he who runs after perish-
able things should also himself be lost.'   But, on the
other hand, she adds, that the virtue of poverty is a
treasure which comprises in itself all other treasures.
She says the ' virtue of poverty ;' for, as Saint Bernard
remarks, this virtue does not consist only in being poor,
but in loving poverty.[14]   Therefore did Jesus Christ
say, " Blessed are the poor in spirit, for theirs is the
kingdom of heaven."[15]   They are blessed because they
desire nothing but God, and in God they find every
good ; in poverty they find their paradise on earth, as
Saint Francis did when he exclaimed, ' My God and my
all.'[16]   Let us, then, as Saint Augustine exhorts us,
'love that one good in which all good things are found,'[17]
and address our Lord in the words of Saint Ignatius,
' Give me only Thy love, with Thy grace, and I am rich
enough.'[18]   ' When we have to suffer from poverty, let
us console ourselves,' says Saint Bonaventure, ' with the

[10] Med. Vit. Chr. c. 12.
[11] Mundanæ divitiæ, velut fœtidissimum lutum, sibi vilescebant.—*Serm.
Ang.* cap. xiii.
[12] Hom. de Vita B.M.
[13] Hist. l. 2. c. 21.
[14] Non paupertas virtus reputatur, sed paupertatis amor.—*Epistola* c.
[15] Beati pauperes spiritu, quoniam ipsorum est regnum cœlorum.—*Matt.*
v. 3.
[16] Deus meus, et omnia.
[17] Ama unum bonum, in quo sunt omnia bona.—*Man.* c. 34.
[18] Amorem tui solum cum gratia tua mihi dones, et dives sum satis.

thought that Jesus and His Mother were also poor like ourselves.'[19]

Ah, my most holy Mother, thou hadst indeed reason to say that in God was thy joy : "and my spirit hath rejoiced in God my Saviour ;"[20] for in this world thou didst desire and love no other good but God. "Draw me after thee,"[21] O Lady ; detach me from the world, that I may love Him alone, who alone deserves to be loved. Amen.

SECTION VIII. *Of Mary's Obedience.*

When the angel Gabriel announced to Mary God's great designs upon her, she, through love for obedience, would only call herself a handmaid : "Behold the handmaid of the Lord."[1] 'Yes,' says Saint Thomas of Villanova, 'for this faithful handmaid never, in either thought or word or deed, contradicted the Most High ; but, entirely despoiled of her own will, she lived always and in all things obedient to that of God.'[2] She herself declared that God was pleased with her obedience, when she said, "He hath regarded the humility of His handmaid ;"[3] for in prompt obedience it is that the humility of a servant, properly speaking, consists. Saint Irenæus says that by her obedience the Divine Mother repaired the evil done by Eve's disobedience : 'As Eve, by her disobedience, caused her own death and that of the whole human race, so did the Virgin Mary, by her obedience, become the cause of her own salvation and of that of all mankind.'[4] Mary's obedience was much

---

[19] Pauper multum consolari potest de paupertate Mariæ et de paupere Christo.—*Spec. B.M.V.* § iv.

[20] Et exsultavit spiritus meus in Deo salutari meo.—*Luc.* i. 47.

[21] Trahe me . . . post te.—*Cant.* i. 3.

[1] Ecce ancilla Domini.—*Luc.* i. 38.

[2] Vere ancilla, quæ neque dicto, neque facto, neque cogitatu unquam contradixit Altissimo ; . . . nihil sibi libertatis reservans, sed per omnia subdita Deo.—*In Annunt. B.M.V.* conc. i.

[3] Respexit humilitatem ancillæ suæ.—*Luc.* i. 48.

[4] Sicut Heva inobediens, et sibi et universo generi humano causa facta est mortis ; sic et Maria Virgo obediens, et sibi et universo generi humano facta est causa salutis.—*Adv. Hær.* l. iii. c. 33.

more perfect than that of all other Saints; since all
men, on account of original sin, are prone to evil, and
find it difficult to do good; but not so the Blessed Virgin. Saint Bernardine writes, that, 'because Mary was
free from original sin, she found no obstacle in obeying
God; she was like a wheel, which was easily turned by
every inspiration of the Holy Ghost.'[5] 'Hence,' continues the same Saint, 'her only object in this world
was to keep her eyes constantly fixed on God, to discover His will, and, when she had found out what He
required, to perform it.'[6] Of her was said, "My soul
melted when He spoke;"[7] that is, as Richard explains
it, 'My soul was as metal, liquefied by the fire of love,
ready to be moulded into any form, according to the
Divine will.'[8]

Mary well proved how ready she was to obey in
all things, in the first place, when, to please God, she
obeyed even the Roman emperor, and undertook the
long journey of at least seventy miles to Bethlehem, in
the winter, when she was pregnant, and in such poverty
that she had to give birth to her Son in a stable. She
showed equal obedience in undertaking, on the very
same night on which she had notice of it from Saint
Joseph, the longer and more difficult journey into Egypt.
Here Silveira asks why the command to fly into Egypt
was given rather to Saint Joseph than to the Blessed
Virgin, who was to suffer the most from it; and he
answers, that it was 'that Mary might not be deprived
of an occasion in which to perform an act of obedience,
for which she was always most ready.'[9] But above

---

[5] In Virgine beata nullum fuit omnino retardativum; proinde rota volu-
bilis fuit, secundum omnem Spiritus Sancti nutum.—*Serm. in Assump. B.M.V.*
art. i. cap. **1.**

[6] Virgo semper habuit continuum aspectum ad Dei beneplacitum promp-
tumque consensum.—*Pro Fest. V.M.* s. 4. a. 3. c. 2.

[7] Anima mea liquefacta est, ut locutus est.—*Cant.* v. 6.

[8] Anima mea liquefacta est per incendium charitatis, parata instar me-
talli liquefacti decurrere in omnes modulos divinæ voluntatis.—*De Laud.
B.M.* l. 4.

[9] Ne Virgini subtraheretur occasio exercendi actum obedientiæ, ad quam
ipsa erat promptissima.—*Lib.* ii. cap. 7, q. 2.

all she showed her heroic obedience when, to obey the Divine will, she offered her Son to death; and this with such constancy, as Saint Ildephonsus says, that had executioners been wanting, she would have been ready herself to have crucified Him.[10] Hence Venerable Bede, explaining our Lord's answer to the woman spoken of in the Gospel, who exclaimed, "Blessed is the womb that bore Thee" .. "Yea, rather, blessed are they who hear the word of God and keep it,"[11] says that Mary was indeed blessed in becoming the Mother of God, but that she was much more so in always loving and obeying the Divine will.[12]

For this reason, all who love obedience are highly pleasing to the Blessed Virgin. She once appeared to a Franciscan friar, named Accorso, in his cell; whilst she was still present, obedience called him to hear the confession of a sick person. He went, and on his return found that Mary had waited for him, and highly commended his obedience. On the other hand, she greatly blamed another religious, who remained to finish some private devotions after the refectory-bell had rung.[13] Our Lord, once speaking to Saint Bridget on the security which is found in obeying a spiritual director, said, 'Obedience brings all Saints to glory;'[14] for, as Saint Philp Neri[15] used to say, 'God demands no account of things done by obedience, having Himself said, "He that heareth you, heareth Me: and he that despiseth you, despiseth Me."[16] The Mother of God herself revealed to Saint Bridget that through the merit of her obedience she had obtained so great power that no sinner, however great were his crimes, who had recourse

---

[10] Parata enim stetit, si deesset manus percussoris.—*Serm.* ii. *de Assump. B.M.V.*

[11] Beatus venter qui te portavit ... Quin immo beati, qui audiunt verbum Dei, et custodiunt illud.—*Luc.* xi. 27, 28.

[12] Et inde quidem beata, quia Verbi incarnandi ministra est facta temporalis: sed inde multo beatior, quia ejusdem semper amandi custos manebat æterna.—Cap. xlix. *in Luc.*

[13] Novarin. Umbra Virg. exc. 79.

[14] Obedientia omnes introducit ad gloriam.—*Rev.* lib. vi. cap. 2.

[15] Bacci. l. 1. c. 20.

[16] Qui vos audit, me audit: et qui vos spernit, me spernit.—*Luc.* x. 16

to her with a purpose of amendment, failed to obtain pardon.'[17]　Our own sweet Queen, then, and Mother, intercede with Jesus for us; by the merit of thine obedience obtain that we may be faithful in obeying His will and the commands of our spiritual fathers. Amen.

SECTION IX. *Of Mary's Patience.*

This world being a place of merit, it is rightly called a valley of tears; for we are all placed in it to suffer, that we may, by patience, gain our own souls unto life eternal, as our Lord Himself says, "In your patience you shall possess your souls."[1]　God gave us the Blessed Virgin Mary as a model of all virtues, but more especially as an example of patience.　Saint Francis of Sales, amongst other things, remarks, that it was precisely for this reason that at the marriage-feast of Cana Jesus Christ gave the Blessed Virgin an answer, by which He seemed to value her prayers but little: "Woman, what is that to thee and to me?"[2]　And He did this that He might give us the example of the patience of His most holy Mother.　But what need have we to seek for instances of this virtue?　Mary's whole life was a continual exercise of her patience; for, as the angel revealed to Saint Bridget, 'as a rose grows up amongst thorns, so did this Blessed Virgin grow up amongst tribulations.'[3]　Compassion alone for the Redeemer's sufferings sufficed to make her a martyr of patience.　Hence Saint Bonaventure says, that 'a crucified Mother conceived a crucified Son.'[4]　In speaking of her dolours, we have already considered how much she suffered, both in her journey to, and during her residence in, Egypt,

---

[17] Pro obedientia mea tantam potestatem obtinui, quod nullus tam immundus peccator est, si ad me cum emendationis proposito convertitur et cum corde contrito, non habebit veniam.—*Rev.* lib. i. cap. 42.

[1] In patientia vestra possidebitis animas vestras.—*Luc.* xxi. 19.

[2] Quid mihi et tibi est, mulier?—*Joan.* ii. 4.

[3] See page 407, note 20.

[4] Crucifixa crucifixum concepit.—*Pro Fest. V.M.* s. viii. s. 2.

as also during the time she lived with her Son in the house at Nazareth. What Mary endured when present at the death of Jesus on Calvary is alone sufficient to show us how constant and sublime was her patience: "There stood by the cross of Jesus His Mother." Then it was that precisely by the merit of her patience, as blessed Albert the Great says, she brought us forth to the life of grace.[5]

If we, then, wish to be the children of Mary, we must endeavour to imitate her in her patience: 'For what,' says Saint Cyprian, 'can enrich us with greater merit in this life, and greater glory in the next, than the patient endurance of sufferings?'[6] God said, by the prophet Osee, "I will hedge up thy way with thorns."[7] To this Saint Gregory adds, that 'the way of the elect is hedged with thorns.'[8] As a hedge of thorns protects a vineyard, so does God protect His servants from the danger of attaching themselves to the earth, by encompassing them with tribulations. Therefore Saint Cyprian concludes, that it is patience which delivers us from sin and from hell.[9] It is also patience which makes saints: "Patience hath a perfect work,"[10] bearing in peace, not only the crosses which come immediately from God, such as sickness, poverty, &c., but also those which come from men—persecutions, injuries, and the rest. Saint John saw all the Saints bearing palm-branches—the emblem of martyrdom—in their hands: "After this I saw a great multitude, and palms were in their hands;"[11] thereby denoting that all adults who are saved must be martyrs, either by shedding their blood for Christ or by patience. 'Rejoice, then,' exclaims Saint Gregory; 'we can be martyrs without the

---

[5] Maria facta est mater nostra, quos genuit Filio compatiendo. †
[6] Quid utilius ad vitam, vel majus ad gloriam, quam patientia?—*De Bono Pat.*
[7] Sepiam viam tuam spinis.—*Osee* ii. 6.
[8] Electorum viæ spinis sepiuntur.—*Mor.* l. 34, c. 1.
[9] Patientia nos servat.—*De Bono Pat.*
[10] Patientia autem opus perfectum habet.—*Jac.* i. 4.
[11] Post hæc vidi turbam magnam . . . et palmæ in manibus eorum.—*Apoc.* vii. 9.

executioner's sword, if we only preserve patience.'[12] 'Provided only,' as Saint Bernard says, 'we endure the afflictions of this life with patience and joy,'[13] O what fruit will not every pain borne for God's sake produce for us in heaven! Hence the Apostle encourages us, saying, "That which is at present momentary and light of our tribulation worketh for us above measure exceedingly an eternal weight of glory."[14] Saint Teresa's instructions on this subject are beautiful. She used to say, 'Those who embrace the cross do not feel it;' and elsewhere, 'that if we resolve to suffer, the pain ceases.' When our crosses weigh heavily upon us, let us have recourse to Mary, who is called by the Church 'the Comfortress of the afflicted;' and by Saint John Damascen, 'the Remedy for all sorrows of the heart.'[15] Ah, my most sweet Lady, thou who wast innocent didst suffer with so much patience; and shall I, who deserve hell, refuse to suffer? My Mother, I now ask thee this favour—not, indeed, to be delivered from crosses, but to bear them with patience. For the love of Jesus, I entreat thee to obtain at least this grace for me from God; from thee do I hope for it with confidence.

Section X. *Of Mary's Prayer.*

There never was a soul on earth who practised in so perfect a manner as the Blessed Virgin the great lesson taught by our Saviour, "that we ought always to pray, and not to faint."[1] From no one, says Saint Bonaventure, can we better take example, and learn how necessary is perseverance in prayer, than from

---

[12] Nos sine ferro martyres esse possumus, si patientiam custodiamus.— *In Evang.* hom. 35.
[13] Patienter et libenter.—*De Div.* s. 16.
[14] Momentaneum et leve tribulationis nostræ . . . æternum gloriæ pondus operatur in nobis.—2 *Cor.* iv. 17.
[15] Omnium dolorum cordis medicamentum.—*De Dorm. B.M.* s. 2.
[1] Oportet semper orare, et non deficere.—*Luc.* xviii. 1.

Mary : ' Mary gave an example which we must follow and not faint;'[2] for blessed Albert the Great asserts, ' that, after Jesus Christ, the Divine Mother was the most perfect in prayer of all who ever have been, or ever will be.'[3] In the first place, because her prayer was continual and persevering. In the very first moment, in which she had the perfect use of reason, which was, as we have said in the discourse on her nativity, in the first moment of her existence, she began to pray. That she might be able to devote herself still more to prayer, when only three years of age she shut herself up in the retirement of the temple ; where, amongst other hours set aside for this exercise, as she herself told Saint Elizabeth of Hungary, ' she always rose at midnight, and went before the altar of the temple to offer her supplications.'[4] For the same purpose, and that she might constantly meditate on the sufferings of Jesus, Odilo says, ' she very frequently visited the places of our Lord's Nativity, Passion, and Sepulture.'[5] More-over, she prayed with the greatest recollection of spirit, free from every distraction and inordinate affection, nor did any exterior occupation ever obscure the light of her unceasing contemplation, as we are assured by Denis the Carthusian.[6]

Through love for prayer, the Blessed Virgin was so enamoured of solitude, that, as she told Saint Bridget, when she lived in the temple she avoided even inter-course with her parents.[7] On the words of the prophet Isaias, " Behold a Virgin shall conceive and bear a Son,

---

[2] Maria indefesse perseverando in oratione exemplum dedit, quam oportet sequi et non deficere.—*Spec. B.M.V.* lect. iv.

[3] Virtus orationis in B. Virgine excellentissima fuit.—*Sup. Miss.* 80. †

[4] Surgebam semper in noctis medio, et pergebam ante altare templi . . . Et sic stando ante altare septem petitiones Domino faciebam.—*Ap. S. Bonav. de Vita Christ.* cap. iii.

[5] Loca Dominicæ Nativitatis, Passionis, Sepulturæ, frequenter invisere cupiebat.—*De Assump.*

[6] Nulla unquam inordinata affectio, distractio, fragilitas, virtuosissimam mentem ejus Virginis a contemplationis lumine revocavit, neque occupatio ulla exterior.—*De Laud. V.* lib. ii. art. 8.

[7] Rev. l. 1. c. 10.

and His name shall be called Emanuel,"[8] Saint Jerome remarks, that the word *virgin*, in Hebrew, properly signifies *a retired virgin;* so that even the prophet foretold the affection which Mary would have for solitude. Richard of Saint Lawrence says that the angel addressed her in these words, " The Lord is with thee," on account of her great love for retirement.[9] For this reason Saint Vincent Ferrer asserts, that the Divine Mother ' only left her house to go to the temple, and then her demeanour was all composed, and she kept her eyes modestly cast down.'[10] For the same reason, when she went to visit St. Elizabeth, " she went with haste."[11] From this, Saint Ambrose says, ' that virgins should learn to avoid the world.' Saint Bernard affirms that, on account of Mary's love for prayer and solitude, ' she was always careful to avoid the society and converse of men.'[12] She was therefore called a turtle-dove by the Holy Ghost : "Thy cheeks are beautiful as the turtle-dove's."[13] ' The turtle-dove,' says Vergello, ' is a solitary bird, and denotes unitive affection in the soul.'[14] Hence it was that the Blessed Virgin always lived solitary in this world as in a desert, and that of her it was said, "Who is she that goeth up by the desert, as a pillar of smoke ?"[15] On these words the Abbot Rupert says, ' Thus didst thou, indeed, loving solitude, ascend by the desert.'[16]

Philo assures us, that ' God only speaks to souls in solitude.'[17] God Himself declares the same thing by

[8] Ecce virgo concipiet, et pariet filium, et vocabitur nomen ejus Emanuel. — *Is.* vii. 14.
[9] Dominus tecum, merito solitudinis quam summe diligebat.—*De Laud. V.* lib. i. cap. 6.
[10] Nunquam exibat e domo, nisi quando ibat ad templum, et tunc ibat tota composita, semper habebat oculos suos ad terram.—*Serm.* ii. *in Vig. Nat. Christi.*
[11] Abiit cum festinatione.—*Luc.* i. 39.
[12] In proposito erat hominum fugere frequentias, vitare colloquia.—*De Laud. V.M.* hom. 3.
[13] Pulchræ sunt genæ tuæ sicut turturis.—*Cant.* i. 9.
[14] Turtur est solivaga, et signat mentis virtutem unitivam.—*Ap. S. Bonav. Dist.* vii. †
[15] Quæ est ista, quæ ascendit per desertum, sicut virgula fumi ?—*Cant.* iii. 6.
[16] Note 7, p. 373. [17] Dei Sermo amat deserta. †

the prophet Osee : " I will lead her into the wilderness : and I will speak to her heart."[18]   ' O happy solitude !' exclaims Saint Jerome, ' in which God speaks familiarly and converses with His own.'[19]   ' Yes,' says Saint Bernard ; ' for solitude, and the silence which is there enjoyed, force the soul to leave the earth in thought, and meditate on the things of heaven.'[20]   Most holy Virgin, do thou obtain us affection for prayer and retirement, that, detaching ourselves from the love of creatures, we may aspire only after God and heaven, where we hope one day to see thee, to praise thee, and to love thee, together with Jesus, thy Son, for ever and ever.   Amen.

" Come over to me, all ye that desire me, and be filled with my fruits."[21]   Mary's fruits are her virtues. ' Thou hast had none like thee, nor shalt thou have an equal.   Thou alone of women hast above all pleased Christ.'[22]

---

[18] Ducam eam in solitudinem, et loquar ad cor ejus.—*Osee* ii. 14.

[19] O solitudo, in qua Deus cum suis familiariter loquitur et conversatur. †

[20] Silentium, et a strepitu quies cogit cœlestia meditare.—*Epist.* 78.

[21] Transite ad me, omnes qui concupiscitis me, et a generationibus meis implemini.—*Eccl.* xxiv. 26.

[22] Nec primam similem visa es, nec habere sequentem.   **Sola sine exemplo** placuisti femina Christo.—*Sedulius, Op. pasch.* l. 2.

VARIOUS PRACTICES OF DEVOTION

THE DIVINE MOTHER.

TOGETHER WITH INSTRUCTIONS AS TO THE MANNER IN WHICH
THEY ARE BEST PERFORMED.

'THE Queen of Heaven is so gracious and liberal,' says
Saint Andrew of Crete, 'that she recompenses her servants with the greatest munificence for the most trifling
devotions.'[1] Two conditions, however, there are: the first
is, that when we offer her our devotions, our souls should
be free from sin; otherwise she would address us, as she
did a wicked soldier, spoken of by Saint Peter Celes-
tine.[2] This soldier every day performed some devotion
in honour of our Blessed Lady. One day he was suffering greatly from hunger, when Mary appeared to him,
and offered him some most delicious meats, but in so
filthy a vessel, that he could not bring himself to taste
them. 'I am the Mother of God,' the Blessed Virgin
then said, 'and am come to satisfy thy hunger.' 'But,
O Lady,' he answered, 'I cannot eat out of so dirty a
vessel.' 'And how,' replied Mary, 'canst thou expect
that I should accept thy devotions, offered to me with
so defiled a soul as thine?' On hearing this the soldier
was converted, became a hermit, and lived in a desert
for thirty years. At death, the Blessed Virgin again
appeared to him, and took him herself to heaven. In

[1] Sanctissima, cum munificentissima sit, pro minutissimis majora retri
buit.—*Serm.* iii. *in Dorm. B.M.V.*   [2] Opusc. cap. 23.

the first part of this work we said that it was morally impossible for a client of Mary to be lost; but this must be understood, on condition that he lives either without sin, or, at least, with the desire to abandon it; for then the Blessed Virgin will help him. But should any one, on the other hand, sin in the hope that Mary will save him, he thereby would render himself unworthy and incapable of her protection. The second condition is perseverance in devotion to Mary: 'Perseverance alone,' says Saint Bernard, 'will merit a crown.'[3] When Thomas à Kempis was a young man, he used every day to have recourse to the Blessed Virgin with certain prayers; he one day omitted them; he then omitted them for some weeks, and finally gave them up altogether. One night he saw Mary in a dream: she embraced all his companions, but when his turn came she said, 'What dost thou expect, thou who hast given up thy devotions? Depart, thou art unworthy of my caresses.' On hearing this, Thomas awoke in alarm, and resumed his ordinary prayers.[4] Hence, Richard of Saint Lawrence with reason says, that 'he who perseveres in his devotion to Mary will be blessed in his confidence, and will obtain all he desires.'[5] But as no one can be certain of this perseverance, no one before death can be certain of salvation. The advice given by the venerable John Berchmans, of the Society of Jesus, deserves our particular attention. When this holy young man was dying, his companions entreated him, before he left this world, to tell them what devotion they could perform which would be most agreeable to our Blessed Lady. He replied in the following remarkable words: 'Any devotion, however small, provided it is constant.'[6] I therefore now give with simplicity, and in a few words, the various devotions which we can offer to our Mother, in order to

[3] Perseverantia sola meretur viris gloriam, coronam virtutibus.—*Ep.* **cxxix.**
[4] Auriemma, Aff. Scamb. p. 1, c. 4.
[5] Qui tenuerit eam perseveranter . . . beatus hic erit in spe . . . quia omnia optata succedent ei.—Lib. ii. cap. 1.
[6] Quidquid minimum, dummodo sit constans.

obtain her favour; and this I consider the most useful part of my work. But I do not so much recommend my dear reader to practise them all as to choose those which please him most, and to persevere in them, with fear that if he omits them he may lose the protection of the Divine Mother. O, how many are there now in hell, who would have been saved had they only persevered in the devotions which they once practised in honour of Mary!

FIRST DEVOTION.

Of the Hail Mary.

This angelical salutation is most pleasing to the ever-blessed Virgin; for, whenever she hears it, it would seem as if the joy which she experienced when Saint Gabriel announced to her that she was the chosen Mother of God, was renewed in her; and with this object in view, we should often salute her with the 'Hail Mary.' 'Salute her,' says Thomas à Kempis, 'with the angelical salutation; for she indeed hears this sound with pleasure.'[1] The Divine Mother herself told Saint Matilda that no one could salute her in a manner more agreeable to herself than with the 'Hail Mary.'[2] He who salutes Mary will also be saluted by her. Saint Bernard once heard a statue of the Blessed Virgin salute him, saying, 'Hail Bernard.'[3] Mary's salutation, says Saint Bonaventure, will always be some grace corresponding with the wants of him who salutes her: 'She willingly salutes us with grace, if we willingly salute her with a Hail Mary.'[4] Richard of Saint Lawrence adds, 'that if we address the Mother of our Lord, saying, "Hail Mary," she cannot refuse the grace which we

---

[1] Salutate eam angelica salutatione frequenter, quia hanc vocem audit valde libenter.—P. 2. *Serm.* ii. *ad Nov.*
[2] Spir. Grat. l. i. c. 67.   [3] Ave, Bernarde.
[4] Libenter nos salutat cum gratia, si libenter salutamus cum Ave Maria. —*Spec. B. V.* lect. 4.

ask.'[5] Mary herself promised Saint Gertrude as many graces at death as she should have said 'Hail Marys.'[6] Blessed Alan asserts, 'that as all heaven rejoices when the "Hail Mary" is said, so also do the devils tremble and take to flight.'[7] This Thomas à Kempis affirms on his own experience; for he says, that once the devil appeared to him, and instantly fled on hearing the 'Hail Mary.'[8]

To practise this devotion : I. We can every morning and evening on getting up and going to bed, say three 'Hail Marys' prostrate, or at least kneeling; and add to each 'Ave' this short prayer : '*O Mary, by thy pure and immaculate conception, make my body pure, and my soul holy.*' We should then, as Saint Stanislaus always did, ask Mary's blessing as our Mother; place ourselves under the mantle of her protection, beseeching her to guard us during the coming day or night from sin. For this purpose it is very advisable to have a beautiful picture or image of the Blessed Virgin.—II. We can say the *Angelus*, with the usual three 'Hail Marys,' in the morning, at mid-day, and in the evening. Pope John XXII. was the first to grant an indulgence for this devotion; it was on the following occasion, as Father Crasset relates it :[9] A criminal was condemned to be burned alive on the vigil of the Annunciation of the Mother of God : he saluted her with a 'Hail Mary;' and in the midst of the flames he, and even his clothes, remained uninjured. Benedict XIII. afterwards granted a hundred days' indulgence to all who recite it, and a plenary indulgence once a month to those who during that time have recited it daily as above, on condition of going to confession and receiving the holy Communion, and praying for the usual intentions. Father **Crasset says** that Clement X. granted other indulgences

---

[5] Si quis veniat ad mensam Matris Domini, dicens Ave Maria, numquid ipsa largitas ei gratiam poterit denegare?—Lib. ii. cap. 7.
  [6] Insin. l. 4, c. 53.
  [7] See note 37, page 124.   [8] Serm. **xxi. ad** Nov.
  [9] Tom. ii. tr. 6, prat. 2.

to those who, at the end of each 'Hail Mary,' add, 'Thanks be to God and to Mary.' Formerly, at the sound of the bell, all knelt down to say the 'Angelus ;' but in the present day there are some who are ashamed to do so; Saint Charles Borromeo was not ashamed to get out of his carriage, or get off his horse, to say it in the street ; and even sometimes in the mud. It is related that there was a slothful religious who neglected to kneel at the sound of the Angelus bell; he saw the belfry bow down three times, and a voice said, 'Behold, wilt thou not do that which even inanimate creatures do ?'[10] Here we must remark that Benedict XIV. directed that in paschal time, instead of saying the 'Angelus,' we should say the 'Regina cœli ;' and that on Saturday evenings, and the whole of Sunday, the 'Angelus' should be said standing.—III. We can salute the Mother of God with a 'Hail Mary' every time we hear the clock strike. Blessed Alphonsus Rodriguez saluted her every hour ; and at night, if the hour had passed without his doing so, angels awoke him, that he might not omit this devotion.—IV. In going out and returning to the house, we can salute the Blessed Virgin with a 'Hail Mary,' that both out of doors and in she may guard us from all sin ; and we should each time kiss her feet, as the Carthusian fathers always do.— V. We should reverence every image of Mary which we pass with a 'Hail Mary.' For this purpose those who can do so would do well to place a beautiful image of the Blessed Virgin on the wall of their houses, that it may be venerated by those who pass. In Naples, and still more in Rome, there are most beautiful images of our Blessed Lady placed along the waysides by her devout clients.—VI. By command of the holy Church, all the canonical hours are preceded by, and concluded with, a 'Hail Mary ;' we should therefore do well to begin and end all our actions with a 'Hail Mary.' I say **all our actions,** whether spiritual, such as prayer, con-

[10] Auriemma, Aff. p. 1. c. 3.

fession and communion, spiritual reading, hearing sermons, and such-like; or temporal, such as study, giving advice, working, going to table, to bed, &c.
Happy are those actions which are enclosed between
two 'Hail Marys.' So also should we do on waking
in the morning, on closing our eyes to sleep, in
every temptation, in every danger, in every inclination
to anger, and such-like; on these occasions we should
always say a 'Hail Mary.' My dear reader, do this,
and you will see the immense advantage that you will
derive from it. Remember also that for every 'Hail
Mary' there is an indulgence of twenty days.[11] Father
Auriemma relates that the Blessed Virgin promised
Saint Matilda a happy death if she every day recited
three 'Hail Marys,' in honour of her power, wisdom,
and goodness.[12] Moreover, she herself told Saint Jane
de Chantal that the 'Hail Mary' was most acceptable
to her, and especially when recited ten times in honour
of her ten virtues.

SECOND DEVOTION.

Of Novenas.

Devout clients of Mary are all attention and fervour
in celebrating the novenas, or nine days preceding her
festivals; and the Blessed Virgin is all love, in dispensing innumerable and most special graces to them.
Saint Gertrude one day saw, under Mary's mantle, a
band of souls, whom the great Lady was considering
with the most tender affection; and she was given to
understand that they were persons who, during the preceding days, had prepared themselves with various devotions for the Feast of the Assumption.[1] The following devotions are some of those which can be used during
the novenas. I. We may make mental prayer in the

---

[11] Viva. App. de Ind. ⸹ ult.   [12] Aff. p. 2, c. 15.   [1] Insin. 1. 4, c. 50

morning and evening, and a visit to the Blessed Sacrament, adding nine 'Our Fathers, Hail Marys, and Glory be to the Fathers.' II. We may pay Mary three visits (visiting her statue or picture), and thank our Lord for the graces He granted her ; and each time ask the Blessed Virgin for some special grace : in one of these visits the prayer, which will be found in this volume, after the discourse on the feast, whichever it may be, can be said. III. We may make many acts of love towards Mary (at least fifty or a hundred), and also towards Jesus ; for we can do nothing which pleases her more than to love her Son, as she said to Saint Bridget : ' If thou wishest to bind thyself to me, love my Son.'[2] IV. We may read every day of the novena, for a quarter of an hour, some book which treats of her glories. V. We may perform some external mortification, such as wearing a hair-cloth, taking a discipline, or the like ; we can also fast, or at table abstain from fruit, or some favourite dish, at least in part, or chew some bitter herbs. On the vigil of the feast we may fast on bread and water : but none of these things should be done without the permission of our confessor. Interior mortifications, however, are the best of all to practise during these novenas, such as to avoid looking at or listening to things out of curiosity; to remain in retirement; observe silence; be obedient ; not give impatient answers ; bear contradictions, and such things ; which can all be practised with less danger of vanity, with greater merit, and do not need the confessor's permission. The most useful exercise is to propose, from the beginning of the novena, to correct some fault into which we fall the most frequently. For this purpose it will be well, in the visits spoken of above, to ask pardon for past faults, to renew our resolution not to commit them any more, and to implore Mary's help. The devotion most dear and pleasing to Mary is, to endeavour to imitate her virtues ; therefore it would be well always to propose to

2 Si te mihi vis devincere, ama Filium meum Jesum.

ourselves the imitation of some virtue which corresponds
with the festival; as, for example, on the feast of her
Immaculate Conception, purity of intention; on her
Nativity, renovation of spirit, to throw off tepidity;
on her Presentation, detachment from something to
which we are most attached; on her Annunciation,
humility in supporting contempt; on her Visitation,
charity towards our neighbour, in giving alms, or at
least in praying for sinners; on her Purification, obedience to superiors; and in fine, on the Feast of her
Assumption, let us endeavour to detach ourselves from
the world, do all to prepare ourselves for death, and
order each day of our lives as if it was to be our last.
VI. Besides going to communion on the day of the
feast, it would be well to ask leave from our confessor
to go more frequently during the novena. Father Segneri used to say, that we cannot honour Mary better
than with Jesus. She herself revealed to a holy soul
(as Father Crasset relates),[3] that we could offer her nothing which was more pleasing to her than the Holy
Communion; for in that Holy Sacrament it is that
Jesus gathers the fruit of His Passion in our souls.
Hence it appears that the Blessed Virgin desires nothing so much of her clients as Communion; saying,
" Come, eat my bread, and drink the wine which I
have mingled for you."[4] VII. Finally, on the day of
the feast, after Communion, we must offer ourselves to
the service of this Divine Mother, and ask her the grace
to practise the virtue, or whatever other grace we had
proposed to ourselves, during the novena. It is well
every year to choose, amongst the feasts of the Blessed
Virgin, one for which we have the greatest and most
tender devotion; and for this one to make a very
special preparation, by dedicating ourselves anew, and
in a more particular manner, to her service, choosing

[3] Tom. ii. tr. 6, prat. 6.

[4] Venite, comedite panem meum, et bibite vinum quod miscui vobis.—
Prov. ix. 5.

her for our Sovereign Lady, Advocate, and Mother.[5] Then we must ask her pardon for all our negligence in her service during the past year, and promise greater fidelity for the next ; and conclude by begging her to accept us for her servants, and to obtain us a holy death.

THIRD DEVOTION.

Of the Rosary and Office of our Blessed Lady.

It is well known that the devotion of the most holy rosary was revealed to Saint Dominic by the Divine Mother herself, at a time when the Saint was in affliction, and bewailing, with his Sovereign Lady, over the Albigensian heretics, who were at that time doing great mischief to the Church. The Blessed Virgin said to him : 'This land will always be sterile until rain falls on it.' Saint Dominic was then given to understand that this rain was the devotion of the rosary, which he was to propagate. This the Saint indeed did, and it was embraced by all Catholics ; so much so that, even to the present day, there is no devotion so generally practised by the faithful of all classes as that of the rosary. What is there that modern heretics, Calvin, Bucer, and others, have not said to throw discredit on the use of beads ? But the immense good which this noble devotion has done to the world is well known. How many, by its means, have been delivered from sin ! how many led to a holy life ! how many to a good death, and are now saved ! To be convinced of this, we need only read the many books which treat on the subject. Suffice it to know that this devotion has been approved of by the Church, and that the Sovereign Pontiffs have enriched it with indulgences. The following are the principal indulgences which may be

---

[5] At the end of the book will be found two formulas for this dedication ; the one for a single person, the other for a family.

gained by those who use beads, to which the Bridgetine indulgences have been attached.

I. A hundred days' indulgence for every 'Our Father,' 'Hail Mary,' and 'Creed.'—*Leo X., July* 10, 1815.

II. For reciting the whole rosary of fifteen decades, besides the above indulgences, one of seven years, and seven quarantines.—*Ib.*

III. If the rosary is said with another person or persons, the same indulgence may be gained.—*Ib.*

IV. Those who say at least five decades of the rosary every day for a year can gain, on a day at their own choice, a plenary indulgence, provided that, truly contrite for their sins, they approach the holy sacraments of Penance and the Eucharist, and pray for the welfare of the Church.—*Clement XI., Sep.* 22, 1714.

V. Those who say at least five decades of the rosary once a week can gain a plenary indulgence on the feast of Saint Bridget (8th of October), on condition that they approach the holy sacraments of Penance and the Eucharist, and in their parish church, or some other church, pray as above.—*Benedict XIV., Jan.* 15, 1743.

VI. Those who are in the habit of saying the rosary as above can, in the article of death, having confessed and received the Holy Communion, gain a plenary indulgence by pronouncing the holy name of Jesus, with sorrow for their sins, at least mentally, if they are unable to do so with their lips.—*Ib.*

VII. Those who say the rosary, as above, every day for a month, can, on a day at their choice within the month, gain a plenary indulgence by going to confession and communion, visiting a church, and praying as above.—*Ib.*

VIII. Those who have the rosary with them, and, contrite for their sins, examine their consciences, and say an 'Our Father' and three 'Hail Marys,' gain an indulgence of twenty days.—*Ib.*

IX. Those who have their rosary with them, and hear mass on any day, hear a sermon, or accompany the Holy Viaticum to a sick person, convert a sinner, or perform any act of piety in honour of our Lord Jesus **Christ, or** of the Blessed Virgin Mary, or of Saint Bridget, and say three ' Our Fathers' and ' Hail Marys,' gain an indulgence of a hundred days.—*Ib.*

X. All the above indulgences are applicable to the souls in purgatory.

Very many other indulgences have been granted to this devotion by various pontiffs : it would therefore be well for all to have the intention to gain all the indulgences which have been granted. The beads must have had the indulgences of Saint Bridget annexed to them by a priest who has received the power to do so. Only the first person who uses them after the blessing can gain the indulgences. If the beads are given away after they have been once used, they must be blessed again. It is also necessary to meditate during the recitation of the rosary on the mysteries which may be found in almost all prayer-books; but it is sufficient for those who do not know them to meditate upon any one of the mysteries of the Passion of Jesus Christ, His scourging, death, &c. The rosary should also be said with devotion ; and here we may call to mind what the Blessed Virgin said to Saint Eulalia, ' that she was better pleased with five decades said slowly and devoutly than with fifteen said in a hurry and with little devotion.'[1] It is, therefore, well to say the rosary kneeling, before an image of Mary ; and, before each decade, to make an act of love to Jesus and Mary, and ask them for some particular grace. It is also preferable to say it with others rather than alone.

As to the little office of the Blessed Virgin, which is said to have been composed by Saint Peter Damian, Pius V. granted indulgences to those who recited it , and the Blessed Virgin has many times shown now acceptable this devotion is to her ; as may be seen in Father Auriemma's little work.[2] She is also much pleased with the Litany of Loretto, for reciting which there is

---

[1] Men. Cist. 11 Maii.   [2] Aff. p. i. cap. viii.

an indulgence of three hundred days each time ; and for those who say it every day, a plenary indulgence on Mary's five principal festivals,—the Immaculate Conception, Nativity, Annunciation, Purification, and Assumption, on the usual conditions.   The hymn, ' Hail, Star of the Sea,' is also very pleasing to Mary ; she desired Saint Bridget to say it every day :[3] but still more is she pleased with the ' Magnificat ;' for we then praise her in the very words in which she herself praised God.

FOURTH DEVOTION.

Of Fasting.

There are many devout clients of Mary who, to honour her, fast on bread and water on Saturdays, and the vigils of her feasts.   It is well known that Saturday is dedicated by the holy Church to Mary, because, as Saint Bernard says, on that day, the day after the death of her Son, she remained constant in faith.[1] Therefore Mary's clients are careful to honour her on that day by some particular devotion, and especially by fasting on bread and water, as did Saint Charles Borromeo, Cardinal Tolet, and so many others.   Nittardo, Bishop of Bamberg, and Father Joseph Arriaga, of the Society of Jesus, took no food at all on that day. The great graces which the Mother of God has dispensed to those who do this are recorded by Father Auriemma in his little work.[2] Let one example suffice : it is that of a famous captain of brigands, who, on account of this devotion, was preserved in life after his head was cut off, and was thus enabled to make his confession ; for the unfortunate creature was in a state

---

[3] Rev. extr. c. 8.
[1] Per illud tristc Sabbatum stetit in fide, et salvata fuit Ecclesia in ipsa sola : propter quod, aptissime tota Ecclesia, in laudem et gloriam ejusdem Virginis, diem sabbati per totius anni circulum celebrare consuevit.—*De Pass. Dom.* cap. ii.
[2] Tom. i. cap. 17.

of sin. After confession he declared that, on account of this devotion, the Blessed Virgin had obtained him so great a grace, and immediately expired.[3] It would not, then, be anything very great, for a person who pretends to be devout to Mary, and particularly for one who has perhaps already deserved hell, to offer her this fast on Saturdays. I affirm that those who practise this devotion can hardly be lost ; not that I mean to say that if they die in mortal sin the Blessed Virgin will deliver them by a miracle, as she did this bandit : these are prodigies of Divine mercy which very rarely occur, and it would be the height of folly to expect eternal salvation by such means ; but I say, that for those who practise this devotion, the Divine Mother will make perseverance in God's grace easy, and obtain them a good death. All the members of our little congregation, who are able to do so, practise this devotion. I say those who are able to do so ; for if our health does not permit it, at least we should on Saturdays content ourselves with one dish, or observe an ordinary fast, or abstain from fruit, or something for which we have a relish. On Saturdays we should always practise some devotion in honour of our Blessed Lady, receive the holy Communion, or at least hear Mass, visit an image of Mary, wear a hair-cloth, or something of that sort. But on the vigils of her seven principal festivals, at all events, her clients should offer her this fast either on bread and water, or otherwise as best they can.

FIFTH DEVOTION.

Of Visiting the Images of Mary.

Father Segneri says,[1] that the devil did not know how to repair his losses in the overthrow of idolatry better than by attacking sacred images through the in-

---

[3] Ap. Auriemma, loc. cit.   [1] Div. di M. p. 2, c. 3.

strumentality of heretics. But the holy Church has defended them even with the blood of martyrs ; and the Divine Mother has shown by prodigies how pleasing to her are the visits paid to her images. Saint John Damascen had his hand cut off for having defended, by his writings, the images of Mary ; but his Sovereign Lady miraculously restored it to him. Father Spinelli relates,[2] that in Constantinople, a veil which covered an image of the Blessed Virgin, on every Saturday drew itself aside, and after vespers again closed of its own accord. The veil of an image of our Blessed Lady, visited by Saint John of God, was once withdrawn in a similar manner ; so much so that the sacristan thought that the Saint was a robber, and kicked him ; but his foot instantly withered.[3] Hence all Mary's clients often visit her images and the churches dedicated in her honour with great affection. These are precisely, according to Saint John Damascen, the cities of refuge in which we can find safety from temptations, and the chastisements which we have deserved for our sins. The first thing that the Emperor Saint Henry used to do, on entering a city, was to visit a church of our Blessed Lady. Father Thomas Sanchez used never to return home without having visited some church of Mary. Let us not think it too much to visit our Queen every day in some church or chapel, or even in our own house, where for this purpose it would be well to have in a retired part a little oratory, with her image, which should be kept decorated with drapery, flowers, tapers, or lamps ; and before it we should also recite her litany, the rosary, &c. For this purpose I have published a little book (which has already been reprinted eight times), of visits to the Blessed Sacrament as well as to the Blessed Virgin, for every day in the month. Some devout client of Mary could also have one of her feasts celebrated in a church or chapel, with greater solemnity than it otherwise would be, and have it preceded by a novena, with exposition of the Blessed Sacrament, and even with sermons.

Here, however, it is well to relate a fact recorded by Father Spinelli, in his book of ' Miracles of the Madonna,' number 65. In the year 1611, on the vigil of Pentecost, an immense concourse of people had assembled at the celebrated sanctuary of Mary, at Montevergine. The people had profaned the feast with dances, excesses, and immodest conduct, when suddenly it was discovered that fire was bursting forth from the house of amusement in which they were assembled, and in less than an hour and a half it was reduced to ashes, and more than 1500 persons lost their lives. Five persons who escaped deposed on oath that they had seen our Blessed Lady herself set fire to the place with two torches. After this, I entreat the clients of Mary to keep away as much as possible from such sanctuaries during festivals, and also, as far as they can, to prevent others from going there; for, on such occasions, the devil gains more profit than the Blessed Virgin derives honour by it. Let those who have this devotion go at a time when there is no concourse of people.

SIXTH DEVOTION

Of the Scapular.

As men esteem it an honour to have persons who wear their livery, so also is our Blessed Lady pleased that her clients should wear her scapular, as a mark that they have dedicated themselves to her service, and that they are members of the household of the Mother of God. Modern heretics, as usual, ridicule this devotion; but the holy Church has approved it by many bulls and indulgences. Fathers Crasset[1] and Lezzana,[2] speaking of the scapular of Mount Carmel, relate, that

---

[1] Tom. ii. tr. 6, par. 4. [2] In Mar. cap. 5, n. 10.

towards the year 1251, the Blessed Virgin appeared to Saint Simon Stock, an Englishman, and giving him the scapular, said, that all who should wear it would be saved from eternal damnation. She said, ' Receive, my beloved son, this scapular of thy order, the badge of my confraternity, a privilege granted to thee and to all Carmelites : whoever dies clothed with it will not suffer eternal flames.' Moreover, Father Crasset relates that Mary appeared to Pope John XXII., and commanded him to make it known that all those who should wear this scapular would be delivered from purgatory on the Saturday after their deaths ; and this he did by a bull, which was afterwards confirmed by Alexander V., Clement VII., and other Pontiffs. Paul V., as we have remarked in the first part of this work,[3] gives us to understand the same thing, and seems to explain the bulls of his predecessors, and prescribes in his the conditions on which the indulgences may be gained. These conditions are : that each one should observe the chastity required in his state of life, and the recitation of the little office of the Blessed Virgin ; those who cannot do so must be exact in keeping the fast-days prescribed by the Church, and abstain from meat on Wednesdays.

The indulgences, moreover, which are annexed to this scapular of Mount Carmel, as also to those of the Seven Dolours, of our Lady of Mercy, and especially to that of her Immaculate Conception, are innumerable, as well partial as plenary, both in life and for the hour of death. For my own part, I have been careful to receive all these scapulars. To that of the Immaculate Conception in particular, very great indulgences have been attached by various sovereign pontiffs.

[3] Page 208.

SEVENTH DEVOTION.

Of joining Confraternities of our Blessed Lady.

Some disapprove of confraternities, because they sometimes give rise to quarrels, and because many join them for temporal purposes. But as churches and the sacraments are not condemned because there are many who make a bad use of them, neither should confraternities be condemned. The sovereign pontiffs, so far from condemning them, have approved and highly commended them, and also enriched them with many indulgences. Saint Francis of Sales,[1] with great earnestness, exhorts all seculars to join them. What pains, moreover, did not Saint Charles Borromeo take to establish and multiply these confraternities. In his synods, he particularly recommends confessors to engage their penitents to join them.[2] And with good reason; for these sodalities, especially those of our Blessed Lady, are so many Noah's arks, in which poor seculars find a refuge from the deluge of temptations and sins which inundate the world. We, from the experience of our missions, well know the utility of these confraternities. As a rule, a man who does not attend the meetings of a confraternity commits more sins than twenty men who do attend them. A confraternity can well be called "a tower of David; a thousand bucklers hang upon it—all the armour of valiant men."[3] The reason for which confraternities do so much good is, that in them the members acquire many weapons of defence against hell, and put in practice the requisite means of preservation in Divine grace, which are seldom made use of by seculars who are not members of these confraternities.

[1] Introd. p. 2, c. 15.
[2] Confessor pro viribus suadebit, ut alicui societati pœnitentes adscribantur.—*Act. Med.* tom. i. p. 4, Instr. conf.
[3] Turris David . . . mille clypei pendent ex ea.—*Cant.* iv. 4.

In the first place, one means of salvation is, to meditate on the eternal truths : "Remember thy last end, and thou shalt never sin."[4] How many are lost because they neglect to do this ! "With desolation is all the land made desolate ; because there is none that considereth in his heart."[5] But those who frequent the meetings of their confraternities are led to think of these truths by the many mediations, lectures, and sermons they there hear : "My sheep hear My voice."[6] In the second place, to save one's soul, prayer is necessary : "Ask, and you shall receive ;"[7] this the brothers of the confraternities do constantly. God also hears their prayers the more readily ; for He has Himself said, that He grants graces more willingly to prayers offered up in common : "If two of you shall consent upon earth concerning anything whatsoever they shall ask, it shall be done to them by my Father :"[8] on which Saint Ambrose says, that 'many who are weak, when united become strong ; and it is impossible that the prayers of many should not be heard.'[9] In the third place, in confraternities the sacraments are more likely to be frequented, both on account of the rules and the example which is given by the other brothers. And thus perseverance in grace is more easily obtained, the sacred Council of Trent having declared, that the holy Communion is 'an antidote whereby we may be freed from daily faults, and be preserved from mortal sins.'[10] In the fourth place, besides the frequentation of the sacraments in these confraternities, many acts of mortification, humility, and charity towards the sick

[4] Memorare novissima tua, et in æternum non peccabis.—*Eccl.* vii. 40.
[5] Desolatione desolata est omnis terra, quia nullus est qui recogitet corde. —*Jerem.* xii. 11.
[6] Oves meæ vocem meam audiunt.—*Joan.* x. 27.
[7] Petite, et accipietis.—*Ib.* xvi. 24.
[8] Si duo ex vobis consenserint super terram de omni re quamcumque petierint, fiet illis a Patre meo.—*Matt.* xviii. 19.
[9] Multi minimi, dum congregantur unanimes, fiunt magni ; et multorum preces impossibile est ut non impetrent.—*In Rom.* xv.
[10] Tamquam antidotum, quo liberemur a culpis quotidianis, et a peccatis mortalibus præservemur.—*Sess.* xiii. cap. 2, *de Euchar.*

brethren and the poor, are performed. Well would
it be if this holy custom of assisting the sick-poor of
the place were introduced into all confraternities. It
would also be of the greatest advantage to introduce,
in honour of the Divine Mother herself, *the secret congregation,* composed of the more fervent brethren. I
will here give, in a few words, the usual exercises of
the secret congregation. I. Half an hour's spiritual
reading. II. Vespers and Complin of the Holy Ghost
are said. III. The Litany of the Blessed Virgin, and
then the brothers, whose turn it is, perform some act
of mortification, such as carrying a cross on their
shoulders, and the like. IV. They then make a quarter of an hour's meditation on the Passion of Jesus
Christ. V. Each one accuses himself of the faults he
has committed against the rule, and receives a penance
for it from the Father. VI. A brother reads out the
little flowers of mortification performed during the past
week, and then announces the novenas which occur,
&c. At the end, they take the discipline during the
space of a 'Miserere,' and a 'Salve Regina,' and then
each one goes to kiss the feet of a crucifix, placed for
this purpose on the step of the altar. The rules for each
brother are : I. To make mental prayer every day. II.
To pay a visit to the Blessed Sacrament and the Blessed
Virgin. III. To make the examination of conscience
in the evening. IV. Spiritual reading. V. To avoid
games and worldly conversations. VI. To frequent
the sacraments, and perform some little acts of mortification, such as the little chain, discipline, &c. VII.
To recommend to God every day the souls in purgatory
and sinners. VIII. When a brother is ill, the others
are all to visit him.—But now, let us return to our
point. In the fifth place, we have already said how
profitable it is for our salvation to serve the Mother of
God : and what else do the brothers do in the confraternity but serve her ? How much is she not praised
there ! How many prayers are not there offered to her !

From the very beginning, the brothers are consecrated
to her service ; they choose her in an especial manner
for their sovereign Lady and Mother ; they are inscribed in the book of the children of Mary ; hence, as
they are her servants and children in an especial manner, in an especial manner are they treated by her, and
she protects them in life and in death.   So that a brother of a confraternity of Mary can say, " Now all good
things came to me together with it."[11]   Each brother
should therefore pay attention to two things : First of
all, to the object he should have in view, which should
be no other than to serve God and His Mother Mary,
and save his soul; secondly, not to allow worldly affairs
to prevent his attendance at the meeting on the appointed days ; for he has there to attend to the most
important business he has in the world, which is his
eternal salvation.   He should also endeavour to draw
as many others as he can to join the confraternity, and
especially to bring back those brothers who have left
it.   O, with what terrible chastisements has our Lord
punished those who have abandoned the confraternity
of our Blessed Lady !   There was a brother who did so
in Naples ; and when he was exhorted to return, he
answered, ' I will do so when my legs are broken, and
my head is cut off.'   He prophesied ; for a short time
afterwards, some enemies of his broke his legs and cut
off his head.[12]   On the other hand, the brothers who
persevere have both their temporal and spiritual wants
provided for by Mary.   " All her domestics are clothed
with double garments."   Father Auriemma[13] relates
how many special graces Mary grants to brothers of the
confraternity, both in life and in death, but more particularly in death.   Father Crasset[14] gives an account
of a young man, who, in the year 1586, was dying.   He
fell asleep ; but afterwards waking, he said to his con-

[11] Venerunt autem mihi omnia bona pariter cum illa.   Sap. vii. 11.
[12] Ap. Sarnelli, Congr. p. 1, § 14.
[13] Tom. ii. cap. 4.
[14] Tom. ii. pr. 5.

fessor, 'O Father, I have been in great danger of damnation, but our Blessed Lady rescued me. The devils presented my sins before our Lord's tribunal, and they were already preparing to drag me to hell; but the Blessed Virgin came and said to them, 'Where are you taking this young man? What business have you with a servant of mine, who has served me so long in my confraternity? The devils fled, and thus was I delivered from their hands.' The same author also relates, that another brother had also, at the point of death, a great battle with hell; but at length, having conquered, filled with joy, he exclaimed: 'O what a blessing it is to serve the holy Mother in her confraternity!' and thus filled with consolation, he expired. He then adds, that in Naples, when the Duke of Popoli was dying, he said to his son: 'Son, know that the little good I have done in this life, I attribute to my confraternity. Hence, I have no greater treasure to leave thee than the confraternity of Mary. I now value more having been one of its members, than being Duke of Popoli.'

EIGHTH DEVOTION.

Of Alms given in Mary's honour.

Clients of the Blessed Virgin are accustomed to give alms to the poor in honour of the Divine Mother, especially on Saturdays. That holy shoemaker, of whom Saint Gregory speaks in his dialogues[1] (his name was Deusdedit), used on Saturdays to distribute all his earnings of the past week to the poor. Hence, a holy soul in a vision saw a sumptuous palace, which God was preparing in heaven for this servant of Mary, but its construction only went on on Saturdays. Saint

[1] Lib. iv. c. 36.

Gerard never refused anything at any time for which he was asked in Mary's name. Father Martin Guttierez, of the Society of Jesus, did the same, and in consequence acknowledged that he had never asked Mary for a grace which he had not obtained. This servant of hers having been put to death by the Huguenots, the Divine Mother appeared to his companions, accompanied by virgins, who, by her direction, wrapped the body in linen, and carried it away.[2] Saint Eberhard, bishop of Saltzburg, practised the same devotion, and, on account of it, a holy monk saw him as a child in the arms of Mary, who said : 'This is my son Eberhard, who never denied me anything.'[3] Alexander of Hales who had the same devotion, being once asked, in the name of Mary, by a Franciscan lay brother, to join the order, immediately complied, gave up the world, and became a friar.[4] Let, therefore, no client of the Blessed Virgin think it too much to give a trifling alms every day in her honour, and to increase it on Saturdays. If they can do nothing else, they should at least perform some other act for the love of Mary ; such as visiting the sick, praying for sinners, and for the souls in purgatory, &c. Works of mercy are very pleasing to the heart of this Mother of Mercy.

NINTH DEVOTION.

Of having frequent recourse to Mary.

Of all devotions, there is none so pleasing to our Mother as that of having frequent recourse to her intercession, seeking her help in all our wants ; for example, when we have to give or ask advice, in dangers, afflic-

------

[2] Ap. P. Pepe, tom. v. lez. 235, in fin. †
[3] Hic est filius meus Eberardus, qui nihil mihi unquam negavit.—*Boll.* 22 *Jun. Vit.* c. 4.
[4] Ap. P. Auriem. tom. i. c. 12.

tions, and temptations; and particularly in temptations against purity. The Divine Mother will then certainly deliver us, if we have recourse to her with the antiphon, 'We fly to thy patronage, &c.;' or with the 'Hail Mary;' or by only invoking the most holy name of Mary, which has particular power against the devils. Blessed Santi, of the Order of Saint Francis, being once tempted with an impure thought, had recourse to Mary: she immediately appeared to him, and placing her hand on his breast delivered him. It is also useful on these occasions to kiss or press to our heart our rosary or scapular, or to look at an image of the Blessed Virgin. It is well also to know that Benedict XIII. granted fifty days' indulgence to those who pronounce the names of Jesus and Mary.

TENTH DEVOTION.

In this tenth and last Devotion I unite several Devotions which may be practised in honour of Mary.

1. To say or to hear Mass, or to have Mass said, in honour of the Blessed Virgin. It is true that the holy sacrifice of the Mass can be offered to God alone, to whom it is offered principally as an acknowledgment of His supreme dominion. But the sacred Council of Trent[1] says that this does not prevent its being, at the same time, offered to God in thanksgiving for the graces granted to the Saints and to His most holy Mother, that whilst we are mindful of them, they may deign to intercede for us. And for this reason at Mass we say, 'That it may avail to their honour, but to our salvation.'[2] Our Blessed Lady herself revealed to a holy soul, that this devotion of offering the Mass, as also of saying three 'Paters,' 'Aves,' and 'Glorias,' in honour of the most

[1] Sess. xxii. cap. 3.
[2] Ut illis proficiat ~d honorem, nobis autem ad salutem.

Holy Trinity, and in thanksgiving for the graces granted
to her, was most pleasing to her; for the Blessed Virgin, being unable fully to thank our Lord for all the
precious gifts He has bestowed on her, rejoices greatly
when her children help her to thank God. 2. To reverence the Saints who are more nearly related to Mary,
as Saint Joseph, Saint Joachim, and Saint Anne. The
Blessed Virgin herself recommended a certain nobleman
to be devout towards her mother, Saint Anne.[3] We
should also honour the Saints who were most devoted
to the Divine Mother, such as Saint John the Evangelist, Saint John the Baptist, Saint Bernard, Saint
John Damascen the defender of her images, Saint Ildephonsus the defender of her virginity, &c. 3. To read
every day a book which treats of the Glories of Mary;
to preach, or at least to try to instil into all, and particularly our relations, devotion to the Divine Mother.
The Blessed Virgin once said to Saint Bridget, 'Take
care that thy children are also my children.' To pray
every day for the most devoted clients of Mary, both
living and dead.

We should also remember the many indulgences
granted by sovereign pontiffs to those who in various
ways honour the Queen of heaven. 1. To whoever says,
'Blessed be the holy and immaculate conception of the
Blessed Virgin Mary,' Pius VI. granted for each time
an indulgence of one hundred days. Father Crasset
says that other indulgences applicable to the souls in
purgatory have been granted to those who after the
word "*immaculate*" add, "*and most pure.*" 2. For the
Salve Regina, forty days' indulgence. 3. For the Litany of Loretto, three hundred days' indulgence. 4. To
those who bow their heads on hearing the names of
Jesus and Mary, twenty days' indulgence. 5. To those
who say five 'Paters' and 'Aves' in honour of the
Passion of Jesus and the sorrows of Mary, many and
great indulgences. Here, for the convenience of devout

[3] Barry, Par. ap. +

souls, I will indicate other indulgences granted by sove
reign pontiffs for other devotions. 1. For hearing Mass
there are many indulgences. 2. For making the acts of
faith, hope, charity, and contrition, with the intention
of receiving the holy sacraments during life and in death,
Benedict XIII. granted seven years' indulgence, and a
plenary indulgence once a month applicable to the souls
in purgatory, and for one's self in the hour of death to
those who have made these acts every day for a month.
3. To those who say fifteen 'Paters' and 'Aves' for
sinners, the remission of a third part of the penalties due
for their own sins. 4. To those who meditate for half
an hour a-day Benedict XIV. granted many indulgences,
and a plenary one once a month, on condition of approaching the sacraments of Penance and the Holy Eucharist. 5. To those who say the prayer 'Anima
Christi' three hundred days' indulgence. 6. To those
who accompany the holy Viaticum five years and five
quarantines, if without a wax-light; and if with one,
seven years and seven quarantines : those who cannot
accompany it, but say a 'Pater' and an 'Ave' for the
intention of the sovereign pontiff, one hundred days.
7. To those who genuflect before the blessed sacrament
two hundred days' indulgence. 8. To those who kiss
the cross a year and forty days' indulgence. 9. To those
who bow their heads at the 'Gloria Patri' thirty days'
indulgence. 10. To priests who before saying Mass say
the prayer 'Ego volo celebrare missam,' fifty years. 11.
To those who kiss the habit of a religious order five
years. Father Viva[4] gives a list of many other indulgences. Those who endeavour to gain these indulgences
must be careful to dispose themselves by an act of contrition.

I omit other devotions which may be found in other
books, such as those of the seven joys, of the twelve
privileges of Mary, and such-like ; and conclude this
work in the beautiful words of Saint Bernardine of

---

4 **Append**. Indulg. in calce Tract. § ult.

Sienna : ' O Lady, blessed amongst all women, thou art
the honour of the human race, and the salvation of our
people. Thy merits have no limits, and thou hast full
power over all creatures. Thou art the Mother of God,
the sovereign Lady of the world, and the Queen of
heaven. Thou art the dispenser of all graces, and the
ornament of the holy Church. Thou art the model of
the just, the consolation of the Saints, and the root of
our salvation. Thou art the joy of paradise, the gate of
heaven, the glory of God. Behold, we have announced
thy praises. We beseech thee, then, O Mother of Mercy,
to supply for our weakness, to excuse our presumption,
to accept our services, to bless our labours, by imprint-
ing thy love in the hearts of all; that after having honoured and loved thy Son on earth, we may praise Him
and bless Him for ever in heaven. Amen.'[5]

CONCLUSION.

And with this, my dear reader and brother, lover of
our Mother Mary, I bid you farewell, and say: Continue with joy to honour and love this good Lady, and
endeavour also to cause her to be loved by as many as
you can: and doubt not, but be fully persuaded, that if
you persevere until death in true devotion to Mary, your
salvation is certain. I conclude, not that I should not
still have much to say on the glories of this great Queen,
but lest I should tire you. The little that I have written will be more than sufficient to make you desire this
great treasure, devotion towards the Mother of God,
which she will fully reward by her powerful patronage.
Accept, then, the desire which I have had in this work,
to lead you to salvation and to sanctity, by inflaming
you with love and ardent devotion to this most amiable
Queen. And should you find that in this I have some-

[5] Serm. de Exalt. B.M.V. in gloria, art. ii. cap. 3.

what helped you by my book, as a charity I beg that you will recommend me to Mary, and ask her for me the grace which I ask her for you, that we may one day be together at her feet, in company with all her other dear children.

And to thee do I turn in conclusion, O Mother of my Lord, and my Mother Mary. I beseech thee graciously to accept my poor labours, and the desire which I have had to see thee praised and loved by all. Thou well knowest how ardently I have desired to complete this little work of thy Glories before the end of my life, which is already drawing to its close. But now I die happy, leaving this book on earth, which will continue to praise and preach thee as I have endeavoured to do during the years which have passed since my conversion, which through thee I obtained from God. O immaculate Mary, I recommend all those who love thee to thee, and especially those who read this little book; and more particularly those who have the charity to recommend me to thee. O Lady, grant them perseverance, make them all Saints, and thus lead them all united to praise thee in heaven. O my most sweet Mother, it is true that I am only a poor sinner, but I glory in loving thee, and hope great things from thee, and amongst others to die loving thee. I trust that in the agonies of death, when the devil will put my sins before me, that in the first place the Passion of Jesus, and then thy intercession, will strengthen and enable me to leave this miserable life in the grace of God, that so I may go and love Him, and thank thee, my Mother, for all eternity. Amen.

PRAYERS.

O Lady, say to thy Son for us, "They have no wine." How bright is the chalice of this inebriating wine! The love of God inebriates us, so as to make us despise the world; it warms and strengthens us to become indiffer ent to temporal things, and inclines us towards, and makes us active in the acquirement of, those things which are invisible.[1]

Thou art a fruitful field filled with virtues, filled with graces. Thou camest forth as a bright and blushing dawn; for original sin being conquered in thee, thou wast born resplendent with the knowledge of truth, and blushing with the love of virtue; the enemy could in nothing prevail against thee, for a thousand bucklers hang upon thee, all the armour of valiant men; for there is no virtue which did not shine resplendent in thee; and whatever was divided amongst all the Saints, thou didst possess united in thyself.[2]

O, our Lady, our mediatress, our advocate, reconcile us with thy Son, commend us to thy Son. Grant, O blessed one, by the grace which thou didst find, by the prerogative which thou didst merit, by that mercy to which thou didst give birth, that He who, through thee, deigned to become a partaker of our infirmity and misery, may also, through thy intercession, make us the partakers of His happiness and glory.[3]

> Lovely Rose, if thou dost deign
> Love to lavish still on me,
> Grant my heart such love to gain
> That it die for love of thee.

----

[1] Dic, Domina rerum, dic pro nobis Filio tuo, Vinum non habent. Calix hujus vini inebrians, quam præclarus est ... inebriat amor Dei ad contemptum mundi: calefacit ... facit fortes ... somnolentos ad temporalia ... et ad invisibilia contemplanda pronos et promptos.—*S. Bern.*, aut quisquis est auctor, *in Salve Reg.* Serm. 4.

[2] Tu es ager plenus, plena virtutum, plena gratiarum ... Tu processisti ut aurora lucida et rubicunda, quia superatis originalibus peccatis in utero matris, nata es lucida cognitione veritatis, et rubicunda amore virtutis ... Nihil omnino profecit inimicus in te, eo quod mille clypei pependerunt ex te, omnis armatura fortium ... Nihil est enim virtutis quod ex te non resplendeat: et quicquid singuli habuere sancti, tu sola possedisti.—*S. Bern.* ib.

[3] Domina nostra, mediatrix nostra, advocata nostr', tuo Filio nos reconcilia, tuo Filio nos commenda, tuo nos Filio repræsenta. Fac, O benedicta, per gratiam quam invenisti, per prærogativam quam meruisti, per misericordiam quam peperisti, ut qui te mediante fieri dignatus est particeps infirmitatis et miseriæ nostræ, te quoque intercedente participes faciat nos gloriæ et beatitudinis suæ.—*S. Bern. Serm.* ii. *de Adv. D.*

My Lady, grant this grace to me,
   To love thee until death ;
And when I die, to call on thee
   Still with my latest breath.

My hope art thou, O Mary blest,
   Sweet star of life's dark sea ;
Ah, guide me safe to port of rest,
   And open heaven to me.

Live Jesus, Mary, Joseph, and Teresa

THE GLORIES OF MARY.

PART THE THIRD.

VARIOUS ADDITIONAL EXAMPLES APPERTAINING TO THE MOST BLESSED VIRGIN MARY,

Discourses, Meditations for several Festivals;

AND MANY DEVOTIONS IN HONOUR OF THIS SAME HOLY VIRGIN.

VARIOUS ADDITIONAL EXAMPLES APPERTAINING TO THE MOST BLESSED VIRGIN MARY.

THERE are some persons who make it a boast that they are free from prejudice, and pride themselves on believing no other miracles than those recorded in the sacred Scriptures, looking upon all others as tales and old women's fables. Here it is well to repeat a just remark made by the learned and pious Father John Crasset.[1] He says, 'that as good people easily believe miracles, so are the wicked always ready to turn them into ridicule;' and he adds, 'that as it is a weakness to give credit to everything, so on the other hand does the rejection of miracles, when they are attested by grave and pious men, either savour of infidelity, because they are thought impossible to God, or of pre-

[1] Tom. ii. tr. 6, prat. 10.

sumption, in denying the credibility of such a class of authors.' We give credit to a Tacitus and to a Suetonius; can we, then, refuse it without presumption to Christian, learned, and tried authors? Father Canisius says: 'There is less danger in believing and admitting that which is related with some appearance of truth by respectable authors, and which has not been rejected by learned men, which is moreover a subject of edification to our neighbour, than in rejecting it with a disdainful and presumptuous spirit.'[2]

EXAMPLES.

1. In Germany a man fell into a grievous sin: through shame he was unwilling to confess it; but, on the other hand, unable to endure the remorse of his conscience, he went to throw himself into a river; on the point of doing so, he hesitated, and weeping, he begged that God would forgive him his sin without his confessing it. One night, in his sleep, he felt some one shake his arm, and heard a voice which said, *Go to confession.* He went to the church, but yet did not confess. On another night he again heard the same voice. He returned to the church; but when he got there, he declared that he would rather die than confess that sin. But before returning home he went to recommend himself to the most Blessed Virgin, whose image was in that church. He had no sooner knelt down than he found himself quite changed. He immediately got up, called a confessor, and weeping bitterly through the grace which he had received from Mary, made an entire confession of his sins; and he afterwards declared that he experienced greater satisfaction than had he obtained all the treasures of the world.[3]

2. A young nobleman who was on a sea voyage began to read an obscene book, in which he took much pleasure. A religious noticed it, and said to him: 'Are

[2] Lib. v. de Deip. c. 18.
[3] Annal. Soc. 1650, ap. Auriem. Aff. Scamb. t. ii. cap. 7.

you disposed to make a present to our Blessed Lady ? The young man replied that he was. ' Well,' the other answered, ' I wish that, for the love of the most holy Virgin, you would give up that book, and throw it into the sea.' ' Here it is, father,' said the young man. ' No,' replied the religious, ' you must yourself make Mary this present.' He did so ; and no sooner had he returned to Genoa, his native place, than the Mother of God so inflamed his heart with divine love that he entered a religious order.[4]

3. A hermit, on Mount Olivet, kept a devout image of Mary in his cell, and said many prayers before it. The devil, unable to endure such devotion to the Blessed Virgin, continually tormented him with impure thoughts ; so much so, that the poor old hermit, seeing that all his prayers and mortifications did not deliver him, one day said to the enemy : ' What have I done to thee that thou tormentest me out of my life ?' On this the devil appeared to him, and replied, ' Thou tormentest me much more than I do thee ; but,' he added, ' if thou wilt swear to keep it secret, I will tell thee what thou hast to give up, that I may no more molest thee.' The hermit took the oath, and then the devil said : ' Thou must no more approach that image which thou hast in thy cell.' The hermit, perplexed at this, went to consult the Abbot Theodore, who told him that he was not bound by his oath, and that he must not cease to recommend himself to Mary before the image, as he had always done. The hermit obeyed, and the devil was put to shame and conquered.[5]

4. A woman, who had carried on a criminal intercourse with two young men, one of whom, through jealousy, had killed the other, came one day in great alarm to confession to Father Humphrey d'Anna, of the congregation of the Pii Operarii, in the kingdom of Naples. She told the father that the wretched youth was no sooner dead than he appeared to her, clothed

[4] Nadasi, Ann. Mar. S.J. 1605.   [5] Bonif. Stor. Verg. l. 2. c. 6.

in black, bound in chains, fire issuing from every part
of his body, and with a sword in his hand which he
had already raised to cut her throat, when she cried
out, calling him by his name, ' Ah, what have I done
to thee, that thou shouldst take my life?' The damned
soul, in a rage, replied, ' What hast thou done to me
indeed, wretch that thou art?—thou hast made me
lose my God.' She then called on the Blessed Virgin;
and at the sound of the most holy name of Mary, the
spectre disappeared, and was no more seen.[6]

5. When Saint Dominic was preaching at Carcas-
sone, in France, an Albigensian heretic, who, for having publicly ridiculed the devotion of the rosary, was
possessed by devils, was brought to him. The Saint
then obliged the evil spirits to declare, whether the
things which he said about the most holy rosary were
true. Howling, they replied, ' Listen, Christians : all
that this enemy of ours has said of Mary, and of the
most holy rosary, is true.' They moreover added, ' that
they had no power against the servants of Mary; and
that many, by invoking in death the name of Mary,
were saved, contrary to their deserts.' They concluded,
saying : ' We are forced to declare, that no one is lost
who perseveres in devotion to Mary and in that of the
most holy rosary, for Mary obtains for those who are
sinners true repentance before they die.'[7] Saint Dominic
then made the people recite the rosary; and, O prodigy,
at every Hail Mary many evil spirits left the body of
the possessed man under the form of red-hot coals ; so
that, when the rosary was finished, he was entirely freed.
On this occasion many heretics were converted.

6. The daughter of a prince had entered a convent
which was not very fervent, and in consequence, though
she was naturally of a good disposition, she advanced
but little in virtue. But having by the advice of a good
confessor begun to say the rosary, meditating at the
same time on the mysteries, she so changed that she

⁶ In Vit. p. Ant. de Collel. c. 32, § 5. †　　⁷ Paciuch. in Sal. Ang. Exc. 3.

became a model for all. The nuns, however, displeased at her seclusion, did all that they could to make her give up the course she had traced out for herself. One day whilst she was saying the rosary, and entreating Mary to help her in the persecution she underwent, a letter fell before her. On the outside was written, 'Mary, the Mother of God, to her daughter Johanna, greeting.' Inside it she read: 'My beloved daughter, continue to say my rosary; avoid intercourse with those who do not help thee to live well; beware of sloth and vanity; banish two superfluous things from thy cell, and I will be thy protectress with God.' The abbot, under whose jurisdiction the monastery was, visited it soon after, and endeavoured to reform it, but without success. He one day saw many devils enter the cells of the nuns, but not into that of Johanna; for the Divine Mother, before whom he saw her praying, drove them away. Having afterwards learnt from her the devotion of the rosary which she practised, and the letter she had received, he ordered all the nuns to do the same; and the account says that the convent became a paradise.[8]

7. For this example see page 172.

8. Blessed Alan relates that there was a lady named Dominica, who for a time said the rosary, but having afterwards given it up, she fell into such poverty that one day in despair she gave herself three stabs with a knife. When she was on the point of expiring, and the devils were already preparing to take her to hell, the most Blessed Virgin appeared to her, and said, 'Daughter, although thou hast forgotten me, I would not forget thee on account of the rosary which at one time thou didst recite in my honour. But now, if thou wilt continue to recite it, I will not only restore thee to life, but will also restore thee the property thou hast lost.' Dominica recovered her health, and, persevering in the recitation of the rosary, regained her property and on her death-bed was again visited by Mary, who

praised her for her fidelity ; and she then died a holy death.[9]

9. In Saragossa there was a nobleman named Peter, a relation of Saint Dominic, but who was a most wicked man. One day when the Saint was preaching he saw Peter enter the church, and begged our Lord to manifest the state of that miserable sinner to the congregation. In an instant Peter appeared as a monster from hell, surrounded and dragged about by many devils. Every one, even his wife, who was in the church, and the servants who accompanied him, began to fly. Saint Dominic then sent him word by a companion that he should recommend himself to Mary, and begin to recite the rosary, which he also sent him. When Peter had received the message he humbled himself, sent to thank the Saint, and then had himself the grace to see the devils who surrounded him. He then confessed his sins with many tears to the Saint, from whom he received the assurance that they were already forgiven. He persevered in saying the rosary ; and became so holy, that one day our Lord made him appear in church in the presence of the whole congregation crowned with a triple crown of roses.[10]

10. In the mountains of Trent there lived a famous robber, who, when he was one day admonished by a religious to change his life, replied that for him there was no remedy. 'No,' said the religious; 'do what I tell you. Fast on Saturdays in Mary's honour, and on that day never molest any one, and she will obtain you the grace not to die at enmity with God.' The poor robber followed this advice, and even bound himself to it by vow ; and that he might not break it, he from that time forward always went unarmed on Saturdays. It so happened that one Saturday he met the officers of justice ; and rather than break his vow he allowed him-

[9] De Psalt. p. 5. c. 67.
[10] Cartag. de Arca Deip. 1. 19. § 114. Should any one wish for other ex amples on the subject of the rosary, he can read those which are in the first part of this work, at pages 59, 90, 182, 209.

self to be made a prisoner without resistance. The judge, seeing that he was an old gray-haired man, wished to save him from death; but, having already received the grace of compunction from Mary, he said that he wished to die in punishment for his sins. He then in the hall of justice made a public confession of all the crimes of his life; and this he did with so many tears, that all who were present wept. He was beheaded, and, a grave being dug, was buried with little ceremony. But afterwards the Mother of God, accompanied by four virgins, was seen to take the body from that place, and wrap it in a rich cloth embroidered with gold. They then carried it to the city gate. There our Blessed Lady herself said to the guards, 'Tell the bishop, in my name, to give honourable burial in such a church to this man, for he was my faithful servant.' This was done. All the people thronged to the place, where they found the body, the rich pall, and the bier on which it was placed. Cesarius relates that from that time all the people of that district began to fast on Saturdays.[11]

11. In Portugal there was a devout client of Mary, who during his life practised the devotion of fasting on bread and water every Saturday, and chose Saint Michael and Saint John as his advocates with the Blessed Virgin. At the hour of his death the Queen of Heaven appeared to him, accompanied by those two Saints, who were praying for him. The Blessed Virgin looked at him with a joyful countenance, and thus answered the prayers of the Saints: 'I will not depart hence without taking this soul with me.'

12. In one of our missions, after the sermon on Mary which it is always customary in our congregation to preach, a very old man came to make his confession to one of the fathers. Filled with consolation, he said, 'Father, our Blessed Lady has granted me a grace.' 'What grace has she granted you?' the confessor asked. 'You must know, father,' he replied, 'that for five-and-

11 Theoph. Rayn. de S. Latr. c. 15.

thirty years I have made sacrilegious confessions, **for** there is a sin which I was ashamed to confess; and yet I have passed through many dangers, have many times been at the point of death, and had I then died, I should certainly have been lost; but now our Blessed Lady has touched my heart with grace to tell it.' This he said weeping, and shedding so many tears, that he quite excited compassion. The father, after hearing his confession, asked him what devotion he had practised. He replied that on Saturdays he had never failed to abstain from milk-diet in honour of Mary, and that on this account the Blessed Virgin had shown him mercy. At the same time he gave the father leave to publish the fact.

13. In Normandy a robber had his head cut off by some enemies, and it was thrown into a ditch; but yet it was afterwards heard to say, ' Mary, give me the grace to go to confession.' A priest hastened to him, and having heard his confession, asked him what devotion he had practised. The robber replied that all he had done was to fast once a week in honour of the Blessed Virgin, and that for this she had obtained him the grace to be delivered from hell by means of that confession.[12]

14. There were two young noblemen in Madrid, of whom the one encouraged the other in leading a wicked life, and in committing all sorts of crimes. One of them one night in a dream saw his friend taken by certain black men, and carried to a tempestuous sea. They were going to take him in a similar manner, but he had recourse to Mary, and made a vow that he would embrace the religious state; on which he was delivered from those blacks. He then saw Jesus on a throne, as if in anger, and the Blessed Virgin imploring mercy for him. After this his friend came to pay him a visit, and he then related what he had seen; but his companion only turned it into ridicule, and he was shortly afterwards

[12] Thom. Cantiprat. de Apib. l. 2. c. 29. n. 24.

stabbed, and died. When the young man saw that his vision was verified, he went to confession, and renewed his resolution to embrace a religious order, and for this purpose he sold all that he had; but instead of giving it to the poor, as he had intended, he spent it in all sorts of debauchery. He then fell ill, and had another vision. He thought he saw hell open, and the Divine Judge, who had already condemned him. Again he had recourse to Mary, and she once more delivered him. He recovered his health, and went on worse than ever. He afterwards went to Lima in South America, where he relapsed into his former illness; and in the hospital of that place he was once more touched by the grace of God, confessed his sins to the Jesuit father, Francis Perlino, and promised him that he would change his life; but again he fell into his former crimes. At length, the same father, going into another hospital in a distant place, saw the miserable wretch extended on the ground, and heard him cry out, 'Ah, abandoned wretch that I am! for my greater torment this father is come to witness my chastisement. From Lima I came hither, where my vices have brought me to this end; and now I go to hell.' With these words he expired, without even leaving the father time to help him.[13]

15. In Germany there was a criminal who had been condemned to death; but he was obstinate, and refused to make his confession. A Jesuit father did all he could to convert him. This good father entreated him, wept, cast himself at his feet; but seeing that all was time lost, he at length said, 'Now, let us recite a Hail Mary together.' The criminal did so, and in an instant began to weep bitterly, confessed his sins with great compunction, and desired to die clasping an image of Mary in his arms.[14]

16. In a city of Spain there was an impious man

13 Bovio, Esemp. d. s. Verg. tom. iii. es. 9.
14 Nadasi, Ann. Mar. S.J. 1618.

who had given himself to the devil, and had never been to confession. The only good thing which he did was to recite a Hail Mary every day. Father Eusebius Nieremberg relates, that when this man was on his death-bed, the most Blessed Virgin appeared to him in a dream, looked at him, and Mary's compassionate eyes so completely changed him, that he immediately called a confessor, and, bitterly sobbing, confessed his sins, and made a vow that if he lived he would become a religious, and thus died.[15]

17. A devout servant of Mary always inculcated on her daughter the duty of frequently reciting the ' Hail Mary,' especially in any danger. One day this girl was reposing after a ball, when she was attacked by a devil, who, in a visible form, was about to carry her off ; he had already seized her, but she had no sooner said ' Hail Mary,' than the enemy disappeared.[16]

18. A woman who carried on an evil intercourse with a priest, one day found him hung in her room. After this she entered a convent, where the devil, under a visible form, so tormented her, that she no longer knew what to do to be delivered from him. A companion of hers advised her to say the Hail Mary. She did so, and the devil exclaimed, ' Cursed be she who taught thee this !' and so saying, he disappeared.[17]

19. A captain, who led a sinful life, was accidentally visited in his castle by a good religious, who, being then enlightened by God, begged him to assemble all his servants. All came with the exception of the valet : he, however, was at last forced to come ; and the Father said to him, ' I command thee, in the name of Jesus Christ, to say who thou art.' He replied, ' I am a devil from hell, who for fourteen years have served this scoundrel, only waiting for the day on which he might omit the seven Hail Marys, which he is in the habit of reciting, to strangle him and carry him to hell.' The

15 Ap. Auriem. tom. i. cap. vi.
16 Bovio. tom. v. es. 7.   17 Cesar. Dial. l. 3. c. 13.

religious then commanded the devil to depart; which he did, instantly disappearing; and the captain cast himself at the father's feet, was converted, and afterwards led a holy life.[18]

20. Blessed Francis Patrizi, who had the greatest devotion to the 'Hail Mary,' used to recite five hundred a day. Mary announced the hour of his death to him, and he died as a saint. After forty years, a beautiful lily grew out of his mouth, and on each of the leaves was written the 'Hail Mary' in letters of gold. This lily was afterwards taken to France.[19]

21. Cesarius relates that a Cistercian lay brother knew no other prayer than the 'Hail Mary,' and recited it continually with the greatest devotion. After his death, a tree grew up on the spot where he was buried, and on its leaves were written these words, 'Hail Mary, full of grace.'[20]

22. Three devout virgins, by the advice of their confessor, one year recited, for forty days, the entire rosary, as a preparation for the Feast of the Purification of Mary. On the vigil, the Divine Mother appeared to the first of the three sisters with a rich robe embroidered with gold, and, thanking her, blessed her. She then appeared to the second with a simple robe, and also thanked her; but she said, 'Lady, why didst thou go to my sister with so much richer a robe?' 'Because,' Mary replied, 'she clothed me with a richer one than thou didst.' She afterwards appeared to the third with a robe of common sacking; on seeing which, the sister asked her pardon for the tepidity with which she honoured her. The following year all prepared themselves well for the same festival, reciting the rosary with great devotion. On the night preceding the feast, Mary appeared to them, resplendent with glory, and said, 'Prepare yourselves; for to-morrow you will go with me to Paradise;' and, in fact, they told their con-

---

[18] Gran. Spec. Ex. d. 8. ex. 60, et Crass. t. ii. tr. 6, pr. 1.
[19] Bolland. 16 Maii. [20] Hom. in Dom. 9. post Pent.

fessor what had happened, received the Holy Communion in the church, and towards the hour of Complin they again saw the most Blessed Virgin, who came to take them, and, amid the songs of angels, one after the other sweetly expired.[21]

23. Father Crasset relates that a military commander told him that once, after a battle, he found a soldier in the camp, who, holding a rosary and Mary's scapular in his hand, asked for a confessor. His forehead was pierced by a musket-ball, which had come out at the back of his head, so that the brain was visible and came out through each opening; so much so, indeed, that naturally he could not live. He raised himself up, made his confession to the chaplain with great compunction, and, when he had received absolution, expired.[22]

24. The same author adds, that this captain also told him that he was present when a trumpeter of his company received a pistol-shot from a man who stood near him. When he examined his breast, where he said he was wounded, he found that the ball had been stopped by a scapular of the Blessed Virgin, which he wore, and had not even touched the flesh. He took it and showed it to all who were present.[23]

25. A noble youth, named Eskill, was sent by the prince, his father, to Hildesheim, a city of Saxony, to study; but he gave himself up to a disorderly life. He afterwards fell so dangerously ill that he received Extreme Unction. While in this state he had a vision: he found himself shut up in a fiery furnace, and believed himself already in hell; but he then seemed to escape from it by a hole, and took refuge in a great palace, in an apartment of which he saw the most Blessed Virgin Mary, who said to him : 'Presumptuous man that thou art, dost thou dare to appear before me? Depart hence, and go to that fire which thou hast de-

[21] Tesor. del Rosar. lib. iv. Mir. 17. Diotal. tom. i. es. vii. †
[22] Crass. tom. ii. tr. 6, pr. 14.　　　　[23] Loc. cit.

served.' The young man then besought the Blessed Virgin to have mercy on him; and then addressed himself to some persons who were there present, and entreated them to recommend him to Mary. They did so, and the Divine Mother replied, 'But you do not know the wicked life which he leads, and that he does not even deign to salute me with a Hail Mary.' His advocates replied, 'But, Lady, he will change his life;' and the young man added, 'Yes, I promise in good earnest to amend, and I will be thy devout client.' The Blessed Virgin's anger was then appeased, and she said to him, 'Well, I accept thy promise; be faithful to me, and meanwhile, with my blessing, be delivered from death and hell.' With these words the vision disappeared. Eskill returned to himself, and, blessing Mary, related to others the grace which he had received; and from that time he led a holy life, always preserving great devotion to our Blessed Lady. He became archbishop of Lunden in Sweden, where he converted many to the faith. Towards the end of his life, on account of his age, he renounced his archbishopric, and became a monk in Clairvaux, where he lived for four years, and died a holy death. Hence he is numbered, by some authors, amongst the Cistercian Saints.[24]

26. A brother of the confraternity of Mary was one day invited by a friend to dine with him. He accepted the invitation, but wished to go, first of all, to a meeting of the confraternity; after which he forgot his promise. His friend was so much offended at this, that, meeting him, he was going to take his life; but, by a just judgment of God, he wounded and killed himself instead. As the brother was believed to be guilty of this crime, he was immediately taken before a court of justice and sentenced to death. He recommended himself to the Blessed Virgin, and she inspired him to beg to be led into the presence of the dead body, and then asked him how he had died. His former friend con-

[24] Manriquez, Ann. Cisterc. 1151, c. 13; 1181, c. 2.

fessed that he had died by his own hands; and the brother was set at liberty.[25]

27. In the year 1604, in Dole, a brother was dangerously ill. One holiday he said : ' Ah, my brothers are all assembled in the confraternity praising Mary, and here am I alone.' He got up, went to the meeting ; the fever immediately left him, and he returned home in perfect health.[26]

28. Another brother of the confraternity, a fisherman in Naples, was ill for several days in consequence of the severity with which he had taken the discipline. As soon as he was somewhat recovered, being poor and having a family, he returned to his usual occupation, but at the same time said to the most Blessed Virgin, Lady, it is on thy account that I have sustained this loss : help me.' Mary did so, and caused him to take, on that occasion, as much fish as he could have taken during the whole time of his illness.[27]

29. Another brother was on the point of being imprisoned for debt. He recommended himself to Mary; and this most Blessed Virgin inspired his creditors to forgive him what he owed them, which they did.[28]

30. A young man, who was a member of the confraternity of the Blessed Virgin, left it, and abandoned himself to a dissolute life. One night the devil appeared to him in a frightful form. He began to invoke our Blessed Lady. ' In vain,' said the enemy, ' dost thou invoke her whom thou hast abandoned; thy crimes have made thee mine.' The young man, trembling, fell upon his knees, and began to recite the formula of the brothers : ' Most holy Virgin Mother,' &c. The Mother of God then appeared. At her presence the devil took flight, leaving a dreadful stench and a hole in the wall. Mary then turned towards the young man and said, ' Thou didst not deserve my help; but I wish

to show thee mercy, that thou mayest change thy life and rejoin the confraternity.'[29]

31. In Braganza there was another young man, who, after giving up the confraternity, abandoned himself to so many crimes that one day, in despair, he went to drown himself in a river; but before doing so, he addressed our Blessed Lady, saying, 'O Mary, I once served thee in the confraternity; help me.' The most Blessed Virgin appeared to him, and said: 'Yes, and now what art thou going to do? Dost thou wish to lose thyself both in soul and body? Go, confess thy sins, and rejoin the confraternity.' The young man, encouraged hereby, thanked the Blessed Virgin, and changed his life.[30]

32. In Spain there was a religious who, in a fit of passion, killed his superior. After committing this crime he fled into Barbary, where he renounced his faith and married. During this time, in which he was leading so wicked a life, the only good thing he did was to say a 'Salve Regina' daily. One day, when he was alone, he said his 'Salve,' and behold Mary appeared to him, reproved him, and encouraged him to change his life, at the same time promising him her assistance. He then returned to his house, where his wife, seeing that he was in affliction, questioned him as to its cause. Weeping, he told her his state, and the vision which he had had. She, moved thereby to compassion, gave him money to return home, and also consented that one of their sons should go with him. He returned to his monastery, and shed so many tears that he was once more admitted into the order, and his son was received with him. He persevered, and died with the reputation of a saint.[31]

33. A student was taught by his master to salute the most Blessed Virgin with these words, 'Hail, O Mother of Mercy!' At his death Mary appeared to him

[29] Lecnero, Sodal. Parth. lib. iii. c. 3.   [30] Auriem. Aff. tom. ii. c. 4.
[31] Auriem. tom. ii. cap. 7.

and said, 'Son, dost thou not know me? I am that Mother of Mercy whom thou hast so often saluted.' The devout servant of the Blessed Virgin then extended his arms, as if to follow her, and sweetly expired.[32]

34. A certain sinner, in the midst of the wicked life he was leading, practised only one devotion; which was, to recite every day the 'Sub tuum præsidium,' 'We fly to thy patronage,' &c. One day the Blessed Virgin so greatly enlightened him, that he gave up his wicked life, embraced a religious order, in which he led for fifty years an exemplary life, and thus died.[33]

35. In Turin, in the year 1610, there was an obstinate heretic, who even on his death-bed would not renounce his errors, notwithstanding all that was said to him by many priests who attended upon him during eight successive days. At length one of them almost forced him to have recourse to Mary, with these words, 'Mother of Jesus, help me.' The heretic, as if awaking from a profound sleep, then said, 'I wish to die a Catholic:' he was thereupon reconciled with the Church, and in two hours expired.[34]

36. Another infidel, in India, was dying, abandoned by all, and having heard the power of Mary so much extolled by the Christians, he had recourse to her. The Blessed Virgin appeared to him and said, 'Behold, I am she whom thou invokest; become a Christian.' He instantly found himself restored to health, was baptised, and many were converted by this prodigy.[35]

37. In the year 1610, in Madrid, there was a man, a very devout servant of Mary, who had especial devotion to an image called 'Our Blessed Lady of Atocha.' He married a woman who, through her suspicions and jealousy, left him no peace. Early every Saturday morning he used to go barefooted to visit the image; but his wife believing that he went elsewhere, on one

[32] Auriem. tom. ii. cap. 8.   [33] De Barry, Ann. Marian. 19 Jul.
[34] De Barry, Par. ap. cap. ii.   [35] Patrignani, Menol. 18 Sept.

occasion in particular, abused him so much, that, in a fit of impatience, he took a rope and hung himself. Just as his soul was departing, being no longer able to help himself, he invoked the help of Mary; when, behold, a most beautiful Lady stood before him, who, coming up to him, cut the rope. The people who were outside the door saw this; and he then related what had taken place. On hearing it, even his wife was moved to compunction, and henceforward they lived in peace, tenderly devoted to the Divine Mother.[36]

38. In the year 1613, a man in Valentia committed a sin which he was ashamed to confess, so that he made sacrilegious confessions. But unable any longer to bear the remorse of his conscience, he went to visit our Blessed Lady of Halle, that she might help him. When he reached the door of the church, which was open, he felt himself forced back by an invisible power. He then determined to make his confession, and immediately was able to enter. He made a sincere confession, and returned home happy.[37]

39. Blessed Adam, a Cistercian, going one evening to visit the most Blessed Virgin in a church, found the door closed, and therefore knelt down outside to make his devotions: he had no sooner done so than the door opened; he entered, and saw the Queen of Heaven in great splendour. She said, 'Adam, come hither: knowest thou who I am?' 'No, Lady,' he replied; 'who art thou?' 'I am,' she said, 'the Mother of God. Know also that, as a reward for thy devotion to me, I will always take care of thee.' Then, placing her blessed hand on his head, she delivered him from a great pain from which the holy man suffered.[38]

40. A devout servant of Mary went one day, without telling her husband, to visit a church of our Blessed Lady, and was prevented by a great storm from returning home at night. She was greatly alarmed lest her

[36] Andrado, del Battes. di n. Don. P. Rho, es. lxxi. †
[37] An. Soc. ap. Auriem. tom. ii. c. 1.
[38] Chronic. Cisterc. 22 Dec.

husband might be angry at it: she, however, recommended herself to Mary, and returned home, where she found her husband very kind to her, and quite in a good humour. By her inquiries she discovered that, the night before, the Divine Mother had taken her form, and attended to all the duties of the household as a servant. She then related all that had taken place to her husband, and they both had ever afterwards the greatest devotion to the Blessed Virgin.[39]

41. A certain cavalier of the city of Dole in France, named Ansald, received in battle a wound from an arrow, which entered so deep into the jaw-bone that it was not possible to extract the iron point which remained. After four years, the poor man, unable any longer to endure the torment, and being besides very ill, thought of having the wound reopened, that the surgeons might again try to extract the iron. He recommended himself to the Blessed Virgin, and made a vow that he would every year visit a devout image of Mary, which was in that place, and make an offering of a certain sum of money, should she grant his prayer. He had no sooner made the vow than he felt the iron drop of its own accord in his mouth. On the following day, ill as he was, he went to visit the image, and scarcely had he placed his offering on the altar when he found himself entirely restored to health.[40]

42. In Spain there was a man who held sinful intercourse with a relation. A devout virgin was in prayer when she saw Jesus on a throne, in the act of sending that sinner to hell; but His most holy Mother said that at one time he had honoured her, and obtained him thirty days in which to repent. By order of the Divine Mother, the young woman told her confessor all that she had seen, and he told the young man, who, on hearing it, immediately confessed his sins with many tears, and promised amendment. Neglecting, however, to shun the society of his guilty partner, who

[39] Auriem. Aff. p. 1. c. 1.   [40] Chron. Dol. 1550. ap. Labb. Bibl. man.

lived in his own house, he relapsed into sin. He again went to confession, again promised amendment; but still relapsed. The father, finding that he did not return, went to his house, but was rudely refused admittance. The last of the thirty days came; the father returned to the house, but in vain; he, however, desired the servants to call him, should any accident occur. At night, indeed, the unfortunate sinner was seized with violent pains; the father was called, and hastened to assist him; but the unhappy man cried out, 'Ah, my heart has been pierced with a lance, and I am dying!' and with a howl of despair he expired.[41]

43. In Milan there was a man named Masaccio, who was such a gambler, that one day he played and lost the very clothes he wore. Enraged at his loss, he took a knife and stabbed an image of the Blessed Virgin; from the wound blood burst forth into his face. He was thereby so much moved that he began to weep, and thanked Mary for having obtained him time to repent, and became a Cistercian. He led so holy a life, that he was even favoured with the gift of prophecy. After spending forty years in religion, he made a holy death.[42]

44. A great sinner was once in prayer at the feet of a crucifix, earnestly entreating that he might receive a sign of pardon; but not receiving it, he addressed himself to Mary in sorrow, who then appeared to him. He saw her present his tears to her Son, saying, 'Son, shall these tears be lost?' He then understood that Christ had already pardoned him, and thenceforward led a holy life.[43]

45. A man advanced in years, during one of our missions, after the usual sermon on the powerful intercession of Mary, came to confession to one of our fathers, named Cesar Sportelli, who lately died in the odour of sanctity, and whose body was found incorrupt many

[41] Lyræus, Tris. Mar. l. 2. m. 8. p. 12. Bovio, Es. e Mir. p. 3, es. 6.

[42] P. Rho Sab. es. xlii. †   [43] P. Sinisc. Mart. di Mar. cons. xxxviii.

months after. Kneeling at the feet of his confessor, he said, 'Father, it is our Blessed Lady who has granted me this grace.' 'That is her employment,' the father replied. 'But you cannot absolve me,' he said, 'for I have never been to confession.' So it was, indeed; for, though a Catholic, he had never made his confession. The father encouraged him, heard his confession, and with great consolation absolved him.

46. Blessed Bernard Tolomeo, the founder of the Olivetan Fathers, who from his childhood was tenderly devoted to Mary, was one day greatly tormented at his hermitage of Ancona, called Mount Olivet, with doubts as to his salvation, and as to whether our Lord had yet forgiven him his sins. The Divine Mother appeared to him, and said, 'My son, why dost thou fear? Take courage, God has pardoned thee, and is pleased with the life thou leadest; persevere, I will help thee, and thou wilt be saved.' The blessed man continued to lead a holy life until his happy death in the arms of Mary.[44]

47. In Germany there was a young woman named Agnes, who had committed the crime of incest in the first degree. She fled to a desert, where she gave birth to a child. The devil then appeared to her under the form of a monk, and made her throw the child into a lake. He then endeavoured to persuade her to throw herself in also. On hearing this, she said, ' Mary, help me !' and the devil disappeared.[45]

48. A soldier made an engagement with the devil, that if he would give him money, he would deliver up his wife to him. To fulfil his promise, he was taking her to a wood, when he passed before a church of the Blessed Virgin. The lady begged her husband to allow her to enter the church to say a little prayer to Mary. Whilst she was there, the Divine Mother herself took her form, and, coming out of the church, got upon her horse. When they reached the wood, the devil cried

[44] In vita B. Bern Tolom. †   [45] J. Major, Magn. Spec. v. B.V. ex. 9

out to the husband, 'Traitor, how is this? instead of bringing me thy wife, thou bringest me the Mother of God, my enemy?' 'And thou,' replied Mary, 'how hast thou dared to think of injuring my devout servant? Depart; go back to hell. And do thou,' she then said, turning to the man, 'change thy life, and I will help thee.' She then disappeared, and the wretched man repented and changed his life.[46]

49. In Mexico there was a wicked woman, who, having fallen sick, repented, and made a vow to Mary, that if she recovered, she would make her the offering of her hair. She got well, and made the promised offering to a statue of the Blessed Virgin. She, however, relapsed into sin; again fell ill, and died impenitent. One day after this had occurred, Mary spoke from the statue to the Jesuit father John Mary Salvaterra, in the presence of a great concourse of people, and said, 'Take this hair from my head, for it belongs to an impure soul, who is already damned; it does not, therefore, become the head of the Mother of purity.' The father obeyed, and without delay threw it into the fire.[47]

50. A Saracen named Petran having made many Christians in Spain slaves, they recommended themselves to the Blessed Virgin. Mary appeared to the Saracen, and said, 'Petran, how dost thou dare hold my devout servants in slavery? Release them immediately; obey.' 'And who art thou,' the Moor replied, 'that I am to obey thee?' 'I am,' she said, 'the Mother of God; and because they have had recourse to me, my will is that thou shouldst set them at liberty.' Petran then felt himself changed; he set the Christians free, and offered himself to the Blessed Virgin. Mary first of all instructed him, then baptised him herself, in a place where a church and Benedictine monastery were afterwards built.[48]

[46] Giac. di Vorag. Leg. Aur. de Ass.   [47] Patrign. Men. 8 Jul.
[48] Eus. Nier. Troph. Mar. l. ii. c. 14.

51. A certain canon was reciting some prayers in honour of the Divine Mother, and whilst doing so fell into the river Seine, and was drowned. Being in mortal sin, the devils came to take him to hell. In the same moment Mary appeared, and said, ' How do you dare to take possession of one who died in the act of praising me ?' Then addressing herself to the sinner she said, ' Now change thy life, and nourish devotion to my Conception.' He returned to life, became a religious, and never ceased to thank his deliverer, and everywhere to propagate devotion to her Immaculate Conception.[49]

52. Once when the monks of Clairvaux were reaping in the fields, and praising the Queen of Heaven, the most holy Mary was seen caressing them, while two other Saints wiped off their perspiration.[50]

53. The brother of a king of Hungary used daily to recite the office of Mary. He once fell dangerously ill, and then made a vow of chastity to the Blessed Virgin if she would restore him to health, and he immediately recovered. His brother, however, afterwards died, and he was going to be married ; but just before the celebration of the nuptials he retired to his room to say his accustomed office. When he came to these words in it, " How beautiful art thou, and how comely !"[51] he saw Mary, who said, ' If I am beautiful as thou sayest, why dost thou now leave me for another spouse ? Know if thou leavest her, thou shalt have me for a spouse, and the kingdom of heaven instead of that of Hungary.' The prince then fled to a desert near Aquileia, where he lived a holy life.[52]

54. Saint John Climacus relates, that there was a devout religious named Carcerio, who used often to recite hymns in praise of Mary, and always saluted her images with a ' Hail Mary.' He afterwards fell into so painful an illness, that, in the paroxysms, he bit his lips and tongue. Thus he had lost his speech, and was

[49] Clictovæus in Ser. Concept. t   [50] Spec. exemp. Laborare, es. vii.
[51] Cant. vii. 6.   [52] Auriem. tom. i. c. 8.

already at the close of his life. But whilst his soul was being recommended to God, the Mother of God appeared to him, and said, ' I am come to cure thee ; for I cannot allow thee to suffer in that mouth with which thou hast praised me so much. So now arise, thou art cured : continue to praise me.' With these words she sprinkled him with some drops of her milk ; he was immediately restored to health ; and during his whole life he never ceased to praise her. At death he was again visited by his lady, and in her arms sweetly expired.[53]

55. When Saint Francis Borgia was in Rome, an ecclesiastic came to speak to him. The Saint being engaged, sent Father Acosta to him ; and he said, ' Father, I am a priest and a preacher, but am living in sin, and I despair of the Divine mercy. I one day preached a sermon against those who are obstinate in sin, and afterwards despair of God's mercy; upon which a person came to confession to me, and having related all my own sins to me, told me that he despaired of the Divine mercy. As it was my duty, I told him that he must change his life, and have confidence in God. On hearing this, the penitent stood up and reproved me, saying : ' Thou who preachest to others, why dost thou not change thy life, and have confidence ? Know,' he added, ' that I am an angel, who have come to help thee ; change thy life, and thou wilt be forgiven.' With these words he disappeared. I gave up my sins for a few days; but an occasion presented itself, and I again fell. On another day I was saying Mass, and Jesus Christ, in the Sacred Host, audibly said these words to me : ' Why dost thou thus ill-treat Me, when I treat thee so well ?' After this I resolved to amend ; but on the next occasion again fell. A few hours ago I was in my room, when a young man appeared before me, and drawing a chalice from under his cloak, and from it a consecrated host, said, ' Dost thou know this

Lord whom I hold in my hand ? Dost thou remember the many graces He has granted thee ? But now receive the punishment due to thine ingratitude ; ' and with these words he drew a sword to kill me. I then cried out, ' For the love of Mary, do not kill me, and I will indeed change my life.' He replied, ' This was the only means which could save thee ; learn to make a good use of it ; it is the last mercy thou wilt receive.' With these words he left me. I immediately came here to entreat you to receive me amongst you.' Father Acosta encouraged him ; and the priest, by the advice of Saint Francis Borgia, entered another Order of strict observance, in which he persevered in sanctity until death.[54]

56. In the year 1228, on a Saturday, a priest was saying Mass in honour of the most Blessed Virgin, when some Albigensian heretics came, and cut out his tongue. In this state he went to the monastery of Cluny, where the good religious welcomed him with the greatest charity, and deeply compassionated the sufferings which he still endured from the loss of his tongue. But the good priest's keenest grief was, that he could no longer say Mass, recite the Divine office, or the office of the Blessed Virgin, as he used to do. On the Feast of the Epiphany he begged to be carried to the church, and there, before the altar of the Blessed Virgin, he begged her to restore him the tongue which he had lost for love of her, that he might be able to praise her as he had formerly done. Behold, Mary appeared to him with a tongue in her hand, and said, ' Since thou hast lost thy tongue for the faith and for the honour thou hast shown me, I now give thee a new one.' When she had said this, she with her own hands put the tongue in his mouth ; and in the same instant the priest, raising his voice, recited the ' Hail Mary.' The monks immediately flocked round him, and the priest declared his wish to remain amongst them to be-

[54] Bovio, Ex. e. Mir. p. 4. es. 5.

come a religious, that there he might always continue to praise his benefactress. The scar remained, so as to make the miracle evident to all.[55]

57. In the year 589 the famous plague, by which men fell dead whilst sneezing, prevailed in Rome. Saint Gregory the Great, when he was carrying the picture of the Blessed Virgin which is preserved in Saint Mary Major's, in procession through the city, in the place now called the Castle of Saint Angelo, saw an angel replacing a sword, reeking with blood, in its scabbard. He then heard the angels singing : ' Queen of Heaven ! rejoice, Alleluia ; for He whom thou didst deserve to bear, Alleluia, is risen again as He said, Alleluia.' Saint Gregory then added, ' Intercede for us with God, Alleluia.' The plague immediately ceased ; and from that time it became the custom to say the Litanies of Saints every year on the twenty-fifth of April.[56]

58. The city of Avignon in France, was once besieged by enemies. The citizens, imploring Mary to protect them, placed at the gate of the city an image of the Blessed Virgin, which they took for the purpose from one of the churches. One of the citizens endeavoured to conceal himself behind the image ; a soldier saw him, and shot an arrow at him, saying, ' Ah, this image shall not save you from death.' But the image presented its knee, in which the arrow remained fixed (as it may be seen to the present day), and thus saved the life of her client. At the sight of this prodigy the enemy raised the siege.[57]

59. In Naples there was a Moor, a slave of Don Octavius del Monaco, who, notwithstanding all the exhortations which were made him to renounce Mahometanism, remained obstinate, but yet he never failed to light every evening, at his own expense, a lamp before an image of Mary which was in the house. He used

---

[55] Cæsarius, lib. vii. Dial. c. xxiv.
[56] Carthagena, de Arc. Deip. l. 19. § 101.
[57] Vincent de Beauvais, Spec. Hist. l. 7. c. 83.

also to say, 'I hope that this Lady will do me some great favour.' One night the Blessed Virgin appeared to him, and told him to become a Christian. The Turk even then resisted ; but Mary, putting her hand on his shoulder, said, 'Resist no longer, Abel ; be baptised, and take the name of Joseph.' On the very next morning he went to be instructed, and with eleven other Turks was baptised on the tenth of August, in the year 1648. It must be here remarked, that when the Divine Mother appeared to him, and had converted him, she was about to depart ; but the Moor took her by the mantle, saying, 'Lady, when I am in affliction, I beseech thee to let me see thee.' She promised him that it should be so ; and, in fact, on an occasion when he was afflicted he called her, and Mary again appeared, and by saying, 'Have patience,' filled him with consolation.[58]

60. A parish priest of Asella, named Baldwin, became a Dominican friar. When he was in the novitiate he had the temptation that he could do more good in the world in his parish. He had already determined to return to it ; but before doing so, he went to take leave of the altar of the rosary. Mary appeared to him with two jars of wine. She gave him to drink of the first ; but the novice had hardly tasted it when he turned away from it ; for although the wine was good, it was full of lees ; the second, however, he said was good wine and pure. 'This,' the Blessed Virgin then said, 'is precisely the difference that there is between a life spent in the world, and one spent under religious obedience.' Baldwin persevered, and died as a good religious.[59]

61. Another novice, also overcome by a temptation, was on the point of leaving his monastery. He stopped to say a 'Hail Mary,' before an image of the Blessed Virgin, when he found himself as it were nailed to

[58] Bovio, Es. e. Mir. p. 4. es. 3.
[59] Chron. Ord. ap. Aur. tom. ii. cap. 7.

the floor, so that he could not rise. He then repented, made a vow of perseverance, was able to rise, asked his master's pardon, and persevered.[60]

62. Blessed Clement, of the order of Saint Francis, one morning delayed going to the common table, that he might finish certain accustomed devotions to the Blessed Virgin ; but she spoke to him from the image, and desired him to go with the others, as she was more pleased with obedience than with all other devotions.[61]

63. Whilst Angela, the daughter of a king of Bohemia, was in a convent, Mary appeared to her, and an angel said, ' Arise, Angela, and fly to Jerusalem, for thy father wishes to give thee in marriage to the Prince of Hungary.' The devout virgin immediately departed ; and on her journey the Divine Mother again appeared to her, and encouraged her to continue. She was then received in Jerusalem amongst the Carmelites ; and was afterwards desired by the Blessed Virgin herself to return to her own country, where she lived a holy life until her death.[62]

64. Saint Gregory relates that there was a young woman named Musa, who was very devout to the Mother of God ; to whom, when she was in great danger of losing her innocence by the bad example of her companions, Mary appeared one day with many Saints, and said, ' Musa, dost thou also wish to be one of these ?' On her answering ' Yes,' she added, ' Well, withdraw from thy companions, and prepare thyself, for in a month thou shalt come.' Musa did so, and related the vision. · On the thirteenth day she was at the point of death, when the most Blessed Virgin again appeared, and invited her to come. She replied, ' Behold, I come, O Lady,' and sweetly expired.[63]

65. Anne Catherine Gonzaga was married to Ferdinand I. Archduke of Austria. On the death of her husband she entered the religious order of the Servants

[60] Auriem. loc. cit.   [61] Ann. Min. ap. Aur. tom. i. cap. 4.
[62] Bovio, Es. e Mir. p. 5. es. 37.   [63] Lib. iv. Dial. cap. 18.

of Mary, and had a chaplet made for herself, on the beads of which were carved the dolours of the Blessed Virgin. She used to say, that for this chaplet she renounced all the other crowns of the world ; and she indeed did refuse to marry the Emperor Rodolph II. When she was told that her younger sister had been crowned empress, she replied, ' My sister may enjoy her imperial crown ; for to me this habit with which my Queen Mary has crowned me is a thousand times dearer.' The most Blessed Virgin appeared to her many times during her life ; and at last this good religious made a holy death.[64]

66. A clerical student was playing at ball with other young men ; and fearing that he might whilst playing lose a ring which had been given him by a lady, went and placed it on the finger of a statue of Mary which was there : he then felt himself inspired to promise the Blessed Virgin that he would renounce the world and choose her for his spouse : he made the promise, and Mary pressed his finger as a sign that she accepted it. After some time he wished to marry another woman. Mary appeared to him, and reproached him with his infidelity ; he therefore fled into a desert, where he persevered to the end in a holy life.[65]

67. Towards the year 850, Berengarius, bishop of Verdun in Lorraine, entered a church in which a priest named Bernier was prostrate before the choir, reciting the office of the Blessed Virgin. The bishop stumbled over him, and in his impatience gave him a kick. In the night the most Blessed Virgin appeared to him and said, ' How didst thou dare to kick my servant whilst he was praising me ? But now,' she added, ' because I love thee, I will that thou shouldst pay the penalty.' His leg immediately withered. He lived and died as a saint ; and after many years his whole body, with the exception of that leg, was found incorrupt.[66]

[64] Marocci, Her. Mar. c. 1. § 15.   [65] Spec. Ex. verb. B. Virg. ex. 3.
[66] Hugues de Flavigny, Chron. Vird. p. 1.

68. A young man who was left in opulence **after** the death of his parents, by gambling and dissipation with his friends lost all that he possessed; he always, however, remained chaste. He had an uncle who, seeing him reduced to poverty by his vices, exhorted him to say every day a part of the rosary, promising him that if he persevered in this devotion he would procure him a good marriage. The young man persevered, and having amended his life, was married. On the evening of his wedding-day he rose from table to go and recite his rosary. When he had finished it, Mary appeared to him, and said, ' Now I will reward thee for the honour thou hast paid me. It is my will that thou shouldst remain a virgin; in three days thou shalt die, and shalt go with me to Paradise.' This really took place; for he was immediately attacked by fever; and having related the vision, he died on the third day in the greatest peace.[67]

69. The devout author of a book in praise of the rosary, called *The Secret of every Grace*, relates that Saint Vincent Ferrer said to a man who was dying in despair, ' Why are you determined to lose your soul, when Jesus Christ wishes to save you?' The man answered that, in spite of Christ, he was determined to go to hell. The Saint replied, ' And you, in spite of yourself, shall be saved.' He began with the persons in the house to recite the rosary; when, behold, the sick man asked to make his confession; and having done so with many tears, expired.

70. The same author relates that in a late earthquake a poor woman was buried under the ruins of a house which was overthrown. A priest had the stones and rubbish cleared away, and under them found the mother with her children in her arms, alive and uninjured. On being asked what devotion she had practised, she replied, that she had never omitted saying the rosary, and visiting the altar of our Blessed Lady.

[67] Cantip. lib. ii. cap. 29, n. 6.

71. He also relates that another woman lived in sin, fancying it was the only means by which she could gain her livelihood. She was advised to recommend herself to Mary by saying the rosary. She did so; and behold one night the Divine Mother appeared to her and said, 'Abandon sin ; and as to thy support, trust in me, I will provide for that.' In the morning she went to confession, changed her life, and the most Blessed Virgin amply supplied her wants.

72. A person who was leading an immoral life had not courage to give it up ; he began to say the rosary, and was converted.

73. Another person who maintained a sinful friendship, by saying the rosary felt a horror of sin ; she fell a few more times into sin, but by means of the rosary was soon quite converted.

74. Another woman bore a bitter hatred to her husband, and was dying. A good priest who was attending her, no longer knowing what to do to convert her, withdrew to say the rosary. When he was at the last decade, she entered into herself, repented, and forgave her husband.

75. Finally, the above-named author relates, that he was once giving a mission to the convicts in Naples. There were some who were obstinate and refused to go to confession. He persuaded them at least to enrol their names in the Confraternity of the Rosary, and to begin to recite it ; they did so ; but scarcely had they recited it once, before they asked to make their confessions, though they had not done so for many years. These more recent examples serve to revive our confidence in Mary, seeing that she is still what she always was to those who have recourse to her.

76. Saint Gregory relates that a holy bishop of Ferentino was inclined from his childhood to give alms to the poor. It happened one day that a nephew of his, a priest, sold a horse for twelve crowns, and having received the money, locked it up in a box. Some poor

persons came to ask an alms of the bishop; and as he had nothing to give them, he broke open the box, and divided the twelve crowns among them. As soon as the nephew discovered it, he was so enraged, that the bishop, no longer knowing how to pacify him, went to a church to have recourse to the Blessed Virgin. Behold, after praying a short time with his arms extended, he saw twelve new golden crowns lying on the hem of his garment; he took them, and gave them to his nephew.[68]

77. A Lutheran lady, at Augsburg in Germany, who was obstinate in her heresy, was one day passing before a Catholic chapel, and out of curiosity entered it, and saw there an image of Mary with the infant Jesus in her arms, and felt inspired to make her an offering. She went to her house and took a piece of silk, which she offered to the Blessed Virgin. On her return home, this good Mother enlightened her to see the errors of her sect; she immediately went to see some Catholics, abjured heresy, and was converted to God.[69]

78. In the city of Cesena there lived two sinners who were great friends. One of them, whose name was Bartholomew, in the midst of his wickedness preserved the devotion of daily reciting the hymn 'Stabat Mater' in honour of Mary in Sorrow. He was one day reciting this hymn, when he had a vision, in which he seemed to stand with his wicked friend in a lake of fire; and he saw that the most Holy Virgin, moved to compassion, extended her hand to him, withdrew him from the fire, and advised him to ask pardon of Jesus Christ, who seemed to forgive him on account of the prayers of His Mother. After the vision, Bartholomew heard that his companion was dead, having been shot; and he thus knew that what he had seen was true. He then renounced the world, and entered the order of Capuchins,

[68] S. Gregor. Dial. lib. i. cap. 9.
[69] An. Soc. 1656, ap. Aur. tom. ii. cap. 7.

where he led a most austere life, and died with reputation of sanctity.[70]

79. Blessed Jerome, the founder of the Somaschi, at a time when he was the governor of a fortress was taken prisoner by the enemy, and was confined in the dungeon of a tower. He had recourse to Mary, and made a vow that if she delivered him, he would make a pilgrimage to Treviso. The Blessed Virgin then appeared to him surrounded by a great light, and with her own hands loosened his chains, and gave him the keys of the prison. When he had gone only a short distance on his road to Treviso in fulfilment of his vow, he found himself in the midst of his enemies : he again had recourse to his protectress, who once more appeared to him, took him by the hand, and having led him through the midst of them, accompanied him to the gates of Treviso, and then disappeared. He made the visit, left his chains at the foot of the altar of Mary, and from that time led so holy a life that he has merited to be ranked by the Holy Church in the number of the blessed.[71]

80. A priest, who had great devotion to Mary in Sorrow, used often to shut himself up alone in a little church, that he might there mourn over the dolours of his Lady ; and out of compassion he would wipe the tears of a statue of the Blessed Virgin in Sorrow with a piece of linen. Now this good priest once fell dangerously ill, and was given up by the physicians. When he was on the point of death, he beheld a most beautiful Lady standing before him ; she encouraged him with kind words, and with a handkerchief gently wiped from his brow the sweat of death, and restored him to health. The priest then said, ' But, Lady, who art thou, who dost treat me with such charity ? ' ' I am,' Mary replied, ' that Lady whose tears thou hast so often dried ; ' and so saying, she disappeared.[72]

81. A noble lady, who had an only son, was in-

[70] P. Sinisc. Mart. di Mar. c. 15.
[71] In vita. †   [72] P. Sinisc. Mart. di. Mar. c. 9.

formed one day that he had been killed. The murderer had by chance taken refuge in her own palace. She then began to reflect that Mary had forgiven the executioners of her Son; and therefore determined that she also would pardon that criminal for the love of the sorrowful Mary. She not only did this, but also provided him with a horse, money, and clothes, that he might escape. Her son then appeared to her, and told her that he was saved, and that for her generous conduct to his enemy the Divine Mother had delivered him from purgatory, in which otherwise he would have had to suffer for a long time, and that he was then going to Paradise.[73]

82. Blessed Bionda performed an act of equal heroism. Some enemies took the life of her innocent and only son, out of hatred to his already deceased father, and with unheard-of barbarity, without her knowledge, gave the heart of the murdered youth to his poor mother to eat. Imitating the example of the most Blessed Virgin, she began to pray for the murderers, and to render them every service in her power. The Divine Mother was so pleased with these acts that she called her to join the third order of the Servites; in which she led so holy a life that she worked many miracles both before and after her death.[74]

83. When Saint Thomas of Canterbury was a young man, he was once in company with other youths, each of whom was perhaps boasting of some foolish love-affair. The holy young man declared that he also loved and was beloved by a great Lady, meaning the most Blessed Virgin. He afterwards felt some remorse at having boasted of this. Being anxious on the subject, behold Mary appeared to him, and with gracious sweetness said, 'Thomas, why fearest thou? Thou hadst reason to say that thou lovest me, and that thou wast loved by me. Assure thy companions of this; and as

[73] P. Tausch de Matre dol. lib. ii. cap. 8.
[74] Ann. Ord. Serv. cent. 2, lib. iv. cap. 14.

a pledge of the love I bear thee, show them this gift which I now bestow upon thee.' The gift was a small box, containing a chasuble of a blood-red colour, as a token that Mary, for the love she bore him, had obtained the grace for him from God, that he should become a priest and a martyr. This was verified ; for he became a priest, then Archbishop of Canterbury in England, where he was first of all persecuted by the King, and had to fly to the Cistercian monastery of Pontigny in France. When there, he was one day mending the hair-shirt which he usually wore ; but not being able to do it well, his beloved Queen appeared to him, and with extraordinary kindness took it from his hands and repaired it as it should be done. After this he returned to Canterbury, and died a martyr, having been put to death on account of the zeal he had shown for his Church.[75]

84. In the Pontifical States a young woman, who was very devout to Mary, met with a captain of bandits. Fearing some outrage, she entreated him, for the love of the most Blessed Virgin, not to molest her. 'Fear nothing,' he replied, ' since you have asked me in the name of the Mother of God; all that I desire is that you should recommend me to her ;' and, in fact, he himself accompanied her along the road to a place of safety. On the following night Mary appeared to the bandit in a dream, and, thanking him for the action he had performed for her love, assured him she would not forget it, and would one day reward him. The robber was afterwards made a prisoner, and condemned to death. The night before the execution was to take place, behold the Blessed Virgin again appeared to him in a dream, and first of all asked him whether he knew her ? He replied that it seemed to him that he had seen her before. ' I am,' she then said, ' the Blessed Virgin Mary, and am come to reward thee for what thou hast done for me. To-morrow thou wilt die ; but

75 Auriemma, Aff. p. 1, c. 1.   Bovio, Es. e Mir. p. 4, es. 36.

thou wilt die with so much contrition that thou wilt go at once to Paradise.' The prisoner awoke, and felt such sorrow for his sins that he began to weep bitterly, at the same time thanking our Blessed Lady aloud. He then begged that a priest might be immediately called; he confessed his sins to him with many tears, related the vision he had had, and entreated him to publish the grace which he had received from Mary. He went with great joy to execution; after which, it is said that his countenance was so peaceful and happy that all who saw him believed that the promise of the Divine Mother had been fulfilled.[76]

85. Blessed Joachim Piccolomini had always a most tender devotion for Mary, and from his childhood was in the habit of visiting an image of our Blessed Lady of Sorrows, which was in a neighbouring church, three times a day; and on Saturdays, in her honour, he abstained from all food; and in addition to this he always rose at midnight to meditate on her dolours. But let us see how abundantly this good Mother recompensed him. In the first place, when he was a young man she appeared to him and desired him to embrace the order of her Servants; and this the holy young man did. Again, in the latter years of his life, she appeared to him with two crowns in her hands: the one was composed of rubies, and this was to reward him for his compassion for her sorrows; the other of pearls, as a recompense for his virginity, which he vowed in her honour. Shortly before his death she once more appeared to him; and then the Saint begged, as a favour, that he might die on the same day on which Jesus Christ had expired. Our Blessed Lady immediately gratified him, saying, ' It is well: prepare thyself; for to-morrow, Good Friday, thou shalt die suddenly as thou desirest; to-morrow thou shalt be with me in heaven.' And so it was; for the next day, during the singing of the Passion according to St. John, at the

[76] P. Recup. de Sign. Præd. c 12

words, " Now there stood by the cross of Jesus His Mother," he fell into the last struggles of death ; and at the words, " He bowed down His head and expired," the Saint also breathed his last : and in the same moment the whole church was filled with an extraordinary light and the most delicious perfume.[77]

86. Father Alphonsus Salmeron, of the Society of Jesus, having always been most devout to the Blessed Virgin, died saying, ' To Paradise, to Paradise ! Blessed are the hours in which I served Mary ; blessed are the sermons, the labours, the thoughts, that I have given to thee, my Lady. To Paradise !'[78]

87. A prince named Farnulfo presented his youthful son Guido, who wished to become a Camaldolese, to Saint Romuald. The holy founder received him with pleasure. Mary one day appeared to this good young man, her servant, with the Infant Jesus in her arms. He, esteeming himself unworthy of so great a grace, stood trembling. The Divine Mother, then drawing nearer to him, said, ' Why dost thou doubt ? what dost thou fear, Guido ? I am the Mother of God ; this is my Son Jesus, who wishes to come to thee.' With these words she placed Him in his arms. Guido had not yet been three years in religion when he fell dangerously ill. Saint Romuald saw the poor youth writhing and trembling, and heard him say, ' O father, do you not see what a number of Moors there are in my cell ?' ' Son,' the Saint said, ' do you remember anything which you have not confessed ?' ' Yes, father,' he replied ; ' I remember disobeying the prior when he told me to gather up some sweepings. I now confess it.' Saint Romuald absolved him, and then the scene changed ; the devils fled, and once more the Blessed Virgin appeared with Jesus ; and at this sight Guido expired, full of consolation.[79]

88. A Cistercian nun in Toledo, named Mary, being

---

[77] Sinisch. Mart. di Maria, cons. 28-30.
[78] In vita. †   [79] Franc. Lelli in vita. †

at the point of death, the Divine Mother appeared to her. The nun then said, 'O Lady, the favour thou dost me in visiting me emboldens me to ask thee another favour: it is, that I may die at the same hour in which thou didst expire and enter heaven.' 'Yes,' Mary replied, 'I will satisfy thee: thou shalt die at that hour; and thou shalt also hear the songs and praises with which the blessed accompanied my entrance into heaven: prepare thyself;' and then disappeared. The nuns, hearing her speaking to herself, thought that she was in delirium; but she related the vision which she had had to them, and the promised favour. She awaited the desired hour; and when she knew, by the striking of the clock, that it had arrived (the writer does not say what hour it was), she said, 'Behold the hour announced to me: I already hear the music of the angels; this is the hour in which my Queen ascended to heaven. Peace be with you; for I now go to see her.' With these words she expired. In the same moment her eyes became bright as two stars, and her face became of a beautiful colour.[80]

89. In the city of Sens in France, towards the eighth century, was living Saint Opportuna, born of parents of royal blood. This holy virgin, who had the greatest devotion to Mary, became a nun in a neighbouring convent, and, being at the point of death one morning towards the dawn, she saw Saint Cecily and Saint Lucy standing before her. 'Sisters,' she said, 'you are welcome: what message does my Queen send me?' They replied, 'She awaits thee in Paradise.' After this the devil appeared to her; and the Saint courageously drove him away, saying, 'Brute beast, what hast thou to do with me, who am a servant of Jesus?' The hour of her death, which she had herself predicted, having arrived, after having received the Holy Viaticum, she turned towards the door, and said,

[80] Menol. Cist. alli Santi d'Agost.

'Behold the Mother of God, who is come to take me. Sisters, to her do I recommend you. Farewell; we shall see each other no more in this world.' Thus speaking, she raised her arms as if to embrace her Lady, and sweetly expired.[81]

61 Surius, die 22 Aprilis.

REPLY TO AN ANONYMOUS WRITER,

WHO HAS CENSURED WHAT THE AUTHOR OF THIS WORK
HAS SAID, IN THE FIRST SECTION OF THE FIFTH
CHAPTER, ON THE SALVE REGINA.

A BOOK* printed in the course of last year (1755) having fallen into my hands, I found towards the end of it
an appendix, in which the author, who is anonymous,
criticises what I have written in the above-quoted part
of my little work. In it I maintain, with Father Piazza,
that all graces come to us through the Divine Mother,
in opposition to that which the celebrated Louis Muratori wrote in his book called *Well-regulated Devotion,*
under the name of Pritanius.

The anonymous writer says that I am mistaken in
my assertion, that Pritanius wrote that the proposition,
that God grants no grace otherwise than through Mary,
was hyperbolical and exaggerated, having dropped from
the lips of some Saints in the heat of fervour. Fearing
that such might have been the case, I have again read
the book; and I see that though Pritanius does not exactly join the above words to the passage in which he
speaks of the Saints, yet from the context it is evident
that he also refers it to the Saints who have spoken on
this subject. Speaking of another proposition, that
Mary commands in heaven, he says, 'Gently; this and
other similar expressions, which have dropped from
the lips of some Saints in their devout fervour, will not
stand when examined by the rules of sound theology.'
Again he says, 'We must hear the Church, and not
the hyperboles of a private author, even though he be

* Lamindi Pritanii redivivi Epistola paraenetica ad P. Bened. Piazza.

a Saint.' He immediately afterwards adds, 'We may also meet with some who assert that no grace comes to us from God otherwise than through the hands of Mary.' Now remark the words, 'We may also meet with some.' He afterwards says, 'To pretend that all the graces which we receive from God pass by Mary, would be a devout exaggeration.'

But even supposing that the dead Pritanius did not say it, there is a living Pritanius who says it in his book (see No. 545), in which, amongst other things, he tells us that ' sometimes the Saints in praising the Blessed Virgin exaggerated, and used tropes.' I now therefore answer him and say, that without doubt hyperbole, under which name tropes are included, cannot be taxed with untruth when it is evident from the context that it goes beyond the truth ; as the case is when Saint Peter Damian says that ' Mary does not pray, but commands.'[1] The same applies to Saint Anselm, when he says that ' she weeps in heaven for those who offend God.' In such cases as these, in which there can be no mistake, tropes are lawful. But such is not the case in proposi tions in which the hyperbole is not evident, and there-fore would be a real deception. But let us come to the principal point in question. To prove it, I do not in-tend to bring forward the intrinsic reasons which would support it. I will only allude here to the reason which I adduced in my book, ' that God is thus pleased to honour His Beloved, who in life honoured Him so much.' Saint Thomas says that ' in proportion to the graces they have merited, the Saints can save many others ; but that our Blessed Redeemer and His most Holy Mother merited so much grace that they can save all men.'[2] Moreover, as she is the universal advocate of all men, it is becoming that all who are saved should obtain salvation by her means. Moreover—and this seems to me a more solid reason—as Mary cooperated by her charity, as Saint Augustine says,[3] in the spiritual

[1] Page 154, note 4.   [2] Page 4, note 5.   [3] De S. Virginit. c. 6.

birth of the faithful, so also God wills that she should coöperate by her intercession in obtaining for them the life of grace in this world, and the life of glory in eternity. For this reason the Church makes us call her, without any limitation, 'OUR LIFE' and 'OUR HOPE.' But that which has and still makes the greatest impression on my mind is, that I see this opinion maintained, not only by so many learned authors, but also by Saints. The anonymous writer believes he has in particular proved that Saint Bernard never meant to assert that all graces come to us by the hands of Mary, but only that through her we received Jesus Christ, who is the source and plenitude of all graces. But I believe, on the other hand, that I shall here evidently prove the reverse by what I now add.

Saint Bernard says that Mary received the plenitude of grace from God. Then explaining in what this plenitude consists, he says that it consists principally in the reception of Jesus Christ, who is the source of all graces, into herself; but then he adds, that in consequence of this, the Blessed Virgin received another plenitude, which is the plenitude of graces; that, as she is the mediatress of men with God, so she might herself dispense these graces to all men. The Saint says, 'Why should human frailty fear to approach Mary? In her there is nothing severe, nothing terrible; she is all sweetness, offering milk and wool to all. Thank Him, then, who has provided you with such a mediatress. She has made herself all to all, to the wise and to the foolish; by her most abundant charity she has made herself a debtor to all. She opens her merciful heart to all, that all may receive of her plenitude; the captive redemption, the sick health, the sinner pardon, the just grace, the angels joy, her Son flesh, that no one may hide himself from her heat.'[4] Remark, therefore, the words, ' that all may receive of her plenitude ;' for they clearly prove that Saint Bernard here speaks, not

Page 189, note 20.

of the first plenitude, which is Jesus Christ—otherwise he could not say that even her Son received His flesh of her plenitude—but of the second, or consequent fulness of grace, as we have already said, which Mary received from God, whereby to dispense to each one of us the graces which we receive. Remark also the words, ' there is no one who hides himself from her heat.' Did anyone receive graces otherwise than through Mary, he could hide himself from the heat of this sun ; but Saint Bernard says that no one can hide himself from the warmth of Mary. Elsewhere he says, 'By thee we have access to the Son, O blessed finder of grace, bearer of life, and Mother of salvation, that we may receive Him by thee, who through thee was given to us ;[5] by which the Saint clearly gives us to understand, that, as we have access to the Father only through the Son, who is the Mediator of justice, and who by His merits obtains for us all graces, so also we only have access to the Son by means of the Mother, who is the mediatress of grace, and by her prayers obtains for us all the graces which Jesus Christ has merited for us.

This is still better explained by that which the Saint afterwards says in his sermon 'Of the Aqueduct,' in the commencement of which he says, that Mary received the first plenitude of grace from God, that is, Jesus Christ, in order that she might impart it to us also. But a little further on he speaks clearly of the second plenitude of graces which she received, consequently of the graces which we receive through her prayers. The Saint says, ' It is true that Mary obtained Jesus Christ, the source of graces, from God ; but this perhaps does not fully satisfy your desires ; for you would wish that she should herself obtain for you, by her intercession, these graces which Jesus Christ merited for you.' The Saint then passes on to exhort us never to cease to honour and have recourse with great

[5] Per te accessum habeamus ad Filium, O Inventrix gratiæ, Mater salutis ut per te nos suscipiat qui per te datus est nobis.—*In Adv. D.* § 2.

confidence to this Divine Mother, saying, that which we desire, God has already granted, by depositing in Mary the plenitude of every blessing; that whatever we receive of hope, grace, and salvation from God, we may see that we have obtained it by the means of Mary, who ascends overflowing with delights.[6] ' She,' the Saint says, ' is a garden of delights' (and remark that he is still speaking of the graces which are actually dispensed to us by Mary's hand), 'upon which that divine south wind has not only breathed in passing, but has so filled with his balmy breath, that its perfumes, that is, the most precious gifts of graces, are sent forth on every side.'[7] And in reference to the first text which I quoted, ' There is no one who hides himself from her heat,' the Saint says : ' Take away the sun, where will be the day ? Take away Mary, what will be left but the darkest night ?'[8]

He then continues to exhort us to recommend ourselves to Mary, and to take her as our advocate with Jesus Christ. He encourages us, saying, that if she prays for us, her Son is certain graciously to hear her; for He hears His Mother, and the Father hears His Son :[9] and he immediately adds, ' My children, she is the sinner's ladder ; she is my greatest confidence ; she is the whole ground of my hope.'[10] Here, when the Saint calls her the sinner's ladder, and the whole ground of his hope, he certainly does so for no other reason than because he considers her as the intercessor for, and the dispenser of, all graces. She is a ladder ; and as we cannot reach the third step of a ladder unless we put our foot on the first, so neither can we reach God otherwise than by Jesus Christ ; nor Jesus Christ otherwise than by Mary. He then calls her his greatest confidence, and the whole ground of his hope : and why ? Because God having willed that all graces should pass

---

6 Page 300, note 66.

7 Hortus deliciarum, quem non modo afflaverit veniens, sed et perflaverit superveniens auster ille divinus, ut undique fluant et effluant aromata ejus, charismata scilicet gratiarum.—*Serm. de Aquæd.*

8 Page 64, note 8.   9 Page 175, note 1.   10 Page 175, note 8.

through Mary, he would have considered himself deprived of grace and hope, had he been deprived of her intercession. He then exhorts us to do as he does; that is, to place all our hopes in Mary; giving us at the same time to understand, that if Mary prays for us, we are certain of salvation. For, as the Father cannot but graciously hear the Son, neither can the Son do otherwise than graciously hear His Mother. On the other hand, he tells us, that if Mary does not pray for us, we shall not obtain salvation; because she will not have provided us with grace, which is all that we require, and the only means by which we are saved. He then concludes, 'What more can we desire? Let us seek for grace, and seek it by Mary; for that which she seeks she finds, and never meets with a refusal.'[11]

Moreover, I have given in my book many other passages, with their references, as well from the writings of the Saints as from other ancient and renowned authors; and I do not see how it is possible to explain them otherwise than according to our opinion. I will here simply give them together, without comment; and my reader may judge how far my opinion is correct.

Saint Sophronius, in a sermon on the Assumption, formerly attributed to Saint Jerome, says, that ' the plenitude of all grace, which was in Christ, came into Mary.'[12] Saint Bernardine of Sienna, that ' all graces of the spiritual life that descend from Christ, their head, to the faithful, who are His mystical body, are transmitted by the means of Mary.'[13] That 'from the moment in which this Virgin Mother conceived the Divine Word in her womb, she acquired a special jurisdiction, so to say, over all the gifts of the Holy Ghost; so that no creature has since received any grace from God, otherwise than by the hands of Mary.'[14] That ' all gifts, all virtues, and all graces are dispensed by

11 Quid nos alia concupiscimus? Quæramus gratiam, et per Mariam quæramus; quia quod quærit invenit, et irustrari non potest. —*Serm. de Aquæd.*
12 Page 4, note 2.   13 Page 135, note 36.   14 Page 135, note 37.

the hands of Mary, to whomsoever, when, and as she pleases.[15] That 'as God was pleased to dwell in the womb of this holy Virgin, she acquired, so to say, a kind of jurisdiction over all graces; for when Jesus Christ issued forth from her most sacred womb, all the streams of Divine gifts flowed from her as from a celestial ocean.'[16] Saint Bonaventure: 'As the moon, which stands between the sun and the earth, transmits to this latter whatever she receives from the former, so does Mary pour out upon us who are in this world the heavenly graces which she receives from God.'[17] Again: 'God will not save us without the intercession of Mary.'[18] Again: 'As a child cannot live without a nurse to suckle it, so no one can be saved without the protection of Mary.'[19] Saint Ephrem says: 'O most holy Virgin, receive us under thy protection, if thou wilt see us saved; for we have no hope of salvation but through thy means.'[20] Saint Germanus: 'What hope can we have of salvation, if thou dost abandon us, O Mary, who art the life of Christians?'[21] Saint Ildephonsus: 'O Mary, God has decided on committing all good gifts that He has provided for men to thy hands; and therefore He has intrusted all treasures and riches of grace to thee.'[22] Saint Antoninus: 'Whoever asks and expects to find graces without the intercession of Mary, endeavours to fly without wings.'[23] Saint Peter Damian: 'All the treasures of the mercy of God are in her hands.'[24] Gerson: 'She is our mediatress, through whose hands God has decreed that all that He gives to men should pass.'[25] The Abbot of Celles: 'She is the dispenser of the Divine graces; for her Son grants nothing but what passes through her hands.'[26] In an-

---

5 Page 136, note 41.   16 Page 135, note 38.   17 Page 134, note 31.

8 Page 145, note 28.   19 Page 145, note 29.

10 Page 149, note 52.   21 Page 146, note 34.   22 Page 137, note 44.

23 Page 144, note 20.   24 Page 344, note 21.

25 Mediatrix nostra, per cujus manus Deus ordinavit dare ea quæ dat homanæ naturæ.—*Serm. de Annunt.*

26 Tu Dispensatrix es gratiarum divinarum: nihil concedit nobis Filius tuus quin pertransierit per manus tuas.—*Op. plen. de B. V. p. 9. cont. 14.*

other place he says : ' Our salvation is in her hands.'[27]
Cassian : ' The salvation of all depends on their being
favoured and protected by Mary.'[28]   Saint Bernardine
of Sienna says the same thing : ' O Lady, since thou
art the dispenser of all graces, our salvation is in your
hands.'[29]   Richard : ' Whatever graces God grants to
His creatures, He wills that they should pass through
the hands of His Virgin Mother.'[30]   Elsewhere he supposes Jesus Christ saying : ' No one comes to Me unless
My Mother draws him by her prayers.'[31]   Richard of
Saint Lawrence, alluding to the words of Proverbs,
" She is like the merchant's ship," says : ' In the sea of
the world all are lost who are not received into this
ship : therefore, as often as we see ourselves in danger
of perishing in the midst of the waves of this sea, we
should cry out to Mary : Lady, save us ; we perish.'[32]
Again he says : ' As we should fall into the abyss if
the ground were withdrawn from under our feet, so
does a soul deprived of the succour of Mary fall first
into sin, and then into hell.'[33]

I add another argument, which has great weight
with me : it is, that the greater part of the faithful have
always recourse to the intercession of the Divine Mother
for all the graces which they desire : whence it appears
that the above pious belief is, we may almost say, the
general belief of the Church.   Of this very argument
—that is, the general belief of the faithful—Petavius[34]
makes use to prove the doctrine, which I consider certain, of the Immaculate Conception of Mary.   To conclude : the above belief, that all graces pass by the
hands of Mary, seeming to me, as also to many other
writers,—such as Segneri,[35] Pacciuchelli,[36] Crasset,[37]

---

[27] Page 144, note 24.   [28] Page 144, note 25.   [29] Page 144, note 26.
[30] Deus quidquid boni dat creaturis suis, per manus Matris Virginis vul'
transire.—*De Laud. B.M.* l. 2. p. 3.
[31] Page 142, note 9.   [32] Page 143, note 14.   [33] Page 145, note 27.
[34] De Inc. l. 14. c. 2. n. 10.   [35] Div. di M. p. 1. c. 5.
[36] In Sal. Ang. exc. 15.   [37] Vér. Dév. p. 1. tr. 1. q. 5.

Mendoza,[38] Nieremberg,[39] Poiré,[40] &c.,—both pious and probable, I shall always rejoice that I have believed it and taught it to others, if for no other reason, at least because it inflames my devotion towards Mary; whereas the opposite opinion cools it, which is certainly not a slight evil.

[38] Virid. s. erum. l. 2. pr. i.
[40] Tr. Cour. tr. 2. c. 10. § 2, 8.

[39] De Aff. B.V. o. v.

A SHORT REPLY

TO THE EXTRAVAGANT REFORM

ATTEMPTED BY THE ABBE ROLLI; A REFORM WHICH IS IN OPPOSITION
TO THE DEVOTION AND LOVE WE OWE TO THE DIVINE MOTHER.

A DEVOUT and learned little work, by Father Ildephonsus Cardoni, of the order of Friars Minor, has lately
fallen into my hands. In it the good father refutes,
with much learning, a book published by the Abbé
Leoluca Rolli, under the title of the *New Project*, &c.,
in which he pretends to reform the various prayers
and devotions of the Catholic Church in honour of the
most Blessed Virgin Mary and other Saints. For the
honour of this Blessed Virgin, and out of the feeling
of especial devotion which I have nourished towards
her from my childhood, I have determined to give in
an abbreviated form the contents of these two works;
that is to say, the wicked propositions of the one, and
the convincing arguments of the other.

In the first place, the Abbé Rolli, speaking of the
miraculous translation by the angels of the holy House
of Loretto from Nazareth into Dalmatia, and from Dalmatia to the property of a good lady named Laureta,
in the diocese of Recanati, in the march of Ancona,
and thence to a hill a mile and a half distant from that
property, where it is now venerated,—the above-named
Abbé calls the history of that translation ' a story which

is told,' as if it was a fable ; whereas the illustrious
Pontiff Benedict XIV., speaking, in his beautiful work
on the feasts of Mary, of this holy house, calls it 'the
dwelling in which the Divine Word assumed human
flesh, and which was translated by the ministry of an
gels.' He then adds, that ' its authenticity is proved as
well by ancient monuments and unbroken tradition as
by the testimony of Sovereign Pontiffs, the common consent of the faithful, and the continual miracles which
are there worked even to the present day.'[1] In fact
Tursellin, in his *History of the House of Loretto,* asserts
that nearly all the Popes after Pius II. have spoken of
its miraculous translation ; and Sixtus V., in the year
1583, instituted an order under the auspices of our
Blessed Lady of Loretto. Notwithstanding this, the
Abbé Rolli, without reason, seems to follow in the
track of Launay, Vergier, Hospinien, and other Pro-
testants who have denied the miraculous translation,
and also Theodore Beza and the Calvinist David Par-
eus, who call the house of Loretto ' the Lauretanian
Idol.' But all these have been refuted with unanswer-
able evidence by many learned Catholic writers—Canisius, Turiano, and Gretser, as Theophilus Raynaud
writes. Tursellin,[2] on the authority of grave authors,
relates the miracle, which is confirmed by Peter Geor-
gio, Jerome Angelita, and by John Bonifacio.[3] He is
referred to by Benedict XIV., who writes, that even
heretics, on entering this holy house, are converted,
and impose silence on those who deny the miracle.[4]

The Abbé Rolli then criticises the titles of ' Tower
of David,' ' Tower of Ivory,' and ' House of Gold,' which
in the litanies are bestowed on the Blessed Virgin. He
calls them affected, almost ridiculous, and unmeaning.
How are they unmeaning ? They indeed mean a great
deal ; for they denote the power with which the Mother

---

[1] De Festis B.M.V. p. ii. c. ccxiv.
[2] Tursellin. in Clyp. Lauret. †
[3] Jo. Bonif. Hist. B.V. †
[4] De Fest. l. 2. c. 16.

of God defends her devout servants, and the ardent
charity of her blessed soul, which rendered her worthy
to become the temple of the Eternal Word; as these
titles are precisely explained by Saint Bernard, Saint
Ephrem, Richard of Saint Lawrence, and others.

Afterwards speaking of the titles, 'Mirror of Justice,' 'Refuge of Sinners,' 'Morning Star,' and 'Gate
of Heaven,' he says that a Catholic hearing these titles
given to the Blessed Virgin must make an act of faith,
and believe that they are only applicable to Jesus
Christ, and not to Mary; just as if they were prejudicial
to faith. He therefore would wish all these litanies
abolished, although they have been recited and sung in
all churches of priests and religious for so many ages,
and this with the approbation of many pontiffs; which
also proves that these titles are not only not affected
and ridiculous, but that they are filled with piety and
tenderness towards our holy Queen, and thus excite us
to greater confidence in her protection. Who can deny
that these litanies, according to the established discipline
of so many years, form a part of the public worship of
the Church?

The Abbé Rolli then takes great pains to discredit
the custom which now exists of singing the Litany of
Loretto when the Blessed Sacrament is exposed, and
expressly calls it an abuse. In this he avails himself
of the opinion of Louis Muratori, who in his book
called *Well-regulated Devotion* does not indeed, as
the Abbé Rolli does, call it an abuse, but says that it
would be worth while to consider whether it might not
be better on this occasion to sing prayers immediately
addressed to Jesus our Saviour. For my part I cannot
understand how it is unbecoming to beg the Divine
Mother to offer her prayers for us to Jesus, exposed in
the Blessed Sacrament. Everyone knows that God has
given us Jesus Christ, that we may have recourse to
Him as to our chief Mediator; but Saint Bernard says
that God has also given us Mary as an advocate with

Jesus Christ: 'Thou desirest an advocate with Him? Have recourse to Mary; the Son will graciously hear His Mother.'[6] In another place the same Saint adds: 'We need a mediator with Christ the Mediator, and we cannot find one more fitting than Mary.'[7] He uses the words 'we need;' that is, another mediator with Jesus Christ is necessary; not indeed with an absolute necessity, but with a moral one, to increase our confidence; for Jesus Christ alone is our Mediator by absolute necessity. Saint Jerome, however, to take away any scruple that might arise when we have recourse to Mary, says that we must go to her, not as to the author of grace (as Calvin falsely said), but only as to an intercessor; and that for this reason we say 'Have mercy on us' to Jesus Christ; but to the Blessed Virgin and the Saints we say, 'Pray for us.' Thus did St. Jerome convince Vigilantius on this point.

The Abbé Rolli is not satisfied with calling the titles bestowed on the Blessed Virgin in the Litany of Loretto affected, almost ridiculous, and unmeaning, but he has also the boldness to attack the sacred Antiphon, 'Hail, Holy Queen,' although he knows that the Holy Church has approved it, by making its recitation in the canonical hours obligatory on all in choir. Luther had already said that this prayer was scandalous, and gave the Blessed Virgin the attributes of God. The heretic Peter Martyr also wrote, that as Jesus Christ was our only Mediator, it was injurious to Him to admit Mary as our advocate and mediatress.

Our Abbé Rolli is not ashamed, in his *New Project*, when speaking of the 'Salve Regina,' to write these words: 'Out of blind respect and party spirit the titles given to the Virgin in the "Salve Regina" are retained.' He says, moreover, that Brother Herman Contratto, whom *he* believes to have been its author, called the Divine Mother 'Our Hope' and 'Our Advocate' only in simple piety and devotion, since Jesus

[6] Page 175, note 7.　　　　[7] Serm. in Sign. Magn.

Christ alone is our only Hope and our only Advocate. It may well be said that this way of speaking differs little from what the above-quoted heretic Peter Martyr said. But since Saint Epiphanius[8] calls the Blessed Virgin our Mediatress, which is the same thing as advocate, and Saint Ephrem[9] calls her the hope of those who are in despair, how does the Abbé Rolli dare to assert that ' these titles are only retained out of blind respect and party spirit ' ? The Church, then, permits the prayer ' Salve Regina ' out of blind respect and party spirit!

The Abbé Rolli then leaves the litany and the 'Salve Regina,' and goes on to speak of the devotions of the scapular, rosary, cords, and girdles of other Saints, calling them all trifling, and, so to say, useless ; when, on the other hand, we know that the Sovereign Pontiffs have approved of these devotions, and enriched them with indulgences. The learned Papebroeck calls those persons wicked who deny that the Sovereign Pontiffs have approved the devotion of devoutly wearing the scapular of Mary by many favours, and that God has approved it by many benefits.[10] Bzovius[11] also, and the Bollandists,[12] speak in high terms of praise of the rosary of Mary, which has also been greatly praised by Leo X., Saint Pius V., Gregory XIII., Sixtus V., and many other pontiffs. Of such religious devotions the learned Pouget writes : ' Those who blame them, in their ignorance blaspheme.'[13]

The Abbé Rolli next vents his fury against those Christians who practise these devotions when in a state of sin, in the hope of receiving mercy from God through their means. He exclaims, ' Such devotees are all damned.' In this, as I have already remarked, he takes Lamindus Pritanius for his master, that is Louis Mura-

---

[8] Serm. de Laud. Deip.
[9] Desperantium consolatio.—*Prec. V. ad Dei Mat.*
[10] Papebroch. par. 2, resp. art. xx. n. 28.
[11] Bzovius ad an. Christi 1213.
[12] Aug. Vit. S. Dom. comm. præv. § 19.
[13] Pouget. Instit. Cath. p. 3, 2 2 c. 10. 2 2.

tori, who, in his book *Well-regulated Devotion*, says, that 'if a Christian, living at enmity with God, trusts that, on account of the confidence which he has in the Blessed Virgin, she by her intercession will not allow him to be surprised by sudden death, and that he will have time to make his peace with God, or hopes for some temporal benefit; such a hope is injurious, superstitious, and contrary to the teaching of the Church, and is wholly to be rejected.' But in this Pritanius and Rolli are in direct opposition with Cardinal Bellarmin, quoted by Benedict XIV. in his book *De Festis*.[14] Cardinal Bellarmin[15] writes, 'that devotions performed in a state of sin, if they do not justify, they at least dispose the soul to obtain justification through the merits of the Divine Mother or of other Saints.' But that which is of the greatest weight, and fully condemns them, is the doctrine of the master of theologians, Saint Thomas, who teaches that 'the devotions of the faithful, although performed in a state of sin, if they do not suffice to obtain their salvation, yet they obtain them three things : first, they accustom them to pious works ; second, they obtain them temporal blessings ; and third, they dispose them for the reception of Divine grace.'[16] The same angelic doctor also teaches 'that although the prayer of a sinner is not in itself worthy of grace, nevertheless it obtains it through the pure mercy of God.'[17] He then adds, that 'it is possible that the prayer of a sinner, even without an efficacious (that is, a firm and enduring) purpose of amendment, may be granted, out of the infinite mercy of God, provided that he is not in so obstinate a state of mind as constantly to reject every exhortation to repentance.'

[14] De Festis B. M. V. p. ii. c. 76.

[15] De Pœnit. lib. ii. c. 7.

[16] Opera ista ad triplex bonum valent ; scilicet, ad temporalium consecutionem, ad dispositionem ad gratiam, et assuefactionem bonorum operum.— *Suppl.* q. 14. art. 4.

[17] Orationem peccatoris Deus audit non quasi ex justitia, sed ex pura misericordia. – 2a 2æ. q. 83. a. 16.

Pritanius also says another thing in his book. He asserts that 'when the Blessed Virgin and the Saints pray for us, they do not offer their own merits, but only the efficacy of the merits of Jesus Christ.' But in this Muratori has been fully refuted by the learned Don Constantine Gaudio, in his book entitled *Defence of the Spotless Devotion*, &c.

The same Pritanius, in another part of his book, says, 'One reason may be alleged, which is, that our prayers will have more power when accompanied by those of the Holy Mother.' But he gives himself an inconsistent answer, and one that in no way corresponds with his learning. He says, 'This reason proves too much, and therefore proves nothing ; otherwise it would never be fitting to pray to Jesus without joining to our prayer the intercession of Mary.' O God, what an answer ! Then it would be unbecoming always to join to our prayers the intercession of Mary when we address ourselves to Jesus Christ ? while the Council of Trent teaches 'that it is good and useful earnestly to invoke the Saints.'[18] But if the intercession of the Saints, and especially that of Mary, is good and useful, it is also good and useful always to obtain it. Therefore Saint Bernard advises and exhorts all to ask for graces from God, and to ask for them through Mary ; for Mary's prayers to God are the prayers of a Mother, and therefore are never refused. The Saint says, 'Let us seek for grace, and seek it by Mary ; for she is a Mother, and cannot ask in vain.'[19] How strange is this ! Louis Muratori, whom I have always venerated, was celebrated throughout Europe, as it appears from his beautiful life, which has been so well written by his nephew ; yet in many parts of his works, as we have already seen, he does not show that piety towards the Mother of God which would have become such a soul as his.

There is no need for me to write at greater length on the propositions above referred to. That which

18 Sess. 25, de Invoc. SS.   19 Serm. de Aquæd.

moved me to write the little I have on this subject, was that I saw the devout prayers and titles commonly given to Mary in her litanies and in the 'Salve Regina' held up to discredit: and also I heard those devotions of the scapular and the rosary of Mary called trifling, which, in fact, are so religious, and which have been dear to me from my childhood. However, should anyone wish to see the reform which the Abbé Rolli pretended to introduce in all these things refuted at length and fully, he can read the work of the Friar Minor Father Cardoni, to which I referred at the beginning of this short treatise.

A SERMON

FOR THE FEAST OF THE ANNUNCIATION OF THE BLESSED VIRGIN MARY.

"The Word was made flesh." *John* i.

SAINT THOMAS calls the mystery of the Incarnation of the Eternal Word 'the miracle of miracles.' What greater prodigy could the world behold, than a woman become the Mother of God, and a God clothed in human flesh? Let us therefore consider to-day these two prodigies.

First point. Mary, by her humility, became the Mother of her Creator.

Second point. The Creator, in His goodness, became the Son of His own creature.

FIRST POINT.

I. God, having determined to manifest to the world His immense goodness, by humbling Himself so far as to become man, to redeem lost man, and having to choose a Virgin Mother, sought amongst virgins the one who was the most humble. He found that the Blessed Virgin Mary surpassed all others in sanctity, as greatly as she surpassed them in humility, and therefore chose her for His Mother. "He hath regarded the humility of His handmaid."[1] 'She did not say,' remarks Saint Lawrence Justinian, 'He hath regarded the virginity or the innocence, but only the humility, of His handmaid.'[2] And before him Saint Jerome had said, that

[1] Page 326, note 30.   [2] Page 327, note 31.

'God chose her to be His Mother more on account of her humility than of all her other sublime virtues.'[3]

II. Now we understand that Mary was that one who was spoken of in the sacred Canticles under the name of spikenard, a small and lowly plant, which, by its sweet odour, drew the King of Heaven, the Eternal Word, from the bosom of His Father, into her womb, there to clothe Himself with human flesh: " While the king was at his repose, my spikenard sent forth the odour thereof ;"[4] which Saint Antoninus thus explains: ' Spikenard, from its being a small and lowly herb, was a type of Mary, who in the highest degree gave forth the sweet odour of her humility.'[5] Before him Saint Bernard had said: ' She was indeed worthy to be looked upon by the Lord, whose beauty the King so greatly desired, and by whose most sweet odour He was drawn from the eternal repose of His Father's bosom.'[6] So that God, attracted by the humility of the Blessed Virgin, when He became man for the redemption of man, chose her for His Mother. He would not, however, for the greater glory and merit of His Mother, become her Son without her consent. ' He would not take flesh from her,' says the Abbot William, ' unless she gave it.'[7] Behold, whilst this humble little Virgin was in her poor cottage, sighing and entreating the Lord, as it was revealed to Saint Elizabeth of Hungary, that He would send the world its Redeemer, the archangel Gabriel came, as the bearer, on the part of God, of the great embassy, and saluted her, " Hail, full of grace ; the Lord is with thee ; blessed art thou among women."[8] Hail, O Mary, full of grace ; for thou art rich in that grace which surpasses the grace given to all men and angels. The Lord is with thee, and always was with thee, assisting thee with His grace. Thou art blessed amongst all women ; for all others fell under the curse of sin ; but thou, as the Mother of the Blessed One, wast preserved from every stain, and always wast, and always wilt be, blessed.

III. What answer does the humble Mary give to a salutation so full of praises? She does not reply; but, astonished at them, is confounded and troubled : " who having heard was troubled at his saying, and thought with herself what manner of salutation this should be."[9] Why was she troubled? was it that she feared an illusion? No, for she was sure that it was a celestial spirit who spoke to her. Her modesty was perhaps troubled at the sight of an angel under a human form, as some have thought? No, the text is clear, " she was troubled at his saying :" to which Eusebius Emissenus adds, 'not at his appearance, but at what he said.'[10] This trouble, then, proceeded entirely from her humility, and was caused by the great praises, which were so far from her own humble estimate of herself. Hence the more she heard herself praised, the more deeply did she enter into the depth of her own nothingness. Saint Bernardine of Sienna writes, that 'had the angel said, O Mary, thou art the greatest sinner in the world, her astonishment would not have been so great ; the sound of such high praises filled her with fear.'[11]

IV. But the Blessed Virgin, I say, already understood the sacred Scriptures ; she well knew that the time foretold by the prophets for the coming of the Messiah had arrived ; she knew that the seventy weeks of Daniel were completed, and that the sceptre of Juda had passed into the hands of Herod, a stranger, according to the prophecy of Jacob ; she also knew that the mother of the Messiah was to be a Virgin. She then heard the angel give her praises, which it was evident could apply to no other than a Mother of God. May not a thought or doubt have entered her mind, that she was perhaps this chosen Mother? No ; her profound humility did not even allow her to have a doubt. Those praises only caused her such great fear, that the angel himself was obliged to encourage her not to fear, as Saint Peter Chrysologus writes : ' As Christ was pleased to be comforted by an angel, so had the Blessed Virgin to be encouraged by one.'[12] Saint Gabriel said, " Fear not, Mary ; for thou hast found grace with God."[13] As if he had said : Why fearest thou, O Mary ? Knowest thou not that God exalts the humble ? Thou in thine own eyes art lowly and of no account, and therefore He, in His goodness, exalts thee to the dignity of being His Mother. " Behold, thou shalt conceive in thy womb, and shalt bring forth a Son : and thou shalt call His name Jesus."[14]

V. In the mean time the angel waits to know whether she is willing to be the Mother of God. Saint Bernard addresses her, saying, 'The angel awaits thy reply ; and we also, O Lady, on whom the sentence of condemnation weighs so heavily, await the word of mercy.'[15] 'Behold, O holy Virgin, the price of our salvation, which will be the blood of that Son now to be formed in thy womb. This price is offered to thee to pay for our sins, and deliver us from death ; we shall be instantly delivered if thou consentest.'[16] 'Thy Lord Himself desires thy consent ; for by it He has determined to save the world. He desires it with an ardour equal to the love with which He has loved thy beauty.'[17] 'Answer, O sacred Virgin,' says Saint Augustine, ' why delayest thou the salvation of the world, which depends on thy consent ?'[18]

VI. But see, Mary already replies to the angel : 'Behold the handmaid of the Lord, be it done to me according to thy word."[19] O admirable answer, which rejoiced heaven, and brought an immense treasure of good things to the world. Answer which drew the only-begotten Son from the bosom of His eternal Father into this world to become man ; for these words had hardly fallen from the lips of Mary before " the

[12] Page 322, note 11.   [13] Page 322, note 12.   [14] Page 322, note 13.
[15] Page 322, note 14.   [16] Page 322, note 15.   [17] Page 323, note 16.
[18] Page 323, note 17.   [19] Page 323, note 18.

Word was made flesh;" the Son of God became also the Son of Mary. 'O powerful *fiat !*' exclaims Saint Thomas of Villanova; 'O efficacious *fiat !* O *fiat* to be venerated above every other *fiat !*[20] for with that fiat heaven came on earth, and earth was raised to heaven.

VII. Let us now examine Mary's answer more closely: "Behold the handmaid of the Lord." By ·this answer the humble Virgin meant: Behold the servant of the Lord, obliged to do that which her Lord commands; since He well sees my nothingness, and since all that I have is His, who can say that He has chosen me for any merit of my own? "Behold the handmaid of the Lord." What merits can a servant have, for which she should be chosen to be the Mother of her Lord? Let not the servant, then, be praised, but the goodness alone of that Lord, who is graciously pleased to regard so lowly a creature, and make her so great. 'O humility,' exclaims the Abbot Guarric, 'as nothing in its own eyes, yet sufficiently great for the Divinity! Insufficient for itself, sufficient in the eyes of God to contain Him in her womb whom the heavens cannot contain!'[21] Let us also hear the exclamations of Saint Bernard on this subject. He says: 'And how, O Lady, couldst thou unite in thy heart so humble an opinion of thyself with such great purity, with such innocence, and so great a plenitude of grace, as thou didst possess?'[22] 'Whence this humility,' continues the Saint, 'and so great humility, O blessed one?'[23] Lucifer, seeing himself enriched by God with extraordinary beauty, aspired to exalt his throne above the stars, and to make himself like God: "I will exalt my throne above the stars of God. . . . I will be like the Most High."[24] O, what would that proud spirit have said had he ever been adorned with the gifts of Mary! He, being exalted by God, became proud, and

[20] Page 324, note 20.   [21] Page 325, note 21.   [22] Page 325, note 22.
[23] Page 325, note 23.   [24] Page 325, note 24.

was sent to hell; but the more the humble Mary saw herself enriched, so much the more did she concentrate herself in her own nothingness; and therefore God raised her to the dignity of being His Mother, having made her so incomparably greater than all other creatures, that, as Saint Andrew of Crete says, 'there is no one who is not God, who can be compared with Mary.'[25] Hence Saint Anselm also says, 'there is no one who is thy equal, O Lady; for all are either above or beneath thee: God alone is above thee, and all that is not God is inferior to thee.'[26]

VIII. To what greater dignity could a creature be raised than that of Mother of her Creator? 'To be the Mother of God,' Saint Bonaventure writes, 'is the greatest grace which can be conferred on a creature. It is such that God could make a greater world, a greater heaven, but He cannot exalt a creature more than by making her His Mother.'[27] This the Blessed Virgin was pleased herself to express, when she said, "He that is mighty hath done great things in me."[28] But here the Abbot of Celles reminds her: 'God did not create thee for Himself only; He gave thee to the angels as their restorer, and to men as their repairer.'[29] So that God did not create Mary for Himself only, but He created her for man also; that is to say, to repair the ruin entailed upon him by sin. We now pass to the second point.

SECOND POINT. *The Creator in His goodness became the Son of His own creature.*

I. Our first father Adam sinned; for, ungrateful to God for the many gifts he had received from Him, he rebelled against Him by eating the forbidden fruit. God was therefore obliged to drive him from before His face, and to condemn him and all his posterity to

[25] Page 329, note 45.   [26] Page 329, note 46.   [27] Page 333, note 65.
[28] Page 333, note 66.   [29] Page 337, note 83.

eternal death. But afterwards pitying him, and moved
by the bowels of His mercy, He was pleased to come on
earth to become man, and thus satisfy the Divine Justice, paying with His own sufferings the punishment
which we deserved for our sins.

II. 'He came down from heaven, and was made
man.' This we are taught by the Holy Church : 'And
He was made man.' O prodigy, O excess of the love
of God,—a God became man! Did a prince of this
world, seeing a worm dead in its hole, wish to restore
it to life ; and were he told that to do so, it would be
necessary that he should himself become a worm, enter
its dwelling, and there at the price of his life make it
a bath in his own blood, and that thus only could its
life be restored, what would the reply of such a prince
be ? 'No,' he would say ; 'what does it signify to me
whether the worm comes to life again or not, that I
should shed my blood and die to restore its life ?' Of
what import was it to God that men should be lost,
since they had merited it by their sins ? Would His
happiness have been diminished thereby ?

III. No, indeed ; it was because God's love for men
was so truly great that He came upon earth and humbled Himself to take flesh from a Virgin ; and taking
the form of a servant became man,—that is, He made
Himself a worm like us : " He emptied Himself, taking
the form of a servant, being made in the likeness of
men, and in habit formed as a man."[30] He is God as
the Father,—immense, omnipotent, sovereign, and in
all things equal to the Father ; but when He was made
man in the womb of Mary He became a creature,—a
servant, weak, and less than the Father. Behold Him
thus humbled in the womb of Mary ; there He accepted
the command of His Father, who willed that after three-
and-thirty years of suffering He should die cruelly executed on a cross : " He humbled Himself, becoming

[30] Semetipsum exinanivit, formam servi accipiens, in similitudinem hominum factus et habitu inventus ut homo.—*Philip.* ii. 7.

obedient unto death, even to the death of the cross."[31]
Behold Him as a child in the womb of His Mother.
He there conformed Himself in all things to the will
of His Father, and, inflamed with love for us, He offered
Himself willingly : " He was offered because it was His
own will."[32] He offered Himself, I say, to suffer all
for our salvation. He then foresaw the scourging, and
offered His body ; He foresaw the thorns, and offered
His head ; He foresaw the nails, and offered His hands
and feet ; He foresaw the cross, and offered His life.
And why was He pleased to suffer so much for us ungrateful sinners ? It was because He loved us : " who
hath loved us, and washed us from our sins in His own
blood."[33] He saw us soiled with sin, and prepared us
a bath in His own blood, that we might thereby be
cleansed, and become dear to God : " Christ also hath
loved us, and hath delivered Himself for us."[34] He saw
us condemned to death, and prepared to die Himself,
that we might live : and seeing us cursed by God on
account of our sins, He was pleased to charge Himself
with the curses which we had deserved, that we might
be saved : " Christ hath redeemed us from the curse of
the law, being made a curse for us."[35]

IV. Saint Francis of Paul had, then, indeed reason,
in considering the mystery of a God made man and
dying through love for us, to exclaim, ' O charity ! O
charity ! O charity !' Did not faith assure us of all
that the Son of God did and suffered for us, who could
ever believe it ? Ah, Christians ! the love which Jesus
Christ had and has for us indeed drives and forces us
to love Him, " for the charity of Christ presseth us."[36]
Tender indeed are the sentiments expressed by Saint

[31] Humiliavit semetipsum, factus obediens usque ad mortem, mortem
autem crucis.—*Philip.* ii. 8.
[32] Oblatus est quia ipse voluit.—*Is.* liii. 7.
[33] Dilexit nos, et lavit nos a peccatis nostris in sanguine suo.—*Apoc.* i. 5.
[34] Dilexit nos, et tradidit semetipsum pro nobis.—*Ephes.* v. 2.
[35] Christus nos redemit de maledicto legis, factus pro nobis maledictum.—
Galat. iii. 13.
[36] Charitas enim Christi urget nos.—*2 Cor.* v. 14.

Francis of Sales on these words of Saint Paul: he says, 'Knowing, then, that Jesus, who was truly God, has loved us, and loved us so much as to die, and to die on a cross, for us, is not this to have our hearts under a wine-press, and to feel them forced and so strongly pressed that love issues from them by the very violence with which they are pressed; and the greater this violence is with which they are pressed, the more sweet and amiable is it.'

V. But here came the tears of St. John, "He came into His own, and His own received Him not."[37] Why did the only-begotten Son of God become man on earth, suffer and die for us, if it was not that we might love Him? 'God became man,' says Hugo of Saint Victor, 'that man might love Him with greater freedom.'[38] 'Jesus Christ,' says Saint Augustin, 'came on earth principally that man might know how much He loved him.'[39] And if a God loves us so much, He requires, with justice, that we should love Him. 'He made known His love,' says Saint Bernard, 'that He might experience thine.'[40] He has shown us the greatness of the love He bears us, that He may obtain our love at least out of gratitude.'

VI. O Eternal Word, Thou camest from heaven on earth to become man and to die for man, that Thou mightest be loved by man; how is it, then, that among men there are so few who love Thee! Ah, infinite Beauty, amiable Infinity, worthy of infinite love, behold me; I am one of those ungrateful creatures whom Thou hast loved so much, but have not yet known how to love Thee; nay even, instead of loving Thee, I have greatly offended Thee. But Thou becamest man and didst die to pardon sinners who detest their sins, and

---

[37] In propria venit, et sui eum non receperunt.—*Joan.* i. 11.

[38] Deus factus est homo, ut familiarius ab homine diligeretur.—*In lib. Sentent.*

[39] Maxime propterea Christus advenit, ut cognosceret homo, quantum eum diligat Deus.—*D. Catech. Rud.* cap. iv.

[40] Notam fecit dilectionem suam, ut experiatur et tuam.—*Serm.* xliii. *in Cant.*

wish to love Thee. Lord, behold me; see, I am a sinner, it is true; but I repent of the crimes I have committed against Thee, and I desire to love Thee; pity me. And thou, O holy Virgin, who by thy humility becamest worthy to be the Mother of God, and as such art also our mother, the refuge, the advocate of sinners, do thou pray for me, recommend me to this Son, who loves thee so much, and refuses nothing that thou askest Him. Tell Him to pardon me; tell Him to give me His holy love; tell Him to save me; that with thee I may one day love Him face to face in Paradise. Amen.

SERMON ON THE DOLOURS OF MARY.

For Friday in Passion Week.

" Now there stood by the cross of Jesus His Mother."[1]

BEHOLD we are about to consider a new kind of martyrdom; we have to consider a Mother condemned to see her innocent Son die as a malefactor on an infamous gibbet. This mother is Mary, who indeed, with too great reason, is called by the Church the Queen of Martyrs; yes, for Mary in the death of Jesus Christ suffered a more cruel martyrdom than all other martyrs; for

    I. Her martyrdom was never equalled.

    II. Her martyrdom was without relief.

FIRST POINT. *Her martyrdom was never equalled.*

    I. The words of the prophet Jeremias explain my meaning in this point : " To what shall I compare thee? or to what shall I liken thee, O daughter of Jerusalem? . . . for great as the sea is thy destruction; who shall heal thee?"[2] No, the acuteness of the suffering of Mary are not to be compared, even with those of all the martyrs united. 'The martyrdom of Mary,' says Saint Bernard, 'was not caused by the executioner's sword, but proceeded from bitter sorrow of heart.' In other martyrs torments were inflicted on the body; but Mary's sorrow was in her heart and soul, verifying in

[1] St. John xix. 25.   [2] Lam. ii. 13.   [3] De Serm. D. in Cana, s. 4.

her the prophecy of Saint Simeon, " Thy own soul a sword shall pierce."[4]

II. Arnold of Chartres writes, that 'whoever had been on Mount Calvary, to witness the great sacrifice of the Immaculate Lamb, would there have beheld two great altars, the one in the body of Jesus, the other in the heart of Mary ; for on that mount, when the Son sacrificed His body by death, Mary sacrificed her soul by compassion.'[5] So much so, says Saint Antoninus, that, whereas other martyrs sacrifice their own lives, the Blessed Virgin consummated her martyrdom by sacrificing the life of her Son, a life which she loved far more than her own, and which caused her to endure a torment which exceeded all other torments ever endured by any mortal on earth.

III. As a general rule, the sufferings of children are also the sufferings of their mothers who are present at and witness their torments. This Saint Augustine declares, when speaking of the mother of the Machabees, who witnessed the execution of her children, martyred by order of the cruel Antiochus : he says, that 'love caused her to endure in her soul all the torments inflicted on each of her children.'[6] Erasmus adds, that ' mothers suffer more at the sight of the sufferings of their children than if the torments were inflicted on themselves.' This, however, is not always true ; but in Mary it was verified ; for she certainly suffered more in witnessing the sufferings of her Son than she would have done had she endured all His torments in her own person. ' All the wounds,' says Saint Bonaventure, ' which were scattered over the body of Jesus were united in the heart of Mary, to torment her in the Passion of her Son ;'[7] so that, as Saint Lawrence Justinian writes, 'the heart of Mary, by compassion for her Son, became a mirror of His torments, in which might be seen faithfully reflected the spittings, the

---

[4] St. Luke ii. 35. [5] De Sept. Verb. tr. 3. [6] Serm. 300. ed. Ben.
[7] Stim. Div. Am. p. i. c. 3.

blows, the wounds, and all that Jesus suffered.'[8]   **We**
can therefore say that Mary, on account of the love she
bore Him, was in heart, during the Passion of her Son,
struck, scourged, crowned with thorns, and nailed to
the very cross of her Son.

IV. The same Saint Lawrence considers Jesus, on
His road to Calvary, with the cross on His shoulders,
turning to Mary, and saying to her, 'Alas, my own
dear Mother, whither goest thou? what a scene wilt
thou witness? Thou wilt be agonised by My sufferings, and I by thine.'[9]   But the loving Mother would
follow Him all the same, though she knew that, by
being present at His death, she would have to endure
a torment greater than any death.   She saw that her
Son carried the cross to be crucified upon it; and she
also took up the cross of her sorrows, and followed her
Son to be crucified with Him.   Hence Saint Bonaventure considers Mary standing by the cross of her
dying Son, and asks her, saying, 'O Lady, tell me
where didst thou then stand—was it near the cross?
No, thou wast on the cross itself, crucified with thy
Son.'[10]   On the words of the Redeemer, foretold by the
prophet Isaias, "I have trodden the wine-press alone,
and of the Gentiles there is not a man with me,"[11]
Richard of Saint Lawrence says, 'It is true, O Lord,
that in the work of human redemption Thou didst suffer alone, and that there was not a man who sufficiently
pitied Thee; but there was a woman with Thee, and
she was Thine own Mother; she suffered in her heart
all that Thou didst endure in Thy body.'[12]

V. To show the sufferings endured by other martyrs, they are represented with the instruments of their
torture; Saint Andrew with a cross, Saint Paul with a
sword, Saint Lawrence with a gridiron; Mary is represented with her dead Son in her arms; for He alone was
the instrument of her martyrdom, and compassion for

[8] De Tr. Chr. Agon. c. 21.   [9] Ib. c. 11.
[10] De Stim. Div. Am. p. i. c. 2.   [11] Is. lxiii. 3.
[12] De Laud. B.M. l. i. c. 5.

Him made her the Queen of Martyrs. On this subject
of Mary's compassion in the death of Jesus Christ,
Father Pinamonti gives expression to a beautiful and
remarkable opinion : he says, that ' the grief of Mary
in the Passion of her Son was so great, that she alone
compassionated in a degree by any means adequate to
its merits the death of a God made man for the love of
man.' Blessed Amadeus also writes, that ' Mary suffered much more in the Passion of her Son than she
would have done had she herself endured it ; for she
loved her Jesus much more than she loved herself.'[13]
Hence Saint Ildephonsus did not hesitate to assert,
that ' the sufferings of Mary exceeded those of all martyrs united together.'[14] Saint Anselm, addressing the
Blessed Virgin, says : ' The most cruel torments inflicted on the holy martyrs were trifling or as nothing
in comparison with thy martyrdom, O Mary.'[15] The
same Saint adds : ' Indeed, O Lady, in each moment of
thy life thy sufferings were such, that thou couldst not
have endured them, and wouldst have expired under
them, had not thy Son, the source of life, preserved
thee.' Saint Bernardine of Sienna even says, that
' the sufferings of Mary were such, that had they been
divided amongst all creatures capable of suffering, they
would have caused their immediate death.'[16] Who, then,
can ever doubt that the martyrdom of Mary was without its equal, and that it exceeded the sufferings of all
the martyrs ; since, as Saint Antoninus says, ' they suffered in the sacrifice of their own lives ; but the Blessed
Virgin suffered by offering the life of her Son to God,
a life which she loved far more than her own.'

SECOND POINT. *The martyrdom of Mary was without
relief.*

I. The martyrs suffered under the torments inflicted on them by tyrants ; but our Lord, who never

---

[13] De Laud. B.V. hom. 5.   [14] Ap. Sinisc. Mart. di Mar. cons. 36.
[15] De Excell. Virg. c. 5.   [16] In Fest. V.M. serm. 13.

abandons His servants, always comforted them in the midst of their sufferings. The love of God, which burnt in their hearts, rendered all these sufferings sweet and pleasing to them. A St. Vincent suffered, when on the rack he was torn with pincers, and burnt with hot iron plates ; but, Saint Augustine says, that ' the Saint spoke with such contempt of his torments, that it seemed as if it was one who spoke, and another who suffered.' A Saint Boniface suffered, when the flesh was torn from his body with iron hooks, sharp reeds were forced under his nails, and melted lead was poured into his mouth ; but, in the midst of all, he could never cease to thank Jesus Christ, who allowed him to suffer for His love. A Saint Lawrence suffered, when roasting on a gridiron ; ' but the love which inflamed him,' says Saint Augustine, ' did not allow him to feel the fire, or even that prolonged death itself.'[17] So that the greater was the love of the martyrs for Jesus Christ, the less did they feel their pains : and in the midst of them all, the remembrance alone of the Passion of Jesus Christ sufficed to console them. With Mary it was precisely the reverse ; for the torments of Jesus were her martyrdom, and love for Jesus was her only executioner. Here we must repeat the words of Jeremias : " Great as the sea is thy destruction : who shall heal thee ?" As the sea is all bitterness, and has not within its bosom a single drop of water which is sweet, so also was the heart of Mary all bitterness, and without the least consolation : " Who shall heal thee ?" Her Son alone could console her and heal her wounds ; but how could Mary receive comfort in her grief from her crucified Son, since the love she bore Him was the whole cause of her martyrdom ?

II. ' To understand, then, how great was the grief of Mary, we must understand,' says Cornelius à Lapide, ' how great was the love she bore her Son.'[18] But who can ever measure this love ? Blessed Amadeus says,

[17] In Joan. tr. 27.   [18] In Thren. l. 12.

that ' natural love towards Him as her Son, and supernatural love towards Him as her God, were united in
the heart of Mary.'[19] These two loves were blended
into one, and this so great a love that William of Paris
does not hesitate to assert, that Mary loved Jesus ' as
much as it was possible for a pure creature to loveHim.'
So that, as Richard of Saint Victor says, ' as no other
creature ever loved God as much as Mary loved Him,
so there never was any sorrow like Mary's sorrow.'[20]

III. " Now there stood by the cross of Jesus His
Mother." Let us stay awhile to consider these words
before concluding our discourse ; but I entreat you to
renew your attention. "There stood." When Jesus was
on the cross the disciples had already abandoned Him ;
they had done so from the moment in which He was
taken in the garden of Olives : " then the disciples all
leaving Him fled."[21] The disciples abandoned Him ; but
His loving Mother did not abandon Him; she remained
with Him until He expired. " There stood by." Mothers fly when they see their children suffer much, and
are unable to give them relief ; they have not then
strength to endure the torment, and therefore fly to a
distance. Mary beheld her Son in agony on the cross ;
she saw that His sufferings were slowly depriving Him
of life ; she desired to relieve Him in that last extremity, but could not ; but with all this she did not fly ;
she did not go to a distance, but drew nearer to the
cross on which her Son was dying : " she stood by the
cross." The cross was the hard bed on which Jesus
Christ had to die. Mary, who stood by its side, never
turned her eyes from Him ; she beheld Him all torn
by the scourges, thorns, and nails ; she saw that her
poor Son, suspended by those three iron hooks, found
no repose. She, as I have already said, would have desired to give Him some relief ; she would have desired,
at least, that He should have expired in her arms; but,
no, even this is forbidden her. 'Ah, cross ! ' she must

19 De Laud. B.V. hom. 5.   20 In Cant. c. 26.   21 Matt. xxvi. 56.

have said, ' restore me my Son ; thou art a gibbet for malefactors, but my Son is innocent.' But wait, O sorrowful Mother ; God's will is that the cross should only restore thee thy Son when He has expired.

IV. Saint Bonaventure, considering the sorrow of Mary in the death of her Son, writes, that ' no grief was more bitter than hers, because no son was as dear as her Son.' [22] Since, then, there never was a son more worthy of love than Jesus, nor any Mother who ever loved as Mary loved, what sorrow can be compared to the sorrow of Mary ? 'Ah, there never has been in the world a more amiable Son than Jesus,' says Richard of Saint Lawrence, ' nor was there ever so loving a Mother. Had there been less love between this Mother and Son, His death would have been less cruel, their griefs would have been diminished ; but the more tender were their loves, the deeper were their wounds.' [23] Mary saw that death approached her Son ; therefore, casting her compassionate eyes upon Him, she seemed to say, 'Ah, Son, Thou already departest, already Thou leavest me ; and art Thou silent ? Give me a last remembrance.' Yes, He did so. Jesus Christ left her a remembrance ; it was this : " Woman," He said, " behold thy son," referring to Saint John, who stood near; and with these words He bade His Mother farewell. He called her woman, that by the sweet name of Mother He might not increase her grief : " Woman, behold thy son ;" he will take charge of thee when I am dead.

V. "There stood by the cross of Jesus His Mother." Let us, in fine, observe Mary, who stood at the foot of the cross and beheld her Son expire. But, O God, what Son was it that died ? It was a Son who from all eternity had chosen her for His Mother, and had preferred her in His love to all men and angels : it was a Son so beautiful, so holy, so amiable ; a Son who had always obeyed her; a Son who was her only love, for He was her Son and her God ; and Mary had to see Him die

[22] Off. de Comp. B.M.   [23] De Laud. B.M. l. 3.

before her eyes, of pure suffering. But, behold, the hour of the death of Jesus has already come; the afflicted Mother saw her Son then enduring the last assaults of death; behold, again, His body already was sinking, His head drooped down on His breast, His mouth opened, and He expired. The people cried out, He is dead, He is dead! and Mary also said, 'Ah, my Jesus, my Son, Thou art now dead!'

VI. When Jesus was dead, He was taken down from the cross. Mary received Him with outstretched arms; she then pressed Him to her heart, and examined that head wounded by the thorns, those hands pierced with nails, and that body all lacerated and torn. 'Ah, Son,' she said, 'to what has Thy love for men reduced Thee!' But the disciples, fearing that with her Son clasped in her arms she would die of grief, out of compassion approached her, and, with reverential determination, removed her Son from her arms, wrapped Him in the winding-sheet, and carried Him away to bury Him. The other holy women accompanied Him, and with them the sorrowful Mother followed her Son to the tomb; where, having herself deposited Him with her own hands, she bade Him a last farewell and retired. Saint Bernard says, that ' as Mary passed along the way, her sorrow and grief were such, that all who met her were thereby moved to tears;' and he adds that ' those who accompanied her wept rather for her than for our Lord.'[24]

VII. My readers, let us be devout to the dolours of Mary. Blessed Albert the Great writes, that ' as we are under great obligations to Jesus Christ for His death, so also are we under great obligations to Mary for the grief which she endured when she offered her Son to God by death for our salvation.'[25] This the angel revealed to Saint Bridget: he said that the Blessed Virgin, to see us saved, herself offered the life of her Son to the Eternal Father: a sacrifice which, as we have already said, cost

[24] De Lam. B.V.   [25] Super Miss. q. 150, resp. ad 148.

her greater suffering than all the torments of the martyrs, or even death itself. But the Divine Mother complained to Saint Bridget, that very few pitied her in her sorrows, and that the greater part of the world lived in entire forgetfulness of them. Therefore she exhorted the Saint, saying : 'Though many forget me, do not thou, my daughter, forget me.'[26] For this purpose the Blessed Virgin herself appeared in the year 1239 to the founders of the order of the Servites, or servants of Mary, to desire them to institute a religious order in remembrance of her sorrows; and this they did. Jesus Himself one day spoke to Blessed Veronica of Binasco, saying, 'Daughter, tears shed over my Passion are dear to me; but as I love my Mother Mary with an immense love, the meditation of the sorrows which she endured at my death is also very dear to me.'[27] It is also well to know, as Pelbart relates it, that it was revealed to Saint Elizabeth of Hungary, that our Lord had promised four special graces to those who are devout to the dolours of Mary: 1st, that those who before death invoke the Divine Mother, in the name of her sorrows, should obtain true repentance of all their sins: 2d, that He would protect all who have this devotion in their tribulations, and that He would protect them especially at the hour of death : 3d, that He would impress upon their minds the remembrance of His Passion, and that they should have their reward for it in heaven: 4th, that He would commit such devout clients to the hands of Mary, with the power to dispose of them in whatever manner she might please, and to obtain for them all the graces she might desire.

[26] Rev. l. iii. c. 30.   [27] Ap. Bolland. 13 Jan.

SERMON FOR THE FEAST OF SAINT JOSEPH.

GOD, in the great love which He bears us, and in
His great desire to see us saved, amongst the many
means of salvation with which He has provided us,
has given us in particular that of devotion towards the
Saints. He wills that they, as His friends, should intercede for us, and by their merits and prayers obtain
graces for us which we do not of ourselves deserve.
Not, indeed, that the merits of Jesus Christ are insufficient to enrich us with every grace, for they are superabundant; but because He is pleased, on the one hand,
to honour His faithful servants by making them co-
operators in our salvation; and, on the other, to increase
our confidence that we shall obtain the graces which
we require, when we seek them through the medium of
the Saints. But who is not aware that, after the Divine
Mother, Saint Joseph is, of all the Saints, the one who
is the dearest to God; and that he has in consequence
great power with Him, and can therefore obtain graces
for his devout clients? Hence we shall see in the two
following points,

I. How great should be our veneration for Saint
Joseph, on account of his dignity.

II. How great should be our confidence in the protection of Saint Joseph, on account of his sanctity.

FIRST POINT. *How great should be our veneration for
Saint Joseph, on account of his dignity.*

I. We should indeed honour Saint Joseph, since
the Son of God Himself was graciously pleased to

honour him, by calling him His Father. 'Christ,' says Origen, 'gave to Joseph the honour due to a parent.'[1] He is also thus spoken of in the gospel : "and His father and mother were wondering at those things which were spoken concerning Him."[2] The Divine Mother also spoke of him under this name, "Thy father and I have sought Thee sorrowing."[3] Since, then, the King of kings was pleased to raise Joseph to so high a dignity, it is right, and a duty on our part, to endeavour to honour him as much as we can. 'He indeed should be greatly honoured by men, whom the King of kings has been pleased thus to exalt.'[4] 'What angel or saint,' says Saint Basil, 'ever merited to be called the father of the Son of God? Joseph alone was thus called.' Hence we can well apply to Saint Joseph the words of Saint Paul, "being made so much better than the angels, as he hath inherited a more excellent name than they."[5] Saint Joseph was more honoured by God, in this name of father, than all the patriarchs, prophets, apostles, and pontiffs ; for all these have the name of servants, Joseph alone that of father.

II. Behold him, as father, made lord of that little family ; little in point of numbers, but great on account of the two great personages who composed it, —the Mother of God, and the only-begotten Son of God made man : "He made him master of His house."[6] Joseph commanded in that house, and the Son of God obeyed : "and He was subject to them."[7] 'This subjection,' says Gerson, 'whilst it shows the humility of Jesus Christ, also shows the greatness of the dignity of Saint Joseph.'[8] 'And to what greater dignity, to what higher degree of exaltation,' continues the same writer,

---

[1] Josephum parentis honore coluit Christus.—*Orig. Hom.* xvii. *Luc.* cap. 2.
[2] Luc. ii. 33.   [3] Ib. 48.
[4] Ab hominibus valde honorandus, quem Rex regum sic voluit extollere. —*Card. d'Ailly de* 12 *Hon. S. Jos.*
[5] Heb. i. 4.   [6] Ps. civ. 21.   [7] Luc. ii. 51.
[8] Et erat subditus illis : quæ subjectio sicut notat humilitatem in Christo, ita dignitatem signat in Josepho.—*Serm. de Nat. B. M. V.*

'can a person be raised, than to that of commanding Him who commands all kings ?'[9]

III. Josue excited the admiration of the whole world when he commanded the sun to stop in its course, that he might have time to conquer his enemies ; and it obeyed, "the Lord obeying the voice of a man."[10] But what comparison can there be between Josue, whom the sun, an inanimate creature, obeyed, and Joseph, who was obeyed by Jesus Christ, the Son of God? As long as Saint Joseph lived, Jesus Christ respected him as a father, and until his death, that is for thirty years, always obeyed him as such : " He was subject to them." So that during all those years the constant occupation of the Saviour was to obey Saint Joseph. During the whole of that time it was Joseph's charge to command, as the head of the family ; and the office of Jesus was, as a subject, to obey Saint Joseph, who had been given to Him by God in place of a father. Hence, on the one hand, Jesus performed no action, did not even take a step, tasted no food, took no repose, but by the orders of Saint Joseph ; and on the other, was all attention in listening to and executing all that Saint Joseph imposed upon Him. Our Blessed Lady said to Saint Bridget, ' My Son was so obedient, that when Joseph said Do this or that, He immediately did it.'[11] Hence John Gerson writes, ' He often prepared the food and drink, washed the vessels, brought water from the fountain, and swept the house.'[12] Saint Bernard, speaking of Saint Joseph, says, ' He was a faithful and prudent servant, whom our Lord made the solace of His Mother, the nourisher of His humanity, and, in fine, the only most faithful coöperator in the great council on earth.[13] Therefore Saint Joseph was

---

[9] Quid sublimius quam imperare ei, qui in femore habet scriptum, Rex regum et Dominus dominantium ?   [10] Josue x. 14.

[11] Lib. vi. Rev. c. 58.   [12] In Joseph. Distinct. 3.

[13] Fidelis servus et prudens, quem constituit Dominus suæ matris solatium, suæ carnis nutricium ; solum denique in terris magni consilii coadjutorem fidissimum.—*Hom.* ii. *sup. Missus.*

not only destined as a relief to the Mother of God, who had so many tribulations on earth; not only was he the supporter of Jesus Christ, but he was also destined to coöperate, in a way, in the redemption of the world, for this was the work of the great council of the Three Divine Persons. God having also given him to His Son in the place of a father, He at the same time charged him to feed and defend this Son from the snares of His enemies: "Take the Child;" as if He had addressed him in the words of the Psalmist, "To thee is the poor man left."[14] Joseph, I have sent My Son on earth; and I have sent Him poor and humble, without the splendour of riches or apparent nobility; hence, in the world, He will be despised, and called the Son of a carpenter: "Is not this the carpenter's Son?"[15] according to thy humble trade; for I have willed that thou shouldst be poor, because I have destined thee to hold the place of a father over My Son, who is poor; for He is not come to reign in the world, but to suffer and die for the salvation of men. On earth, then, thou wilt hold My place of father over Him, and be His guardian: "To thee is the poor man left." I abandon Him into thy hands. He will be persecuted, and thou wilt have thy share in His sufferings; guard Him with care, and be thou faithful to Me. 'Therefore,' says Saint John Damascen, 'God gave Saint Joseph the love, the care, and the authority of a father over Jesus: He gave him the affection of a father, that he might guard Him with great love; the solicitude of a father, that he might watch over Him with care; and the authority of a father, that he might feel sure that he would be obeyed in all that he arranged as to the person of this Son.'

V. Having, then, made him, as St. Bernard says, a coöperator in the work of redemption, He willed that he should be present at the birth of Jesus, that he might be a faithful witness of the glory which the

[14] Ps. x. 14.   [15] Matt. xiii. 55.

angels gave to God on this occasion; and also that it had been revealed to the shepherds, who, when they came to visit the Saviour who had been announced to them, related all to Mary and Joseph.   Again, that he might be a witness of the coming of the kings, who, guided by a star, had come from afar to adore the Holy Child, as they themselves said: "for we have seen His star in the East, and are come to adore Him."[16] God also willed that Joseph, together with Mary, should offer Him the new-born babe, as they did "they carried Him to Jerusalem to present Him to the Lord;"[17] and then sacrificed Him to death for the salvation of the world, according to the Scriptures, in which the Passion of Jesus Christ had already been foretold, and which were well known to Mary and Joseph.

VI. God then seeing that, through jealousy, and fear of losing his kingdom, Herod wished to gain possession of the Divine Child to take His life, sent an angel to Saint Joseph, to desire him, in His name, to take the Child and His Mother and fly into Egypt: "Arise, and take the Child and His Mother, and fly into Egypt; and be there until I shall tell thee: for it will come to pass that Herod will seek the Child to destroy Him."[18] Behold, Joseph, faithful and obedient to the voice of God, arose in the night (the very same night on which he received notice from the angel, as interpreters explain it), took the Child and His Mother, and journeyed towards Egypt.   Joseph, without loss of time, gathered together as many instruments of his trade as he could carry, which were required to enable him to support his poor family in Egypt.   Mary, on the other hand, took the child in her arms, and the poor linen for the use of her Son; and they set out alone, without a servant, as poor pilgrims on a journey which was so long and full of dangers, having to pass through so many desert places before they could reach

Egypt ; a country in which they had no relations or friends, and where they would only find barbarous and unknown people. When they got there, Saint Joseph, as Saint Bernard says, laboured night and day to support his Holy Spouse and the Divine Child. Having afterwards returned from Egypt, according to the new command of the angel,—" Arise, and take the Child and His Mother, and go into the land of Israel,"[19]—Joseph at once left Egypt, and returned into Judea. But he was again told by the angel not to remain in Judea, for fear of Archelaus, who reigned there in the place of Herod his father, who was dead : he went therefore to dwell in Nazareth, in the parts of Galilee, and remained there in the company of his beloved Jesus, living in poverty on the small profits of his humble trade, until the time of his death.

VII. During this time it was, that, having gone with Mary and with Jesus, who was then about twelve years of age, to visit the Temple, he returned home and met Mary, whom he believed to have been accompanied by Jesus, but Jesus had not returned ; therefore for three days Joseph constantly wept, for he was separated from Jesus, the love of his heart ; but that which caused him the greatest affliction was the fear that Jesus had left him on account of some displeasure which he might have caused Him, and therefore that He no longer considered him worthy to have charge of so great a treasure, as Lanspergius writes.[20] He was, however, afterwards consoled when he heard from Jesus Himself that He had remained in the Temple for affairs which concerned the glory of God. From that time he attended on Jesus until his death, when it was his happy lot to expire in the arms of Jesus and Mary, who attended upon him in that last moment: hence Saint Francis of Sales says, that 'it is certain that, like the Blessed Virgin his spouse, he died of love.'

---

[19] Matt. ii. 20.   [20] Exeg. Dom. ii. post Nat D.

SECOND POINT. *How great should be our confidence in the protection of Saint Joseph, on account of his sanctity.*

I. We should have great confidence in the protection of Saint Joseph, because, on account of his sanctity, he was very dear to God. To form an idea of the sanctity of Saint Joseph, we need only know that he was chosen by God to hold the place of a father over the person of Jesus Christ. Saint Paul writes, "Who also hath made us fit ministers of the new testament;"[21] which, as Saint Thomas explains it, means, that 'when God chooses any one for a particular charge, He gives him the graces which fit him for it.'[22] God having, then, chosen Saint Joseph to fill the charge of a father over the person of the Incarnate Word, we must certainly believe that He conferred upon him all the gifts of wisdom and sanctity which became such an office. Nor should we doubt that He enriched him with all the graces and privileges granted to other Saints. Gerson[23] and Suarez say, that amongst other privileges he had three, which were special to him. 1. That he was sanctified in his mother's womb, as Jeremias and the Baptist; 2. that he was at the same time confirmed in grace; 3. that he was always exempt from the inclinations of concupiscence,—a privilege with which Saint Joseph, by the merit of his purity, favours his devout clients, delivering them from carnal movements.

II. In the Gospel, Saint Joseph is called just, "whereupon Joseph her husband, being a just man."[24] What is meant by a just man? Saint Peter Chrysologus says, that 'it means a perfect man, one who possesses all virtues.' So that Joseph was already holy before his marriage; but how much must his sanctity have increased after his union with the Divine Mother! The example alone of his holy spouse sufficed to sanctify

---

21 2 Cor. iii. 6.   22 Pars 3, q. 27, a. 4.
23 S. de Nat. B.M.   24 Matt. i. 19.

him. But since Mary, as Saint Bernardine of Sienna says,[25] is the dispenser of all the graces which God grants to men, in what profusion must we not believe that she showered them down upon her spouse, whom she loved so much, and by whom she was so tenderly loved ! How much must the sanctity of Saint Joseph have increased by his conversations and familiarity with Jesus, during the many years he lived with Him ! If the two disciples going to Emmaus were inflamed with Divine love by the few moments which they spent in company with our Saviour, and by His words; so much so, that they said, " Was not our heart burning within us whilst He spoke in the way ?"[26]—what flames of holy love must we not suppose to have been enkindled in the heart of Saint Joseph, who for thirty years conversed with Jesus Christ, and listened to His words of eternal life ; who observed the perfect example which He gave of humility and patience, and saw the promptitude with which He obeyed and helped him in his labours, and in all that was needed for the household ! What a furnace of Divine love must this burning charity of Jesus have enkindled in the heart of Joseph—a heart which was entirely free from all earthly affections ! It is true that his love for Mary was also very great ; but this love did not divide his heart, as is too often the case, according to the word of the Apostle, "but he that is with a wife is solicitous for the things of the world, how he may please his wife, and he is divided."[27] No, for love for his spouse filled him still more with Divine love. Hence, we cannot doubt that, during the time which Joseph spent with Jesus Christ, he advanced in such a degree in sanctity and merits, that he surpassed the merits of all the other Saints.

III. Admitting this, the Apostle writes, that in the next life Jesus Christ " will render to every man according to his works."[28] What great glory must we

---

[25] Pro Fest V.M. s. 13, a. 2, c. 3.
[26] Luc. xxiv. 32. [27] 1 Cor. vii. 33. [28] Rom. ii. 6.

not suppose that He bestowed upon Saint Joseph, who
served and loved Him so much whilst he lived on earth !
At the last day our Saviour will say to the elect, " I
was hungry, and you gave Me to eat . . . . I was a
stranger, and you took Me in : naked, and you covered
Me."[29] These, nevertheless, have fed Jesus Christ, have
lodged Him or clothed Him, only in the persons of the
poor ; but Saint Joseph procured food, a dwelling, and
clothes, for Jesus Christ in His own person. Moreover,
our Lord has promised a reward to him who gives a
cup of water to the poor in His name : " for whosoever
shall give you to drink a cup of water in My name . . .
he shall not lose his reward."[30] What, then, must be
the reward of Saint Joseph, who can say to Jesus Christ,
' I not only provided Thee with food, with a dwelling,
and with clothes ; but I saved Thee from death, delivering Thee from the hands of Herod.' All this helps
to increase our confidence in Saint Joseph ; it makes us
reflect that, on account of so many merits, God will refuse no grace which Saint Joseph asks of Him for his
devout clients.

IV. Saint Bernardine of Sienna adds, that ' we cannot doubt that Christ not only does not refuse to Saint
Joseph in heaven that familiarity and reverence which,
as a Son towards His father, He accorded him when He
lived on earth, but rather, that it is now perfected.'[31]
Remark the words, *familiarity and reverence;* that
Lord, who, on earth, revered Saint Joseph as His father,
will certainly deny him nothing that he asks in heaven.
Besides this, we may add that, although on earth Saint
Joseph had not the authority, by nature, of a father
over the humanity of Jesus Christ, he nevertheless had
it, at least in a certain manner, as the spouse of Mary,
who, as the real Mother of the Saviour, had authority

---

[29] Matt. xxv. 35. [30] Marc. ix. 40.
[31] Dubitandum non est, quod Christus familiaritatem, reverentiam atque
sublimissimam dignitatem quam sibi exhibuit dum ageret in humanis, tanquam filius patri suo, in cœlis utique non negavit, quin potius complevit et
consummavit.—*S. de S. Joseph.* art. iii.

over Him : he to whom the tree belongs has also a right to its fruit. This caused Jesus, when on earth, to respect and obey Saint Joseph as His superior. This also causes Jesus, now in heaven, to consider the prayers of Saint Joseph in the light of commands.[32]

V. Let us now listen to what Saint Bernard writes of the power of Saint Joseph to dispense graces to his devout servants : 'To some of the Saints power is granted to succour in particular necessities; but to Saint Joseph power is granted to succour in all necessities, and to defend all who, with devotion, have recourse to him.' That which Saint Bernard wrote as his opinion, Saint Teresa confirmed by her own experience : she says, 'It would seem that to other Saints our Lord has granted power to succour in some particular necessity; but experience proves that Saint Joseph succours in all.' Of this we are certain ; for, as on earth Jesus Christ was pleased to be subject to Saint Joseph, so in heaven He does all that the Saint asks. Let us therefore imagine that we hear our Lord, when He sees us afflicted in the midst of our miseries, address us all in the words in which Pharaoh addressed his people at the time of the famine in Egypt : "Go to Joseph,"[33] if you desire consolation. By our Lord's grace, there is not at present a Christian in the world who is not devout to Saint Joseph ; but, amongst them all, those receive the most abundant graces who recommend themselves to him the most frequently and with the greatest confidence. Let us therefore never pass a day without many times recommending ourselves to Saint Joseph, who, after the most Blessed Virgin Mary, is the most powerful of all the Saints with God. Let us never allow a day to pass without offering him some particular prayer ; but especially during the novena for his feast, let us redouble our prayers, and fast on the vigil ; and let us seek from him the graces which are useful

---

[32] Dum pater orat natum, velut imperium reputatur.—*Gerson, Jos. Orat.*
[33] Gen. xli. 55.

for our souls; for he will always obtain them for us. In particular, I exhort you to ask for three special graces : for the forgiveness of your sins, the love of Jesus Christ, and a good death.   As to the forgiveness of sins, I thus argue; when Jesus Christ lived in this world in the house of Saint Joseph, could a sinner who desired to obtain the forgiveness of his sins from our Lord, have found a more efficacious means to obtain this consolation than through Saint Joseph?   If, then, we desire to be pardoned by God, let us have recourse to Saint Joseph, who, now that he is in heaven, is more loved by Jesus Christ than he was loved by Him on earth.   Let us also ask Saint Joseph for love towards Jesus Christ; this I firmly believe to be the particular grace which Saint Joseph obtains for those who are devout to him—tender love towards the Incarnate Word; and the Saint merited this by the tender love which he himself bore Him on earth.   Let us also ask him for a happy death : all know that Saint Joseph is the patron of a good death; for he had the happiness to die in the arms of Jesus and Mary; therefore his devout servants should hope with confidence that, at their death, Saint Joseph will visit them, accompanied by Jesus and Mary, and that he will help them.   Of this there have been many instances.

VI. Boverio relates that in the year 1541 brother Alexius of Vigevano, a Capuchin lay-brother, was dying, and begged the brothers to light some tapers : they asked him why?   He replied, that it was because Saint Joseph and the most Blessed Virgin would shortly come to visit him.   He had scarcely pronounced these words when he exclaimed, ' Behold Saint Joseph and the Queen of Heaven; kneel down, my fathers, and welcome them !' and so saying, he sweetly expired on the 19th of March, the day which is consecrated in honour of Saint Joseph.   Saint Vincent Ferrer, Father Patrignani,[34] and others, relate that a merchant in the

---

[34] Div. di S. Gius. l. 2, c. 7.

city of Valencia used every year, on Christmas-day, to invite to dinner an old man and a woman nursing a child, in honour of Jesus, Mary, and Joseph. This good man appeared after his death to a person who was praying for him, and told him that at his death Jesus, Mary, and Joseph had visited him, and said: 'In life thou didst receive us into thy house in the person of those three poor persons; we are now come to receive thee into our house;' and they then took him to Paradise. In the Franciscan legendary, on the 14th of February, it is related that Sister Prudentiana Zagnoni, who had great devotion to Saint Joseph, was favoured at her death with the vision of Saint Joseph, who came close to her bed with Jesus in his arms. She began to converse first with Saint Joseph, then with Jesus, thanking them for so great a favour, and in this sweet company breathed forth her happy soul. In the history of the Discalced Carmelites it is also related that when the Venerable Sister Anne of Saint Augustine, a Carmelite nun, was dying, some of her sisters saw Saint Joseph and Saint Teresa, who attended upon her, and that the servant of God was filled with joy. A nun in another convent saw her ascend to heaven between Saint Joseph and Saint Teresa. Father John de Allosa, in his book on Saint Joseph, relates, that a religious of the order of Saint Augustine appeared to a companion, and said, 'that God had delivered him from hell on account of the particular devotion which he had had for Saint Joseph.' He then declared that the Saint, as the adopted father of Jesus Christ, had great power with Him.

NOVENA OF MEDITATIONS

FOR THE

NINE DAYS PRECEDING THE FEAST OF THE PURIFICATION OF MARY ; TO COMMENCE ON THE 24TH OF JANUARY.

These Meditations are on the Litany of Loretto, and can be used for the Novenas preceding the principal Festivals of the Divine Mother.

First Day.

I. 'HOLY MARY, pray for us.'—Since, in the Litany of our Blessed Lady, the Church teaches us to ask this good Mother so many times to pray for us, it will be well before meditating upon the titles by which she is invoked, to consider the great power which her prayers have with God. Blessed is that person for whom Mary prays. Jesus rejoices when His most Beloved Mother prays to Him, that He may have the pleasure of granting her all she asks. One day Saint Bridget heard Jesus speak to Mary and say, 'My Mother, thou well knowest that I cannot do otherwise than grant thy prayers; therefore ask of Me what thou wilt.'[1] And He then added, 'Since thou, when on earth, didst deny Me nothing, it is becoming, now that I am in heaven, that I should deny thee nothing that thou askest Me.'[2] Saint Bernard says, 'To be heard by the Son is to be graciously heard.'[3] Mary has only to speak, and her Son grants her all that she asks. Let us, therefore, pray to this Divine Mother, without ceasing, if we wish to secure our eternal salvation ; and let us address her in the words of Saint Andrew of

---

[1] Rev. lib. iii. c. 24.   [2] Ib.   [3] A Filio audiri est exaudiri.

Crete : ' We beseech thee, therefore, O Holy Virgin, **to**
grant us the help of thy prayers with God ; **prayers**
which are more precious than all the treasures of **the**
world ; prayers which obtain for us a ve.'y great abundance of graces ; prayers which confound all enemies,
and triumph over their strength.'[4]

II. ' HOLY MARY.'—The name of Mary is a name
of salvation. This name came not of earth, but from
heaven ; hence St. Epiphanius says, that it was not
given to Mary by her parents, but was imposed on her
by the express will of God. Therefore it is that, after
the name of Jesus, the name of Mary is above every
other name ; for God has filled it with grace and sweetness, that every blessing may be obtained by him who
names it. Saint Bernard says, ' O Mary, thou canst
not be named without inflaming the heart of him who
does so with love for thee.'[5] Blessed Henry Suso used
to exclaim, ' O Mary, what must thou thyself be, since
thy very name is so amiable and gracious?'[6] That name
is filled with blessings. Saint Bonaventure says[7] that
the name of Mary cannot be invoked without profit to
him who does so. Above all, this name has power to
overcome the temptations of hell. Ah, my Lady, had
I always invoked thee in my temptations, I should not
have fallen. For the future I will never cease to invoke thee, saying, ' Mary, help me : Mary, succour me.'
And do thou obtain me the grace always to invoke thee
in time of spiritual danger.

III. ' HOLY MOTHER OF GOD.'—If the prayers of
the Saints are very powerful with God, how great must
be the power of those of Mary ! The former are the
prayers of servants, the latter the prayers of a mother.
Saint Antoninus says, that the prayers of Mary have
the force of a command with Jesus Christ. Hence
he concludes, that it is impossible for the Son not to
grant a grace for which the Mother asks.[8] Saint Ber-

---

4 In Dorm. S.M. s. 3.　　5 Depr. ad Glor. V.　　6 Dial. c. 16.
7 Spec. B.V. lect. 9.　　8 P. 4. tr. 15. c. 17. § 4.

nard, therefore, exhorts us to ask for every grace which
we desire from God through Mary.' 'Let us seek for
grace, and seek it by Mary.' And why? 'Because she
is a mother, and is always graciously heard.'[9] O great
Mother of God, pray to Jesus for me. Behold the
miseries of my soul, and pity me. Pray, and never
cease to pray, until thou seest me safe in Paradise. O
Mary, thou art my hope ; abandon me not. ' Holy
Mother of God, pray for us.'

Second Day.

I. 'MOTHER OF DIVINE GRACE.'—Saint Anselm calls
Mary 'the Mother of all graces ;'[10] and Blessed Raymond Jordano, 'The treasurer of Divine grace.'[11]
Hence Saint Bernardine of Sienna writes, that 'all the
gifts and graces which we receive from God are dispensed by the hands of Mary, to whom, when, and as
she pleases.'[12] This she herself says : " With me are
riches . . . that I may enrich them that love me."[13]
' Our Lord has deposited all the riches of His graces
in my hands, that I may enrich those who love me.'
Then, my Queen, if I love thee, I no longer shall be
poor as I now am. After God, I love thee above all
things ; do thou obtain me greater tenderness and love
for thy goodness. Saint Bonaventure tells me that all
whom thou willest are saved ; therefore will I address
thee with the same Saint, ' O salvation of all who call
upon thee, save me from hell ;' but first of all, save me
from sin, which alone can take me to hell.

II. ' MOTHER MOST PURE.'—This Virgin Mother, all
fair and pure, renders all her servants pure and chaste.
Saint Ambrose writes, that when Mary was on earth
her presence alone inspired all those who looked at her
with a love of purity.[14] She was called a lily amongst
thorns : " As the lily among thorns, so is my love

---

[9] De Aquæd.   [10] Mater gratiarum.—*Psalt. B.V.* p. 2.
[11] Thesauraria gratiarum.—*Cont. de V.M.* in prol.
[12] In Fest. B.V. s. 5. c. 8.   [13] Prov. viii. 18, 21.   [14] Inst. Virg. c. 7.

among the daughters."[15] 'All other virgins,' says
Denis the Carthusian, 'were thorns either to themselves or to others; but the Blessed Virgin was so
neither to herself nor to others, for she inspired all
those upon whom she looked with pure and holy affec
tions.'[16] Frigenius, who wrote the life of Saint Thomas
Aquinas, relates that it was an ordinary saying of the
Saint, that 'even the images of this chaste turtle-dove
extinguish sensual desires in those who look at them
with devotion.' The venerable John D'Avila says,
'that many who were tempted against purity had preserved themselves chaste by devotion to our Blessed
Lady.'[17] O, how especially powerful is the name of
Mary in conquering all temptations to this vice! O
most pure Mary, deliver me from it. Grant that in
my temptations I may always have recourse to thee,
and invoke thee as long as the temptation lasts.

III. 'MOTHER UNDEFILED.'—Mary was that spotless
woman who always appeared beautiful and without
stain in the eyes of God: "Thou art all fair, O my
love, and there is not a spot in thee.'[18] Hence she was
made the sinner's peacemaker, as she is called by Saint
Ephrem, 'Hail, peacemaker of the whole world!'[19]
This she also says herself in the sacred Canticles, "I
am become in His presence as one finding peace."[20]
Saint Gregory says,[21] 'that if a rebel appeared before
his offended king to appease him, instead of doing so
he would provoke him to greater anger.' Hence Mary
being destined to treat of peace between God and men,
it was not becoming that she should appear as a sinner
and as an accomplice in Adam's sin; and therefore our
Lord preserved her from every stain. Ah, my immaculate Queen, fair dove, and the beloved of God, disdain
not to cast thine eyes on the many stains and wounds
of my soul; see me, and pity me. God, who loves thee
so much, denies thee nothing; and thou knowest not

---

[15] Cant. ii. 2.
[16] In Cant.
[17] Audi fil. c. 14.
[18] Cant. iv. 7.
[19] Ave orbis conciliatrix.—De Laud. Dei Gen.
[20] Cant. viii. 10.
[21] Past. p. i. c. 11.

how to refuse those who have recourse to thee. **O** Mary, to thee I have recourse ; pity me. ' Mother inviolate, pray for us.'

Third Day.

I. ' MOTHER MOST AMIABLE.'—Richard of Saint Lawrence says, ' that Mary was amiable in the eyes of God Himself.'[22] Mary was so beautiful in the eyes of God that He was enamoured of her beauty. " How beautiful art thou, my love! how beautiful art thou !"[23] Hence He called her His only dove, His only perfect one : " One is my dove ; my perfect one is but one."[24] ' It is certain,' as Father Suarez says,[25] ' that God loved Mary more than all the other Saints together ; and with reason ; for she alone loved God more than all men, and all angels have ever loved Him.' O most beautiful Mary, O most amiable Mary, thou hast gained the heart of God ; take also my poor heart, and make me a saint. I love thee ; in thee is my confidence. ' Most amiable Mother, pray for us.'

II. ' MOTHER OF OUR REDEEMER.'—Saint Bonaventure calls Mary ' the Mediatress of our salvation ;'[26] and Saint John Damascen ' the Saviour in a certain manner of the world.'[27] For two reasons Mary can be called the Saviour of the world and our Mediatress; that is, the mediatress of grace, as Jesus Christ is the mediator of justice. First, on account of the consent which she gave at the Incarnation of the Eternal Word ; for by that consent, Saint Bernardine says, ' she procured us salvation.'[28] Secondly, by the consent which Mary gave to the death of her Son, in which she expressed her willingness that He should be sacrificed on the cross for our salvation. I remind thee, then, O Mother of my

[22] Fuit Beata Virgo amabilis oculis ipsius Dei.—*De Laud. B.M.* 1, 5.
[23] Cant. iv. 1.   [24] Cant. vi. 8.   [25] De Inc. p. 2, d. 18, s. 4.
[26] Maria mediatrix nostræ salutis.—*Spec. B.V.* lect. 9.
[27] Salvatrix mundi.—*Men. Græc.* 15 Aug.
[28] Per hunc consensum omnium salutem procuravit.—*Pro Fest. V.M.* s. 3, a. 2. c. 2.

Saviour, that thou didst once offer the life of thy Son to God ; save me now by thy intercession.

III. 'VIRGIN MOST VENERABLE.' — Saint Anselm says, 'that when we say that Mary is the Mother of God, we speak of a dignity which is above every other dignity that can be named or thought of, after that of God ;' therefore he says, ' O Lady, nothing equals thee ; for all is either above thee, and this is God alone, or beneath thee, and this is all which is not God.'[29] In fine, Saint Bernardine writes, 'that God alone can know the greatness of Mary.'[30] Blessed Albert the Great says, 'that Mary could not be more closely united to God without becoming God. This great Mother of God is, then, indeed worthy of our veneration, since God Himself could not have made her greater than He did when He made her His Mother. O Mother of God, my Mother Mary, I adore thee, and would wish thee to be adored by all hearts, as that exalted Lady which thou art. Pity a poor sinner who loves thee, and trusts in thee. ' Virgin most venerable, pray for us.'

Fourth Day.

I. 'VIRGIN MOST RENOWNED.'—The Holy Church proclaims that this Divine Mother is ' most worthy of every praise ;'[31] for, as Saint Ildephonsus says, 'all praise which is given to the Mother redounds to the honour of the Son.'[32] With reason, then, did Saint George of Nicomedia declare, 'that God accepts the praises which are lavished on Mary, as if they were bestowed on Himself.'[33] The Blessed Virgin promises Paradise to him who endeavours to make her known and loved : " they that explain me, shall have life everlasting."[34] Therefore, Richard of Saint Lawrence

[29] De Conc. B.V.
[30] Tanta fuit perfectio Virginis, ut soli Deo cognoscenda reservetur.—*Pro Fest. V.M.* s. 4. a. 3. c. 1.
[31] Brev. Rom.   [32] De Virginit. B.M. c. 12.
[33] Tuam enim gloriam Creator existimat esse propriam.- *Or. in Ingr. B.V.*
[34] Ecclus. xxiv. 31.

writes, that 'all who honour her in this world will be honoured by her in the next.'[35] Saint Anselm says, 'that as Mary, by becoming the Mother of God, was the means of the salvation of sinners, so are sinners saved by proclaiming her praises.'[36] All cannot be preachers, but all can praise her, and speak to relations and friends in familiar conversation of the merits of Mary, of her powers and mercy, and thus lead them to devotion towards this Divine Mother. O Queen of Heaven, from this time forward I am determined to do all that I can to cause thee to be venerated and loved by all. Accept my desire, and help me to execute it; in the mean time inscribe me in the number of thy servants, and never permit me again to become a slave of Lucifer.

II. 'VIRGIN MOST POWERFUL.'—And who amongst the Saints is as powerful with God as His most holy Mother? She obtains all that she pleases. 'Thou willest,' says Saint Bernard, 'and all is done.' Saint Peter Damian even says, 'that when Mary asks graces from God, she does not ask, but, so to say, commands; for her Son honours her by refusing her nothing.'[37] Thus does the Son honour His beloved Mother by granting her whatever she asks, even in favour of sinners. Hence Saint Germanus says, 'Thou, O Mother of God, art omnipotent to save sinners, and needest no other recommendation with God, for thou art the Mother of true life.'[38] O Mary, thou canst make me a saint; I rely on thee.

III. 'VIRGIN MOST MERCIFUL.'—Mary is as clement and merciful towards those who have recourse to her intercession as she is powerful with God. Saint Bernard says, 'that since the power to save us cannot be wanting to Mary, as she is the Mother of God, so neither can the will be wanting to her, for she is our Mother.'[39] Who is there that ever had recourse to Mary and was abandoned? 'Let him cease to praise thy mercy,' says

---

[35] De Laud. B.M. l. 2. p. 1.   [36] De Excell. V. c. 1.   [37] In Nat. B.V.
[38] In Dorm. B.V. s. 2.   [39] In Assumpt.

the same Saint Bernard, 'who remembers having **ever** invoked thee without being graciously heard.'[40] Saint Bonaventure writes, 'that Mary has so great a desire to be invoked by us, that she may dispense her favours to us in greater abundance, that she is not only offended by those who speak ill of her, but also by those who neglect to ask her for graces.'[41] Thus, to obtain her help, we are not obliged to entreat this Mother of Mercy much; it is enough to ask for it with confidence. 'Her mercy,' says Richard of Saint Victor, 'comes to our aid before we invoke it:' and he tells us why: 'It is because she cannot know and see our miseries without relieving them.'[42] See, then, O Mary, see my miseries, and help me. 'Virgin most merciful, pray for us.'

Fifth Day.

I. 'VIRGIN MOST FAITHFUL.'—Blessed is he who by his prayers watches at the gates of Mary, as the poor wait at the door of the rich to obtain relief. "Blessed is the man," Mary says, "that heareth me, and that watcheth daily at my gates."[43] O that we were as faithful to serve this Divine Mother, as she is faithful to relieve us when we pray to her! Mary promises that all who serve and honour her shall be free from sin and obtain eternal life: "They that work by me shall not sin. They that explain me shall have life everlasting."[44] She invites all to have recourse to her, and promises them every grace which they desire: "In me is all grace of the way and of the truth; in me is all hope of life and of virtue; come over to me, all ye that desire me."[45] Saint Lawrence Justinian applies to Mary that other text of Ecclesiasticus, "her bands are a healthful binding;"[46] and then adds, 'wherefore bands, unless to bind her servants, that they may not

---

40 In Assumpt.   41 In Spec. Virg.   42 In Cant. c. 23.
43 Prov. viii. 34.   44 Ecclus. xxiv. 31.   45 Ib. 25, 26,
46 Ecclus. vi. 31.

stray in the fields of sin.'[47]   Mary binds her servants,
that they may not give themselves too much liberty,
which would cause their ruin.   O Mother of God, in
thee do I place all my confidence ; thou must preserve
me from falling any more into sin.   My Lady, abandon
me not, obtain me the grace rather to die than to lose
the grace of God.

II. 'CAUSE OF OUR JOY.'—As the dawn is a cause
of joy, after the darkness and gloom of night, so was
the birth of Mary, who is our dawn, a cause of joy to
the world, which, before the coming of Jesus Christ,
had been, for four thousand years, immersed in the
darkness of sin.   A holy father says, ' that in the birth
of Mary the dawn appeared.'[48]   The dawn is the forerunner of the sun, and Mary was the precursor of the
Incarnate Word, the Sun of Justice, the Redeemer, who,
by His death, delivered us from eternal death.   With
reason the Church sings, on the nativity of Mary, 'Thy
birth, O holy Mother of God, announced joy to the
whole world.'   And as Mary was the beginning of our
joy, so is she also its completion ; for Saint Bernard
says, 'that Jesus Christ deposited the whole price of
our redemption in the hands of Mary ; that every grace
which we receive, we may receive it from her.'[49]   O
Mother of God, thou art my joy and my hope ; for
thou deniest thy graces to no one, and thou obtainest
all that thou willest from God.

III. 'VESSEL OF SINGULAR DEVOTION.'—Devotion,
as Saint Thomas[50] teaches, consists in the readiness
with which our will conforms itself to the will of God.
This was the principal virtue which rendered His most
Holy Mother so dear to God.   This also was the signi-
fication of the answer which our Lord gave to the woman who called the womb which bore Him blessed :
   Yea rather, blessed are they that hear the word of

[47] De Laud. B.M. l. 2. p. 3.
[48] Nata Virgine surrexit aurora.—*S. Pet. Dam. Serm. de Assump.*
[49] De Aquæd.   [50] 2a 2æ, q. 82. a. 1.

God, and keep it."[51]   By this, according to **Venerable**
Bede, our Lord meant that Mary was more blessed by
the union of her will with that of God than by being
His Mother.   That flower which always turns towards
the sun is a real type of Mary.   The Divine will was
alone the aim and satisfaction of the heart of Mary ; as
she herself proclaimed, " My spirit hath rejoiced in God
my Saviour."   O blessed art thou, my Lady, who wast
always, and in all, united to the Divine will.   Obtain
me the grace to spend the rest of my life in constant
uniformity with the will of God.

Sixth Day.

I. ' MYSTICAL ROSE.'—Of Mary it is said, in the
sacred Canticles, that she was the enclosed Garden of
God, " My sister, my spouse, is a garden enclosed."[52]
Saint Bernard writes, ' that our Lord planted all the
flowers which adorn the Church in this garden ; and
amongst others the violet of humility, the lily of purity,
and the rose of charity.'[53] ' A rose is red, and of a fiery
colour,' says Blessed Raymond Jordano ; ' which denotes
love of God and our neighbour ;'[54] therefore, on account
of the ardent love with which the heart of Mary was
always inflamed towards God and us, she is called a
rose. And where can we find an advocate who is more
earnest in the affair of our salvation, or who loves us
more than Mary ? ' We acknowledge,' says Saint Augustine of her, ' that one alone is solicitous for us in
heaven.'[55] O my dear Mother, could I but love thee
as thou lovest me ! I will not, however, cease to do all
that I can to honour and love thee. My most sweet
Lady, do thou obtain me grace to be faithful to thee.

II. ' TOWER OF DAVID.'—Mary is called in the sacred

---

[51] Luc. xi. 28.   [52] Cant. iv. 12.   [53] Depr. ad Glor. V.
[54] Rosa rubicunda, per Dei et proximi charitatem ; nam igneus color designat charitatem.—*Op. plen. de V.* p. 14. cont. 43.
[55] Te solam, O Maria, pro Sancta Ecclesia sollicitam præ omnibus sanctis
scimus.—*Ap. S. Bonav. Spec. B. V.* lect. 6.

Canticles the Tower of David : " Thy neck is as the tower of David ; a thousand bucklers hang upon it ; all the armour of valiant men."[56]   Saint Bernardine says, that the tower of David stood on high, that is, on Sion ; therefore Mary is called the tower of David, to denote the height of the perfection of this great creature : ' As Sion was a very elevated spot, so was the Blessed Virgin most exalted.'[57]   Therefore of Mary it is said in the Psalms, that the very beginning of her sanctity was more exalted than the mountains : " The foundations thereof are in the holy mountains."[58]   Saint Gregory[59] explains it to mean that the Divine Mother was more holy in the first moment of her life than any of the Saints were at the moment of their death.   Ah, my Queen and Mother, I rejoice in thy greatness, and am willing rather to sacrifice my life than that thy glory should be diminished in the least degree, were such a thing possible.   O, that I could only by shedding every drop of my blood cause all nations of the earth to adore and love thee as the great Lady which thou art !

III. ' TOWER OF IVORY.'—Thus is Mary also called, " Thy neck is as a tower of ivory."[60]   Mary is called a neck ; for she is the mystic neck through which the vital spirits, that is, the Divine help which preserves in us the life of grace, are transmitted from Jesus Christ the Head to us the faithful, who are members of the mystic body of the Church.   Saint Bernardine says, ' The life-giving graces flow from Christ the Head, through the Blessed Virgin, into His mystic body.'[61]   The Saint then adds, ' that from the time when Mary conceived the Incarnate Word, she received the great honour from God, that no one should receive any grace otherwise than through her hands.'   In fine, ivory is greatly esteemed, and is strong.   Hence the Abbot

---

[56] Cant. iv. 4.
[57] Sion locus erat eminentissimus, sic Beata Virgo altissima. —*Pro Fest. V.M.* s. 4. a. 2. c. 3.   [58] Ps. lxxxvi. 1.
[59] In 1 Reg. l.   [60] Cant. vii. 4.   [61] In Fest. B.M. s. 5. c. 8.

Rupert writes of Mary, that 'as a tower of ivory she is beloved by God, and terrible to the devil.'[62] Then, O my sovereign Lady, because thou art so beloved of God, thou canst obtain us every grace ; and because thou art terrible to the evil spirits, thou canst deliver us from all their snares. Have mercy on us, who glory in living under thy protection.

Seventh Day.

I. 'House of Gold.'—Gold is a symbol of love. Therefore Blessed Albert the Great calls Mary 'a golden temple of charity.'[63] And with reason; for Saint Thomas says, that 'as all in the temple was covered with gold, so was everything in the beautiful soul of Mary filled with sanctity.'[64] Mary was the house of gold which Eternal Wisdom, that is, the Divine Word, chose for His dwelling on earth : " Wisdom hath built herself a house."[65] 'This House of God,' says Richard of Saint Lawrence, 'is so rich that it can relieve all our wants.'[66] O Mary, thou lovest God so much, and therefore thou desirest to see Him loved by all. This is the grace which above all others I ask of thee, and which I hope from thee : obtain me great love for God.

II. 'Ark of the Covenant.'—Hesychius calls Mary ' an ark more spacious than that of Noah ;'[67] for in the ark of Noah only two animals of every kind were received, but under the mantle of Mary the just and sinners find place. This was one day revealed to Saint Gertrude ;[68] for she saw a multitude of wild beasts, lions, leopards, and the like, who took refuge under the mantle of Mary ; and she not only did not drive them away, but with her benign hands caressed them, that they

---

[62] Sicut turris eburnea Deo amabilis, diabolo terribilis.—*In Cant.* l. 6.

[63] Templum aureum charitatis.—*Bibl. Mar.* iii. *Reg.* n. 4.

[64] Nihil erat in templo quod non auro tegeretur; nihil erat in Virgine quod non sanctitate plenum esset.—*S. in Purif. ex Ep.*

[65] Prov. ix. 1.

[66] Domus Dei, cujus tanta est abundantia, quod nostram potest replere inopiam.—*De Laud. B.M.* l. 12.

[67] Arca Noe largior.—*De S.M. Deip.* hom. 2.   [68] Insin. l. 4. c. 50.

might not fly away. The animals which entered the ark remained animals ; but sinners who are received under the mantle of Mary do not remain sinners. She is certain to change their hearts, and to render them dear to God. The Blessed Virgin herself said to Saint Bridget, 'However much a man may have sinned, if he returns to me with a real purpose of amendment, I am ready at once to receive him ; neither do I pay attention to the sins with which he is laden, but only to the good disposition in which he comes ; and then I do not disdain to anoint and heal his wounds, for I am called and truly am the Mother of Mercy.'[69] O Mother of Mercy, will I then say to thee, in the words of Saint Bernard, ' Remember that it has never been heard of in any age, that any sinner who had recourse to thee was rejected by thee.' I, a miserable sinner, have recourse to thee and trust in thee.

III. ' GATE OF HEAVEN.'—Mary is called the ' Gate of Heaven,' because, as Saint Bonaventure declares, ' no one can enter heaven unless by Mary, as through a door.'[70] Our Queen says, " My power is in Jerusalem."[71] Richard of Saint Lawrence adds : ' commanding what I will, and introducing whom I will.'[72] I can obtain whatever I please for my clients, and introduce all whom I please into Paradise. Hence, Saint Bonaventure writes, that ' those who enjoy the favour of Mary are recognised by the citizens of heaven ; and those who bear her stamp, that is, have the grace to be her servants, are inscribed in the Book of Life.'[73] For this reason, Bernardine de Bustis[74] calls Mary ' the Book of Life,' and says that whoever, by his devotion, is written in this book, is certain to be saved. Ah, my Mother, in thee do I repose my hope of eternal salvation. I love thee ; do thou save me ; never allow a servant of thine who loves thee to go to blaspheme thee in hell.

[69] Rev. l. 2. c. 23 ; l. 6. c. 117.
[71] Ecclus. xxiv. 15.
[73] Psalt. maj. Ps. xci.
[70] Exposit. in cap. i. Luc.
[72] De Laud. B.M. l. 4.
[74] Marial. p. 2. s. 2.

Eighth Day.

I. ' MORNING STAR.'—Saint John Damascen calls Mary ' the Star which indicates the rising of the sun.'[75] As the morning star precedes the sun, so does devotion towards the most Blessed Virgin precede the sun of Divine grace; for Saint Germanus says[76] that ' devotion in a soul towards Mary is a sign either that it is already in a state of grace, or that it will very soon be so.' Our Lady is also called ' the Star of the Sea' by the Church; for, as Saint Thomas explains it, ' as mariners, in tempestuous weather, are guided by the star of the sea into port, so are souls guided by Mary over the sea of this world into Paradise.'[77] Hence Saint Bernard warns us, saying, ' If you do not wish to be lost in the storm of temptations, turn not your eyes from this star of salvation.' He then continues, ' if you follow Mary, you will not go astray; if Mary protects you, you cannot fear to be lost; if Mary favours you, you will reach Paradise.'[78]

II. ' HEALTH OF THE WEAK.'—Mary is called by Saint Simon Stock ' the medicine of sinners;' and by Saint Ephrem, not only medicine, but health itself: ' Robust health for those who have recourse to her.'[79] Hence those who have recourse to Mary, not only find in her a remedy, but health itself; and this she herself promises to all who seek her: " He that shall find me shall find life, and shall have salvation from the Lord."[80] Neither let us fear that, on account of the bad odour of our wounds, she may refuse to take care of us: she is our Mother; and as a mother does not shrink from dressing the wounds of her child, neither does this celestial physician refuse to heal her servants who have recourse to her. Wherefore Saint Bernard says, ' O

[75] Stella demonstrans solem.—*Men. Græc.* 15 *Mart.*
[76] De Zona Deip.   [77] In Sal. Ang.
[78] Super Missus, hom. 2.
[79] Salus firma recurrentium ad eam.—*De Laud. Dei Gen.*
[80] Prov. viii. 35.

Mother of God, thou dost not disdain a sinner, however loathsome he may be : if he sends up his sighs to thee, thou wilt deliver him with thine own hand from despair.'[81]

III. 'REFUGE OF SINNERS.'—Thus is Mary called by Saint Germanus ; he says, 'She is the ever-ready refuge of sinners.'[82] Yes, of all sinners ; for as the Abbot of Celles says, 'she can despise no sinner, but receives all, and welcomes all, the moment they have recourse to her.'[83] Hence Saint John Damascen affirms, that Mary is not only the refuge of the innocent, but also of the wicked, who implore her protection : 'I am a city of refuge to all who fly to me.'[84] Therefore Saint Anselm exclaims, 'Thou embracest with maternal affection a sinner who is even despised by the whole world, nor dost thou cease thine embrace until thou hast reconciled him with his Judge.' By this the Saint gives us to understand, that a sinner being hated by God is also odious and abominable to all creatures ; but if he has recourse to Mary, the refuge of sinners, not only she does not despise him, but embraces him with affection, and does not leave him until her Son Jesus Christ, who is our Judge, has forgiven him. Since, then, O my Lady, thou art the refuge of all sinners, thou art also my refuge. Thou, who despisest no one who has recourse to thee, despise me not, who recommend myself to thee : 'Refuge of sinners, pray for us.' O Mary, pray for us, and save us.

Ninth Day.

I. 'COMFORTRESS OF THE AFFLICTED.'—Saint Germanus says, 'O Mary, who, after thy Son, is as solicitous for the whole human race as thou art? who protects us in our trials as thou dost?'[85] Who, O Mary,

---

[81] Depr. ad Glor. V.

[82] Refugium paratissimum peccatorum.—*De Zona Deip.*

[83] Tu es tutissimum refugium ; a te nullus peccator despicitur ; omnes peccatores recipis, nec moram in hoc facis. - *Op. plen. de V.* p. 9. cont. 14.

[84] De Dorm. B.M. s. 2.

[85] Quis, post Filium tuum, curam gerit generis humani sicut tu ? quis ita nos defendit in nostris afflictionibus ?--*De Zona Deip.*

watches over our interests as thou dost? who is solicitous as thou art for us in our afflictions? 'No,' replies
Saint Antoninus; 'no Saint can be found who compas-
sionates us in our miseries as does this most tender
Lady, the Blessed Virgin Mary.'[86] And as the miseries
which afflict us the most are disorders of the soul,
blessed Henry Suso calls Mary 'the most faithful comfortress of sinners.'[87] We need only show Mary the
wounds of our souls, and she immediately helps us by
her prayers, and consoles us. Nay, even as Richard
of Saint Victor writes, her compassion anticipates our
wants, and she relieves us before we invoke her.[88] Let
us say, then, with Saint Bonaventure, 'O Mary, console
us always, but especially at the hour of our death;
come at that last hour and receive our souls, and present them thyself to thy Son, who will judge us.'

II. 'HELP OF CHRISTIANS.'—Saint John Damascen
calls Mary 'the prepared and always ready-help of
Christians, by which they are delivered from dangers.'[89]
The help of Mary is, as Saint Cosmas of Jerusalem[90]
writes, 'all powerful to deliver us from sin and hell.'
Saint Bernard,[91] addressing Mary, says, 'Thou art an
invincible warrior in defence of thy servants, fighting
against the devils who assail them.' For this reason
she is called an army in the sacred Canticles: "thou
art . . . terrible as an army set in array."[92] Ah, my
Queen, had I always had recourse to thee, I should
never have been conquered by my enemies; from henceforth thou shalt be my strength: in my temptations I
will always have recourse to thee; from thee do I hope
for victory.

III. 'QUEEN OF MARTYRS.'—With reason is Mary

[86] Non reperitur aliquis Sanctorum ita compati infirmitatibus nostris, sicut mulier hæc, Beata Virgo Maria.—*P.* 4. t. 15. c. 2.

[87] Consolatrix fidelissima peccatorum.—*Dial.* c. 16.

[88] Velocius occurrit quam invocetur.—*In Cant.* c. 23.

[89] Auxilium promptum et paratum Christianorum, eripiens nos a periculis.—*Paracl. B.V.*

[90] Hymn. 6. in depr. ad Deip.

[91] Tu bellatrix egregia.—*Depr. ad Glor. V.*

[92] Cant. vi. 3.

called the Queen of Martyrs, for her martyrdom in the
death of her Son on the cross exceeded the sufferings
of all the martyrs. "There stood by the cross of Jesus
His Mother."[93] Mothers fly from their children when
they see them dying and are unable to help them.
Mary did not fly, but remained with Jesus until she
saw Him expire. "She stood by the cross," and whilst
Jesus was in His agony she offered the life of her Son
to the Eternal Father for our salvation; but in doing
so she also was in an agony, and experienced a torment
greater than any death. O my afflicted Mother, be
graciously pleased, by the merit of the sorrows which
thou didst endure at the foot of the cross, to obtain
me true sorrow for my sins, and love for Jesus my
Redeemer; and by the sword which transpierced thy
heart when thou didst see Him bow down His head
and expire, I beseech thee to help me at the hour of
my death, and then to obtain me eternal salvation, that
I may love thee with thy Jesus for ever.

MEDITATION FOR THE SECOND OF FEBRUARY.

*For the Feast of the Purification of Mary, and the
Presentation of Jesus.*

I. When the time had come in which, according to
the law, Mary was to be purified in the Temple, and to
present Jesus to the Eternal Father, she, accompanied
by Saint Joseph, directed her steps towards Jerusalem.
Joseph took two turtle-doves, which were to be offered,
and Mary took her beloved Infant. She took the Divine
Lamb to offer it to God, as a token of the great sacrifice
which He would one day accomplish on the cross. My
God, I also unite my sacrifice to that of Mary: I offer
Thee Thy Incarnate Son; and by His merits I beseech
Thee to grant me Thy grace. I do not deserve it; but

Jesus sacrificed Himself to Thee to obtain it for me. For the love of Jesus, then, have mercy on me.

II. Behold, Mary entered the Temple, and in the name of the whole human race made the oblation of her Son. But, especially on this day, Jesus offered Himself to His Eternal Father. 'Behold Me, O Father,' He said; 'to Thee do I consecrate My whole life; Thou hast sent Me into the world to save it: accept My blood and My life; I offer them without reserve to Thee, for the salvation of the world.' Unfortunate should I have been, my dear Redeemer, hadst Thou not satisfied the Divine Justice for me. I thank Thee with my whole soul, and I love Thee with my whole heart. And whom shall I love, if I do not love a God who sacrificed His life for me?

III. This sacrifice was more precious in the sight of God than if all men and angels had offered Him their lives. Yes, because it was in this offering of Jesus alone that the Eternal Father received infinite honour and an infinite satisfaction. Jesus Christ said one day to blessed Angela of Foligno, 'I offered Myself for thee, that thou mightest offer thyself to Me.' Yes, my Jesus, since Thou hast offered Thy life to Thy Eternal Father for me, I offer my life and my entire self to Thee. Hitherto, with the greatest ingratitude, I have despised Thee; but Thou hast promised no more to remember the outrages of a sinner who repents of having offended Thee. My Jesus, I grieve for having offended Thee, and wish that I could die of grief. I was dead by sin; from Thee I hope for life, and my life shall be to love Thee, O Infinite Good. Make me love Thee; I ask for nothing more. Dispense the riches of this world to those who desire them; I desire nothing but the treasure of Thy love. My Jesus, Thou alone art sufficient for me. O Queen and my Mother Mary, through thee do I hope for every grace.

MEDITATION FOR THE 25TH OF MARCH.

For the Feast of the Annunciation of Mary.

I. When God was pleased to send His Son on earth, that by becoming man He might redeem lost man, He chose Him a Virgin Mother, who, amongst all virgins, was the most pure, the most holy, and the most humble. Behold, whilst Mary was in her poor dwelling, beseeching God to send the promised Redeemer, an angel stood before her and saluted her, saying, " Hail, full of grace ; the Lord is with thee ; blessed art thou among women." And what was the conduct of this humble Virgin when she heard so honourable a salutation ? She was not elated, but was silent and troubled, considering herself indeed unworthy of such praises : " she was troubled at his saying." O Mary, thou art so humble, and I am so filled with pride ; obtain for me holy humility.

II. Think you that these praises caused Mary at least to suspect that she might be the destined Mother of the Redeemer ? No ; they only caused her to conceive a great fear of herself ; so much so, indeed, that the angel had to encourage her : " Fear not, Mary ; for thou hast found grace with God." He then announced to her that she was the chosen Mother of the Redeemer of the world : " Behold thou shalt conceive in thy womb, and shalt bring forth a Son, and thou shalt call His name Jesus." Blessed art thou, O Mary ; how dear wast thou to God, and how dear art thou still to Him ! Have pity on me.

III. 'And now, O holy Virgin,' says Saint Bernard,[1] 'why dost thou delay thy consent ? The Eternal Word awaits it to clothe Himself with flesh and become thy Son. We also await it, who in misery are condemned to eternal death. If thou consentest, and acceptest to become His Mother, we shall be made free. Quickly,

[1] De Laud. V.M. hom. 4.

O Lady, answer. Delay not the salvation of the world, which depends on thy consent.' But let us rejoice, for Mary already hears the angel : " Behold the handmaid of the Lord ; be it done to me according to thy word." ' Behold,' she says, 'the slave of the Lord, who is bound to do all that her Lord commands.' If He chooses a slave for His Mother, it is not she who is to be praised, but the goodness of that Lord alone, who is thus graciously pleased to honour her. O most humble Mary, thou by this thy humility didst so enamour thy God that thou didst draw Him to thee, so as to become thy Son and our Redeemer. I know that thy Son refuses thee nothing that thou askest Him. Ask Him to forgive all the offences which I have committed against Him ; ask Him to grant me perseverance until death. In fine, recommend my soul to Him ; for thy recommendations meet with no denial from a Son who loves thee so much. O Mary, thou hast to save me ; thou art my hope.

MEDITATION FOR THE 2D OF JULY.

The Feast of the Visitation of Mary.

I. Mary set out from Nazareth to go to the city of Judea, in which Saint Elizabeth resided ; a distance, according to Broccardus, of upwards of seventy miles, or at least seven days' journey. Her spouse Saint Joseph alone accompanied her. The holy and tender Virgin hastened her steps, as Saint Luke tells us : " Mary, rising up in those days, went into the hill country with haste." Tell us, O holy Lady, why didst thou undertake so long and arduous a journey, and why didst thou so hasten thy steps ? ' I went,' she replies, ' to exercise my office of charity : I went to console a family.' Since, then, O great Mother of God, thy office is to console and dispense graces to souls, ah, be graciously pleased also to visit and console my soul. Thy visit sanctified the house of Elizabeth : come, O Mary, and sanctify me also.

II. Behold, the Blessed Virgin is already arrived at the house of Elizabeth. She was the Mother of God, but yet she was the first to salute Elizabeth : " and she entered . . . and saluted Elizabeth.' Elizabeth, enlightened by God, knew that the Divine Word had become man, that He had become the Son of Mary ; therefore she called her blessed amongst women, and blessed the Divine fruit which she carried in her womb : " Blessed art thou among women, and blessed is the fruit of thy womb." At the same time, filled with confusion and joy, she exclaimed : " And whence is this to me, that the Mother of my Lord should come to me ?" But what does the humble Mary reply to these words ? She says : " My soul doth magnify the Lord ;" as if she had said, ' Ah, Elizabeth, thou dost praise me ; but I praise my God, who hath been graciously pleased to exalt me, who am His poor servant, to the dignity of being His Mother :' " He hath regarded the humility of His handmaid." O most holy Mary, since thou dispensest so many graces to those who ask thee for them, I beseech thee to grant me thy humility. Thou esteemest thyself as nothing before God ; but I am worse than nothing, for I am a sinner. Thou canst make me humble ; do so, for the love of that God who made thee His Mother.

III. But what took place at the first sound of the voice of Mary saluting Elizabeth ? " When Elizabeth heard the salutation of Mary, the infant leaped in her womb, and Elizabeth was filled with the Holy Ghost." The infant John exulted with joy on account of the Divine grace which was then conferred upon him. Elizabeth was filled with the Holy Ghost ; and Zachary, the father of the Baptist, had shortly afterwards the consolation of recovering his speech. So that it is indeed true, O my Queen and Mother, that it is through thee that Divine graces are dispensed, and through thee that souls are sanctified. Then, my own most dear Queen, do not forget me thy poor servant; for I love thee and have placed all my hopes in thee. Thy prayers are ever graciously heard by God, who loves thee so much. Hasten, therefore, my mother; pray for me, and make me a saint.

MEDITATION FOR THE 15TH OF AUGUST.

The Feast of the Assumption of Mary into Heaven.

I. Mary died; but how did she die? She died entirely detached from all created things; she died consumed by that Divine love which during her whole life had always inflamed her most holy heart. O holy Mother, thou hast already left the earth; do not forget us miserable pilgrims who remain in this valley of tears, struggling against so many enemies who wish to drag us to hell. Ah, by the merits of thy precious death be graciously pleased to obtain us detachment from earthly things, the forgiveness of our sins, love of God, and holy perseverance; and when the hour of death arrives, help us from heaven with thy prayers, and obtain for us that we may kiss thy feet in Paradise.

II. Mary died, and her most pure body was carried by the holy Apostles and placed in the sepulchre, where it was guarded by angels for three days; after which it was transported to Paradise; but her beautiful soul entered the blessed kingdom in the very moment in which she expired, accompanied by innumerable angels, and also accompanied by her Son Himself. When she had entered heaven, she humbly presented herself before God, adored Him, and with immense feeling thanked Him for the many graces which He had bestowed upon her. God embraced her, blessed her, and declared her

Queen of the universe, exalting her above all the angels and saints.[2] But now, if, as the Apostle says, the human mind cannot comprehend the immense glory which God has prepared in heaven for His servants who have loved Him in this world, how great must be the glory which He bestowed on this most holy Mother, who on earth loved Him more than all the saints and angels, and loved Him with all her strength; so that when Mary entered heaven she alone could say to God, 'O Lord, if on earth I did not love Thee as much as Thou deservedst, at least I loved Thee as much as I could love Thee.'

III. Let us rejoice with Mary at the glory with which God has enriched her. Let us also rejoice for ourselves; for at the same time that Mary was made Queen of the world, she was also made our advocate. She is so compassionate an advocate, that she accepts the causes of all sinners who recommend themselves to her; and she also has such great power with our Judge, that she gains all causes which she defends. Our Queen and advocate, our salvation is in thy hands; if thou prayest for us, we shall be saved. Only tell thy Son that thou willest that we should be with thee in Paradise. He refuses thee nothing that thou askest. O Mary, our life, our sweetness, and our hope, pray to Jesus for us.

MEDITATION FOR THE 8TH OF SEPTEMBER.

The Feast of the Nativity of Mary.

I. Before the birth of Mary the world was lost in the darkness of sin. 'Mary was born, and the dawn arose,' says a holy father.[3] Of Mary it had already been said, "Who is she that cometh forth as the morn-

---

[2] Exaltata est sancta Dei Genitrix super choros angelorum ad cœlestia regna.
[3] Nata Virgine surrexit aurora.—*S. Pet Dam. Serm. de Assump*

ing rising?"[4] As the earth rejoices when the dawn appears, because it is the precursor of the sun, so also when Mary was born the whole world rejoiced, because she was the precursor of Jesus Christ, the Sun of Justice, who being made her Son, came to save us by His death; hence the Church sings, 'Thy nativity, O Virgin Mother of God, announced joy to the whole world; for from thee arose the Sun of Justice, who has given us life eternal.'[5] So that when Mary was born, our remedy, our consolation, and our salvation came into the world; for through Mary we received our Saviour.

II. This child being, then, destined to become the Mother of the Eternal Word, God enriched her with such great grace, that in the first moment of her Immaculate Conception her sanctity exceeded that of all the saints and angels together, for she received grace of a higher order—one which corresponded with the dignity of Mother of God. O holy child! O full of grace! I, miserable sinner that I am, salute and adore thee. Thou art the beloved one, the delight of God; pity me, who on account of my sins have been hateful and abominable in His sight. Thou, O most pure Virgin, knewest from thy very childhood so well how to gain the heart of God, that He never did and never will refuse thee anything, and grants thee all that thou askest. My hopes are therefore in thee; recommend me to thy Son, and I shall be saved.

III. When Mary was destined to be the Mother of God, she was also destined to become the mediatress between God and sinners. Hence the angelic Saint Thomas says 'that Mary received sufficient grace to save all men;'[6] and therefore Saint Bernard calls her 'a full aqueduct, that of her plenitude we all may partake.' O my Queen, mediatress of sinners, perform thy office; intercede for me. My sins shall not prevent me from trusting in thee, O great Mother of God; no, I trust

[4] Cant. vi. 9.　　　　[5] Brev. Rom. in Nat. B.M.V.
[6] Exp. in Sal. Ang.

in thee ; and so great is my confidence, that were my salvation in my own hands, I would place it in thine. O Mary, receive me under thy protection ; for that is all my desire.

MEDITATION FOR THE 21st OF NOVEMBER.

The Feast of the Presentation of Mary.

I. The holy child Mary had hardly attained the age of three years when she entreated her holy parents to take her to the Temple, according to the promise which they had made. The appointed day having arrived, the immaculate young Virgin left Nazareth with Saint Joachim and Saint Anne ; a choir of angels also accompanied that holy child, who was destined to become the Mother of their Creator. 'Go,' says Saint Germanus, 'go, O Blessed Virgin, to the house of the Lord, to await the coming of the Holy Ghost, who will make thee the Mother of the Eternal Word.'[7]

II. When the holy company had reached the Temple of Jerusalem, the blessed child turned to her parents, and kneeling, kissed their hands, asked their blessing, and, without looking back, ascended the steps of the Temple, and renouncing all earthly things, and all that the world could give her, she offered and consecrated herself without reserve to God. The life of Mary in the Temple was thenceforward but one continual exercise of love and offering of her whole self to her Lord. She advanced from hour to hour, nay even from moment to moment, in all virtues, fortified, it is true, by Divine grace, but always exerting herself with her whole strength to correspond with this grace. Mary herself said, in a vision to Saint Elizabeth of Hungary, 'Thou thinkest, perhaps, that I obtained grace and virtues without effort. Know that I received no graces from

---

[7] Encom. in S. Deip.

God without great labour, constant prayer, ardent desires, and many tears and mortifications.[8]

III. Thus in the Temple the tender Virgin Mary prayed without ceasing. And seeing that the human race was lost and hateful to God, she principally prayed for the coming of the Messiah, and ardently desired to be the servant of the happy virgin who was to become the mother of God. But, O holy Lady, know that on account of thy prayers the Son of God hastens His coming into the world to redeem the world ; and moreover know that thou art that blessed one who art chosen to be the Mother of thy Creator. O beloved of God, most holy child, thou prayest for all, pray also for me. Thou didst consecrate thy entire self from thy very childhood to the love of thy God ; obtain that I, during the time that I have yet to be on earth, may live for God alone. On this day, in union with thee, I renounce all creatures, and consecrate myself to the love of my Lord. I also offer myself to thee, my Queen, to serve thee always. Accept me as thy servant in an especial manner, and obtain me the grace to be always faithful to thee and to thy Son, that I may one day praise thee, and love thee for all eternity in heaven.

MEDITATION FOR THE 8TH OF DECEMBER.

The Feast of the Immaculate Conception of Mary.

I. It was indeed becoming that the three Divine Persons should preserve Mary from original sin. It was becoming that the Father should do so, because Mary was His first-born daughter. As Jesus was the first-born of God, " the first-born of every creature,"[9] so also was Mary, the destined Mother of God, always considered by Him as His first-born daughter by adoption, and therefore He always possessed her by His

[8] Ap. S. Bonav. Med. Vitæ Chr. c. 3.   [9] Colos. i. 15.

grace: "The Lord possessed me in the beginning of His ways." For the honour, therefore, of His Son, it was becoming that the Father should preserve His Mother from every stain of sin. It was also becoming that He should do so, because He destined this His daughter to crush the head of the infernal serpent, who had seduced man, as we read in Genesis, "she shall crush thy head." How, then, could He permit that she should first be the slave of this infernal serpent? Moreover, Mary was also destined to become the advocate of sinners; therefore it was also becoming that God should preserve her from sin, that she might not appear guilty of the same fault of men, for whom she was to intercede.

II. It was becoming that the Son should have an immaculate Mother. He Himself chose Mary for His Mother. It is impossible to believe that a son who could have a queen for his mother would choose a slave. How, then, can we imagine that the Eternal Word, who could have an ever-immaculate Mother, and one who had always been the friend of God, would have one defiled by sin, and at one time the enemy of God? Moreover, as an ancient author says, 'the flesh of Christ is the flesh of Mary.'[10] The Son of God would have felt horror to have taken flesh of a Saint Agnes, a Saint Gertrude, or of a Saint Teresa, because these holy virgins were defiled by sin before baptism; and therefore the devil could then have reproached Him with being clothed with flesh which had once been subject to him. But as Mary was always pure and immaculate, our Lord felt no horror at becoming man in her chaste womb.[11] Besides, Saint Thomas says,[12] that 'Mary was preserved from every actual sin, even venial;' for otherwise she would not have been a becoming Mother of God; but how much less would she have been so, had she been defiled by original sin, which renders the soul hateful to God?

[10] Caro Jesu caro est Mariæ.
[11] Non horruisti Virginis uterum.
[12] P. 3. q. 27. a. 4.

III. It was becoming the Holy Ghost, that this His most beloved spouse should be immaculate. As men who had already fallen into sin were to be redeemed, He willed that this His spouse should be redeemed in the more noble way; that is, by being preserved from falling into sin. And since God preserved the body of Mary after her death, how much more should we believe that He preserved her soul from the corruption of sin? Hence the Divine Spouse calls her, in the sacred Canticles, " an enclosed garden, a sealed fountain;"[13] for an enemy never entered the blessed soul of Mary. Therefore He praised her, calling her all beautiful, always His friend, and all pure : " Thou art all fair, O my love, and there is not a spot in thee."[14] Ah, my most beautiful Lady, I rejoice in seeing thee, by thy purity and thy beauty, so dear to God. I thank God for having preserved thee from every stain. My Queen, since thou art so loved by the most Holy Trinity, disdain not to cast thine eyes on my soul, which is so defiled by sin, that, seeing it, thou mayest obtain me pardon and eternal salvation from God. Behold me, and change me. Thou, by thy sweetness, hast drawn so many hearts to thy love, draw also my heart, that from henceforward it may love no other than God and thee. Thou well knowest that I have placed all my hopes in thee, my dear Mother; abandon me not. Help me always with thine intercession in life, and especially at the hour of my death; grant that I may die invoking and loving thee, that I may love thee for ever in Paradise.

[13] Cant. iv. 12.

MEDITATION.

For the Feast of Saint Joseph.

I. To understand how powerful is the intercession of Saint Joseph with Jesus Christ, we need only know what the Gospel says, " and He was subject to them."[15] For thirty years, then, the Son of God attentively obeyed Joseph and Mary. Joseph had only to indicate his will by a word or a sign, and he was immediately obeyed by Jesus. This humility of Jesus in obeying, teaches us that the dignity of Saint Joseph was above that of all the Saints, with the exception of the Divine Mother.

II. Let us now attend to what Saint Teresa says of the confidence which we should have in the protection of Saint Joseph : she says, ' Our Lord seems to have granted power to other Saints to help in one necessity ; experience proves that this Saint helps us in all ; and that our Lord wishes us to understand, that as on earth He was subject to him, so also in heaven He refuses him nothing that he asks. Other persons whom I advised to recommend themselves to him have experienced this. I never knew anyone who served him, by practising some particular devotion in his honour, who did not always progress in virtue. I entreat those who do not believe what I say, to try it themselves. I cannot understand how it is possible to think of the Queen of Angels, and of all the labours which she underwent during the childhood of Jesus, without returning thanks to Saint Joseph for all the services he rendered at that time to the Mother and the Son. '[16]

III. We should especially be devout to Saint Joseph, in order that the Saint may obtain us a good death. He, on account of having saved the infant Jesus from the snares of Herod, has the special pri-

[15] Luc. ii. 51.   [16] Vita, ch. 6.

vilege of delivering dying persons from the snares of the devil. Moreover, on account of the services which he rendered for so many years to Jesus and Mary, having by his labours provided them a dwelling and food, he has the privilege of obtaining the special assistance of Jesus and Mary for his devout clients at death. My holy protector, Saint Joseph, on account of my sins I deserve a bad death; but if thou defendest me, I shall not be lost. Thou wast not only a great friend of my Judge, but thou wast also His guardian and adopted father; recommend me to thy Jesus, who loves thee so much. I place myself under thy protection; accept me for thy perpetual servant. And by that holy company of Jesus and Mary, which thou didst enjoy on earth, obtain that I may never more be separated from their love; and, in fine, by the attendance of Jesus and Mary, which thou hadst in death, obtain for me, that at my death I also may have the special assistance of Jesus and Mary. Most holy Virgin, by the love which thou didst bear to thy holy spouse Saint Joseph, help me at the hour of my death.

PRAYERS TO THE DIVINE MOTHER

SUNDAY.

Prayer to the most Blessed Virgin Mary, to obtain the Forgiveness of our Sins.

BEHOLD, O Mother of God, at thy feet a miserable sinner, a slave of hell, who has recourse to thee and trusts in thee. I do not deserve that thou shouldst even look at me; but I know that thou, having seen thy Son die for the salvation of sinners, hast the greatest desire to help them. I hear all call thee the refuge of sinners, the hope of those who are in despair, and the help of the abandoned. Thou art, then, my refuge, my hope, and my help. Thou hast to save me by thy intercession. Help me, for the love of Jesus Christ; extend thy hand to a miserable creature who has fallen, and recommends himself to thee. I know that thy pleasure is to help a sinner to thy utmost; help me, therefore, now that thou canst do so. By my sins I have lost divine grace, and with it my soul; I now place myself in thy hands. Tell me what I must do to recover the favour of my Lord, and I will immediately do it. He sends me to thee that thou mayest help me; and He wills that I should have recourse to thy mercy, that not only the merits of thy Son, but also that thy intercession may help me to save my soul. To thee, then, I have recourse; do thou, who prayest for so many others, pray also to Jesus for me.

Ask Him to pardon me, and He will forgive me; tell Him that thou desirest my salvation, and He will save me; show how thou canst enrich those who trust in thee. Amen. Thus I hope, thus may it be.

MONDAY.

Prayer to the most Blessed Virgin Mary, to obtain holy Perseverance.

O Queen of Heaven, I, who was once a miserable slave of Lucifer, now dedicate myself to thee, to be thy servant for ever; I offer myself to honour thee, and serve thee during my whole life; do thou accept me, and refuse me not, as I should deserve. O my Mother in thee have I placed all my hopes, from thee do I expect every grace. I bless and thank God, who in His mercy has given me this confidence in thee, which I consider a pledge of my salvation. Alas, miserable wretch that I am, I have hitherto fallen, because I have not had recourse to thee. I now hope that, through the merits of Jesus Christ and thy prayers, I have obtained pardon. But I may again lose Divine grace; the danger is not past. My enemies do not sleep. How many new temptations have I still to conquer! Ah, my most sweet Lady, protect me, and permit me not again to become their slave: help me at all times. I know that thou wilt help me, and that with thy help I shall conquer, if I recommend myself to thee; but this is what I fear, I fear that in time of danger I may neglect to call upon thee, and thus be lost. I ask thee, then, for this grace: obtain that, in the assaults of hell, I may always have recourse to thee, saying, Mary, help me. My Mother, permit me not to lose my God.

TUESDAY.

Prayer to the Blessed Virgin Mary, to obtain a good Death.

O Mary, how shall I die? Even now, that I think

of my sins, and of that decisive moment on which my salvation or eternal damnation depends, of that moment in which I must expire and be judged, I tremble and am confounded. O my most sweet Mother, my hopes are in the blood of Jesus Christ and in thy intercession. O comfortress of the afflicted, do not, then, abandon me, cease not to console me in that moment of so great affliction. If I am now so tormented by remorse for sins committed, the uncertainty of pardon, the danger of relapse, and the rigour of divine justice, what will become of me then? Unless thou helpest me, I shall be lost. Ah, my Lady, before death obtain me great sorrow for my sins, thorough amendment, and fidelity to God during the remainder of my life. And when my last moment arrives, O Mary, my hope, help me in the great distress in which I shall then be; encourage me, that I may not despair at the sight of my sins, which the devil will place before me. Obtain that I may then invoke thee more frequently; so that I may expire with thy most sweet name and that of thy beloved Son on my lips. Nay more, my Lady, but forgive my boldness, before I expire do thou come thyself and comfort me with thy presence. Thou hast granted this favour to so many of thy devout servants, I also desire and hope it. I am a sinner, it is true; I do not deserve so great a favour; but I am thy servant, love thee and have full confidence in thee. O Mary, I shall expect thee; do not disappoint me of this consolation. At least, if I am not worthy of so great a favour, do thou help me from heaven, that I may leave this life loving God and thee, to love thee eternally in Paradise.

WEDNESDAY.

Prayer to the most Blessed Virgin Mary, to obtain Deliverance from Hell.

My most beloved Lady, I thank thee for having

delivered me from hell as many times as I have deserved it by my sins. Miserable creature that I was, I was once condemned to that prison, and perhaps already, after the first sin, the sentence would have been put into execution, if thou, in thy compassion, hadst not helped me. Thou, without even being asked by me, and only in thy goodness, didst restrain Divine Justice; and then, conquering my obduracy, thou didst draw me to have confidence in thee. O, into how many other sins should I have afterwards fallen, in the dangers in which I have been, hadst not thou, my loving Mother, preserved me by the graces which thou didst obtain for me! Ah, my Queen, continue to guard me from hell; for what will thy mercy, and the favours which thou hast shown me, avail me if I am lost? If I did not always love thee, now at least—after God—I love thee above all things. Never allow me to turn my back on thee and on God, who, by thy means, has granted me so many graces. My most amiable Lady, never allow me to have the misfortune to hate thee and curse thee for all eternity in hell. Wilt thou endure to see a servant of thine, who loves thee, lost? O Mary, what sayest thou? I shall be lost if I abandon thee. But who can ever more have the heart to leave thee? How can I ever forget the love thou hast borne me? My Lady, since thou hast done so much to save me, complete the work, continue thy aid. Wilt thou help me? But what do I say? If at a time when I lived forgetful of thee thou didst favour me so much, how much more may I not hope for now that I love thee and recommend myself to thee! No, he can never be lost who recommends himself to thee; he alone is lost who has not recourse to thee. Ah, my Mother, leave me not in my own hands, for I should then be lost; grant that I may always have recourse to thee. Save me, my hope, save me from hell; but, in the first place, save me from sin, which alone can condemn me to it.

THURSDAY.

Prayer to the most Blessed Virgin Mary, to obtain Heaven.

O Queen of Paradise, who reignest above all the choirs of angels, and who art the nearest of all creatures to God, I, a miserable sinner, salute thee from this valley of tears, and beseech thee to turn thy compassionate eyes towards me, for whichever side they turn they dispense graces. See, O Mary, in how many dangers I now am, and shall be as long as I live in this world, of losing my soul, of losing heaven and God. In thee, O Lady, I have placed all my hopes. I love thee, and sigh to go soon to see thee, and praise thee in heaven. Ah, Mary, when will be that happy day on which I shall see myself safe at thy feet, and contemplate my Mother, who has done so much for my salvation? When shall I kiss that hand which has delivered me so many times from hell, and has dispensed me so many graces, when, on account of my sins, I deserved to be hated and abandoned by all? My Lady, in life I have been very ungrateful to thee; but if I get to heaven, I shall no longer be ungrateful; there I shall love thee as much as I can in every moment for all eternity, and shall make amends for my ingratitude by blessing and thanking thee for ever. I thank God with my whole heart, who gives me firm confidence in the blood of Jesus Christ and in thee, and the conviction that thou wilt save me; that thou wilt deliver me from my sins; that thou wilt give me light and strength to execute the Divine will; and, in fine, that thou wilt lead me to the gate of Paradise. Thy servants have hoped for all this, and not one of them was deceived. No, neither shall I be deceived. O Mary, my full confidence is that thou hast to save me. Beseech thy Son Jesus, as I also beseech Him, by the merits of His Passion, to preserve and always increase this confidence in me, and I shall be saved.

FRIDAY.

Prayer to the most Blessed Virgin Mary, to obtain Love towards her and Jesus Christ.

O Mary, I already know that thou art the most noble, the most sublime, the most pure, the most beautiful, the most benign, the most holy—in a word, the most amiable of all creatures. O that all knew thee, my Lady, and loved thee as thou dost merit! But I am consoled when I remember that in heaven and on earth there are so many happy souls who live enamoured of thy goodness and beauty. Above all, I rejoice that God Himself loves thee alone more than He loves all men and angels together. My most amiable Queen, I, a miserable sinner, love thee also; but I love thee too little. I desire a greater and more tender love towards thee; and this thou must obtain for me, since to love thee is a great mark of predestination, and a grace which God only grants to those whom He will save.

I see also, my Mother, that I am indeed under great obligations to thy Son. I see that He merits infinite love. Thou, who desirest nothing else but to see Him loved, hast to obtain me this grace above all others; obtain me great love for Jesus Christ. Thou obtainest all that thou willest from God ; ah, then, be graciously pleased to obtain me the grace to be so united to the Divine will that I may never more be separated from it. I do not ask of thee earthly goods, honours, or riches. I ask thee for that which thy heart desires most for me. I wish to love my God. Is it possible that thou refusest to second this my desire, which is so pleasing to thee ? Ah no, thou already helpest me ; already thou prayest for me. Pray, pray, and cease not to pray until thou seest me safe in heaven, beyond the possibility of ever more losing my Lord, and certain to love Him for ever, together with thee, my dearest Mother.

SATURDAY.

Prayer to the most Blessed Virgin Mary to obtain her Patronage.

O my most holy Mother, I see the graces which thou hast obtained for me ; and I see the ingratitude of which I have been guilty towards thee. An ungrateful soul is no longer worthy of favours ; but I will not on this account distrust thy mercy, which is greater than my ingratitude. O my great advocate, pity me. Thou dispensest all the graces which God grants to us miserable creatures, and for this purpose He has made thee so powerful, so rich, and so benign. He has done so, that thou mightest succour us in our miseries. Ah, Mother of mercy, leave me not in my poverty. Thou art the advocate of the most miserable and guilty criminals who have recourse to thee ; defend me also, who recommend myself to thee. Say not that my cause is too difficult to be gained ; for all causes, however desperate, when defended by thee are gained. In thy hands, then, do I place my eternal salvation ; to thee do I intrust my soul : it was lost ; thou, then, by thy intercession hast to save it. I wish to be inscribed amongst thy most devoted servants ; reject me not. Thou seekest the miserable, to relieve them ; abandon me not, who am a wretched sinner, and who have recourse to thee. Speak for me ; thy Son does all that thou askest Him. Take me under thy protection ; that is all that I ask. Yes ; for if thou protectest me, I fear nothing. I do not fear my sins ; for thou wilt obtain me a remedy for the evil they have done me. I do not fear the devils ; for thou art more powerful than all hell. I do not even fear Jesus my Judge Himself ; for by a single prayer of thine He is appeased. I only fear that by my negligence I may cease to recommend myself to thee, and thus be lost. It is true that these graces are too great for me, who have not deserved them; but they are not too great for thee, who art so much loved by God. Hence He grants thee all that thou askest. Thou hast only to speak, and He denies thee nothing. Pray, then, to Jesus for me; tell Him that thou protectest me; and then He is sure to pity me. My Mother, in thee do I trust; in this hope I shall live in peace, and in it I wish to die.

Live Jesus our love, and Mary our hope!

LITTLE ROSARY

OF THE SEVEN DOLOURS OF MARY.

INCLINE unto mine aid, O God, &c.
    Glory be to the Father, &c.

> My Mother! share thy grief with me,
> And let me bear thee company
> To mourn thy Jesus' death with thee.

FIRST DOLOUR. I pity thee, O afflicted Mother, on account of the first sword of sorrow which pierced thee, when in the Temple all the outrages which men would inflict on thy beloved Jesus were presented before thee by Saint Simeon, and which thou already knewest by the sacred Scriptures; outrages which were to cause Him to die before thine eyes, on an infamous cross, exhausted of His blood, abandoned by all, and thyself unable to defend or help Him. By that bitter knowledge, then, which for so many years afflicted thy heart, I beseech thee, my Queen, to obtain me the grace that during my life and at my death I may ever keep the Passion of Jesus and thy sorrows impressed on my heart.

Our Father, Seven Hail Marys, and the Strophe, are repeated after each Dolour.

SECOND DOLOUR. I pity thee, my afflicted Mother, for the second sword which pierced thee, when, soon after His birth, thou didst behold thy innocent Son threatened with death by those very men for whose salvation He had come into the world; so that in the darkness of night thou wast obliged to fly secretly with Him into Egypt. By the many hardships, then, which thou, a delicate young woman, in company with thine exiled Child, didst endure in so long and fatiguing a journey through rough and desert countries, and during thy residence in Egypt, where, being unknown and a stranger, thou didst live for so many years in poverty and contempt,—I beseech thee, my beloved Lady, to obtain me grace to suffer with patience until death, in thy company, the trials of this miserable life; that I may thus in the next escape the eternal punishments of hell, which I have deserved.

Our Father, &c.

THIRD DOLOUR. I pity thee, my sorrowful Mother, on account of the third sword which pierced thee in the loss of thy dear Son Jesus, who remained absent from thee in Jerusalem for three days. No longer seeing thy Beloved by thy side, and not knowing the cause of His absence, I can well imagine, my loving Queen, that during those nights thou didst not repose, and didst only sigh for Him, who was all thy treasure. By the sighs, then, of those three days, for thee too long and bitter, I beseech thee to obtain me the grace, that I may never lose my God; that so, always clinging to Him, I may leave the world united to Him.

Our Father, &c.

FOURTH DOLOUR. I pity thee, my sorrowful Mother, for the fourth sword which pierced thee, in seeing thy Son condemned to death, bound with cords and chains, covered with blood and wounds, crowned with a wreath of thorns, falling under the heavy weight of the cross which He carried on His wounded shoulders, going as an innocent Lamb to die for love of us. Thine eyes met His, and His met thine; and your glances were as so many cruel arrows, which wounded your loving hearts. By this great sorrow, then, I beseech thee to obtain me the grace to live in all things resigned to the will of my God, and to carry my cross cheerfully in company with Jesus, until my last breath.

Our Father, &c.

FIFTH DOLOUR. I pity thee, my afflicted Mother, for the fifth sword which pierced thee, when on Mount Calvary thou didst behold thy beloved Son Jesus slowly dying before thy eyes, amid so many torments and insults, on that hard bed of the cross, where thou couldst not administer Him even the least of those comforts which are granted to the greatest criminals at the hour of death. I beseech thee, by the agony which thou, my most loving Mother, didst endure together with thy dying Son, and by the sadness which thou didst feel, when, for the last time, He spoke to thee from the cross and bade thee farewell, and left all of us, in the person of Saint John, to thee as thy children; by that constancy with which thou didst then see Him bow down His head and expire, I beseech thee to obtain me the grace, from thy crucified Love, to live and die crucified to all earthly things, that I may spend my life for God alone, and thus one day enter Paradise to enjoy Him face to face.

Our Father, &c.

SIXTH DOLOUR.—I pity thee, my afflicted Mother, for the sixth sword which pierced thee, when thou didst see the sweet heart of thy Son pierced through and through. He was already dead, and had died for those ungrateful creatures, who, even after His death, were not satisfied with the torments they had inflicted upon Him. By this cruel sorrow, then, which was all thine, I beseech thee to obtain me the grace to dwell in the heart of Jesus, wounded and opened for me; in that heart, I say, which is the beautiful abode of love, in which all souls who love God repose; and that, living there, I may never think of or love anything but God. Most sacred Virgin, thou canst obtain this for me; from thee do I hope for it.

Our Father, &c.

SEVENTH DOLOUR.—I pity thee, my afflicted Mother, for the seventh sword which pierced thee on seeing thy Son in thy arms already dead, no longer fair and beautiful as thou didst receive Him in the stable of Bethlehem, but covered with blood, livid and all lacerated with wounds, so that even His bones were seen; thou didst then say, 'My Son, my Son, to what has love reduced Thee!' And when He was borne to the sepulchre, thou wouldst thyself accompany Him, and place Him with thy own hands in the tomb; and bidding Him thy last farewell, thou didst leave thy loving heart buried with thy Son. By this martyrdom of thy beautiful soul, do thou obtain me, O Mother of fair love, the forgiveness of the offences which I have committed against my beloved God, and of which I repent with my whole heart. Do thou defend me in temptations, do thou assist me at the moment of my death, that, saving my soul through the merits of Jesus and thine, I may one day, after this miserable exile, go to Paradise to sing the praises of Jesus and of thee for all eternity. Amen.

Our Father, &c.

Pray for us, O most sorrowful Virgin:

That we may be made worthy of the promises of Christ.

Let us pray.

O God, at whose Passion, according to the prophecy of Simeon, a sword of sorrow did pierce through the most sweet soul of the glorious Virgin and Mother Mary; grant that we, who commemorate and reverence her dolours, may experience the blessed effect of Thy Passion, who livest and reignest world without end. Amen.

Benedict XIII. granted two hundred days' indulgence for every 'Our Father' and every 'Hail Mary,' to those who recite this little Rosary in the churches of the Servites of Mary. He also granted the same favour to all who recite it in any place whatever, on Fridays or any day during Lent. To those who recite it on other days he granted one hundred days for every 'Our Father' and 'Hail Mary.' To those who recite it entire, seven years. To those who recite it for a year, a plenary indulgence, applicable to the souls in purgatory.[1]

*For the various Indulgences granted to the recitation of the Rosary of the Seven Dolours, the reader is referred to the last English edition of the Raccolta, p. 220.—*Ed.

1 Sinisc. in fin. prat. iii. page 8. ?

LITTLE ROSARY OF MARY IMMACULATE,

V. Incline unto mine aid, O God.

R. O Lord, make haste to help me.

Glory be to the Father, and to the Son, and to the Holy Ghost: as it was in the beginning, is now, and ever shall be, world without end.   Amen.

After this an 'Our Father' is recited, in honour of the Eternal Father, and in thanksgiving for all the graces bestowed on Mary, and is followed by four 'Hail Marys.'   The same is repeated in honour of the Son, and again in honour of the Holy Ghost.   After each 'Hail Mary' are added these words : 'May the Immaculate Conception of Mary be ever praised.'

After each fourth 'Hail Mary' is recited the following verse :

> As 'mid the thorns the lily fair
> Art thou, Virgin Immaculate,
> From sin preserved by Him whose care
> Did thee His Mother blest create.

V. In thy Conception, O Virgin, thou wast Immaculate.

R. Intercede for us with the Father, to whose Son thou didst give birth.

Let us pray.

O God, who by the Immaculate Conception of the Blessed Virgin didst prepare a worthy dwelling for Thy Son, we beseech Thee, who by the prevision of the death of this same Son didst preserve her from all stain, to grant that we may, through her intercession, come to Thee cleansed from all sin ; through Jesus Christ our Lord.   Amen.

Note. The little Rosary of the Immaculate Conception, to the recital of which his Holiness Pope Pius IX. has granted Indulgences, is somewhat different from the above.   The reader is referred to the last English edition of the *Raccolta*, p. 400.—ED.

DEDICATIONS AND PRAYERS.

DEDICATION OF ONE'S SELF TO MARY.

MOST holy Virgin Mary, Mother of God, I., N., although most unworthy to be thy servant, yet moved by thy wonderful compassion, and by my desire to serve thee, now choose thee, in presence of my guardian angel and of the whole celestial court, for my especial Lady, Advocate, and Mother : and I firmly purpose always to love and serve thee for the future, and to do whatever I can to induce others to love and serve thee also. I beseech thee, O Mother of God, and my most compassionate and loving Mother, by the blood which thy Son shed for me, to receive me into the number of thy servants, to be thy child and servant for ever. Assist me in all my thoughts, words, and actions in every moment of my life, so that every step that I take, and every breath that I draw, may be directed to the greater glory of my God ; and through thy most powerful intercession, may I never more offend my beloved Jesus, but may I glorify Him, and love Him in this life, and love thee, my most beloved and dear Mother, and thus love thee and enjoy thee in heaven for all eternity. Amen.

My Mother Mary, I recommend my soul to thee, and especially at the hour of my death.

DEDICATION OF A FAMILY TO MARY.

Most Blessed Virgin, Immaculate Queen and our Mother Mary, refuge and consolation of all miserable creatures ; prostrate before thy throne, with my whole family, I choose thee for my Lady, Mother, and Advocate with God. I dedicate myself, **with all who belong to**

me, for ever to thy service, and beseech thee, O Mother
of God, to receive us into the number of thy servants,
by taking us all under thy protection, helping us in life,
and still more at the hour of our death. O Mother of
Mercy, I appoint thee as Lady and Ruler of my whole
house, of my relations, of my interests, and of all my
affairs. Disdain not to take charge of them : dispose
of all as it pleases thee. Bless me, then, and all my
family, and do not permit that any of us should offend
thy Son. Do thou defend us in temptations, deliver
us from dangers, provide for us in our necessities, counsel us in our doubts, comfort us in our afflictions, assist
us in our infirmities, and especially in the sorrows of
death. Never allow the devil to glory in having in his
chains any of us who are now consecrated to thee ; but
grant that we may go to heaven to thank thee, and together with thee to praise and love Jesus our Redeemer
for all eternity. Amen. Thus may it be.

ABBREVIATED PRAYER OF SAINT EPHREM TO THE BLESSED VIRGIN MARY.

O Immaculate and wholly-pure Virgin Mary, Mother of God, Queen of the world, hope of those who
are in despair; thou art the joy of the Saints ; thou art
the peacemaker between sinners and God ; thou art the
advocate of the abandoned, the secure haven of those
who are on the sea of the world ; thou art the consolation of the world, the ransom of slaves, the comfortress
of the afflicted, the salvation of the universe. O great
Queen, we take refuge in thy protection : 'We have
no confidence but in thee, O most faithful Virgin.'
After God thou art all our hope. We bear the name
of thy servants; allow not the enemy to drag us to hell.
I salute thee, O great Mediatress of peace between men
and God, Mother of Jesus our Lord, who is the love of
all men and of God, to whom be honour and benedic-
tion with the Father and the Holy Ghost. Amen.[1]

[1] De Laud. Deip.

PRAYER OF SAINT THOMAS AQUINAS.

O most blessed and most sweet Virgin Mary, full of mercy, to thy compassion I recommend my soul and body, my thoughts, actions, life, and death. O my Lady, help and strengthen me against the snares of the devil; obtain me true and perfect love, with which to love thy most beloved Son and my Lord Jesus Christ with my whole heart, and after Him to love thee above all things. My Queen and Mother, by thy most powerful intercession, grant that I may persevere in this love until death, and after death be conducted by thee to the kingdom of the blessed.

PRAYER OF THE DEVOUT BLOSIUS TO THE BLESSED VIRGIN MARY.

Hail, Mary, hope of those who are in despair, help of the destitute! Hail, thou whom thy Son so greatly honours, that whatever thou askest, thou dost at once obtain; whatever thou willest is at once done. To thee are the treasures of the kingdom of heaven intrusted. Grant, O Lady, that amid the storms of this life I may always remember thee. To thy charitable mercy I commend my soul and body. O my sweet protectress, direct and protect me in every hour, in every moment of my life. Amen.[2]

ANOTHER PRAYER BY THE SAME DEVOUT WRITER.

Hail, most benign Mother of Mercy! Hail, our Comfortress, Mary the desire of our hearts! who is there that loves thee not? Thou art our light in doubts, our comfort in sorrows, our relief in distress, our refuge in dangers and temptations. Thou, after thy only-begotten Son, art our certain salvation; blessed are those who love thee, O Lady. Incline, I beseech thee, the ears of thy compassion to the prayers of this thy servant, a miserable sinner, and dispel the darkness of

[2] Par. An. Fid. p. 2, c. 4.

my vices by the rays of thy sanctity, that I may please thee.[3]

Mother of God, remember me.—*Saint Francis Xavier.*

O Virgin and Mother, grant that I may always remember thee.—*Saint Philip Neri.*

Holy Virgin Mary, Mother of God, pray to Jesus for me.—*The same Saint.*

O Lady, grant that Jesus may never cast me off.—*Saint Ephrem.*

O Mary, may my heart never cease to love thee, and my tongue never cease to praise thee.—*Saint Bonaventure.*

O Lady, by the love which thou bearest to Jesus, help me to love Him.—*Saint Bridget.*

O Mary, be graciously pleased to make me thy servant.—*Saint Jane de Chantal.*

O Mary, I give myself to thee without reserve; do thou accept and preserve me.—*Saint Mary Magdalen de Pazzi.*

O Mary, abandon me not until death.—*Father Spinelli.*

Hail, Mary, my Mother. —*Father Francis Brancaccio.*

Holy Mary, my Advocate, pray for me. —*Father Sertorio Caputo.*

> Thy name of Mary, to my ear,
> O Mother Mary, sounds more sweet
> Than sweetest melody ;
> It brings such peace and joy so dear,
> That I would ever more repeat
> A word so sweet to me.

Our Blessed Lady revealed to a devout soul that she was much pleased at being honoured by her servants with the following devotion:

---

[3] Par. an. fid. p. 2, c. 4.

I thank Thee, O Eternal Father, for the power given to Mary, Thy daughter. *Our Father, Hail Mary, Glory be to the Father, &c.*

I thank Thee, O Eternal Son, for the wisdom given to Mary, Thy mother. *Our Father, Hail Mary, Glory be to the Father, &c.*

I thank Thee, O Eternal and Holy Spirit, for the love given to Mary, Thy spouse. *Our Father, Hail Mary, Glory be to the Father, &c.*

To thee do we cry, O Queen of Mercy, return, that we may behold thee dispensing favours, bestowing remedies, giving strength. Show us thy compassionate looks, and we shall be saved.[4]

O sovereign Lady of all things, Saint of saints, splendour of the world, glory of heaven, acknowledge those who love thee ; hear us, for thy Son honours thee by denying thee nothing.[5]

Run, hasten, O Lady, and in thy mercy help thy sinful servant, who calls upon thee, and deliver him from the hands of the enemy.[6]

Who will not sigh to thee ? We sigh with love and grief, for we are oppressed on every side. How can we do otherwise than sigh to thee, O solace of the miserable, refuge of outcasts, ransom of captives ? We are certain that when thou seest our miseries, thy compassion will hasten to relieve us.[7]

O, our sovereign Lady and our Advocate, commend us to thy Son. Grant, O blessed one, by the grace

[4] Ad te clamamus, regina misericordiæ . . . revertere ut intueamur te largientem beneficia, conferentem remedia . . . ponentem fortitudinem . . Ostende nobis faciem miserationum tuarum, et salvi erimus.—*Serm.* ii. *sup. Salve Reg. int. Op. S. Bern.*

[5] Domina rerum, Sancta sanctorum, virtus nostra et refugium, decus mundi, gloria cœli . . . agnosce omnes te diligentes. Audi nos ; nam te Filius nihil negans honorat.—*Ib. Serm.* iii.

[6] Curre, festina, Domina, et tuum nequissimum servum ac infidelissimum ad te clamantem parcendo adjuva, et eripe de manibus inimici, et periculis tui hostis.—*S Bonav. Stim. Am.* p. iii. c. 19.

[7] Quis ad te non suspirabit ? Amore etiam suspiramus, et dolore : undique namque nos angustiæ premunt. Quomodo ergo nunc non suspiramus ad te, quæ solatium es miserorum, refugium expulsorum, liberatio captivorum ? . . Non dubito, quod si nostras aspexeris miserias, non poterit tua miseratio suum retardare officium.—*Ib.* loc. cit.

which thou hast merited, that He who through thee was graciously pleased to become a partaker in our infirmity and misery, may also, through thy intercession, make us partakers in His happiness and glory.—*St. Bern.*

In thee from my whole heart I have placed my hope.—*St. John Damascen.*

It is not possible, O Lady, that thou shouldst abandon him who has placed his hopes in thee.—*St. Bern.*

Thou hast only to will our salvation, and then it is not possible that we should not obtain it.—*St. Anselm.*

Hail, Daughter of God the Father; hail, Mother of God the Son; hail, Spouse of God the Holy Ghost; hail, Temple of the whole Trinity.—*Simon Garcia.*

> O Virgin fair,
> What loveliness is thine !
> Mother Divine,
> Such beauty rare
> Enslaves this heart of mine.

Thanks be to God and to Mary.

May all things be to the eternal glory of the most Holy Trinity and of Immaculate Mary.

Live always Jesus our love, and Mary our hope, with Saint Joseph and Saint Teresa our advocates !

ACCLAMATIONS IN PRAISE OF MARY.

O most sacred Virgin Mary, O Queen of angels, how beautiful, accomplished, and perfect, has Heaven made thee ! O that I could appear to God as thou appearest to me. Thou art so beautiful and gracious that with thy beauty thou ravishest hearts. When thou art seen, everything appears deformed, all beauty is eclipsed, every grace is lost sight of; as the stars disappear at the rising of the sun.

When thy tenderly devoted servant, Saint John Damascen, contemplated thee, and when he saw that thou wast so beautiful, it seemed to him that thou hadst taken the flower and that which was best in every creature, and therefore he called thee 'the loveliness of nature,'[8] the grace and comeliness of every creature. Saint Augustine, the bright light of doctors, contemplated thee, and thou didst appear to him so fair and beautiful, that he called thee the countenance of God, and it did not seem to him adulation.[9] Thy devout son Albert the Great[10] contemplated thee, and to him it seemed that all the graces and gifts which were in the most celebrated women of the old dispensation, were all in a much higher degree in thee : the golden mouth of Sarah, which, smiling, rejoices heaven and earth; the sweet and tender look of the faithful Lia, with which thou didst soften the heart of God, hardened against sinners; the splendour of countenance of the beautiful Rachel, for with thy beauty thou dost eclipse the sun; the grace and demeanour of the discreet Abigail, by which thou didst appease an angry God; the vivacity and strength of the valiant Judith, for by thy power and thy grace thou dost subdue the most ferocious hearts.

In fine, O sovereign Princess, from the immense ocean of thy beauty the beauty and grace of all creatures flowed forth as rivers. The sea learnt to curl its waves, and to wave its crystal waters from thy golden hair, which gracefully floated over thy shoulders and ivory neck. The crystal fountains and their transparent depths learnt their tranquil and steady flow from the serenity of thy beautiful brow and placid countenance. The lovely rainbow, when in full beauty, learnt with studious care its graceful bend from thy eyebrows, thus better to send forth its rays of light. The morning-star itself, and the sweet star of night, are sparks from thy beautiful eyes. The white lilies and ruby roses stole their colours from thy lovely cheeks. Envious purple and coral sigh for the colour of thy lips. The most delicious milk and sweetest honey are distillations from

---

[8] Venustas naturæ.—*In Nat. B.M.* s. 1.

[9] Si formam Dei te appellem, digna existis.—s. 208, ed. B. app.

[10] De Laud. B.M. l. 6. c. 9.

the sweet honeycomb of thy mouth. The scented jas-mine and fragrant Damasc rose stole their perfume from thy breath. The loftiest cedar and the most erect, the fairest cypress, were happy when they beheld their image in thy erect and lofty neck. The palm-tree, emulous and jealous, likened itself to thy noble stature. In fine, O Lady, every created beauty is a shadow and trace of thy beauty. And thus I wonder not, O sovereign Princess, that heaven and earth place themselves under thy feet; for such are they, and thou art so great, that to be only under thy feet enriches them, and they esteem themselves happy and blessed in kissing them. Thus did the moon rejoice when the evangelist Saint John saw her under thy feet, and the sun increased in splen-dour when it clothed thee with its rays of light. The Evangelist, blinded by the brilliancy of thy light, was lost in wonder and ravished out of himself at the sight of so stupendous a miracle of beauty, in which the beauty of heaven and earth was concentrated, and he said,[11] "There appeared a great sign in heaven." A great miracle appeared in the heavens—a miracle which filled the angels with astonishment, and caused the earth to tremble. That miracle was, a woman clothed from head to foot in light and splendour. The resplend-ent sun itself chose her for his Mother, and placed him-self in her womb; the fair moon covers her feet as san-dals edged with silver; a multitude of stars crown her brow, and, emulating one with another, bind her locks together, and form upon her head a diadem of precious gems: "and on her head a crown of twelve stars."

Thus, O most sacred Virgin, the Saints, considering thee in the midst of such splendour more beautiful than the sun, and more fair than the moon, which are the ornament and concentration of all beauty; and con-sidering the acclamations of joy which attend thee in heaven, can never cease their astonishment at thy beauty,

---

[11] Signum magnum apparuit in cœlo; mulier amicta sole, et luna sub pedibus ejus, et in capite ejus stellarum duodecim.—*Apoc.* xii. 1.

.nd can only exclaim and burst forth in acclamations of wonder and astonishment. Saint Peter Damian exclaims in his admiration, ' O holy and most holy of all Saints, richest treasure of all sanctity.' Saint Bernard: ' O admirable Virgin, O woman honour of all women, the best, the greatest that the world ever possessed. Saint Epiphanius : ' O heaven, greater and vaster than the heavens themselves ; O Virgin, truly full of grace.' And the Catholic Church, in the name of all, exclaims, ' O most clement, most pious, and most sweet Virgin Mary.'

And I also, O heavenly Princess, with thy permission, although I am the least of thy servants, I will also make my acclamations of wonder and astonishment. O gracious and beautiful heaven, more vast than the heavens themselves, for they cannot contain God, who is immense, but He concealed Himself in thy womb ; O richest of all treasures, in which was deposited the treasure of our redemption ; O Mother of sinners, under whose mantle we are defended ; O consolation of the world, in which all who are afflicted, infirm, and disconsolate, find consolation ; O beautiful eyes, which steal hearts ; O coral lips, which imprison souls ; O generous hands, filled with lilies, and which always distribute graces ; O pure creature, who appearest a God, and whom I should have taken for a God, had not faith taught me that thou art not so, although thou hast a splendour, and I know not what of Divine sovereignty ; O great Lady, empress of heaven, enjoy for a thousand eternities the greatness of thy state, the immensity of thy greatness, and the happiness of thy glory. We only beseech thee, O compassionate Mother, not to forget us, who glory in being thy servants and children. And since in thee are deposited all graces, and the best and most privileged of all created things, grant, O Lady, that we, thy devout children, may be favoured more beyond comparison than are all other men on earth. The whole world should know that the dear children of Mary are the best of heaven and earth: they are the spoilt children, who enjoy all the choicest possessions of their Mother; they are the beloved Benjamins, who being caressed in the bosom of the Queen of Heaven, are doubly favoured and doubly caressed by the Majesty of God. This I hope, O most beautiful Rachel; and this I am confident that thou wilt do, O sovereign Princess. In the name of what thou art, do it; for all heaven prostrate at thy feet beseeches thee, and with importunity asks it of thee. Say only yes, pronounce only a loving consent; be it done, be it done, *fiat, fiat!* O men, of what are you thinking? How can you love earthly, deceitful, and lying creatures, which betray you and cause you to lose your souls, your bodies, Paradise, and God! And why do you not love the most loving, the most amiable, the most faithful Mary, who, after having enriched you with consolations and graces in this life, will obtain you from her Divine beloved Son the eternal glory of Paradise? O Mary, Mary, more beautiful than all creatures, lovely after Jesus above all loves, more dear than all created things, gracious above every grace, pity this miserable heart of mine; miserable because it does not love thee; and it ought to love thee. Thou canst inflame it with thy holy love. Turn, O Mary, thy loving eyes upon me; look at me, and draw me to thee; and grant that after God I may love no other but thee, most gracious, most amiable Mary, Mother of Jesus, and my Mother.

The End.

If you have enjoyed this book, consider making your next selection from among the following . . .

Prices guaranteed through December 31, 1995.

Ven. Jacinta Marto of Fatima. *Cirrincione* 1.50
Reign of Christ the King. *Davies* 1.25
St. Teresa of Ávila. *William Thomas Walsh* 18.00
Isabella of Spain—The Last Crusader. *Wm. T. Walsh* 20.00
Characters of the Inquisition. *Wm. T. Walsh* 12.50
Philip II. *William Thomas Walsh.* H.B. 37.50
Blood-Drenched Altars—Cath. Comment. Hist. Mexico. . 18.00
Self-Abandonment to Divine Providence. *de Caussade* . . . 16.50
Way of the Cross. *Liguorian* 75
Way of the Cross. *Franciscan* 75
Modern Saints—Their Lives & Faces, Bk. 1. *Ann Ball* . . . 18.00
Modern Saints—Their Lives & Faces, Bk. 2. *Ann Ball* . . 20.00
Saint Michael and the Angels. *Approved Sources* 5.50
Dolorous Passion of Our Lord. *Anne C. Emmerich* 15.00
Our Lady of Fatima's Peace Plan from Heaven. Booklet. .75
Divine Favors Granted to St. Joseph. *Pere Binet* 4.00
St. Joseph Cafasso—Priest of the Gallows. *St. J. Bosco* . . 3.00
Catechism of the Council of Trent. *McHugh/Callan* 20.00
Padre Pio—The Stigmatist. *Fr. Charles Carty* 13.50
Why Squander Illness? *Frs. Rumble & Carty* 2.00
Fatima—The Great Sign. *Francis Johnston* 7.00
Heliotropium—Conformity of Human Will to Divine. . . . 11.00
Charity for the Suffering Souls. *Fr. John Nageleisen* 15.00
Devotion to the Sacred Heart of Jesus. *Verheylezoon* 13.00
Sermons on Prayer. *St. Francis de Sales* 3.50
Sermons on Our Lady. *St. Francis de Sales* 9.00
Sermons for Lent. *St. Francis de Sales* 10.00
Fundamentals of Catholic Dogma. *Ott* 20.00
Litany of the Blessed Virgin Mary. (100 cards) 5.00
Who Is Padre Pio? Radio Replies Press 1.50
Child's Bible History. *Knecht* 4.00
The Life of Christ. 4 Vols. H.B. *Anne C. Emmerich* 55.00
St. Anthony—The Wonder Worker of Padua. *Stoddard* . . . 4.00
The Precious Blood. *Fr. Faber* 11.00
The Holy Shroud & Four Visions. *Fr. O'Connell* 2.00
Clean Love in Courtship. *Fr. Lawrence Lovasik* 2.50
The Secret of the Rosary. *St. Louis De Montfort* 3.00
The History of Antichrist. *Rev. P. Huchede* 3.00
Where We Got the Bible. *Fr. Henry Graham* 5.00
Hidden Treasure—Holy Mass. *St. Leonard.* 4.00
Imitation of the Sacred Heart of Jesus. *Fr. Arnoudt* 13.50
The Life & Glories of St. Joseph. *Edward Thompson* . . . 13.50

At your bookdealer or direct from the publisher.

Prices guaranteed through December 31, 1995.

NOTES

NOTES

NOTES